CW00457575

SUFISM

Sufism

A NEW HISTORY OF
ISLAMIC MYSTICISM

Alexander Knysh

PRINCETON UNIVERSITY PRESS

PRINCETON & OXFORD

Copyright © 2017 by Princeton University Press

Requests for permission to reproduce material from this work
should be sent to Permissions, Princeton University Press

Published by Princeton University Press,
41 William Street, Princeton, New Jersey 08540

In the United Kingdom: Princeton University Press,
6 Oxford Street, Woodstock, Oxfordshire OX20 1TR

press.princeton.edu

All Rights Reserved

Library of Congress Cataloging-in-Publication Data

Names: Knysh, Alexander D., author.
Title: Sufism : a new history of Islamic mysticism / Alexander Knysh.
Description: Princeton ; Oxford : Princeton University Press, 2017. |
    Includes bibliographical references and index.
Identifiers: LCCN 2017016916 | ISBN 9780691139098 (hardcover : alk. paper)
Subjects: LCSH: Sufism—History. | Mysticism—Islam—History.
Classification: LCC BP189 .K695 2017 | DDC 297.4--dc23 LC record available at
https://lccn.loc.gov/2017016916

British Library Cataloging-in-Publication Data is available

This book has been composed in Miller

Printed on acid-free paper. ∞

Printed in the United States of America

10 9 8 7 6 5 4 3 2 1

To my ever-curious grandson

Alexander Knysh Jr.

CONTENTS

ILLUSTRATIONS AND DIAGRAMS

THE AUTHOR has used a simplified transliteration of Arabic, Persian, and Turkish names and terms that makes no distinction between emphatic and nonemphatic consonants (usually conveyed in specialized academic books by Latin letters with dots underneath). Macrons (short stroke marks above Latin vowels) to differentiate between the long and short vowels of the Arabic alphabet have not been used either. The Arabic letter *'ayn* is conveyed by a single quotation mark ('). The Arabic *hamza* in the middle or at the end of a word is marked by a closing quotation mark ('). The simplified transliteration was adopted by the author to facilitate the reception of the book by the reader with no prior knowledge of academic transcription conventions. Some exceptions apart, the author has adhered to the spelling of Muslim names and terms that is current in the English-speaking media. The dates are given according to the Common Era calendar (henceforth CE) preceded by the Muslim, Hijra(h), calendar equivalents.

ACKNOWLEDGMENTS

THIS BOOK owes its existence to the support of several academic institutions as well as the suggestions, insights, and help of the author's friends and colleagues. First, I am deeply indebted to the Helsinki Collegium for Advanced Studies whose administration kindly hosted me as a visiting fellow of the European Association of Institutes for Advanced Studies (EURIAS) in 2014–15. I am grateful to my colleagues at EURIAS for awarding me a generous research grant that allowed me to focus on my research for this book. Second, I would like to gratefully acknowledge the assistance and encouragement of my colleagues at the Saint Petersburg State University, especially the Rector's office and the leadership of the Oriental Faculty (*Vostochnyi fakul'tet*) whose commitment to advancing Islamic studies deserves the highest praise. Third, I thank the administrators of the University of Michigan for facilitating the completion of my book by granting me an academic leave in the fall of 2016. As far as individuals are concerned, I would like to extend my heartfelt thanks to Fred Appel, my editor at Princeton University Press, for his patient and benevolent guidance and encouragement. Had it not been for him, this book would have never seen the light of the day. I would also like to thank the anonymous reviewers of the manuscript of my book for their judicious and constructive analysis of its content and helpful suggestions for its improvement. My special thanks goes to Mrs. Evyn Kropf of the Hatcher Graduate Library of the University of Michigan for her help with identifying and copying the manuscript pages that were used as illustrations for my book. Last but not least, I am grateful to my wife Anna Knysh for her creative contributions to my thinking about Sufism, Islam, and religion in general. In particular, I cannot thank her enough for her assistance with the index, tables, and illustrations as well as her intellectual companionship throughout our married life. I dedicate this book to the youngest male member of our family, Alexander Knysh Jr. (better known as "Sashul'ka"). As the author, I bear full responsibility for any factual or printing errors that may have crept into my text.

For permission to quote material in my epigraphs, I gratefully acknowledge the following publishers: *Reassembling the Social: An Introduction to Actor-Network Theory* by Bruno Latour (2007), Oxford University Press; *Holy Terrors: Thinking about Religion after September 11*, Second Edition by Bruce Lincoln (2006), The University of Chicago Press; *Globalized Islam: The Search for a New Ummah* by Oliver Roy (2004), Columbia University Press and C. Hurst & Co., Ltd.

SUFISM

Introduction

How else can any past, which by definition comprises events, processes, structures, and so forth, considered to be no longer perceivable, be represented in either consciousness or discourse except in an "imaginary" way?

HAYDEN WHITE, *THE CONTENT OF THE FORM*

THIS BOOK IS ABOUT SUFISM, the ascetic-mystical stream in Islam that emerged at the very early stage of this religion's development and that subsequently took a wide variety of devotional, doctrinal, artistic, and institutional forms. Sufism's internal diversity has produced an equally wide variety of its assessments by both insiders and outsiders. They range from soberly detached and critical to empathetically enthusiastic and apologetic. Our study of the phenomenon of Sufism itself and its conceptualizations by various actors with vastly different intellectual and devotional agendas will reveal a great deal not just about Sufism but also about human beings' religious imagination more generally. What lies beyond this imagination does not concern us here. We leave it to believers, philosophers, and theologians to explore and appreciate.

Our task is to examine how Sufism has been imagined and, in the case of insiders, practiced based on this imagination, by various parties and actors since its inception up to the present. Our approach to the subject is inspired, in part, by Hayden White's (b. 1928) aforementioned statement about history as a product of imagining and emplotment[1] of facts and figures. The continual imagining and emplotting of the historical vicissitudes of the ascetic-mystical movement in Islam by insiders and outsiders allow us to discover ever-new nuances and aspects pertaining to it. The process of imagining and emplotting is also revealing of the changing cultural, societal, and aesthetic assumptions current in the societies whose members seek to conceptualize and explain the phenomenon of Sufism and the actions and statements of its followers. Excluding or delegitimizing one party to this collective act of imagining (for example, academic and nonacademic Orientalists, non-Muslim anthropologists of Muslim societies, or the Muslim fundamentalists/Salafis[2]) in favor of the other inevitably impoverishes our understanding of Sufism and Islam generally.[3] Moreover, as will be shown, in describing the ascetic-mystical stream in Islam, different actors with different intellectual backgrounds and sometimes incompatible methodologies and goals feed off each other's discourses, thus creating epistemological bricolages that are as fanciful and illuminating as they are puzzling or occasionally incredible.[4]

As some postmodernist[5] critics of history writing have claimed, cogently, "history is always history for someone, and that someone cannot be the past itself, for the past does not have a self."[6] Like all historians, historians of Sufism are not neutral observers: they always "take a stand within the world, [are] occupied with it, fascinated by it, overjoyed or horrified by it."[7] Prompted by their all-too-human (and humane) "care"[8] for the world, historians of Sufism "transform into ultimately imagined narratives a list of past events that would otherwise be only a collection of singular statements and/or a chronicle."[9] In other words, like all historians, students of Sufism are on a mission of emplotting disparate events and statements related to the object of their concern in order to convey their personal understanding of it, on the one hand, and perhaps also to teach us a certain moral-ethical lesson, on the other. This being so, they are usually deeply, inextricably, and passionately invested into their own storytelling.[10] The historians' act of arranging of events, statements, dates, and actors—usually depicted without any plot or logic in chronicles, literary works, or other historical documentation—has an obvious aim: to give these disparate pieces of historical evidence some "unity of significance."[11] How exactly this raw historical evidence is emplotted into narratives remains uncertain. Hayden White has discussed its transformation into history writing mostly in literary terms, arguing that a "narrative account is always a figurative account, an *allegory*" aimed at the translating or "carrying over" of meanings from one discursive community to another.[12] Whereas one does not have to agree with White on the predominantly literary nature of history writing, one can hardly deny that the success or failure of arranging raw historical evidence into a story depends, in the end, on its resonance or lack thereof with cultural and intellectual preferences of the members of the society in which a given historical account has been produced.[13] The same, of course, is true of any literary work.

It is probably in the spirit of such postmodernist conceptualizations of Western ("bourgeois") historiography as a work of fiction par excellence that in his seminal book on Sufism Carl Ernst has presented its modern understanding in the West as "an invention of late eighteenth-century European Orientalist scholarship."[14] Bearing in mind its origins in the subaltern studies, which purposefully aim at dislodging Western intellectual paradigms, we should take Ernst's deconstructive[15] statement cum grano salis, as the saying goes.[16] Sufism, no matter how fancifully construed and emplotted, was and still is quite real for its followers, opponents, and students, both inside and outside the Sufi tradition. What Sufis of Islam's "classical age" (the ninth to twelfth centuries CE) said, implied, or wrote about Sufism in Arabic, Persian, Turkish, or the other "languages of Islam" was diligently translated by the oft-criticized Orientalists of western and eastern Europe as well as Russia into the languages of their native cultures. In the process, the Orientalists *inevitably* couched the original Sufi ideas and practices into the cultural codes intelligible to their own societies.[17] The same applies to other phenomena within Islam, such as law, discursive theology, or the biography of the Prophet (*sira*).[18]

The repackaging of Muslim discourses into one or the other European cultural idiom was, in our view, largely a natural process by which European intellectuals sought to comprehend and convey to others a complex, multifaceted foreign culture and religion. In order to be understood and appreciated by the European and Russian reading publics of a given age, Islam and its various trends, including Sufism, had to be defined, classified, and presented in the intellectual conventions that would make sense to the intended recipients. Presenting Sufism on its own terms, namely, as it was professed by countless Sufi teachers and their disciples, was simply not an option for European and Russian scholars of Islam. First, there was no one uniformly accepted, transregional metanarrative about Sufism and Sufis in the premodern and modern Muslim world. There were, of course, numerous textbooks of Sufism or even dynastic histories composed from a Sufi perspective,[19] but they were socially, linguistically, and culturally specific to the regions where they originated and, to boot, hardly representative of the internally diverse Sufi movement in Islam as a whole. Mentions by Sufi authors and teachers of their predecessors reveal a genealogy of their thought and practice, but do not provide a comprehensive picture of how, when, and why Sufism had arisen and developed in time and space. Second, as already mentioned, when translated literally into Western languages, Sufi teachings and biographies would have no doubt fallen flat on European audiences. It is in this sense that a general notion of Sufism had to be "invented," or, rather, imagined and emplotted, by European Orientalists for an average European intellectual to understand and relate to his or her own cultural and intellectual background and life experience.

In weaving a coherent and accessible narrative about Sufism for European audiences, leading experts on "Oriental studies" from the nineteenth to the early twentieth centuries first had to undertake the painstaking task of collecting, editing, and annotating Sufi texts. After this intellectual spadework had been accomplished, they would venture some general observations that have become grist to the mill of present-day critics of Orientalism.[20] Finally, as we shall see throughout this book, medieval and modern Muslim writers both sympathetic and unsympathetic to Sufism tended to detach it from the rest of the Muslim tradition by presenting it being either its culmination or aberration. Therefore, to hold Westerners responsible for doing exactly the same, as Carl Ernst does,[21] is seeing the situation with one eye only, to borrow an image used by the great Muslim mystic Ibn (al-)'Arabi (d. 638/1240).[22]

On balance, one can submit that the biases[23] of Orientalist scholarship, although obvious to everyone with a modicum of knowledge of the subject, are no more or less severe than the biases of Sufis writing about their own doctrines and practices today as in the past. All writers, both insiders and outsiders, were, and still are, equally and deeply embedded in their own sets of power relations, cultural and social assumptions, and "oppressive [discursive] practices."[24] Like Muslim scholars advocating their fields of intellectual endeavor (for example, jurisprudence and theology), Sufi teachers were and still are eager to assemble a certain concept of Muslim ascetic-mystical piety and to present it as the only correct, orthodox one.[25] Equally obvious and unavoidable are biases of Sufism's Muslim opponents whose views of Sufism will be discussed in detail later on in this book. One, then, wonders what "an unbiased and authentic" account of Sufism, which Ernst implies is possible,[26] might look like.[27] In the end, the question boils down to whose biases are more preferable (or less distorting)—those of insiders or those of outsiders to the Sufi tradition? Some tentative answers to this question will be proposed in the present study.

To reiterate, what the European and Russian Orientalists of the nineteenth and early twentieth centuries did was to repackage for their respective reading publics, with various degrees of success and accuracy, the diverse Sufi and anti-Sufi discourses internal to the Muslim community at various stages of its evolution. In pursuing this educational goal (which was consonant with the spirit of the European Enlightenment), European students of Sufi texts[28] carefully preserved and reproduced the hidden and not-so-hidden biases inherent in their sources.[29] Simultaneously, they also injected into their renditions of original Muslim sources their own intellectual preferences and world-orientational convictions.[30] As should be abundantly clear from the recent critical examinations of Orientalism,[31] the Western scholars' biases were, in large part, shaped by the analytical categories that they used, because these categories were specific social-cultural constructs with particular genealogies of their own.[32] Thus, the very notion of "religion" itself, which had grown out of the specific experiences of Christian Europe, was widely used as "the fundamental yardstick or paradigm-case for the study of 'other religions.'"[33] The same applies to such categories as "mysticism" and "rational/irrational"[34] that are of direct relevance to our study of Sufism. An unreflective, summary application of such distinctly (western) European categories to non-Abrahamic traditions of India and the Far East has been even more problematic due to the vast disparity in the cultural and social sensitivities of Eastern and Western societies.[35]

Besides, as Edward Said and his numerous followers have shown, some practitioners of Orientalist scholarship in the nineteenth to early twentieth centuries did indeed pursue sometimes covert and sometimes obvious political and ideological agendas aimed at facilitating and justifying European colonization of the Muslim lands.[36] For example, a number of politically and ideologically engaged Orientalists in the service of the European and Russian colonial governments tended to exaggerate the militant, anti-Christian "resistance potential" of Islam generally and Sufism in particular.[37] In so doing, they followed, perhaps unwittingly, in the footsteps of medieval Christian detractors of Islam and Muslims.[38]

This said, the views of various cohorts of European students of Islam (summarily described by Said as "Orientalists") differed significantly, determined as they were by their professional responsibilities and various audiences to whom they addressed their discourses.[39] The situation in which nineteenth- and twentieth-century Orientalists found themselves is not dissimilar to that of today's Islamologists in Europe, the United States, and Russia, who, when called upon to comment on an "Islamic" event, wittingly or not, adjust their comments to the expectations and levels of understanding peculiar to their audiences. Thus, a Western scholar of Sufism today, when asked by state officials to explain why his or her study is important and how it is relevant to state policy toward various Muslim communities located inside and outside his or her native country, is likely to present a different image of Sufism from the one that he or she would in a lecture addressed to an audience of experts on the subject, in a college classroom, or while speaking to journalists. Any scholar who wants to be understood by a nonspecialist auditorium is under pressure to avoid nuances and prolixity, going straight to the heart of the matter, as it were.[40] This factor inevitably detracts from the complexity of the issues discussed, not to mention accuracy of his or her analysis. The image of Islam and Muslim societies is likely to be substantially different (usually more nuanced and self-reflective) in the scholar's academic works addressed to his or her intellectual peers. In short, one should keep in mind the diversity of consumers of Orientalist expertise, in addition to the sociopolitical positions and predilections of the experts. The experts have to weigh and adjust constantly and consciously their public pronouncements about Islam and Muslims or risk stepping on many sensitive toes and facing public outrage.

Finally, scholars, who in the nineteenth and early twentieth centuries served as colonial administrators, did indeed pursue definite professional goals (as do scholars today who are working for Western and Russian governments and think tanks). However, their discourses, in our opinion, should not be lumped together with those of academic Orientalists, who were under no immediate pressure to produce actionable or ideologically driven analyses.[41] So, before launching into a diatribe against their predecessors, today's experts on Islam and Muslim societies, who have taken Said's critique of Orientalism to heart, should determine which group of the Orientalists they are targeting in order not to paint them all with one brush. They should also take a long and hard look at their own knowledge production and knowledge deployment practices that are always situational, determined as they are by concrete circumstances, audiences, and venues. In short, every critical deconstruction of Orientalism should begin at home.

As for the role of nineteenth- and twentieth-century Orientalists in reconstructing Sufism's evolution in time and space, without their painstaking efforts our knowledge of the ascetic-mystical tradition in Islam today would have been much poorer and less comprehensive than it is.[42] We can agree or disagree with their descriptions of Sufism and/or Islam, but we should be grateful, not disdainful toward them, despite prejudices, errors, and blind spots that were as unavoidable in their time and age as they are in ours.[43] In the present book, the legacy of European and Russian Orientalists is treated as the fruit of the collective intellectual discovery[44] of Sufism that they shared with Sufis and Muslims generally, for no one, in our opinion, has the monopoly on exploring a subject that interests and excites them, even if, in hindsight, this exploration may appear to have been incomplete or biased. Richard King argues, and we agree, that a fruitful and illuminating study of religions by outsiders is possible, despite the cognitive gap between the subject and the object of study and with the proviso that academic scholars should not "claim ultimate jurisdiction in these matters."[45]

As for the "invented" character of Sufism in Orientalist discourses that Ernst and others have pointed out, it is no less or no more real or invented than such widely used concepts as "asceticism,"[46] "religion,"[47] "Neoplatonism,"[48] "Judeo-Christian tradition,"[49] or "Islam" itself.[50] All these intellectual abstracts and constructs, whether external or internal to the phenomenon in question, are made real (realized) by the actors who take them to heart, discuss, debate, teach, or implement. Sociologists and anthropologists have shown that to exist and to have staying power, ideas and practices have to be constantly enacted or performed by various groups of actors.[51] If a certain idea or practice is no longer enacted/performed by one group, it either vanishes or, as Bruno Latour has suggested, "the *other* actors have taken over the relay"[52] to sustain it in a different type (or site) of performance. The actors are, in other words, the real agents, not the abstracts and practices themselves. However, abstracts, constructs, and practices do matter as motivations, frameworks, and sources of arguments insofar as they are being reimagined, emplotted, and debated by various categories of participants who thereby help to sustain them. In this respect, the notions of "Sufism" and "Islam" are not different from any other abstractions created by human beings to serve as explanatory tools.[53]

Having just mentioned "Islam" alongside "Sufism," in the chapters that follow we treat the latter as "Islam in miniature." In other words, all the features of the encompassing larger tradition (Islam) are reflected in its ascetic-mystical stream (Sufism), albeit on a relatively smaller scale. We submit that, like Islam or any other religion for that matter, Sufism comprises the following major components:[54]

1. Teachings (discourses), both hegemonic and counterhegemonic, stabilizing and destabilizing, widely accepted and marginal;
2. Practices, defined by the teachings (discourses) and instrumental in the production and maintenance of certain world outlooks, values, lifestyles, cosmologies, and social orders;

3. Community of intellectual and, in the case of Sufism, also spiritual commitment that constitutes a source (and, occasionally, the primary source) of identity/subjectivity[55] for its followers;

4. Institutions that ensure the continuity of the Sufi stream of Islam by creating a propitious milieu for the cultivation, performance, and reproduction of its teachings/discourses and practices;

5. Leaders, who interpret the foundational teachings/discourses, supervise rituals, secure the functioning of institutions, and determine the overall direction of the religious tradition and/or community that they guide and represent.

The aim of this book is to explore these dimensions of the ascetic-mystical stream of Islam, or Sufism, without sliding into either unbridled partisanship or adverse criticism of the subject and of its conceptualizations by both insiders and outsiders.[56] As the hope of reaching "the heights of complete 'objectivity'" is unreachable by definition,[57] scholars, according to the British Buddhologist Richard King, should frankly acknowledge "their own 'pre-judgments,'" then attempt "to provide a balanced and fair portrayal of that in which they are claiming expertise," even if this attempt may entail expressing "alternate opinions" and challenging "perspectives offered by the religious traditions themselves."[58] Our hope is that the relative impartiality of our approach to Sufism and Islam generally is assured by our lack of any personal stake in either. The American philosopher and psychologist William James (1842–1910), citing the great Muslim theologian al-Ghazali (d. 505/1111),[59] has argued that "to understand the causes of drunkenness, as a physician understands them, is not to be drunk."[60] Likewise, to understand Sufism, one does not have to "imbibe" and "digest" its principles with a view to implementing them in practice. On the contrary, to maintain a modicum of objectivity, one should remain immune to Sufism's potent allure. This detached, nonparticipatory kind of understanding, limited and limiting as it may appear, does have the right to exist. This is exactly our position: that of an outsider looking inside the "Abode of Islam/Sufism" without embroiling him or herself in debates about its true essence or what constitutes correct or incorrect Muslim or Sufi doctrine and practice.

This said, one can never hope to avoid having personal intellectual preferences, simply because they are humanly inescapable. Our approach to Sufism and Islam has been shaped by our lifelong academic study of Islam and Muslim societies. In the course of this study we have grown increasingly weary of the rampant ideological partisanship that has been the hallmark of the field of Islamic studies over that past few decades.[61] While being cognizant of the fact that partisan approaches to Islam and the Muslims in the academic world and beyond are unavoidable under the current geopolitical and cultural conditions, we have endeavored, to the extent this is possible, to steer clear of ideologically and personally driven debates over Islam's and Sufism's true nature and orthodoxy (or a lack thereof). This does not mean that they are ignored. On the contrary, these debates are given serious consideration as long as they are germane to the issues raised in this book.[62] For us, these debates are but evidence that should be treated objectively and impartially, not arbitrated, nor taken sides with or against. It is certainly true that any serious scholar of Sufism and/or Islam is not immune to a certain level of empathy for his or her subject. Nevertheless, our overall position is to try to keep our personal preferences to ourselves as much as possible.

On the methodological plane, we are not wedded to any particular theory for its own sake. Conversant with the latest methodologies offered by sociologists, anthropologists, literary critics, cultural historians, and adepts of so-called subaltern studies, we employ this or that method and theory only as long as it sheds new light on the aspects of the subject that would otherwise have remained invisible or underappreciated. At the same time, we are convinced that none of the methods or theories mentioned or applied in the narrative that follows is sufficient to explain such as a complex and multifaceted phenomenon as Sufism, not to mention Islam as a whole. New theories offered by social sciences and the humanities can indeed be of great help in that they allow the investigator to see one and the same event, personality, or concept from a variety of vantage points, which occasionally, but not always, can be quite illuminating. Furthermore, Islam and Islamic studies should not, in our opinion, be the limit in telling a comprehensive story of Sufism and its five components enumerated above. Methods used and insights obtained in academic fields and contexts outside Islamic studies proper often prove to be extremely helpful in exploring the ascetic-mystical stream of Islam. Therefore, in this book we will be drawing parallels between Sufi Islam and other religious traditions as well as Sufism and secular ideological systems.[63] This perspective should help us to avoid the common trend among scholars of Islam to focus on "things Islamic," while ignoring rich opportunities for comparative analysis offered by other religions and cultures. The lack of such a comparative perspective, as will be shown, is in part a result of the ideological self-censure performed by scholars out of a misguided (in our opinion at least) sense of political correctness or for apologetic considerations.

The main objective of this book is to give an accessible, while also nuanced, account of Sufism as a system of thought and action. The chronological scope is from Sufism's beginnings in the second/eighth century to the present day. Because our approach to Sufism is novel in many respects and departs from the traditional historicist and positivist perspective that we adopted in our earlier works, we have titled our study *Sufism: A New History of Islamic Mysticism*. Whether this title accurately reflects the content is for the reader to judge.

In order not to digress from the plot lines in the main body of this book, a definition of several key concepts that inform our analytic framework is in order. We treat Sufism as an ascetic-mystical movement, stream, or trend within Islam (both Sunni and Shi'i). Our choice of the hyphenated definition indicates our reluctance to separate strictly and unequivocally "ascetic" beliefs and practices from those commonly understood as "mystical."[64] This separation takes its origins in Max Weber's concept of early Islam as "this-worldly asceticism of a warrior group" that was later somehow "adulterated by Sufism which catered for the emotional and orgiastic needs of the masses."[65] Basing himself on this initial axiom, Weber defined Sufism as "other-worldly mysticism" that was derived "from Hindu and Persian sources" and that "in no case did constitute 'asceticism' in the special sense of the term which we have employed."[66] Although adopted by a number of present-day Islamologists,[67] such a neat and occasionally useful dichotomy is, in our opinion, unsustainable.[68] The same applies to Weber's concurrent dichotomy of "ascetic virtuoso" versus "mystical virtuoso."[69]

Renouncing this world often entails reorienting oneself to the world to come and, as a consequence, attempts to experience visionary glimpses or even somatic sensations of its glories and pleasures (for example, seeing God, partaking of paradisiacal fruits, drinks, and delicacies, embracing houris, and such) already in this life.[70] The purpose of ascetic self-discipline and self-imposed strictures is, as numerous Sufi masters have argued for centuries, to purify the soul and to prepare it for a vision of or communion/communication with God here and now.[71] That this originally Platonic idea was adopted by some early Christian thinkers (for example, by Justin Martyr, 100–165 CE) is evidenced by their descriptions of "the soul's return to God through purification (*askēsis*) followed by contemplative vision (*theōria*)."[72] In other words, the desire to "starve out or punish the animal elements of the human condition" exhibited by early Christian monks (those "athletes of Christ")[73] has always been supported by "a highly articulated [mystical] theology."[74]

Therefore, distilling asceticism and mysticism into two "ideal types"[75] may be helpful and elegant at first sight, but, at closer look, fails to account adequately for the messiness and originality of the thought and practice of real-life "spiritual athletes." After examining the statements of early Muslim heresiographers, the German Islamologist Bernd Radtke (b. 1944) has unequivocally linked the ascetic practices and self-imposed strictures of early Muslims to their mystical aspirations and goals.[76] In fact, the two usually went hand in hand and were inseparable. The early Muslim heresiographers cited by Radtke considered both ascetic feats and mystical aspirations of the first Muslim pietists to be equally objectionable insofar as they had the potential to entice some gullible members of the Muslim community into thinking of themselves as God's beloveds, thereby causing them to neglect their religious duties. Much later, the renowned advocates of Sunni "orthodoxy" Ibn Taymiyya (d. 728/1328) and al-Dhahabi (d. 748/1348) also conflated asceticism and mysticism by mentioning certain individuals who acted simultaneously "on the basis of the asceticism and Sufism of the philosophers."[77] At the same time, Muslim scholars such as Ibn Khaldun (d. 808/1406)[78] believed that "philosophizing Sufis" had corrupted "the originally pious tradition of *zuhd*" with their mystical metaphysics.[79] This view was reproduced by Western students of Islam, such as Louis Massignon (1883–1962) and Christopher Melchert, both of whom have argued that asceticism is not the same as mysticism and vice versa. According to Massignon, for example, by diluting the originally pure ascetic tradition of Islam with Neoplatonic metaphysics, later followers of Sufism sacrificed its suprarational, emotional impulse and directness. As a result, Sufism turned into a sterile scholastic theology.[80] As for the Sufis themselves, they have never tired of emphasizing an intimate link between the Sufi's "action(s) and elegant deeds of devotion," on the one hand, and the "divinely-inspired knowledge" bestowed on him by God, on the other.[81] In any event, the very dynamic of merger and separation of asceticism and mysticism in insider and outsider accounts of Sufism is indicative of the two being, essentially, conterminous and complementary.

Similar conclusions about the relationship between ascetic and mystical belief and behavior have been reached by scholars of Christianity. Thus, the major expert on Western Christian mysticism Bernard McGinn (b. 1937) has argued that "rather than being something added on to mystical experience, mystical theory in most cases *precedes and guides* [emphasis ours—A. K.] the mystic's whole way of life."[82] This way of life, as McGinn's multivolume project demonstrates, invariably requires that Christian devotees engage in ascetic exercises and rigorous self-discipline (defined as "monasticism," "penance," and "absolute poverty") with a view to "attaining the 'loving knowledge of God.'"[83] In other words, the ascetics' arduous feats of perseverance and self-disciplining strictures, according to McGinn, inevitably produce "visualizations," "contemplations," and ecstatic "trances." Thus, both ascetic practice and mystical longing for God are equally necessary for the devotees to achieve their destination.[84] A similar opinion was articulated by Vladimir Lossky (1903–1958) in his study of the mystical aspects of Eastern Orthodox Christianity. In his rather apologetic description of Russian Orthodoxy, he argued, among other things, that mystical theology constitutes the very core of its faith and practice.[85] In sum, ascetic life and mystical theology are inseparable and feed off each other. The conclusions reached by McGinn and Lossky, as well as numerous other scholars of Christianity, apply neatly to the ascetic-mystical tradition in Islam. Like their Christian brothers-in-spirit, medieval Muslim devotees organically combined, albeit in varying degrees, ascetic practices (or "bodily regimes/praxis" as they are often dubbed in today's Western scholarship[86]) with mystical speculations about God and his relations with his human creatures.[87]

Should one still insist that there is an obvious heuristic validity to the asceticism-mysticism dichotomy, we can suggest that the former is more about disciplining the human appetitive soul or *anima*[88] (by means of vows, vigils, fasting, and other self-imposed rigors and penances),[89] whereas the latter is more about imagining and experiencing "symbolic" cosmologies[90] as well as an often ingenious linking of concrete ascetic actions to broader, and loftier, cosmic contexts and goals.[91] Concisely put: asceticism is primarily about body, whereas mysticism is primarily about mind; however, the two are usually merged organically in one and the same personality and are thus inseparable, except for heuristic purposes. To go against one's natural instincts one has to have a really good cause.[92] Therefore, in unison with McGinn, Lossky, and others, we submit that one cannot engage in ascetic "bodily regimes" without a mystical theology or metaphysics (that is, a "symbolic universe"),[93] no matter how rudimentary, unstructured, or illogical. Whereas discoursing about mystical experience usually falls within the rubric of "mysticism" or "mystical theology,"[94] with asceticism being commonly conceived as practice par excellence, separating them may distract us from their organic coexistence and interdependence.[95] As already mentioned, subduing one's appetitive nature demands a really good cause, in our case, either salvation or intimacy/union with

God. However, we admit that occasionally such a separation may come in handy for educational purposes, for example, framing Sufism as a sequential progression from simpler to more sophisticated forms of belief and practice.

Nevertheless, one has to acknowledge that differences between "asceticism" or "renunciation of the world" (Arab. *nusk*; *taqashshuf*; *zuhd [fi 'l-dunya]*) and "mysticism" (*'irfan*; *kashf*; *hikma*) were as real for medieval Muslim scholars as they are for modern-day Islamologists.[96] Moreover, recent scholarship on the subject has suggested that one could pursue a rigorous type of ascetic piety without ever engaging in mystical speculations or attaching oneself to a Sufi community or spiritual lineage (*silsila*).[97] Such assumptions notwithstanding, the two more often than not go hand in hand,[98] which, in our view, warrants bringing them together in a hyphenated phrase. The usefulness and viability of numerous other terms and concepts pertinent to the ascetic-mystical movement in Islam are discussed in what follows. In particular, the ideologically driven contractions and expansions of the term "Sufism" itself constitute the subject matter of chapter 1 of this book.

This study has been inspired, in large part, by the author's editorial work for E. J. Brill's monumental *Encyclopedia of Islam* (*EI*). To its erudite, eloquent, and perceptive contributors he owes a profound debt of gratitude. In the process of editing submissions to the section "Sufism" of the *Encyclopedia of Islam*'s third edition (*EI3*), he has had a unique chance to observe the overall evolution of the academic field of Sufi studies, a subfield of Islamic studies, or "Islamology/Islamologie," as it is sometimes dubbed in the European and Russian academe. One important advantage of his editorial duties was that they allowed the author to discover new scholarship on Sufism and Islam generally. This does not mean that the insights of the contributors to the *EI3* have been simply integrated into this monograph. Most of the entries edited by the author were too narrow in their focus to serve as the foundation of a general analytic survey of Sufism such as the one intended here. The author's task was to synthesize disparate facts about Sufism in order to produce, hopefully, a cohesive and comprehensive whole.

The Gist

1. In exploring various manifestations of the phenomenon called "Sufism" (*tasawwuf*), one should bring together both "internal" and

"external" perspectives on it that are often being intricately engaged in conversations with one another.

2. Sufism is "Islam in miniature" with the major features of Sufism present in Islam and vice versa. This being the case, Sufism, like Islam, comprises all the major components of a religious tradition, namely, teachings/discourses, practices, communities, institutions, and leaders.

3. The author has strived to steer clear of both barefaced apologetics and theological criticism of Sufism, seeking impartiality and objectivity as far as humanly possible.

4. The author takes a holistic approach to Sufism by refusing to separate its ascetic and mystical elements, in particular Sufi teachings from Sufi practices. The two always go hand in hand and are reciprocal. Hence, the author's use of the hyphenated adjective "ascetic-mystical" in describing and analyzing various components and manifestations of Sufism.

5. The book summarizes the major insights that the author has acquired in working as an editor of the *Encyclopedia of Islam*'s third edition (E. J. Brill, Leiden and Boston), the seminal reference for the field of Islamic studies today.[99]

CHAPTER ONE

How and Why Sufism Came to Be

Scriptural Grounds and Authoritative Precedents

Sufis never tire of insisting that their teachings and practices are rooted in the Qur'an, the Prophet's exemplary "custom" (*sunna*), and the moral-ethical standards set by the first two generations of Muslims.[1] Indeed, the Muslim scripture features many passages encouraging Muslims to behave modestly, remember God often, love him as he loves his creatures, not for a moment to be distracted by commerce or other mundane concerns from remembering him, and, in general, to prefer the world to come to the deceptive allure of the imperfect, transient, and treacherous earthly existence.[2] The Qur'an constantly presents righteous fear of God (*taqwa*), a major characteristic of ascetic-mystical piety in the Abrahamic religions, as a sine qua non for all faithful.[3] Some Qur'anic passages may be interpreted as praising the world-renouncing and God-fearing demeanor of Christian monks.[4] To the pious and God-fearing "friends of God" (*awliya'*) among the Muslims themselves God promises his loving care and protection.[5] Moreover, the Qur'an implies that these pious individuals constitute a special category of believers whose wholehearted devotion to God has absolved them from the horrors of the Judgment Day described so vividly in the Muslim holy book.[6] Unlike ordinary believers, "none should fear for them, nor shall they sorrow (or grieve) [on the Day of Judgment]."[7] In general, the Qur'an insists that fear of God and the resultant avoidance of this life's sensual enticements is "the proper deportment of the faithful."[8]

Similar ideas abound in the Prophet's "exemplary way" (*sunnat al-nabi*) as recorded in the Hadith.[9] The Hadith depict the Prophet as a paragon of piety and renouncer of worldly delights: he goes hungry for two days, breaking his fast on the third day only, eats frugally, never allows himself the food he enjoys most (for example, wheat bread), washes and mends his own clothes, engages in supererogatory (additional) acts of piety,[10] keeps night vigils, and so on.[11] Even more significantly, he receives his first divine revelation while being in a contemplative retreat on the mountain outside Mecca,[12] to which he retires to escape mundane disturbances and to engage in pious meditation and ascetic self-discipline (*tahannuth*).[13] In an oft-quoted Hadith, the Prophet encourages his followers "to be in this world as though you were a traveler or passerby and count yourself from among the dead."[14] In a similar vein, he consistently discourages gaiety and laughter, while advising sadness and contrition in anticipation of the Day of Judgment.[15] Collections of reports about the life of the primeval *umma* ascribe analogous ascetic, world-renouncing inclinations to some of the Prophet's closest companions,[16] including his successors ("caliphs") at the head of the nascent Muslim state.[17] In sum, Muslim ascetics-mystics who consider the Prophet and his companions to be their forerunners have no trouble finding scriptural and other authoritative evidence to legitimize their world-renouncing and self-abnegating beliefs and practices. Not surprisingly, Western observers, too, have discovered in the history of the early Muslim community elements of "this-worldly asceticism," although, in line with the Western perception of Islam as the religion of the sword, they tended to describe it as being of a predominantly "martial," "warrior" character.[18]

On the other hand, Muslim opponents of ascetic-mystical practices have had no difficulty finding the Qur'anic verses and the Prophet's pronouncements that contain exactly the opposite message. These foundational sources of Islamic faith and practice describe human beings as creatures whom God destined to enjoy the good things of this life, albeit in moderation: "O Children of Adam! Wear your beautiful apparel at every place of prayer. Eat and drink, but waste not by excess, for God loves not the wasters" (7:31).[19] The Qur'an depicts its followers as the community (*umma*) of the "just mean" or "the middle way" (*wasat*)[20] who should be keeping balance between worshiping God and enjoying the licit pleasures of this life.[21] Being wealthy is not shameful as long as one shares his or her riches with less fortunate members of the *umma* and fulfills his or her duties toward God.[22] In contradistinction to Christian monastic celibacy, Muslim men, no matter how pious, are encouraged to marry and have children, whom they are obligated to support by pursing a gainful employment.[23]

In accord with the aforementioned principle of the just or golden mean, Muslims should avoid extremes, including all manner of self-imposed strictures, purposeless wandering,[24] or voluntary poverty.[25] The Prophet is quoted saying, "When God favors a person with property, He likes the person to show it."[26] A good number of the Prophet's closest companions were wealthy, and some very rich indeed.[27] The Prophet himself was a trader, whom God granted his job to rescue him from poverty.[28] The same Qur'anic passage that contains an apparently favorable mention of the God-fearing Christian monks is also critical of their self-abnegating "excesses."[29] A later tradition has the Prophet declare, "There is no monasticism (*rahbaniyya*) in Islam; the monasticism of this community is *jihad*."[30] A similar attitude, albeit on purely rational grounds, is demonstrated by the first Arab-Muslim philosopher Abu Yusuf Ya'qub al-Kindi (d. around 252/866). He rejects the self-imposed strictures practiced by the Hindus, Manichaeans, and Christian monks, all of whom "resist the urge for sex, weaken themselves through hunger and thirst, withdraw from the world in cloisters . . . give up daily affairs, limit themselves to a small amount of unpalatable food, and to wearing painful and uncomfortable clothes." For al-Kindi, "all such behavior is just a form of self-oppression and self-harm" that, unlike medical surgery, dietary avoidance of tasty food, or swallowing a bitter medicine, does not help one to prevent a greater pain. This being the case, concludes al-Kindi, ascetic excesses are unnecessary, harmful, and irrational.[31] Contradicting his own conclusions about Islam's alleged focus on otherworldly mystical contemplation discussed in the introduction to this book, Max Weber occasionally presented "the Muslim tradition" as encouraging "the luxurious raiment, perfume, and meticulous beard-coiffure of the pious" and discouraging "every type of monasticism, though not all asceticism."[32] Weber's confusion is understandable: both the Qur'an and the "Muslim tradition" (especially, the Sunna of the Prophet) do indeed carry contradictory messages regarding the proper attitude to worldly life to be practiced by the faithful.

On the one hand, the Qur'an asks, "What is the life of this world except the enjoyment of delusion" (3:185) and lauds "those who repent, those who praise [God], those who journey,[33] those who prostrate themselves in worship, those who command what is right and forbid what is wrong, those who keep God's bounds" (9:112). On the other, sura 55 ("The Beneficent") recounts for the believers the numerous material blessings bestowed on them by God—a message brought home by the constantly repeated refrain: "Which of your Lord's bounties will you [two] deny?"[34] In short, in and of themselves wealth and enjoyment of life are not evil or improper. Wealth can and should be enjoyed as long as it has been properly "purified" by paying alms or spent "in the path of God" (Q 2:261–65).[35] Yet the surest way to God, according to the Qur'an, is to obey and worship him: "[women] who are faithful, surrendered themselves [to God], obedient, penitent, worshipful, journeying, who have been married and [who are] virgins" (66:5). Whereas the meaning of the word "journey" / "journeying" in this list of meritorious acts and character traits is not quite clear, it may well have referred to the practice of "pious wandering" that some devout early Muslims shared with itinerant Christian ascetics and monks.[36] The presence of those in the region is so amply attested as to absolve us from belaboring the issue any further.[37]

Such ambiguous scriptural references and contradictory historical precedents have been grist for the mill of heated debates over the legitimacy of the ascetic-mystical strain of Islam almost since its very inception.[38] As one can expect, the legitimacy (or lack thereof) of world-renouncing and world-denigrating attitudes to mundane existence depends heavily on the personal inclinations and intellectual background of the interpreter, or, simply put, is in the eye of the beholder. Therefore, the issue of legitimacy or illegitimacy of the ascetic-mystic interpretation of Islam stands little chance of ever being resolved, because its resolution depends on the sort of ideological glasses the beholder happens to sport. What one cannot deny is that the Muslim scripture and the precedent-setting history of the early Muslim community contain evidence that yields itself to disparate, if not diametrically opposed, understandings. The only constant is the will to interpret this evidence, and this has never been in short supply.

Why? The Argument from the "Temperament"

After discussing some scriptural and historical precedents for the rise of ascetic-mystical tendencies in the early Muslim community, the logical question arises as to why some Muslims were inclined to adopt and cultivate world-renouncing attitudes and mystical aspirations in the first place. An interesting explanation was proposed by the American scholar Marshall Hodgson (1922–1968), who argued that to thrive and expand a religion should be able to accommodate the widest possible spectrum of human temperaments.[39] According to Hodgson, if some believers are not allowed to practice, within a given religious environment, the type of piety[40] that resonates with their temperamental disposition, they are likely to be lost to this religion as they will be compelled to seek a more accommodating environment elsewhere. In our case, if a Muslim of world-renouncing and mystical propensities cannot find his or her "temperamental niche" in Islam, he or she is likely to turn to another religion. All the more so because in the Middle East and Eurasia, such accommodations were available in monastic Christianity, Manichaeism, or Buddhism. In Hodgson's view, Muslims of different personal inclinations took vastly different approaches to the historical act of Islam[41] by interpreting it "in all the directions that the full range of human temperament might suggest."[42] Relevant to our subject, to successfully compete with its religious rivals, Islam had to develop its own version of world-renouncing piety in order to capture and retain within its fold individuals of an ascetic-mystical "temperament."[43]

Accepting Hodgson's explanation hardly resolves the issue, because it raises a number of fraught questions. One can ask, for example, whether Hodgson's theory of accommodation of different temperaments by religious traditions holds true for the ascetic-mystical stream in Judaism? Can we confidently argue, for instance, that Judaism or, rather, its learned leaders, the rabbis, were indeed interested in drawing into the ranks individuals of ascetic-mystical propensities regardless of their ethnic background? Experts on Judaism are likely to answer this question in the negative, citing the fact that Judaism was and still is hardly interested in casting the widest possible net to "catch" outsiders (non-Jews) of various temperaments and to keep them within its fold.[44]

The example of Judaism just cited does not necessarily negate Hodgson's thesis. It only problematizes its universal applicability. After all, one may argue, in many respects, Judaism is unique, being intimately linked as it is to the ethnic identity of "the Children of Israel." Other religious traditions, one can argue, were and are much more interested than Judaism in attracting new followers and keeping the existing ones within their bounds. Therefore, they willy-nilly have to be responsive to temperamental needs of both extant followers and new recruits. If so, then Hodgson indeed has a point. Furthermore, his thesis seems to find confirmation in our own quotidian experience that tells us that people do possess different psychological predispositions and, therefore, are likely to seek congenial environments to nurture them. If, following Hodgson, individuals with certain personal inclinations can find such an environment in Islam, they are likely to stay within its fold. Conversely, if the conditions offered by Islam turn out to be unconducive to their needs, they are likely to be attracted to a religious tradition that is more welcoming to their temperament.

Plausible as Hodgson's thesis may appear at first blush, one must point out that in the overwhelming majority of cases in the premodern and even modern epochs people were brought up Muslims or Sufis, not "programmed" automatically to look for a religious identity suitable for their psychological needs. Ergo, instead of seeking accommodation outside Islam, they were much more likely to deliberately create and cultivate their preferred religious attitude within the confines of their native community of religious commitment. The way Hodgson frames the issue may indicate that his thesis was shaped, probably unconsciously, by his very Western (and even more so American!) concept of a free individual exercising his or her own free choice that resonates with his or her innate inclinations and convictions (or "temperament," in Hodgson's own parlance). In the final account, Hodgson's thesis concerning "temperaments" is acceptable in principle with the following proviso: ascetically and mystically inclined Muslims actively and consistently sought to carve out an "ecological niche" for themselves within their own religious and social environment. That they could easily justify their efforts by invoking Islam's foundational texts and authoritative historical precedents has already been demonstrated.

Let us now turn to some other explanations of the rise and persistence of the ascetic-mystical movement in Muslim societies during the first centuries of Islam and throughout the rest of its history.

The Vexed Issue of the Origins

It is a widely known fact that on the eve of Islam the Middle East and North Africa were home to several highly developed and sophisticated traditions of ascetic-mystical piety. Judaism was one such tradition.[45] Even more prominent in this respect was Christianity[46] which had inherited its ascetic, world-renouncing attitudes not only from Judaism but also from the pagan traditions of the Greco-Roman world, especially the Cynics and Stoics.[47] Given the well-documented, and natural, tendency of human collectivities to borrow ideas, technologies, and practices from one another,[48] it stands to reason that certain members of the early Muslim community found something attractive in the behavior and beliefs of the Christian monks and desert hermits of Egypt, Syria, Arabia, and Mesopotamia.[49] The fact that early Sufis admired the devout and self-abnegating beliefs and practices of Christian monks of various denominations is abundantly attested in medieval Sufi literature.[50] The exact factors that prompted early Muslims to borrow ascetic and mystical beliefs and practices from their neighbors remain an intriguing and, to some, also vexing question. As mentioned in the previous section, Hodgson has attributed the rise of ascetic-mystical beliefs and practices in the early Muslim community to the temperamental inclinations of some of its members who, in his view, would have otherwise been lost to other religions, in particular to Christian monasticism.

The British scholar of early Christianity and Islam, Margaret Smith (1884–1970), not only recognized the Christian roots of Muslim ascetic-mystical piety but also pointed out the possible role of the Christian wives of the Arab conquerors in steering their Muslim children toward "the habits of life of the Christian solitaries and monks."[51] According to Smith, the high opinion that Muslim ascetics and mystics had of the beliefs and practices of Christian monks in the Middle East was "genetically" inherited, as it were, or, to be more precise, transmitted and reproduced through household upbringing and socialization.

Other Western scholars of Sufism focused their attention on the tumultuous socioeconomic conditions of the early Muslim state. They construed these conditions as the primary reason why some early pious Muslims attempted to escape from this imperfect world into an "internal immigration," that is, into a life of seclusion, social aloofness, and mystical meditation.[52] The ubiquitous presence of Christian monasteries and itinerant monks in Egypt, Syria, and Mesopotamia made contacts between early Muslims and all manner of Christian devotees not just possible, but, in fact, unavoidable.[53] Denying Muslim-Christian interactions and mutual borrowings in these areas is counterintuitive and goes against the grain not only of historical evidence but of human nature as well.

Although the assumption about the borrowing or imitating by some pious members of the early Muslim community of monastic practices and beliefs seems entirely plausible, it has not met with a uniform acceptance by students of Sufism.[54] The reasons for this puzzling fact are purely ideological. Admitting foreign, especially Christian, influences on Islam and its ascetic-mystical stream in particular could be easily construed by some members of the public both inside and outside the Muslim community as casting doubt on Islam's self-sufficiency and ability to develop its own "vaulted spiritually" and "sophisticated philosophy" that Sufi Islam is often seen as representing.[55] Unsurprisingly, some modern-day admirers of Sufism, Muslims and non-Muslims alike, find suggestions about Sufism's "foreign roots" offensive to "the majesty that was Islam"[56] and thus erroneous.[57]

The assumption that Sufism has organically emerged from the pristine sources of Islam, is captured in the famed assertion by the French Isla-mologist Louis Massignon, according to which, "The Qur'an, through con-stant recitation, meditation, and practice, is the source of Islamic mysti-cism, at its beginning and throughout its growth."[58] The fact that Massignon's thesis sounds more rhetorical than factual and that his own investigations seem to have vitiated it[59] is ignored by the advocates of Su-fism's "Qur'anic roots."[60]

Massignon was no doubt right about the centrality of the Qur'an to the Muslim intellectual and spiritual universe generally and the Sufi version of it in particular,[61] but this is hardly the whole picture. The fact that Sufi beliefs and practices are couched in Qur'anic terminology[62] does not au-tomatically imply that they take provenance in the Qur'an alone. On the contrary, as a Western scholar of (proto-)Sufism has aptly remarked, "If the Qur'an is the ground of [Islamic] mysticism, then Qur'anic piety itself builds, in important ways, on Christian foundations,"[63] albeit, one should add, thoroughly adapted to the Qur'an's overall Weltanschauung.[64] As re-gards asceticism-mysticism, the Qur'anic references to monks and their beliefs and practices, which have been cited above, are evidence enough that monasticism and Christianity more generally were already part and parcel of the Qur'an's symbolic universe.[65] The scriptural evidence con-cerning monasticism being, as shown, ambivalent, there is little wonder that early Muslims paid close attention to the monks' beliefs and practices in order to determine which of these were acceptable and which had better be avoided. For comparison, the whole project of "the Jesus movement" consisted in recasting the Jewish tradition according to the precepts and demands of the new cult.

If we abstract ourselves for a moment from the ideological underpin-nings of the fraught debate over the origins of Sufism, we will have to ac-knowledge the improbability of the very idea that Islam, whose sources were so deeply rooted in the pre-Islamic belief systems of the Mediterra-nean region, could have remained immune to ascetic-mystical trends in the local versions of Christianity.[66] The same, perhaps to a lesser extent, is true of Judaic, Neoplatonic, Manichaean influences as well as those as-sociated with the amorphous esoteric/gnostic tradition known as "Hermeticism."[67]

This said, the debt that (proto-)Sufism[68] owes to the beliefs and prac-tices of its pre-Islamic ascetic-mystical precursors can indeed be cited by its opponents to undermine its credibility in the eyes of certain groups of

Muslims.[69] This being the case, the unwitting or deliberate obfuscation of the obvious (which occasionally amounts to self-censure) is driven primarily by polemical or apologetic considerations. The only way to achieve a modicum of objectivity in this matter is for scholars of Sufism to disengage, deliberately and consciously, from the pro- or contra-Sufi polemical agendas. To what extent this is possible in practice is a different matter.

In this connection, one may ask if Christianity's dependence on Judaism for its texts and forms of worship in any way diminishes its stature as a world religion? More pertinent to our purpose, does the acceptance of some Manichaean ideas (for example, the strict separation of spirit and matter and the notion of body as a vessel of vices) by the early medieval monks of Mesopotamia and Syria[70] demote them to the status of blind imitators of Mani or render them less authentically Christian? If the answer is "no," then why should not the same apply to Islam in general and (proto-)Sufism in particular? Seen from this vantage point, the ongoing debates over the Islamic or non-Islamic roots of ascetic-mystical Islam are but a product of today's polemical and apologetic agendas. It is true that these debates have improved our knowledge of the subject, in particular, of the religious and cultural background of the primeval ascetic-mystical movement in Islam. In the final account, however, by insisting on the "autochthonous" Islamic/Qur'anic origins of such a complex and variegated phenomenon as Sufism, we run the risk of ignoring the obvious for the sake of a wrongly construed notion of political correctness.

To return to Hodgson's thesis about the role of the human temperament in the formation of religious traditions. If we admit that the availability of temperamental accommodations within a religious tradition does matter and that, to be competitive, early Islam (or, to be more exact, its followers) sought to expand its recruitment base by creatively adopting and adapting the ascetic-mystical beliefs and practices current in the Mediterranean basin in late antiquity, then the question arises why this ascetic-mystical piety has turned out to be so successful and persistent in the long run? Hodgson's "temperament thesis" is insufficient to answer this question. In fact, empirical observations show that "natural-born" ascetics and mystics are but a tiny minority not only in any human collectivity of our own epoch but also in the premodern age. As our subsequent discussion is bound to demonstrate, Sufism's popular appeal and recruitment capacity were far broader than Hodgson's thesis seems to admit. At work were deeper and complex social mechanisms that scholars of Islam have been at pains to account for.

The Issue of Motivation: Sufism as Escapism and Passive Protest?

Writing in 1896, the influential Russian Ukrainian scholar Agafangel Krymskii (1871–1942) stated, poignantly: "[My] painstaking study of the spirit of Sufi writings has driven me to the conclusion that the reasons for the spread of the Sufi doctrine can be limited to socio-economic [conditions]. . . . The periods of the greatest flourishing of Sufism coincide with the times of the most horrendous suffering of the popular masses."[71] Krymskii's statement captures the gist of the materialist-Marxist explanation of the rise and flourishing of the ascetic-mystical movement in Islam. It is informed by Marx's famous axiom that declares religion to be "the opium of the people," that is, their illusory consolation and last recourse against the injustices and cruelties of everyday life that is characterized by the exploitation of underprivileged social classes by privileged ones.[72] According to Krymskii, following the upheavals and turmoil caused by the Arab conquests, the emerging ascetic-mystical movement helped the downtrodden and disenfranchised populace to cope with rampant injustices of the dynastic-military rule of, first, the Umayyads, and later of the 'Abbasids. Seen from this vantage point, the early ascetic-mystical movement in Islam ([proto-]Sufism) was a natural escape route for the oppressed Muslim masses from the intolerable realities of their daily existence. That this explanatory paradigm is not confined to Sufism is confirmed by the statement of a renowned scholar of early Christian asceticism and monasticism in Syria and Iraq, who argues that:

> In the disorderly conditions of the Orient [during the first centuries of the Christian era], which was leading even toward the growing impoverishment of the masses . . . Syrian monasticism acted as a rescue squad. In the ocean of human need and suffering it prepared its huts, cells and monasteries as islands within which the afflicted could find understanding, care and help. Nor did it shrink back from using its prestige to challenge the civil powers in the interest of the suppressed and rightless ones.[73]

Examples of such materialist explanations of the emergence of ascetic-mystical movements in the Mediterranean world and beyond can be easily multiplied.[74] In reference to the early history of Islam and Sufism in particular, this explanation requires some adjustments, though. The first Muslim ascetics and mystics (proto-Sufis) were hardly the most indigent and downtrodden members of the Muslim community. Many of them were merchants, stall-keepers, traders, and craftsmen and, thus, part of the "middle class," if this term is appropriate for the age in question. Others were religious professionals: Qur'an readers, Hadith collectors, preachers, and jurists.[75] Nevertheless, one can still argue that their exemplary self-abnegating behavior inspired the downtrodden masses to (re-)focus their thoughts on the future life and its rewards, while forgetting about their sufferings here and now. Even with this adjustment the argument still rests on the Marxist idea that religion's primary raison d'être is to "compensate" human beings for the frustrations in their earthly life by relegating their rewards to the hereafter.[76] In both explanations, frustrations and sufferings, from which Christian monasticism and Sufism allegedly served as "shelters," were seen as having been caused by large-scale social and political transformations and the attendant social injustices, dislocations and insecurity. In this scenario, otherworldly oriented ascetic-mystical movements emerge as crisis management devices of sorts, if not exactly "opium of the people."[77]

One can hardly deny that ascetic and mystic trends in Islam do indeed appear at the times of momentous historical transitions, in the case of the Muslim world, from the Arab-Muslim conquests of the Mediterranean region to the increasingly authoritarian rule of the first Muslim dynasty (661–750), the Umayyads, and later on from the Arab-dominated empire to the more cosmopolitan and inclusive 'Abbasid one (750–1258). As advocates of the materialistic theory would argue, the conquests brought in their wake considerable, even unheard of, wealth to some Arab-Muslim clans with the resultant disparities in the living standards both among the Arabs and between the Arabs and the new Muslims of non-Arab descent (*mawali*).[78] These disparities resulted in protest movements, whose participants, in accordance with the Marxist theory, couched their grievances and aspirations in a religious idiom, because, in that age and time, religion was the only means of expression available to them.[79] However, according to classical Marxism, in reality, the underlying nature of these grievances and aspirations was socioeconomic, not religious.[80] Alongside militant religious movements such as Shi'ism and Kharijism,[81] there appeared "piety-minded" Muslims who consciously or unconsciously embodied passive protest against the socioeconomic inequities of imperial rule. The "piety-minded" practiced various forms of rejection of this world and its values, including withdrawal from society and its corrupt and corrupting ways.[82] This was (proto-)Sufism.[83] With time, the movement of passive protest grew into Sufism sensu stricto, as it was articulated and codified in Sufi manuals, textbooks, and biographies of the tenth to eleventh centuries

CE,[84] complete with its own institutional structures, authorities, distinctive identity, dress code, teachings, and practices. Gradually but inexorably, Sufism's original antiestablishment and world-denying impulse is dulled by the economic and social imperatives that every religious movement inevitably has to contend with. To preserve themselves as a distinctive group, the movement's leaders begin to make compromises. In the process, some of the movement's initial values and ideas are either lost entirely or drastically revised.[85] Adjusted in this way and augmented by Max Weber's seminal ideas of "charismatic revolution" and "routinization of charisma,"[86] the materialistic explanation of the rise of Sufism in early Islamic societies packs considerable explanatory power. It is hardly surprising that it keeps reappearing in various guises in general and specialized studies of Sufism.[87]

To Be Distinct: Viri Religiosi

Speculating about the origins of world-renouncing tendencies in Christianity, some Western historians have suggested that the mass conversion of Roman subjects to Christianity under and after Constantine the Great (r. 306–37) "created a need for some believers to distinguish themselves from the believing masses."[88] Consequently, some particularly scrupulous Christians of "the first call" adopted a life of self-denial and special moral-ethical demeanor in an effort to set themselves apart from the rest of their allegedly less sincere and more opportunistic coreligionists. Applying a similar rationale to nascent Islamic asceticism-mysticism, the German scholar Bernd Radtke has suggested that it, too, may have emerged among some particularly scrupulous members of the Muslim community who wanted to dissociate themselves from the rapidly increasing number of Muslims in the aftermath of the military and political successes of the early Muslim state. In line with the same logic, the emergence of ascetic-mystical trends within early Muslim society can also be construed as a Muslim parallel to the rejection of "the growing power of the ecclesiastic hierarchy" by some scrupulous early Christians.[89]

Apparently taking his cue from such explanations of the origins of Christian asceticism, Radtke has described the early Muslim ascetics and mystics as *viri religiosi*[90]—a Latin term for men and women who have taken vows of strict piety and chastity to become, as it were, full-time religious professionals and, thus, "dead to this world."[91] Radtke's thesis is in tune, albeit indirectly, with the Marxist (materialistic) explanation of the rise of ascetic-mystic trends in Islam cited above.[92] Or, rather, the two theses seem to complement each other by presenting ascetic-mystical movements in a given religion as a reaction of certain pious or religiously scrupulous individuals to the predominance of mundane concerns and aspirations among members of the ruling elite as well as the religious establishment associated with it.[93] In other words, disturbed by the sight of the rampant debasement of the lofty ideals of the religion's formative age, some devout idealists chose to withdraw from the world either into the desert or into self-righteous groups of like-minded individuals, creating a "counterculture" and "alternative community"[94] of sorts.

The Quietist Revolt of Religious Virtuosi?

The thesis outlined above does not explain why certain individuals may react to the inequities and injustices of this world in a specifically "renunciant" way.[95] An influential response to this obvious question, which has been adopted by many students of Islam, was provided by Max Weber. He introduced the notion of "religious virtuosi"—individuals possessed of a special type of the psychological makeup and ample imagination that render them "spiritually attuned" to the higher religious truths that elude the majority of believers.[96] In Weber's theory, the virtuosi constitute a small cohort of individuals whose heightened charisma and spiritual drive can be harnessed to launch a social and spiritual reform here and now or to inspire their followers to dedicate themselves to a life of moral self-improvement, self-abnegation, and introspection.[97] The path of introspection and self-abnegation was taken by Muslim ascetics-mystics, whereas moral self-improvement was pursued by all manner of Muslim reformers and political activists. The exact configurations of movements launched and led by charismatic leaders depend on what Weberians call "religious markets," which vary dramatically in terms of their social composition and expectations entertained by potential constituencies.[98] The fact that the ascetic-mystical trend gained acceptance in certain quarters of Muslim society can be explained by the presence of an authoritative precedent (monastic Christianity), on the one hand, and the conscious desire of certain individuals to juxtapose their frugal and self-abnegating lifestyle to the ostentatious luxury and pomp of the ruling class. According to a typical Marxist-Weberian explanation of the rise of Sufism, the *baraka*-infested[99] men of Islam tended to follow in the footsteps of the mystics of Christianity and the Buddhist monks of Asia because, in Weber's terms, their lack of involvement in and disesteem for the world of labor had to be financed by a laity that is itself completely immersed in profane routines. Like academics, saints are unproductive workers who were maintained out of general revenue, charity, or patronage.[100]

For better or worse,[101] many scholars of Sufism today and before continue to see its rise and evolution through the prism of Weber's theory of charismatic individuals or religious virtuosi whom this theory portrays as being engaged in symbolic exchanges with their lay constituencies. In the case of Sufi masters (*shaykhs*) they are trading their *baraka* for livelihood.[102]

Constructing a Composite Answer

As an attentive reader may have noticed, the diverse explanations of the origin and continual relevance of the ascetic-mystical movement in Islam documented in this chapter are not necessarily mutually exclusive. If anything, they seem to complement one another, giving us an opportunity to arrange them in various combinations and then to assign one or the other explanation a greater or lesser role in the overall scheme of things. Moreover, the very fact that these diverse explanations are available enables us to critically examine, accept, reject, or adjust them, as the case may be. For example, we can construct the following composite answer by employing the elements of the explanatory models outlined above.

Let us start with differences in the human temperaments (inclinations) and their religious accommodations suggested by Marshall Hodgson. Empirical observations make it impossible to deny: people in general, and those whom we happen to know personally, exhibit different attitudes to life, intellectual preferences, and emotional reactions. Some are more self-centered, others more extravert; some are inclined to contemplation, others to action; some are more open to new ideas, others are more doctrinaire or conservative; some are patient and persevering, others are less so, and so on. If we cast a look at the picture of Sufism as it emerges from the writings and statements of Sufis themselves as well as non-Sufi chronicles and eyewitness accounts, we will find the gamut of these temperamental and psychological types amply represented. Does this nullify Hodgson's explanation that privileges, wittingly or unwittingly, only one psychological type, that of a reclusive, otherworldly ascetic-mystic? Probably not. One can, for instance, argue that initially the ascetic-mystical movement attracted the pensive, introverted type, while later, as Sufism flourished, gained popularity and became institutionalized, it cast its net wider, as it were, thereby allowing a wider variety of temperamental types to "get entangled" in it. An even closer look suggests that people of quite different psychological types seem to have been represented in the movement al-most from its very outset.[103] In other words, in order to attract the greatest possible number of followers the early ascetic and mystical movement in Islam had to diversify internally from the very beginning to accommodate a variety of dissimilar human temperaments and inclinations. At any rate, such a scenario seems plausible, to us at least.

One common feature that early ascetic-mystics of varied temperaments seem to have shared is intense piety. If we define piety as a strongly, sin-cerely, and emotionally held commitment to religious values and striving to achieve perfection in fulfilling one's duties toward God, we will imme-diately realize that such individuals need not be "full-time" ascetics and mystics who are commonly seen as the precursors of Sufism. Individuals of ascetic-mystical inclinations were found among other groups of Muslim *viri religiosi*, such, for instance, as the followers of Ahmad Ibn Hanbal (d. 241/855),[104] whom Muslim historiography has routinely portrayed as being suspicious of, if not outright hostile toward contemporary Sufis.[105] As we have argued elsewhere,[106] in our reconstruction of Sufism's history we are heavily dependent on later Sufi authors who, for one or the other reason, appropriated certain renowned individuals as forefathers of Su-fism, while wittingly or unwittingly neglecting others.[107] For our argu-ment, it is important that not all ascetics-mystics of early Islamdom were to become precursors of Sufism. Some resembled them in significant ways (for example, Ibn Sirin, d. 110/728, and Sufyan al-Thawri, d. 161/778),[108] but have not made it into the standard biographical collections of early Sufi masters. Even if they have, they were not recognized as such by the later generations of both Sufis and non-Sufis.

The normative and selective nature of Sufi historiography notwith-standing, it is impossible to deny that early Muslim ascetics and mystics were motivated by their strongly held and deeply internalized religious convictions that served as the primary motivation for their thought and action. Some possessed charisma, others did not, but the fact remains obvious—the early Muslim devotees were driven by a religious sentiment that expressed itself in a wide variety of ways, such as despondency, self-loathing, fear of God, constant contemplation of the truths of the revela-tion, supererogatory acts of piety, indifference to mundane preoccupations of the lay majority and, last but not least, an intense and constant intro-spection and fear of God (*taqwa*). Despite the diversity of their tempera-ments (as manifested in their demeanor), they shared a common concern for salvation in the hereafter and sought to actualize the presence of God already in their earthly life (in addition to winning God's pleasure through acts of piety and altruism). So, perhaps, the commonality of such objectives and dispositions should be taken as primary, the diversity of individual temperaments being less immediately relevant to the formation and persistence of Sufism as a distinctive trend within Islam.

The other explanatory theses outlined above have as much to do with personal motivations of early Muslim ascetics and mystics as with their position vis-à-vis Muslim society at large. It is not easy to ascertain to what extent their behavior was a simple reaction to societal ills and dramatic metamorphoses of the *umma*, such as, for example, the transition from the largely informal, personality-based rule of the Prophet's first successors to the heavy hand of the centralized imperial state; institutionalization and co-optation of religious specialists by the imperial rulers; and, ultimately, the emergence of a professional learned class. On the one hand, one should not view the co-optation of various strands of Islamic thought and practice into power structures by the ruling elite as a deliberate and concerted strategy on its part. On the other, one cannot deny that such co-optation did take place judging by the fact that many early Muslim ascetics and mystics left government-controlled cities to avoid the far-reaching clutches of the state bureaucracy, viewing it as both "oppressive" and "impious."[109] However, why exactly their escapism took the world-renouncing and passivist twist is not so obvious. After all, many pious individuals (for example, the Kharijis and some Shi'i groups) chose to take up arms against the oppressive state and to withdraw to the fringes of the empire, launching deadly attacks on its forces and representatives when possible. They, too, led a frugal, pious life and demonstrated a high level of ascetic self-abnegation,[110] yet they were not (and still are not) seen as an integral part of the ascetic and mystical movement that eventually led to the formation of Sufism. Is this because they were declared dangerous heretics and rebels and were thus ineligible to be included into Sufi biographical works whose authors sought to present Sufism as part and parcel of the Sunni community and "orthodoxy"? This question should once again remind us of the highly selective, apologetic nature of the normative Sufi literature, whose aim was to strip the Sufi tradition of "undesirable" social, political, and doctrinal elements and to emphasize continuities, rather than ruptures, between the old and new styles of ascetic-mystical piety.

To sum up. The charismatic revolution in Arabia gave rise to the fledgling Muslim state that embarked on successful conquests. The dramatic expansion of Muslim military and political might across the Mediterranean region and beyond resulted in the creation of a multiethnic and culturally diverse society. It needed to forge a distinctive and vibrant culture of its own. This culture, understood as doctrines, practices, communal ethos, institutions, and leadership patterns, evolved under the influence of the religious and cultural ferment to which the Muslim imperial state had fallen heir. The growing complexity of Muslim life, which was now controlled, especially in urban centers, by a ramified military and bureaucratic apparatus, had to be matched by the complexity and sophistication of its cultural and spiritual expression. In response to this societal need, Islamic asceticism-mysticism evolved naturally out of the Mediterranean cultural milieu to form an integral part of Muslim societies. It served the *umma* well for many centuries. Up to this day they are still being fondly remembered by Muslims and non-Muslims alike as the "Golden Age of Islam."[111]

Sufism as a Meeting Place of "Creative Imaginations"

To conclude our discussion of the emergence of the ascetic and mystical stream of Islam and of its various conceptualizations by modern-day scholars, we would like to once again turn to Marshall Hodgson's seminal *Venture of Islam*, in which he identified "the *mystical* component in personal piety" as the mystic's desire to achieve "objective ultimacy . . . in subjective inward experience [and] in maturing *selfhood*." By cultivating his/her own self, "the seeker of cosmic commitment," continued Hodgson, could "find ever more comprehensive meanings in the environment."[112] Hodgson identified this type of world-outlook and devotional style as "inventive" or "imaginative."[113] His observations concerning the nature and role of the human imagination in Muslim societies can be extrapolated to the human condition as a whole.

This was done, for example, by the well-known Dutch British Islamologist Patricia Crone (1945–2015), who used the terms "inventive" or "imaginative" to describe the faculty of the human mind that, in her opinion, can account for the evolution of the entire human species.[114] Taking her cue from modern neurology, on the one hand, and from the influential examination of culture by the American anthropologist Clifford Geertz (1926–2006),[115] on the other, Crone has argued that human beings are forced "to supplement their genetic deficiencies with culture," because "their genetic programming has stopped giving them specific instructions and started to give them general instructions to be inventive instead." "What we invent, in other words culture," Crone argues, "is not an unexpected bonus of high intelligence, but on the contrary what our intelligence is for: we could no more survive without it than could beavers without tails or cats without claws."[116] The principles—which we call "culture" but that are, according to Crone, in essence, human beings' "survival strategy"—allow members of the human species to organize themselves into complex hierarchical and functional communities, be they religious, social, military, or otherwise. These principles have to be, in Crone's own words, *invented* or *made up*. As a result, she concludes, "all human societies are strung around figments of the human imagination."[117] By way of fine-tuning Crone's thesis one can add that, once appropriated, taken to heart, and deployed by human beings of various psychological and intellectual dispositions, these "figments of imagination" become "actionable" and, consequently, real and tangible in their effects.

If one were to apply Crone's and Geertz's ideas to the ascetic-mystical version of Islam, one would argue that, having originated in the imaginative faculty of its founding fathers, it gradually acquired concrete practical, doctrinal (discursive), artistic, and institutional dimensions that constitute the abstraction we call "Sufism."

What factors, then, account for Sufism's abiding importance for the functioning of Muslim societies? The answer may lie in its ascetic (self-disciplining) component, on the one hand, and in its ability to offer a loftier, transcendent meaning to human life, on the other. Concerning the former one can argue that resistance to natural human instincts and appetites (through ascetic self-control and self-denial) is at the very heart of cultural integration and function of all human collectivities.[118] In other words, a deliberate and self-reflexive disciplining of natural, "animal-like" human instincts have transformed primeval tribal life into a qualitatively new mode of human coexistence and cooperation that we call "society." Because strictures and deprivations will not be endured by humans except for the sake of a lofty and worthy purpose, they seek justification in the form of ascetic-mystical universes of meaning that leaders of world-renouncing communities duly create and maintain.[119] Such group leaders are central to any collective endeavor in that they are defining who its members are, what they should be, and what they have been. These are constantly at work, justifying the group's existence, invoking rules and precedents, and measuring up one definition against all the others.[120]

Granted that the social implications of ascetic-mystical thought and practice, overseen and maintained by permanently active leaders, are essential for the proper, civilized functioning of human societies, the persistence of asceticism-mysticism in various guises and social contexts across the centuries becomes not just fully understandable but also indispensable.

Narrowing down the focus of our narrative to Sufism proper, some investigators have defined it as a heightened piety and acute perception of divine presence shared by individuals of certain temperamental inclinations;[121] others described Sufism as a distinctive voice within Islam's polyphony of faith and practice;[122] still others imagined it in terms of the old-fashioned but still useful concept of "tradition" that rises, grows, and undergoes change as it progresses through time and space.[123] In the present chapter, we have also witnessed how Sufism was envisioned through the lenses of Max Weber's sociology or the materialist-Marxist ones adopted, among others, by Agafangel Krymskii. Original depictions of Sufism's rise and evolution have been offered by Margaret Smith, Christopher Melchert, Bernd Radtke, Nile Green, Ahmet Karamustafa, and Bryan Turner. These and other academic conceptualizations of Sufism differ from one another, reflecting the optics adopted by different observers in different times and under different circumstances. By imagining and reimagining Sufism over and over again academic scholars display no less creativity and inventiveness than the Sufis themselves. These academic (re-)imaginings of Sufism resonate well (and remarkably so!) with the Sufi paradox of "imagination within imagination."[124] Recasting the Sufi spiritual cosmology[125] from its original meaning into a more academic mold, the outsiders to the Sufi tradition try to "imagine" how this spiritual cosmology was and is "imagined" by its proponents or, rather, how the proponents want it to be "imagined"—remember the normative and selective character of the Sufi literary corpus. One can agree or disagree with Carl Ernst's thesis that Sufi conceptualizations ("imaginings") of Sufism are more authentic and less biased than those of the European Orientalists.[126] This does, however, not change the fact that the respective imaginings of Sufism by Sufis and by Orientalists reflect completely different levels of abstraction and conceptualization; they also pursue quite different goals, attuned as they are to the intellectual interests, religious and social backgrounds, and cultural tastes of their respective audiences. To present the nineteenth-century Western public with an "indigenous" or "authentic" (that is, internal) image of Sufism would have been a futile, unrewarding task. To be comprehensible and coherent, the image had to be couched in the Western intellectual and cultural conventions of the age. It took a century of painstaking Western study to develop a more accurate image of Sufism and to prepare the Western public for engaging with it. This is a consideration that Carl Ernst and Edward Said before him seem to have missed in their poignant criticisms of Western Orientalist scholarship.[127] The fact that today, as before, Western students of Sufism and Islam generally are interested in more than just recounting the story of Sufism as narrated by Sufis themselves is not only natural. It is inevitable. In repackaging Sufism's history for consumption by Western audiences, the outsiders inevitably make choices and ask questions of their material that are different from those made and asked by the insiders. The outsiders use narrative strategies and conceptual frameworks that the insiders often consider inappropriate or even downright incorrect. In particular, instead of accepting Sufi discourses at face value the outsiders tend to detect in them normative, apologetic, and self-serving undertones. Therefore, it is naive to expect images and histories of Sufism produced by the two groups to be in harmony, although certain overlaps between them are inevitable due to the commonality of the source-base. And this, in our view at least, is fine, as long as the efforts of the insiders and outsiders are self-reflective, self-critical, persuasive, well informed and well documented. On the other hand, attempting to pass for an insider without being one may turn out to be more detrimental to our understanding of Sufism and Islam than the real or perceived misdeeds of the Orientalists.

Conclusion

In sum, the phenomenon called "Sufism," which has been so painstakingly and elegantly designed by the human imagination, or rather, by a long series of individual imaginations, is real in the sense that it has long-ranging and tangible sociopolitical, practical, cultural, and institutional (material) implications. Sufism's followers imagine it to be the only correct way to God and therefore feel obligated to defend it; occasionally, as we will see, they are even ready to give their lives for the sake of its ideals and values. Sufism's opponents, on the contrary, imagine it to be a gross violation of the correct Islam of its pious forebears (al-salaf al-salih) and, consequently, attack it without mercy.[128] Outsiders see it as an important variant of an ascetic-mystical lifestyle and belief system that is particularly fascinating due to its perceived or real antiestablishment, free-thinking, and liberating aspects or because of its multifarious beneficial roles in Muslim societies across the centuries.[129] Regardless of all these conceptualizations, in the end, Sufism stands tall—an imposing monument to human creativity, a whole-hearted and often disinterested commitment to a lofty spiritual ideal and to achieving perfection in word and deed. Sufism's continual relevance today shows that its founders and their numerous followers designed, built, and imagined well.

CHAPTER TWO

What's in a Name?

HOW DEFINITIONS OF SUFISM HAVE BECOME
A SITE OF POLEMICAL PARTIS-PRIS

IN THE PREVIOUS CHAPTER, we have touched upon the role of modern-day ideological and cultural struggles and identity politics in shaping both Muslim and Western discourses about Islam and Sufism in particular. In the present chapter, we will show that the very category "Sufism" can easily become a site of heated debates that result in its politically, culturally, and theologically driven contractions and expansions. This is hardly surprising, because all scholarship begins and ends with definitions of the subject(s) explored. Although, as one scholar has opined, "Sufism is perhaps the most difficult of the terms to define,"[1] its definitions feature in practically every academic study or theological tractate relevant to the subject.[2] Obviously, in addition to one or the other facet of Sufism per se, each such definition reflects the intellectual or devotional stance of the defining subject.[3] As argued in the introduction to this book, like all human beings, scholars are not neutral observers: they always "take a stand within the world,"[4] deeply immersed as they are in its flow and flux. Consequently, they are always eager to fashion the subject of their investigation, consciously or unconsciously, according to their personal convictions, educational and ethnic backgrounds, and life experiences.[5] Furthermore, scholars, like all humans, are not just "solitary observers of the world"; they live in an environment richly populated by other human beings whose judgments, tastes, and preferences influence how they perceive and represent things.[6] Hence, the profusion of various definitions of one and the same phenomenon, on the one hand, and the persistence of certain elements (themes) out of which these definitions are being constructed, on the other.

These general observations are fully applicable to definitions of Sufism.[7] What is less obvious is how exactly and why such definitions are being constructed and articulated. Some, but by no means all, instances of the defining process are the subject of this chapter. We will focus, in particular, on reasons and dynamics of inclusion in or exclusion from Sufism of certain characteristics or phenomena. As already stated, the process of definition reflects both obvious and not-so-obvious ideological and intellectual predilections of defining subjects. It goes without saying that ideologically driven constructions and adaptations of the object(s) defined are not unique to Sufism. In the field of Islamic studies, they are richly attested for the notion "Islam," beginning with a very pertinent to our inquiry and hotly disputed question of whether Sufism should be considered its integral and legitimate part.[8] This question will occupy us later in this book. Leaving it aside for the time being, let us review how the concept "Sufism" can be contracted and expanded in response to various intellectual, cultural, and ideological concerns.

Sufism versus 'Irfan

Whether the Shi'i version of the ascetic-mystical trend in Islam should or should not be called "Sufism" is an old question. In the 1960s, the renowned French scholar of Iranian mysticism[9] Henry Corbin (1903–1978) noticed that the mere mention of the words "Sufism" (*tasawwof*) and "Sufi" (*soufi*) before some high-ranking Shi'i clerics of Qumm in prerevolutionary Iran "caused a shadow to cross their faces."[10] Taking heed of this obvious unease on the part of his interlocutors, Corbin quickly "adopted authoritative Iranian distinctions between 'true' and 'false' Sufis. . . . Righteous ones were unambiguously involved with gnostic mysticism (*'erfan*), while tricksters, imposters, and clowns were counteracting the *shari'a*."[11] The malefactors, in the dominant Shi'i theological discourse, were identified as either Sunni Sufis or their misguided Shi'i imitators. In short, "Sufism" has become a term of opprobrium in the context of modern-day Iran. "Since Sufism," points out the contemporary Iranian academic Nasrollah Pourjavady, "developed as a form of Sunnism . . . it follows that the Shiites were opposed and at times even hostile to the Sufis."[12] Paradoxically, even "philosophical theologians (*hukama'*)"—who had drawn heavily and consistently on the Sufi metaphysics of the likes of Ibn (al-)'Arabi (d. 638/1240) and his disciple Sadr al-Din al-Qunawi (d. 673/1274),[13] as well as their later commentators—were suspicious if not outright hostile to Sufism due to its Sunni origins.[14] Hence the uneasiness, on the part of many contemporary Iranian thinkers,[15] about calling the great poet Jalal al-Din Rumi (d. 672/1273) a "Sufi" (as Rumi would probably have had no compunctions being designated), preferring instead a more "respectable," in the Shi'i milieu, word "gnostic" (*'aref* or *'arif*).[16]

This uneasiness has persisted despite the attempts of Iranian dervish brotherhoods, especially Dhahabiyya and Ni'matullahiyya, to attribute the secondary saintly "moonlight" of their spiritual leaders to the primary "solar" glare of the Twelve Shi'i imams, the Prophet, and his daughter Fatima.[17] That this stratagem was not entirely successful is evidenced by the fact that Iran's greatest Safavid ruler, Shah 'Abbas the Great (965/1557–1037/1628) humiliated his erstwhile supporters from among the Turkoman dervishes, members of the Safawiyya (Sefeviyya) Sufi order, by assigning them to "baser types of employment." He, of all people, would have found the title "The Grand Sophi" attributed to him by some European travelers to be "an insult."[18] Be this as it may, the subsequent centuries of Safavid rule witnessed the suppression and gradual decline of Sufi institutions, both Shi'i and Sunni, in Shi'i Iran.[19] Although justified on doctrinal grounds as a fight against heretics, persecution of Iranian Sufis was driven by considerations of power harbored by the shahs or prominent Shi'i clerics seeking to assert control over the religious life of Safavid society. Thus, Matthijs van den Bos attributes the suppression of the Ni'matallahiyya Sufi order under Shah 'Abbas's successor to "Ne'matollahi political intrigues" rather than their "heretical" doctrines and practices per se.[20] At the same time, the Safavid rulers "tolerated the individualistic and apolitical Sufism of the literati and of the mystic virtuosi,"[21] who "produced the tradition of *'irfan* or gnostic philosophy."[22] Following Said Amir Arjomand, van den Bos argues that "a different Sufism flourished in his [Shah 'Abbas the Great's] polity. *'Erfan* . . . philosophically oriented and respected 'gnostic wisdom,' was [seen as] unrelated to 'Sufi order Sufism' (*tasavvof*)."[23] On the one hand, *'irfan* was viewed by the Safavid state, ever wary of popular millenarian uprisings,[24] as elitist, inward-looking and thus socially and politically "benign." On the other, the metaphysical teachings of *'irfan* could easily be blended with the Shi'i esoteric metaphysics and doctrine of the imamate.[25] As a result, both Shi'i mystical theologians and legal scholars—such as Mulla Sadra Shirazi (d. 1050/1640) and Muhammad Baqir Majlisi (d. 1110/1698), who would not otherwise see eye to eye—sought to sever "high Sufism and gnostic philosophy" from the popular *tasawwuf/tasavvof* of Iran's Sufi orders by presenting them as refuges of "charlatans and tricksters."[26] In the end, the Iranian scholarly establishment condemned *tasawwuf/tasavvof* as a playground of "libertine and wandering dervishes" and used their clout with the Safavid state authorities to outlaw it.[27] The ambivalent attitude to Sufism and Sufis in Iran has persisted until today, giving them a bad name quite literally, as Corbin's experience with the scholars of Qumm has eloquently demonstrated.[28] As a result, in the Iranian Shi'i milieu, the "nobler" metaphysical, cosmological, and gnoseological aspects of Sufism were excluded from this notion and renamed as "wisdom" (*hikma*), "transcendental philosophy" (*hikmat-i muta'aliyya*),[29] or "divine gnosis" (*'erfan/'irfan*).[30] Simultaneously, the notion of Sufism (*tasawwuf / tasavvof*) per se was demoted to the antisocial behavior and crude superstitions of the "antinomian ignoramuses." Iranian religious authorities routinely indicted them as "heretics, Sufis, lovers—[*'ushshaq*], i.e., those who believed in the Sufi doctrine of divine love,"[31] in other words, misguided imitators of the heretical Sunnis.[32]

At the same time, already in the eighth/fourteenth century, Iranian Shi'i thinkers such as Haydar Amuli (Amoli; d. after 787/1385), endeavored to integrate the ideas of Sunni Sufis, especially Ibn (al-)'Arabi and his commentators, with the Shi'i concept of the imamate, the mainstay of Shi'i doctrine and identity. In particular, Ibn (al-)'Arabi's momentous concept of "perfect man" and "spiritual pole" of the universe was identified with the Shi'i imams or their descendants.[33] The imams being the conduit to salvation for the Shi'is, the ramifications of this Shi'i reimagining of the Sunni-Sufi ideas of pole-hood (*qutbiyya*) and "sainthood" (*walaya/wilaya*)[34] are obvious.[35] As one can surmise from a Shi'i interpretation of Rumi's intellectual legacy by the modern Shi'i thinker 'Abd al-Karim Soroush/Sorush,[36] in contemporary Iran the unease about associating refined mystical philosophy and poetry with Sufism persists unabated. In religious seminaries of Qumm, Najaf, Karbala, Mashhad, and other Shi'ite theological institutions, studying *'irfan/hikmat* is either part of the official curriculum or at the very least encouraged.[37] The same is true of philosophical faculties of Iranian universities.[38] However, looking up these disciplines under the name "Sufism" (*tasawwuf/tasavvof*) is, for obvious reasons, futile. The artificial, ideologically induced nature of the Shi'ism-Sufism dichotomy has been vividly demonstrated by the works of the major experts on Iranian Sufism[39] and need not be belabored here any longer.

What is noteworthy is that this dichotomy was accepted and legitimized by an outsider, the French Islamologist Henry Corbin,[40] who emphasized "the esoteric quality of Shi'ism" and its resultant affinity with "high," that is, philosophical Sufism. For Corbin, both Sufi and Shi'i "philosophy" were the two kindred expressions of "Islamic esotericism" (*l'ésoterisme de l'Islam*),[41] which he considered to be the true essence of the

Muslim religion (its "perennial core") in contrast to its accidental "temporal and social, or historical and sociological" manifestations.[42] After painting this bifurcated picture of Islamic asceticism-mysticism, Corbin has resolutely opted for its spiritual, esoteric, and eternally relevant side over its temporally and socially contingent one. Corbin's "esoteric" thesis has informed the view of Islamic mysticism espoused, among others, by the influential Iranian American scholar S. H. Nasr (b. 1933).[43]

This fact, in our view, confirms the premise stated earlier in this book that Sufism serves as a meeting place of discourses and imaginations, both Muslim and Orientalist, that is, internal and external to the Islamic tradition. It is in such meeting places that various visions of Sufism are being (re-)negotiated, (re-)adjusted, and (re-)articulated by various actors based on their personal religious or secular convictions and intellectual tastes. This conclusion should alert us to the danger of juxtaposing too rigidly internal and external discourses about Sufism,[44] not to mention endorsing the former as integral to the tradition, while summarily debunking the latter as somehow "prejudiced" or "unauthentic."[45] Seeing resonances and dialogues rather than ruptures and discontinuities in the discursive fields gravitating around Sufism seems more constructive and fruitful.

It is important to point out that the desire to separate "philosophical Sufism"[46] from its "less sophisticated" or outright "vulgar" manifestations in collective or individual practices and rituals of Sufi communities ("brotherhoods") is not unique to Shi'i or pro-Shi'i scholars. Thus, William Chittick, the major American expert on the legacy of the Andalusian Sufi Muhyi al-Din Ibn (al-)'Arabi, has unequivocally stated that "Western scholarship and much of the later Islamic tradition have classified Ibn [al-] 'Arabi as a 'Sufi', though he himself did not."[47] It is obvious from Chittick's account of the Andalusian thinker that the American scholar does not want to see Ibn (al-)'Arabi as "just Sufi."[48] Instead, Chittick is eager to depict him primarily as "the greatest of all Muslim philosophers."[49] This treatment of a major Sufi thinker jibes well with the Shi'i theological and academic misgivings (exemplified, respectively, by Mulla Sadra and S. H. Nasr) over "lumping together" the sublime metaphysical *'irfan/hikma* and the popular, rough-around-the-edges "Sunni-style" Sufism. We deal here with yet another demonstration of an uncanny convergence of outsider and insider perspectives on Sufism. It is true that both Chittick and Nasr adhere to the same traditionalist/perennialist philosophy,[50] but what matters is the fact that, for them, Sufism has become the site of an intellectual and spiritual quest and, eventually, tryst. Seen from this perspective, their being insiders or outsiders to the Sufi tradition is almost irrelevant. What matters is that the abstraction "Sufism" has facilitated a meeting of similar minds that transcends the scholars' dissimilar personal backgrounds.

"In Texts We Trust"

Now, the study of Sufism in the West started with Sufi texts[51] that, quite naturally, furnish a much more intellectually sophisticated image of Sufism than the one reconstructed by means of observing routine, quotidian actions and rituals of real-life Sufis. Tellingly, a recent study of Islam presents Sufism itself as a giant, cosmic text that enshrines the unspoken but potentially discoverable divine intent with regard to creation.[52] Such text-based concepts are indicative of how Sufism has been perceived and construed by both academic insiders and outsiders over the past two centuries. Field studies are much less in vogue with scholars of Sufism. There are several reasons for that. One is that up-close-and-personal observations, if conducted in a noncommittal and unprejudiced manner, often result in stripping Sufism of its aura of mystery and exoticism, which is so vital to its appeal to various educated audiences. For example, an impartial and incisive gaze might reveal the elaborate, if invisible, mechanism of submission of Sufi "aspirants" (*murids*) to the authority of Sufi masters claiming sublime but unverifiable truths. As a result, Sufism may lose at least some of its luster. In other words, an impartial investigator working "in the field" soon begins to see Sufis as ordinary people or groups of people doing ordinary things and having all-too-familiar (and so human!) feelings, concerns, fears, aspirations, and moral failings.[53] Viewed from this vantage point, the ethereal, idealized image of Sufi life carefully assembled by Sufi authors and sympathetic armchair scholars in the West dissipates and gives way to a much more down-to-earth, unromantic one of a hard-nosed field anthropologist. The anthropologist's "objectivist" stance vis-à-vis the subject has the potential to disillusion his/her audience, unless one has preprogrammed oneself to see only what one wants to see, ignoring the seamy, quotidian side of the phenomenon. This fact helps to explain, at least in part, why a text-based approach has dominated both internal and external imaginings and conceptualizations of Sufism until today. Far from being a mere tribute to the "outdated" and much-reviled "philological approach,"[54] the predilection for texts on the part of students of Sufism is dictated, at least in part, by an unconscious human longing for fascination and enchantment. If our assumption is correct, then the candid field descriptions of living Sufism (and Sufis) are more likely to produce disenchantment in the audience than those that depict Sufism on the basis of its normative, idealized texts.

This said, one cannot deny that today's academics studying Muslim societies do pay much more attention than before to "performative" manifestations (or embodiments) of Sufism in everyday ritual and pedagogical activities as well as routine, repetitive, meditative techniques.[55] However, even such ritual-focused studies still depend heavily on textual sources,[56] rather than empirical field data sensu stricto.[57] The old Orientalist habit of "overreliance on texts and underreliance on observations"[58] persists. Calls to overcome the text-based habits of Sufism scholarship[59] are yet to bear fruit, although we do have studies of certain Sufi communities by field anthropologists and ethnographers who strive to break away from reliance on texts and texts alone.[60] In the end, however, the predominance of texts in the study of Sufism is completely understandable: they tell a more coherent (and thus more analyzable and readable) story than either oral accounts or field observations. Moreover, the texts contain more enchanting and fascinating power than ethnographic distillations of raw "on-site" actions and sayings of actual Sufis, because authors of the texts have already packaged a certain chunk of "raw" Sufi theory and practice for the reader-writer to consume, repackage, and disseminate, in his or her turn, to various audiences.

The accuracy of our observations notwithstanding, there's no denying that field studies of Sufism and Sufi-related phenomena are still rather scarce. Furthermore, they are too narrowly focused and technical to change the overall perception of Sufism by the Western and Muslim publics at large. Hence, the widespread visions of Sufism, especially in the West, as first and foremost a treasure trove of wisdom, be it poetic, spiritual, didactic, or metaphysical,[61] rather than a regimented discipline, self-imposed deprivations and vows, unquestioning submission to the often authoritarian will of the spiritual master, routine pedagogical and ritual activities, and so on. The Romantic, intellectualist, liberal-minded vision of Sufism continues to rule supreme in the Western mentality, overshadowing Sufism's more quotidian aspects that are not as congenial to the tastes and expectations of, for the most part, liberal Western audiences attracted to the exotic promise of "Islamic mysticism."[62]

Rooted in the "armchair" philological methods employed by both Western and Western-trained Muslim scholars for the past two centuries, as well as the intellectual and cultural preferences of their respective audiences,[63] textual, but decontextualized, imaginings of Sufism and the Sufis continue to dominate the perception of the ascetic-mystical movement in Islam by Westerners, including Muslims residing in the West.[64] As a result, a great mass of yet unprocessed but potentially significant "live" material pertaining to "Sufism observed"[65] remains outside the purview of Sufi studies.[66] This is regrettable, because Muslims, among whom actual Sufis have lived and are living today, often see their behavior and outward appearances, and not their texts, as the primary markers of their Sufi identity.[67] In the final analysis, although our discussion began with examining the epistemological dichotomy of sublime mystical wisdom and "on-the-ground" Sufism within the Shiʻi theological and intellectual milieu, we have discovered a similar preference for the intellectual/textual over the quotidian/routine in Western accounts of Sufism more generally.[68] This preference is determined by the nature of sources at scholars' disposal, by the scholars' intellectual commitments and tastes as well as by the expectations and interests of their audiences. To capture the attention of the Western reader, accounts of Sufism should fascinate and enchant, and they do. As long as this is the case, Sufism will be defined and perceived by Westerners primarily as "wisdom," "metaphysics," "philosophy," and as a "message of love, harmony, and beauty,"[69] with the practical, quotidian, and routine remaining largely in the shade. This vision may be heartwarming and fascinating, but is it accurate?

Walaya/Wilaya *Contested*

The dichotomies Sufism/*ʻirfan* and Sufism/philosophy are not the only cases when the definition of Sufism is shaped by intellectual and doctrinal convictions of those who define it. A similar process is evident in the vicissitudes of the notion of *walaya* ("spiritual authority" in the sense of "the right and responsibility to guide the faithful"), which is commonly translated into European languages as "sainthood."[70] In Shiʻi Islam *walaya* constitutes "the most important article of Shiʻi faith."[71] In Sunni theology, it occupies an important, albeit by no means central, place, being especially important for Sufism.[72] It makes perfect sense that *walaya* is construed differently by Sunnis and Shiʻis due to their cardinal disagreement over who is to be considered the legitimate heir to the Prophet and rightful leader of the Muslim community (*umma*).[73] In Sunni Islam, *walaya* can be earned by, or bestowed by God upon, any person (including even apparently undeserving or unlikely ones) regardless of their kinship, literacy, or social standing.[74] In Shiʻism *walaya* is "an *aristocratic privilege* reserved to Alid descendants"[75] that performs both an initiatory and sanctifying function.[76] In other words, in Sunni Islam it is more or less "merit-based," whereas in Shiʿism it is genealogically inherited and available only to the prophets and Shiʿi imams.[77] So, when Sufis and Shiʿis talk about *walaya* their common use of the same word should not obscure the deep dogmatic gulf that separates them. For many, but not all Sunnis, *walaya* is obviously and undeniably part of Sufism (insofar as it is believed to be possessed by a particular Sufi master), whereas claimants to *walaya* within the Shiʿi milieu (whether or not they explicitly designate themselves as "Sufis")[78] inevitably encroach on the unique genealogical prerogative of the Shiʿi imams and their descendants (*sayyids* or *imam-zadehs*).[79] Attempts by some Shiʿi mystical orders to present their masters as basking in or borrowing from the resplendent glow of the Shiʿi *walaya* (namely, that of the Prophet, his daughter Fatima, and the Twelve imams)[80] have proved unsuccessful in the end, because they came into conflict with a major tenet of the Shiʿi creed.

Therefore, although *walaya* is an integral part of both Sunni *tasawwuf* and Shiʿi *ʿirfan/hikma*, its understanding and implications in each tradition are distinct, if not outright incompatible. It is true that Shiʿi followers of certain Iranian spiritual lineages (for example, Niʿmatullahiyya and Nurbakhshiyya)[81] would occasionally attribute *walaya* to their leaders,[82] but they were always doing this at their own peril, because their claims inevitably clashed with the Shiʿi axiom that *walaya* is the sole prerogative of the imams and prophets.[83] As a result, the Shiʿi religious establishment of Iran would periodically "call the bluff" of Iranian Sufi masters by denouncing them as heretics who had arrogated the God-given right of the imams to guide the community.[84]

As already noticed, such denunciations were usually doctrinal manifestations of struggles for religious authority among various groups of claimants who used the doctrine of *walaya* as an argument to advance their respective causes and defeat their opponents.[85] The long history of state-sponsored persecutions against dervish orders and individual Sufi masters in modern Iran bears ample evidence to the abiding uneasiness of Sufi-Shiʿi relations, periods of rapprochement and even familial intimacy between certain Sufi leaders and the courtly circles of the Safavid or Qajar dynasties notwithstanding.[86]

In sum, including or excluding *walaya* from the definition of Sufism is a serious theological statement with long-ranging implications. In Shiʿi contexts, for claimants of *walaya* the implications of exclusion/inclusion could be dire. Our discussion of *walaya* logically leads us to the related phenomenon of the so-called cult of "saints" or "friends of God" (*awliya'*) and its links to Sufism.

Sufism and the Cult of God's Friends

Writing in the 1960s, the British expert on Sufi orders, Spencer Trimingham, whose work remains influential today, argued that,

> The word *tasawwuf* conjures up to the mind of the average modern Arab thoughts of speculative abstractions and obscure or erotic poems, on the one hand, and of gross superstition, filthy ragged dervishes, orgiastic dances, and venal charlatan shaikhs caricatured in current literature and magazines, on the other.[87]

In trying to explain this widespread rejection of Sufism by the Arab intelligentsia and youth of the age, Trimingham has suggested that,

> Few objected outright to Sufism as an individual spiritual discipline, even though they may have thought it a waste of time, but the form it had taken . . . especially . . . the power the *baraka*-exploiters wielded over their adherents.[88]

Among the practices that the modern-day critics of Sufism find particularly repugnant, argues another prominent scholar of Sufism, Martin van Bruinessen, are:

> Visits to the tombs of saints, especially when their purpose is to demand intercession or help . . . the attribution of miraculous powers to Sufi shaykhs and the traffic in magical objects as amulets; and the unconditional surrender of the individual devotee to a Sufi master.[89]

Such criticisms notwithstanding, the cult of "God's friends" or "saints" (*awliya' Allah*), or, to be more precise, the belief in their miraculous and intercessory powers by some Muslims, is found throughout the Muslim world unless it is prohibited by state authorities on doctrinal grounds.[90] Opponents of this belief and practices associated with it, namely, supplication or animal sacrifice at the tombs of "God's pious friends" (*awliya' Allah al-salihun*), routinely condemn them as a grave violation[91] of the principle of God's oneness (*al-tawhid*). The critics maintain that God being the sole worthy object of worship, seeking help from or addressing prayers to anyone other than the Creator amounts to heresy or even unbelief.[92] Bearing in mind the fact that the majority of living or dead "friends of God," who

FIGURE 2.1. Sufi shrines and tombs in the district (*raion*) of Shamakhi in Azerbaijan (Shamaxı, Kələxana türbələri). The image was kindly provided by the well-known Azeri photographer Irada Gadirova.

enjoy such popular adulation, have ties to a Sufi order or a Sufi spiritual lineage (*silsila*), the question arises as to whether belief in their intercessory powers (and the attendant practices associated with their graves) should be included in the definition of Sufism. Ibn Taymiyya and his foremost disciple Ibn Qayyim al-Jazwiyya (d. 751/1350) thought that they should not.[93] In so doing, they anticipated the modern-day criticism of the cult of living and dead Sufi teachers by many centuries. Ibn Taymiyya's attitude is finely captured in the following paraphrase by Muhammad Memon of the gist of his treatise against various heretical excesses of the age:

> In themselves, the Sufi ideas are very beautiful, a source of spiritual and intellectual satisfaction. But the trouble is the excesses committed in the name of Sufism.[94]

Of these "excesses," Ibn Taymiyya singles out the cult of Sufi saints and their tombs as being the most egregious one.[95] Thus, the influential Sunni theologian and jurist has effectively excluded this widespread and popular phenomenon from his definition of what constitutes correct or orthodox Sufism.[96]

Whereas Ibn Taymiyya had his reasons for doing so,[97] there are as many reasons to suggest that it is, in fact, an integral part of Sufi doctrine and practice. As a justification of its inclusion, one can argue that not only does Sufism supply God's friends for the general populace to venerate and supplicate, but it also furnishes a comprehensive doctrine aimed at ascertaining their special status in the Muslim community.[98] Articulated for the first time in the late ninth to early tenth century CE by the Arab-Iranian mystic and theologian al-Hakim al-Tirmidhi (d. circa 295–300/907–12),[99] the theory of "sainthood" (*walaya* or *wilaya*) was elaborated by the subsequent generations of Sufis, most notably by Ibn (al-)'Arabi and his followers.[100] Throughout the Middle Ages and into the modern period, deceased ("horizontal") "friends of God" belonging to various Sufi lineages (*silsilas*)[101] as well as their living (or "vertical") counterparts served as powerful symbols of local identities[102] in the same way as Christian saints had from late antiquity onward.[103] In modern times, the cult of God's friends was denounced by some Muslim reformers, both Sufi[104] and non-Sufi,[105] for a variety of reasons. One of them is the adoption by some Muslim reformers of the late nineteenth to early twentieth century of the stridently negative attitude toward saints and their supernatural powers.[106] In the societies of western Europe, a similar attitude had made itself felt much earlier, during the "long" Christian Reformation of the fourteenth to seventeenth centuries[107] to be reinforced, later on, with the anticlerical, secularist attitudes championed by the major figures of the European Enlightenment.[108] Now, whether this rejection of the intercessory powers of the *awliya'* is homegrown—as Muhammad b. 'Abd al-Wahhab's Arabian campaigns against "idolatry" (*shirk*) seem to indicate[109]—or borrowed from Christian Europe is a moot point. Regardless, the iconoclastic efforts by various groups of Muslims to condemn material and doctrinal manifestations of anthropolatry are both obvious and ubiquitous today and in the recent past.

As opposition to saint- and shrine-centered Islam had been growing in the early twentieth century in the aftermath of Islamic reformist-modernist critiques of the status quo, Sufi leaders faced the choice of either acknowledging or denying that the popular belief in "God's friends" and the rites attendant to it are part of Sufism.[110] Whereas medieval pro-Sufi scholars could afford to dismiss Ibn Taymiyya's criticism of the belief in the supernatural powers of departed *awliya'* and supplications at their graves without justifying their position,[111] in the postreformist environment this nonchalant attitude was no longer tenable. One reason was that opponents of Sufism accused its leaders of deliberately and unscrupulously inculcating in their followers "outdated," "idle" superstitions, especially the cult of living and dead saints, in order to gain both the material advantages and high social status that they did not deserve. Worse still, in the eyes of Salafi and

FIGURE 2.2. Tomb of an anonymous Sufi saint from Baghdad (Piribağdad, Pir-i-Bağdat) in the district of Shamakhi, Azerbaijan (Shamaxı, Göylər kəndi). The image was kindly provided by the well-known Azeri photographer Irada Gadirova.

Wahhabi detractors of Sufism, Sufi beliefs and practices associated with the cult of *awliya'* were but a manifestation of "polytheism" (*shirk*) similar to that espoused by the pre-Islamic Arabian tribes in the age that the Qur'an and the Prophet condemned as one of crass "ignorance" (*jahiliyya*).[112] Hence, the pressure on Sufi leaders, today as never before, either to exclude the belief in God's friends and their miraculous powers from the definition of "correct" Sufism or to recognize it as integral to the Sufi tradition, citing scriptural evidence in support of this theological position. As we have shown elsewhere, Sufi leaders have resorted to one of these strategies depending on the concrete circumstances in which they found themselves.[113] However, with a few notable exceptions,[114] to avoid controversy and recrimination, Sufism's modern-day advocates have tended to minimize or even deny its association with such "objectionable" beliefs and practices. In the process, they have redefined the concept of "correct" Sufism to absolve it of what the reformist-modernist discourse has condemned as "popular superstitions,"[115] especially "grave worship." As a consequence, Sufism was recast as a technique for the "purification the soul" (*tazkiyat al-nafs*) or achieving a moral-ethical perfection (*ihsan*)[116]—the precepts that are accepted as appropriate and even necessary by every pious Muslim whether Sufi or not.[117] In this way, the more controversial and visible aspects of Sufism's public presence have been either obfuscated or, at the very least, rendered accidental to its definition. Subsumed under the much broader, nebulous rubric of "soul purification" and "self-improvement/perfection," Sufism has become subtly "privatized,"[118] that is, relegated from the public sphere to that of the individual Sufi's internal struggle with his or her restive, instinct-driven ego (*nafs*). On the one hand, this move to internalize Sufism jibes well with the public sensitivities of the modern age, especially in the West, where religion is a private, even confidential concern of every citizen. On the other, it does not contradict the rich tradition of historical Sufism, an important strain of which emphasizes the necessity for the Sufi to combat constantly and valiantly the vicious dictates of his or her lower, "animal-like" self, while concealing his or her efforts from outsiders.[119] The discursive move just described is both subtle and effective, albeit probably not sufficient to placate Sufism's staunch detractors who reject Sufi teachings and practices as a matter of principle. One conclusion is inescapable: Sufism, or rather its denizens, are flexible and adjustable to new situations and environments, either favorable or adverse. In this game of constant readjustment, the expansion and contraction of Sufism's (re-)definition has a vital role to play. It assures its survival in the face of adverse criticism and gives its followers ammunition to repulse their detractors in private and in public.

The process of obfuscating Sufism's public displays is part of the attempts, by both insiders and sympathetic outsiders, to foreground its gnoseological and metaphysical aspects at the expense of the quotidian, ritualistic, and routine.[120] Here, once again, we observe a meeting of the intellectual agendas of the insiders (Sufi or pro-Sufi theologians) and outsiders (Western and Western-trained academic scholars of Sufism).[121] Deliberately or not both groups tend to portray Sufism as a lofty spiritual and intellectual pursuit innocent of beliefs or practices commonly considered "irrational" or "vulgar." Rectified from and elevated above such unseemly characteristics, the notion of Sufism is expanded to include *falsafa*. On the one hand, we witness a subtle, or at least nonobvious, discursive contraction of Sufism that relieves it of "objectionable" legacy, in this case, the beliefs and practices associated with the supernatural and intercessory powers of *awliya'*. At the same time, the notion of Sufism is expanded in a different direction to absorb the desirable elements of *falsafa*, a worthy and sophisticated intellectual discipline in the eyes of both Muslim and Western intellectuals.

The reasons for the insiders to resort to this dual discursive move are more or less clear. They seek to burnish Sufism's image tarnished, as it were, by the reformist-modernist questioning of both its "rationality" and its "orthodoxy." What is at stake for outsiders, one might ask? The reasons for their uneasiness about Sufism's affinity with "anthropolatry" (especially in its public displays) are rather complex. On the one hand, one can argue that conceptualizations of Sufism by Western and Western-trained academics spring from their preference for philosophically sophisticated discourses uncontaminated by the natural messiness of everyday human existence. In their view, the "irrational and naïve superstitions" associated with Sufism on the ground turn out to be incompatible with the lofty sophistication of Sufi ontological and gnoseological discourses enshrined in Sufism's literary corpus.[122] At the very least, popular Sufi beliefs and rituals strike them as "illogical" and "contradictory,"[123] despite their being, according to a field anthropologist, "deeply ingrained in the religious psyche of the neighborhood" due to the "spiritual benefits" that they portend to its inhabitants.[124] Whereas the anthropologist reveals a typical ethnographic respect for performative aspects of Sufism, they are of little interest to scholars of Sufi texts, such as William Chittick or Andrei Smirnov, who are, as far as we can tell, still in the majority. These two scholars' professional affiliations with philosophy departments may have played a role in their conceptualizations of Sufism as a sophisticated intellectual and textual tradition par excellence. However, one should not discount other, less obvious factors that are definitely at work in academic conceptualizations of Sufism but that run much deeper.

Steeped as they are in the vicissitudes of the history of Western Christianity, Western-born or Western-trained scholars of Muslim societies unwittingly tend to see Islam's evolution through Christian lenses.[125] To reiterate, there is nothing unusual or inherently sinister about this approach to the history of a religious and cultural Other, because, as has already been noticed, Western scholars of Islam were and still are but translators of foreign cultures and texts into the linguistic and cultural idioms of their own societies.[126] This is a fact whether we like it or not. Taking as our starting point the Cartesian axiom (cited by Michel Foucault) about all knowledge being but a fruit of "comparison of two or more things with each other,"[127] let us now find out what is being compared to what and why.

It stands to reason that to explain to a Western audience why some Muslim groups reject the ritualistic side of Sufism, especially one associated with saints and their tombs, a suitable Western parallel needs to be found. It made perfect sense for a curious, but not necessarily prejudiced, Western translator of Islamic culture to draw a comparison between antisaint and antishrine attitudes of latter-day Islam and the violent confrontations between Europe's Protestants and Catholics over what appear to be similar issues. The Catholic-Protestant quarrel, as we know well, was in large part about the trappings of worship (for example, decoration of churches and altars) and the role of human beings (priests and saints) and figural representations (icons, paintings, relics, and such) as mediators between believers and God.[128] To these theological "flashpoints," one should add the issue of education and the language of the Scripture, but we will set them aside for now. In short, at some point in the history of Western discourses about Islam, a number of Western scholars of Muslim societies ("Orientalists") came to construe the beliefs and practices of Europe's Catholics as somehow analogous to those of the Sufis. The cult of saints, their tombs and relics, routinely associated with Sufism in popular narratives and in texts, appear to have warranted such an analogy. Correspondingly, the anti-Sufi position of certain reform-minded modernists, as well as fundamentalist Salafis, seemed like a replay, within the Muslim context, of the antisaint and antishrine attitudes of Europe's Protestants.[129]

Eminently pertinent to our argument is the fact that the parallels between Catholics and Protestants, on the one hand, and Sufis and their (Salafi) critics, on the other, have been drawn not only by Western scholars (outsiders)[130] but also by Muslim religious scholars (insiders) familiar with Protestantism through books or thanks to "the omnipresent Pentecostal churches" and missions in Africa and elsewhere.[131] Thus, whenever the Nigerian religious reformer Abubakar Gumi (1922–1992), who opposed the Sufi notion of *walaya*, says that "every believer is a saint" or that one's faith (*iman*) is not dependent on how many fasts or prayers one performs,[132] or when a Senegalese reformer Cheikh Touré (b. 1925) attacks visits of tombs of Sufi *awliya*[133] and adulation of living Sufi teachers by their followers as vestiges of "polytheism" (*shirk*),[134] they without doubt are drawing upon a certain understanding of the Protestant creed and its incompatibility with the Catholic one. One Tanzanian author, Muhammad Ghassany, writing in 2003, explicitly referred to the antisaint and antishrine attitudes in today's Muslim societies as "Protestant Islam" (*Uprotestanti wa Kiislamu*).[135] These remarkable facts once again corroborate our earlier suggestion that Sufism serves as a meeting place of discourses and imaginations that are both internal and external to Islam. They cross-pollinate and intertwine, feeding off one another in often subtle, unpredictable but always fascinating ways.

Academic ruminations on parallels between the Sufi-Salafi conflict and its Catholic-Protestant predecessor vary. Whereas some scholars see Sufi-Salafi confrontations today as a close replay, many centuries later, of the fateful collision between Europe's Catholics and Protestants, others consider it a phenomenon largely, if not wholly, indigenous to Islam and thus uniquely Islamic. They suggest that the process was internal not only to Islam but also to Sufism: at some point in time a more rational and sober Sufi version of Islam challenged and partly supplanted the traditional one practiced before the advent of the modern age and Western technological, political, and cultural domination. Proponents of this view argue that in the eighteenth century, if not earlier, the "saint-based" and "superstition-laden" ("vulgar") Sufism of old gradually transformed itself into a more "streamlined," "rational," or even outright "modern" one.[136] This new interpretation of Sufism in some quarters of Muslim societies, which academic scholars have dubbed "neo-Sufism," led to its being stripped of objectionable, heterodox features, including the pantheistic theosophy of Ibn (al-)'Arabi and his followers, "ecstatic Sufi practices," "pacifism," and, last but not least, the worship of saints and their tombs.[137] Thanks to this internal self-purification, Sufi institutions and leaders managed to adapt themselves to the demands of the age and embarked on the social-moral reconstruction of Muslim society, which can be likened to an "autochthonous Islamic Enlightenment."[138] With time there emerged what can be dubbed "Sufi Wahhabism"—a puritanical and activist strain of Sufism that was ready to engage its "saint-focused" counterpart, violently if need be.[139]

This thesis, while elegant and packing considerable explanatory force, has met with opposition. Marshalling evidence from nineteenth-century Sufi sources (mostly African), its critics have argued that the transition assumed by the proponents of the neo-Sufism thesis has never occurred or occurred on the institution-building (not doctrinal) level only and, then again, only in certain places (for example, sub-Saharan Africa).[140] In short, argued the critics, the parallels between the European religious and intellectual developments in the sixteenth to eighteenth centuries and those in evidence in the Muslim world of the past century and a half do not stand up to scrutiny. They are but a Eurocentric illusion.[141]

Whatever side one may choose to take in this academic debate, what is hardly in doubt is that some Sufi masters of the nineteenth and twentieth centuries indeed expressed reservations about popular excesses associated with the cult of departed "friends of God."[142] In other words, the definition of "correct" Sufism offered by such Sufis bracketed certain beliefs and practices, especially ones centered on tombs of "God's friends," as being outside the pale as it were. Whether this intra-Sufi critique indeed should be qualified as an element of "neo-Sufism," or as a "Protestant" turn within Sufism, is a different matter.[143]

One possible way out of this conundrum is to relegate the cult of Sufi *awliya'* and its accoutrements to "folk Islam,"[144] while simultaneously foregrounding Sufism's theological and philosophical dimensions as its "true essence." This intellectualist, "philosophizing" trend in Sufi studies is exemplified by William Chittick's aforementioned designation of Ibn (al-)'Arabi as "the greatest of all Muslim philosophers."[145] A slightly different view is taken by Shahab Ahmed, who argues that Sufism and *falsafa* coexisted harmoniously, while being a mutually enriching, integral part of everyday religious learning and discourse at least in some areas of the premodern and early modern Muslim world.[146]

In short, both abstractions, namely, Greek-inspired *falsafa* and Sufism, are creatively readjusted to meet the sensibilities of present-day Western or Westernized intellectuals interested primarily in Sufism's intellectual and philosophical dimensions. One interesting outcome of this "philosophizing approach" is in evidence in some recent "histories of Islamic philosophy" or "histories of Islamic theology"[147] that, unlike more conventional Western works of the same genre,[148] include chapters devoted to mystical thinkers, like Ibn (al-)'Arabi and his Iranian followers, thereby downplaying the fact that such thinkers were usually critical of Muslim admirers of "Greek wisdom."[149] The objective of these new histories is to demonstrate that medieval Islamic philosophical thought was not entirely "epigonic," that is, indebted to "Greek wisdom" (*al-hikma al-yunaniyya*) and reliant heavily on its methods and terminology.[150] Once Sufi teachings of Ibn (al-)'Arabi and his school have been identified as "philosophical," Islam's ability to produce original philosophical thinking (in the European sense of the word) is strongly vindicated. In the process, however, Sufism loses its quotidian, disciplinary regimens and routine devotional practices, whereas *falsafa*, in its turn, is redefined as being mystical-metaphysical par excellence. In principle, this approach is no more and no less plausible than placing under the rubric "Christian philosophy" such Christian mystics as Pseudo-Dionysius the Areopagite (late fifth to early sixth centuries), Meister Eckhart (d. 1327), Santa Theresa of Ávila (d. 1582), Saint John of the Cross (d. 1591), Jakob Böhme (d. 1624), or Angelus Silesius (d. 1677), so that they would find themselves rubbing shoulders with Anselm of Canterbury (d. 1109), Peter Abelard (d. 1142), Saint Thomas Aquinas (d. 1274), Duns Scotus (d. 1308), and William of Ockham (d. 1374).

These examples, and one can adduce more, show the elasticity of the definition of Sufism that can be contracted or expanded in response to various intellectual and doctrinal agendas. They also demonstrate, once again, the close intertwining and cross-pollination of insider and outsider discourses around the notion of Sufism.

Sufism and Occult Sciences

In the popular imagination of medieval Christendom, magic and occult sciences were often perceived as "possessed of an aura of menace, something dangerous to have from a social, legal, or even soterial standpoint."[151] Modern Western academics, motivated by the sober rationalist spirit of the European Enlightenment, were not impressed by this "irrational fear." Moreover, until very recently,[152] they have treated occult sciences, including letter and astral magic and prognostication, with open disdain. Within the field of European Islamology, this dismissive attitude toward the irrational has been transposed onto Muslim "magic and talismanery" (*'ilm al-sihr wa 'l-tilsamat*), "the science of the magical properties of [Arabic] letters" (*'ilm asrar al-huruf*), and occult sciences (*'ulum al-ghayb*) as a whole.[153] Throughout the twentieth century, these subjects were seen by European and American academics as undeserving of serious consideration.

Typical in this respect are the "unvarnished" Western assessments of the work of the highly regarded Muslim prognosticator and "lettrist"[154] Ahmad al-Buni (d. 622/1225 or 629/1232) as "stupid, formalistic arithmetic"[155] or "a collection of both muddled and dreary materials for the magical use of numbers and letter-squares."[156] As in the case with the cult of Sufi *awliya'*, the epistemological roots of this dismissive attitude toward Islamic magic sciences on the part of European Orientalists hark back to the Weltanschauung produced by the European Enlightenment. Indeed, both phenomena are often bracketed together by Muslim critics of both Sufism and occultism as well as outside observers.[157] One consequence of this bracketing by critics is the deliberate obfuscation, in pro-Sufi literature, of the close connection between letter magic, divination techniques, and other forms of occult sciences, on the one hand, and Sufism on the other. This long-standing and time-tested connection has only been brought to light recently thanks to the efforts of Western scholars such as Steven Katz (Jewish and comparative mysticism),[158] Pierre Lory and Jean-Charles Coulon (the Muslim world as a whole),[159] Jonathan Katz (North Africa),[160] Noah Gardiner (Egypt, North Africa, and Anatolia during the Mamluk epoch), and Matthew Melvin-Koushki (early Timurid Iran).[161] Thus, the studies of Jonathan Katz, Melvin-Koushki, and Gardiner have shown that in the thirteenth to fifteenth centuries CE Sufis and occultists (whom Gardiner identifies as physicians, alchemists, astrologers, "lettrists," and even as would-be *mahdis*), such as Ahmad al-Buni, Sayyid Husayn al-Akhlati (d. 799/1397), Muhammad al-Kumi and Muhammad al-Zawawi (both fl. in the first half of the ninth/fifteenth century), Badr al-Din al-Simawi (d. 819/1416), Ibn Turka (d. 835/1432), and 'Abd al-Rahman al-Bistami (d. 858/1454), not only moved in the same cultural and devotional spaces but also read the same books and shared the same audiences.[162] They, as the saying goes, wore two hats in being simultaneously (and quite comfortably) occultists and Sufi theorists.[163] Their spiritual pedigrees (*silsilas*) feature such great heroes of early Sufi literature as Ma'ruf al-Karkhi, Sari al-Saqati, al-Junayd, Abu Yazid al-Bistami, and Abu Husayn al-Nuri as well as later founders of the major Sufi brotherhoods, such as Abu Madyan Shu'ayb, Abu 'l-Hasan al-Shadhili, Abu 'l-'Abbas al-Mursi, Ibn 'Ata' Allah al-Sikandari (al-Iskandari), Abu Najib al-Suhrawardi, and Shihab al-Din 'Umar al-Suhrawardi.[164] Further to the point, Sufi biographical sources credit a number of earlier Muslim mystics with expertise in letter magic, for example, Dhu 'l-Nun al-Misri (d. 245/860) and Husayn b. Mansur al-Hallaj (d. 309/922), and some are believed to have composed treatises on this subject, for example, the aforementioned al-Hakim al-Tirmidhi and Sahl al-Tustari (d. 283/896).[165] The "Greatest Master" of Sufism, Ibn (al-)'Arabi (d. 638/1240) not only dabbled in numerology and prognostication but also devoted several long chapters of his giant "encyclopedia of Islamic esotericism," *The Meccan Revelations* (*al-Futuhat al-makkiyya*),[166] to the magical and metaphysical properties of Arabic letters. The French scholar Denis Gril, who has rendered these chapters into French,[167] has proposed that they serve as the key to Ibn (al-)'Arabi's entire worldview.[168] Finally, both the Greatest Master and his contemporary Ahmad al-Buni underwent training at the hands of the same master—'Abd al-'Aziz al-Mahdawi (d. 621/1224) of Ifriqiya (Tunis), to whom Ibn (al-)'Arabi dedicated his *Meccan Revelations*.[169] They read the same books and shared many common assumptions about God, the universe, and the place of human beings in it. Further to the point, in an influential Sufi work by the Egyptian Shaykh Ibn 'Ata' Allah al-Iskandari (d. 709/1309), al-Buni is mentioned as a companion of Abu 'l-Hasan al-Shadhili (d. 656/1258),[170] the eponymous founder of the most popular North African and Egyptian Sufi order.[171]

One can argue that in the premodern epoch and to a lesser extent today, Sufism's popularity with the masses sprang in great part from its affinity with occult sciences rather than its sophisticated but often highly recondite metaphysics and gnoseology. A talisman or a Qur'anic phrase written on a piece of paper by a charismatic Sufi master was of much greater significance to the ordinary Muslim than volumes of obscure mystical speculations.[172] In other words, were it not for its close association with occult sciences, Sufism would not have enjoyed the same popularity as it did and still does. No wonder that premodern and early modern Sufi authors who mentioned occult interests of Sufis in their biographies did not see any contradiction in their dual pursuit of Sufism and occultism. After all, the alchemist's use of the philosopher's stone[173] to transform base metals into gold and silver is akin to the Sufi master's application of a subtle spiritual elixir to the disciple's psyche to transform his or her "animal soul" (*nafs*) to "the soul at peace/rest" that, according to the Qur'an, comes to God "well-pleased and well-pleasing" (89:27–28).[174]

Nevertheless, in standard accounts of Sufism's history, including our own, one looks in vain for any mention of links between Sufi teachings and practices, on the one hand, and occult sciences on the other. All of these are "woven into an elaborate vision of reality"[175] that sets Sufis apart from their non-Sufi coreligionists. Only now such links begin to catch the attention of Western scholars as they abandon the deep-seated Enlightenment-induced prejudice against occultism and thaumaturgy. Yet as Islamic intellectual history shows, in the premodern times, Sufism was intimately associated with occultism. As an example, one can cite the fate of the famous Andalusi Sufi exegete Ibn Barrajan (d. 536/1141), who may have fallen victim to his interest in the science of letters. At least, accusations of practicing and conversing about "lettrism" (*'ilm al-huruf*) were used as a pretext for his condemnation by a group of Maghribi jurists at Marrakesh.[176]

Now, if someone thinks that the distrust of all manner of occultism is characteristic of the "enlightened" Western mindset, they are mistaken. A promising Shafi'i scholar and preacher, Muhammad b. al-Naqqash, whose career was cut short by an untimely death in 762/1361, informs us (in referring to al-Buni's occult legacy) about "a weak-minded community of little knowledge who busied themselves with these letters."[177] His words resonate eerily with the damning verdict on al-Buni's books passed by the modern-day Western scholars mentioned at the beginning of this section. In a similar vein, the famous Hanbali preacher and theologian Ibn Taymiyya accused al-Buni and his ilk of being "star-worshippers in the thrall of devils."[178] The Hanbali guardian of Sunni orthodoxy[179] scathingly ridiculed "the masters of invocatory prayer to the stars, who invoke a star from among the stars and worship it and converse with it and invoke it and fabricate [things] for it from foodstuffs, costume and incense and praise such as are appropriate to it [viz. the star] . . . calling that the spiritual science of the stars."[180] Ibn Taymiyya attributed such "heterodox" pursuits, along with the esoteric teachings of the Andalusian Sufis Ibn (al-)'Arabi and Ibn Sab'in (d. 668 or 669/1269 or 1271), to the "pernicious influences" of the "Shi'i esotericists" (al-batiniyya), that is the Isma'ilis.[181] The renowned North African historian and judge Ibn Khaldun (d. 808/1406) argued that, its religious trappings notwithstanding, the occult science of letters was in reality a form of sorcery (sihr) and, as such, an illicit encroachment on God's monopoly to know and manipulate the unseen (al-ghayb).[182] The Egyptian biographer and jurist al-Sakhawi (d. 902/1497), a harsh critic of the unitive doctrines of Ibn (al-)'Arabi and his followers,[183] insisted that it was their preoccupation with the "pernicious science of letters" that had caused them first to adopt esoteric interpretations of the Qur'an (ta'wilat) and then to concoct the heretical doctrine of the unity of being (wahdat al-wujud). Strong misgivings about the science of letters were expressed by the Andalusian jurist Abu Ishaq al-Shatibi (d. 790/1388), who opined that its "foreign" (that is, Hellenistic) origins render it incompatible with the beliefs and practices of the primeval Muslim community led by the Prophet and his successors.[184]

Cognizant of the close link between the occult sciences and Sufism, Ibn Khaldun endeavored to separate the two[185] with a view to forging a socially and religiously acceptable version of Sufism. To this end, he detached the original Sufism of the classical age (understood primarily as an exemplary moral-ethical uprightness and a rigorous world-renouncing self-discipline)[186] from its later "distortions" at the hands of "Sufi philosophers" (mutafalsifat al-sufiyya).[187] Ibn Khaldun specifically mentions al-Buni, Ibn al-Farid, Ibn Barrajan, Ibn Qasi, and Ibn (al-)'Arabi and his commentators, Ibn Sawdakin and Sa'd al-Din al-Farghani.[188] Ibn Khaldun's goals have been examined elsewhere and should not detain us here.[189] Germane to the present discussion is the definition of Sufism that Ibn Khaldun strove to promote. Contrary to the recent tendency in Western academia to conflate Sufism and philosophy, he wanted to draw a sharp borderline between the two with the aim of promoting Sufism as primarily a moral-ethical self-discipline (which is consistent with the current apology for Sufism as being primarily a technique for soul purification and self-improvement). Consequently, Ibn Khaldun's definition of Sufism denudes it of metaphysical and gnoseological dimensions. Moreover, and surprisingly in step with modern Enlightenment-induced sensitivities, he strips Sufism of the features (especially occult speculations on the thaumaturgic and metaphysical properties of letters and numbers) that almost six hundred years later were dismissed by German Orientalists as "stupid, formalistic arithmetic" and "a collection of both muddled and dreary materials." This remarkable convergence of the minds is yet another example of how Sufism can serve as a meeting place of intellectual agendas and imaginations for observers of vastly different backgrounds and historical epochs. It is also another eloquent testimony to the elasticity of Sufism's definition that is subject to expansions and contractions in response to intellectual and devotional preferences of various actors.

Is an Objective Definition of Sufism Possible in Principle?

The examples furnished above show that the decision to include or not to include certain characteristics or phenomena into the definition of Sufism is determined by the observers' religious and intellectual convictions, upbringing, ethnic identity, ability for self-reflection, professional training, academic and social positions, and so on. All of these and numerous other subjective factors shape decisively what Marshall Hodgson has described as "scholarly precommitments." They manifest themselves "in the questions he [the scholar] poses[190] and in the type of category he uses, where, indeed, bias is especially hard to track down because it is hard to suspect the very terms one uses, which seem so innocently neutral."[191]

Sufism is but one of many show windows for human religious, ideological, and personal "precommitments" that result in what has been dubbed by Michel Foucault "discursive fields" or "discursive formations."[192] Due to Sufism's enmeshment in a variety of conterminous discourses, such as "Islam," "mysticism," "occultism," "philosophy," "fundamentalism," and so on, and in light of the emotional pull it packs and intellectual challenges it presents to its adepts, opponents, and outside observers, it can be characterized as being discursively "fertile." As will be shown throughout this book, its discursive fertility has not been curtailed by the advent of modernity. Moreover, one can venture to predict that it will remain high for the foreseeable future.

Our own position regarding the definition of Sufism is to advocate inclusion over exclusion. Events, personalities, and practices that various insiders and outsiders associate with Sufism deserve to be included into its definition unless there are compelling reasons not to do so. The expansive definition that we tentatively suggest here does not necessarily invalidate more narrowly focused, normative definitions as long as they are viewed as such, that is, attempts by a certain actor or group of actors to legitimize and authenticate their concept of Sufism. In the polyphony of discourses generated by the notion of "Islam,"[193] Sufism has an influential and meaningful part to play. One should not forget, however, that, in addition to being a discursive voice in the choir of Islamic discourses, Sufism has established its highly visible and tangible presence in the very texture of Muslim life. It is represented by brick-and-mortar structures, be they tombs of revered Sufi *awliya'*, memorial mosques dedicated to them, cenotaphs and shrines (*maqams*; *mazars*), Sufi lodges (*zawiyas*; *ribats*), or even full-fledged "monasteries" (*khaneqahs*) that thrived during the premodern period and have survived in the modern age. Supported by charitable donations of God-fearing and impious rulers, government and military officials, merchants and their wives, they can still be seen throughout the width and breadth of the Muslim world. Parallel to Sufism's brick-and-mortar presence, Sufi ideals have manifested themselves in the comportment, rituals (both collective and individual), and dress code(s) of its adherents. These buildings, behaviors, gestures, and costumes, along with the teachings enshrined in the vast body of Sufi literature, constitute the phenomenon that we call "Sufism." Whether real or noetic, "invented" or "imagined" by well- or ill-meaning actors with various degrees of competency, Sufism is here to stay.

A Tentative (Functionalist) Definition

The possibility of producing a comprehensive definition of Sufism remains as elusive as ever before, especially since the terms of debate over what exactly constitutes it continue to change and to involve new actors with new goals, for example, government agencies seeking to domesticate or instrumentalize both Sufism and its organizations as a counterweight to more activist and politically engaged versions of Islam.[194] This conclusion is as obvious as it is discouraging. It implies that any quest for a comprehensive and universally acceptable definition of Sufism by either insiders or outsiders is futile. The various definitions of Sufism examined above seem to confirm this pessimistic conclusion. This is not to deny that progress in our understanding of Sufism's teachings and practices in their historical evolution is not only possible but also obvious. We know about them much more and better than either Sufis or Western academic scholars who lived one century ago.[195] The burden of proof lies on the shoulders of those who deny that this is indeed the case.

At this stage of our own research and that of our colleagues specializing in Sufi studies, it seems reasonable to assume that a working definition of Sufism should be based on its social functions. Articulated and applied by the Polish British anthropologist Bronislaw Malinowski (1884–1942) and his British colleague Alfred Radcliffe-Brown (1881–1955), this structural-functionalist approach to religion purports to demonstrate how social and cultural institutions, religion included, serve basic human needs and function in society as a whole.[196] Seen through the prism of this approach, Sufism's social roles can be defined as ranging from education, moral and spiritual upbringing of the masses to promotion of various forms of artistic creativity (from music and poetry to painting and architecture), and provision of food and shelter to travelers, widows, and orphans. It can also be defined as a means of spiritual solace to the oppressed and downtrodden. Armed with popular appeal, reputation for integrity, and spiritual authority (Weber's "charisma"), individuals with various degrees and forms of Sufi affiliation are favorably positioned to mediate often conflictual relations between rulers and their subjects, competing sociopolitical factions, tribes, families, and individuals. Such mediatory, educational, artistic, and other functions inevitably place Sufism and its followers within a complex network of social and cultural relations in a given collectivity from which it cannot be neatly extricated. In fact, detaching Sufism and Sufis from the cobweb of these social relations and ties is bound to distort the nuanced and eminently complex picture of their functioning within Muslim communities. The better we understand the multifarious contexts within which concrete Sufis are embedded and operate, the more accurate and comprehensive our conception of Sufism will be.

Another consideration is in order here. Through the actions, performances, and ideas of its followers, Sufism has been involved not only in dialogues with various other strands of Islamic tradition, such as *fiqh*, *kalam*, *falsafa*, poetry, occultism, and so on, but also with ideas and practices of non-Muslim religions and philosophical systems, especially (Neo)platonism, Christianity, Judaism, Gnosticism, Manichaeism, Buddhism, and Hinduism. By the logic of inclusion suggested earlier, students of Sufism should not restrict themselves to the cozy confines of the Islamic tradition but should venture beyond it for parallels and examples of mutual enrichment and intersection among various intellectual and devotional traditions.

In the spirit of the functionalist approach outlined above, formulating a working definition of Sufism requires that we identify the major ideas, practices, and values ("constants") that are shared by Sufi communities worldwide. Whereas these communities are extremely diverse both culturally and historically, and their experiences, teachings, and practices are often "apparently *contradictory* and mutually *non-commensurate*,"[197] they can still be integrated into the abstraction "Sufism" in the same way as the experiences, teachings, and practices of various groups of Muslims living in vastly dissimilar conditions and epochs still cohere into the abstraction "Islam."[198] The list of Sufism's "constants" that follows is by definition incomplete and possibly faulty. However, it can, at the very least, serve as a basis for further elaborations, additions, and corrections. Here it is:

- The recognition by Sufism's followers or sympathetic outsiders (and the energetic denial by its detractors) of the supersensory, intuitive, revelatory knowledge and experience of God and the world that Sufis present as God-given and concerned with the esoteric (that is, accessible to the elect few) aspect of the revelation;
- The acceptance of claims to such knowledge not only by the Sufis themselves but also by the Muslim masses, which accounts for the popularity of claimants with Sufi affiliations and, more generally, for the respectability and wide circulation of Sufi doctrines and practices;
- The promise, by possessors of this special knowledge, to impart it to their followers by means of certain meditative techniques and bodily regimes becomes an important recruitment tool that assures the persistence and reproduction of Sufi beliefs and practices across time and space;
- The attainment of this highly valued knowledge requires a radical transformation of the seeker's self that is commonly envisioned as a staged progress ("way") to God that requires meeting certain conditions ("stations") and experiencing certain psychological phenomena ("states");
- The transformation of the self can be achieved individually; however, much more commonly it is pursued collectively by like-minded individuals within the framework of Sufi institutions, that is, "spiritual brotherhoods" (*tariqa*) and their lodges (*zawiya/ribat/ khaneqah*);
- The idea, shared by the overwhelming majority of Sufism's followers, that the transformation of the self requires that a spiritual master (*shaykh, murshid, pir*) with a respectable Sufi "pedigree" (*silsila*) supervise and guide the "aspirant" (*murid*) on the way to his or her goal;

- The mutual obligations of the master and the aspirant constitute the spiritual and disciplinary "glue" that hold together Sufi communities that can be internally diverse, hierarchical, and spatially dispersed;
- Perceived by their followers as bearers of God-given, salvific knowledge and experience (*ma'rifa*; *'irfan*), the Sufi masters acquire the status of God's elect friends (*awliya'*); placed, in the popular imagination, well above fallible and sinful human beings the *awliya'* acquire the reputation of miracle workers and dispensers of beneficial blessing (*baraka*); this reputation and their being, both inside and outside society, render Sufi masters and saints perfect mediators in conflicts among its various segments and competing interests.

This list, as mentioned, is by definition incomplete, and can be expanded and fine-tuned practically ad infinitum. Rendering it complete and all-comprehensive is not our goal. What we would like to emphasize here is that Sufism does indeed meet certain essential societal and existential human needs by helping to alleviate insecurity and precariousness of everyday human existence, fulfilling the desire for authoritative and inerrant guidance, accommodating the human aspiration for the transcendent source of life and goodness, and, ultimately, for achieving redemption and salvation in the afterlife. We explore the ways in which Sufism's diverse representatives have fulfilled these tasks, as well as the societal, political, and intellectual implications of their actions "in the world," in the chapters that follow.

CHAPTER THREE

Discourses

Discourse or Tradition?

Each religious or political movement requires doctrines, practices, individuals, and rules to sustain it. Collectively called "tradition," scholars of religion use this polysemic and occasionally amorphous term to analyze the functioning of various religious communities and societies.[1] Some critically minded sociologists have argued that "tradition" is but an arbitrary and highly problematic heuristic device that scholars employ to introduce the theme of continuity and order into a usually chaotic profusion and dispersion of beliefs, personalities, practices, and ways of knowledge transmission. Structured around the concept of the origin (the diverse components of which are often downplayed) and influence (to establish causality), tradition, Michel Foucault (1926–1984) has argued, "Enables us to isolate the new against a background of permanence, and to transfer its merit to originality, to genius, to the decision proper to individuals." Moreover, tradition, Foucault has suggested, "links, at a distance and through time . . . such defined unities as individuals, *oeuvres*, notions, or theories."[2] By stressing both constancy and evolution, the concept of tradition "makes it possible to group a succession of dispersed events, to link them to one and the same organizing principle."[3] In our own opinion, the function of this organizing principle is to squeeze the vivacity, diversity, discreteness, inconsistency, and unpredictability of human behavior and thought into a ready-made structure.[4] As with any intellectual premise, the concept of tradition is vague and malleable, allowing for a wide variety of uses, often incompatible. However, if we abandon it altogether, as Foucault has himself acknowledged, we will be left face to face with a chaotic "population of dispersed events."[5] To find a way out of this predicament, we take seriously his advice to be self-reflexive and self-critical in using such broad, "catch-all" analytical categories, but we do not dismiss them altogether insofar as they are useful for describing the phenomena we want to convey to our audience. Categories such as "tradition" are necessary for our narrative to be coherent and comprehensible. The alternative is to descend into the "primeval chaos" of unconnected events, personalities, institutions, and doctrines, without any hope of making sense out of them.

In the field of Islamic studies, we find not only the Islamic tradition per se, but also its various subsets qualified by such epithets as "theological," "philosophical," "legal," "rationalist," "fundamentalist," or by eponymous designations, such as "Ash'ari," "Maturidi," "Hanafi," "Shafi'i," "Maliki," "Hanbali," "Avicennan," and so on. The principal subject of the present chapter is Muslim exegetical tradition with special reference to its allegorical-esoteric subset as represented by Sufism.[6] Sometimes such derivative traditions are designated as "schools of thought," for example, "theological schools of thought," namely, Ash'arism, Maturidism, and Hanbalism. In the present chapter, we will be dealing with the "Akbarian school of thought," that is, one that draws its inspiration from the intellectual legacy of Sufism's "Greatest Master" (*al-shaykh al-akbar*) Ibn (al-)'Arabi (d. 638/1240). Another "school of thought" that will occupy us is "Kubrawi," which is named after the sobriquet of the Central Asian Sufi thinker Najm al-Din (al-)Kubra (d. in or shortly after 617/1220). Overall, our use of the term "tradition" as opposed to "school of thought" usually indicates that the former refers to both doctrine and practice, whereas the latter to doctrine or discourse par excellence.

When scholars of Islam talk about Sufi tradition, they usually subsume under this category teachings, practices, communities, and institutions without clearly differentiating among them.[7] This usage may be justified in the light of Foucault's warning about the dangers of classifying products of human thought under such neat rubrics as "literature," "politics," "philosophy," "religion," and such,[8] because he viewed them, rightly, as arbitrary and anachronistic and thus potentially misleading. On the other hand, a lack of differentiation among the tradition's subsets may occasionally muddle the narrative, thereby confusing the reader. To avoid this, in the introduction to this book we proposed that the Sufi tradition, defined as an ascetic-mystical movement or stream in Islam, be treated under five principal rubrics: 1. Discourses; 2. Practices; 3. Community; 4. Institutions; 5. Leaders. As with any analytical schema, this pigeonholing of real-life Sufism is reductive and open to criticism along the lines suggested by Foucault and his followers. However, the proposed rubrics do, in our opinion at least, capture the most salient features of the phenomenon in question and are therefore useful for the purpose of communicating the gist of our findings to the reader.

The first component of the Sufi tradition, "discourse," is also in itself problematic. Is it synonymous with Sufism's teaching(s), doctrine(s), and literature(s)? One can argue that to some extent it is. Why, then, one may ask, should we use it? The advantage of this term, in our opinion, is that not only does it denote oral or written instruction, textual production, and formulation of creed (that is, normativity), but it also implies a certain fluidity and lack of stability, in other words, dynamic and vivacious open-endedness. It also implies an audience that discourse is supposed to edify or influence in some way, for example, transform one's entire worldview and lifestyle (existence).[9] Most importantly, the word "discourse," as we understand it, conveys open-endedness and fluidity, that is, the process of an ongoing renegotiation and readjustment of the tradition's elements and symbols by various agents in response to changing conditions of their own existence, their own preferences, and expectations of their audiences.[10] The edifice of Sufism's history shows both a certain level of stability of Sufi discourse and, simultaneously, its mutability at the many hands of its architects. This, at first sight paradoxical, combination of stability and malleability (and the resultant openness to change) explains why the Sufi tradition has persevered, by constantly readjusting itself, in response to sometimes rather adverse historical, sociopolitical, and ideological conditions. We will now examine the evolution of Sufi discourse with a special focus on exegesis, because not only does it contain the keynotes of Sufi thought and practice generally, but also it anchors them firmly in the authority of the Muslim scripture.

The Qur'an and Hadith as a Source of Mystical Inspiration, Contemplation, and Language

The good of a book lies in its being read. A book is made up of signs that speak of other signs, which in their turn speak of things.

UMBERTO ECO, *THE NAME OF THE ROSE*

As discussed in chapter 1, many Sufi concepts, terms, and practices hark back to the Qur'anic text and the sayings (Hadith) of the prophet Muhammad,[11] which endows them with legitimacy in the eyes of both Sufis and Muslims generally. The use of the Scripture by the Sufis is consistent with the goals and textual practices of their counterparts in other religions insofar as "mystics across traditions and cultures have always assumed that the sacred texts of their traditions are authentic centers of divine, transcendent, ultimate truth ... and the mystical quest is, quite literally, the discovery or rediscovery of the mysteries encoded in scripture."[12] Given the centrality of scripture to ascetic-mystical Weltanschauung and experience, it is hardly surprising that "the mystical exegesis of canonical texts constitutes a large, if not the largest, segment of what is usually identified as the collective body of [the] world's mystical literature."[13] This fact explains our choice of esoteric-mystical exegesis as the fulcrum of our discussion of Sufi discourses and gnoseological claims made on their basis.

In light of the foregoing general observations about the role of exegesis in ascetic-mystical traditions, it is hardly surprising that Sufi literature virtually brims with Qur'anic and prophetic references and allusions. Combined with the cardinal principles of Sufi theory and practice, Sufi exegesis lies at the heart of both a distinctly Sufi expressive idiom and vision of the world more generally. In devising and articulating ascetic-mystical conceptions of knowledge (gnoseology) and cosmology, medieval Sufi thinkers put the Qur'an and Hadith to a wide variety of creative uses.[14] Whereas in principle any Qur'anic verse or saying of the Prophet potentially yields itself to an allegorical-esoteric interpretation, some are richer in relevant meanings than others. Over the centuries Sufi theorists have consistently deployed them as proof texts.[15] Among these semantically and symbolically rich passages are: Q 17:1, alluding to the Prophet's night journey and ascension to heaven (al-isra' wa 'l-mi'raj);[16] Q 18:13–25, the story of the Seven Sleepers [of the cave];[17] Q 53:1–16, describing the Prophet's audiences with God or his angelic messenger, Gabriel; Q 18:60–82, featuring the momentous encounter between the prophet Moses (Musa) and a mysterious personage identified by Muslim exegetes as al-Khadir (Khizir);[18] Q 3:35–44; 19:16–29; 66:12, and so on, relating the story of Mary (Maryam) and her son Jesus ('Isa).[19] Moses's direct encounters and conversations with God, depicted in Q 7:142–43, 20:9–15, and 20:17–22, have also inspired numerous mystical elaborations.[20] In a similar vein, Qur'anic passages that allude to God's immediate, immanent presence among his human servants have drawn the attention of many Sufi exegetes. Whereas Q 2:115 and 235 portray God, respectively, as being ever-watchful ("God knows what is in your hearts")[21] and omnipresent ("whithersoever you turn, there's God's face"), Q 50:16 goes even further by declaring him to be nearer to a human servant than "his jugular vein."[22] Especially attractive to Muslim ascetics-mystics is the famous "Light Verse" (Q 24:35) that depicts God as the sublime and all-permeating light. The Light Verse has proved to be a particularly fertile starting point for mystical meditations on the theme of light and darkness, creation, prophethood, divine nature, and guidance as well as the cosmic disjuncture between spirit and matter.[23] One can also read it as symbolic of what Marshall Hodgson calls "a unitive idea of total reality," namely, God's luminous presence in the empirical universe that, in his view, is reminiscent of the ideas articulated in the Gospel of Saint John.[24] When taken to heart by the faithful, continues Hodgson, the similes of the Light Verse convey "the full impression of brilliance and purity, of detachment from any local or transient involvement, and withal of perfect security and dependability"; it invites "the further consideration which [the entire] Qur'an itself often suggests."[25] On a more humane, microcosmic plane, ascetically-mystically minded exegetes have interpreted the niche, in which the Qur'anic lamp is said to be shining, as the heart of the prophet Muhammad or that of any God's faithful servant.[26] After surveying such exegetical elaborations, the Hungarian Islamologist Ignaz Goldziher (1860–1925) has remarked that in Sufi interpretations of this symbolically "fecund" verse, one allegory is being "heaped on another."[27]

In their obvious fascination with the imagery of the Light Verse, the two Western scholars (that is, outsiders) were certainly not alone. Long before them insiders from among early Sufis masters had explored its allegorical potential, suggesting, among other things, that its underlying message is that God guides whom he wishes with his light.[28] Drawing on a selection of Qur'anic passages,[29] they identified such divinely guided individuals as the pious, God-fearing servants of God (awliya' Allah) who devote themselves single-mindedly to worshipping him and doing his will.[30] In return for their unshakeable loyalty and single-minded devotion, God has granted them a superior, unique insight into his deepest mysteries and has promised them unconditional salvation in the hereafter.[31] As a result, they have become, at least in the eyes of their followers, the natural guides of and protectors of humankind. To substantiate this vision of God's elect, Sufi theorists marshaled numerous relevant passages culled from the Qur'an.[32]

The Qur'an was the most important source of Sufi concepts and terms. But it was not the only one. Sufis mined the giant corpus of the Prophet's sayings (Hadith) for ideas that resonated with their aspirations and general worldview.[33] Particularly fertile for esoteric-mystical speculations were the so-called sacred or holy Hadith (hadith qudsi),[34] in which God speaks in the first person through the prophet Muhammad.[35] Some of these Hadith describe God as being intimately close to his servant to the point of becoming the servant's hearing, sight, hand, and foot;[36] rushing forth to fulfill his needs;[37] being always present in his servant's thoughts;[38] and being "more intense in yearning" to meet his faithful worshipper than the worshipper himself.[39] Moreover, God's entire purpose in creating this world is to give his human servants a chance to know and love him.[40] Pertinent to our discussion of Sufi engagements with the divine word is the Hadith that asserts that those of God's servants who constantly ponder on the hidden meanings of the Qur'an are God's elect[41]—a theme that we will be dealing with throughout the rest of this chapter. Whereas references to prophetic Hadith are particularly prominent in Ibn (al-)'Arabi's writings,[42] it is also richly attested in the writings of earlier and later Sufis.[43] As in the Qur'an, the vast and diverse corpus of the Prophet's sayings constitutes an important source of Sufi terms, themes, and arguments not just in the context of Sufi exegetical works but also in Sufi apologetic and polemical discourses more generally.[44]

Its importance for Sufi discourse notwithstanding, the Hadith corpus (Sunna) still takes a back seat to the Qur'an that has served as the principal starting point and frame of reference for Sufi disquisitions about God, the cosmos, and the vicissitudes of humanity in this world and in the hereafter. The process has never been unidirectional, though, that is, from the Qur'an as the source to the esoteric-mystical discourse as the product. Rather, mystical (gnostic) ideas, for which Sufis have diligently mined the Qur'anic text, in their turn, shaped, often decisively, their perceptions of and approaches to the Muslim scripture. An important caveat is in order here. Seen objectively and dispassionately over the *longue durée*, Sufi ideas did not originate exclusively in the Qur'an and the Sunna, as some Muslim and Western scholars have implied.[45] Couched in Qur'anic and Prophetic (Sunnitic) terminology, they had antecedents in the Judeo-Hellenistic environment of the Mediterranean basin.[46] This is hardly surprising, for the Qur'an, as has been shown by recent scholarship, was itself a product of the Mediterranean cultural and intellectual melting pot.[47] The same, one might add, equally applies to Christianity and Western culture.

The Beginnings of Mystical Exegesis

Religion tunes human actions to an envisaged cosmic order and projects images of cosmic order into the plane of human experience.

CLIFFORD GEERTZ, *INTERPRETATION OF CULTURES*

Not only does the Qur'an encourage its followers to practice a pious, penitent, and worshipful behavior in this world,[48] it also provides explanations as to how human experience fits into the overall cosmic order of things. Thus, Q 7:172, which figures prominently in Sufi discourses, describes the pre-eternal covenant or pact (*mithaq*) between God and his human servants[49] during which they appeared before God as an assemblage of disembodied souls. While in this disembodied state, God demanded that the souls (described as "human atoms or specs")[50] bear witness to his sovereignty or lordship (*rububiyya*), and they complied. However, according to Sufi elaborations of this passage,[51] once the souls acquired desiring bodies prone to sin and inequity, they forgot their primordial pledge and therefore are in need of constant reminders about it by divinely commissioned messengers and prophets.[52] After the cessation of the prophetic era, the role of admonishers and guides has devolved upon God's faithful and pious "friends" (*awliya'*).[53] They consider life in this world to be but a test of human loyalty to the primordial covenant between God and the disembodied human race. Reminiscences of the day of the covenant (*yawm al-mithaq*) compel the *awliya'* to abstain from the glitter of mundane existence and to strive to return to the state of the pristine faithfulness to their Lord that they demonstrated during that momentous meeting with him in pre-eternity. The world-renouncing demeanor advocated by both the prophets and the *awliya'* is to be achieved by minimizing the corruptive drives of the human lower soul (*nafs*) that "prompt [the believer] to evil" (*ammara bi-su'*; Q 12:53). If successful, the ascetic-mystic's lowly, "appetitive" self is transformed into a soul "at peace" (*al-mutma'inna*; Q 89:27) that by its very nature is incapable of disobeying its Lord.[54] The Sufi tradition offers ample means to this end: a life of renunciation of worldly pleasures, of pious meditation, and of a constant remembrance of God (*dhikr*),[55] as explicitly enjoined in Q 8:87, 18:24, and 33:41. Finally, verses describing some ocular and auditory experiences of the prophet Muhammad[56] have motivated Sufis to try, as it were, "to recapture the rapture" experienced by the founder of Islam[57] by seeking a direct encounter with God, especially since the Qur'an repeatedly calls upon the faithful to emulate his ways in minute detail.[58]

Although Sufi thinkers have drawn consistently on the Qur'anic imagery and couched their discourses in Qur'anic terminology, Sufi interpretations of the Scripture (as well as Sufi practices, values, and beliefs generally) have been frequently condemned as heretical by influential representatives of the Sunni and Shi'i religious establishments, occasionally resulting in persecution of their authors.[59] Today, as in the past, Sufism's critics frequently accuse its followers of overplaying allegorical aspects of the Qur'an and of claiming to know its real meaning, while disregarding the text's literal sense. Sufis usually respond by profusely quoting Qur'anic verses and Prophetic Hadith that, in their opinion, justify their exegetical methods and conclusions.[60] Typical in this respect is the following statement of Ibn (al-)ʿArabi:

> Know that everything that is expressed in my discourses and works originates from the treasury of the Koran because the keys to its understanding have been handed over to me.[61]

Whereas some Muslims may find such statements disturbing or even outrageous,[62] the centrality of the Qur'an to Sufism as the source of inspiration and ideas as well as the main proof-text for the Sufi Weltanschauung is hardly in doubt. Sufi discourses are literally suffused with Qur'anic images, terminology, allusions, and reminiscences.[63]

How exactly did early Muslim ascetics-mystics approach the Qur'an? The Francophone scholar of Christian (Chaldean) background Paul Nwyia (1925–1980), who followed in the footsteps of the renowned French Catholic Islamologist Louis Massignon (1883–1962), has shown that Sufi engagements with the Qur'an were quite distinct from those of conventional Sunni interpreters, for example, Muqatil b. Sulayman (d. 150/767), who was concerned primarily with historical, philological, and legal aspects of the Muslim revelation.[64] Exegetical glosses attributed rightly or wrongly to the sixth Shiʿi imam Jaʿfar al-Sadiq (d. 148/765)[65] show no concern, on the part of this esoterically minded exegete, with the historical circumstances of the battle of Badr mentioned in the Qur'an and elucidated in its numerous exoteric commentaries. When the text says that, at Badr, "God supported him [Muhammad] with the legions you [his followers] did not see" (Q 9:40), (Pseudo-)Jaʿfar interprets the legions not as angels (as Muqatil and other exoterically minded exegetes would do), but as the spiritual virtues that the seeker of God acquires on the way (tariq) to his Creator, namely, "certitude" (yaqin), "trust" (thiqa), and submission to his will (tawakkul). Likewise, (Pseudo-)Jaʿfar interprets the Qur'anic injunction for the believers to "purify My [God's] House (namely, the Kaʿba) for those who shall circumambulate it"[66] as a call on the seeker of God (murid) to "purify [his] soul from any association with the disobedient ones and anything other than God."[67] In a similar vein, (Pseudo-)Jaʿfar explains the Qur'anic phrase "those who stay in front of it [the Kaʿba]" not as a reference to the ritual standing performed by pilgrims during the hajj, but rather as an invitation for the believers to seek the company of "the [divine] gnostics (ʿarifun), who stand on the carpet of intimacy [with God] and service to Him." Here once again the notion of the divinely bestowed and inspired "gnosis," or mystical knowledge (maʿrifa), comes to the fore. (Pseudo-)Jaʿfar unequivocally attributes it to God's elect servants,[68] which sets his esoteric exegesis apart from the conventional one of Muqatil and other exoterically minded interpreters, who did not attribute special insight into the meaning of the Qur'anic text to any particular group of believers. Such claims, as we shall see, were to become a hallmark of Sufi exegesis ever since.[69]

For the early Muslim advocates of the ascetic-mystical version of Islam, oral and written commentaries on the Qur'an became the preferred arena for arguing that accomplished Sufi masters had access to its underlying secrets. In later Sufi gnoseology this esoteric, divinely inspired "realization" (*tahqiq*) of the divine word is presented as a special type of cognition (*ma'rifa*; *kashf*) that God bestows upon the realizer as a favor, either deserved or not. This cognition (or "gnosis" as it is often rendered into European languages by Western scholars) is consistently juxtaposed by Sufis with both the received wisdom (*naql*) transmitted from one learner to another[70] and the knowledge one acquires by exercising one's rational faculty (*'aql*).[71] Both have their uses in the believer's life. However, in the final account, Sufis have insisted, they are inadequate to lead their adherents to a true realization of God's message in the Qur'an as well as in its giant replica, the cosmos.[72] Learning from predecessors and following blindly injunctions of prior authorities becomes a blinker of sorts for the seeker of true knowledge, a constraint, or even "a collar around the neck."[73] Likewise, the intellect has an important function to play in restraining the person's appetitive soul (*nafs*) and discerning right from wrong,[74] but is, in the final account, an inadequate tool to plumb the unfathomable depths of the revelation.[75] For (Pseudo-) Ja'far as for later Sufi exegetes, a divinely inspired "realization" (*tahqiq*) of the Qur'anic word is the only sure way to obtain the supersensory awareness (*ma'rifa*) of the true nature of God (*haqq*) and his creation (*khalq*).[76]

Claims to Privileged Knowledge of the Revelation as a Hallmark of Sufi Exegetical Discourse

Homo hierarchicus *enshrines a notion of cosmic responsibility, of the unique, precious value of each individual's keeping his place. This sense of significance is often lacking among societies possessing a more egalitarian view.*

JONATHAN Z. SMITH, *MAP IS NOT TERRITORY:*
STUDIES IN THE HISTORY OF RELIGIONS

The earliest extant book of Sufi exegesis was assembled by a prolific Sufi teacher from the city of Nishapur in the Iranian province of Khurasan named Abu 'Abd al-Rahman al-Sulami (d. 412/1021). Titled *True Realities of Commentary (Haqa'iq al-tafsir)*, al-Sulami's work is our principal source for understanding the earliest stages of allegorical-esoteric exegesis in Islam.[77] Its major representatives cited by al-Sulami—al-Hasan al-Basri (d. 110/728), Ja'far al-Sadiq (d. 148/765), Sufyan al-Thawri (d. 161/778), and 'Abdallah b. al-Mubarak (d. 181/797)—were not Sufis sensu stricto, because Sufism as a distinctive and free-standing set of communities, teachings, and practices was yet to emerge. Nevertheless, these highly revered early Muslims were subsequently co-opted into Sufism by its later proponents who portrayed them as the founding fathers of Sufism before this name itself had gained wide currency and popular recognition.[78] Although the preoccupation of this cohort of Muslim devotees with the allegoric aspects of the Muslim scripture is plausible, the authenticity of their exegetical logia, collected and transmitted by al-Sulami a century and a half later, should not be taken for granted. The problem is particularly severe (and intriguing) in the case of the sixth Shi'i imam Ja'far al-Sadiq[79] to the extent that some modern scholars attribute the exegetical material transmitted in his name to a certain Sufi teacher, who "flourished in [the] fourth/tenth century."[80] Ja'far al-Sadiq's role as a doyen of the primeval allegorical-esoteric exegesis is difficult to ascertain, especially because his exegetical statements, transmitted by al-Sulami, are devoid of any recognizably pro-'Alid themes.[81] Be this as it may, scattered throughout al-Sulami's voluminous *Haqa'iq al-tafsir*, they help us to reconstruct the principles of allegorical-esoteric exegesis in Islam that continue to motivate its adherents until today.[82] According to these principles, the Qur'an contains four levels of meaning: *'ibara* (literal), *ishara* (allegorical or allusive), *lata'if* (subtle), and *haqa'iq* (real).[83] Each of them has its own addressees, respectively: the commoners (*'awamm*), the religious elite (*khawass*), God's friends (*awliya'*), and the prophets (*anbiya'*).[84] This fourfold categorization is complicated and potentially confusing; subsequent Sufi commentators usually speak of just two levels: the outward, or exoteric (*zahir*), and the inner, or esoteric (*batin*). In this way, the moral-ethical, historical, and legal aspects of each Qur'anic passage were subsumed under the rubric outward, or exoteric, whereas its allegorical, mystical, and anagogical senses fell under the rubric inner, or esoteric.[85] The former is the domain of the common believers (*ahl al-zahir*), including "scholars of outward [divine] prescriptions" (*'ulama' al-rusum*), the latter exclusively of the Sufi "friends of God" (*awliya'*) or "gnostics" (*'arifun [bi-llah]*).[86]

Sufi claims to a superior, privileged understanding of God's word are brought into a sharp relief in the writings of Abu 'l-Qasim al-Qushayri (d. 465/1072) of Nishapur who is famous primarily as the author of the

Al-Qushayri's Epistle on Sufism (*al-Risala al-Qushayriyya fi 'ilm al-tasawwuf*), a treatise that combines elements of Sufi biography with those of a Sufi manual.[87] The main objective of both the *Epistle* and al-Qushayri's other major works, especially the Qur'anic commentary *Subtleties of Allusions* (*Lata'if al-isharat*), is to advocate the teachings, values, and practices of a "moderate," "Junayd-style"[88] Sufism. Combining elements of Sufi "science" (*'ilm hadhihi 'l-ta'ifa*), Hadith scholarship, Shafi'i jurisprudence, Ash'ari theology, and allegorical-esoteric exegesis,[89] this multivolume opus seeks to demonstrate the complete harmony between Sufism and the creeds and juridical theory of Sunni Islam. Simultaneously, al-Qushayri shows how Sunni Muslims in general stand to benefit from the values and insights of Sufism—an endeavor brought to fruition by Abu Hamid al-Ghazali (d. 505/1111) half a century later.[90] Started in 437/1045,[91] al-Qushayri's massive exegesis consistently correlates the exegete's progress from a literal to a subtler meaning (*lata'if*) of the Qur'anic text with the stages of the Sufi's self-perfection and self-purification during his experiential journey to God (*tariq*). Al-Qushayri draws the same parallel in his *Epistle*. Here the discussion of each Sufi term or concept is preceded by apposite Qur'anic statements that emphasize its different implications for Sufi seekers at various stages of progress toward their Lord.[92] According to al-Qushayri, the foremost masters (*shuyukh*) of the Sufi community (*ta'ifa*) are privy to the Qur'an's most profound and subtle mysteries. His commentary on Q 9:122 eloquently describes his hierarchical conception of the knowledge of Qur'anic mysteries and of the various classes of knowers whom God grants access to these mysteries:

> He [God] arranged the Muslims according to ranks. The masses are like subjects of the king. The *hadith* collectors are like the treasurers of the king. The people of the Qur'an are like the guardians of the registries and valuables [of the king]. The jurists are the king's trustees, because the jurist [adjudicates][93] for God. The scholars of the roots (*'ulama' al-usul*)[94] are like the chiefs and commanders of the armies. The *awliya'* are like pillars of the [palace's] gate, while the lords of hearts (*arbab al-qulub*) and the people of purity (*ashab al-safa'*) are like the elect of the king and his companions.[95]

Al-Qushayri argues that one's comprehension of the mysteries of the Qur'an, as well as one's progress on the path to God, depends on one's ability to combine personal piety and feats of ascetic self-abnegation with sound doctrinal convictions and correct implementation of God's moral-ethical imperatives. Giving preference to one over the other leads to failure. Even when this felicitous balance of spiritual perfection, sound creed, and pious actions is struck by the exegete, he or she would still need divine assistance (*tawfiq*) to plumb the deepest mysteries of the sacred text. The same goes, according to al-Qushayri, for the seeker's (*salik*) quest for intimacy with God. Only after the aspiring traveler (*murid*) has become God's chosen friend and beloved (*murad*) can he hope to achieve the ultimate goal, be it proximity to God, purity in thought and action, or a divinely induced veridical knowledge (*ma'rifa*) of the true reality (*haqiqa*) of the divine word.[96] In the end, only the cream of the cream of the Sufi community, "the lords of [mystical] hearts" and "people of purity," in al-Qushayri's parlance, are destined to obtain the veridical realization of the true sense of the divine writ because it is revealed to them directly by its author himself.

In parallel to the traversal of the stages of the Sufi path (*tariq*) by the Sufi seeker,[97] al-Qushayri presents the exegete's immersion into the meaning of the Scripture as a movement, first, from the intellect to the heart, next to the spirit (*al-ruh*), then to the innermost secret (*al-sirr*) and, finally, to the secret of secrets (*sirr al-sirr*) of the Qur'an.[98] Al-Qushayri's own engagement with the scripture exhibits his deep reverence for, and meticulous attention to, every detail of the Qur'anic diction, from the entire verse to every single letter in it. Typical in this regard is his interpretation of the *basmala*.[99] The Sufi exegete endows every letter of this oft-repeated Qur'anic phrase with an allegorical-esoteric significance: The *ba'* stands for God's gentleness (*birr*) toward his "righteous friends" (*awliya' salihun*); the *sin*—for the secret (*sirr*) that God entrusts to his "chosen and purified ones" (*asfiya'*); the *mim*—for God's bestowal of grace (*minna*) upon "those seeking intimacy" with him (*ahl wilayatihi*).

Whereas such "lettrist" reflections are not unique to al-Qushayri,[100] there is one feature that sets him apart from both his predecessors and successors. For al-Qushayri, the *basmala* at the head of each Qur'anic chapter (*sura*) is not a simple repetition of the same underlying message(s), because, in his opinion, the Scripture is too sublime and perfect to allow for a simple repetition. Therefore, al-Qushayri argues, the *basmala*'s meaning changes according to the major themes embedded in each individual sura.[101] Thus, in discussing the symbolism of the *basmala* of sura 7, al-Qushayri implicitly links it to the themes of submission (*islam*), humility, and reverence required of the true believer as opposed to the rebellious behavior of the Devil (*Iblis*), both themes being an important motif of this particular chapter.[102] Al-Qushayri's interpretation of the *basmala* of sura 15 is quite different. The omission of the letter *alif* in the *basmala* of that sura without any apparent reason, either grammatical or morpho-logical, in al-Qushayri's opinion, symbolizes God's seemingly "illogical" elevation of Adam above the angels,[103] despite his base natural composi-tion (clay) and their elevated status in the heavenly hierarchy, as described in the sura.

Fascinated as he is with the esoteric and spiritual dimensions of the divine word, al-Qushayri pays little heed to its historical and legal refer-ences, treating them primarily, if not exclusively as allegorical windows onto Sufism's ideas, practices, and moral-ethical values. Thus, in discuss-ing the spoils of war (*ghanima*) mentioned in Q 8:41 al-Qushayri argues: "*Jihad* can be of two types, that is, the external one [waged] against the infidels and the internal one [waged] against [one's] soul and Satan. In the same way as the lesser *jihad* involves [the seizure of] spoils of war after victory, the greater *jihad*, too, brings the spoils of war of its own, that is, taking possession of his soul by the servant of God after it has been held hostage by its two enemies—[lowly] passions and Satan."[104] A similar ap-proach to the Qur'anic themes is evident in al-Qushayri's explanation of the Qur'anic command to fast during the month of Ramadan, which re-quires that the ordinary believer abstain from food, sex, and drink during the daytime. According to al-Qushayri, when applied to the perfected Sufi seeker this injunction demands, in addition to a regular fasting, that he abandon mundane affairs altogether to concentrate his thoughts solely and exclusively on God. Although abstention is demanded in both cases, in the second it is not just external or formal (*zahir*), but internal or pro-found (*batin*) as well.

Now, anticipating our comparative discussion of allegorical-esoteric exegesis in chapter 4 of this book, it should be pointed out that al-Qushayri's approach to the Scripture has influential predecessors not only among Muslim thinkers, such as al-Sulami and the exegetical authorities he quoted, but outside Islam as well. The name that immediately comes to mind is Philo of Alexandria (d. 45 CE), whose work "is nearly synonymous with allegorical exegesis" in the Judaic exegetical tradition.[105] Like al-Qushayri, Philo was prone "to piece together the allegorical meaning [of the Hebrew Bible] while accepting also the literal, even if he will nearly always give preference to the former."[106] For example, he interpreted God's words addressed to Abraham in Genesis 12:3, "in you all of the tribes of the earth will be blessed," as an allegory of the "transformation of the bad passions [of the human soul] into good ones." This transforma-tion, argued Philo, is achieved by keeping the mind, the governor of the soul, in a healthy (that is, worshipful and pious) condition.[107] This kind of allegorical-esoteric explanation of the Torah immediately conjures up al-Qushayri's Qur'anic glosses cited above, which, in their turn, are representative of Sufi exegesis generally.

Despite its overall "moderate" and moral-ethical character, al-Qushayri's exegesis is not devoid of certain visionary and ecstatic elements that characterize the "bolder" type of allegorical-esoteric exegeses to be discussed further on. These "bolder" aspects of al-Qushayri's engagement with the Scripture can be described as "unitive,"[108] that is, alluding to the possibility of an ecstatic or cognitive union between God's chosen servants and their Lord. As an example, one can cite al-Qushayri's interpretation of Q 7:143. Here the divinely chosen servants are exemplified by the prophet Moses (Musa) who requests that God appear to him only to be humbled by the sight of a mountain crumbling to dust, after God has shown himself to it. During this paradigmatic encounter, Moses's very personality is "erased" in an act of (self-)annihilation in God usually described in Sufism by the term *fana'*.[109] In al-Qushayri's poetically articulated gloss,

> Moses came to God as [only] those passionately longing and madly in love would do. Moses came without Moses. Moses came, yet nothing of Moses was left to Moses. Thousands of men have traversed great distances, yet no one remembers them, while Moses made [only] a few steps and [school]children will be reciting until the Day of Judgment: "When Moses came."[110]

Such moving exegetical interventions notwithstanding, al-Qushayri's exegesis should still be classified as "moderate," because the exegete strives to achieve a balance between daring flights of the mystical imagination and respect for the letter of the revelation, or, in the Sufi parlance, between the external moral-ethical and legal dispensation (*shari'a*), on the one hand, and its inward dimension, or true reality (*haqiqa*), on the other. In sum, al-Qushayri's influential oeuvre bears an eloquent testimony to his triple credentials: a Sufi master, a Shafi'i *faqih*, and an Ash'ari theologian.[111]

The world of Sufi exegesis is rich and variegated. The same applies to Sufi uses of the Qur'an more generally. One cannot hope to exhaust this vast topic in one book chapter. The best one can do is to highlight some of its most salient features by citing representative works of the genre. Noteworthy in this regard is Rashid al-Din Ahmad al-Maybudi's (d. 530/1135) *The Unveiling of Mysteries* (*Kashf al-asrar*) that, in its turn, is based on the Qur'anic commentary by the renowned Hanbali mystic of Herat, 'Abdallah al-Ansari al-Harawi (d. 481/1089), as al-Maybudi explicitly states in the introduction.[112] William Chittick has identified the second major source of Maybudi's commentary as *The Repose of Spirits: Explaining the Names of the All-Opening King* (*Rawh al-arwah fi sharh asma' al-malik al-fattah*) by Ahmad b. Mansur Sam'ani (d. 534/1140) of Merv (Mary) in today's Turkmenistan.[113] According to Chittick, "Maybudi uses at least as much material from Sam'ani as he does from Ansari" and, like its two antecedents, al-Maybudi's "Unveiling" is written in Persian.[114] Born in a family renowned for its learning and piety in the town of Maybud (the province of Yazd in Iran), al-Maybudi, like al-Qushayri, combined the conventional education of a Shafi'i jurist and Hadith collector (*muhaddith*) with a strong inclination to contemplative mysticism and ascetic lifestyle.[115] As with other "moderate" Sufi commentaries, al-Maybudi's *Kashf al-asrar* contains conventional historical, philological, and legal exegeses along with discussions of the Qur'an's "allusions" (*isharat*), "symbols" (*rumuz*), and "subtleties" (*lata'if*).[116] The Iranian commentator describes his method as consisting of three "stages" (sing. *navbat*). The first is a translation of selected Qur'anic verses from Arabic into "literal Persian" (*farsi-ya zahir*); the second, a conventional historical, philological, and juridical commentary in Persian; while the third is an exploration of allegorical-esoteric aspects of the Scripture. The last "stage," as mentioned, draws heavily on al-Ansari's mystical commentary, which, in its turn, is based on al-Sulami's *True Realities of [Qur'an] Interpretation* (*Haqa'iq al-tafsir*) and the (proto-)Sufi pious individuals cited therein. No less significantly, al-Maybudi also makes extensive use of al-Qushayri's *Subtleties of Allusions* (*Lata'if al-isharat*) that is "sometimes quoted word for word in Arabic, and at other times rendered in Persian."[117] One can thus say that al-Maybudi belongs to the allegorical-esoteric exegetical tradition originating among the major representatives of Sufism in late fourth-/tenth-century Khurasan.

As befits a "moderate" commentator, al-Maybudi avoids interpretations that depart too far from the literal meaning of the Qur'an. His treatment of the potentially controversial anthropomorphic features of God, the provenance of good and evil, and divine predetermination of all events is that of a middle-of-the-way theologian of both Ash'ari and traditionalist leanings.[118] In this respect, al-Maybudi follows in the footsteps of his eminent predecessor al-Qushayri, although al-Qushayri's commitment to Ash'arism appears to be much stronger in comparison.[119] Al-Maybudi explains the necessity to practice allegorical-esoteric exegesis by the presence in the Qur'an (Q 3:7) of the "obscure" or "ambiguous" verses (*mutashabihat*) alongside the "clear" or "unequivocal" ones (*muhkamat*). The meaning of the "obscure" or "ambiguous" verses is known to God alone.[120] This is not to say that the spiritual elite of the Muslim community (*khassa*) should not try to unravel the mysteries of the *mutashabihat*. On the contrary, the Sufi "gnostics" (*'arifan*), according to al-Maybudi, "are given illuminative vision (*dada-yi mukashafa'i*) so that every veil between their hearts and the truth is lifted."[121] "Firmly rooted in knowledge,"[122] they have obtained all of its varieties: "The knowledge of the Shariah, the knowledge of the Tariqah, and the knowledge of the Haqiqah."[123] They are thus the only ones capable of discovering (*istinbat*) the hidden subtext of the revelation through exegetical unveiling (*ta'vil kashfi*) granted to them by God.[124] In this respect, al-Maybudi's Persian exegesis is in full agreement with its Arabic forerunners. They all insist that the exegete has to be divinely aided and inspired, which, in its turn, presupposes pursuing the ascetic-mystical regimen aimed at purifying the heart of the interpreter to prepare it for divine tidings.[125]

It is against this background that one should consider al-Maybudi's explanation of the various functions of the "ambiguous verses" of the Qur'an as summarized by Annabel Keeler:

1. They challenge human beings to use their rational and spiritual faculties, thereby separating them from animals;
2. They distinguish the spiritual elite from the mass of ordinary believers;
3. They humble wise men by making them aware of their weakness as they seek, in vain, to reach the unfathomable depths of the divine word;
4. They motivate interpreters to obtain a spiritual realization of the true reality (*haqiqat*) of the scripture instead of senselessly fulfilling its outward commands (*shari'at*);
5. They guard the mystery of the divine word, which surpasses human understanding, while encouraging God's servants to accept it unconditionally and unquestioningly.[126]

Despite the apparent uniqueness of al-Maybudi's exegesis, in the end, his approach to the Qur'an and the *muhkamat/mutashabihat* dichotomy is typical not only of Sufi exegesis but also of the Sufi Weltanschauung as a whole.[127] Whether or not one should classify him as a full-fledged Sufi is not that important.[128]

A distinct and highly influential vision of the Qur'anic revelation was articulated by the renowned Sunni theologian with ascetic-mystical propensities Abu Hamid al-Ghazali (d. 505/1111)[129] in his *Jewels of the Qur'an* (*Jawahir al-Qur'an*). Although not exegetical in the conventional sense of the word, this treatise aims at bringing out layers of meaning embedded in Qur'anic chapters and verses from an allegorical-esoteric vantage point.[130] As with al-Maybudi, who may have availed himself of al-Ghazali's insights in his own exegesis,[131] the latter considered the deepest and subtlest dimensions of the revelation to be the exclusive domain of Sufi gnostics (*'arifun*). In other respects, al-Ghazali's *Jewels* is innovative and suffused with symbolism. For example, he offers an allegorical classification of Qur'anic verses based on their contents. To show his deep reverence for the wisdom of the divine word, he correlates its narratives with various types of precious stones, pearls, and rare substances.[132] Thus, the knowledge (*ma'rifa*) of God is symbolically described as the "red sulfur"—the elusive and much-sought-after element that, according to medieval alchemy, transforms base metals into gold. The awareness that Sufi gnostics have of God's essence, attributes, and actions is likened to three sorts of corundum. Below this realm of the supreme knowledge of God available to a handful of divinely chosen knowers lies one pertaining to the Sufi path. It comprises the verses of the Qur'an that al-Ghazali relates to the major stages of the believer's progress to God. He describes this progress by the common Sufi topos of "polishing the mirror of one's heart." In Sufi lore, the act of "polishing" actualizes the divine nature (*lahut*) that resides in the "heart of hearts" (*sirr al-sirr*) of each human individual.[133] Al-Ghazali calls the Qur'anic verses related to the knowledge of the mystical path "shining pearls." The fourth type of knowledge corresponds to the verses that depict the condition of human beings after they have finally met God face to face, that is, at the time of the resurrection, reckoning, reward, and punishment as well as afterward, when humans will witness the beatific vision in the hereafter. This category, which al-Ghazali likens to green emeralds, comprises one-third of the Qur'anic suras. The fifth category of verses, in al-Ghazali's classification, depicts the condition of "those who have traversed [the path to God]," on the one hand, and "those who have denied God and deviated from His path," on the other. Al-Ghazali compares this group of verses to gray ambergris and fresh, blooming aloe wood. To the sixth category of verses belong "the arguments of the infidels against the truth and a clear evidence of their humiliation by undeniable proofs." In al-Ghazali's topology, such verses are associated with the "greatest antidote" (*tiryaq akbar*)—the essential cure for ills and vices of the human soul. The final category of verses deals with the stages of the journey of believers to their Creator and the management of its "vehicle," the human body, namely, what exactly constitutes its licit and illicit means of sustenance and procreation from the vantage point of the divine dispensation. Al-Ghazali allegorizes this category of verses as the "strongest musk."

Upon establishing the principal types of divine knowledge and thematic categories of Qur'anic verses associated with them, al-Ghazali proceeds to classify the outward and inward sciences of the Qur'an. To the
former belongs (a) the art of Qur'an recitation represented by readers and
reciters of its text; (b) the knowledge of the Qur'anic language and gram-
mar, which according to al-Ghazali is represented by philologists and
grammarians; and (c) the science of the outward exegesis (al-tafsir al-
zahir) of the Qur'an, which its practitioners, the exoteric 'ulama', consider
to be the consummate knowledge available to the faithful. Although al-
Ghazali duly concedes that ordinary Muslims should observe the outward
sciences of the Qur'an and respect their learned keepers, he denies that
they contain the ultimate understanding of the divine word available to
human beings. In his view, this ultimate understanding becomes possible
only through the "sciences of the kernels of the Qur'an" ('ulum al-lubab)
as opposed to what he calls its outer "shell" (sadaf). In the final analysis,
al-Ghazali, like al-Qushayri and al-Maybudi, attributes the knowledge of
the Qur'an's "kernels" exclusively to the Sufi gnostics ('arifun).

According to al-Ghazali, the mystical seeker's goal is to realize the
allegorical-esoteric underpinnings of the divine revelation. Inscribed on
the Preserved Tablet (al-lawh al-mahfuz),[134] its mysteries are revealed to
the divinely inspired gnostics in their sleep. As any knowledge received in
a dream, it requires interpretation, therefore, in al-Ghazali's own words,

> The [esoteric] interpretation of the Qur'an (ta'wil) occupies the place
> of the interpretation of dreams (ta'bir).

The exegete's task, argues al-Ghazali, is to "comprehend the hidden
connection between the visible world and the invisible" in the same way as
an interpreter of dreams explains the true import of a dream or vision to
the uninitiated. He brings this idea home in the following programmatic
statement:

> Understand that so long as you are in this-worldly life you are sleeping,
> and you will wake up only after you have died at which time you will be
> able to see the manifest truth face to face. Before that time, it is impos-
> sible for you to attain to the [true] realities [of being], except when they
> are couched in the form of imagination-inspiring symbols.

To gain this inspired, veridical understanding of the true reality of
God's word one must, according to al-Ghazali, renounce this world and
focus one's thoughts exclusively on God and the afterlife. Those who seek
"the vanities of this world, eating what is unlawful and pursuing [their]

carnal desires" are barred from gaining a glimpse of the Qur'an's innermost meaning. Because their corrupt and sinful egos inevitably distort their perception of the Scripture's "kernel," they see nothing in the Qur'an but contradiction and incongruence. According to the standard Sufi view already familiar to us, which al-Ghazali fully endorses, the comprehension of Qur'anic allegories and allusions by different people corresponds to their level of spiritual and intellectual purity and perfection. In commenting on the special virtue of the "Opening" sura of the Qur'an (al-fatiha; Q 1), which many exegetes consider to be the key to paradise, al-Ghazali argues that whereas ordinary believers imagine paradise to be a place to satisfy their lowly cravings for food, drink, and sex, the perfected Sufi gnostic sees it as a realm of refined spiritual pleasures and "pays no heed to the paradise of the fools."[135] Al-Ghazali expresses similar ideas in his *Niche for the Lights* (*Mishkat al-anwar*)[136]—a deeply mystical reflection on the gnoseological and ontological implications of the Light Verse (Q 24:35) that, as has been mentioned earlier in this chapter, was and still is one of the most "fertile" Qur'anic passages for Sufi exegetes.

In his monumental exploration of Muslim faith and practice titled *The Revivification of the Sciences of Religion* (*Ihya' 'ulum al-din*),[137] al-Ghazali links "the various methods toward mindful reading [of the Qur'an]" to ten requirements that the reader/reciter needs to observe:

1. Understanding the majesty and grandeur of the divine speech;
2. Exaltation of the divine speaker in one's soul and action;
3. Being present with God in one's heart (*hudur al-qalb*) to the exclusion of anything else;
4. Pondering (*tadabbur*) attentively the meaning(s) of the divine speech;
5. Making every effort to understand it (*tafahhum*);
6. Removing obstacles to the proper understanding, namely, sinful actions, pride, reliance on personal opinion, passionate drives of the soul (*nafs*) and, rigidity and zealotry in defending one's method or school of thought (*madhhab*);
7. Viewing oneself as the only addressee of the divine word to whom God is speaking in person (*takhsis*);
8. Opening oneself to the effects of divine outpourings and changing one's internal state in response to differing tenors and modalities of the verses heard (*ta'aththur*);
9. Ascending through various degrees of awareness of God in an effort to reach the stage of a full absorption into the divine speaker,

which, in turn, should make one oblivious of the very act of reading or listening to the Scripture;

10. Disavowal (*tabri'*) of one's own ability and power and viewing oneself as the lowest of the low in this life and the life to come.[138]

Al-Ghazali's exegetical principles are conveniently captured in his description of Sufi gnostics' (*'arifun*) spiritual journey during which

> they ascend from the foothill of metaphor (*majaz*) to the waystation of the true reality (*haqiqa*). When they complete their ascension, they witness directly that there is nothing in existence except God Most High.

In line with this unitive ontological position, the famous Qur'anic phrase, "Everything perishes save His face" (Q 28:88), should be, according to al-Ghazali, understood as meaning:

> Everything except God, when considered from the viewpoint of its essence, is but a pure nonexistence (*'adam mahd*).

In the final account, argues al-Ghazali, God is the only true reality of the entire universe.[139] The rest is nothing but the reality's multifarious and fleeting manifestations in the events and entities of the material universe. This ontological conception and its gnoseological implications, as we shall see in chapter 4, hark back to various versions of (Neo)platonic cosmologies of the Hellenistic epoch. Within the framework of Islamic intellectual history proper, al-Ghazali's ontology prefigures the unitive speculations of Muhammad al-Daylami (d. 593/1197), Ruzbihan Baqli (d. 606/1209), Ibn (al-)'Arabi (d. 638/1240), and Ibn (al-)'Arabi's numerous followers, who, like al-Ghazali, relied on allegorical-esoteric exegesis to explicate and justify, on scriptural grounds, their deeply mystical perception of the cosmos and the place that the human race occupies in God's scheme of things. One important result of this collective exegetical engagement with the Scripture is the Sufi cosmology and gnoseology that we know today.

The Qur'an as a Touchstone and Sounding Board of Mystical Experiences

The intellectual legacy of the Persian Sufis Shams al-din Muhammad al-Daylami and Ruzbihan Baqli constitutes a distinctive and influential trend in Sufi exegesis. It is characterized by "intense visions and powerful ecstasies interpreted in terms of a Qur'anically based metaphysics."[140] The prevalence of such elements in the exegetical works of these two Sufis has

prompted some Western investigators to suggest that their profoundly esoteric and experiential character sets them apart from the more "moderate"
types of Sufi exegesis discussed earlier in this chapter.[141] However, this
epistemological distinction is more a matter of emphasis than quality. The
borderline between "esoteric-ecstatic" and "moderately esoteric" types of
exegesis is blurry and easily crossed by exegetes depending on their state
of mind at a particular moment in time.

Al-Daylami, a little known but original and prolific author, composed
a mystical commentary, *The Verification of Mystical Gnosis* (*Tasdiq al-
ma'arif*),[142] in addition to a series of mystical treatises describing his visionary experiences.[143] Al-Daylami's works creatively mingle early Sufi
exegetical dicta borrowed from al-Sulami's *True Realities of [Qur'anic]
Commentary* with the author's own elaborations. Al-Daylami's exegesis
reveals, in the words of a Western investigator of his legacy, his preoccupation with "the visionary world of the mystic," which "is seen as totally real
and fully identical with the spiritual world of the invisible realm."[144] In
terms of narrative composition, the same investigator has described al-
Daylami's method as one of "a continuous yet eclectic commentary on selected Koranic verses from all suras presented in sequence."[145] One distinctive feature of al-Daylami's method is his consistent use of the Qur'an
as the "touchstone" to verify the authenticity of his mystical experiences
and cosmological visions by tracing them to their true source (that is, God
or Satan).[146] In his personal engagements with the Qur'an the exegete
avails himself of the verses that are commonly used by Sufis to validate
their thought and behavior. Among them are the already familiar Light
Verse (24:35), the verse of the "[the Prophet's] Ascension" (17:1), and the
entire text of sura "Ya Sin" (Q 36).[147] Al-Daylami's meditations on these
and other Qur'anic passages, either in a wakeful state or in a dream, allow
him to gain glimpses of the world of spirits (*'alam al-arwah*), of the dominion of divine kingship (*malakut*), or even of the afterlife.[148] His mystical experiences being "based on a mystical reading of the Qur'an," al-
Daylami records them "autobiographically and employs them as a way of
narrating"[149] the major themes of his mystical Weltanschauung. As one
might expect of a Sufi, in addressing the validity of various forms of cognition, that is, theological, philosophical, and mystical, al-Daylami refutes
the theological and philosophical ones in order to present his own "visionary cosmology" as the surest way to obtain the true meaning of both the
Qur'an and of human experience of the world generally.[150]

The works of al-Daylami's contemporary Ruzbihan (al-)Baqli al-Shirazi
(d. 606/1209), especially his commentary *The Brides of Explanation of the*

True Realities of the Qur'an ('Ara'is al-bayan fi haqa'iq al-Qur'an), testify to the author's propensity to visions, dreams, powerful ecstasies, and ecstatic utterances that have "earned him the sobriquet 'Doctor Ecstaticus' (*shaykh-i shattah*)."[151] The German-American scholar of Sufism Annemarie Schimmel (1922–2003) has described Ruzbihan's diction as influenced "by the poets of Iran during the eleventh and twelfth centuries, filled with roses and nightingales, pliable and colorful."[152] Like al-Daylami's *Verification of Mystical Gnosis*, Ruzbihan's *Brides* is composed in Arabic and consists almost equally of earlier exegetical material—mostly borrowed from al-Sulami and al-Qushayri—and of the author's own glosses.[153] Although he draws on the previous tradition of allegorical-esoteric exegesis, Ruzbihan's uses of the Qur'an are bolder, in the mystical sense, than those of the Sufi exegetes mentioned above. Not only does he constantly invoke the Scripture to describe his personal interactions with of God, but he also claims to have symbolically "eaten" it, along with the Jewish Torah and the Christian Gospel.[154] Whereas Ruzbihan has used this "culinary" metaphor to underline his internalization of the divine writs of the three Abrahamic religions, his boldness and self-confidence cannot but impress.

Qur'anic imagery and vocabulary virtually permeates Ruzbihan's ecstatic visions. In one memorable passage, he compares his condition in the presence of God with that of Zulaykha, Potiphar's wife, in the presence of Joseph (Yusuf).[155] Couched in the Qur'anic idiom, such expressions of mutual love and (com)passion between God and his mystical lover constitute a major hallmark of Ruzbihan's esoteric worldview. According to Carl Ernst's pertinent observation, the very title of Ruzbihan's commentary— *The Brides of Explanation*—"invokes the unveiling of the bride in a loving encounter as the model of initiation into the esoteric knowledge of God."[156] Moreover, Ruzbihan believed that love makes all the difference when it comes the seeker's comprehension of the true reality (*haqiqa*) of the Qur'an. It may even allow the lover to have a vision of his divine beloved clothed in "the form of Adam."[157] Only the Sufi gnostic who listens to it with the "hearing of love and passionate desire (*sama' 'ishq wa-mahabba*)," as opposed to the "hearing of [rational] understanding (*sama' fahm*)," can gain mastery (*tasarruf*) of both the Qur'an's clear verses ('*ibarat*) and those containing allegorical allusions (*isharat*).[158] Enamored with God and perfected through their faithful worship of him, such saintly individuals (*awliya'*), who, according to Ruzbihan, number either 428 or 427, were placed by God in the midst of humankind to serve as guides and guarantors of the covenant between the Creator and his creatures.[159] They form a complex hierarchy of God's chosen "men of the unseen" (*rijal al-ghayb*) that roughly corresponds to that described by Ibn (al-)'Arabi at the beginning of chapter 73 of his *Meccan Revelations* (*al-Futuhat al-makkiyya*), as will be discussed further on.

In sum, Ruzbihan's visionary and ecstatic experiences, inspired in part by those of his controversial predecessor Husayn b. Mansur al-Hallaj (d. 309/922),[160] are thoroughly and consistently couched in the Qur'anic language and imagery. For Ruzbihan, as for his fellow Sufis before and after him, the Qur'an serves as a powerful means of transforming the mystic's personhood and preparing it for an ultimate ecstatic encounter and union with the Divine. Like al-Daylami, Ruzbihan uses exegesis to assert that "illuminated" Sufi friends of God enjoy special access to inward, "real" aspects of the divine word and the universe as a whole. The experience they derive from mystical contemplation on the Qur'anic text transforms their selves, raising them above the crowd of ordinary believers and potentially exposing them to the censure of "ignoramuses."[161] As already pointed out, this has been a characteristic feature of Sufi engagements with the Qur'an since the very beginning.

Elaboration of Unitive Metaphysics and Gnoseology: Ibn (al-)'Arabi and His School

The double metaphor of the world as a text and a text as a world has a venerable history. To interpret means to react to the text of the world or to the world of a text by producing other texts.

UMBERTO ECO, *THE LIMITS OF INTERPRETATION*

The subsequent evolution of Sufi exegesis is dominated by two powerful personalities: Ibn (al-)'Arabi (d. 638/1240) and his followers and Najm al-Din Kubra (d. in or shortly after 617/1220), the founder of the Kubrawiyya school of Sufism that was active in the eastern lands of Islam.[162]

Ibn (al-)'Arabi's influence on Sufi thought has been so broad and pervasive that one can confidently speak of pre- and post-Ibn (al-)'Arabi Sufism. Drawing on the rich tradition of Maghribi and Andalusi mysticism represented by Ibn Masarra al-Jabali (d. 319/931), Ibn Barrajan (d. 536/1141), Ibn al-'Arif (d. 536/1141), Ibn Qasi (546/1151), and Abu Madyan Shu'ayb (d. 594/1197), to name but the most important ones, he managed to create a powerful mystical paradigm that became dominant among eastern Sufis as well.[163] Of Ibn (al-)'Arabi's intellectual forebears in the Muslim West, mention should be made of Ibn Barrajan, whom one of his Andalusian biographers described as "the Ghazali of al-Andalus."[164] For our purpose, he deserves a special notice as the author of at least one, possibly two, commentaries on the Qur'an and a lengthy treatise on the "most beautiful names of God" (*al-asma al-husna*)—a recurrent theme in the Qur'an (see, for example, 7:180, 17:110, and 20:8).[165] As with other ascetic-mystical exegetes, Ibn Barrajan viewed the realization (*tahqiq*) of the Qur'anic message by the mystic as his or her progressive emersion into its depths. This emersion eventually results in what the Andalusi Sufi master calls "the superior reading" (*tilawa 'ulya*) of the Qur'an. In the process, the personality of the mystic is transformed under the overwhelming influence of the divine word, causing him or her to pass from its literal meaning (*'ibra; i'tibar*) to its underlying message (*ma'bur ilayhi*), as it is enshrined in the unseen realm.[166] Ibn Barrajan describes this passage as "the act of worship" (*ta'abbud*)[167] to emphasize that only by submitting to God unequivocally and single-mindedly can one advance beyond a literal understanding of his word, delving into its underlying truth accessible only to the elect few.[168] The invisible, spiritual world of the divine command (*al-amr*) lying beyond the created physical universe (*al-khalq*), the only connection between the two are God's special signs (*ayat khassa*). Manifested in the natural objects and phenomena, on the one hand, and in the Qur'anic text, on the other, they serve as bridges between the two separate realms. In the course of contemplating God's signs in the phenomenal world, the mystical exegete eventually crosses over (*mu'tabir*) from their outward meaning to their underlying sense. In so doing, the exegete plucks the fruit of wisdom (*hikma*) that Ibn Barrajan defines as the supreme awareness of the unseen realities of, simultaneously, divine word and creation.[169]

This intellectual and spiritual awareness is the fruit of the dual act of contemplating nature (for example, by retreating into the countryside)[170] and a constant remembering/reciting (*dhikr*) of the text of the Qur'an. Thanks to such exercises, the mystic, in his capacity of both contemplator and reciter, acquires a veridical insight into the very kernel of the divine world and word, which transforms him or her into a human replica of the "universal servant" (*'abd kulli*)—a microcosmic compilation of all realities of existence that corresponds to the universal intellect of Neoplatonic cosmology.[171] This enlightened entity seems to refer to the principle of existence and prophethood, similar to the old Sufi notion of the Muhammadan Reality (*al-haqiqa al-muhammadiyya*) or Muhammad's light-nature (*nur Muhammad*).[172] The universal servant is the vital bridge between God's sublime, unfathomable uniqueness and the profusion of divine attributes and properties in the world of empirically perceived multiplicity. Adam (and individual human beings generally) is but a "partial or particular servant" (*'abd juz'i*).[173] In Ibn Barrajan's exegesis, the universal and particular servanthood is linked, albeit inexplicitly, to two types of revelation and two levels of understanding the divine word, the "Tremendous Qur'an" (*al-Qur'an al-'azim*) and the "Exalted Qur'an (*al-Qur'an al-'aziz*)."[174] The former contains the sum total of divine names and attributes in an undifferentiated, general (*mujmal*) manner. The latter presents them in a detailed, differentiated way (*mufassal*), namely, as the concrete Qur'anic verses, which "serve as entry points into the higher, more condensed reaches of the Tremendous Qur'an."[175] Ibn Barrajan's exegesis displays the following unique features that, in his works, coexist with more traditional exegetical elements:

1. Insistence on the necessity of a constant recollection (*dhikr*) and contemplation (*tafakkur*) of the Qur'an as a means of achieving a total and undivided concentration on its underlying messages.[176]
2. Awareness of subtle correspondences between the phenomena of the physical universe and the "signs" (*ayat*) of the Scripture.
3. Conviction that the heart of the universal servant, which seems to be both the creative principle (universe in miniature) and the principle of prophethood, encompasses the totality of existence in the same way as it is contained in the "Guarded Tablet" mentioned in the Qur'an (85:22).[177]
4. Belief that the divine word permeates the innermost reality of human nature, which makes it possible for the faithful servant of God to achieve a cognitive and experiential union with him.[178]

In sum, Ibn Barrajan's entire symbolic universe is constructed around several pivotal correspondences between the text and the universe that the influential Italian scholar Umberto Eco (1932–2016), quoted at the beginning of this section, has described as a major keynote of the antique and medieval Weltanschauung.[179] It is against this background that we should read the following summation of Ibn Barrajan's Qur'an commentary, whose Arabic title *Idah al-hikma bi-ahkam al-'ibra* the editors of this work have rendered into English as *Wisdom Deciphered, the Unseen Discovered*:

> The human being ... is the comprehensive (*mujmal*) reflection of the Universal Servant; the universe is the unpacked and differentiated (*mufassal*) cosmic reflection of the Universal Servant; while revelation resembles both human being and creation and comprises both differentiated and undifferentiated modes of divine self-disclosure ... the Tremendous Qur'an and the Exalted Qur'an.[180]

As with other allegorical-esoteric exegetes, Ibn Barrajan restricts the superior realization of the divine word to a small group of divinely chosen individuals, whom he calls "God's pious friends" (*awliya' Allah al-salihun*), "possessors of sound intellects and contemplation" (*ulu al-albab wa 'l-tafkir*),[181] "lovers of God" (*muhibbun*),[182] and "truthful or veracious ones" (*siddiqun*).[183] Being privy to divine mysteries (*ma'rifa*), however, by no means absolves them from performing God's external commands (*ahkam al-'ilm*), whose foundation is the Qur'an and the Sunna of the Prophet.[184] Ibn Barrajan's ideas were further elaborated in the teachings of his Andalusian compatriot Ibn (al-)'Arabi and his numerous followers.

Ibn (al-)'Arabi's relations with the Qur'an are complex and variegated. He is credited with a multivolume Qur'anic commentary, *The General and the Detailed in the Mysteries of the Meanings of the Divine Revelation* (*al-Jami' wa 'l-tafsil fi asrar ma'ani 'l-tanzil*), which seems to have been lost. However, his entire corpus of writings, including his influential masterpieces—*The Ringstones of Wisdom*[185] (*Fusus al-hikam*) and *The Meccan Revelations* (*al-Futuhat al-makkiyya*)—are, in essence, but running commentaries on the Qur'an and the Sunna.

Ibn (al-)'Arabi's approach to the Qur'an should be considered against the background of his overall worldview, according to which the true reality of God and the cosmos is concealed from ordinary human beings behind the veil(s) of distorting appearances.[186] The presence of the veil(s) renders inscrutable the true reality of the divine essence. In fact, one can perceive it exclusively thanks to variegated manifestations of its existential potentialities, or "names"[187] that alone render it accessible to the human senses.[188] Therefore, the entire universe consists of sites of manifestation of the divine names (*tajalliyat*; *mazahir*). In Ibn (al-)'Arabi's own words:

> God says, "In that there [are] signs for a people who reflect."[189] But reflection upon the Essence of God is impossible, so there remains only reflection upon engendered existence. That to which reflection becomes connected is the Most Beautiful Names or features (*simat*) of the temporary originated things. The names, all of them, are the root of engendered existence.[190]

God grants glimpses of the underlying reality behind his "most beautiful names" only to "the people of the true reality" (*ahl al-haqiqa/al-haqq*) or "divine gnostics" (*'arifun*).[191] As the first step, they experience a spiritual awakening that, in its turn, results in a revelatory insight, or "unveiling" (*kashf*; *makashafa*).[192] The "people of the true reality" and "unveiling" (*ahl al-kashf*) are the only ones capable of deciphering the true sense behind the symbols that constitute both the Qur'anic text and the empirical universe.

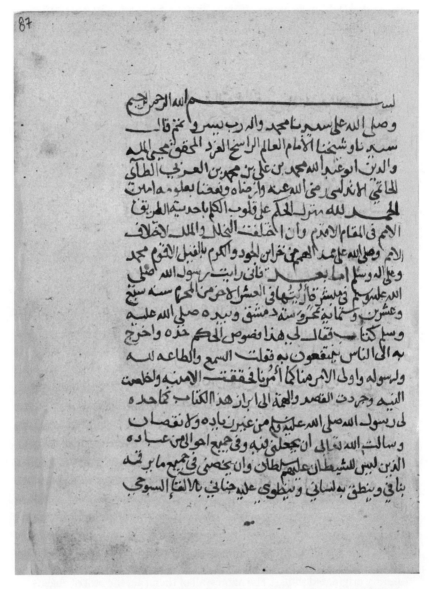

FIGURE 3.1. Opening of Ibn al-ʿArabī's Fuṣūṣ al-ḥikam, pp. 87 and 88 in Isl. Ms. 512, Special Collections Library (University of Michigan Library), Ann Arbor.

Thus, summarizes Ibn (al-)ʿArabi,

> The world is but the giant text [of the Qurʾan] (*mushaf kabir*) that God has uttered upon us ... The world is but letters written and inscribed in the unfurled parchment of existence; writing on it is eternal and never ceases.[193]

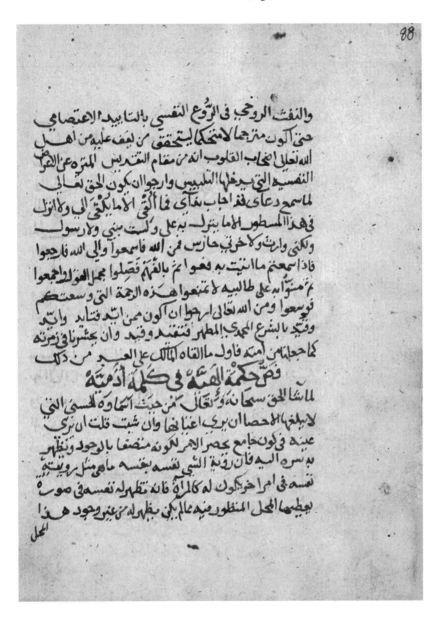

Elaborating on this symbolically fertile image, Ibn (al-)'Arabi argues that
by reciting the primordial, existential Qur'an inscribed in the Preserved
Tablet, God brings the universe into existence.[194] Elsewhere and repeatedly, Ibn (al-)'Arabi talks about how God "breathes" the world into existence.[195] In sum, for Ibn (al-)'Arabi and for his fellow gnostics ('arifun),
both the Qur'an and the universe are but God's "uttering" or "writings"—

assemblages of sounds and symbols pointing to the true realities of existence (*haqa'iq*) that, in the final account, take their origin in and are somehow identical with the Truly Real One (*al-haqq*). Lying above and beyond
the comprehension of human beings in its inexhaustible richness of potentialities and sublime inscrutability, the Truly Real One makes itself known
to its human worshippers through incessant manifestations that Ibn
(al-)'Arabi allegorizes as divine "exhalations" imbued with existential potentialities. Using a Qur'anic idiom, he describes them as "[God's] most
beautiful names."[196] Whether or not Ibn (al-)'Arabi's consistent use of this
Qur'anic designation is inspired by Ibn Barrajan's discussions of the manifestations of the divine signs in natural phenomena, as mentioned above,
is not that important. What matters is that the letters of the "cosmic
Qur'an," as Ibn (al-)'Arabi never tires of saying,[197] are means and tools of
creation, or to be more precise, of the incessant regeneration of the universe (*khalq jadid*) by the ever active Truly Real One.[198]

On the microcosmic level, the Prophet and his successors, the Sufi
gnostics, whom Ibn (al-)'Arabi, like Ibn Barrajan before him, designates as
"lovers of God," are the carriers of the Qur'an (*hamalat al-Qur'an*).[199] Unlike short-sighted exegetes, who rush quickly from the outward (*zahir*)
sense of a verse to its inward (*batin*) meaning, discarding the former in the
process, the "folk of God" (*ahl Allah/ahl al-haqq*)[200] "cross over" (*ta'bir*)[201]
from the outward sense to the inner one, while "carrying" the former with
them into the new exegetic realm. In other words, they refuse to make a
final judgment regarding the verse's obvious import (*'ibara*), despite their
realization of its nonobvious, inward (*batin*) aspects. In this way, they preserve both the verse's ambiguity and literal sense—an exegetical stance that
the Greatest Master calls "seeing things with two eyes."[202]

Because Ibn (al-)'Arabi apparently considered himself to be the foremost gnostic (*'arif*) of his age, and possibly of all times, as well as the spiritual "pole" (*qutb*) of the universe in his epoch,[203] he saw no reason to legitimize his understanding of the Scripture by citing any prior exegetical
authorities. He believed that his own insights into the multiple senses of
the Scripture came to him directly from God and, as such, were incontro-
vertible.[204] This belief is attested by Ibn (al-)'Arabi's commentaries on selected Qur'anic suras included in his large poetic collection,[205] in which
Ibn (al-)'Arabi presents himself as an explicator of the spiritual quintes-
sence (*ruh*) of the suras in question. The Greatest Master of Sufi gnosis
considers his spiritual unveilings to be a fruit of the mystical moment
(*warid al-waqt*) in which he happens to find himself. Responding to his
critics, whom he describes as "possessors of theories (*ashab al-afkar*) and

interpreters of transmitted reports (*al-muta'awillin al-akhbar al-warida*) according to their own rational arguments (*adilluhum al-'aqliyya*),"[206] Ibn (al-)'Arabi denies that his own personality adds anything to what comes to him from the divine source.[207] His insights into the realm of divine realities and mysteries of the Scripture are direct, accurate, and inerrant.

Ibn (al-)'Arabi is also original and even controversial in using poetry for exegetical purposes—after all, in Muslim culture this art was associated with pre-Islamic paganism. Furthermore, his occasional imitation of the meter and rhythm of the Qur'an no doubt raised scholarly eyebrows both during his lifetime and after his death.[208] Yet, at the same time, Ibn (al-)'Arabi's repeated claim to be a simple mouthpiece of God[209] has effectively absolved him of the necessity to justify his unusual interpretations of the Qur'an or to comply with the conventions of the Muslim exegetical tradition, exoteric or otherwise.

Ibn (al-)'Arabi's exegesis can be subdivided into three distinctive levels: the metaphysical-cosmological; the analogical (microcosmic/macrocosmic), built around implicit or explicit correspondences between the universe and the human organism; and the existential-experiential that rests on his claim to possess an intuitive, supersensory comprehension of the underlying unity of God, man, and the universe.[210] In the *Ringstones of Wisdom (Fusus al-hikam)*—Ibn (al-)'Arabi's controversial meditation on various facets of prophethood and human-divine relations more generally—his uses of the Qur'an are particularly daring, even scandalous. Its verses effectively serve him as show windows for his unitive metaphysics and esoteric gnoseology. As a scholar of his legacy has aptly pointed out, Ibn (al-)'Arabi's approach to the Qur'an "may be considered an Islamic religious genre in its own right."[211] The scholar then describes this genre as "Sufi metaphysical story-telling."[212] Earlier, another European scholar, Ignaz Goldziher, jestingly referred to Ibn (al-)'Arabi's exegesis as "an allegorical hermeneutics superhighway."[213] More recently, Kristin Zahra Sands has observed that the "close attention to the etymological and grammatical possibilities of the text which distinguishes Ibn 'Arabi's approach to Qur'anic interpretation" is based "on the assumption that all the possible meanings which the Arabic language allows for any word or group of words in the Qur'an are valid."[214] Ibn (al-)'Arabi's own idea concerning the necessity of "seeing things with two eyes"[215] resonates well with Sands's assessment.

In the history of Islamic theological thought Ibn (al-)'Arabi has gained notoriety for his shocking exegetical paradoxes that, his opponents have argued, make a mockery of the literal sense of the Scripture.[216] As an example one can cite his rendition of the story of Aaron (Harun), Moses (Musa), and the golden calf.[217] Contrary to the literal meaning of the Qur'anic narrative, Ibn (al-)'Arabi portrays Aaron and the apostatized worshippers of the golden calf as being wiser than Moses, who "naively" scolds them for lapsing into idolatry. Unlike Moses, who is blinded by his overriding preoccupation with delivering the monotheistic message to his people, his biblical opponents realize that God can be worshipped in everything, because every object, including the golden calf, is but "a site of divine self-manifestation (ba'd al-majali al-ilahiyya)."[218] In Ibn (al-)'Arabi's audacious interpretation of the story, the original Qur'anic condemnation of idolatry is completely inverted: the idolaters become "gnostics," who "know the full truth concerning idolatry, but are honor-bound not to disclose this truth, even to the prophets, the apostles and their heirs, for these all have their divinely appointed roles in curbing idolatry and promoting the worship of God *in their time and their situation*."[219] The ultimate truth, however, is that God is immanently present in all things and can thus be worshipped in any object or site without his oneness being compromised.

In this exegetical gloss, and throughout Ibn (al-)'Arabi's *Ringstones*, his unitive vision of God and the world is illustrated by Qur'anic narratives describing the vicissitudes of the prophetic missions from Adam to Muhammad. As we have just seen, a non-Sufi is likely to find his exegesis not just far-fetched, but scandalous. Using the familiar stories of the Qur'anic prophets, Ibn (al-)'Arabi impregnates them with ideas and associations that appear to be completely alien to the original Qur'anic universe. To some extent, this is true of any posterior reading of the Qur'an, but in the case of Ibn (al-)'Arabi the contrast between the literal, historically bound meaning and his exegetical flights of fantasy is particularly conspicuous. In this way, Ibn (al-)'Arabi is effectively, although not necessarily deliberately, creating a new scripture, one that showcases his elaborate unitive metaphysics and mystical gnoseology. The content of this new scripture, as will be shown further on, bears a striking resemblance to various versions of (Neo)platonism.

In Ibn (al-)'Arabi's mind, as already mentioned, his exegetical elaborations are by no means his personal readings of the sacred text. He sees his glosses of the Qur'an as the only true understanding of God's intended message to humankind.[220] Nor, as already mentioned, does he pretend to be an independently minded speaker or writer. Like the prophet Muhammad, he is but a mouthpiece of God who utters only that which his "direct tasting"[221] of the "true realities of existence" (haqa'iq al-wujud) dictates him—nothing more and nothing less. At the same time, Ibn (al-)'Arabi readily concedes that his fellow travelers on the Sufi path (*ahl al-tariq*)[222] may occasionally enjoy similar insights. Such acknowledgments abound not only in his *Meccan Revelations*[223] but in his autobiographical writings as well.[224] If we abstract ourselves for a moment for the innumerable details and digressions of Sufism's foremost exponent, we will find out that one of his major goals in the *Futuhat*[225] and, to some extent also the *Fusus*, is to erect a complex mystical ontology with the attendant hierarchy of knowledge and knowers. He does this by availing himself systematically and deliberately of carefully selected and creatively reimagined verses and themes of the Qur'an.

The keynotes of Ibn (al-)'Arabi's unitive metaphysics and mystical gnoseology were taken up and developed by his foremost disciple, Sadr al-Din al-Qunawi (d. 673/1274) in his exegetical tracts *Key to the Unseen of [Absolute] Unity and Its Dispersal [in the Entities of the Physical World] (Miftah ghayb al-jam' wa tafsilihi)*[226] and *Impossibility of Exposition in the Interpretation of the Mother of the Qur'an (I'jaz al-bayan fi ta'wil umm al-Qur'an).*[227] The latter work of this "famously difficult" student of Ibn (al-)'Arabi[228] is a lengthy disquisition on the metaphysical, epistemological, and psychological implications of the "Opening" sura of the Qur'an (*al-fatiha*) that, according to al-Qunawi, captures the very gist of the entire Muslim scripture. The author's indebtedness to his teacher[229] is made obvious from the outset[230] when he states that

> God has made the primeval macrocosm (*al-'alam al-kabir*)—from the viewpoint of its [outward] form—a book carrying the images of the divine names ... and He [God] has made the perfect man—who is but a microcosm (*al-'alam al-saghir*)—an intermediate book, from the viewpoint of [its] form, that combines in itself the presence of the names [i.e., the universe] with the presence of the named [i.e., God].[231]

One of the goals of al-Qunawi's exegesis is to impose some order on Ibn (al-)'Arabi's often fanciful flow of associations, elaborations, and digressions.[232] According to an eloquent personal assessment of the leading scholar and advocate of Ibn (al-)'Arabi's legacy in the West today,

> If Ibn 'Arabi's writings dazzle because of the non-stop rush of inspirations, Qunawi's soothe because of his calm and reasonable exposition of metaphysical principles. ... Even when Qunawi speaks of visionary affairs that are inaccessible to reason, he presents the discussion in an eminently rational and lucid manner.[233]

FIGURE 3.2. Opening of Ṣadr al-Dīn al-Qūnawī's Tafsīr al-Fātiḥah, pp. 70 and 71 in Isl. Ms. 252, Special Collections Library (University of Michigan Library), Ann Arbor.

وفي وقت ظهوره في عالم الشهادة عليها فإذا كان كذلك فما ... فما لنسبة مرآة الانقطاع ...
ارادة منظمة وموصل وجامع ولذا اعتبرنا كون ... ماعل المنطق أي كل ... طلب سابع واما
نسبة من القدرة من حيث كونه ... فرآ بب ان ... فرى الآمر والكون لي آية ... ولهذا كان الاب ...
على قول كن معز أو صورة أو صاحب ماعلامى ... واستوى اسم من الكام وهو الناطق بيننا ...
التر الحكيم ثم سر الكن وكل كام صادر من حكم لا الانظار الا بحكم الانب ... المذكورة منفصلة ...
عليم البرين واقتضاه كل النظر العقلي على النظم ... الكام والبرج ... ونبين عليكم ... اخبار
ما يكشف لك ... مرآته وداكا هو ان كان ... اي ... جعل العالم الكبر الاعلى من جهة ...
كتابا حاملا ... وصور ... العلم المودع ... العقل الاول ... وجعل الانسان الكامل الذي
هو العالم الصغير من حيث الصورة ... أوسط جامعا بين جهة العالم ... وحضرة المعلى حصل الترا ...
العزيز على الملوك على صورة النبين ... بخط سرى سورة ... فالقرآن العزيز ... ان تمهج حرمة
... كمال الطاهر ... بالانسان والغاية ... النظم ... القرآنية من عبرة انزال وانفصال ... وكان كل
... نائبة هو مرتبة الله ... لكن كان الغاية أو النبع الاعلى وذلك الآية الآية ... محتا على عدد
الحروف ... الاصلية ... فاوقها الكمرة العينية العلية ... وتجاها حضرة المظهور والشهادة ولها ...
ظاهر والوجه الكوني النجمي والجناب الكبر وساير التنزيه ... الصورة ... وحضرة الحكم والوجه ... والاجماع ...
ولها الوسط ... وساحها الآن ... وعن بين مرآ الكفرة الوسطى حضرة بينها ... ومن الغيب المصون ...
الاقوى وان تمهج كتابا ... عالم الارواح واللوح المحفوظ المصون المحجوب وعن ... وحضرة الآربعة ...
الاسم الظاهر ومرتبة الشهادة أقرب وهي من مستوى القصد ... بمنزلة على الانبياء والكتب ... فالكتب الآربعة
المذكورة ... حدا ول بحد أحكام مرتبة النابية المستورة ... وأما المشاهد الوجودية ... لقطيلة ...
الاعتبارية العلمية فإن علمها بترتيب علام النبأ ... الاصلية ... ماينجها من الآية المستورة في العلوم المكية و
أجروبية والملكوتية ... على الوجود ذات مظاهر مرتبافي الآسماء والمسمع ... في علم الاحصر وفي المراتب
الاحس وغيره ... قوحضرة ... فان حكم ذلك المرتبة العلية يكون فيه على انظر وابن ... وليس بكلام وما

It is against the background of al-Qunawi's propensity to systematize and streamline Ibn (al-)'Arabi's often convoluted discourses that we should see his famous description of the five realms of existence, or "universal divine presences,"[234] which he associates with "the universal divine books [that] are five in number."[235] Al-Qunawi's presences range from the unfathomable divine mystery or, in Richard Todd's translation, the "Nonmanifest" (al-ghayb), to the visible, material world. These two polar presences are connected by the middle one that encompasses them all.[236] The five presences, namely, the divine mystery, the spiritual, imaginal and corporeal realities, and the perfect man,[237] correspond to the five revealed books that, in their turn, correspond to the five levels of mystical awareness represented by various classes of human beings.[238] Those who can actualize the "subtle particle" (raqiqa) or the "divine secret" (al-sirr al-ilahi or sirr al-rububiyya)[239] cast by God into their souls when he breathed life into them will achieve perfection, thereby realizing the full potential of the human condition allotted to them.[240] According to al-Qunawi, the greatest of all truth verifiers (al-muhaqqiqun)[241] from among the divine brethren (al-ikhwan al-ilahiyun)[242] of the age is no one other than the "perfect man" (al-insan al-kamil). His cosmic function is to serve as the "conspectus" or "synopsis" (nuskha mukhtasira)[243] of all the realities and realms of the created universe.

As with the universal servant of Ibn Barrajan, we are dealing here with the indeterminate and transcendent absolute reality that lies behind and beyond the concrete entities of existence, both noetic and corporeal, and that manifests itself through a staged descent or emanation (fayd) into the realm of the admixture of spirit and matter.[244] What al-Qunawi does, following the lead of his teacher Ibn (al-)'Arabi—who, in his turn, built on the ideas of Ibn Barrajan—is to highlight the role of the perfected human being as the isthmus (barzakh) and "mediator" (wasita) between the noetic-spiritual and corporeal-empirical realms of existence, or, in other words, between the unseen and the visible.[245] Having "realized his identity with the 'common measure' of existence, he 'flows through all things' and sustains all world from the highest to the lowest of the low."[246]

On the microcosmic plane, these ideas can be traced back to the widely used (Neo)platonic and Gnostic concept of the human soul trapped in the world of matter and striving toward its source in an effort to realize the cognitive potential seeded in it by the divine design. At the same time, as Todd correctly points out, the (Neo)platonic elements in al-Qunawi's oeuvre are not necessarily borrowed directly from the books of the "ancient sages" (al-hukama' al-awa'il)[247] themselves. Rather, Todd argues,

Many of these concepts had simply merged into the general framework of medieval Islamic thought; a process helped in large measure by their having been Islamized through their incorporation within philosophical and scientific compendia such as the *Rasa'il Ikhwan al-Safa'* [*Epistles of the Brethren of Purity*].[248]

Overall, al-Qunawi's description of the hierarchies of the divine presences (*hadarat*) and their gnoseological and scriptural parallels and implications, as well as the role of Sufi gnostics in exemplifying and explicating them, can be seen as a fitting tribute to Ibn (al-)'Arabi's unitive cosmological psychology outlined above. Al-Qunawi thus represents the first stage in the formation of the Akbarian school of thought,[249] whose pervasive influence will be examined in the subsequent narrative. In discussing the vicissitudes of Ibn (al-)'Arabi's ideas one should keep in mind James Morris's highly important caveat:

> As with "Aristotelianism" or "Platonism" in Western thought, Ibn 'Arabi's writing[s] were only the starting point for the most diverse developments, in which reference to subsequent interpreters quickly became at least as important as the study of the Shaykh himself.[250]

Morris's statement is eminently pertinent to the role of 'Abd al-Razzaq al-Qashani or Kashani (d. between 730–36/1329–35), a native of the Iranian province of Isfahan, who is considered, alongside al-Qunawi, to be a major follower and exponent of Ibn (al-)'Arabi.[251] As with al-Qunawi, al-Qashani, too, saw his task in presenting lucidly and coherently Ibn (al-)'Arabi's often ambiguous and unstructured cosmological and gnoseological deliberations, so as to render them accessible to an average educated reader or listener[252] interested in the subject. The fact that al-Qashani has indeed excelled in popularizing Ibn (al-)'Arabi's teachings is attested by the fact that his commentary, originally titled [*Allegorical-Esoteric*] *Commentaries on the Qur'an* (*Ta'wilat al-Qur'an*), was, and often still is, taken by many to be a work of Ibn (al-)'Arabi himself.[253]

A systematic and self-reflective thinker,[254] al-Qashani provides an exposition of his exegetical method in the introduction to his allegorical-esoteric commentary that ranks among the major works of this genre alongside al-Qushayri's *The Subtleties of Allusions* (*Lata'if al-isharat*), Ruzbihan Baqli's *The Brides of [the Qur'an] Exposition* (*'Ara'is al-bayan*), or *The Source of Life* (*'Ayn al-hayat*) started by Najm al-Din Kubra, continued by his student Najm al-Din Daya (d. 654/1256), and completed by 'Ala' al-Dawla al-Simnani (d. 736/1336).[255] Citing the famous prophetic

Hadith that attributes two aspects to each Qur'anic verse, the outward (*zahr*) and the inward (*batn*), al-Qashani identifies the explication of the former as *tafsir* and of the latter as *ta'wil* (lit. "tracing something back to its origin").[256] By defining his own exegetical method as *ta'wil*,[257] he wittingly or not contradicts his master's teaching: Ibn (al-)Arabi, unlike other Sufis, viewed *ta'wil* primarily as a rational process and, thus, inferior to the supersensory, intuitive unveiling (*kashf*) granted to the exegete directly by God.[258] Al-Qashani's choice of the term may indicate that, by al-Qashani's time, the *tafsir/ta'wil* dichotomy had become widespread and accepted, at least in Sufi circles.[259] Seeking to set himself apart from conventional exegetes, he preferred the term *ta'wil* over *tafsir* that, in the minds of his contemporaries, usually conjured up long-winded and technical ruminations on the historical circumstances, stylistic and linguistic minutia, and legal-moral implications of the Scripture. This is not to say that the binary opposition *tafsir/ta'wil* was unequivocally accepted by every Muslim exegete. Such renowned Qur'an commentators as al-Tabari (d. 310/923) and al-Baydawi (d. shortly before or after 691/1292) used the word *ta'wil* to designate their conventional historical-cum-philological-legal-ethical commentaries. Much later, the renowned Indian reformer Shah Wali Allah (d. 1176/1762) considered *ta'wil* to be a normal historical and contextual commentary.[260]

In the introduction to his *Ta'wilat*, al-Qashani provides a memorable self-reflective description of his personal relationship with the Qur'an. It finely captures the nature of mystical engagement with the divine word to which many Sufis would eagerly subscribe:

> For a long while, I made the recitation (*tilawa*) of the Qur'an my habit and custom and meditated on its meaning with the [full] strength of my faith. Yet, in spite of my assiduousness in reciting its passages (*awrad*), my chest remained constrained, my soul troubled and my heart was closed to it. However, my Lord did not divert me from reciting the Qur'an until I had grown accustomed and habituated to it to begin tasting the sweetness of its cup and its drink. It was then that I felt invigorated, my breast opened up, my conscience expanded, my heart felt at ease, and my innermost self was liberated. . . . Then there appeared to me from behind the veil such meanings of every verse that my tongue is incapable of describing, no capacity able to capture and count, and no force can resist.[261]

Al-Qashani's programmatic statement bears a striking resemblance to the exegetical method of the Christian theologian and biblical commentator Hugh of Saint Victor[262] (d. 1142), according to whom,

From study (*lectio*) man must go to meditation (*meditatio*) by which the soul tries to discover the Divine thoughts hidden under the veil of both creatures and the Scriptures and to achieve purity of life and strive after loving contemplation (*contemplatio*).[263]

That this parallel is not accidental will be shown in chapter 4 of this book.

The French scholar of Sufism, Pierre Lory, has identified five different levels of metaphysical psychology that operate in al-Qashani's commentary:

1. The level of the divine essence that is ineffable and eludes any definition;
2. Various spiritual realms "sandwiched" between the ineffable and inscrutable divine essence and the world of empirical witnessing (*'alam al-shahada*); they correspond to the exegete's psychological and cognitive states, which allows him to make sense simultaneously of both the Scripture and the cosmos;
3. Astral correspondences (for example, between sun and the spirit, moon and the human heart, and such) as well as micro-macrocosmic correspondences reflecting;
4. The various stages of the mystic's progress on the path to God;
5. And psychological states that the mystic experiences in the course of his spiritual ascension toward the Truly Real One.[264]

Lory's classification seems to be unnecessarily detailed. Some levels and correspondences he mentions overlap. Moreover, all of them can be subsumed under the rubric of micro- and macro-cosmic correspondences, which, of course, was not unique to al-Qashani and the Sufis. Similar correspondences were identified and actively explored by thinkers of different denominations around the Mediterranean basin and beyond.[265] What al-Qashani did was transpose, deliberately and consistently, this ancient parallelism onto the mystic's personal engagement with the Qur'anic text. As Lory has pointed out, al-Qashani frequently uses the word "application" (*tatbiq*) to denote resonances between a given Qur'anic verse and the personal experiences of an individual mystical exegete. In such instances, al-Qashani juxtaposes *tatbiq* and *ta'wil*, the latter being, as mentioned, a general method employed by the exegete to elucidate the more universal, symbolic, and impersonal connotations of a given verse.[266]

Unlike some authors of "moderate" Sufi commentaries discussed above, al-Qashani consistently omits those passages of the Qur'an that, in his view, do not call for an esoteric interpretation (*kull ma la yaqbal al-ta'wil 'indi aw la yahtaj ilayhi*).[267] With five centuries of Sufi exegesis behind him, he no longer feels obligated to pay tribute to the trivia of the conventional *tafsir*, focusing instead only on those aspects of the sacred text that resonated with his esoteric-mystical convictions and experiences. Even such favorite "Sufi" verses as Q 7:172 and Q 85:22 are passed over in silence, possibly because al-Qashani believed that their interpretative potential had been exhausted by his predecessors.[268] Addressed to his fellow Sufis, the people of (supersensory) unveiling (*ahl al-kashf*),[269] spiritual self-exertion (*ahl al-mujahada*), and (passionate) love of God (*ahl al-shawq*),[270] al-Qashani's exegesis brims with terminology and thematic keynotes already familiar to us from Ibn (al-)'Arabi's unitive metaphysics and mystical gnoseology. In many cases, this terminology is left unexplained, indicating that al-Qashani must have assumed its prior knowledge by his audiences.[271] Al-Qashani is completely at home with all the major exegetical themes articulated by his predecessors: the emanationist metaphysics with its tripartite division of existence into the realm of empirically perceived realities (*'alam al-shahada* or *'alam al-mulk*); the intermediate realm of divine sovereignty (*al-malakut*); the purely spiritual dominion of divine power (*al-jabarut*);[272] the major stages and spiritual states of the mystic's journey to God; the parallelism between the universe (the macrocosm) and its human counterpart (the microcosm); the elaborate symbolism of the letters of the Arabic alphabet and numerology; and so on.

Here is a typical instance of al-Qashani's method of "application" (*tatbiq*) of the Qur'anic revelation to the microcosmic experience of the individual mystical seeker.[273] In a gloss on Q 17:1 he writes (the Qur'anic verses are italicized):

> *Glory be to Him, who carried His servant*, that is—Him who purified [his servant] from material attributes and deficiencies associated with [his] created nature by the tongue of the spiritual state of disengagement [from the created world] (*al-tajarrud*) and [bestowed upon him] perfection at the station of [absolute] servanthood ... *by night*, that is, in the darkness of bodily coverings and natural attachments, because ascension and rise can only occur by means of the body; *from the Holy Mosque*, that is, from the station of the heart that is protected from being circumambulated by the polytheism of beastly, animal-like carnal passions ... *to the Farthest Mosque*, that is, the station of the [pure] spirit that lies the farthest from the corporal world.[274]

The same method is at play in the story of Moses (Musa) and the burning bush (Q 20:10–23). The fire of the bush, according to al-Qashani, alludes to God's "holy spirit" (= presence); the two sandals, which Moses is commanded to remove, refer to his soul and body; whereas the concern for their well-being, which resides in the baser part of his heart, is represented by Moses's feet. Likewise, the staff that Moses sheds at God's command is an allusion to his carnal soul, while his right hand, which, in the Qur'anic narrative, becomes white, refers to his intellect, and so on.[275]

As mentioned earlier, al-Qashani's Christian counterparts pursued similar exegetical methods, albeit with a distinctly Christian turn that was dictated by Jesus's preaching of love and his divine-human nature. Thus, according to Hugh of Saint Victor's interpretation of the biblical "Song of Songs," the bridegroom mentioned therein is no one other than

> God [whereas] the bride is the soul. The bridegroom is at home when he fills the mind with inward joy; he goes away when he takes away the sweetness of contemplation. But by what similitude is the soul said to be the bride of God? She is the bride because she is joined to him by a chaste love. She is the bride, since by the breath of the Holy Spirit she is made fertile with the offspring of the virtues.[276]

Both similar and different in tenor and content, such cross-cultural parallels can be multiplied and extended to Judaism, as we have already seen in comparing Philo of Alexandria's exegesis to that of al-Qushayri.

To return to al-Qashani, in the passages just cited and throughout his massive exegesis, correspondences between Qur'anic images and Sufi psychology, epistemology, and ontology are consistently and imaginatively pursued, leaving little room for the ambiguity of reference and referent, as well as for the general opacity of discourse, which are so characteristic of Ibn (al-)'Arabi's oeuvre. Thus, in al-Qashani's commentary, the esoteric exegetical tradition of the previous centuries receives a systematic and lucid articulation. The method of "inspired" allegorical-esoteric interpretation harking back to Ibn (al-)'Arabi and his Andalusian predecessor Ibn Barrajan is being streamlined, finalized, and routinized.[277] Its subsequent (re-)application by such consequential Sufi exegetes as Badr al-Din Simawi (d. 820/1420), Isma'il Haqqi al-Brusawi/Bursevi (d. 1137/1725), Shah Wali Allah (d. 1176/1762), and Ibn 'Ajiba (1224/1809), to name but a few, evinces a remarkable continuity of and faithfulness to the tradition. Anticipating the discussion that follows, one can say that their collective contributions to this tradition lie in presenting, with various degrees of freshness and creativity, a number of exegetical topoi to support the exegetes' cosmological and gnoseological assumptions. The symbolic intellectual universe created and maintained by this combination of topoi and proof-texts functioned extremely well for many centuries, at least for the interested parties. No wonder that certain Muslim thinkers today often bemoan the marginalization of this sophisticated and harmonious Sufi discourse due to the importation into the Muslim intellectual universe of European ideas and values.[278] Their complaints may well be justified. However, the prevalence and persistence of tried old ideas that constitute the Sufi discourse (and Islamic discourses generally) may be construed by less sanguine observers as a lack of originality, if not outright stagnation of Muslim intellectual activity. This fact, the sceptics would argue, has eventually resulted in the inability of the Muslim world to respond effectively to the variegated intellectual and cultural challenges posed by the rise of Western-style modernity.[279] We will revisit this issue later on.

Let us now consider some members of the aforementioned cohort of later Sufi exegetes more closely. Isma'il Haqqi al-Brusawi (1063/1652–1137/1725), a prolific and influential Ottoman scholar born near Edirne and buried in Bursa (present-day Turkey),[280] shows great admiration for Ibn (al-)'Arabi's intellectual legacy, treating him as second only to the Prophet himself.[281] Predictably, Ibn (al-)'Arabi's cosmological psychology serves as the predominant frame of reference for Isma'il Haqqi's own ruminations regarding the cosmos, prophesy, and the destiny of human beings in this world and the world to come. In Isma'il Haqqi's cosmology, the Truly Real One (*al-haqq*)[282] is conceived as an inscrutable "thing-in-itself" that makes use of the entities and phenomena of the universe as the arena for its all-encompassing and ever-active imagination (*khayal*). In this scheme of things, human beings are but "figments" of the imaginative faculty of the Truly Real One.[283] They enable it to realize and contemplate its inexhaustible existential potentialities, or attributes (also called "the most beautiful names"), as in a giant mirror. In the personality of the supreme gnostic (*'arif*), the perfect man (*al-insan al-kamil*) of the age, all these dispersed attributes and names of the Truly Real One converge to manifest themselves in the figure of its human representative or vicegerent (*khalifa*).[284] In an image borrowed from Ibn (al-)'Arabi's *Ringstones*,[285] Isma'il Haqqi presents this earthly *khalifa*, the perfect man (*al-insan al-kamil*), as the pupil (*insan*) in the "eye" of God.

In and of itself, the Truly Real One is unknown and unknowable (*ghayb-i mutlaq*), but it is divided into two halves (*shatr*). One half is self-contained, self-sufficient, and inscrutable. It "excludes any company," that is, any possibility or hint of plurality. The second half, on the other hand, contains seeds of plurality and thus is subject to particularization (*ta'ayyun*),[286] resulting in the Truly Real One's self-realization in the infinite events and entities of the cosmos, which, as mentioned, is nothing other than the site of God's perpetual (self-)imagining (*khayal*).[287] This cosmology is so recognizably Akbarian[288] that no further evidence is necessary. It is abundantly obvious that Isma'il Haqqi's massive Qur'an commentary *The Spirit of the Explanation* (*Ruh al-bayan*) draws heavily and consistently on Ibn (al-)'Arabi's thought, although the authorities he cites are quite diverse. In addition to al-Sulami, al-Qushayri, al-Ghazali, Ibn (al-)'Arabi, al-Qunawi, and a few other members of the Akbarian school of thought, Isma'il quotes the great Persian poets Musharrif al-Din Sa'di (d. 691/1293), Jalal al-Din Rumi (d. 672/1273), and 'Abd al-Rahman Jami (d. 898/1492).[289] He also avails himself of the mystical commentary of Najm al-Din Kubra and his followers,[290] which may indicate that by Isma'il Haqqi's age the Akbarian and Kubrawi traditions had effectively merged into one giant exegetical *summa*. The mention of the "wise sayings" (*hikam*) of Ibn 'Ata' Allah al-Iskandari (d. 709/1309), the principal liturgical book of the Shadhiliyya Sufi order of Egypt and North Africa,[291] points to the internationalization of Sufi thought during the late Ottoman epoch. With the increased mobility of the modern era, Sufi ideas and texts now travel freely and intertwine in various combinations, with the core set of themes and exegetical procedures remaining stable, because numerous ethnically and culturally diverse contributors to Sufi discourse take them for granted and keep building on.

As already mentioned, this conceptual core and the imagery and terminology associated with it are predominantly Akbarian. Their presence in Isma'il Haqqi's Qur'an commentary is truly pervasive.[292] Taking his lead from Ibn (al-)'Arabi and al-Qunawi, Isma'il Haqqi attributes (in a very [Neo]platonic way) the imperfections of the empirical universe to the admixture of the perfect light of the sphere of pure existence (*wujud mahd*) with the pitch-darkness of nonexistence (*'adam*). In a similar vein, he declares human souls virtuous or sinful based on the amount of divine light they have received and absorbed in pre-eternity.[293] The hierarchies of Qur'anic meanings and their respective knowers from rank-and-file believers to inspired friends of God and recipients of divine unveiling (*ahl al-kashf*) are constantly mentioned to explain variations in human understanding of the Qur'an.[294]

In Isma'il Haqqi's *Spirit of the Explanation*, mystical exegesis (*tafsir ishari*) is offered alongside other types of Qur'an commentary. This seems to have been a general trend in the exegetical discourses of the Ottoman epoch. The Moroccan mystic of the Darqawa Sufi order Ibn 'Ajiba names as many as eleven types of Qur'an commentary (*tafsir*) in his own *The*

Widespread Sea (*al-Bahr al-madid*).[295] Ibn 'Ajiba's sources, carefully identified by the translators of the fifty-fourth "portion" (*hizb*)[296] of the *al-
Bahr al-madid*, include both al-Qushayri's and (al-)Baqli's[297] commentaries,[298] which testifies to the Moroccan Sufi's loyalty to the long-standing
tradition of allegorical-esoteric exegesis analyzed above. At the same time
Ibn 'Ajiba sees no harm in people reading the Qur'an according to their
needs and level of comprehension. For him, *tafsir* is:

> The noblest of all sciences, because it is the place where elevated
> thought and profound understanding can be expressed. . . . It is exoteric
> for whoever is exoteric and esoteric for whoever is esoteric.[299]

At the same time, Ibn 'Ajiba does not downplay the substantial differences between the esoteric as opposed to exoteric readings of the Qur'an:

> Interpretation of the people of esoteric allusions (*ahl al-isharat*) de-
> parts from the outward meaning of expression. It consists of symbols
> and subtleties. The meanings of an *aya(t)* become unveiled to them
> after they have ascertained how the expression's [literal] meaning is to
> be understood.[300]

As with Isma'il Haqqi's reference to a Shadhili prayer book from North
Africa, Ibn 'Ajiba's use of Baqli's allegorical-esoteric *tafsir* from Iran (despite its misattribution) indicates that Sufi ideas and writings circulated
freely well outside the geographical areas in which they had originated.
The same exegetical topoi and methods can be found throughout the vast
swath of land and sea from West Africa to Indonesia.[301] This fact seems to
speak in favor of Reinhard Schulze's controversial thesis regarding early
modern and modern *Islamischer Internazionalismus*.[302] However, the
process of an active exchange and cross-pollination of esoteric discourses
certainly predates the advent of modernity. Thus, as Marshall Hodgson has
pointed out, in the late Middle Ages:

> Thomas Aquinas was read from Spain to Hungary and from Sicily to
> Norway. Ibn al-'Arabi was read from Spain to Sumatra and from the
> Swahili Coast to Kazan on the Volga.[303]

On the face of it, such a remarkable ubiquity and uniformity of intellectual preoccupations implies resilience and stability. However, as mentioned before, these same characteristics can be construed by critically
minded observers as signs of stagnancy and complacency on the part of
the learned custodians of Islamic scholarly discourse.

Najm al-Din Kubra and the Kubrawi
School of Sufi Exegesis

The school of Qur'anic commentary associated with the Central Asian Sufi master Najm al-Din Kubra (d. in or shortly after 617/1220) and his foremost followers Najm al-Din Daya (al-)Razi (d. 654/1256) and 'Ala' al-Dawla Simnani (d. 736/1336) is sometimes treated as a separate tradition.[304] However, this perception has more to do with its distinctive spiritual lineage than with its underlying conceptual framework. Whereas the Akbarian tradition owes its name to Ibn (al-)'Arabi's honorific title,[305] the Kubrawi one is derived from Najm al-Din Kubra's sobriquet.[306] There are some differences between the two exegetical traditions in their respective approaches to the Qur'an and Sufism generally, but, for the most part, they are similar and overlap to a considerable degree. After all, both grew out of the same school of Sufism that had emerged in Baghdad and spread to Iran and Central Asia, where it found a cohort of such eloquent exponents as al-Kalabadhi, al-Sarraj, al-Sulami, al-Qushayri, and al-Ghazali, to name but the most prominent ones.[307]

The Kubrawi school is represented by a number of mystical treatises, including the collective exegetical work that was started by Kubra himself, continued by Daya (al-)Razi, and completed by Simnani, although "it is possible that there are two different continuations to Kubra's commentary, one by Simnani and the other by Daya."[308] In any event, this collective commentary remains unpublished, and our exposition of its keynotes relies, in large part, on an illuminating study of Simnani's oeuvre by Jamal Elias.[309]

Like his predecessors, Simnani seeks to establish a hierarchy of Qur'anic senses and their respective knowers. The four levels of meaning of the Qur'an that he discerns correspond to the four levels of existence.[310] The Scripture's exoteric dimension is associated with the realm of humanity (*nasut*); its esoteric dimension with that of divine sovereignty (*malakut*); its limit[311] (*hadd*) with that of divine omnipotence (*jabarut*); and its point of ascent (*muttala'*; cf. the Greek *anagōgē*[312]) with that of divinity (*lahut*).[313] These realms, in their turn, correlate with several levels of the human comprehension of the Qur'an—that of the ordinary believer (*muslim*), who uses his faculty of hearing; that of the faithful one (*mu'min*), who benefits from his divinely induced insight; and that of the righteous one (*muhsin*), whose knowledge is more profound than the *mu'min's* and, therefore, should not be disclosed to anyone except with a divine permission (*idhn*).[314] The ultimate realization of the Qur'an's underlying sense belongs to the witness (*shahid*) who should keep it secret, because, if disclosed to the uninitiated, it may plunge them into confusion or even outright unbelief.[315] The theme of the danger contained in the deeper meanings embedded in the Qur'an is an old one. Attributed variously to 'Ali b. Abi Talib and the foremost companion of the Prophet and early Qur'an commentator 'Abdallah b. 'Abbas (d. ca 68/687),[316] this theme is widely used by both Sunni and Shi'i exegetes who espouse an allegorical-esoteric approach to the Scripture.[317]

In sum, mystical commentaries on the Qur'an that originate in the eastern lands of Islam are keen to show that God's purpose in sending down the revelation is to cleanse the hearts and souls of his servants from mundane distractions and thereby, eventually, to lead them to salvation. To this end, God has supplied them with subtle centers (*lata'if*) that reside in their bodies. They alert the elect men of God to his immanent presence in the world, thereby prompting them to experience "a complete revelation of the true nature of reality."[318] Once again, the insistence on the presence in the Qur'an of a deeper, esoteric meaning, which God imparts exclusively to his chosen folk (*awliya' Allah*; *'arifun*; *hukama'*; *al-khassa*; *al-muhaqqiqun*; *ahl al-ishara wa 'l-fahm*; *ahl al-mawajid*, and so on),[319] is brought home forcefully and unequivocally. This view is shared by both Sunni and Shi'i mystics, despite their disagreements over the sources from which divine gnostics draw their privileged knowledge.

The Shi'i ta'wil *in an Akbarian Garb*

To avoid the impression that allegorical-esoteric exegesis was confined to representatives of Sunni Islam, it is essential to point out that mystically minded Shi'i thinkers have also developed their own sophisticated version of *ta'wil* and a cosmology and gnoseology built thereon. Naturally, these were articulated within the overall framework of the Shi'i doctrine of the imamate.[320] Among the foremost representatives of this Sufi-Shi'i synthesis are the Iranian thinkers Haydar-i Amuli (Amoli) (d. around 787/1385) and Mulla Sadra Shirazi (d. 1050/1640), who had numerous followers.[321] As discussed in chapter 2, they made extensive use of Ibn (al-)'Arabi's cosmological and gnoseological concepts to develop an esoteric-allegorical and unitive dimension of Shi'i theology. Despite Ibn (al-)'Arabi's Sunni background, Haydar-i Amuli has no compunctions about paying tribute to his work in a statement whose boldness no doubt raised the hackles of at least some of his Shi'i peers:

The book that descended (*nazil*) for the sake (*min ajl*) of the Prophet—
blessings on him—is the Qur'an; [the book] that descended for the sake
of the Greatest Master[322] is the *Ringstones of Wisdom*, and the book
that descended for our own sake is *The Greatest Ocean*.[323]

While this statement draws a parallel between his own exegetical work,
The Greatest Ocean and the Vast Sea (*al-Muhit al-a'zam wa 'l-bahr al-
hidamm*),[324] and Ibn (al-)'Arabi's controversial masterpiece (as well as the
Qur'an itself!), elsewhere, Haydar-i Amuli explicitly acknowledges that he
used the esoteric commentary (*ta'wil*) of the Kubrawi Sufi Najm al-Din
Daya al-Razi (d. 654/1256) as a template for his own.[325] Thus, one can
argue that Haydar-i Amuli drinks from the two major streams of esoteric-
allegorical exegesis simultaneously. However, his primary source and inspiration is definitely Ibn (al-)'Arabi, whom he describes as "the greatest
and noblest teacher of all teachers, past and present."[326] Although Haydar-i Amuli often cites the sayings of 'Ali b. Abi Talib and other imams as
his proof-texts,[327] his metaphysical and gnoseological discourses are nevertheless informed primarily by the thought-world and terminology of Ibn
(al-)'Arabi's *Ringstones* and *Meccan Revelations*. The only difference is that
in discussing Ibn (al-)'Arabi's famous concept of the Seal of Muhammadan
sainthood, whom the Greatest Master implicitly identified with his own
persona,[328] Haydar-i Amuli unequivocally attributes this honor to 'Ali b.
Abi Talib, as, in his words, "any reasonable person" would do.[329]

As with the Sunni mystical exegetes examined above, Haydar-i Amuli's
intellectual enterprise in his Qur'an commentary and in his other major
works can be described as establishing hierarchies of meanings, knowledge, and knowers:

> Know that the summit of all knowledge consists of three [types]: The
> knowledge of the True Reality (*al-haqq*), the knowledge of the world
> (*al-'alam*) . . . and the knowledge of humankind (*al-insan*). Whosoever
> has attained these three [types] of knowledge has attained the knowl-
> edge of [the realms of] divine ownership (*mulk*), divine sovereignty
> (*malakut*), and divine power (*jabarut*).[330]

Whereas Haydar-i Amuli duly recognizes that the complete knowledge
of the outward and inward aspects of the world and the divine revelation
is unique to the Prophet,[331] he, nevertheless, claims to be able to obtain
glimpses of this superior knowledge through unveiling and direct tasting
(*bi-tariq al-kashf wa 'l-dhawq*).[332] The individuals whom Haydar-i Amuli
calls "possessors of the inward aspect (*batin*) [of the Qur'an]" and "people

of the [Sufi] path" (*ahl al-tariqa*) gain their veridical knowledge of the Scripture by practicing a parallel exegesis (*ta'wil*) of two books. He calls one "the collected Qur'anic" (*al-qur'an al-jam'i*), the other—"the book of the heavenly horizons [or spheres]" (*al-kitab al-afaqi*). By collating (*tatbiq*) these two holy writs the inspired exegetes can see God manifest himself in "the vestment of letters, words, and chapters" of the Qur'anic text, on the one hand, and "in the form of manifestations of His names and actions" on the "cosmic horizons," on the other.[333] In the final account, however, there is nothing in existence but God. Commenting on Q 57:3,[334] Haydar-i Amuli states this explicitly and unequivocally:

> If it is firmly established that there is no one in existence but Him alone, then it inevitably follows that He is the first and the last, the manifest and the hidden, and thus no differentiation can be imagined either within His essence or his attributes. For He is indeed the first in the essence[335] of the last and the last in the essence of the first. And the same applies to His being manifest and hidden, as we have stated so many times and from so many various perspectives.[336]

Seeing God simultaneously as both indivisible and dispersed in the things and phenomena of the empirical universe[337] is the privilege of "divine messengers, prophets, friends of God (*awliya'*), and God's chosen (*asfiya'*) [folk]." Only they can comprehend allusions (*isharat*) assembled in God's two books, the cosmos and the Qur'an.[338] This, of course, is nothing but a restatement of Ibn Barrajan's and Ibn (al-)'Arabi's Qur'an-universe analogy, on the one hand, and of Ibn (al-)'Arabi's insistence that one should read the text of God's word and God's creation both literally and allegorically ("seeing with two eyes"), on the other.[339] Moreover, taking his cue from Ibn (al-)'Arabi's manuscripts that contain numerous visual aids, Haydar-i Amuli includes in his commentary complex diagrams representing the visible and invisible world, divine names, heavenly spheres, heaven and hell, prophethood, absolute sainthood (*al-walaya al-mutlaqa*), and so on.[340] In so doing, he says, he hopes to convey these complicated concepts to people who lack the revelatory insight that God bestows exclusively on his chosen friends (*awliya'*).[341]

The Qur'an, according to Haydar-i Amuli, contains mysteries, which he calls "seven [layers of its] inner meaning" (*batn*). They can be extracted from the literal Qur'anic text exclusively by practitioners of allegorical-esoteric exegesis, whom Haydar-i Amuli predictably identifies with "those firmly grounded in knowledge" mentioned in Q 3:7.[342] Although Haydar-i Amuli occasionally says that he is eager to share his divinely inspired unveilings with his fellow Shi'is through his writings and diagrams, he still insists (somewhat self-contradictorily) that this magnificent knowledge can be overwhelming and therefore had better be concealed from the ordinary believers (*'ammat ashab al-din*).[343] In sum, as with his Sunni counterparts, for Haydar-i Amuli, mystical gnosis is the exclusive prerogative of God's friends and vicegerents (*awliya' Allah wa khulafa'uhu*).[344]

Despite the fact that Haydar-i Amuli and later Shi'i mystical thinkers, especially Mulla Sadra Shirazi, paid due tribute to the epistemological and soteriological preeminence of the Shi'i imams, their metaphysics and gnoseologies inevitably clashed with the Shi'i doctrine, according to which the imams of the 'Ali-Fatima lineage are the only ones capable of extracting the hidden sense of the Scripture by means of the revelatory knowledge (*'ilm*) bestowed upon them by God.[345] For the Shi'is, the imams are "the living and speaking Qur'an,"[346] so any real or perceived attempt by someone inside or outside the Shi'i community to create an alternative hierarchy of exponents of the Qur'an's hidden subtext could easily be construed as heresy by Shi'i men of religion (*rijal*).[347] This factor, however, has not deterred Shi'i admirers of mystical *hikma* (*'irfan*) from building and defending hierarchies of privileged knowledge and knowers (apart from the imams). In so doing they inevitably have run the risk of being denounced as heretics by defenders of Shi'i orthodoxy (as discussed in chapter 2 of this book). However, for many Shi'i thinkers of esoteric-mystical propensities, the temptation has proved too irresistible and the rewards too great to forgo.

Sufi Exegesis Today: Old Themes and Claims in the New Age

> Polonius: *What do you read, my lord?*
> Hamlet: *Words, words, words.*[348]

The Naqshbandi-Haqqani (Rabbani) *tariqa(t)* of Shaykh Muhammad Nazim (al-)Haqqani al-Qubrusi/Kibrisi (d. 2014),[349] founded in 1973, is often considered to be a new, modern form of Sufism.[350] The American scholar of Sufism Marcia Hermansen has identified Shaykh Nazim's *tariqa(t)* as a "hybrid" movement that combines features of "New Age" religions with loyalty to the spirit and letter of the Qur'an.[351] One of the *tariqa(t)*'s most distinctive features is the emphasis that its late leader Shaykh Nazim placed on "the imminent coming of the Last Days of the world and the appearance of the anticipated Islamic Messianic figure, the

Mahdi."[352] Such millennial expectations are, of course, not new and abound already in the works of Ibn (al-)'Arabi and his followers, including those discussed earlier in this chapter.[353] For a variety of reasons, the Naqshbandi-Haqqani (Rabbani) *tariqa(t)* has gained a large and diverse following in the West (especially in England since 1974, Germany, and in the United States since 1990).[354] It now boasts a truly international outreach. The founder of the *tariqa(t)* Shaykh Muhammad Nazim al-Haqqani (who gave it its current name "Haqqaniyya") was born in the Turkish part of Cyprus and was educated in Istanbul. One of Haqqaniyya's most active branches today is led by Shaykh Nazim al-Haqqani's son-in-law, Shaykh Hisham Kabbani (b. 1945), currently based in Michigan.[355] Shaykh Hisham Kabbani's son, Nour (Nur) Kabbani (b. 1971 in Beirut), a medical doctor, is actively promoting the teachings of his father's *tariqa* across the United States.[356]

The founder of the *tariqa* was inducted into a branch of the Naqsh-bandiyya order in Damascus by the Sufi master 'Abdallah Fa'iz (Faizi) al-Daghestani (d. 1973),[357] whom both Shaykh Nazim and Shaykh Hisham style "the Grandshaykh" in their oral and written sermons.[358] Despite some critics' claims to the contrary,[359] Shaykh Nazim, Shaykh Hisham,[360] and now also Shaykh Hisham's son Shaykh Nour, depict themselves as modern-day proponents of Sufi gnosis, practices (*dhikr*), and spirituality. They make extensive use of the Qur'an and prophetic Hadith in their sermons, hundreds of which are now available online.[361] As with the premodern and modern Muslim exegetes examined earlier in this chapter, over the past several decades these Sufi teachers have been actively engaged in constructing hierarchies of knowledge and knowers.[362] A brief overview of their literary and oral production shows that one major theme invoked by the spiritual masters of the Naqshbandiyya-Haqqaniyya-Rabbanniyya[363] is the enormity and profundity of the knowledge contained in the Qur'an. Thus, according to the founder of the order, Shaykh Nazim:

> Everything must be found in the Holy Quran. Everything that everyone does must therefore be found in the Holy Quran. If a person says that his meeting or association is not mentioned in the Holy Quran, there will be danger for him [*sic*] Iman, for his belief. Yes, if Allah Almighty says that everything is in the Quran, it must then be so. . . . You cannot say "how can this be?" You must believe in it. You must believe in the endless Power of Allah Almighty, in Kudratallah.[364] You have been created weak; therefore do not try to measure huge things with your small

mind. . . . This is why the Prophet, on whom be peace, gave "Thafseer" or explanations of the Holy Quran for a period of over twenty years. Without this giving you cannot enter into these Oceans. This is why you are not able to read Quran Kareem or the Hadees (Traditions) of the Prophet and give an interpretation as to its meaning. You have not been authorised to do this. Therefore you must not try to give meanings to this. Today, however, people who are not authorised are giving all types of meanings and interpretations of the Hadees of the Prophet, on whom be peace, and they say, "I know Thafseer, I know the explanation."[365]

The theme of authorization voiced by Shaykh Nazim is important. It unequivocally goes against the grain of the insistence by some modern-day liberal thinkers that:

[All] Muslims have an equal right to understand the Scripture according to their ability and skill. Whether the text is read in Arabic or in translation, aiming at some understanding of God's word is not a sin; on the contrary, it reflects obedience to the Qur'anic command to think and reflect on its meanings.[366]

Shaykh Nazim's discourses are deliberately and consistently geared toward bucking the trend, now in evidence across the Muslim world and in the Muslim diaspora, toward democratizing access and interpretation of the Muslim scripture.[367] Contrary to this democratizing tide, he would like to restrict the prerogative to interpret the Qur'an and Sunna to the elect friends of God (*awliya' Allah*), thereby excluding "unworthy" commentators, be they lay thinkers or religious scholars. By virtue of their God-given insight, argues Shaykh Nazim, the *awliya'*, who in the online English translations of his orations are designated "[Sufi] Saints,"[368] are aware that every single letter of the Qur'an is "like an ocean" of various senses. According to Shaykh Nazim, just one combination of three "mysterious letters" *alif-lam-mim*, which precedes some Qur'anic suras,[369] can be interpreted by the saints in 24,000 different ways. To be more exact, each of the three letters can yield up to 24,000 meanings to every saint, in addition to the meanings that numberless combinations of these letters can produce. Having said this, Shaykh Nazim rhetorically exclaims, "How, then, is it that these ordinary people[370] give only a very few meanings and say that, it is the interpretation? We cannot accept it because they cannot give as much as a Saint."[371] "In the early days," continues Shaykh Nazim, "the learned people did not allow the others to interpret the Holy Quran because they knew that they did not have the knowledge to do so."[372] Qualified knowers,

FIGURE 3.3. Shaykh Hisham Kabbani at the Fenton Lodge on
February 21, 2016, Michigan. Courtesy of Talia Gangoo.

the "Saints," were then (and should be today) the only legitimate "carriers of the Qur'an" (*hamalat al-Qur'an*). They form a hierarchy of the elect people of God headed by the "spiritual pole" (*qutb*) of the universe, who is capable of removing falsehood from the entire world with just "one Divine Breath."[373] Under the guidance of such a divinely enlightened Sufi master his disciples can "traverse the seven levels of heavenly knowledge."[374]

Shaykh Hisham is in full agreement with his teacher:[375]

> *Awliya'ullah*,[376] Grandshaykh[377] and Mawlana Shaykh,[378] say that Allah revealed to the Prophet(s)[379] on each letter of the Qur'an, he revealed it in 12,000 oceans of knowledge. And they say that all that is written in bookstores, libraries, from *'ulama*, etc., if you add together and know, it is but a drop in the ocean of the knowledge of the Prophet(s).[380]

The fact that Shaykh Nazim and Shaykh Hisham are not unique in their praise of the superiority of Sufi *awliya'* over other categories of believers is attested by the discourses of a modern Turkish Sufi master, Muzaffer Ozak (1916–1985),[381] who calls God's friends "the elite of the elite" of the Muslim community. They enjoy "the acceptance and approval" of both God and his creatures who "hold these beings in honor." Furthermore, according to Ozak, "immersed in the ocean of Unity," Sufi *awliya'* are incapable of committing sinful acts or disobeying their Lord as they reside "entirely with Allah, wholly with Him."[382] It goes without saying that the *awliya'* are the only ones qualified to interpret the ambiguous verses (*mutashabihat*) of the Qur'an.[383] Thanks to the supernatural insight granted to them by God they roam like lions in the forest of human hearts.[384]

To emphasize the special cognitive abilities of Sufi *awliya'* Shaykh Nazim and Shaykh Hisham often quote verse 76 from sura 12 ("Joseph"/ "Yusuf"), according to which "Above every possessor of knowledge there is a [greater] knower."[385] As in the premodern and early modern Qur'anic exegeses analyzed earlier in this chapter, the "higher knowers"[386] of the Qur'an and Islam are not the ordinary members of the Muslim learned class (*'ulama'*) but divinely appointed and inspired gnostics (*'arifun*). The *'ulama'* are proficient only in the external aspects of the Divine Law (*shari'a*), whereas the *'arifun* are privy to the mysteries of its true reality (*al-haqiqa*). The type of knowledge possessed by the gnostics is so sublime that it may disturb the uncouth minds of the common believers.[387] As such it has to be kept secret from the uninitiated—a theme that we have already encountered in connection with the exegetical principles of Haydar-i Amuli.

In his multivolume *Encyclopedia of Islamic Doctrine*, Shaykh Hisham argues that the saints (*awliya'*) receive their superior knowledge as a gift (*karama*) from God.[388] This gift entails the ability to acquire various types of supersensory perception, such as inspiration (*ilham*), veridical vision (*ru'ya*), unveiling (*kashf*),[389] piercing insight (*firasa*), glad tidings (*mubashshira*), direct witnessing (*mushahada*), and direct conversation with God (*mukhataba*).[390] Commenting on the Qur'anic verse 4:69 ("Whoso obeys God and his Messenger, they are those unto whom God has shown favor, of the prophets, the *siddiqun*,[391] the martyrs and the righteous. The best of company they are!"), Shaykh Hisham identifies the *siddiqun* with the spiritual masters of his own *tariqa(t)*, stressing the dual spiritual lineage of Shaykh Nazim: from the first caliph Abu Bakr, on the one hand, and the fourth caliph 'Ali (via the sixth Shi'i imam Ja'far al-Sadiq), on the other. He then concludes:[392]

> O students of Mawlana Shaykh Nazim! We are lucky and blessed to be connected to such a wali, who is connected to the Golden Chain[393] through two big oceans, Sayyidina[394] Abu Bakr as-Siddiq and Sayyidina 'Ali (may Allah be pleased with him) . . . "two oceans coming together and between them a divider." Those two places of knowledge that come together, as mentioned in Surat ar-Rahman.[395]

The highest-ranking saint of the present age is the "Muhammadan Inheritor." Not only has he inherited the supreme knowledge of the Qur'an and Islam from the Prophet himself, but he is also charged by God with dispensing it to the remaining 123,999 living saints (there are 124,000 in all) of whom 7,007 are followers of the Naqshbandiyya *tariqa(t)*.[396] For the followers of the Naqshbandiyya-Haqqaniyya, there is no doubt about Shaykh Nazim's having been the "Muhammadan Inheritor," as well as "[the] Sultan of Saints" of his age.[397]

In his comments on the last sura of the Qur'an (114; "Mankind" or "People") Shaykh Hisham argues: "In every century, there must be someone that these [divine] manifestations appear in these [*sic*] inheritors that inherit from the Prophet(s). *This is what we call the qutb.*"[398] He identifies the spiritual pole or axis of the age (*qutb*) as his own teacher, Shaykh Muhammad Nazim (al-)Haqqani, then proceeds to talk about how one becomes a saint. As the first step, one should reach the level of a full submission to God and annihilation in the divine presence, whereupon:

> Allah brings you up a wali. When you annihilate in the divine presence, you will be dressed in the attributes of the divine presence, so when you

appear among human beings, you will be like a spotlight. A king. A wali is a king. . . . You will be such that wherever you will go you will be like a magnet attracting people to you without doing anything. . . . Like a person in the stadium under a big spotlight. Like a spotlight and all the insects and bugs are attracted to the light. Why people run to you, they don't know that is Haqiqat al-Juzbah.[399]

Despite similarities in tone and content, Shaykh Nazim's and Shaykh Hisham's orations exhibit certain important differences as well. The former often uses Qur'anic verses and references to comment on the events inside and outside the Muslim word, especially to criticize Muslim and Western rulers for their greed, haughtiness, and tyranny. For instance, in an extended comment on Q 13:24, Shaykh Nazim lambastes, in the same breath, the "kings of lamp oil"[400] and democracy ("the way of dogs"),[401] while calling on the Muslim Brothers,[402] Sufis, Salafis, Shi'is, and other Islamic parties and factions to abandon their "invented names" and self-centered ambitions in order to rejoin the community of Islam as "people of their Lord" (*rabbaniyun*).[403] Shaykh Nazim's call evinces his desire to unify the *umma* in the face of the rampant disunity and internecine hostility that, in his view, have afflicted the Muslims in the modern age. Significantly, he uses the obscure but evocative Qur'anic term *rabbaniyun* to bring the message home.[404] In his other politically focused statements, Shaykh Nazim is harshly critical of the uprising of Egypt's masses during the "Arab spring" of 2011. In one memorable sermon, he admonishes ordinary Egyptian Muslims to stay at home, heeding the advice of the Qur'anic ant to its brethren in which it forewarns them about the approaching armies of Solomon's (Sulayman's) "hosts, men and jinn" who are bound to trample the ants underfoot. "Enter your homes," says Shaykh Nazim, citing the Qur'an (27:18), "lest [the prophet] Sulaiman and his army crush you, while they perceive not."[405]

Obviously, Shaykh Nazim's reference here is to the armed forces of Egypt's President Mubarak, which the Sufi interpreter predicts, correctly as it has turned out, will crush the popular rebellion that started on the Tahrir Square in Cairo in the winter of 2010. Examples of Shaykh Nazim's political preferences and of his creative uses of the Qur'an to substantiate them are as numerous as they are varied.[406] However, this kind of politically and socially driven exegesis is by no means unique to him. It can be found in the orations of another neo-Sufi master of Turkish background with a Western following, the Jarrahi-Khalwati Shaykh Muzaffer Ozak (1916–1985), who bemoaned the unraveling of political and moral-ethical fabric of the *umma* due to its collective neglect of "the spirit of the Qur'an."[407]

Compared to Shaykh Nazim's frequent invocations of past and present political events,[408] Shaykh Hisham's commentaries on Qur'anic passages are more in line with the traditional themes of the premodern Sufi exegesis discussed earlier in this chapter. He talks, for example, about various stages of divine self-manifestation, in particular the elusive relation between the unique divine essence symbolized by the divine epithet "One" (*ahad*) and its potentially divisible aspect described by the epithet "Single" (*wahid*). Whereas the former designates the unfathomable and inscrutable divine mystery,[409] the latter belongs to the realm of the divine names that carry in themselves seeds of multiplicity. It is this aspect of the divine essence that gives rise to both noetic (spiritual) and physical forms of existence.[410] As one might expect, Shaykh Hisham attributes the knowledge of the true realities of the divine names to the highest-ranking members of the invisible hierarchy of saints (*awliya'*) who have "one leg in *dunya*[411] and one in *akhira*."[412] Protected by God from human gazes (for no one knows their true identity), these "seekers of the [Sufi] way" are "endowed with perfect knowledge of Allah, *ma'rifa ullah*."[413]

These themes ring familiar, reminiscent as they are of Ibn (al-)'Arabi's invisible hierarchy of divine gnostics (*rijal al-ghayb*)[414] with the spiritual pole of the universe (*al-qutb*) at its very top.[415] The same is true of the theme of the "divine presences" and their association with God's "most beautiful names" discussed by Shaykh Hisham.[416] Even the circular diagrams by which Shaykh Hisham illustrates his deliberations on the metaphysical effects of the divine names and attributes are remarkably similar to those found in Ibn (al-)'Arabi's *Futuhat*[417] and *The Initiation of Circles* (*Insha' al-dawa'ir*).[418] In his *sohbet*s (*suhbas*)[419] disseminated via various Internet resources, especially YouTube, Shaykh Hisham uses an exegesis of the Light Verse (24:35) to elucidate various levels of God's self-revelation to his human servants. As in premodern Sufi exegeses, they correspond to the spiritual level of each intended recipient. Thus, the ordinary believer receives the divine manifestations in his heart (*qalb*); the Sufi seeker (*murid*)—in the secret recess (*sirr*) of his spiritual core; the advanced friend of God (*wali*)—in its secret of secrets (*sirr al-sirr*). After this exalted cognitive stage comes the place of concealment (*maqam al-khafa'*) accessible only to the prophets and the perfected saints. And even this is not the end of the spiritual journey toward the truth, because there exists a greater mystery (*maqam al-akhfa*)[420] of which even the prophet Muhammad gained only a partial, incomplete knowledge.[421]

This is not to say that Shaykh Hisham totally avoids references to contemporary cultural, political, and scientific developments. A chemist by training,[422] in his commentaries on the Qur'an he discusses modern scientific theories and discoveries. Typical in this regard is his exegesis of sura 78 (al-Naba'; "The Tidings" or "The Great News"), which contains numerous references to the creation of human beings, heavenly bodies as well as astronomical and natural phenomena as they were understood in the seventh century CE. Commenting on 78:8, "And have We[423] not created you in pairs?," Shaykh Hisham has the following to say:

> If you think a little bit, a tiny bit, about how Allah designed male and female, in his power of "kun fayakoon."[424] How they come together to bring generations? That mechanism is beyond imagination. They speak of scientific discovery, what scientific discovery!? Stem cells. What, they invented the dynamite? They are using what is there. Can they bring a non-living stem cell and give it life. They are using what exists. And they are still using it and they have to plant it and place it where it is necessary in order to grow (the womb). They say about the moon, that there is no living species on the moon. Why? Because it is too cold no one can live on the moon, no one live on mars [sic]. Who told them? Who told them no one can live on the moon. If they cannot see, then they are stupid. Who told them there is no one inside the moon? How do we know there is not life inside the moon? Why do we have to believe them? Look at DNA. Can they see it with their eyes? It might be Allah put something on the moon, living thing that they cannot see. Now they are making experiments, now they find that one DNA can take the information of 1 million books. And that DNA is a complete plan of your entire lifetime from the time of your creation in your mother's womb until you die. How much you will breathe, speak, walk, work. Every action you will ever do in your life is written there. Like a blueprint. They say if the temp [is] too low you die. Who dies?[425] How are they preserving these stem cells and embryos? At –30 C. [W]hy then Allah will not create creation[s] on the moon and they are living? They pull it out of the freezer and fertilize the egg, and it comes living. Who gave them that knowledge? They say Allah cannot do it but they can do it![426]

In the subsequent narrative Shaykh Hisham uses verse 7 of sura 78, "And We have made you sleep for rest (sabat)," to engage the Big Bang theory, arguing that, had it not been for God's power to counter, that is, "to put to rest (sabat)," the overwhelming force of the Big Bang, it would have kept expanding ad infinitum and, thus, no creation would have ever taken place. Mulling over the word "sleep" (*nawm*) mentioned in the same verse, Shaykh Hisham brings into play the common Muslim belief that sleep is "a kind of death" from which one may return or not return depending on God's will.[427] This theme gives Shaykh Hisham another occasion to showcase his version of elitist Sufi gnoseology:

> Awliya-Ullah,[428] they have been freed by Allah at any time they have reached that state, in their life, "*muutu qabl an-tamut*."[429] Because he controlled his ego, made his ego to die. Awliya, inheritors of sahaba,[430] died before their death, [which] means their spirits are freed from the cage of the body. They do this and they are able to say, "Read this *awrad*,[431] and you will be safe, read the Quran and you will be ok." They see what is ahead of the mureed[432] in order to warn them, give them a hint, in order to protect them.[433]

Thus, Shaykh Hisham defines the inspired, revelatory knowledge of the *awliya'* as a gift from God in return for their fidelity to his commands and their humility and self-abnegation. In other words, their symbolic death to this world is rewarded by a vigorous life of the spirit in contemplation of divine mysteries and the events of the life to come. As with Ibn (al-)'Arabi and numerous other Sufi exegetes,[434] one association in its train produces another one, which, in its turn, produces another one, and so on and so forth.

Our final example is taken from the publicly available commentaries on the Qur'an by Shaykh Hisham's son, Shaykh Nour (Nur) Kabbani (Qabbani). According to his personal Facebook page, he was "born in Beirut in 1971, where he was raised by his parents, Shaykh Hisham Kabbani and Hajjah Naziha Adil Kabbani, daughter of the late As-Sayyid Shaykh Muhammad Nazim Adil an-Naqshbandi (d. 2014), Chief Scholar of Hanafi Fiqh in Turkey and founder of the Naqshbandiyya Nazimiyya Sufi Order."[435] Judging by Shaykh Nour's active involvement in the dissemination of the teachings of the order, he is likely to succeed his father at the helm of this organization when the time comes. A fluent and engaging speaker of both English and Arabic, Shaykh Nour's exegesis focuses on moral and ethical issues that are common to Friday sermonizing at American congregational mosques. At the same time, Shaykh Nour is eager to pursue what he calls "the inner meaning of the holy Qur'an." His approach to the Scripture is to the fore in his extensive commentary on sura 12 ("Yusuf") posted in cyberspace.[436]

The exegete starts out by reading the story of Joseph (Yusuf) in Arabic and English, whereupon he proceeds to elucidate its inner meaning. Focusing on Joseph's famous encounter with Potiphar's wife, Zulaykha,[437] whom Shaykh Nour calls, respectively, the "Ruler" and "the Wife," Shaykh Nour identifies these biblical-Qur'anic personages with the Spirit/Soul (*ruh*) and the human "Ego" (*nafs*). Joseph himself is allegorized as the "Heart" (*qalb/sirr*). In the scene of the seduction of Joseph (the heart) by the "Wife" (the sensual human ego), the two find themselves in a dark room, from which Joseph manages to escape guided by the light of the spirit, exemplified by the "Ruler," that is, the owner of the household, who cracks open the door of the dark room. In Shaykh Nour's interpretation, the seductive machinations of the ego (Zulaykha) fail to distract the heart (Joseph) from the spirit (light) symbolized by the owner of the household (Potiphar). After receiving the light of divine guidance, both the heart and the ego repent their carnal desires and become morally upright. In further elaborating the story Shaykh Nour talks about "the women of the city," who were gossiping following Zulaykha's misadventure. Zulaykha invites them to her house, where they witness the appearance of Joseph (the heart) wrapped up into the light of divine guidance.[438] The sight is so overpowering that they immediately repent their evil thoughts and gossips, while uttering words of submission to God, which the exegete describes as an instance of Sufi *dhikr*.[439] As a reward from God for their act of sincere repentance, they begin to see angels, exemplified by the figure of Joseph.[440] Like Zulaykha herself, in Shaykh Nour's interpretation, the women of the city symbolize human carnal desires, whereas the knives handed to them by Zulaykha's servants exemplify means of gratifying their cravings.[441] In the end, both Zulaykha and the women are guided aright by the divine light embedded in the worshipful and God-fearing human heart (that is, Joseph).

As with any scriptural exegesis, Shaykh Nour's interpretation of the Qur'an draws on a set of symbols (mythologems) that itself is, at least in part, a product of scriptural hermeneutics. His goal is to show how exactly "God acted on the mundane events to make them signify something else."[442] This approach is allegorical insofar as, to use Goethe's definition, "Allegory transforms experience into a concept, and a concept into an image, but so that the concept remains always defined and expressible by the image."[443] In this particular case, it cannot be defined as open-ended, because Shaykh Nour deliberately seeks to tame the incessant profusion of associations[444] that we find in the esoteric-mystical exegesis of

Ibn (al-)'Arabi and his ilk discussed earlier in this chapter. Ibn (al-)'Arabi's exegesis, to use Umberto Eco's definition, is a product of "strong Neoplatonism" with its concept of "a One that is not only unknowable and obscure but, who, being independent of any determination," contains all of possible existents and references, and "is consequently the place of all [possible] contradictions."[445] Thus, although Shaykh Nour identifies his interpretation of the Qur'an as pertaining to the spiritual method of his Sufi order ("*tariqa* meaning"), what he offers, in fact, is a moral-ethical exegesis in which the buoyant and polyvalent Qur'anic symbolism is "tamed" in order to avoid an incessant and unpredictable exploration of what Eco has called "the inexhaustible profundity of the Scriptures."[446] In Shaykh Nour's exegesis the limits of allegories are made clear from the outset (for example, Zulaykha can only be an allegory of the human ego (*nafs*) and nothing else[447]), then pursued throughout the rest of the exegesis. The exegete's controlling authority is unambiguously and forcefully asserted to forestall what Eco has defined as "hermeneutic drift" or "unlimited semiosis."[448]

Conclusions

Within the context of the Sufi tradition, which, as we already know, consists of teachings (discourses), practices, community, institutions, and leaders, Sufi approaches to and uses of the Qur'an fall within the ambit of both teachings (discourses) and practices. As a set of discourses, Sufi exegesis has shaped Sufi cosmology and gnoseology that lie at the heart of ascetic-mystical world-outlook, values, and practical actions (rituals and meditative techniques). Throughout the history of the ascetic-mystical movement in Islam, as has been shown, its leaders have been making elaborate claims to a privileged access to Qur'anic mysteries through what they called "unveiling" (*kashf*), "veridical realization" (*tahqiq* or *tahaqquq*), "direct tasting" (*dhawq*), or "direct witnessing" (*mushahada*). Such claims have set them apart not only from ordinary believers but from exoterically minded Muslim scholars as well.[449] This feature of Sufism has rendered it, on the one hand, attractive to Muslims at large and, on the other hand, objectionable in the eyes of those who themselves wanted to be seen as the only legitimate custodians and exponents of the revelation. Such exponents and custodians have been, for the most part, non-Sufi members of the *'ulama'* class in both Sunni and Shi'i communities.

Of late, several Muslim movements and schools of thought, such as liberal modernizers, Salafis (fundamentalists) of various stripes, secularists, and Gulf-area Wahhabis, have been harshly critical of Sufism generally and of allegorical-esoteric interpretations of the Qur'an by Sufis more specifically. An acrimonious polemic has ensued over correct ways to engage and understand the Scripture. It continues unabated today.[450]

As far as Sufi practices are concerned, acts of reciting, contemplating, and internalizing the Qur'an play a key role in Sufi training and (self-) disciplining. Hearing a verse of the Qur'an, as attested by numerous Sufi biographies, would occasionally precipitate one's conversion to a Sufi version of Islam or, at the very least, make one acutely aware of God's immediate presence[451] both inside and outside his or her own self.[452] Once the conversion or the heightened awareness of divine presence has taken place, the Scripture becomes the seeker's inseparable companion that guides his or her acts of worship and everyday transactions, a powerful protection from being distracted from God by the flux and flow of everyday existence. This process is deeply transformative for the person in question, because it affects his or her entire worldview and public demeanor. Such transformations of the believer's entire world-outlook are neither uncommon nor unique to Islam.[453] The rationale for and exact circumstances of conversion and the role in it of the Scripture and its exegesis are always unique and personal and thus elude a convenient generalization. In any event, it seems that the presence of the Scripture facilitates the process, but is insufficient in and of itself.

After examining the evolution of allegorical-esoteric exegesis in Islam since its inception until today, we can propose the following conclusions:

- Muslim thinkers have demonstrated the same "midrashic-haggagic" preoccupation with extracting all possible connotations and allusions of the Scripture that one finds in either rabbinic Judaism[454] or in Christian theologies.[455]
- The samples of Sufi exegesis examined in this chapter have shown the tendency on the part of Sufi masters (*shaykhs*) to make use of Qur'anic imagery, characters, and topoi in order to create and populate a universe of meaning that they invite their followers (*murids*) to enter and settle in. As we have observed, the masters deliberately and consistently positioned themselves as the indispensable guides of both their followers and the common believers to the unfathomable mysteries of this "imaginal,"[456] supersensory universe of true realities.
- Since its very inception in the eighth century CE, Sufi exegesis has served as a construction site for hierarchies of knowledge and knowers of the Qur'an and, by extension, of Islam, God, and the

cosmos. Whether intentional or not, this hierarchy building has resulted in the elevation of Sufi gnosis (*ma'rifa*) and, by association,
its divinely inspired custodians (*'arifun*), above other types of exegesis and exegetes.

• The consistent and unapologetic departure of Sufi exegetes from
  the literal meaning of the Qur'anic text has created grounds for a
  potential relativizing of the revelation to the point of evacuating its
  historically conditioned (contextual) sense(s) altogether.[457] Consequently, allegorical-esoteric-experiential exegesis cultivated by the
  Sufi intellectual elite has introduced instability into this critical field
  of Islamic epistemology. This fact was acutely perceived not only by
  medieval critics of Sufism, such as Ibn al-Jawzi (d. 597/1201),[458]
  'Abdallah al-Fishtali (d. 660/1261),[459] Ibn Taymiyya
  (d. 728/1328),[460] al-Shatibi (d. 790/1388),[461] or today's Salafis of
  various persuasions, but also by scholars generally sympathetic to it,
  such as Jalal al-Din al-Suyuti (d. 911/1505). All of them have shown
  an obvious unease over uncontrolled and random flights of fantasy
  and imagination that mystically minded commentators were so
  eager to pursue.[462] Thus, opposition to Sufism in the past and today
  is fed, at least in part, by the opponents' realization of the potentially destabilizing effect that Sufi exegetical discourses may have on
  how the Muslims understand and observe the principal source of
  their faith and practice.

• Sufi exegetical discourse, on the other hand, evinces a relatively
  high degree of stability across the centuries; it has found its most
  vivid expression in the use of the same sources, as well as similar
  imagery, terminology, and topoi, by practically every esoterically
  minded commentator including Shi'i ones. These paradigmatic
  sources of Sufi exegesis are al-Sulami's (d. 412/1021) collection of
  early exegetical dicta and their later systematization and elaboration by 'Abd al-Karim al-Qushayri (d. 465/1072) in his massive
  allegorical-esoteric *tafsir*.

• The growing doctrinal sophistication of the ascetic-mystical stream
  of Islam prompted its adherents to develop an elaborate metaphysics and gnoseology that were aimed at placing experiences of individual ascetics-mystics into a broader cosmological framework.
  This development came to fruition in the works of Ibn (al-)'Arabi
  and his followers as well as those of the Kubrawiyya school of Iranian and Central Asian Sufism. Combined, these two strands of Sufi
  exegetical thought have created what one might call, after Gavin

Flood, "a cosmological psychology"[463] that has been reproduced by Sufi masters in various shapes and forms ever since and that is still in evidence today.

- The rise of New Age variants of Sufism along the lines of Shaykh Nazim's branch of the Naqshbandiyya-Haqqaniyya or Muzaffer Ozak's Jarrahiyya-Khalwatiyya has brought about a number of changes in the subject matter of exegesis and introduced new elements not found in the works of its earlier practitioners. One novel feature is the strong emphasis that the commentators affiliated with the Naqshbandiyya-Haqqaniyya place on the exclusive ownership of the deeper meaning of the Qur'an by members of their own Sufi lineage. Some indications of this exclusivity can be detected already in the discourses of Simnani, who belonged to the Kubrawiyya Sufi order, or in those produced by the loosely structured Akbariyya school of mystical thought, but it is not nearly as pronounced as in the recent exegetical discourses of the leaders of the Naqshbandiyya-Haqqaniyya. This tendency may reflect the acute competition among various neo-Sufi communities[464] whose leaders sometimes resort to dramatic claims and grandiose predictions in an effort to "outbid" their competitors in the busy "market" of latter-day spirituality.[465] Another salient characteristic of modern Sufi exegesis is the preoccupation of some of its practitioners with contemporary political, social, scientific, and cultural developments. This preoccupation seems to cater to the expectations and sensibilities of today's educated audiences, both Eastern and Western. Whatever one may think of the validity of this new exegetical turn, it has definitely resonated with the target audiences of neo-Sufi brotherhoods steeped as they are in Western cultural codes, yet eager to partake of the gnoseology, metaphysics, and promise of intellectual and experiential reorientation offered by the modern-day versions of the ascetic-mystical stream of Islam.

CHAPTER FOUR

Sufism in Comparison

THE COMMON FERMENT OF HELLENISM

Antecedents and Parallels to Sufi
Cosmological Psychology

*The Scriptures had potentially every possible meaning, but their reading
had to be governed by a code, and that is why the Fathers proposed the
theory of the allegorical senses. In the beginning, the senses were three
(literal, moral, mystic or pneumatic); then they became four (literal,
allegorical, moral, and anagogical).*

UMBERTO ECO, *THE LIMITS OF INTERPRETATION*

THE ABOVE STATEMENT by Umberto Eco indicates that the multilayered
readings of the Qur'an practiced by Sufi exegetes, as well the Sufi "cosmological psychology"[1] as a whole, have a venerable history in Mediterranean
religions and cultures. The levels of meaning that the Christian church
fathers found in the Judeo-Christian scriptures correspond neatly to the
four possible readings of the Qur'an postulated by Muslim exegetes,[2] some
of whom we have discussed in the previous chapter. As far as cosmological
psychology is concerned, after surveying the history of Sufi thought as reflected in allegorical-esoteric exegesis, one cannot but agree with Samuel
Taylor Coleridge's (1772–1834) praise of (Neo)platonism[3] as:

The most beautiful and orderly development of the philosophy that endeavors to explain all things by an analysis of consciousness, and builds
up a world in the mind of materials furnished by the mind itself.[4]

What Coleridge said about (Neo)platonism two centuries ago is eminently pertinent to Sufi cosmology and gnoseology. This is hardly surprising, because they grew organically out of ancient Greek Platonism—the shared legacy of all three Abrahamic religions or, to be more precise, their intellectual elites. Initially elaborated by the Middle Platonists, such as Antiochus of Ascalon (fl. circa 90 BCE), Eudorus of Alexandria (fl. circa 25 BCE), Alcinous (second century CE),[5] and Clement of Alexandria (d. circa 215),[6] (Neo)platonic ideas received the most authoritative and influential articulation in the teachings of Plotinus (d. 270 CE) and his major followers, Porphyry (d. 305) and Proclus (d. 485).[7] The Latin and Arabic renditions of their works had a lasting paradigmatic impact on Christian,[8] Jewish, and Muslim theologies,[9] especially the mystical strands within each of them. During the first centuries of the Common Era, Christian (Neo)platonism was represented by such consequential thinkers as Clement of Alexandria, Origen (d. 253 or 254), Gregory of Nyssa (d. 395), Evagrus Ponticus (d. 399), and Pseudo-Dionysius (fl. around 500).[10] In the Middle Ages various Christianized types of (Neo)platonism were developed by Hugh of Saint Victor (d. 1142), Richard of Saint Victor (d. 1173), Thomas Gallus (d. 1246), Bonaventure (d. 1274), and, of course, Thomas Aquinas (d. 1274), whose thought is still influential among Catholics today.[11] It is noteworthy that some of these Christian thinkers and exegetes lived approximately at the same time as al-Ghazali, Ahmad al-Maybudi, Ruzbihan (al-)Baqli, Najm al-Din (al-)Kubra, and Ibn (al-)'Arabi, whose exegesis, and the cosmologies and gnoseologies build thereon, have been discussed in the previous chapter.

Plotinus, who regarded himself as "a faithful interpreter of Plato,"[12] is the key figure in this pervasive (Neo)platonization of Mediterranean thought. He created an elaborate cosmological psychology that easily yielded itself to a variety of interpretations, of which mystical ones have eventually taken pride of place.[13] This is hardly surprising if we take into account the fact that Plotinus is credited with giving an "inward" spin to Plato's hierarchal structures of metaphysics by presenting them not only as an objective reality "out there" but also as being simultaneously *inherent in* and *internal to* the soul.[14] Hence, the seminal idea, shared by the majority of Mediterranean religions and cultures, that each human individual is but a microcosm, a universe in miniature.[15] Its gist was conveniently captured by the Muslim thinker Ahmad Sam'ani (d. 534/1140) who talked about each human being as "a container of the meanings of the cosmos" and "an abridged translation . . . of the macrocosm."[16]

Another cardinal concept of the (Neo)platonic worldview postulates the realm of intelligible or spiritual (pneumatic) existence that constitutes "the source and model of the physical universe."[17] Departing from Plato and availing himself of Aristotle's idea of "god as a self-thinker," Plotinus argued that "by thinking itself" the divine absolute, whom he defined simply as "One" (Gk. *hen*), incessantly generates or radiates the intelligible-spiritual and material realms of existence through a staged emanation of existential potentialities inherent in it. These noetic[18] potentialities are transformed into empirically perceived forms of existence (entities) by means of the Universal Intellect and the Universal Soul, which Plotinus calls "hypostases."[19] The (Neo)platonic[20] triad of Being-Life-Intellect would shape how medieval and modern thinkers of vastly different backgrounds understood the origin and functioning of the universe. In this "cosmic drama," Plotinus's One had the central part to play. It was the very principle of all unity and being,[21] rather than a definable entity or intellect:

> The One is the ultimate source of all, including the universe, which is then prefigured in the [universal] Intellect and transmitted through [universal] Soul to become manifest as our physical universe.[22]

What role is allotted to human beings in this Platonist drama? According to Plotinus himself:

> The human individual mirrors this structure to which we are related at each level. For each of us has a body, soul, an intellect, and even something within us that relates to the One.[23]

In other words, the cosmic aspiration of the Universal Being toward its originator, the Universal Soul, and of the Soul toward its originator, the Universal Intellect, is reflected on the microcosmic level in the aspiration of every human individual to the intelligent source of being from which he or she once emerged. The higher, spiritual aspect of the human soul aspires toward its fountainhead, the Intellect,[24] and even beyond, but is weighed down by its "natural duty to body," which causes the soul's alienation from its original source.[25] Plotinus encouraged his followers to make a return or, rather, ascent to the original source of their existence and intellection, which he considered the abode of every human individual's "true self."[26] Plotinus envisioned this process as "a cognitive activity, a form of contemplation, weaker at each successive level"[27] due to the soul's progressive entanglement in the distracting appetitive desires and mundane needs of the physical body.

Already for Plato and later also for Plotinus, the ability of the souls to climb the rungs of the ladder leading to the higher, intelligible realm of existence, where they would contemplate the beauty of their own selves and various sciences as well as the notion of beauty itself,[28] is the unique privilege of the elect few. Being "[al]most godlike" and "keep[ing] company with God," the elect souls are rewarded by gaining glimpses of the splendor of the true reality of all existence.[29] According to Plato and Plotinus, these souls belong exclusively to philosophers, which is quite understandable given both thinkers' high regard for philosophy as the ultimate human achievement and perfect state of mind. Taking their cue from Socrates, Plato and Plotinus suggested that in "a rehearsal for life after death," the philosopher should rid himself of all bodily distractions in this world in order "to contemplate the realities of the intelligible world which can only be approached by means of pure reason."[30] Such purified souls-intellects "must think thoughts that are immortal and divine."[31] As for ordinary, nonphilosophical souls, they are by their very nature incapable of independent thinking and intellectual ascent and thus doomed to remain in the netherworld, "feeding on opinion."[32]

Now, although Plotinus himself "was a resolute intellectualist,"[33] he did not think that the act of knowing alone could bring the soul back to its source.[34] In his interpretation of Plato's teachings, *eros* has a critical, even cosmic role to play.[35] The One (*hen*) is "at once, lovable, love, and love of himself"—an idea that opens up a possibility for the seeker and the sought to unite, becoming truly one,[36] in what Plotinus called the "flight of the alone to the Alone."[37] This possibility was duly explored by Plotinus's followers, such as Alcinous, who declared that the goal of the perfected philosophical souls is to be assimilated to "the god of the heavens and not the god above the heavens,"[38] the latter being the unknowable and transcendent One. Overall, already for Plotinus himself, "all things are one" and "we are all and one"—the terse cosmological adages that prefigure the controversial unitive metaphysics of Muslim mystics such as (al-)Baqli, Ibn (al-)'Arabi, al-Qunawi, al-Qashani, and others discussed in the previous chapter.[39]

Pertinent to our discussion of Sufi exegesis is the fact that for Plotinus and his followers, especially Proclus, Plato's writings themselves were "an illumination according to the beneficent purpose of the higher powers."[40] Differently put, the (Neo)platonists treated Plato's works as a divine scripture of sorts, as Proclus himself eloquently confirms by saying: "All that Plato tells us, we must take 'as given': our task is only to interpret."[41] "Where the two revelations," he continues, "appear to conflict . . . the appearance is due to the crudity of our interpretation."[42] Enough said.

Now, many thinkers among Jews, Christians, or Muslims found the ideas of Plato, Plotinus, and their followers to be highly germane to their own intellectual pursuits.[43] For one thing, Plotinus's tripartite doctrine of emanation was perfectly suited to account for the experience of a human seeker striving toward a higher, perfect reality beyond the physical realm. This striving could be presented as the return journey of human souls to God facilitated by a progressive acquisition by the seeker of ever-larger and subtler amounts of divine knowledge. This journey, as some Western scholars have suggested,[44] was imagined by ancient and medieval Mediterranean thinkers as primarily, if not exclusively, internal experience—a soul's ascent through layers of an internalized cosmic hierarchy into the presence of God and, simultaneously, the soul's progressive discovery of its true, original self.[45] This internal spiritual-intellectual journey can be construed as an alternative of sorts to the more common "ordering" of the human self through fulfilment of legal obligations and assumption of social responsibilities.[46] Seen in this light, the two types of "ordering" of the self, namely, through the observance of laws/social conventions and through experiential/mystical quest, are not necessarily mutually exclusive. In fact, they may occasionally complement each other. Nevertheless, a one-sided emphasis on the cognitive-experiential side of the "ordering" at the expense of observance of social and legal rules may occasionally bring about accusations of heresy against certain imprudent mystical seekers of the divine Absolute and its hidden mysteries.[47]

The erotic overtones of the experiential journey toward the source of one's existence, mentioned above in connection with Plotinus, were eagerly taken up by monotheistic thinkers of ascetic-mystical propensities.[48] They creatively recast the main themes and images of (Neo)platonism into the vocabulary of their respective scriptures (Judaic, Christian, or Muslim).[49] Thus, Clement of Alexandria (d. circa 215), whom many scholars of early Christianity consider to be "the founder of Christian mysticism,"[50] would combine the language of Greek philosophy with that of the Christian sacred texts.[51] This tendency became more pronounced with his followers, especially Origen (d. 253 or 254), who had studied in Egypt with the same teacher as Plotinus.[52] Summarizing Origen's contribution to the Christian tradition, Bernard McGinn describes him as "first and foremost an exegete, perhaps the greatest that Christianity has ever known."[53] Unlike many Platonists who sought to learn the truth about the self and the world by observing human society and engaging in metaphysical contemplations, Origen was convinced that one's main task was to discover the meaning of the self, God (Jesus Christ), and the universe through a close reading the Judeo-Christian scriptures. This discovery, according to Origen, should begin by an examination of the grammatical aspects of the text to be followed by a study of its historical references. After this preliminary work has been accomplished, the reader (seeker) is ready to ascend to "the level of spiritual meaning."[54] While at this stage, the exegete is advised to treat the events and persons of the Old Testament as "types" (typoi, 1 Cor. 10:11) and "allegories" (allēgoroumenoi; literally, "things spoken allegorically" in Gal. 4:24) of realities, past and present.[55]

The ultimate objective of the reader's (seeker's) exegetical ascent to "spiritual realities" is "to realize the Bible's teaching through our own ascension to God."[56] Especially pertinent to our discussion of Muslim exegesis is the fact that Origen's "ascent" (anagōgē) corresponds neatly to the stage called muttala' or matla' ("ascent" or "lookout point") in the Muslim exegetical hierarchy of the layers of reading, as discussed throughout the previous chapter. Long before the Muslim exegetes, Origen envisioned the reader's[57] engagement with the Scripture to be a major prerequisite for his spiritual progress toward God, on the one hand, and the true meaning of his inmost self, on the other. He was definitely one of those "Christian writers" implied by the French biblical scholar Marguerite Harl (b. 1919) when she said:

> The Bible furnished Christian writers citations corresponding to a verbal and gestural thematizing of the encounter with God. . . . Citation makes it possible for the experience of a single person not to remain isolated: it authenticates individual experience by situating it within the collective experience of the people of God.[58]

In line with his single-minded preoccupation with the various meanings embedded in the Judeo-Christian scriptural canon, Origen uses its imagery to describe the soul's exegetical-mystical ascent, portraying it as a reflection of the major themes of the three books ascribed to Solomon:

1. The Book of Proverbs teaches the believer proper manners of virtuous and moral living.
2. Ecclesiastes instructs him in enlightened knowledge of the nature of things and of how they are to be used as God intended.
3. The Song of Songs is a book that instills love and desire of celestial

and divine things under the image of the Bride and the Groom, teaching how we come to fellowship with God through oaths of love and charity.[59]

Anticipating by many centuries Sufi speculations about the allegorical significance of biblical characters and their actions, Origen interprets Moses's and his people's departure from Egypt as the believer's moral transformation and repentance of sins; their subsequent flight from Pharaoh and his army is an allegory of the believer's constant warfare against demonic temptations; the light and abundance of the Promised Land symbolize, for him, the enjoyment by the seeker of God's luminous presence in this world and the hereafter.[60] As one can see, Origen's allegorical exegesis demonstrates clear parallels with the Sufi interpretations of the Qur'an discussed in the previous chapter.[61] Likewise, his spirited glosses on the biblical Song of Songs[62] prefigure in remarkable ways the oft-cited Sufi images of loving union and spiritual intoxication of the human lover with the divine beloved.[63] As already mentioned, for Origen, the soul's journey to God, at once cognitive (*gnōsis*) and visual (*mystikē theōria*),[64] has a clear erotic dimension. The quest of the seeker is driven by "the power of yearning desire implanted in the soul by God" who himself is nothing but Eros.[65] This notion gives rise to the famous formula: "Love is a form of knowing" (*amor ipse intellectus est*).[66] Its message has informed Christian mystical discourses ever since.

Around 500 CE, the allegorical-esoteric exegetical tradition adumbrated above had reached a high point in the work of Dionysius the Areopagite, the still-unidentified mystical thinker who probably resided in Syria. He brought to new levels of sophistication the (Neo)platonizing trend in Christian theology[67] initiated by Justin and Irenaeus in the second century CE and further elaborated by Clement of Alexandria and Origen.[68] As did his predecessors, Pseudo-Dionysius taught that "mystical secrets of sacred scripture . . . can only be gradually revealed to the real 'lovers of holiness,'"[69] because their longing for God is stronger and purer than that of the "lower strata" of people.[70] This elitist vision of human beings' striving toward their origin, the utterly inscrutable godhead manifesting itself in the multiplicity of the physical universe,[71] anticipates the Muslim discourses that would appear several centuries later in the same geographical area.[72] Similarly paradigmatic and influential is Pseudo-Dionysius's hierarchical vision of the structure of the universe that we have repeatedly encountered in our discussion of Sufi exegeses earlier in this chapter. The universal hierarchy encompasses the levels or stages of manifestation of the inscrutable Absolute that, in their turn, contain the pneumatic powers of purification, illumination, and perfection.[73] These powers enable the aspiring soul of the divinely guided seeker to return to its creator. Pseudo-Dionysius's tripartite division of the universe and its correlation with the stages of the soul's progress toward God anticipate the widely known and discussed division of the Sufi path to God into three stages: *shari'a* (law = purification), *tariqa* (path to God = illumination), and *haqiqa* (true reality = perfection, culminating in union with God).[74] According to Pseudo-Dionysius, the archetypal mystic (symbolized by Moses),[75] undergoes first purification (*katharsis*), then gains contemplation (*theōria*) of the place (not the essence) of God, and finally attains union with him (*henōsis*).[76] "Here," says Pseudo-Dionysius, "being neither oneself, nor someone else, one is supremely united to the Unknown by an inactivity of all knowledge, and knows beyond the mind by knowing nothing."[77] This depiction of the experience of the archetypal mystical seeker cannot but conjure up the image of Moses coming to God "without Moses," his very personality "erased" in an act of an ecstatic (self-)annihilation in God, as described in al-Qushayri's *Subtleties of Allusions*. Remarkably, both the Christian and the Muslim exegetes have chosen the same biblical personality to convey essentially the same message, albeit couched in the terminology of their respective religious traditions.[78]

Noteworthy is the role of love in the psycho-cosmological universe painstakingly assembled by Pseudo-Dionysius. It is set in motion and operates thanks exclusively to the driving force generated by *erōs/apapē*. In his own words:

> All things must desire, must yearn for, must love, the Beautiful and the Good. Because of it and for its sake, subordinate is returned to superior, equal keeps company with equal, superior turns providentially to subordinate. . . . The cause of all things loves all things in the superabundance of his goodness, that because of this goodness, he makes all things, brings all things to perfection, holds all things together, returns all things.[79]

Thus, for Pseudo-Dionysius, "God is both the object of the yearning of all things to return to him and that very yearning itself as participated in by all levels of the individual hierarchies."[80] The uplifting process that brings chosen human beings into the presence of or to a union with God is called *anagōgē*,[81] a term that appears to be the exact equivalent of the Sufi *matla'/muttala'*, as has already been mentioned in connection with Origen's description of the seeker's ascent to God by means of an allegorical-esoteric reading of the Scripture. In the end, however, Pseudo-Dionysius insists that the unfathomable and inscrutable divine essence eludes the grasp of even the most determined mystical seeker. His or her "glass ceiling," is, according to Pseudo-Dionysius, nothing but a total "absence of knowledge" (*agnōsia*), which he holds to be the (only) "true *gnōsis* of God." This concept rings very familiar to every student of Ibn (al-)'Arabi who, too, insisted that on reaching the end of his or her mystical quest the accomplished seeker is thrown into "bewilderment" (*hayra*), that is, the "state of finding and knowing God and of not-finding and not-knowing Him at the same time."[82] Ibn (al-)'Arabi's statement resonates neatly with Pseudo-Dionysius's insistence on "the necessity of both affirmation and negation (how can something be negated unless it [be] first affirmed)"[83] or his concept of "dissimilar similarity," that is, a characteristic attendant to every single manifestation of God in the material universe.[84] These ideas, too, dovetail with Ibn (al-)'Arabi's assertion that "every existent thing other than God dwells in a never-never land of affirmation and negation, finding and losing, knowing and not knowing."[85] Although separated by hundreds of years and a deep religious-cultural divide, both thinkers seem to agree that the true reality of existence is concealed from ordinary believers and revealed only to the elect, and even then nothing can be taken for certain. Even the most advanced knowers remain hesitant and even perplexed regarding that which they perceive or learn. For Ibn (al-)'Arabi, they are perfected Sufi "finders" from among the "people of unveiling," "gnostics," and "[truth]verifiers" (*kummal; ahl al-kashf wa'l-wujud; 'arifun; muhaqqiqun*).[86] For Pseudo-Dionysius, they are "lovers of holiness" and "perfect mystics" exemplified by the prophet Moses himself.[87]

Pseudo-Dionysius's teaching inspired later generations of Christian mystics, such as Thomas Gallus,[88] who consistently elevated superintellectual wisdom (*nosse*) above the knowledge derived from books and rational consideration (*scire*).[89] In describing the mystic's ascent to the remote, majestic deity, Thomas Gallus "places the experience of affective love above all cognition"[90] and treats the angelic hierarchies of the spiritual world as the inner powers of the soul to be energized and set in order by the mystic whose goal is to achieve a loving union with the divine.[91] As did Pseudo-Dionysius, Thomas Gallus viewed "the Song [of Songs] as a key to unlock the central message of the Bible, citing hundreds of correlative texts from the Old and New Testaments to underline the message he discovers."[92]

The profound and long-lasting impact of Dionysian thought, sometimes described as "the Dionysius renaissance,"[93] on Christian mystical theology has been a recurrent theme in European scholarship on medieval and early modern Christendom. Thanks to Pseudo-Dionysius, as well as his predecessors and followers, the emanationist metaphysics and gnoseology of (Neo)platonism was adapted to the Christian doctrine of the Trinity and couched in carefully selected biblical images and terminology.[94] The Song of Songs was a major, although by no means sole, focus of exegetical endeavor on the part of such thinkers as Richard Saint Victor (d. 1173), Thomas Gallus (d. 1246), and Bonaventure (d. 1274), to name but a few.[95] For Bonaventure in particular, the created world was but a symbol or image reflecting the higher truth of the sublime and magnificent divinity. While the majority of believers will discover it (and thus be redeemed) at the end of time when Christ returns, "some blessed people can journey to God within themselves and experience a vision of the Lord that is a precursor of what is to come."[96] In Bonaventure's memorable allegory, the physical world is identified with Jacob's ladder (*scala*),[97] which the blessed aspirant endeavors to climb:

> Placing our foot on the first rung, we behold the material world as a mirror through which we pass over into God as the Hebrews passed over from Egypt and Christ [from this world] into the realm of the Father.[98]

In sum, the physical and human existence in this world is but a reflection of the cosmic order of divine self-manifestations. Spiritually and gnostically endowed individuals can attain their place of origin and experience it directly by ascending the stages of the divine Absolute's (Plotinus's "One") gradual descent into the materiality of physical being. Because the Scripture "describes the entire universe" (*sic dexcribit totum iniversum*), the enlightened traveler[99] must simultaneously navigate the hierarchies of existence and the contents of the divine writ. In other words, the soul's mystical ascent to the divine presence, as well the ecstatic, supersensory wisdom it acquires in the course of its journey, "is a kind of interpretation of the cosmos—a kind of reading."[100] The notion of a simultaneous reading of the cosmos and the Scripture, which Bonaventure shared with many of his predecessors and successors, such as Meister Eckhart (d. 1328),[101] Jakob Böhme (d. 1624),[102] and Angelus Silesius (d. 1677), corresponds perfectly to the vision of Bonaventure's older contemporary Ibn (al-)'Arabi:

> The world is but the giant text [of the Qur'an] (*al-mushaf al-kabir*) that God has uttered upon us. ... The world is but letters written and inscribed in the unrolled parchment of existence; writing on it is eternal and never ceases.[103]

General Observations

The translation of the gospel of Christianity, and, after it, the gospel of
Islam, into terms of Hellenic metaphysics was, indeed, unavoidable.
Christianity and Islam made their epiphanies in a Hellenizing world in
which they could no more avoid an encounter with Hellenic philosophy
than they could avoid one with the Roman Imperial Government.

ARNOLD TOYNBEE, *AN HISTORIAN'S APPROACH TO RELIGION*

In the spirit of Arnold Toynbee's message cited above, the goal of this chapter was to demonstrate that Sufi cosmological psychology and the exegetical methods devised to support it take their origins in various versions of
(Neo)platonism and systems of thought and belief associated with it, for
example, Hermetism.[104] In the same way as "the [Christian] Church could
not afford to rebuff" the intellectual needs of the philosophically educated
upper stratum of Mediterranean societies,[105] the region's new religion,
Islam, did not remain immune to the allure of Hellenic thought and eventually took it on board after reshaping it in accordance with Islamic principles and values. Sufism was an important part of this process of the do-
mestication by the Muslim intellectual elite of various strands of Hellenic
thought that permeated the cultures of the late antique world around the
Mediterranean basin.[106] Whether this process occasionally involved "mis-
translation,"[107] or, on the contrary, a systematic and organic integration of
two systems of thought that complement, not contradict, each other,[108] is
a matter of personal opinion. Be this as it may, the fusion and adjustment
of the prophetic religions of the region, on the one hand, and Hellenic
metaphysics and gnoseology, on the other, was inevitable. The similarities
in this respect between ascetic-mystical Islam and its predecessors pointed
out in this chapter should be sufficient to demonstrate this point. Those
who disagree with this conclusion should prove that the coincidences documented above are merely accidental and that, therefore, the roots of Sufi
cosmology and gnoseology lie elsewhere. As already mentioned in chapter
1 of this book, the presence of extraneous elements in Judaism, Christianity, or Islam must not be taken as a sign of their "slavish dependence" on
outside influences—a notion that is highly problematic for a variety of reasons. Rather, it is their absence that would have been truly puzzling, for
ideas do travel, intertwine, and crossbreed, especially in the same geographical area—this is a simple but undeniable fact of civilized human
existence.

Naturally, Sufi thinkers were not the only Muslims fascinated with (Neo)platonism in its various guises. The intellectual leaders of the Isma'ili community developed their own sophisticated interpretation of the (Neo) platonic doctrine of emanation as well as the complex gnoseology attendant to it, including an allegorical-esoteric exegesis.[109] Cultivated in secret by the intellectual elite of the Isma'ili community, it was revealed piecemeal to its rank-and-file members depending on their level of maturity and preparedness to cope with the "higher truths" of existence.[110] The emphasis on the esoteric (inner) aspects (*batin*) of the revelation as opposed to its exoteric (external) message (*zahir*) is common to the Sufis, Twelver Shi'is, and Isma'ilis, as Henry Corbin's studies have abundantly demonstrated, his partiality for esoteric aspects of religion notwithstanding.[111]

Whereas the elegance of the doctrinal (discursive) foundations of Sufism is fascinating, their social and institutional implications are no less intriguing, if often less obvious. Claims to superior knowledge and the ability to reveal it to those seeking it are both enticing and contagious. One can argue that the dual claim that Sufi teachers lay to the inspired knowledge of the Scripture, on the one hand, and of the hierarchically structured cosmology, on the other, may have come as a Sunni response to the attribution by the Shi'is of the similar divinely given competences to the imams of the 'Ali-Fatima line.[112] It is hardly accidental that the imams are called *awliya'* in Shi'i theology; the same term is commonly applied to Sufi knowers of God (*'arifun*) and spiritual leaders (*murshdun*) in Sunni Islam.[113] This suggestion is especially plausible, because in Isma'ilism and Twelver Shi'ism claims to privileged knowledge have been used to justify the exclusive right of their respective leaders to both spiritual and political guidance of the community.[114] It would be very tempting to argue that in contradistinction to the imams of the Shi'i community, Sufi *awliya'* were not interested in the political implications of their gnoseological claims, being content with moral-ethical guidance of their followers. However, as the rich history of Sufism shows, attempts to assume political leadership have not been entirely alien to certain Sufi *shaykhs* under propitious social and geopolitical conditions.[115]

What role do the cosmological psychologies of Sufism discussed in this and previous chapters play in the real world with its power relations, struggles for economic and social advantage, and domination? As we have shown, these Sufi discourses are a result of a long and laborious process of the construction of a distinctive cosmology and gnoseology by Sufi leaders who availed themselves of the conceptual bricks and blocks left behind by

Hellenism. Numerous known and anonymous hands were hard at work in this collective construction project, contributing ever-new concepts, nuances, and adjustments. The idea of a wholesale and deliberate borrowing of (Neo)platonic ideas and value systems by Sufi thinkers does not stand up to scrutiny, because the building blocks had to be rearranged in novel combinations to meet the needs of a new, increasingly more sophisticated society and the religious tradition that undergirded it. Nevertheless, as with their Jewish and Christian counterparts, Muslims of ascetic-mystic propensities could not resist the attraction of Greek wisdom in its Hellenistic form. The elaborate Platonic and (Neo)platonic imagery and concepts were simply too elegant and powerful to be ignored.[116] All the more so, because they were readily translatable and adaptable according to one's particular needs and tastes. The translation activity under the early 'Abbasids was no doubt important,[117] but no less important was the fact that the Qur'an itself contained gnostic, mystical, and visionary elements,[118] which facilitated the integration of the rich Hellenistic philosophical-spiritual legacy into the ascetic-mystical stream of Islam, as well as into certain variants of Shi'ism. Gradually but inexorably, the collective effort of several generations of ascetically and mystically minded Muslims resulted in the creation of the complex and multilayered Sufi cosmology and gnoseology discussed in the previous chapter. Supported by a highly imaginative, if occasionally far-fetched and even scandalous exegesis, it captivated the minds and hearts of many Muslims. To enter and navigate successfully such a complex universe of meaning and symbols, specially trained and certified guides acting within institutionalized structures were necessary. This necessity has given rise to patterns of Sufi leadership, ethos, practices, and institutions that are the subject of the chapter that follows.

CHAPTER FIVE

Practices, Ethos,
Communities, and Leaders

*Religion, by fusing ethos and world view, gives to a set of social values
what they perhaps need most to be coercive: an appearance of objectivity.
In sacred rituals and myths, values are portrayed not as subjective
human preferences but as the imposed conditions for life implicit in a
world with a particular structure.*

—CLIFFORD GEERTZ, *INTERPRETATION OF CULTURES*

Sufi adab *as the Foundation of Sufi Practice*

Trite as this may sound, in discussing Sufi practices and ethos[1] it is very
important to keep in mind their normative nature.[2] Authors of numerous
books on the good manners of Sufis (*adab al-sufiyya*)[3] do not, as a rule,
describe how actual Sufis behaved in real situations. Rather, they usually
tell their readers how they *should* behave or *should have* behaved. This is
not to say that such normative books are unrevealing of Sufis' actual behavior. Occasionally they are, especially when some moot points of the Sufi
etiquette are elucidated or when the author wants to demonstrate how one
should not have acted under given conditions.[4] Finally, we have critical or
outright hostile accounts of Sufi public activities and comportment that
can serve as a counterbalance to the normative and idealized image of Sufis
in Sufi literature.[5] Therefore, forming a general notion of how Sufis of old
actually behaved is possible in principle. Much better attested are Sufi rituals and public activities today thanks to recent "on-site" anthropological
studies in various areas of the Muslim world and among Sufi (or neo-Sufi)

communities in the West,[6] as well as availability of video clips depicting Sufi activities on the Internet.

As any successful religious movement, Sufism has generated a large amount of rule books. Sufi rules of good manners and proper conduct (*adab*)[7] fall into two major categories: (a) how one should behave oneself toward God; (b) how one should deal with various categories of people both inside and outside one's Sufi community. Definitions abound. Abu Hafs al-Haddad (d. circa 265/879), an ascetic-mystic of Nishapur (Iran), defined the former aspect of *adab* as "fulfilling God's orders with the utmost sincerity (*ikhlas*)[8] and maintaining correct behavior both outwardly and inwardly with fear of God (*khawf*) and awe (*hayba*) of Him." The other aspect of *adab*, according to Abu Hafs, consists of proper ways of keeping company with people, showing kindness to them in times of tribulation, exercising sound judgment[9] when making choices, and being generous and forgiving to others as much as one can.[10] In the terse definition of an early Sufi master Ibn 'Ata',[11] "Good manners is that you adhere to good deeds."[12] However, when pressed for what exactly he had in mind, Ibn 'Ata' added, "This means that you treat God properly both inwardly and outwardly."[13] So, whereas Abu Hafs's definition of good manners is broad enough to be practiced by all believing Muslims, Ibn 'Ata' adds to it a specific Sufi twist (internality), upping the ante, as it were. Nevertheless, the distinction between the Muslim ethos generally and the one unique to the Sufis is not always clear. Yes, Sufis are people of good manners. However, their good manners are special, because they emphasize interiority over exteriority—a feature that, they believe, renders them distinct from the rest of the Muslims.[14]

The great Maghribi thinker 'Abd al-Rahman Ibn Khaldun (d. 808/1406) stated this idea with his characteristic directness: outward actions of the body's limbs fall into the category of "outward jurisprudence" (*fiqh al-zahir*), whereas the actions and motives of the heart are the domain of "inward jurisprudence" (*fiqh al-batin*).[15] The latter regulates the believer's "pious striving" (*jihad al-taqwa*) aimed at conquering one's base passions and acquiring both external and internal manners (*adab*) that are pleasing to God and conducive to salvation (*najat*).[16] Quoting al-Ghazali (d. 505/1111), Ibn Khaldun then added that whereas the outward jurisprudence allows the believer to enjoy piously the benefits (*masalih*) of earthly existence, the internal one secures him the benefits of the hereafter.[17] The pious striving is followed by several advanced stages of self-perfection, namely, that of "striving for uprightness" (*mujahadat al-istiqama*) and that of "striving for unveiling" (*mujahadat al-kashf*). In any event, the first stage with the *adab* attendant to it is indispensable for attaining the ones that follow.[18]

Sufi teachers are in agreement that good manners have to be internalized in order to effect a complete harmony between one's external comportment (*adab al-zahir*) and one's internal (spiritual) state vis-à-vis both God and human beings (*adab al-batin*).[19] An oft-quoted Sufi saying brings home the importance of *adab*:

> All of Sufism is [nothing but] *adab*.[20] For each mystical moment (*waqt*)[21] there is an *adab*; for each [spiritual] state[22] there is an *adab*; for each station[23] [of the mystical path] there is an *adab*. Whoever follows *adab* will achieve the status of the real men (*rijal*) [of the mystical path].[24]

Coincidence of inward convictions and outward actions constitutes sincerity (*ikhlas*) and truthfulness (*sidq*), the primary Sufi virtues that are indispensable for achieving the goal of the Sufi path, alongside renunciation of the world (*zuhd*), obtaining God's pleasure (*rida*), and the taming of one's lower self (*mujahadat al-nufus*).[25] Raising the stakes even higher, the Sufi ethos may demand that all normal human attachments be severed (*qat' al-'ala'iq*), including familial duties, professional responsibilities, and mundane possessions.[26] The sincere seeker of God has to empty his or her hands and heart of worldly possessions and to embrace poverty (*faqr*) willingly and happily, because it is

> a distinctive feature of the friends of God (*awliya'*), a decoration of the pure ones (*asfiya'*),[27] and the special feature with which God—praise be to Him—distinguishes His elect ones from among the righteous and the prophets. The poor (*fuqara'*) are the elect servants of God . . . and carriers of His secrets among His creatures. Through them God protects His creatures, and it is due to their supplications that He bestows livelihood upon humankind.[28]

Thus, being poor in the inner (spiritual) sense is not just having one's hands free of worldly possessions, but also maintaining, through a close self-scrutiny, the sense of a constant existential need for God and God alone (or, put differently, "being independent of anything save God").[29] This, according to al-Ghazali, is absolute poverty, which is different from that which one experiences after having lost one's worldly possessions.[30] Al-Ghazali's discourse already contains the seeds of an allegorizing approach to human actions and rituals, which, as we have seen already, was to become a distinguishing feature of later Sufi cosmological psychology.[31] Initially, however, Muslim ascetics-mystics were concerned primarily with immediate practical implications of being poor. "Poverty," wrote Abu 'Abd al-Rahman al-Sulami (d. 412/1021),[32] quoting an earlier Sufi teacher, "is renunciation of the world and the ego-self (nafs), and holding them both in disdain."[33] Only after this initial stage of the mystical path is properly "conquered" by the seeker, he or she should try to make it his or her internal conviction. Therefore, the true Sufi is one who has achieved perfection in poverty by internalizing it, abandoning self-reliance, putting his trust in God (tawakkul), and focusing himself completely on his Creator.[34] For the ideal Sufi, wealth and poverty become equal, or rather, he or she becomes indifferent to both.[35] Says al-Sulami:

> [The Sufi] associates with people, behaving with integrity, manifesting neither wealth nor poverty. He is among people as one of them, indiscernible from them except by the steadfast discipline of his journeying. . . .[36] He discloses his outer manner to people, while safeguarding from them his inner state. . . . Outwardly he follows a livelihood, while inwardly he puts his trust [only in God].[37]

The same process of internalization should be applied to all other internal states and external actions of a Sufi aspirant (murid[38]): fear of God (taqwa); scrupulousness in food, drink, and companionship (wara'); renunciation of the world (zuhd); sadness (huzn); humility (hushu'); modesty (tawadu'); trust in God (tawakkul[39]); patience (sabr); gratitude [to God] (shukr); uprightness (istiqama); sincerity (ikhas); truthfulness (sidq); shame or diffidence (haya); and so on.[40] While most of these virtues and behaviors are incumbent on every pious Muslim, only the elect folk of God (namely, accomplished Sufi masters) achieve perfection in performing them. This level of performative excellence eludes ordinary believers, preoccupied as they are with mundane concerns. The Sufis deemed themselves superior to other Muslims, because they thoroughly and consciously avoided reprehensible character traits, such as envy (hasad), backbiting (ghiba), carnal desire (shahwa), and so on.[41] Occasionally, they were even able to reshape seemingly blameworthy qualities in such a way as to turn them into virtues.

Take jealousy (ghayra), for example. It is obviously an evil character trait for an ordinary believer to possess. However, according to al-Qushayri's master Abu 'Ali al-Daqqaq (d. 495/1015),[42] this is not the case with Sufis who "grow jealous when they observe other people remember God Most High mechanically, [because] they [the Sufis] cannot tolerate this sight and are aggravated by it."[43] For some Sufi masters, even a call to the prayer uttered perfunctorily by a distracted muezzin may become "deadly poison" and a cause for anger.[44] Thus, while jealousy, and the zeal it engenders, is reprehensible for ordinary believers, for the Sufi seeking God's pleasure it becomes a positive quality. Consumed by jealousy and zeal, the Sufi devotes "all of his spiritual states and breaths to no one but God Most High."[45] As a result, he may occasionally feel irritated by the lack of a similar single-minded dedication to God on the part of ordinary believers, whom he may be tempted to censure or threaten. Examples of this kind can be multiplied, but the conclusion is obvious: the Sufis, or rather Sufism's educated spokesmen, have been deliberately and carefully shaping a distinctive, inward-oriented ethos that would set them apart, and above, ordinary believers, including representatives of the learned class ('ulama'). The author of the first full-fledged Sufi manual to reach us, Abu Nasr al-Sarraj al-Tusi (d. 378/988),[46] unequivocally admits as much:

> With respect to good manners (*adab*), people can be divided into three categories: The people of this world, most of whose manners have to do with eloquence, rhetoric, and the study of various sciences, names of rulers, and poetry of the Arabs.[47] The second category comprises men of religion, who acquire their good manners by subjugating their [base] souls, restraining their limbs [from prohibited things], observing the rules of the Divine Law, and abandoning passions and appetites. The third category is the elite (*khususiyya*); their manners consist of purifying their hearts, scrutinizing their inner thoughts, being faithful to their pacts, observing [the conditions required by] every [spiritual] moment (*waqt*),[48] paying little attention to tempting thoughts, and implementing the rules of decent behavior in their striving [toward God], while being in His presence and entering the stations of proximity [to Him].[49]

Effectively, Sufis have created not just their own ethos but also an entire way of life peculiar to them: they took to wearing rough patched garments (*khirqa*), living in lodges (*khanaqa*; *khanegah*), listening to music or dancing during "mystical concerts" (*sama*'; *majlis al-dhikr*), withdrawing into forty-day seclusion (*chilla*) for meditation, traveling without provisions, begging for food and shelter, and so on. While some Muslim scholars routinely denounce such actions as "heretical innovations" (*bida*'),[50] Sufis see them as "praiseworthy customs" (*mustahsanat*) aimed at purifying and subduing one's appetitive soul and preparing it for receiving outpourings of divine grace and intimacy.[51] These customs constitute a distinctly Sufi codex of proper behavior (*adab sufi*)[52] that remains as actual for modern-day Sufis as it was for their predecessors.[53] "Just as the whole life in the monastic orders," notes Fritz Meier, "fundamentally came to be subjected to *regulae, constitutiones* and *consuetudines*,[54] so the whole of Sufism came to be [ruled by the norms of Sufi] *adab*."[55] One can easily take issue with Meier's parallel,[56] arguing that monastic communities in Christianity were centralized and closely regulated under the aegis of the papacy in Rome, whereas Sufi institutions were not subject to any overarching authority, not to mention the general differences between Christianity and Islam, such as the absence in Islam of the institution of ordained priesthood and monkhood.[57] However, details apart, Meier's comparison is correct, in our view, as long as we accept the fact that (a) like-minded people united by shared values and beliefs tend to form communities and establish rules governing their behavior within and outside them; (b) Weber's idea that the institutionalization and rationalization of every sphere of human activity, including the religious one, is an inevitable element of civilized life.[58] If Meier's parallel is acceptable in principle, then one is justified in posing the question as to whether or not (or to what extent) monasticism can be considered to be part of "mainstream Christianity." Answering it should give us a clue to the fraught issue of Sufism's alleged "heterodoxy" and "foreignness" to Islam as religion. Before the onset of the Reformation no one seems to have doubted that monasticism was an integral part of mainstream Christianity and the Church, and yet its distinctness from ordinary forms of religious devotion was properly acknowledged. So, one may argue, was Sufism before the rise of so-called Salafism that, as has been shown earlier in this book, is sometimes seen as analogous to Christian Protestantism. To what extent Orientalists are responsible for exaggerating the Sufism-versus-Islam dichotomy is a different question altogether.[59]

To return to the topic of *adab*. As already mentioned, Sufi teachers had different understandings of its practical implications. Some limited *adab* primarily to ritual activities and occasional supererogatory acts of piety (especially additional fasting in the months Rajab and Sha'ban), whereas others included into this notion interactions with peers and masters, eating habits, listening to music, traveling, dress codes, vows, night vigils as well as family matters (especially marriage versus celibacy), leaving practically no aspect of the seeker's life unregulated or discretionary.[60] The tendency to regulate everything is evident in al-Ghazali's *Revivification of Religious Sciences* (*Ihya' 'ulum al-din*), a detailed blueprint for the pious and godly life of a Muslim actively seeking salvation. This massive theological summa specifies in meticulous detail ways of relieving and cleaning oneself, avoiding impurity, dealing with one's neighbors, buying and selling, and so on, while at the same time recommending how one should resist ills of the soul, such as onslaughts of evil thoughts, hypocrisy, anger, greed, and illicit sexual passion.[61] Al-Ghazali wanted his *Revivification* to be a guide for the entire Sunni community on the implicit understanding that only few of its members would be capable of living up to the stringent requirements laid down therein.[62] The overall context of al-Ghazali's oeuvre indicates that he considered Sufis to be the ideal bearers and implementers of the demanding moral-ethical codes explicated in his *Revivification*.[63] So, whereas his statements were "not intended for [any] particular group, but for all Muslims in general, he wished to educate Muslims as such to be Sufis."[64] In other words, in an ideal world, al-Ghazali would have liked to see every Muslim act and think as a Sufi.

A similar position was taken by his Maghribi follower Ibn 'Abbad al-Rundi (d. 792/1390).[65] It is in this sense that we should understand Fritz Meier's statement, based partly on his analysis of al-Ghazali's texts,[66] that "the concept of good behavior involved views and feelings which were not found on one side only, but bound together both camps [that is, Sufis and non-Sufis], indeed could extend to bind together people of very different lines of thought."[67] "Consequently," concluded Meier, "one must be on guard not to postulate oppositions that do not exist."[68]

Meier's statement clearly contradicts the idea that European Orientalists consistently sought to juxtapose Sufism to Islam, as Carl Ernst and some of his students have argued so vigorously of late.[69] Whereas some Orientalists may have indeed been guilty of this "sin," others were certainly not. In the case in point, Meier, like al-Ghazali and Ibn Khaldun long before him,[70] recognizes Sufi ethics as an integral part of Muslim ethics as a whole. Sufis, he argues, set a very high standard of piety for the rest of the community, then invited their fellow Muslims to try to attain it. To this end, they furnish detailed guidelines aimed to demonstrate how this standard should be achieved by each individual believer.[71] Whether every Sufi has always been able to live up to it is a different question. The long lists of mistakes and slippages (*zalal*) committed by ascetics-mystics from different epochs indicate that they have not.[72] However, in the end, this fact does not affect the validity of Meier's call[73] not to create dichotomies where they do not exist.

Allegorizing Practices and Implements

The force of a religion in supporting social values rests, then, on the ability
of its symbols to formulate a world in which those values, as well as the
forces opposing their realization, are fundamental ingredients. It
represents the power of the human imagination to construct, in which, to
quote Max Weber, "events are not just there and happen, but they have a
meaning and happen because of that meaning."

—CLIFFORD GEERTZ, *INTERPRETATION OF CULTURE*

While living a pious and godly life was eminently important for Sufi teachers and their followers, at least some of them have consistently sought to allegorize their actions in order to tie them to the overarching cosmological and gnoseological hierarchies outlined in chapters 3 and 4 of this book. This consistent transference of everyday physical actions to a loftier cognitive and cosmological plane created by the collective Sufi imagination is one of the features that sets Sufis aside from their fellow believers. In the Sufi universe of meaning, richly furnished as it is with symbols and allegories,[74] even the items of the Sufi's daily costume are subject to the same sublimating procedure. Thus, according to Fritz Meier, "the border of the neck of the [Sufi's] patched frock" becomes "the sword belt of the profession of God's oneness," while the cap on the Sufi's head is understood as "the crown of reverence" symbolizing his having freed himself from arrogance and pride.[75] By wearing black, the Sufi implicitly announces the death of his base ego (*nafs*), while the round tambourine that he holds in his hand during a Sufi "concert" (*sama'*) alludes to the "circle of all things in existence."[76] The five bells of the tambourine, in their turn, signify prophethood, sainthood, messengership,[77] deputyship,[78] and leadership[79]—notions that are central to Sufi cosmology, epistemology, and soteriology. In a similar vein, the Sufi's tearing off of his clothing during an ecstatic dance at a session of *sama'* symbolizes his renunciation of mundane matters and concerns for the sake of God.[80]

In sum, whereas Sufis do share many virtues, practices, and ethical-moral character traits with the Muslim community as a whole, they spiritualize and allegorize them in ways that are unique to their path to God (*tariq*). Preferably, Sufi teachers never tire of saying, both outward and inward senses should be duly observed. As a typical example of this dual concern, one can cite al-Ghazali's interpretation of the prophetic Hadith, according to which "Angels will not enter a house in which there is a dog."[81] In line with the Sufi propensity to allegorize, al-Ghazali interprets the house as the heart of the true believer, as well as a natural abode of the angels (that is, virtues). The "dog" stands for reprehensible passions and instincts of the human ego, such as anger, lust, hatred, envy, pride, and vainglory.[82] At the same time, al-Ghazali is careful to point out that these images feed off one another, as it were, therefore, in preferring allegory over reality, as the Isma'ilis (al-batiniyya) do, one should never neglect what lies behind it, namely a concrete, physical house or a concrete, physical dog.[83] In practice this means, although al-Ghazali does not say so explicitly, that one should expel real dogs from one's physical house, while also banishing from one's heart its allegorical "dogs," that is, base passions, drives and evil thoughts.[84] Basically the same sentiment is voiced by the doyens of the popular Shadhiliyya Sufi order of Egypt and North Africa, Abu 'l-'Abbas al-Mursi (d. 686 /1287) and Ibn 'Ata' Allah al-Iskandari (d. 709/1309). They insist that if Sufis are duly attentive to their outward actions, God will eventually grant them a superrational, intuitive insight into their allegorical and esoteric dimensions.[85]

Nevertheless, the almost irrepressible desire to allegorize has occasionally prevailed, despite the charges of critics, already mentioned in chapter 3, that Sufis are prone to depart completely from the original meaning of either text or practice.[86] Their allegorical-esoteric inclination comes to the fore in Ibn (al-)'Arabi's interpretations not just of the desirable moral-ethical behavior but also of the main duties of Islam, such as the canonical prayer, alms giving, fasting, and the hajj.[87] Thus, according to Ibn al-'Arabi, when the Shari'a demands that the praying person conceal his or her private parts, the true sense of this injunction can be grasped only by a Sufi gnostic endowed with intuitive unveiling (kashf). Ibn (al-)'Arabi insists that this divinely enlightened individual should conceal the knowledge that he or she receives through such an unveiling, because it belongs to the realm of divine mysteries (asrar al-haqq) and may turn out to be detrimental to simple minds. Among these mysteries, continues Ibn (al-)'Arabi, is God's immediate presence both in the world and in the secret recesses of every person's soul.[88] The need to conceal this fact springs from the concern, which Ibn (al-)'Arabi shared with many Sufi gnostics, that undeserving individuals might misinterpret it, thereby straying from the path of righteousness and propriety prescribed to them by the Shari'a.[89] This is, according to Ibn (al-)'Arabi, the true import of the divine injunction that the person in prayer cover his or her private parts.

Now, should one for a moment decide to step back from the Sufi vision of things and review them in a more impartial light, one is likely to discover that secrecy is but a social and cultural capital that Sufis have always wanted to protect from outsiders. When deployed properly by respected Sufi masters it brings to them a wealth of tangible and not-so-tangible benefits from comfortable material well-being to high social stature. The air of secrecy is maintained by the deliberate use of a suggestive, portentous language meant, simultaneously, to entice and confuse, to attract and push back, to reveal and conceal. Of this language, Ibn (al-)'Arabi was and still is an unsurpassed master. Here are a few more examples.

In the spirit already familiar to us from his allegorical-esoteric exegesis discussed in chapter 3, Ibn (al-)'Arabi interprets the trivial legal requirement that a praying woman should cover her head by allegorizing the woman as the human soul (a common metaphor in Sufism)[90] and her head as "headship" in the sense of self-sufficiency, sovereignty, and independence. These mundane aspirations symbolized by the woman's head are reprehensible for a humble servant of God. Therefore "the head" should be "covered" in the presence of God, who alone is the true possessor of unconditional and unlimited self-sufficiency, sovereignty, and independence.[91] In a similar vein, the wife's request that her husband allow her to go on a pilgrimage to Mecca (*hajj*) unaccompanied by him is allegorized by Ibn (al-)'Arabi, as the human soul embarking on a quest for knowledge. While in principle this quest is praiseworthy (knowledge, even incomplete and faulty, is still better than ignorance, argues the exegete) and the wife ("soul") should be allowed to travel in search of it, there is a danger that she may grow prideful due to her being more knowledgeable than her peers. Moreover, she might be lost in her quest without the husband by her side. The husband in Ibn (al-)'Arabi's interpretation is identified with either the human intellect (*'aql*), which resonates with the rationalist stance of the Mu'tazilis, or with the revealed law (*shar'*), which speaks to the nomocentric teachings of their opponents, the Ash'aris.[92] The advantages and disadvantages of letting the wife ("soul") embark of the hajj ("quest for knowledge") should thus be carefully weighed up by the husband (either "the intellect or the law") before making a decision. Similar allegorical-esoteric explanations are offered in the discussion of the rules for washing corpses, in which the washer's ("teacher's") actions are allegorized as imparting knowledge ("teaching") to the dead ("ignorant individuals").[93]

As for the canonical obligations incumbent on the Muslims, Ibn (al-)'Arabi sees them as reflective of the major stations on the Sufi path to God:

> The stations of this [Sufi] path are similar to the duties of the Shari'a, such as prayer, alms-giving, fasting, hajj, jihad and so on. In the same

way that every religious obligation requires the knowledge peculiar to it, so do the etiquette (*adab*) and actions (*a'mal*) [of the Sufis].[94]

Such allegorical transpositions of ritual activities to mystical gnoseology have cosmological implications. Thus, in Ibn (al-)'Arabi's interpretation, the three basic times for the ritual prayer (*salat*)—daytime, night, and the in-between periods of morning light and evening glow—are transformed into allegories of the three levels of existence (*wujud*) and the cosmic realms associated therewith. The daytime corresponds to the (empirical) world of witnessing, the night to the world of the unseen, and the in-between period to the intermediate world, or the "isthmus" (*barzakh*)—a key conception of Ibn (al-)'Arabi's cosmology.[95] This passage caught the attention of the major American expert on Ibn (al-)'Arabi's legacy, William Chittick, who remarked that, for the Greatest Master, "The prayers (*salawat*) of the various times of day leave different traces in the worshipper in keeping with the specific domains of *wujud* to which each corresponds."[96] The *barzakh*, in particular, is the abode of allegorical allusions and veridical dreams. Here knowledge appears to the dreamer as milk, religion as chain, and faith as bond.[97]

In a similar vein, the triple throwing of pebbles by pilgrims during the hajj is interpreted by Ibn (al-)'Arabi as an allusion to three divine presences (*hadarat*): that of the divine essence, that of the intelligible (*ma'nawiyya*) divine attributes, and that of divine actions.[98] The standing of the pilgrims on the plain of 'Arafat, which constitutes the acme of the hajj, prompts Ibn (al-)'Arabi to discuss the nature of Sufi gnosis (*ma'rifa*), which he describes as both the knowledge of God's oneness and the gnostic's self-knowledge—themes that are already familiar to us from chapter 3 of this book.[99] In short, by fusing ethics, rituals, juridical norms, gnoseology and cosmology Ibn (al-)'Arabi gives his favorite ideas, which are often but not always unique to him, an air of objectivity and universality[100] while also vindicating them by the uncontestable authority of the divine word.

Many more examples can be adduced, but the overall conclusion is obvious: ignoring al-Ghazali's warning against excessive reliance on allegorical interpretation at the expense of the literal meaning of events, objects, or sacred texts, Ibn (al-)'Arabi's allegorical-esoteric treatment of the basic Muslim duties and scriptural references to them exhibits a typical characteristic of the "Hermeneutic drift." According to Umberto Eco's (1932–2016) definition, it implies that "no contextual structure holds any longer: not only is the interpreter entitled to shift from association to association, but also in doing so every association becomes possible."[101] One should, however, point out that, in contradistinction to the Peircean theory of "un-limited semiosis" examined by Eco as his case study,[102] Ibn (al-)'Arabi's "semiotic drift"[103] is neither arbitrary nor incessant. It takes place within the framework of his overall system of cosmology, gnoseology, and soteriol-ogy. Like the compass, Ibn (al-)'Arabi's allegories eventually point in the same direction—his concept of God contemplating himself in the mirror of the cosmos and of the role that human beings play in this incessant and ever-changing divine self-reflection. Therefore, Ibn (al-)'Arabi's ultimate "signified" is not being "continually deferred and delayed,"[104] although, as we have repeatedly observed elsewhere, it always remains highly ambigu-ous, open-ended, and elusive.[105] Intentionally or otherwise, Ibn (al-)'Arabi pursues his goal of concealment of his true intentions by rendering the flow of his associations well-nigh incomprehensible to outsiders not thor-oughly steeped in the conceptual world of "philosophical Sufism."[106] Spe-cial training and lengthy explanatory glosses are required to master the keynotes of his Weltanschauung, which makes the Akbarian stream of Sufism particularly arcane and elitist in much the same way as the teach-ings of Isma'ilism and its various hypostases, such as Druze, Hurufis (hurufiyya), and ahl-i haqq, are surrounded by an aura of mystery and kept secret from the uninitiated.[107] It is hardly surprising that Ibn (al-)'Arabi himself has occasionally been seen by his critics as a dissimu-lating Isma'ili thinker.[108] As far as his overall contribution to Islamic tra-dition is concerned, Ibn (al-)'Arabi's recondite speculations about ritual actions and moral-ethical virtues (his "Hermeneutic drift," as it were) have proved to be too abstruse to serve as an adequate discourse for com-munity and institution building. Over the past eight centuries his ideas have remained the exclusive domain of a relatively small intellectual elite, Sufi or otherwise,[109] whereas the much more lucid and accessible rules of Sufi adab mentioned earlier in this chapter have become effective training manuals for Sufi teachers, novices, and associated members (muhibbun) of Sufi communities.[110] Among them, al-Qushayri's Epistle on Sufism and al-Ghazali's Revivification, which, as we have seen, intri-cately combine allegorism and literalism, have remained the preferred guides for moral-ethical edification until today. Overall, however, our thesis that Sufis have a pronounced tendency to internalize and allegorize both Muslim rituals and ascetic-mystical practices still stands. This ten-dency, which has been a distinctive feature of Sufi life since the very be-ginning, should be added to our list of Sufism's characteristics found at the end of chapter 2.

Leaders and Their Followers

Any group needs some people defining who its members are, what
they should be and what they have been. These are constantly at
work, justifying the group's existence, invoking rules and
precedents, and measuring up one definition against all the
others.

—BRUNO LATOUR, *REASSEMBLING THE SOCIAL:*
AN INTRODUCTION TO ACTOR-NETWORK THEORY

In his magisterial *Venture of Islam*, Marshall Hodgson has identified relationships between the Sufi master (*shaykh*; *pir*) and his disciple (*murid*) as the essential bond that kept together otherwise very internally diverse and loosely structured Sufi communities.[111] Emerging almost simultaneously with the ascetic-mystical movement in early Muslim societies, this bond subsequently shaped Sufism's evolution from informal circles of similarly minded individuals to hierarchically structured institutions known as "Sufi ways or paths" (*turuq/tara'iq sufiyya*).[112] Obedience to the will of the master was required of all members of Sufi communities, which are sometimes called "lineages" or "chains" (Arab. *salasil*; sing. *silsila*) to emphasize their provenance from the Prophet and his companions.[113] Mutual obligations of teachers and students were stipulated in the *adab* literature peculiar to every Sufi collectivity and were strictly observed by their members.[114] As we have seen in chapter 3, the Sufi teachers' role as guides of their followers (*murids*) rested on an elaborate array of gnoseological claims combined with promises of spiritual and cognitive advancement and, eventually, salvation.

On the social plane, Hodgson has argued, *"piri-muridi* discipline" came to serve Sufi communities as a "vehicle for public outreach."[115] A Sufi master trained a group of students who subsequently returned to their towns and villages to become Sufi teachers in their own right with coteries of devoted disciples, and so on and so forth. Thus emerged a network of Sufi centers that produced new cohorts of teachers reaching outlying areas of the Muslim ecumene and beyond. This system of reproduction and expansion has proved successful and determined the important social roles that Sufism played throughout the late Middle Ages and into the modern era.[116] That Hodgson's observations are accurate is attested by Sufis themselves, including the Naqshbandi master Shaykh Hisham Kabbani, whose exegesis was addressed in chapter 3 of this book. Firmly convinced of the

FIGURE 5.1. A throng of Sufi disciples during an annual pilgrimage to the shrine of prophet Hud (Qur'an sura 11) in Hadramawt, June 18, 2013. Courtesy of Ali Hussain.

critical role of Sufi masters in sustaining and propagating ascetic-mystical Islam, he argues:

> Following a trustworthy person is essential to our spiritual path. Such a person is needed to lead us, to guide us and be a beacon for us on that [Sufi] way. . . . He establishes the disciple's connection [to the Prophet]. The disciple's obligation is to maintain his connection to his shaykh, to

hold tightly to the hand of the one within his reach. The shaykh maintains the further connection to the previous shaykhs and [all the way] to the Prophet.[117]

The long and complex history of *"piri-muridi* discipline" spans a whole gamut of communities, historical periods, and geographical regions, and we cannot address it here in detail. The same goes for Hodgson's point about Sufism's public "outreach" that was spearheaded by charismatic Sufi leaders, these "spiritual hoplites of Islam" who penetrated every nook and cranny of the Muslim world.[118] Therefore, our discussion of this important aspect of Sufism's history and present is perforce cursory and short on specifics.

Many outsiders and insiders interested in Sufism have noticed that *"piri-muridi* discipline" is built on a strong personal and emotional bond between the student and his master. Sufi teachers see this bond as a prerequisite for a successful relationship. The contemporary Sufi teacher Shaykh Muhammad Hisham Kabbani never tires of insisting that the disciple "must love his shaykh with extraordinary love . . . and must not look to any other than his shaykh."[119] Shaykh Hisham's admonition is not new. It harks back to the hundreds of sayings to the same effect found in Sufi *adab* literature from the eleventh to twelfth centuries CE and duly reproduced in Sufi manuals ever since. In addition to love, these manuals instruct Sufi aspirants (*murids*) to submit unconditionally to the will of their mentors, "as the sick person gives himself to the doctor to be cured."[120] The numerous and varied functions of Sufi *shaykhs* as teachers, intermediaries, and institution builders have also been examined in our own studies and those of our colleagues and need not be detailed here.[121] These functions have never been static. They are best seen as a dynamic and multidirectional process that originated in primeval ascetic-mystical communities of the Middle East, Iran, and Central Asia to evolve differently in different parts of the Muslim world and the Muslim diaspora. Patterned on the paradigmatic interactions between the Prophet and his companions (as imagined by Sufi teachers),[122] the vicissitudes of *"piri-muridi* discipline" and of social roles of Sufi masters more generally reflect the principal stages of the evolution of Sufism as a distinctive stream of Islamic belief and practice, or "piety," to use Hodgson's favorite term.

Conceptualizing the Shaykh-Murid *Dyad*

The fact that relationships between Sufi masters and their students changed over time was not lost on medieval Muslim scholars. Hodgson's and Meier's examinations of the topic in the middle of the twentieth century[123] faithfully reflect the observations made by insiders (both Sufis and their critics) in the Middle Ages.[124] Once again, we witness a meeting of minds of insiders and outsiders facilitated by their common interest in Sufism, as argued in chapter 2 of this book. This said, one should not downplay serious differences in the ways in which premodern insiders and modern-day outsiders conceptualized the evolution of "*piri-muridi* discipline" across the centuries. The approach to Sufism taken by Hodgson,[125] Meier, and other Western scholars of Sufism[126] is informed, consciously or not, by the Western academic discipline of "comparative societies and religions" formulated, among others, by the French sociologists Émile Durkheim (1858–1917) and Marcel Mauss (1872–1950). Inspired by newly discovered explanatory paradigms, these intellectuals encouraged their colleagues to examine any religious phenomenon within the complex network of sociocultural practices and institutions surrounding it.[127] With the possible exception of Ibn Khaldun, whom some consider rightly or wrongly to be "the father of sociology" and "critical historiography,"[128] this approach was unique to modern-day Western outsiders looking inside the "house of Islam." We will now examine intellectual bricolages that resulted from the intertwining of both insider and outsider visions of the *shaykh-murid* bond in Sufism.

In a series of now-classic studies of the transformation of Muslim asceticism-mysticism from informal circles of like-minded individuals to full-fledged organizations ("brotherhoods" or "orders"), Fritz Meier (1912–1998) makes extensive use of numerous Sufi writings to show how the office of the Sufi *shaykh* evolved from that of an informal "educator" (*shaykh al-ta'lim*), whom anyone could visit and leave at will, to that of a strict and demanding trainer (*shaykh al-tarbiya*).[129] The latter, whom Meier compares to a strict and demanding schoolmaster monitoring closely the progress of his wards,[130] was the product of several centuries of Sufism's evolution that, one can add, remains the predominant model of Sufi pedagogy today.[131] Unlike the *shaykh*-the-educator, the training master required of his wards (*murid*s) absolute loyalty and unquestioning submission.[132] Not so in the "good old days," argues Meier citing an array of medieval sources, showing that *murid*s were free to contradict or question the master's instructions or leave him for another one, as they saw fit. In the later period, *murid*s were obligated to obey the master humbly and unconditionally by fulfilling his occasionally authoritarian commands. In other words, while *shaykh al-ta'lim* was a caring adviser, *shaykh al-tarbiya* was a demanding and occasionally harsh supervisor.[133] According to Meier,[134] "the master of training" wielded full control over his students' lives:

> He had his students withdraw in spiritual retreat, kept them occupied with the formula of recollection of God (*dhikr*), which he had "implanted" in them, ordered them to diminish their food, speech and sleep, etc., and in this way drilled them under his supervision until they became perfected (*kamil*) and could now themselves be models for others.[135]

Once again, we are witnessing a fascinating example of a dialogue between an Orientalist outsider and a Sufi insider. Let us explain why. The major source of Meier's idea of the transformation of the Sufi master-disciple relationship is the renowned Maghribi Sufi master Ibn 'Abbad al-Rundi (d. 792/1390), who had not only detected the momentous transition from the *shaykh*-the-educator to the *shaykh*-the-trainer, but also dated it to around the year 500/1107.[136] As many Sufi masters before him,[137] Ibn 'Abbad bemoaned the progressive decline of the original Sufi values, viewing the change in the pedagogical role of the Sufi master as one its major signs.[138] Accepting Ibn 'Abbad's idea in principle, Meier suggests, cogently, that the transformation was a drawn-out and uneven process. First, according to Meier, it had started earlier (in the fourth/tenth century) than claimed by Ibn 'Abbad and, second, it was never unidirectional or final: the *shaykh*'s personality was often critical in how he dealt with his disciples; it shaped decisively his instructional methods.[139] Moreover, in discussing various types of Sufi teachers and patterns of their interactions with their followers, Meier suggests that they should not be pressed into the rigidly dichotomous classification proposed by Ibn 'Abbad al-Rundi,[140] especially since Ibn 'Abbad implicitly acknowledges that in his own age the same *shaykh* could perform the function of both trainer and educator, thus wearing, as it were, two hats simultaneously.[141]

Although Meier never explicitly addresses this issue, from the large body of evidence that he and his student Bernd Radtke have assembled,[142] one can surmise that the need for a closely monitored, systematic training was occasioned by the exponential growth of the body of Sufi knowledge to be imparted to the beginner,[143] on the one hand, and by the proliferation of distinctive schools and methods among Sufis, on the other. Indeed, by the fourth/tenth century ascetic-mystical communities that medieval sources identify as "Sufi" must have acquired a particular, recognizable identity that rested on shared values, ethos (*adab*), ritual practices, and corpus of oral and written narratives. These and other factors, especially an acute rivalry among various Sufi communities and their leaders, necessitated a closer supervision of the trainees by an instructor eager to instill in his wards the "correct" teachings and practices of his own *silsila*, while simultaneously protecting them from "faulty" or "deviant" ones of rival Sufi masters and their aficionados.[144] In the words of a Sufi *shaykh* quoted by Meier, the goal of this close supervision was to help the novice "to avoid the tortuous paths of self-deception." In practice this meant the aspirant's (*murid*) complete submission to his "master of discipline" (*mu'addib*) who would subject him to systematic training (*riyada*), while monitoring closely his thoughts, dreams, emotional impulses, and actions.[145] The master-trainer would also meticulously determine the amount of various ascetic and meditative exercises his follower should undertake.[146]

Whereas Ibn 'Abbad was speaking from within the Sufi tradition, as it were, his contemporary Ibn Khaldun (d. 808/1406)[147] was an outsider with some Sufi connections and interests, especially later in his life when he assumed the coveted position of head of the Baybarsiyya *khanaqa*—a large and well-endowed Sufi monastery in Egypt.[148] However, there is no evidence that he personally was attracted to Sufi teachings, practiced Sufi discipline, or adhered to a particular Sufi *silsila* or *tariqa*.[149] His deliberations regarding Sufism and Sufis were shaped by his overall approach to life, which can be characterized as a combination of positivism and pragmatism of a rather detached, objective nature. In his survey of Sufism's evolution from its inception until his own age, titled *The Cure of the Enquirer* (*Shifa' al-sa'il*), Ibn Khaldun presents himself as a level-headed, if occasionally sympathetic and nuanced observer.[150] The gist of his argument can be rendered as follows. Whereas the Sufis of old were engaged in the improvement of their morals and purifying their souls of mundane concerns and sinful passions, in recent times Sufism has become a refuge for individuals who indulge in metaphysics, philosophy, and occult speculations that have precious little to do with the original Sufi teachings and practices.[151] Most disturbingly, for Ibn Khaldun, such "philosophizing Sufis" tend to make exaggerated claims about their relations with God in order to attract a large popular following.[152]

Ibn Khaldun's discussion in the *Shifa'* of the role of the *shaykh* is at once similar to and different from that offered by either Ibn 'Abbad or Meier. Before summarizing Ibn Khaldun's argument in this rather long-winded and repetitive opus, we should mention that it was written in response to two interrelated issues that were being debated by Maghribi thinkers of the age. The first was the necessity of a spiritual guide for a beginner embarking on the Sufi path. The second was the possibility of one's mastering Sufi theory and practice on one's own exclusively from books and without the master's supervision.[153] To address these issues effectively, Ibn Khaldun places them in the broader context of Sufism's evolution. Following in the footsteps of Ibn 'Abbad and his authorities, including a certain 'Abd al-Rahman al-Saqalli,[154] he is forging what may be designated a metanarrative of Sufism's history. In so doing, he consciously or unconsciously becomes an investigator who draws on Sufi literature and his own "field" observations to construct a panorama of Sufism's evolution across the ages.

It is important to point out that, in principle, Ibn Khaldun has no problem with acknowledging the validity of the supersensory cognition claimed by the Sufis. He considers it be the product of veridical insight (*kashf*), divine inspiration (*ilham*), and direct witnessing (*mushahada*) that God grants to his elect folk.[155] At the same time, as we have pointed out elsewhere,[156] he rejects excessive claims made by some later Sufi thinkers who had adopted metaphysical and cosmological speculations as well as recondite letter magic and numerology to conceal under the guise of Sufism what, in Ibn Khaldun's opinion, were heretical, non-Islamic, or at the very least non-Sunni, ideas and practices.[157]

Ibn Khaldun's criticisms of Sufi metaphysics and numerology should not distract us from our immediate task that consists of finding out how the great Maghribi scholar evaluated the role of the Sufi master in guiding his student to perfection (*ihsan*) in thought and deed. Ibn Khaldun viewed the presence of the master as desirable but not essential for two initial stages of what he called "spiritual striving" (*mujahada*) on the path to God. The first stage required that the seeker (*murid*) adopt fear of God (*taqwa*) as his or her guiding principle, the second—that he or she be upright (*istiqama*) in every mundane action he or she undertakes.[158] By applying himself to the study of the Qur'an, Sunna, and moral-ethical works, Sufi or otherwise, the seeker can learn the rules and practices pertaining to these two types of *mujahada* on his or her own. Thus, for the beginner on the mystical path the presence of a teaching master (*shaykh mu'allim*), while beneficial, is not absolutely required.[159] However, when it comes to the third, and the highest, stage of spiritual progress, which involves unveiling (*kashf*) and direct witnessing (*ittila'*; *mushahada*) of divine realities, the training teacher (*mu'allim murabbi*), more commonly called *shaykh*,[160] becomes indispensable.[161] Remarkably, to explain his conclusion, Ibn Khaldun argued that this advanced stage of spiritual striving was nothing short of a "special law" (*shari'a khassa*), being the exclusive domain of

perfected Sufi gnostics ('arifun).[162] Entering this stage may lead a successful seeker to the supreme happiness (sa'ada kubra) in the afterlife that
surpasses anything held in store for ordinary believers, no matter how
righteous and upright. This stage of the mystical path has its own rulings,
manners, and requirements that go beyond and above the ambit of received wisdom ('ulum or ma'arif kasbiyya).[163] Being of a subtle and intuitive nature, the knowledge associated with this sublime stage is impossible
to obtain without the help of a master who has already conquered it, experiencing in the process its numerous dangers, temptations, and pitfalls.[164]
It is to this experienced master-psychologist possessed of a special insight
into the mysteries of the Sufi path that the seeker should entrust himself
completely to become the proverbial dead body in the hands of the
washer.[165] Barring this, the unwary seeker is likely go astray to the point
of losing his mind, or, worse still, falling into the embrace of the Devil.
This, according to Ibn Khaldun, is what has happened to heretical sects
and individuals claiming divine inspiration. In short, in the absence of an
experienced, knowledgeable master (shaykh muhaqqiq 'arif), and prod-
ded on by misguided and misguiding "heresiarchs," unwary seekers may
be tempted to claim being one with God (al-hululiyya) or knowing the
hidden sense of the revelation (al-batiniyya). As a result, the more deluded ones are bound to fall into outright antinomianism and atheism
(al-ibahiyya).[166]

As mentioned, Ibn Khaldun was an outsider to Sufism. Yet he was well
read in its literature. At least he quotes its classics who lived in the fourth/
tenth to seventh/thirteenth centuries, especially al-Muhasibi, al-Qushayri,
al-Ghazali, and al-Suhrawardi.[167] In any event, he felt competent enough
to chip into the ongoing debates about the role of Sufi books as opposed to
that of Sufi masters in training Sufi novices. These debates involved such
Maghribi and Andalusian luminaries as Ibn 'Abbad al-Rundi and Abu
Ishaq al-Shatibi (d. 790/1388).[168] What is remarkable is that the same
ideas and sources were still in use in Sufi circles in the eighteenth and
nineteenth centuries (twelfth and thirteenth centuries according to the
Hijra calendar)[169]—a striking testimony to the durability and stability of
the Sufi textual canon that we shall revisit later on.

All the texts we have just mentioned and numerous others from the
same age depict Sufism not just as a special doctrine and practice within
Islam but also as an exclusive sports club of sorts.[170] Joining the club requires abilities that commoners can hardly hope to obtain. No wonder,
therefore, that the commoners were many, while the high-achieving ath-

letes were few.[171] Like professional sportsmen, the "spiritual athletes" of Sufism submitted themselves willingly and unconditionally to the rigorous discipline, dietary restrictions, and constant supervision by an experienced and decorated mentor. Unlike usual paths of righteousness, which pious individuals could enter and navigate on their own, travelers on the path of supersensory unveiling (*suluk kashfi*) could not do without an experienced guide.[172] To recompense the master for this precious guidance the *murid* felt obligated to serve him and his relatives, usually taking care of household chores and manual tasks both inside and outside the *shaykh*'s household.[173] Abu 'l-Najib al-Suhrawardi's (d. 563/1168) "Rule for [Sufi] Novices," a pioneering work of this kind, describes the disciple's "companionship" (*suhba*) of a Sufi master as follows:

> Accompanying the teacher (*ustadh*) requires the fulfillment of all his commands and prohibitions. In reality, companionship is nothing but service. Someone asked Abu 'Uthman al-Maghribi:[174] "How many [teachers] have you accompanied?" He answered: "I have not accompanied them, rather, I served them!"[175] It is incumbent [upon the disciple] to serve his teacher, to be patient under his command, not to contradict him, either inwardly or openly, to accept his instruction and have recourse to it in everything that one encounters, and to revere him[176] in private and in public. . . . [For] it is said: "The master (*shaykh*) is like a prophet in his community." . . . It is also said that whosoever asks his teacher "Why?" will never succeed.[177]

Abu 'l-Najib's nephew, Abu Hafs 'Umar al-Suhrawardi (d. 632/1234),[178] another source used by Ibn Khaldun, goes even further than his uncle by ascribing to the Sufi master the same role that Jibril, the angel of revelation, performed for the prophet Muhammad by passing to him divine instructions.[179] "The rank of shaykhhood," says al-Suhrawardi, "is the highest rank of the Sufi path (*tariqat al-sufiyya*) and is the representative (*niyaba*) of prophethood."[180] His Persian translator and commentator 'Izz al-Din Mahmud Kashani (d. 735/1334) speaks of the *shaykh* as "the lower lord" (*al-rabb al-adna*) as opposed to the "higher lord" up in heaven.[181] In his capacity of the "superintendent of souls" (*mushrif 'ala 'l-bawatin*),

> he has the right of free disposal of the program of his disciples, determining what they should wear and when they should fast, when they should work and when they should they should beg, as well as ensuring

that they persist in their litanies, pray the proper supererogatory prayers, and hold fast to their recitation of the Qur'an.[182]

In sum, one can say that Sufi literature portrays Sufi *shaykh*s as God's ambassadors in the post-prophetic age.[183] Had it not been for their presence amid the Muslims they would have collectively gone astray.[184] According to al-Ghazali, the *murid* needs the *shaykh*'s directorship as much as a blind man needs a guide while walking along a precipitous riverbank.[185] Anyone who wants to embark on the Sufi path without a *shaykh* has no religion (*la din lahu*).[186] Finally, the Sufi master Ahmad b. Idris (d. 1253/1837), one of the most influential figures of nineteenth-century Islamdom,[187] has argued:

> When it comes to fathers, they are two kinds, the father of the body and the father of the heart, and the latter is more noble, the better, the greater, because whereas the father of the body is the educator of the coarse gloom-laden body which is the cause of man's death, the father of the heart is the educator of the spirit, the luminous framework which is the cause of man's [eternal] life.[188]

Essentially the same ideas are being taught to their students by present-day Sufi masters, including Shaykh Muhammad Hisham Kabbani who says:

> The shaykh will lift him [the disciple] up through a path filled with difficulties, train him through worship and guide him to a state of complete self-effacement. Only this will elevate him to the Divine Presence.[189]

The exalted stature of the *shaykh* vis-à-vis his followers demands that they constantly show him signs of respect. When the *shaykh* speaks, they should fall silent, for his words are actually not his; they are dictated to him directly by God.[190] This being so, a diligent disciple may even occasionally wet himself out of fear of missing a single word from the master's mouth while answering the call of nature.[191] Centuries fly by, but the ethos of discipleship remains unchanged. Thus, according to Shaykh Muhammad Hisham Kabbani, today as before, in the presence of the master the disciple should avoid "yawning, laughing, raising his voice, talking without authorization, extending the feet"; instead, "he should always be sitting in a respectful manner," being attentive to the master's every word or movement.[192] Similar rules abound in the numerous medieval books of Sufi *adab* examined by Meier and other modern-day scholars mentioned at the beginning of this chapter.

Even the fundamental Islamic duty of submitting oneself to God (*islam*) is reimagined in Sufi didactic literature as the requirement that the disciple surrender wholeheartedly and willingly to the will of his master.[193] For his disciples, as already mentioned, the *shaykh* is the spiritual father without whose permission they can neither frequent other masters nor marry, travel, or make any other important decisions.[194] He is also a healer of his followers' souls; his beneficial effect on them is often likened to the doctor's treatment of his patients.[195] This age-old image remains actual today. In the words of Shaykh Hisham Kabbani:

> As the sick person gives himself to the doctor to be cured. So too does the disciple, sick in conduct and behavior, submit to the shaykh's experience in order to be healed.[196]

The student's failure to respect his master is punishable by the disappearance of God's invisible presence from his heart or by his permanent negligence of God's commands. "No deprivation (*hirman*) can be greater than this," says Ibn (al-)'Arabi, who, contrary to his usual propensity for allegorizing, is quite unambiguous on this issue.[197]

On a more personal level, an eloquent and moving attestation of reverence for the *shaykh* is given by al-Qushayri in respect to his own master Abu 'Ali al-Daqqaq (d. 405/1015) of Nishapur:[198]

> As a beginner I would never enter into the presence of my master Abu 'Ali unless I was fasting. I would also perform a full ablution. How many times did I come to the door of his school only to turn back out of my lack of resolve to enter! When I overcame my timidity and entered the school, I would be assaulted by numbness in the midst of it to such an extent that one could stick a needle into me without my taking notice of it. . . . Sometimes I would think to myself: "If God were to send a messenger to His creatures during my lifetime, could I possibly have felt for him the same respect that I had for Abu 'Ali—may God have mercy on him?"[199]

Summarizing his examination of the history of Sufi pedagogical practices, Meier has proposed that (a) from the sixth/eleventh century on normative Sufi literature refocuses from an informal self-education by the beginner to his voluntary submission to the training regimen peculiar to an experienced Sufi teacher, as a result of which (b) the distance between the two increases dramatically, elevating the *shaykh* to the position of God's deputy on earth and spiritual pole (axis) of the universe (*qutb*), at least in the eyes of his students.[200] In the words of Meier,

> The rank of shaykh [now] entails priestly traits and autocratic authority. The novice, on the other hand, is demoted to being a poor sinner devoid of [his own] will.[201]

Note the use of the term "priestly" by Meier—a clear reference to ordained priesthood in the Christian church, which has no close parallel in Islam where induction into the *'ulama'* class was much less formal, even spontaneous. As argued earlier in this book,[202] the mention by a Western scholar of a distinctly Christian term should not be automatically seen as his deliberate attempt to "Christianize" Islam by depriving it of its specificity.[203] It is more likely that Meier's use of this Christian concept was aimed at rendering a Sufi reality understandable to an audience steeped in European Christian culture and history. With the benefit of hindsight, we may quibble over this usage, but we can hardly deny the accuracy of the underlying reality it describes.

This said, the picture is more complex than Meier's statement might suggest. Obligations within the *shaykh-murid* tandem were reciprocal, not one way. In his *Epistle on Sufism* al-Qushayri repeatedly emphasizes that the master should treat his follower "with compassion and kindness, [while] the one who is followed[204] should be treated with compliance and respect."[205] Later Sufi manuals contain a special section that defines how *shaykh*s should deal with (*adab*) their disciples in various circumstances and venues.[206] The manuals often describe relationships between *shaykh* and *murid*s as mutually accommodating, tender, and emotional,[207] similar to those of the father and his children.[208] The persistent use of this "familial" metaphor by Sufi theorists indicates that they wanted interactions between members of Sufi communities to be built on mutual trust, respect, tenderness, and compassion.[209] In short, the two sides of the master-disciple tandem are so closely bound together that it is impossible to imagine one without the other.[210] Such close ties between the mentor and his ward were not, however, unique to Sufism. They are in evidence in the relationships between a physician and his patient, a Shi'i imam and his followers, a craftsman and his apprentice(s), as well as a philosopher and his students. Meier even suggests that the Sufi rules (*adab*) regarding the teacher-disciple relationship may have been patterned on one or all of those and vice versa,[211] but this hypothesis is impossible to ascertain.

Meier is absolutely right in pointing out the progressive formalization of Sufi training through the obligatory imposition on novices of *dhikr* formulas that they should repeat a certain number of times during the day and night;[212] practices of voluntary retreat (*khalwa*) for meditation and penance; duties of service to the master and the community as a whole (*suhba*; *khidma*);[213] and so on. The same applies to the elaborate rites of passage adopted by the majority of Sufi communities,[214] such as the formal investiture of the disciple with a patched frock (*khirqa*),[215] the cropping of one's hair during an elaborate initiation ceremony,[216] and the bestowal upon the graduating novice of the litany (*wird*; *hizb*) that is unique to the Sufi community into which he or she is being inducted.[217] These Sufi rituals are highly consequential in that their enactment induces "a set of moods and motivations—an ethos—and defines an image of cosmic order—a world view."[218] In other words, Sufi *adab* decisively and profoundly shapes the lives of Sufi communities,[219] creating and maintaining a universe of meaning and practical action that makes it distinct from conterminous world-orientational systems and discursive formations, such as theology, jurisprudence, belles-lettres, and *falsafa*. Calling the Sufi universe "Islamic mysticism," "asceticism-mysticism," "*tasawwuf*," "*tariqa*," "*haqiqa*," "*hikma*," or "*'irfan*" does not change this undeniable fact.[220]

Following in the footsteps of Meier, some modern-day Western scholars have come to view the formalization and codification of interpersonal relationships within Sufi communities as an unavoidable and predictable consequence of what Max Weber called "rationalization" or "routinization."[221] Others, taking a statist approach, attribute the progressive institutionalization of Sufi life to government interference aimed at bringing Sufi institutions under state control in order exploit more effectively the social, economic, and political (legitimizing) potential of Sufi groups and institutions.[222]

Whereas Weber's ideas concerning various types of charisma, charismatic authority, and its inexorable routinization with time[223] remain useful, they do not necessarily account exhaustively and satisfactorily for the evolution of the *shaykh-murid* bond that was and still is so central to the Sufi version of Islam. The same goes for Bruce Lincoln's influential discussion of the nature of religious authority.[224] Perhaps one reason for this is that such explanations are based primarily on non-Islamic evidence, with a partial exception of Weber, whose knowledge of Islam was, however, rather sketchy, imprecise, and biased to boot.[225] What the Weberian model misses is the significant nuances of a given historical and cultural context. The same, to some extent, applies to the conceptualization of Sufism by medieval Muslim writers. It is true that at some point in Sufism's history Muslim authors, whether Sufi or not, became aware of changes in the status of the *shaykh* and in the nature of his interactions with his followers. Not only had these changes been, mostly unconsciously, documented in early Sufi literature, but they could also have been observed firsthand by anyone interested in the subject.[226] This awareness brought about reflective conceptualizations of Sufism's evolution that were informed to a considerable degree by the medieval Muslim perception of history as a decline of the mores of the primeval community (*umma*) from the original high standard of piety and devotion to a progressively imperfect condition.[227] In the medieval Muslim mentality, the gold standard of Islam was firmly associated with the life and rule of the Prophet and his companions. What came next was and still is seen by the majority of Muslims as a process of decline and distortion of the originally perfect teachings and practices of the pious ancestors of Islam.[228] This paradigm was and still is pervasive and applied to various streams of Islam, not just Sufism. It lies behind the phenomenon of Salafism that is discussed in the last chapter of this book.

Whereas Western scholars of Islam have readily acknowledged the decline, they explained it differently from Muslim scholars by using the realities of modern western European societies as their preferred benchmark.[229] Because they viewed Sufism generally and *piri-muridi* discipline more specifically through the prism of the Weberian categories of routinized or traditionalized charisma, they, however, had trouble explaining its continual ability to produce talented and creative individuals, the ability that is so well attested by Sufism's long history.[230] More generally, the idea of Sufism's decline, that has been the staple of Western Islamology since Arthur J. Arberry (1905–1969),[231] is fraught with questions. Indeed, if the process of routinization, as well as the "decadence" and "paralysis" attendant to it,[232] were real, would not the constant (re-)appearance of Sufi movers and shakers of different backgrounds and aspirations have introduced a destabilizing factor interfering with the smooth reproduction of the charisma of the office? In a similar vein, what were the mechanisms that kept the tradition with its various constituents stable, while allowing it to thrive, adjust, and self-reform?[233] Had Weber been working with Islamic materials and Sufism in particular, might not his conclusions have been substantially different?[234] All these questions beg for answers that we cannot address in this book, except very tentatively.

We do not suggest that Weber's model of the charisma of the office is entirely irrelevant or inapplicable to Sufism. After all, one cannot deny that the prestige of later Sufi teachers did indeed rest, at least in part, on the authority of their predecessors who were eulogized and idealized in hundreds Sufi biographies and hagiographies.[235] What Weber and his followers among scholars of Islam do not explicitly tell us is that the Sufi master did not simply inherit his authority and prestige to enjoy for the rest of his life. The inheritance demanded of the heir a great deal of work to preserve and maintain it. The history of Sufi intuitions and spiritual lineages teaches us[236] that each incoming Sufi leader had to reposition himself, often decisively, vis-à-vis the concrete spiritual lineage or institution he had inherited. The exact parameters of this repositioning were determined by his changing constituencies, on the one hand, and geopolitical realities on the ground more generally, on the other.[237] What we can say with confidence is that the new *shaykh*'s success or failure depended in large part on his resourcefulness and creativity as displayed in his public orations, written works, training style, and daily comportment. In other words, each Sufi leader faced the challenging task of carving out a unique niche of his own within the large and diverse body of the Sufi tradition—an exercise in which his personal skills, acumen, and genealogy, or his lack thereof, played a decisive part. His being part of a venerable, charismatic family would definitely facilitate his task, but, in principle, he could do without it to assert himself as a respectable teacher with a *silsila* of his own.[238] In either case, the Sufi normative literature discussed earlier in this chapter alongside a large corpus of authoritative precedents and a cohort of distinguished predecessors were at the new leader's disposal in this undertaking, the outcome of which was always dubious, dependent as it was on a complex combination of objective and subjective factors.

To reiterate, among numerous and often accidental factors that determined the *shaykh*'s success or failure, his personality, pedigree, and attitude to life played the critical role. Therefore, one should not construe Weber's routinization as a unidirectional, irrevocable, and predictable process. Failures were as common as successes but remained underreported because they did not fit in to the normative and idealized mold of the Sufi literary canon and oral tradition. Successes were remembered and broadcast by all means available to Sufi communities, from hagiographies (*manaqib*) and miracle narratives (*karamat*) in the past to the Internet and YouTube today. Because the oral and written Sufi tradition is in most cases our only source for reconstructing Sufism's history, we can only venture guesses about the incidence of successful as opposed to unsuccessful bids by Sufi masters to secure a following and to maintain the authority and public respect they have inherited from their predecessors (if any). This statistic simply does not exist, so we can only venture guesses.

Sufi Leaders and Their Claims

Seen against the historical and cultural background outlined in this and previous chapters, the emergence in Islam of religious leaders claiming special knowledge and insight by virtue of which they can guide their followers to this-worldly bliss and serenity and, eventually, salvation, was not just logical. It was unavoidable. Thus has arisen the class of professional Sufi masters (*shaykhs*) and saints (*awliya'*). In the Western academic environment shaped by the theories of Michel Foucault, Pierre Bourdieu, Edward Said, and their numerous followers, human endeavors tend to be interpreted as a disguised or undisguised quest for, or exercise of, power and domination.[239] Through the Foucauldian prism, the societal implications of the Sufi gnoseological and soteriological claims outlined above may indeed appear to be just another example of the ubiquitous and inexorable working of carefully masked or obvious power relations. This view may be correct in principle, but it fails to do justice to the complexity of human aspirations. "Power" is too general a concept to account for construction, justification, and performance by Sufi masters of their claims to knowledge and guidance across the centuries. Commanding respect and awe, being listened to in silence by a captive and respectful audience without necessarily "dominating" or "exploiting" it,[240] is a motivation that does not fit neatly into the narrowly conceived grid of power relations envisioned by neo-Marxian sociologists of various stripes. Furthermore, seeking, obtaining, and maintaining real political and social power usually entails responsibility, conscious manipulation of individuals and institutions, self-control, and, occasionally, even peril. For today's Sufis, claims to superior knowledge of, and ability to guide aspirants through, the complex hierarchically arranged realms of existence are, in general, a much safer bet. The elaborate system of practice and the universe of meaning attendant to it, so ingeniously constructed by many hands over many centuries, are now securely in place and ready to be used by those who position themselves as the inheritors of the great *awliya'* of the past. Grounded firmly in the spiritual genealogies of Sufism's saintly custodians, the system looks imposing and even unassailable to many, albeit by no means all,[241] insiders and outsiders. To challenge the *awliya'*'s gnoseological and soteriological claims, one has to deconstruct, stone by stone, the foundations of the sophisticated cosmological psychology of Sufism that the imagination of Islam's finest minds driven by the noblest aspirations has managed to assemble. However, even if one should succeed in this laborious and painstaking task, what will one be able to offer in return?

The Decline Thesis in Sufism's History

Given the fact that unlike Fritz Meier or Marshall Hodgson, Ibn 'Abbad al-Rundi and Ibn Khaldun were not familiar with Weber's theory of the progressive formalization of charismatic authority, the coincidence of their ideas about the process is remarkable. At the very least, it calls in doubt Carl Ernst's thesis about Sufism being an "invention" of eighteenth- and nineteenth-century Orientalists who selectively used historical data and their Eurocentric prejudices to construct its image.[242] If Sufism was indeed "invented," this happened long before the dawn of the "Orientalist age."[243] The invention was done by Muslim thinkers without the help of modern intellectual tools and analytic frameworks. When European Islamologists like Snouck Hurgronje (1857–1936), Arthur Arberry (1905–1969), Fritz Meier (1912–1998), or Louis Massignon (1883–1962) talked about Sufism's "corruption" at the hands of unscrupulous *shaykh*s, formalization of Sufi spiritual discipline (from the eleventh century CE onward),[244] or the adulteration by later Sufis of the "primeval" mystical experience with speculative metaphysics borrowed from external sources, especially "Hellenistic philosophy,"[245] they were not saying something unprecedented or uniquely "Eurocentric." The same is true of the Swedish bishop Tor Andrae (1885–1947), who bemoaned the progressive decline of Sufi spirituality—an idea that he derived from his close investigation of original Sufi sources.[246] Even Hodgson with his rigorous self-reflection and aversion to blanket generalizations implicitly admits the decline thesis by mentioning "corruption and localism" in later Sufism—a tribute to the constant refrain of Muslim sources themselves, not to outsiders' arbitrary Eurocentric biases.[247] In sum, these and many other Islamologists simply repeated, in their own native tongues and cultural idioms,[248] what earlier Muslim writers had thought and said about Islam and Sufism in particular in Arabic, Persian, and Turkish. The insiders and outsiders may have had different reasons for saying this, but the upshot of their argument is quite similar: in the course of its historical development Sufism has grown more formalized and regimented; the original freshness and directness of interaction among its followers was, to some extent, lost, and it took on board a panoply of extraneous ideas that were not always consonant with its original aspirations and practices. In repackaging this pessimistic vision of Sufism for their audiences, European Islamologists wittingly or not implemented a typical phenomenological approach to religion: scholars should take very seriously how members of a given religious tradition actually "see things" themselves.[249] That this approach remains widely accepted today, as it was yesterday, is evidenced by the following statement of the influential Canadian philosopher Charles Taylor (b. 1931):

> Making sense of agents does require that we *understand* [emphasis of the original] their self-descriptions . . . [for] interpretative social sciences cannot by-pass the agents' self-understanding.[250]

In other words, the aforementioned Islamologists and their numerous colleagues before and after them sought to develop an "empathy" with their object of study that was encouraged by the European phenomenological theories of the age. They may also have been motivated by Weber's method of "understanding" (*Verstehen*) that, like phenomenology, requires that the investigator abstract him or herself from their own intellectual position in order to comprehend what items in a certain chain of causality mean, not to the investigator personally, but to the actors or believers themselves.[251] Even if these European scholars were wrong about Sufism's "decline" or "adulteration by foreign elements,"[252] they should not be summarily accused of "inventing" its history. It was invented well before by medieval Muslim thinkers, Sufis and non-Sufis alike. The Westerners simply adapted it, with various degrees of empathy, skill, and accuracy, to the intellectual and cultural expectations of their European audiences. We have every right to disagree with their conclusions, but we should be aware of the fact that in doing so we are also, to some extent, disagreeing with their sources.

A noteworthy feature of premodern discourses about Sufism, such as those offered by al-Qushayri, Ibn 'Abbad, al-Shatibi, and Ibn Khaldun among others, is that they presented it as a process, not something static and given once and for all.[253] One should of course not forget that Ibn Khaldun was an exceptional individual, whose sense of history should not be automatically extrapolated to other Muslim thinkers.[254] Even with this caveat, his observations about the progressive decline and adulteration of authentic Sufi values and practices were by no means unique to him. They had been a staple of Sufi discourse almost since its very inception.[255] In any event, there is no doubt that Ibn Khaldun, Ibn 'Abbad al-Rundi, al-Shatibi, and others involved in the discussions of the vicissitudes of Sufism did try to place their subject into a meaningful historical perspective, thereby creating a metanarrative of its evolution across time, although not within a meaningful geographical scope. Furthermore, they treated Sufism as a subject in its own right that was, to a degree, self-sufficient and distinct from other versions of Islam, for example, jurisprudence, philosophy, or speculative theology.[256] They also knew well what made Sufism distinct, which, in our view at least, undermines the argument advanced by some critically minded postmodernist scholars that such notions as "mysticism" and "religion" are but modern Western or Orientalist conceptions arbitrarily transposed onto the experiences of non-Western societies.[257] This view is thrown into sharp relief by Jonathan Z. Smith, a prominent American scholar of comparative religion, who has argued:

> Man, more precisely, western man, has had only the last few centuries in which to imagine religion. . . . Religion is solely the creation of the scholar's study. It is created for the scholar's analytic purposes by his imaginative acts of comparison and generalization. Religion has no independent existence apart from the academy.[258]

Contrary to the assumption of Jonathan Z. Smith and his deconstruction-minded colleagues, the Muslim scholars mentioned above were scholars of religion in that they, too, created and deployed large concepts for "analytic purposes." Their investigative assumptions may have been different from ours, but to expect them to be exactly like us would be naive. Contrary to what postmodernist critics of Orientalism try to convince us, Muslim scholars of religion acted very much like their modern Western counterparts: "[They] eagerly collected, catalogued, compared, and attempted to systematize myths, rituals, and other noteworthy customs and habits" of both Muslims and other people.[259] Yes, they used different terms and concepts, but they often arrived at essentially the same conclusions as the European Orientalists would. It is also true that they were not embedded in the Western academy, as Smith has rightly pointed out, but is this indeed a necessary precondition for thinking about religion critically and analytically? In any case, to deny them the ability to conceptualize and discuss their own religion and other religions is, ironically, the worst kind of Orientalism.

Now, what the works of medieval Muslim scholars of religion do not display in comparison to Western Islamology is the awareness of the broader geographical and cultural contexts outside their immediate environments. Yes, they had access to books produced well outside their homelands, but only in rare instances[260] would they travel to observe how Islam and other religions were practiced by their followers in remote geographical areas. The global vision that informs the modern study of religion requires the means of communication, knowledge production, and mobility that are a product of a later age, the period that we describe by the highly ambiguous and problematic term "modernity."[261] To develop this broader, globalist view, one also needed access to modern intellectual tools as well as comparative and sociological perspectives on Islam and Muslim societies. As we have seen, European Islamologists had internalized and attempted to implement these perspectives with various degree of success over the course of the nineteenth and twentieth centuries. Their inevitable prejudices, misconceptions, and blind spots notwithstanding,[262] their broader vision of Sufism and Sufis was informed by the achievements of the European "theorizing about religion that has conspicuously engaged practically every major Western thinker of any note since the 1500s—Spinoza, Locke, Hume, Kant, Hegel, Marx, Durkheim, Max Müller, Freud, and many others."[263] There is no denying that the historical-critical method of studying the Bible from Friedrich Schleiermacher (1768–1834) and the Strauss-Baur School to Martin Dibelius (1883–1947) and Karl Barth (1886–1968)[264] radically changed European perceptions of not only their own Judeo-Christian scriptures but also of other religious canons, including Islam's.[265] The collective efforts of these and other investigators,[266] Ivan Strenski argues, following Jonathan Z. Smith, have led to a radical redefinition of the human self and its religious commitments:

> Like art and economic life, religion became the object of a disciplined academic or systematic program of self-reflection—what can be called "science." Only in the past century and a half there has been anything called a "science of religion."[267]

In accordance with the same Weberian logic that we have observed in relation to Sufism's evolution, Western scholarship about Sufism has itself become routinized and institutionalized. It is now a professionalized site of knowledge production about religion(s).[268]

Nevertheless, the epistemological divide between premodern and modern conceptualizations of Islam generally and Sufism in particular, albeit undeniable, should not be exaggerated. Discussions of the vicissitudes of Sufism by premodern Muslim intellectuals, Sufi and non-Sufi alike, demonstrate that they did not take their religion for granted, as is often implied by modern postcolonial theorists who are eager to present Western conceptualizations of religion as colonial, Eurocentric, and hegemonic constructs.[269] Premodern Muslim inquirers were consciously committed to understanding their religion, its history, its internal divisions, and its specificity vis-à-vis other religions and intellectual systems, especially Judaism, Christianity, and Greek philosophy.[270] In particular, Muslim doxographers,[271] such as al-Ash'ari, al-Malati, Ibn Hazm, 'Abd al-Qahir al-Baghdadi, al-Shahrastani, Ibn al-Jawzi, al-Shatibi, to name but the most prominent, examined Sufi theories and practices as well as their relations with other schools of thought in Islam, including traditionalist, legal, rationalist-theological, and Shi'i.[272] Moreover, some of these writers also discussed, often quite competently, non-Islamic religions, usually in order to demonstrate their inferiority to Islam.[273] The same, however, applies to many modern Western studies of Islam that are covertly or overtly biased against it, so the widely held thesis regarding a decisive epistemological break with premodern conceptualizations of religion, as advocated by many postcolonial Western thinkers mentioned above, is not as ironclad as it may appear. Furthermore, like premodern Muslim scholars of religion, many Western experts on Islam were and still are but theologians.

In sum, we suggest that reflection and self-reflection focused on religion was an important concern of Muslim religious specialists well before the rise and institutionalization of the European study of "comparative religions" or Islamology more specifically. Moreover, as we could see, premodern Muslim thinkers dealt with very real problems. However, to reiterate, their investigations were not, and could not have been, based on a cross-cultural, cross-regional, and cross-disciplinary approach that, at least in theory, would not "allow one individual religious perspective to hold a privileged place"[274] and to be used as the benchmark to measure the veracity of this or that religious doctrine or practice. This relatively detached, noncommittal approach took a long time to gestate. Only about three hundred years ago, religion came to be perceived by some Western thinkers as a universal intellectual problem that they tried to resolve by drawing on an ever-growing body of knowledge about both Christian and non-Christian religions assembled through textual study or travel.[275] From that point on, for Western scholars of religion(s) one or the other form of comparative perspective became a necessity. It boils down to a simple axiom that by knowing only one religion, one knows none.[276] It stands to reason that Western scholars of non-Western societies, despite their predominantly philological training, could not remain immune to the major intellectual fashions of their intellectual milieu, including sociology, anthropology, and comparative religious studies. The direct or indirect influence of these new disciplines, which were internally diverse and often polemical,[277] informed the work of Western scholars of Sufism. For example, the careful discussion of the formalization of *piri-muridi* discipline in later Sufism by Fritz Meier and Marshall Hodgson was dictated, at least in part, by their awareness of the potent Weberian theses of the routinization of charisma and charisma of the office.

Theorizing religion within the conceptual framework of comparative religious studies enabled Western scholars of Islam to furnish a compelling and comprehensive picture of Sufism's evolution across time and space. This approach is modern in the sense that it allowed them, to the extent possible, to depart from the age-long storage of hostile stereotypes of Islam and Muslims that had steadily accrued over the course of the Christian Middle Ages[278] to articulate a more balanced view of Islam and its subdivisions, including Sufism. It enabled a new type of intellectual and emotional appreciation, theretofore impossible. As for Sufism, here we once again have an instance of its being a meeting place of discourses and creative imaginations for both insiders and outsiders. These encounters have produced fascinating discursive bricolages and intellectual conversations, some of which we have examined in this chapter.

World-Rejecting Mysticism versus Inner-Worldly Asceticism

Given the ubiquitous presence of the Weberian explanatory paradigms in the academic field of Islamic studies, it would be instructive to test their applicability to Sufism. One such paradigm seems to be particularly relevant. It postulates the highly consequential dichotomy of world-rejecting mysticism versus inner-worldly asceticism.[279] Examining its accuracy gives us yet another chance to put Sufism's history in conversation with Western perspectives on ascetic-mystical movements in Islam and other religions. For example, if we accept the Weberian classification of "roads to salvation,"[280] postulating the predominantly ascetic, world-renouncing nature of early Sufi piety, Sufism at its beginnings will appear to us as a typical religious attitude of "a world-fleeing ascetic."[281] However, as already mentioned, Max Weber himself, although by no means an expert on Sufi history, recognized that Sufism was internally diverse and combined contemplative and mystical elements with inner-worldly activism and even militancy.[282] Throughout his massive sociological oeuvre Weber's analysis oscillates uneasily between denying and recognizing Sufism's inner-worldly, reform-oriented potential[283]—a predicament that he himself has created by postulating two ideal types of ascetic-mystical behavior in line with his overarching thesis of the world-transformative functions of ascetic Calvinism.[284] Nevertheless, in the end, the very logic of Weber's thesis, which emphasizes the uniqueness of Western European Christianity vis-à-vis other religions, prompts him to relegate Sufism to the status of "orgiastic, spiritualistic, contemplative" (that is, "world-renouncing") religious attitude, rather than viewing it as an Islamic form of inner-worldly asceticism, that is, one eager to get involved in mundane affairs in order to change them.[285] If Albert Hourani's and Bryan Turner's conclusions are correct, Weber's views, as well as the ideas of his Western European confreres who were critical of monastic withdrawal from the world (for example, Rousseau, Compte, Spenser, and Durkheim), may have shaped the anti-Sufi attitudes of Muslim reformers of the early twentieth century, steeped as they were in the Western European thought of the age, including Weber's "Protestant ethics thesis."[286] Thus, we may have here another instance of a dialogue between insider and outsider discourses about Islam that, as we shall soon see, had drastic and long-ranging implications for the vicissitudes of Sufism in the twentieth century and today.

The predicament of being in the world while at the same time striving to transcend it, as described—somewhat self-contradictorily—by Weber,[287] was intimately familiar to premodern Sufis. They realized that to sustain oneself and one's family, one had to engage with the world and earn a livelihood.[288] It was the extent and consequences of this fraught engagement with mundane realities that troubled them, causing them to spill much ink in an effort to forge a compromise between dealing with society and avoiding its treacherous enticements and distractions.[289] Moreover, medieval Sufi writers themselves actively strove to find a solution to this dilemma well before the criticisms of Sufi passivity and aloofness were voiced by such prominent Muslim reformers and modernizers as 'Abdo, al-Shawkani, Ibn Badis, Rashid Rida, and Ahmad b. Musa,[290] to name but a few.

In his momentous *Revivification of Religious Sciences*, al-Ghazali argues that flight from the world is much easier than confronting it head on, and thus less meritorious. The goal of breaking the soul and overcoming its drives, according to al-Ghazali, is best achieved through living in the midst of ordinary people and being subject to abuse and maltreatment at their hands. This is part of being in the world and mixing (*mukhalata*) with its denizens as opposed to seeking retreat or seclusion (*'uzla*) from society.[291] The correct way, concludes al-Ghazali, is that the inhabitants of Sufi lodges (*ribatat*) should not simply abandon their lodges in order to serve people of the marketplace. Rather, they should respect the pursuits and values of the worldlings, while praying for and dispensing divine blessings to them.[292] Ibn Khaldun brings home the same message, quoting a saying of the Prophet that encourages his followers to strike a delicate balance between being pious and meeting the inevitable demands of human nature.[293] About four hundred years later, the prolific Maghribi Sufi writer Ibn 'Ajiba (d. 1224/1809) invokes the same idea—a clear indication that it remained as actual in his times as it had been during the lifetime of Ibn Khaldun and al-Ghazali. Commenting on Q 25:20, which describes the biblical and Qur'anic prophets as "eating food and walking in the markets," he argues that this passage accurately describes the true Sufi "friends of God" (*awliya'*): they, too, should frequent the markets and eat food of the people of the bazaar if only for the sake of experience, instruction, and reflection. For, not just in the peaceful calm of their cells but also in the hustle and bustle (*ziham*) of the marketplaces, they should learn to catch the glimpses of God's earthly presence, thus drawing ever closer to him. From the viewpoint of God's ubiquitous presence, being in the crowd or in retreat makes no difference. Ibn 'Ajiba then goes on to conclude:

> The [spiritual] seeker (*murid*) needs to train his thought in both isolation (*'uzla*) and in the crowd (*khalta*),[294] in solitary retreat (*khalwa*) as well as in the open (*jalwa*). He should not limit himself to meditating in isolation so that, when he finds himself in the crowd, his spiritual state (*hal*) would not undergo change thereby exposing its weakness. Isolation is necessary at the beginning, before one enters the realm of [subtle mystical] meanings. After one has entered this realm, he should choose the crowd over isolation, so that his heart would achieve equanimity in both the crowd and solitude. Isolation from people is the isolation of the weak, whereas isolation in the midst of people is the isolation of the strong.[295]

This statement serves as a compelling insider corrective to Weber's dichotomy of inner-worldly asceticism versus otherworldly mysticism. Similar attitudes have been encouraged by Muslim proponents of ascetic-mystical piety beginning with the Malamatiyya and, in the subsequent centuries, by the leaders of the Naqshbandiyya and Shadhiliyya Sufi brotherhoods.[296] This is how Sufi theorists themselves envisioned the ideal behavior of an ascetic-mystic. By disseminating, orally or in writing, discourses about bodily regimens and good manners, the states and stages of the mystical path, cosmologies and gnoseologies specific to Sufism, not to mention Sufi biographies and hagiographies, these theorists were striving to establish Sufism as a community (*ta'ifa*; *qawm*) of intellectual and practical commitment that was somehow distinct from the rest of the *umma*, either Sunni or Shi'i. In other words, objectively the learned custodians of the Sufi tradition have asserted its existence as a distinctive subset of the larger Muslim tradition. As a result of this effort to carve out a special niche for Sufism within the broader framework of Muslim life, much ambiguity and confusion has arisen that is still evident today in how Sufism is perceived by both insiders and outsiders.[297] As with Ibn (al-)'Arabi's famous (and some would say notorious) ambiguity over whether God is identical with or distinct from his creation ("He/"not He"),[298] resolving this dilemma, if, in fact, it needs resolving, is a matter of the perspective that one chooses to adopt. This subtle dynamic of distinctness-identity should be borne in mind when trying to conceptualize Sufism. The fact that Sufi theorists today as before continue to debate whether Sufism and Islam are identical or different is an eloquent proof that the creators and sustainers of the Sufi tradition have succeeded in asserting this distinctness without, however, postulating it as a full-fledged, free-standing alternative to other manifestations of Muslim belief and practice. Had it been otherwise, we would not have studied Sufism as a distinctive stream of Islam.

While discussing Sufi thinkers' metaphysical and gnoseological engagements with the Qur'an, we have identified their main vectors and objectives. Deliberately or not, the Sufi elite was creating a unique universe of meaning aimed at supporting the hierarchy of individuals capable of gaining glimpses of a sacred, revelatory knowledge (ma'rifa/kashf) of God and the world. This knowledge was, and still is, presented as being beyond and above the ken of the vast majority of ordinary believers.[299] The same applies to Sufi conduct and ways of worshipping (or, rather, interacting with) God that, too, were presented as the domain of the divinely chosen and initiated few. As a result, the standard of exemplary ascetic-mystical behavior is set so high as to leave little hope for a commoner to ever reach it. If he or she would still want to try, he or she had to attach themselves to a respected teacher (shaykh; murshid; pir) and to dedicate himself or herself single-mindedly to fulfilling his commands.[300] A less demanding option was to become an associated member of a Sufi community gravitating around a charismatic master.[301] In either case, the role of the Sufi teacher was of essence. In the same way, the mystical knower ('arif) is indispensable for extracting and imparting to his followers the hidden mysteries of the revelation, the shaykh/murshid/pir is essential in assisting his followers to navigate the practicalities of the ascetic-mystical path to God. Naturally, the regimens and precepts ascribed to venerable Sufi masters of old and the guidelines provided by founders of various Sufi lineages (silsila) have other important functions to play, such as creating lasting communities of a shared spiritual and behavioral commitment, textual communities, and, in the final account, also stable and influential social institutions. Sufi exegesis, metaphysics, and gnoseology, as well as Sufi practices and institutions, all are geared to maintaining an identity that is distinct from various other identities available to Muslims. Seen from this perspective, the widely circulated Sufi maxim that Sufism is Islam and Islam is Sufism seems problematic and, actually, contrary to the goals of Sufi theorists, who, consciously or not, were at pains to elevate Sufi teachings and practical discipline above all other religious and social persuasions. Subjectively, they may have sincerely seen Sufism as the true Islam, but objectively their vision was exclusivist nonetheless.

General Observations

Our examination of Sufi teachings and practices from different epochs and geographical areas demonstrates a remarkable stability and uniformity of the Sufi tradition. As pointed out in chapter 1, Sufi ideas did indeed have legs and were able to traverse vast distances and different historical epochs—"from Iran to West Africa," as Bernd Radtke has perceptively pointed out.[302] And even this giant swath of land and sea was not the limit. Today as before, Sufis and Sufi institutions can be found as far as Siberia in the north and the Indonesian archipelago in the south.

When insider and outsider views of Sufism are juxtaposed to prove that the former are more authentic and correct, while the latter less so,[303] this is but a conscious or unconscious exercise in "Orientalism-bashing" inspired by Edward Said's now paradigmatic critique of Western study and imagining of Islam and the Muslims.[304] Looked at dispassionately and objectively, conceptualizations of Sufism by both insiders and outsiders seem to have been congruent. This is evident in how both groups construed the long-term transformation of the critical *shaykh-murid* (*pir-murid*) relationship and of Sufism's evolution from informal circles to institutions more generally. At the same time, as has been shown, Meier's (and to some extent Hodgson's) interest in this subject may have been dictated, at least in part, by their familiarity with Weber's concept of "routinization of charisma," which they applied to realities they found in Sufi literature.

After examining Ibn Khaldun's writings one can argue that long before the emergence of European Orientalism, Sufism was already conceptualized and historicized by outside observers, who engaged in what can be described as a premodern version of religious studies. Given the fact that Ibn Khaldun's discourses about Sufism were driven by his personal convictions and larger intellectual agendas, his concept of Sufism is no less or no more "invented" than those of Meier's or Hodgson's. Both Ibn Khaldun and

Ibn 'Abbad, on the one hand, and Meier and Hodgson, on the other, use the *piri/muridi* bond as the starting point for their metanarratives on Sufism. In the process, it becomes Hayden White's "trope" that selectively represents the entire historical evolution of Sufism as envisioned by premodern Muslims and modern Western observers.

CHAPTER SIX

Sufism's Recent Trajectories

WHAT LIES BEHIND THE
SUFI-SALAFI CONFRONTATION?

Religion spawns organization: to propose a new interpretation of the
invisible entities is to propose a new way of doing things.

—PATRICIA CRONE, *PRE-INDUSTRIAL SOCIETIES:*
ANATOMY OF THE PRE-MODERN WORLD

AFTER EXAMINING SOME major components of the Sufi tradition in
their historical evolution, we should be clear that its creators and advocates
have succeeded in rendering it an attractive and respectable option for
Sunni Muslims and, to a lesser extent, for Shi'is as well.[1] By the eleventh
century CE, Sufism had become an essential part of Muslim life not just in
the lands where Muslims were in the majority but also in those in which
they lived as a minority.[2] Although often perceived by many Muslims and
Westerners as conservatives staunchly opposed to change,[3] some leading
Sufis of the modern age, such as the Damascene polymath 'Abd al-Ghani
al-Nabulusi (d. 1143/1731), advocated a greater freedom of social inter-
course and public entertainment (especially musical performances, coffee
drinking, and smoking in coffee shops) for both men and women, often
against a stiff opposition of conservative members of the religious establishment.[4] Whereas other Sufi leaders would occasionally adopt a less le-
nient, legalistic position on such issues, for example, Muhammad al-Sanusi
(d. 1276/1859) or Shamil (Shamwil; d. 1287/1871),[5] the fact remains: Sufis
or individuals with Sufi affiliations were active players in the life of their
societies, often assuming leadership roles on intellectual, cultural, and
sociopolitical planes.[6] Indeed, from the eighteenth century on, Sufism in

its regional and institutional forms has come to serve as a major vehicle for reform and spiritual rejuvenation of some, although by no means all, Muslim societies.[7] Even those Muslim leaders who rejected Sufism for doctrinal or personal reasons were often affiliated with Sufi institutions or individual Sufi masters. Moreover, they made use of Sufi concepts and organizational structures, which is hardly surprising given Sufism's ubiquitous presence in every nook and cranny of Muslim life.[8] In other words, blanket generalizations about Sufism being conservative or, on the contrary, innovative and prone to modernize hardly do justice to the wide variety of interactions between individuals posing or perceived as Sufis and their sociopolitical environments.

The vicissitudes of various Sufi communities across time and space have been examined in a large corpus of academic and nonacademic literature that need not be discussed here.[9] In each case, as just mentioned, the actions and beliefs of any given community were shaped by a panoply of local and global factors that have to be taken into account to grasp the why, what, and how of the community's trajectory, before deciding what role Sufism played in the choices its leaders made.[10] What follows is a brief outline of some general vectors of Sufism's evolution in recent times based on the study of concrete cases either by our colleagues or ourselves. Naturally, our choice of evidence and analytic frameworks is, perforce, subjective or, to use Hayden White's terminology, "tropical."[11] In other words, we select concrete evidence based on our preconceived notion of the object, analyze it, and extrapolate our conclusions to larger contexts. The conclusions become a synecdoche of sorts for a much greater and complex whole. While such an approach obviously fails to do justice to the richness and complexity of each case discussed in what follows, it still allows us to detect and highlight certain general tendencies in Sufism's evolution over the past century.

Sufism as a "Mainstay for Muslim Social Order"

In his magisterial *Venture of Islam*,[12] Marshall Hodgson identifies several characteristics of Sufism in the premodern age that, in his mind, explain its pervasive presence across the breadth and width of the Muslim world. One of them has been examined in chapter 5 of this book under the rubric of *piri-miridi* discipline.[13] Another feature identified by Hodgson is *dhikr*, a ritualized invocation or recollection of God's name by devotees. It constitutes a centerpiece of Sufi self-discipline and meditation and, when performed collectively at specified times, functions as a community-building and sustaining device as well as a source of a distinctive identity, in the same way as any public rituals usually do.[14] Now, according to Hodgson, in addition to *dhikr*'s important roles as a technique of focusing the mind of performers on God and rendering them oblivious of the flow and flux of daily existence, this practice furnishes them with an alternative means and space, a Sufi lodge (*khanaqah*; *ribat* or *zawiya*), for expressing emotionally and uninhibitedly their acute experience of God's presence in their lives, or as the case may be, their gratitude for his loving care and grace.[15] According to Hodgson, "the dhikr sessions of mystical worship" were attended by commoners "for the sake of pious edification or a sheer blessing."[16] To this important function, one may add the performances' entertainment value that no one who has ever attended them would deny.[17] In the premodern and early modern age, with public entertainment of any kind rare or nonexistent, Sufi-led and sponsored *dhikr* performances served as an effective means of public outreach and recruitment tools for Sufi communities. To the same category, that is, public outreach, popularization, and recruitment, belongs the sponsorship by Sufi communities of pilgrimages to tombs or cenotaphs of Qur'anic prophets,[18] Sufi *awliya*', and heroes of early Islam located in various regions of the Muslim world.[19] "The celebration of a great saint's birthday at his tomb," notes Hodgson, "became a major local festivity, in which every inhabitant took part."[20] Finally, in rural and sparsely populated areas, Sufi lodges were often the only centers of Islamic education to which local peasants and tribes sent their children to learn the basics of Islam and elements of Sufi moral-ethical discipline under the guidance of a popular *shaykh* or his lieutenants. Thus, the children benefited doubly from their sojourn at a Sufi institution: by acquiring basic religious education and principles of moral-ethical behavior (*adab*), while also partaking of the *shaykh*'s blessing (*baraka*) and charisma (*karama*).[21] Upon his death, the Sufi master would often become, in Hodgson's parlance, "the protecting genius of the village," whose tomb symbolized his invisible but beneficial presence in the midst of its inhabitants who honored it "as the locus of his blessed power."[22] Throughout the Muslim world, Sufi shrines and lodges served as a social safety net of sorts, providing accommodation for wayfarers and pilgrims, food for the poor, and psychological consolation for the oppressed and downtrodden.[23] Due to the high respect that Sufi leaders enjoyed among the masses, they were often courted by military and secular rulers who employed them as advisers, spiritual counselors, legal experts, and judges.[24]

Taking into account all these varied roles, Western anthropologists have often depicted Sufi *shaykhs* as brokers in dealings between the popu-

FIGURE 6.1. Mawlawi dervishes dancing at Konya, Turkey, summer 2010. The author's photograph.

lace at large and powers that be.[25] Also important were the roles that popular Sufi teachers played in mediating in conflicts between various segments and clans of local populations.[26] All these factors explain what Hodgson has called, using a term borrowed from Christian history, "the catholic appeal of Sufism."[27] As with Meier, who used the term "priestly authority," one can hasten to accuse Hodgson of a Eurocentric bias, but one can hardly disagree with him when he adds, "a tradition of intensive interiorization re-exteriorized its results and was finally able to provide an important basis for social order."[28] Nor can one take issue with his subsequent conclusion that "the Sufis succeeded in combining a spiritual élitism with a social populism—even though to a considerable degree, at the expense of a certain vulgarization."[29]

The felicitous ability of Sufism in its various guises to meet the needs of both a refined intellectual and an ordinary villager, as well as the social groups located in between these poles (contrary, for example, to the uncompromising and self-conscious elitism of the Muslim *falasifa*) should probably be seen as the key to its historical success.[30] Last but not least, in the wake of the fall of Baghdad to the Mongols in 656/1258 and the breakup of the political unity of Islamdom that had preceded it, Sufi communities and institutions fulfilled the role of an institutional and ideological glue that held together the Muslim world's diverse and often mutually hostile constituent parts. Although "everywhere . . . burdened with the weight of endowed property and popular superstition,"[31] Sufism managed to sustain its consolidating and animating social, intellectual, and spiritual force over the centuries.[32] In sum, to use Hodgson's well-known metaphor, until very recently in historical terms the Sufi component of the "venture of Islam" has been an almost unqualified success.[33] However, under the pervasive impact of what Hodgson calls "the Great Western Transmutation," Sufism became an important target of Islamic reformist movements because of its pervasive and salient presence in Muslim societies.[34] The whole paradigm of Muslim life under this new geopolitical condition had to change, and with it, Sufism as well.

Modernity on the Doorstep: Sufism Stands Accused

Whether or not we accept Hodgson's terminology and line of thinking generally, there is no doubt that with the advent of the geopolitical, social, and economic condition that we designate by an elastic and contested term "modernity," Sufism's status in Muslim societies as a mainstay of the international social order[35] has come under critical scrutiny from a variety of quarters.[36] Criticisms of Sufism, as we have argued already in this study, were due to its prior social success and its ubiquitous presence in Muslim societies.[37] Enmeshed deeply and inextricably into the very fabric of Muslim life, Sufism with its doctrines, practices, institutions, literature, and leadership structures was a potent symbol of the *ancien régime*, of the status quo that reformers of various stripes sought to change or even to abolish altogether.[38] Here are some examples of the anti-Sufi rhetoric that, as we shall see, was found in Muslim communities across the globe throughout the twentieth century.

Citing their own experiences with *tariqa* Sufism, the Indonesian reformers Ahmad al-Fatani (1856–1908) and Ahmad Khatib al-Minankabawi (1860–1916) summarily dismissed the adepts of the local Sufi orders (primarily the Naqshbandiyya and the Qadiriyya) as "victims of foolishness, potential enemies of public safety, and lust-maddened rural simpletons."[39] They warned their coreligionists against being entrapped by those "tricksters who sold religion to the world, seeking livelihood by using the name tariqa."[40] Entering a "corrupt *tariqa*," argued another Indonesian scholar, Muhammad b. Jamal al-Din al-Lunggi, also known as Cik 'Id (1875–1926), himself a Sufi of the Ahmadiyya-Idrisiyya order,[41] is wrong, among other things, because of Sufism's apathy toward the affairs of this world. In his words, its adepts "have moved away [from this world] with their dhikr dances and their twirling and their killing of the self with their jumping and stamping and such things that are nothing other than a danger to this life and that to come."[42] About the same time, and thousands of miles away, a learned Moroccan vizier accused the local Sufi leader Muhammad al-Kattani (1873–1909) of "enticing foolish minds and seducing the common people" by his claims to sainthood (*walaya*) and knowledge of the esoteric sense of the Shari'a(t).[43] Today, as at the beginning of the twentieth century, many critics of Sufism will gladly subscribe to the words of these Indonesian and Moroccan intellectuals. Moreover, they will add to them their own anti-Sufi grievances, many of which will be discussed later in this chapter.[44]

Over the past century and a half, advocates of Islamic reform explained its necessity by the Muslim world's political, military, and economic weakness in the face of European technological supremacy and cultural and political domination. Many, but by no means all, of the reformers held Sufism at least partly responsible for the Muslim plight, because Sufism, in their opinion, was and is at odds with the modern conditions to which the majority of humankind has acceded. Because of this premise, discussions about the vicissitudes of Sufism in the modern era are often being conducted in conjunction with the phenomenon of modernity. Modernity's exact nature and provenance, as well as its impact on Muslim thought and practice generally and Sufism in particular, have generated many volumes, the contents of which need not be rehearsed here.[45] Without delving into details, the change in the perception of Sufism among various Muslim groups and classes was (and still is) a direct result of the change in the ideological and cultural orientations of Muslim societies. This change, in its turn, came on the heels of the dramatic political, economic, and social transformations on a global scale over the past several centuries. The same factors, which, from the second half of the nineteenth century onward, have animated calls for reform among concerned Muslim intellectuals across the Muslim world, have caused some of them to critically reassess Sufism's place in their societies. To be sure, already in the premodern Muslim world criticisms of Sufi teachings and practices as well as individual Sufis were not unusual. They can be found in the works of Ibn al-Jawzi,[46] Ibn Taymiyya,[47] Lisan al-Din Ibn al-Khatib,[48] Ibn Khaldun, and a number of less distinguished scholars from Iran to Yemen.[49] One factor that makes modern criticisms of Sufism distinct from their premodern antecedents is the existence today of viable alternatives to Sufi interpretations of Islam. As with institutionalized Christianity,[50] Sufism's doctrinal premises, social status, and ritual practices remained stable until the arrival of new, alternative ideologies that came to vie with its theretofore unshakable authority for the attention of various segments of the *umma*. In the majority of cases, and in contradistinction to the European and Russian experiences of the eighteenth and nineteenth centuries,[51] secularism in one form or the other, even when forcibly imposed from above, failed to establish itself as a viable alternative to religion. This failure was due in large part to the level of social and technological development of Muslim societies in that age.[52] Even today, to galvanize the masses for action, challenges to the status quo in the Muslim world have to be couched in a predominantly or even exclusively Islamic idiom.[53] Scholars of Islam and Muslim societies have spilled much ink trying to describe these new Islamic alternatives to the religious and political establishments associated with the *ancien régime*.[54] Some of them also have tried to explain why leaders of these emerging alternative movements tended to assume an anti-Sufi stance.[55] We have already answered this question, at least partly, by suggesting that premodern and early modern Sufism was too closely linked to the status quo in the majority of Muslim societies. To change it and to dislodge the ruling elite committed to its maintenance, one willy-nilly had to mount an attack on Sufism and its followers. Whether we call the ideological and sociological alternatives to Sufi versions of Islam "Salafi," "Islamist," "fundamentalist," or "neo-fundamentalist"[56] is not that important, especially because the answers offered by investigators are often unconvincing or even outright tautological such as, for example, Roxanne Euben's characterization of "Islamic fundamentalism" as "a modern response to modernity."[57] What is important is that the appearance in new Islamic discourses of anti-Sufi themes points to certain deeper societal subcurrents that, in their turn, are reflective of the geopolitical realities of the world we live in. Overall, these realities do not bode well for the majority of Muslims, with the exception of those who live in the countries rich in natural resources. Seen in a global perspective, the current position of the *umma*, the worldwide "imagined community" of the Muslims,[58] is hardly favorable and, worse still, its prospects do not look much brighter today than they did during the colonial era.

The global Muslim community may be imagined or even outright fictitious,[59] but the perception of its plight is quite real for many Muslims, some of whom are eager to stake their lives on alleviating it. They begin their task by asking: "Who is to blame?" For reasons just outlined, Sufism has ended up on the black list of the culprits,[60] alongside "heretical" Sunni sects, popular superstitions (*khurafat*), Greek philosophy, Shi'ism (for some, but not all members of the Sunni majority, especially the jihadi groups operating in Iraq, Syria, and Yemen),[61] Russia, the West led by the United States as well as, closer to home, corrupt government officials of the Muslim states and docile religious scholars subservient to them.[62]

Because this book is about Sufism, we will discuss in detail the criticisms that its opponents level at its followers. They are as numerous as they are remarkably similar across the Muslim world and in societies in which Muslims are a minority. To begin with, let us consult the notes of a Muslim fighter found on a battlefield.

The Salafi Creed on the Battlefield

Most [religious] traditions possess a large discursive repertoire that knowledgeable actors can deploy ... to identify their immediate campaign with a sacred and transcendent cause, while representing themselves as heroic defenders of the faith against demonic, infidel, or apostate opponents.

—BRUCE LINCOLN, *HOLY TERRORS: THINKING ABOUT RELIGION AFTER SEPTEMBER 11*

In late August–early September of 1999, when the so-called Russian antiterrorist operation in Daghestan, an autonomous southern republic of the Russian Federation, was in full swing following its invasion by a group of Islamist fighters (*mujahideen*) from the neighboring republic of Chechnya,[63] a Russian anthropologist came into possession of the lecture notes that apparently belonged to a Daghestani Muslim trained in a rebel camp in either Chechnya or Daghestan.[64] The notes were later published in the Russian academic journal *Vestnik Evrazii* (*Eurasian Courier*) under the title "Kredo wakhkhabita" ("A Wahhabi's Creed").[65] They provide an illuminating glimpse into the ideological underpinnings of the militant movement in the Northern Caucasus that Russian and Western academics and mass media routinely describe as "Salafi" or "Wahhabi." The lecture notes appear to be part of a crash course on "true" or "pure" (Rus. *chistyi*) Islam[66] taken by the author in conjunction with his military training—a practice widely attested in the Russian media coverage of the Islamic insurgency in the Northern Caucasus.[67] Written in Russian, the lecture notes contain numerous quotations from the Qur'an and the prophetic Hadith, occasionally with a parallel Arabic text. The course consists of the following major units: "Islam," "Innovations [in Religion]" (*bid'a*), "Jihad," "The Saved Community" (*al-firqa al-najiya*),[68] "Hypocrisy and Its Types," and "An Appeal to the Leaders and Rulers of the Muslim World." Evidence of this kind merits closer examination, especially because "Wahhabism" is routinely viewed as the archenemy of Sufism and is officially banned in Daghestan and the other Muslim republics of Russia as a "pernicious and subversive ideology."[69] Flyers enumerating authors whose works were prohibited for distribution through either state or private channels were being handed to book vendors in Daghestan's capital of Makhachkala and other urban centers of the republic in the late 1990s and early 2000s. Among the proscribed authors were Ibn Taymiyya, Sayyid Qutb, Nasir al-Din al-Albani, Salih b. Fawzan al-Fawzan,[70] 'Abd al-'Aziz b. Baz, Muhammad b. Jamil Zinu,[71] and a few local authors.[72]

The first unit of the course provides a brief definition of Islam based on its principal sources, the Qur'an and the Sunna of the prophet Muhammad. Special emphasis is placed on the role of jihad and on safeguarding the correct Islamic creed and practice, which are identified as strict monotheism and avoidance of any innovations in doctrine and practice of Islam—a standard Salafi-Wahhabi thesis.[73] Following this rather brief positive definition, the author of the notes furnishes a much longer list of acts and beliefs that he and his instructors consider to be contrary to Islam. Labeled as manifestations of "polytheism" or "idolatry" (*shirk*), they include:

- Supplication (*du'a*) addressed to, or recourse to, anything or anyone other than God be they dead or alive;
- Sacrifice devoted to anyone or anything but God;
- Vows and oaths made to anyone but God;[74]
- Circumambulation of any object (e.g., a grave or a bonfire) other than the House of God;[75]
- Pinning one's hopes on anything or anyone but God;
- Acts of worship dedicated to anything or anyone other than God;[76]
- Submitting oneself to adjudication or legislation based on anything other than the Law of God (*al-shari'a*);[77]
- Dissatisfaction with God's rulings as stipulated in the Shari'a(t);
- Putting one's faith in various "ungodly" teachings and ideologies, such as atheism, communism, socialism, "Jewish masonry," democracy, secular way of life, and nationalism;[78]
- Abandonment of Islam or conversion to a non-Muslim religious creed;
- Helping the infidels, namely, the Jews, the Christians, and the Communists;
- Failure to declare these groups infidels;

- Attempts to effect a separation of religion and state under the pretext that Islam provides no guidelines for state politics, which amounts to calumny against God and his Prophet;
- Belief in the veracity of astrologists, witch doctors, soothsayers, fortune-tellers, and other individuals who claim to know the unseen, which is the exclusive prerogative of God;[79]
- Adhering to the Sufi doctrine of the unity of being, which postulates that the entire universe is identical with God.[80]

Pertinent to our discussion of the anti-Sufi attitudes commonly espoused by Muslims of Salafi-Wahhabi persuasion, the author of the notes enumerates the following deviations from the correct practice of Islam's pious forebears (*al-salaf*) that are commonly associated with Sufism:[81]

- The celebration of the Prophet's birthday (*mawlid*)—a practice borrowed from Christianity by the "heretical Shi'i sect of the Fatimids" and adopted by Sufi brotherhoods;[82]
- Recitations of Sufi poetry and Sufi chants (*dhikr*) accompanied by drumbeat and dances;
- Celebrations of "birthdays" of Sufi *shaykh*s and scholars;
- Seeking the blessing (*baraka*) of "holy" sites, monuments, dead and living individuals, or [their] photographs;[83]
- Supererogatory prayers and vigils;
- Loud declarations of one's intention (*niya*) before the prayer;[84]
- The reading of the "Opening" sura (*al-fatiha*) over the deceased and/or holding a wake over them;
- Celebration of noncanonical holidays, such as the Prophet's "night journey and ascension" (*al-isra' wa-l-mi'raj*) or commemoration of the Prophet's emigration (*hijra*) to Medina;
- The construction of buildings and monuments over the graves of religious scholars and Sufis and the practice of converting them into mosques.[85]

On the positive side, the battlefield notes contain a special section describing the beliefs and fate of the "saved host,"[86] whose members are identified as faithful adherents of the Prophet's Sunna.[87] Their emergence, according to the notes, was predicted by the Prophet in an oft-quoted Hadith about the seventy-three sects of Islam, of which only one is destined to achieve salvation. Given the sorry state of Muslim belief and practice, the author of the notes argues that the members of the saved host are but a tiny minority in the world today.

To avoid any deviations from the true or pure Islam defined in the preceding unit, its champions should form a righteous community (*jama'at*)[88] while rejecting "bogus *tariqats*"[89] that split the Muslim community into mutually hostile groups and introduce innovations into Muslim religious practice thereby departing from the Qur'an and the Sunna of the Prophet.[90] The major task of the members of the *jama'at* is to "enjoin the right and to prohibit the wrong," even if this means declaring an armed jihad against miscreants.[91]

Sufis and Anti-Sufis

To anyone with a modicum of knowledge of Salafi-Wahhabi ideology, the articles of the "battlefield creed" from Daghestan will not come as a surprise. Inspired by the writings of Ibn 'Abd al-Wahhab and his Saudi commentators,[92] they can be heard from any mosque pulpit or in a classroom of a religious college in Saudi Arabia, the Gulf, and beyond.[93] Because we are primarily interested in the Wahhabi-Salafi position vis-à-vis Sufism, rather than the Salafi-Wahhabi doctrinal package as a whole, we will focus specifically on how the battlefield notes deal with Sufism and the Sufis.

The list of the "blameworthy innovations" (*bida'*; sing. *bid'a*)[94] cited above leaves little doubt that the author and his instructors hold Sufis, both past and present, responsible for serious transgressions against their understanding of the correct Islamic creed (*'aqida*).[95] On the doctrinal level, the notes squarely condemn the doctrine of the unity (oneness) of being (*wahdat al-wijud*), whose origin is attributed to the "head of all Sufis."[96] This unnamed individual is accused of teaching that "God is identical with a dog and a pig" and that he (God) "is nothing but a priest in the church." This seems to be a veiled reference to Ibn (al-)'Arabi (d. 638/1240), whose controversial intellectual legacy we have examined in a special monograph.[97] The other unnamed Sufi master mentioned in the creed is held responsible for professing a complete unification of God and man. Since, according to the notes, he was condemned to death for this blasphemy by Muslim men of learning, this cannot be anyone but the famous (or infamous—depending on one's perspective) Sufi martyr Husayn b. Mansur al-Hallaj (d. 309/922).[98] The presence of these Sufis in the creed is hardly surprising given the strident condemnation of both Sufi masters by Ibn Taymiyya,[99] who is held in high regard by the majority of present-day Salafi-Wahhabi authors.[100]

As far as religious rituals are concerned, the Sufis are accused of encouraging the innovation of singing, dancing, and drumbeating during their devotional assemblies (*adhkar*). More seriously, Sufi *shaykh*s are re-sponsible for splitting the initially united *umma* into numerous mutually hostile brotherhoods and factions blindly loyal to their leaders. Even when Sufism and Sufis are not explicitly condemned, they are implicated by as-sociation as it were, because the practices denounced in the creed are often sponsored by Sufi communities,[101] for example, the celebration of the Prophet's birthday (*mawlid*)[102] and of the "weddings" of God's friends (*awliya'*);[103] visits to and worship at their tombs; seeking the blessing and help of dead and living saintly persons (*tawassul*); engagement in super-erogatory prayers, fasts, and vows; and observance of noncanonical holi-days such as the Prophet's "night journey and ascension" or his *hijra* to Yathrib (Medina).[104]

Noteworthy is the mention in the battlefield notes of the custom of seeking help from a photograph.[105] It apparently refers to the famous Naqshbandi precept of *rabita*—the spiritual bond between the Sufi *shaykh* and his disciple that requires of the latter to keep the image of his master constantly in his mind's eye.[106] To this end, some nineteenth-century Sufi treatises from the Caucasus provided detailed descriptions of the physical appearances of the foremost Sufi masters in the area.[107] Today such de-scriptions are replaced by photographs of Sufi masters, which their disciples are expected to carry at all times.[108] Thus, members of the Mah-mudiyya branch of the Shadhiliyya-Naqshbandiyya, headed by Said (Sa'id)-Afandi of Chirkey (al-Chirkavi) in Daghestan,[109] "are known for their use of photographs to better imagine the physical traits of their mas-ter."[110] On occasion, a photograph of a Sufi master, commonly called *ustadh* in Daghestan and Chechnya-Ingushetia, may trigger a person's conversion to a certain Sufi lineage (*tariqat, wird,* or *silsila*).[111]

Taken for granted by Muslim communities of the Caucasus in the past, such beliefs and practices now irritate, even enrage, local supporters of the Salafi-Wahhabi creed (*'aqida*),[112] who consider the majority of *tari-katisty*[113] to be misguided purveyors of *bid'a*.

The "battlefield notes" is just one of many examples of the Salafi-Wahhabi discontent with Sufism. In a Salafi newspaper published in Chechnya in December 1999,[114] Sufi masters are accused of pretending to have knowledge of the unseen (*al-ghayb*), which non-Sufi scholars con-sider to be the exclusive prerogative of God;[115] of surreptitiously inserting themselves between the believers and God to act as mediators between them; of claiming infallibility and divine protection from sin; and of ne-glecting the duty of jihad by collaborating with ungodly Muslim state au-thorities and non-Muslim enemies of the *umma*.[116] Some Salafi-Wahhabi

FIGURE 6.2. Said-Afandi of Chirkey (al-Chirkavi), head of the
Mahmudiyya-Shadhiliyya Sufi brotherhood in Daghestan. Assassinated
by a female suicide bomber in August 2012, his photographs have been
widely circulating in the Northern Caucasus over the past two decades.
Courtesy of the collection of Dr. Shamil Shikhaliyev.

objections may appear trivial, but are, in fact, symbolically significant
and capable of provoking violent confrontations between the opposing
parties.[117] Whereas evenhanded religious leaders of Daghestan such as
Akhmad-kadi (Ahmad-Qadi) Akhtaev (1942–1998) attempted to steer a
middle course between the two groups of believers, holding both equally
responsible for misinterpreting the Muslim creed,[118] in his videotaped
sermons and on pages of Daghestani newspapers the leader of Daghestani Salafis-Wahhabis, Bagauddin (Baha' al-Din) Muhammad Kebedov

(b. 1947)[119] accused Sufis of violating no fewer than one hundred rulings of the Shari'a(t).[120] The gravest of them, the eyes of Kebedov, is the assertion that Sufi *shaykhs*: (a) possess supernatural, God-given power and knowledge; (b) are divinely protected from error and delusion (that is, infallible in their thoughts and actions); (c) are capable of interceding before God for their followers; and (d) are worthy of unquestioning submission and obedience.[121]

Shifting his attention to the Daghestani social and political scene, Kebedov voiced his discontent with the fact that the *tarikatisty* have full control over the religious life of the republic, while depriving their ideological competitors of access to media outlets or membership in the republican Directory for Religious Affairs (DRA).[122] Neutral observers have confirmed that this accusation is not groundless. Both the republic's media outlets and the DRA are indeed monopolized by religious leaders with pro-Sufi views and Sufi credentials. Some are *murids* of Said-Afandi or other local Sufi masters.[123]

Tensions between Sufis and their opponents have tangible behavioral and social implications in the Muslim societies of the Northern Caucasus. Thus, before the crackdown on their movement by the Daghestani authorities in 1998–1999,[124] the local Wahhabis-Salafis routinely condemned their Sufi counterparts from the pulpits of mosques, refused to pray or eat with them, to marry their daughters, or attend their funerals. The Sufis paid them in kind by refusing to have any social interactions with them. They routinely branded the Salafis as grievous innovators who had abandoned the religious precepts of their forebears and, moreover, attempted to impose upon their communities an "alien," "bigoted heresy" that breeds "vicious sedition" and leads Muslims on the "false path."[125] Sufi leaders (*ustadhs*) had no compunctions about using their political connections and control over the republican DRA, as well as the majority of Islamic teaching institutions and mosques in the republic, to oust their Salafi-Wahhabi opponents from the Daghestani social and religious scene.[126] Similar events occurred in Chechnya, where the balance of power initially favored the pro-Salafi-Wahhabi party of Ichkeria[127] due to the active role that its members played in the armed resistance to the Russian federal troops as well as the generous funding it received from foreign donors.[128]

The rift between the Salafis-Wahhabis and the Sufis grew deeper following the denunciation of Wahhabism by several authoritative scholars of Daghestan,[129] including the republic's major Sufi teacher Said (Sa'id) Afandi Atsayev of the Avar village of Chirkey.[130] Until his assassination by a female suicide bomber in August 2012, Said-Afandi had the largest coterie of *murid*s in the entire Caucasus. His public lectures and sermons were widely disseminated via various media, including the Internet. They contain detailed denunciations of Wahhabism that are too long to be discussed here in detail.[131] We will highlight a few major points of Said-Afandi's anti-Wahhabi and anti-Salafi discourses. Most of them deal with practical, mundane matters, but some are theological in nature, such as a rather standard disparagement of the "Wahhabi sect" for its espousal of an anthropomorphic image of God.[132] Said-Afandi is particularly upset about the Salafi-Wahhabi denial of the intercessory powers of the Prophet (*shafa'a*), which they, in his words, consider "less effective than a walking stick one leans on."[133] He insists that the ability to intercede on behalf of one's followers is not restricted to the Prophet, but also possessed by his heirs, the Sufi *awliya'* who can serve as channels of communication to God for ordinary believers. Denying their intercessory and mediatory role, argues Said-Afandi, is not unlike denying the necessity of electric wires for transmission of electricity or TV for reception of images.[134] He also accuses his opponents of summarily excommunicating (*takfir*) their opponents—a practice, he argues, that is bound to stoke the fires of "a dirty [religious] strife" (Rus. *griaznaia smuta*) among the Daghestani Muslims.[135] In sum, according to Said-Afandi and his numerous followers,[136] Salafism-Wahhabism is a foreign implant that has been deliberately cultivated by the "godless West," especially the British Empire, whose rulers were eager to destroy its major geopolitical rival, the Ottomans, by depriving them of the control over the principal sanctuaries of Islam, Mecca and Medina. Because Sufism was a foundation of Ottoman power, it fell victim to the British anti-Sufi propaganda.[137]

While on the face of it Said-Afandi appears to be defending the supernatural power of the Prophet, which allows him to intercede on behalf of his community and that Salafi-Wahhabi leaders flatly reject, implicitly he defends the exclusive right of Daghestan's Sufi masters to be guides and educators of the local Muslims. This right, according to the Daghestani *ustadh*, devolved upon them through their adherence to the spiritual chain of succession (*silsila*) stretching back to the Prophet himself.[138] As we have noted repeatedly, the claim to special knowledge and authority to guide followers to salvation is crucial for the successful functioning of Sufism as a discipline that demands that adepts submit themselves unconditionally to their spiritual preceptor. Seen in this light, Said-Afandi's apology for the privileged knowledge of Sufi *shaykh*s and their God-given "right to guide"[139] the believers is just another evidence of this claim being as actual today as it was in premodern and early modern Muslim societies.[140] Inevitably, this claim clashes with the Salafi-Wahhabi insistence on God's being the sole source of knowledge and guidance for the faithful.[141] In a similar vein, Said-Afandi's Sufi claims also contradict the Salafi-Wahhabi idea that salvation is open to all believers on an equal basis, or, put differently, "everyone [is] equidistant from God" regardless of their personal origin and status.[142]

Heated polemical exchanges between Sufis and their Salafi-Wahhabi critics are not unique to the Caucasus. Today they take place with various degrees of intensity in practically every Muslim country as well as in Muslim communities residing outside the Muslim world proper. It is hardly surprising that both insiders and outsiders construe them as evidence of the longstanding and intractable conflict between these two interpretations of Islam.[143] However, in and of itself, this general observation does not carry far, for behind the apparent universality of the Salafi-Sufi conflict we find a myriad of indigenous factors that shape, often decisively, its concrete sociopolitical manifestations. In what follows we will examine several regional, historical, and cultural contexts in which this conflict has unfolded over the past several decades.

Daghestan and Chechnya

Islam is recast as a strategic factor only post hoc, *when there is a coincidence between ethnic and religious affiliations, for example, Muslim Chechens versus Orthodox Russians, or Christian Moluccans against Muslim immigrants from Borneo.*

—OLIVER ROY, *GLOBALIZED ISLAM:*
THE SEARCH FOR A NEW UMMAH

Our discussion begins with Daghestan—the probable homeland of the author of the battlefield notes. This former Soviet autonomous republic consists of a congeries of communities divided along ethnic and kinship lines, language, customs, historical experiences, and geographical locations (that is, highlanders versus lowlanders; inhabitants of the coastal areas as opposed to mountain communities of the hinterland; and so on).[144] The Daghestanis speak at least thirty-two different languages and constitute fourteen officially recognized nationalities, which were created, often arbitrarily, by the Russian and Soviet authorities.[145] The fact that they have ended up within the confines of the same autonomous republic is purely accidental—Daghestan's central plateaus and areas south of the Terek River are occupied by the Turkic-speaking Kumyks;[146] its southern areas, inhabited by the Lezgi nationality, could as well have been part of the Turkic-speaking republic of Azerbaijan; its northwestern areas—part of Chechnya; and its northeast—an integral component of the Turkic-speaking Nogay population of the steppe. Throughout the republic, Russian cultural and linguistic influence is predominant, especially in the urban centers and the capital Makhachkala.[147]

Before the Russian conquest, the motley populations of Daghestan used Arabic and Azeri Turkic as their lingua franca. After the Russian Empire had taken control of this rugged area around the middle of the nineteenth century after overcoming a fierce resistance of the local communities, Arabic remained the language of jurisprudence, culture, and administration until the late 1920s.[148] Islam in its Sunni Shafi'i, Hanafi, and Sufi forms has served as an important source of common identity for Daghestani Muslims as it was for their coreligionists in the Central and Western Caucasus (Circassia).[149]

During the first decades of the nineteenth century, the Russian colonization of Chechnya and Daghestan triggered a wave of rebellions among the local Muslim communities. Initially successful, they led to the creation in the 1830s–1850s of a jihad- and Shari'a-based state under the leadership (imamate) of three successive Avar warriors: Ghazi-Muhammad, Hamzat Bek, and Shamwil (Shamil).[150] Under Shamil, who relied heavily on Chechnya's warlike population, the North Caucasian imamate achieved the peak of its power only to be destroyed by a Russian expeditionary force in 1859. These dramatic events, known in Russian historiography as "the First Caucasus War," continue to inspire those Chechens and Daghestanis who seek independence from Russia and the establishment of an independent polity governed by the Shari'a(t).[151] In the aftermath of the fall of Shamil's imamate, both Daghestan and Chechnya witnessed several uprisings against Russian rule, although on a much smaller scale. Led by charismatic leaders with Sufi connections, they failed to achieve their goals.[152] Nevertheless, resistance to the Russian political and cultural domination of the region under religious banners continued after the Soviet takeover. It was suppressed by the fledgling communist state only in the late 1920s.[153] From that time on, Daghestan became part of the Soviet state with Soviet-style administrative, cultural, economic, and ideological practices aimed at erasing differences among the local nationalities and creating an internationalist, classless, and harmonious communist society united by a sense of common purpose and destiny.[154]

After the collapse of the Soviet Union in 1991, the Northern Caucasus experienced a major sociopolitical turmoil[155] that was accompanied, among other things, by the emergence of ethnic nationalist movements whose leaders demanded greater autonomy and, in the case of Chechnya, independence from the Russian Federation.[156] The Russian government under President Boris Yeltsin (1931–2007) responded positively to the demand for greater autonomy, but rejected independence out of fear that it would lead to the disintegration of the Russian federal state. In December 1994, following the declaration of independence by the Chechens led by the charismatic Soviet-era general Dzhokhar Dudayev (1944–1996), the Russian government sent a large, but poorly prepared and led military contingent to restore federal control over the rebellious republic. The Russian invasion triggered a bloody and ferocious Russo-Chechen war that lasted for two years (1994–96).[157] Faced with the overwhelming military superiority of a weakened but still powerful Russian state,[158] the Chechen separatists appealed to their fellow Muslims worldwide for financial and military support.[159] The appeal brought fruit, especially in view of the horrific devastation wreaked by the hostilities upon the Chechen civilian population and infrastructure. The independent government of Chechnya (called "Ichkeria" at the time) received substantial financial and moral support from Muslim NGOs.[160] In the meantime, the war attracted a number of foreign fighters (*mujahideen*) from the Arab world, as well as the Maghrib, Turkey, and Central Asia, who viewed it as yet another front in an epic battle between the Muslims and the meddling Christian West.[161] Launched as a movement for national liberation, the Chechen uprising gradually acquired a distinctive Islamic character with nationalist slogans giving way to the Islamist calls for the creation of a transnational and transregional Shari'a state and unification of the Muslims of the Caucasus into "the Caucasus Emirate."[162] Many Chechen field commanders and their fighters embraced Salafism-Wahhabism as their ideology of choice.[163] Sufis became their principal rivals in the struggle over which version of Islam the Chechens should embrace following the republic's declaration of independence from Russia in 1996.[164] After Chechnya had finally returned under Russia's tutelage in the early 2000s, the leaders of the republic adopted Sufism as the state ideology.[165]

The situation was different in Daghestan. After the fall of the Soviet Union, the republic's leaders did not seek independence from Russia. Recruited among former Communist Party and Komsomol apparatchiks, they were ready to settle for a broad autonomy within the Russian Federation.[166] For this, there were several reasons. Unlike a mono-ethnic Chechnya, especially after the exodus of its Russian-speaking population in the late 1990s, Daghestan's ethnic composition is extremely diverse.[167]

Throughout its existence, first under Russian and then Soviet rule, its territorial and political integrity has depended on the ability of both central
and local authorities to balance the aspirations of its ethnically, economically, and culturally diverse constituencies. Failure to maintain this balance threatened to bring about political fragmentation and interethnic violence. Under Soviet rule, the centralized state and party apparatus in
Moscow served as the vital arbitrator and diffuser of interethnic tensions
in the republic.[168] Alongside the coercive force of the Soviet state, the
Marxist-Leninist doctrine of supraethnic brotherhood of all the laboring
masses (the so-called proletarian internationalism) was cultivated by the
Communist Party as an ideological safeguard against ethnic conflicts and
separatism.[169] Nevertheless, Islam continued to play an important, if officially unacknowledged, role as a source of identity and cohesion.[170] Any
attempts by a Daghestani ethnic group to assert its ethnic exclusivity or
impose its will on the neighboring peoples invited a prompt and decisive
interference of the Communist Party and the Soviet state.[171] Nevertheless,
some Daghestani nationalities (for example, the Avars and Dargins) enjoyed more favorable treatment than others (for example, the Kumyks,
Nogays, Lezgis, and Laks).[172]

If we delve deeper into the region's history, after the collapse of the
resistance movement led by Shamil (Shamwil) in 1859, the Russian state
instituted the so-called popular-military form of governance (*voenno-
narodnoe pravlenie*) in the mountainous areas of central and western Daghestan. It granted a considerable level of autonomy to local village communities under the supervision of those of Shamil's former lieutenants and
military commanders (*na'ib*s and *dibir*s) who had agreed to submit to
Russian rule. The more uncompromising elements left the area to settle in
the Ottoman Empire.[173] Whereas the major urban centers of Daghestan
gradually succumbed to Russification and secularization, remote village
communities in the mountains were largely left to their own devices. The
Russian plan envisioned the creation of a congeries of egalitarian communities of free villagers (*jama'at*s) ruled by elected elders. In real life, the
leadership of such communities often fell into the hands of the former
nobility (the *bek*s and *khan*s) who came from the clans (*tukhum*s) that had
controlled the village communities before the Russian conquest. Thus, the
oft-claimed "egalitarian" character of Daghestani mountaineer communities is not only a relatively recent phenomenon; it is, largely, a historical
fiction.[174]

Leaders of Daghestani communities in villages and towns wore two
hats, as it were. In addition to administrative functions, they also per-

formed religious services as legal scholars (*fuqaha'*) and spiritual guides (*shaykhs* or *ustadhs*). In fulfilling this dual function, they availed themselves of the norms of the Shari'a(t) and the local *'adat* (customary law) to mediate conflicts in the communities under their jurisdiction.[175] For about a century and a half, such leaders constituted an informal judicial and spiritual authority that coexisted peacefully within the official structures of the Russian, and later Soviet, state. Although the village leaders usually abstained from openly challenging Russian and Soviet state structures in the region, they served as an important bulwark against Russification, Sovietization, and de-Islamization of the local populations. Following the Soviet drive to collectivize the agricultural sector of the economy and animal husbandry, many rural Daghestani communities (*jama'ats*) relatively smoothly morphed into Soviet-style collective farms (*kolkhoz*).[176] Despite the considerable efforts on the part of Soviet authorities to eradicate religious beliefs and practices among the Daghestani Muslims, they were preserved and reproduced thanks to the parallel structures of authority just described.[177] To propitiate secular state administrators and Communist Party functionaries of the republic, some pacifistically minded Sufi masters, such as Hasan Hilmi al-Qahi (Khasan-efendi Kakhibskii, 1852–1937),[178] argued that (a) "Soviet power liberates working masses from social and national oppression," which is exactly what "the Prophet Muhammad and his companions strove to achieve"; and (b) "in accordance with the Prophet's teaching, Soviet power seeks to establish peace and brotherhood among nations."[179]

In addition to the canonical Islamic rituals, Daghestani villagers practiced visits to the shrines of local holy men and women and performed *dhikr*, according to the rules of one of several regional Sufi brotherhoods.[180] Contrary to the commonly held stereotypes about the uncontested doctrinal and ritual predominance of Sufism in the area,[181] participation in *dhikr* assemblies did not necessarily mean active membership in a Sufi *tariqat* or *wird*.[182] The number of active, practicing members of the main local *tariqats* of the region (namely, the Naqshbandiyya, Qadiriyya, and Shadhiliyya) was and still is relatively insignificant compared to the overall number of the Daghestani Muslims. In general, loyalty was demanded by[183] and given to a concrete Sufi *ustadh* (in his capacity of a spiritual councilor, arbitrator of disputes, and expert on Islamic law) rather than the doctrines and practices of a particular Sufi institution (*tariqat*) or spiritual lineage (*silsila; wird*).[184]

Now, let us briefly examine the role of Sufism in Daghestani society over the past two centuries. Since the beginning of the Russian expansion into the areas in the early 1800s, both Russian and Western historians and colonial administrators have considered Sufism to be a major (if not the major) mobilizing ideology behind the mountaineers' resistance to the Russian conquest of the Northern Caucasus that persisted intermittently from the 1820s through the 1870s. Following the spread in the Caucasus of the teachings of the Naqshbandiyya-Mujaddidiyya-Khalidiyya brotherhood during the first two decades of the nineteenth century, it was used by three successive religious leaders of the mountaineers (Ghazi Muhammad, Hamzat Bek, and Shamil) to launch and sustain the local struggle against the Russian military advance and the colonial administration that came on its heels.[185] According to the proponents of the Sufism-as-resistance thesis, Shamil in particular was successful in transforming the precepts of the Naqshbandiyya-Khalidiyya into the effective ideological and organizational foundation of his religious polity, the imamate. More specifically, the scholars have argued that Shamil astutely exploited the Naqshbandi-Khalidi emphasis on the strict observance of the Shari'a and the brotherhood's hostility toward both non-Muslims and Muslim deviators (especially, the Shi'a) to consolidate his grip on power and to establish a centralized and efficient jihad state. Because Shamil's spiritual disciples, the *murids*, allegedly constituted the military backbone of this state, the movement itself was dubbed *muridizm* by contemporary Russian observers. What more evidence of Sufism's central role in Shamil's resistance movement would one need? By the same logic, following the collapse of Shamil's imamate, the mountaineers' continuing struggle against Russian domination was construed by both Western and Russian scholars as being Sufi in its inspiration and organization. In particular, the 1877 rebellion of the Khalidi-Naqshbandi *shaykh* 'Abd al-Rahman al-Sughuri (al-Thughuri; d. 1882) has frequently been cited by historians as a typical example of the key role that Sufism played in motivating anti-Russian insurgency in the Caucasus.[186] As a proof, they cite the fact al-Sughuri's disciples Najm al-Din Gotsinski (al-Hutsi) and Uzun Hajji[187] spearheaded a powerful "Sufi" rebellion in Daghestan, this time against the Soviets in 1920–21. Following the capture and execution of imam Gotsinski in 1925, the Daghestani Naqshbandiyya seems to have lost its militancy and maintained a low profile socially and politically throughout the Soviet rule that ended in 1991.[188]

In Chechnya, the collapse of Shamil's imamate in 1859 led to the shift of the resistance base from the Naqshabndiyya-Khalidiyya networks to the originally pacifistic local branch of the Qadiriyya brotherhood founded by the Chechen preacher Kunta Hajji (d. circa 1868).[189] Despite his avowed pacifism and inward orientation, for which Kunta Hajji was ostracized by

Shamil himself,[190] the stridently anti-Muslim policies of the Russian military officials in the area eventually forced Kunta Hajji's followers to turn their pacifistic movement into a vehicle of the Chechen-Inghush resistance to Russian colonial rule.[191] The Kunta Hajji *tariqat*'s numerous offshoots (known locally as *wird*s) survived the czarist-era repressions and played a pivotal role in helping the Chechens and the Ingush to survive the horrendous trials following their massive expulsion to Kazakhstan by Stalin's regime in 1944.[192]

Western proponents of the Sufi thesis, such as Alexandre Bennigsen, Chantal Lemercier Quelequejay, Marie Bennigsen-Broxup, Moshe Gammer, Anna Zelkina, and others, have argued that in the 1960s to 1980s Sufi brotherhoods in Chechnya and Daghestan served as the principal organizational vehicle and ideological motivation of the mountaineers' resistance to the atheistic rule of the Soviet state. Driven underground by the KGB, the leaders of the Sufi *wird*s never relinquished the hope of restoring Islam as the law of the land. This, so goes the argument, was hardly surprising, because the overwhelming majority of Daghestani, Chechen, and Ingush Muslims belonged to one or the other Sufi *wird*, which rendered Sufism the major bulwark against communist indoctrination and integration of the mountaineers into Soviet society. As we have argued elsewhere, this standard and widely accepted account of the central role of Sufism in the mountaineers' struggle against Russian and later also Soviet domination of the Northern Caucasus is problematic for several reasons.[193]

First, we find no evidence of a widespread network of Sufi lodges and *waqf*s associated with them, as was, for example, the case in Tripolitania, Cyrenaica, and Sudanic Africa, where these institutions were part of the hierarchically structured and socially and economically dominant Sufi brotherhoods, such as the Sanusiyya, Qadiriyya, Tijaniyya, and Muridiyya, throughout the late nineteenth and early twentieth centuries.[194] By making use of these resources, the Sanusiyya, Qadiriyya, several branches of the Idrisiyya, and the Tijaniyya, for example, were able to mount a relatively effective armed resistance to the colonial encroachments of the British, Italians, and the French.[195] Similar conditions did not obtain in the Northern Caucasus. This is not to say that individual Sufi masters there were unable to rally their followers against the Russian colonial advances in the region. Rather, we argue that the rebels being members of a Sufi lineage was not their primary motivation or source of legitimacy. In other words, their Sufi convictions and practices were purely accidental to their political and military decisions and actions. Moreover, and, this is our second point, the Daghestani resistance leaders mentioned earlier were not full-fledged *shaykh*s of the Naqshbandiyya-Khalidiyya in the Caucasus,[196] as is widely believed. Rather, they were disciples of two preeminent Sufi *shaykh*s of the area, Muhammad al-Yaraghi and Jamal al-Din al-Ghazighumuqi. The former apparently blessed the Daghestani-Chechen *ghazawat*[197] (possibly, for personal reasons), while the latter warned his disciples against pursuing it for both religious and military reasons.[198] The fact that the rebellious imams ignored their teacher's advice indicates that there was nothing intrinsically militant about the tenets of the Naqshbandiyya-Khalidiyya or, at the very least, that they yielded themselves to different, if not diametrically opposed, interpretations.[199] Our conclusion is further confirmed by the aforementioned transformation of the initially peaceful Qadiriyya of Chechnya and Ingushetia into a major organizational vehicle of active or passive opposition to Russian and later Soviet rule. Finally, we find no obvious link between the relatively standard moral-ethical precepts of the Naqshbandiyya-Khalidiyya[200] and the jihad-based ideology of anti-Russian resistance that, along with the enforcement of Shari'a(t) norms, constituted the chief legitimizing factor and raison d'être of Shamil's imamate as well as its earlier and subsequent reincarnations. If the Naqshbandi-Khalidi spiritual precepts and moral discipline were indeed the ideological foundation of anti-Russian resistance,[201] then they must have been recast by Shamil and his predecessors and successors beyond recognition to suit their military and political goals.

Elsewhere, we have tried to explain the persistence of the Sufi explanatory thesis in Russian and Western studies of the Northern Caucasus by tracing its origins back to the French colonial historiography of Algeria, whose creators, too, considered the local Sufi brotherhoods to be the bulwark of "obscurantism" and "fanaticism," in other words, the main obstacle to the French *mission civilisatrice* in the area.[202] The fact that Sufi leaders and institutions were blacklisted by both Russian and French colonial authorities as actual or potential troublemakers seems ironic today when numerous political scientists and policy makers routinely depict Sufism as a pacifistic, inward-oriented (and thus politically harmless) alternative to Salafi-Wahhabi social and political activism.[203]

Let us now sketch out the current religious and political situation in Daghestan in order to determine what role, if any, Sufi teachings, practices, leaders, or communities (*tariqat*s) may have played in the local societies following the disintegration of the Soviet state in the early 1990s. Because the situation in Daghestan is shaped by an intricate intertwining of numerous elements, a diagram is needed to clarify relationships among the actors and factors involved (see figure 6.3).

DAGHESTAN

SOVIET PERIOD: 1920s–1986

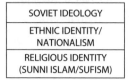

PERESTROIKA: 1986–1991

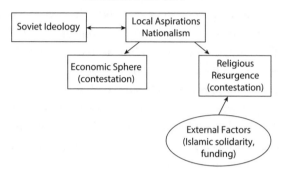

POST-SOVIET CHAOS, CONFLICT & CONSOLIDATION IN DAGHESTAN 1991–2016

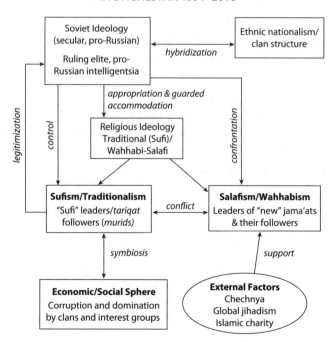

FIGURE 6.3. Daghestan diagram.

1. Soviet Period.

- Throughout the Soviet period (1920s–1986), Daghestan witnessed a curious coexistence of several ideologies. The official doctrine of the Soviet state cultivated an identity based on the Soviet value system with special emphasis on the equality of all members of society regardless of their regional provenance or social status in the name of "proletarian internationalism." This new, supraethnic and supranational (Soviet) identity was supposed to override and supplant the traditional affiliations of the Daghestani population (and the Soviet population generally), which were based on kinship, ethnicity, region, and religion. Eventually all Soviet nationalities were supposed to morph into a "new historical entity"—the Soviet people unencumbered by the "obsolete" loyalties and divisions that had prevailed in "bourgeois" or "feudal" societies.[204]

- In reality, ethnic identity (Avar, Lak, Lezgi, Dargin, Kumyk, Chechen, and so on) not only survived the communist social engineering, but was also reinforced even more, because access to resources and subsidies provided by the "Federal Center" in Moscow was spread unevenly among Daghestani ethnic groups at the republican level with some enjoying preferential treatment. The same applied to access to state power. On the regional level, affiliation with a given clan or family (and its traditional religious commitments that stubbornly refused to be overridden by proletarian internationalism) continued to be the most precious asset that frequently took precedence over loyalty to the Communist Party or the Soviet state.

- As in the nineteenth century (described above), the religious identity of the majority of the Daghestani populations was based predominantly on the Sunni Islam of the Hanafi or Shafi'i *madhhab*s and traditional (hereditary) association—often very loose— with several local Sufi *silsila*s (*wird*s) and their leaders.[205] The knowledge of Arabic was highly valued and constituted an important social and cultural asset for those lucky few who managed to learn it in Moscow or Leningrad.[206] Despite severe persecutions under the Soviet regime, the surviving Daghestani *'ulama'* and Sufi *ustadh*s managed to maintain the Muslim identity of the majority of the population via informal educational networks, especially home-based religious schools or *hujra*s.[207] This identity was periodically renewed by means of collective participation of Daghestani Muslims in the rites of passage (births, religiously officiated marriages, and funerals), prayers, festivals, and *dhikr* assemblies.[208]

- Throughout the 1970s, efforts by the local and central Soviet authorities to resettle various Daghestani communities from remote mountain areas to the plains resulted in an unprecedented admixture of various ethnic groups and deracinated elements in villages and towns on the plains. This transformation, which, to some extent, mirrored similar developments in other areas of the Muslim world,[209] led to the rise of a generation of young men and women whom some Daghestani observers[210] have called "new Muslims" or "new Dagestanis."[211] Subject to the new, unfamiliar living conditions marked by more impersonal, atomized, and "rationalized" (in the Weberian sense of the word) social intercourses, the traditional, localized patterns of religious belief and practice began to erode. The relatively cosmopolitan environment of the new settlements demanded new ways of doing things. Exposed to new ideas and practices, the postwar generation of the "new Daghestanis" began to forge their own version of Islamic doctrine, practice, and morality. Local historians and political scientists consider the 1960s and 1970s to be the turning point in the transformation of the local forms of religiosity. This transformation gave rise to new patterns religious and social life and a specific world outlook that its critics later summarily dubbed "Salafism-Wahhabism."[212] The critics represented the republic's secularized ruling establishment, on the one hand, and the traditional religious authorities, the Hanafi and Shafi'i *'ulama'* and Sufi *ustadh*s, on the other. For obvious reasons, both groups felt threatened by the assertive, well-educated, and vocal leaders of the new Muslim movement.[213] Their fears grew even stronger with the advent of the Soviet reformist initiative announced by the last Soviet president and, previously, the general secretary of the Communist Party of the USSR, Mikhail Gorbachev (b. 1931). Popularly known as perestroika (literally, "reconstruction" or "renovation"), it brought about long-ranging changes that its author could not foresee, eventually leading to his own downfall.

2. Perestroika: 1986–91.
  - The perestroika period witnessed the weakening and, occasionally, collapse of Soviet state structures and the discredit of the authority of the Communist Party and the "internationalist proletarian" ideology associated with it. As a result, the former Soviet

republic of Daghestan witnessed an explosive and often violent release of competing local aspirations, which one scholar aptly described as "the division of spoils of the Soviet Empire."[214] Contestation among and within the local elites (which were extremely competitive, territorial, and divided along ethnic, clannish, and regional lines) focused on the political, economic, and religious sphere with the more numerous and compact nationalities (such as Avars and Dargins) enjoying advantage over smaller and dispersed ones.[215]

- Activities of foreign religious missionaries, many of whom arrived from the Arab Middle East, especially the Gulf, Jordan, and Syria, became an important factor during the chaos and disorientation brought about by Gorbachev's perestroika. Their interpretations of Islam that were largely new to the locals fell on a fertile ground, as the majority of Daghestanis (this is equally true of the Chechens and Ingush) were already eager to rediscover implications of their Islamic identity. In being reintegrated into the imaginary worldwide Islamic *umma*, many local Muslims hoped to improve their material lot by benefiting from the financial support of international Islamic charities.[216] A massive influx from Saudi Arabia and the Gulf of the Salafi-Wahhabi ideas advocating the pristine teachings and practices of the first Muslim community[217] undermined the positions of the traditional Muslim authorities of the Caucasus societies and, by implication, those of the post-Soviet ruling officialdom associated with them.[218] Fueled by generous injections of cash from the Gulf and availability of Salafi-leaning or outright Salafi-Wahhabi education in the Middle East and south Asia, the imported brand of "true" (*istinnyi*) Islam was embraced by many Daghestani Muslims. It became a major ideological escape route for many young men and women from the grim realities of the last years of Soviet rule.[219] The major selling point of the Salafi-Wahhabi creed (*'aqida*) in Daghestan, as elsewhere, was its promise to "transform the humiliated, the downtrodden, disgruntled young people, the discriminated migrant, or the politically repressed into a chosen sect (*al-firqa al-najiya*) that immediately gains privileged access to the Truth."[220] Bearing in mind the fact that Sufi leaders, as we have seen throughout this book, also promise to guide their followers to the religious truth, this earthly bliss, and, eventually, salvation, a clash between the local version of Islam (either Hanafi, Shafi'i, or Sufi-based) and the new Muslims' movement, empowered by Salafi ideas, was simply inevitable. The same, to a large extent, is true of Chechnya, whose quasi-independent status vis-à-vis Russia between 1996 and 1999 gave free rein to foreign missionaries of various Salafi-Wahhabi persuasions to disseminate their creeds among the primarily youthful local constituencies eager for new ideological orientations and certainties.[221]

3. Post-Soviet Chaos, Conflict, and Consolidation.

• In Daghestan and Chechnya, the post-Soviet period witnessed the persistence of the Soviet mentality and modus operandi, namely, the instinctive suspicion on the part of the post-communist ruling elite of ideological pluralism and its readiness to use raw force, intimidation, and bribery to silence the opponent. Encouraged by the weakness of the "Federal Center" (the Russian federal government in Moscow), authoritarian inclinations and clannish loyalties of the Northern Caucasus elites became even more pronounced than in the Soviet era.[222]

• In Daghestan, the former communist functionaries and administrators smoothly transformed themselves into the new ruling class under then-fashionable democratic slogans.[223] These former Soviet apparatchiks retained their traditional subservience to Moscow, viewing the central government of the Russian Federation as the indispensable guarantor of their rule and a source of subsidies that were necessary to secure basic living standards for the republic's impoverished populations and to keep afloat its traditionally feeble and inefficient economy. The support of the Federal Center was particularly vital for Daghestan, which, unlike Chechnya, has scarce oil resources.[224] It also explains why Daghestani leaders were not so eager to cut loose from Russia after the dissolution of the Soviet Union.

• In Chechnya, on the contrary, the Soviet-style "patrocracy" (Rus. *patrokartiia*) was largely displaced by the ambitious professionals, former military officers, and freelance intellectuals, who were almost uniformly opposed to continuing Russian rule and wanted to leave the Russian Federation.[225] Riding on the wave of Chechen nationalism and the long-standing opposition of the Chechens to Russian rule, they managed to outflank the old guard. In their aspirations, they were aided by the incoherent Russian internal policy under President Yeltsin. As a result, a conflict broke out that led to Yeltsin's ill-advised military campaign

against the popular Chechen militias rallied around the former
Soviet general Dzhokhar Dudayev (1944–1996). The Russo-
Chechen war (1994–96) that ensued discredited those elements of
Chechen society that were ready to strike a deal with the Russian
federal authorities and to settle for autonomy within the Russian
state.[226] After wresting power from the pro-Russian elite, the new
generation of Chechen leaders was ready to go it alone in the hopes
of benefiting from the republic's oil resources and economic ties
with the wealthy countries of the Middle East, including Turkey.

- In both Daghestan and Chechnya, the role of ethnicity and clannish solidarity[227] increased as Communist Party loyalty and the
  official ideology of Soviet internationalism had become discredited and irrelevant to the daily lives of the former Soviet citizens
  (see figure 6.3). Simultaneously, religion became a vital marker of
  identity and source of legitimization for the ruling establishments
  of both Chechnya and Daghestan.

In the course of the momentous transformations outlined above there
emerged a symbiosis between the republican state structures and the
traditional religious authorities—'ulama' and Sufi shaykhs or ustadhs. It
has found its most vivid manifestation in the makeup of the Spiritual Directory of the Muslims of Daghestan (DUMD), whose members were
closely affiliated with popular Sufi masters, the aforementioned
Naqshbandi-Shadhili shaykh Said (Sa'id) Afandi (Apandi) of the Chirkey
village (aul) being the most powerful and influential of them all. An ethnic
Avar, Said-Afandi as well as half a dozen of his fellow Naqshbandi Sufi
masters of Avar, Dargin, and Kumyk background[228] established themselves as the paramount religious leaders of Daghestan.[229] They enjoyed
the support of the republican authorities and were effectively in control of
DUMD, the supreme religious governing body in the republic.[230] This is
not to say that the opponents of religious authorities associated with
DUMD were necessarily adherents of Salafism-Wahhabism. Some Naqshbandi shaykhs, such as Ramazavov of the town of Khasaviurt; Babatov of
the village of Kiakhulai; and Karachaev, Gadzhiev, and Iliasov of Makhachkala refused to recognize the legitimacy of DUMD and harshly criticized
it. Thus, one can speak of oppositional or rival trends within not just the
Daghestani Sufi establishment generally but also within the same Sufi silsila, the Naqshbandiyya. Moreover, the disagreements were primarily over
control of resources and appointments, not about religious matters per se.
This phenomenon, of course, has been typical of institutional (tariqa) Su-

fism almost since its inception. No matter how spiritual and high-minded they may appear to their followers or sympathetic outsiders, Sufi masters have remained competitive, territorial, and jealous of one another—a characteristic they share with the overwhelming majority of humankind.

The Weight of the Past and the Clash of New and Old Islams

The recent sociopolitical role of Sufism in Daghestan has important historical precedents. Here we find two different patterns of the interaction between Sufi leaders and the state. They are represented by two principal branches of the Naqshbandiyya in the area: one associated with the aforementioned 'Abd al-Rahman al-Sughuri or al-Thughuri (d. 1882), the other with the *shaykh* Mahmud al-Almali (d. 1877).[231] The former is considered, rightly or wrongly, as an advocate of the activist, jihad-oriented trend in the local Naqshbandi tradition. His son, Muhammad Hajji, was declared by his followers the leader (imam) of an anti-Russian uprising in Daghestan and Chechnya in 1877, and, after its failure, was executed by the Russian administration. Although 'Abd al-Rahman initially opposed the uprising, his prior support of Shamil's *ghazawat* and a prominent role he had played in Shamil's imamate made him a convenient symbol of the anti-Russian rebellion. Regardless of the fact that his own role and that of the Naqshbandiyya *tariqat* in the 1877 rebellion remain obscure,[232] it is popularly believed to have been considerable, if not decisive.[233] As we know well, popular perceptions do matter.

An alternative pattern of Sufi-state interaction is exemplified by the branch of the Naqshbandiyya *tariqa* inaugurated by Mahmud al-Almali (d. 1877). Named "Mahmudiyya" after its founder, its leaders, especially the popular *shaykh* Sayfullah-kadi (Sayf Allah al-Qadi; d. 1920),[234] consistently demonstrated restraint and even docility vis-à-vis the Russian state authorities in the region and were not averse to occasionally cooperating with them.[235] The close relations between the recent Naqshbandi leaders of Daghestan, especially the aforementioned Said-Afandi of Chirkey, and the authorities of the republic reflect the continuity of this pacifistic, collaborative trend in the local Naqshbandi tradition.[236] It is hardly surprising that Said-Afandi belonged to the same branch of the *tariqat* as Sayfullah-kadi and considered himself to be Sayfullah-kadi's spiritual inheritor and beneficiary.[237]

In sum, the history of the Naqshbandiyya *silsila* of Daghestan offers its present-day followers two diametrically opposed patterns of interaction with state authorities of the republic and of the Russian Federation more generally. Taking their cue from the pacifistic trend exemplified by Mahmud al-Almali and Sayfullah-kadi—the first Sufi *shaykh*s of Daghestan to combine the Naqshbandi and Shadhili spiritual lineages[238]—some Daghestani Sufi leaders today have consciously opted for cooperation with the predominantly secular, pro-Russian government of the Republic of Daghestan. In return, the authorities have granted them an almost exclusive control over the religious officialdom, represented by the republic's Spiritual Directory (DUMD), which is responsible for appointments to religious posts, disseminating religious education, and distributing funds allocated to it by the republican authorities.[239] The Directory's overall philosophy can be described as gradualist—while the enforcement of the norms of the Shari'a(t) and long-term goal of the creation of an Islamic state in Daghestan are given lip service, the republic's religious leaders content themselves with a step-by-step re-Islamization of the public sphere and education and, then again, within the limits set for them by the republic's secular leadership and the government of the Russian Federation.

Given the overall situation in Daghestani society in the post-Soviet era, as just outlined, it is hardly surprising that the "new Muslims" who oppose the rule of the pro-Russian elite tend to couch their criticism of the status quo in anti-Sufi rhetoric. As already mentioned, the leader of the Daghestani Salafis-Wahhabis Baha' al-Din Muhammad Kebedov (a.k.a. Bagauddin Magomed Kebedov) of Kizyliurt went on record by accusing Sufis of violating one hundred rulings of the Shari'a(t). After the activities and publications of Kebedov's party were banned by the republican parliament in December 1997, it went underground and has remained in opposition ever since. Kebedov himself fled to Chechnya where he was received with open arms by local warlords and politicians such as Shamil Basaev, Zelimkhan Yandarbiev, Movladi Udugov, and the Arab *mujahid* al-Khattab from Saudi Arabia (nicknamed "Black Arab" by the Russian media), who were seen by ordinary Chechens and Daghestanis as militant "Wahhabis" or "Salafi-Takfiri jihadists" par excellence.[240] Kebedov's Daghestani followers took an active part in the 1999 incursion into the Botlikh, Tsumadin, and Novolak districts of Daghestan of the Islamist militias led by Shamil Basaev and al-Khattab.[241] After the expulsion of Basayev's and Khattab's *mujahideen* to Chechnya by Russian armed forces in September 1999, the Daghestani Salafi communities either followed them or went underground and started an undeclared war against their persecutors, the local police, Russian federal troops, and secret service (FSB) operatives.[242]

Started as the Chechen-led incursion of several detachments of *mujahideen* into Daghestan, the war now shifted back to Chechnya, where it continued unabated for several years with much devastation and heavy casualties on both Russian and Chechen sides.[243] Throughout the 2000s, the pro-Russian republican authorities of Daghestan and the Russian federal troops operating in the area kept announcing the discovery of yet another cache of weapons and "extremist Wahhabi" literature and video and audio cassettes. Such reports indicate that in their struggle against their enemies Salafis-Wahhabis of the Northern Caucasus availed themselves of both military and ideological means.[244] Until the pacification of Chechnya under Ramzan Kadyrov (b. 1976) in the mid-2000s, life in the republic was being shaped decisively by the bloody confrontation between the Russian military contingent stationed in the republic and the Chechen *mujahideen* seeking independence from Russia for the sake of building an Islamic polity, the Caucasus Emirate. Already at the beginning of this military conflict, political power shifted from the followers of the largely pro-Russian population of the Chechen plains to the warlike clans of the mountainous Ichkeria.[245] Pertinent to our subject, the largely pro-Russian population of the Chechen plains have been traditionally associated with the Naqshbandiyya *tariqat*, whereas the warlike clans of the mountainous Ichkeria adhered to various branches of the Qadiriyya founded by Kunta Hajji; there are around thirty branches (*wird*s) of this *tariqat* in Chechnya. Some observers have gone as far as to present, inaccurately it seems, this transition of power as a decisive triumph of the activist Qadiriyya over the pacifist Naqshbandiyya.[246] Interestingly, the situation seems to have been exactly the opposite under Shamil's imamate.[247]

In the course of their unequal struggle against the Russian state, the Chechen *mujahideen* were supported by Muslim charities worldwide. This support often came in the form of both funding and ideology, the latter being for the most part of Salafi-Wahhabi inspiration.[248] The majority of non-Chechen fighters in Chechnya were Salafis-Wahhabis of various ethnic backgrounds who professed a global jihad and viewed the local religious customs and traditions as gross "aberrations" of "true Islam" that must be corrected or extirpated.[249] As in other areas of the Muslim world, their righteous anger often targeted local sanctuaries and saints' tombs.[250] At one point, the Salafis attempted to destroy the tomb of Kunta Hajji's mother at the village of Gehi—a major Chechen sanctuary that attracts hundreds of pilgrims from across Chechnya and Ingushetia.[251] Chechen Wahhabis led by the former Chechen president Zelimkhan Yandarbiev,

Shamil Basayev, Arabi Barayev, and 'Abd al-Malik Mejidov (Medzhidov) became the principal opponents of President Aslan Maskhadov, who relied on the support of traditional leaders, including the chief mufti of Chechnya, Ahmad (Akhmet) Kadyrov, an *ustadh* of the Qadiriyya *tariqat*, who later threw in his lot with the Russians and was assassinated by his Salafi-Wahhabi enemies.[252] In 1996, the leaders of the two major Sufi *tariqat*s of Chechnya joined forces in order to challenge the ideological and political ascendancy of their Salafi-Wahhabi opponents.[253] The conflict between the two factions came to a head in the Chechen town of Gudermes in the summer of 1998 when an armed confrontation between a Salafi-Wahhabi detachment and the fighters loyal to President Maskhadov (1951–2005) resulted in heavy casualties on both sides.[254] In sum, whereas the disagreements between the two sides of the confrontation were (and still are) largely over strategic sociopolitical goals and means to achieve them, they have been routinely couched in a religious idiom that stresses the incompatibility of Sufi and Salafi-Wahhabi versions of Islam.[255] Presented this way, the conflict acquires a lofty and even transcendent significance. To say that you are fighting to fulfill the will of God and defend pure Islam is not the same as saying you are fighting to improve your personal earthly lot or the political fortunes of your clan or your comrades-in-arms. Therefore, when Olivier Roy says, "Islam is never a strategic factor as such,"[256] he has a point.

Over the past decade Chechnya has remained relatively peaceful under the local strongman Ramzan Kadyrov, who has shown himself to be a staunch supporter and promoter of the "traditional Chechen" Islam that is closely associated with the local branch of the Qadiriyya order established by Kunta Hajji Kishiev.[257] In line with the thinking current among numberless policy makers and political analysts worldwide, Kadyrov and the religious officials of Chechnya loyal to him promote the rituals and teachings of Sufi Islam as an alternative to Salafi-Wahhabi militancy and extremism.[258] With the blessing and encouragement of the all-powerful ruler of Chechnya, the stirring sounds of the vocal Qadiri *dhikr* are now ringing across the breadth and width of the land. Grounded in the pacifistic, otherworldly oriented preaching of Kunta Hajji, Sufism serves not only as a means to legitimize Kadyrov's rule[259] but also, more subtly, to justify his conciliatory stance vis-à-vis the Federal Center in Moscow. After all, as we have argued elsewhere, Kunta Hajji preached peace with Russia to the war-weary Chechens following the collapse of Shamil's jihad state.[260] In a cruel irony of fate, Kunta Hajji's pacifism did not save him from the suspicions of the Russian military administrators who exiled him to northern

Russia, which led to his premature death of illness and malnutrition.[261] Incensed by this injustice, his followers subsequently adopted a more aggressive policy toward the Russian military and civilian presence in the Northern Caucasus, for which the Russian authorities paid dearly in human life and materiel.[262] Originally a vehicle of inward-oriented self-reflection and self-improvement, Kunta Hajji's Sufism transformed itself into a basis of resistance, both passive and active, to Russia's colonial rule and cultural domination. It confirms our earlier observation that actions of a Sufi-based movement, or any Islamic movement for that matter, are decisively determined by its sociopolitical environment and personalities of its leaders. Seeing Sufism (or Islam as a whole) as a self-sufficient motivating factor and actor is nothing but delusion. Its precepts and organizational structures can be used toward different ends by different actors. These ends can be pacifist, neutral, or militant.

Turning now to Daghestan, as already mentioned, in 1998–99 the Spiritual Directory of the Muslims and Republican Parliament of Daghestan declared the "Wahhabi sect" to be enemy number one of the Daghestani state and of "traditional Islam." Salafi-Wahhabi educational institutions and presses were shut down, while the movement's suspected sympathizers denied religious appointments not only in the religious governing bodies of the republic, but as *muftis*, *qadis*, and *khatibs* of urban and village mosques as well. The chief religious official of Daghestan, Abubakarov, who was a follower of Shaykh Said-Afandi of Chirkey, went as far as to declare that "a believer who kills a Wahhabi will go to Paradise, as will a believer killed by a Wahhabi."[263] The opponents responded violently by assassinating both men in 1998 and 2012, respectively. These dramatic events are indicative of the deadly consequences that Sufi-Salafi doctrinal and ritual disagreements are bound to produce under favorable (if one can use this adjective) sociopolitical conditions.

Hadramawt: Between Genealogical Privilege and Demands for Egalitarianism

Our second case study takes us to Hadramawt, an eastern province of the Republic of Yemen, which until 1990 had been part of the People's Democratic Republic of Yemen (PDRY), a client state of the Soviet Union in the Arabian Peninsula from 1969 until 1990.[264] In the early 1970s, the radical Communist-Maoist rulers of the PDRY launched a violent atheist campaign against Islam, destroying or desecrating saints' tombs and arresting and murdering religious scholars or forcing them to emigrate.[265] However,

it soon became obvious to the iconoclasts that Islam was too deeply entrenched in South Yemeni society to be eradicated overnight even with the
harshest of measures.[266] The state policy toward Islam had to be changed,
and it was, gradually. Muslim scholars, who remained in the country, were
left alone as long as they refrained from challenging directly the secular
ideology promoted by the ruling elite educated in the Soviet Union or the
Socialist countries of Eastern Europe. One should point out that the ideological precepts of the Yemeni Socialist Party (YSP), which were alien and
incomprehensible to the overwhelming majority of the Yemeni population,
bore a close resemblance to the Soviet ones, as described in the previous
section of this chapter in connection with Daghestan and Chechnya. Like
other aspects of social, political, and economic life of the PDRY, its leadership's atheistic attitude to religion was inspired by the official Soviet ideology. After studying Marxism-Leninism in the countries of the Soviet bloc,
Yemen's Socialists were eager to create a Soviet Socialist republic on the
southern tip of the Arabian Peninsula. They justified their policies toward
Islam and its local exponents by citing the Marxist-Leninist doctrine of
class struggle and proletarian revolution. Seen through this ideological
prism, the members of Yemen's religious establishment would appear
to be backers of the "feudal, comprador classes" or a "parasitic religious
aristocracy."[267] This ideological cliché seemed to be particularly actual for
the province of Hadramawt where the overwhelming majority of men of
religion came from the local families that claimed descent from the
Prophet via his cousin 'Ali and his daughter Fatima. Collectively known as
al-sada,[268] they had often occupied positions of authority in the governments of the local sultans before and after British rule,[269] while also playing important roles in the transmission and preservation of Islamic learning not just in Hadramawt, but throughout the Muslim world as well.[270]
A British visitor to Hadramawt in 1959 observed:

> The sherifs' whole position rested on their descent, ritual competence,
> and the belief in their power to bring blessing, education, and knowl-
> edge of Islamic law.[271]

It is hardly surprising that after the departure of the British and the
communist takeover of the country in 1968–69,[272] the secular-minded
leaders of the YSP came to see the sada as dangerous ideological and political rivals in the struggle for the hearts and minds of the local population.[273] Using their newly acquired political power, Yemen's communists
visited severe reprisals on prominent representatives of the sada stratum,[274] forcing many into exile to North Yemen and Saudi Arabia.[275] We

have examined the fortunes of the *sada* of Hadramawt elsewhere and will not repeat ourselves.[276] Interestingly, the Socialists were not the first to accuse the Hadrami *sada* of claiming a special status in Hadrami society in order to derive the tangible economic and social advantages that came with it.[277] During the first decades of the twentieth century, opposition to the religious and cultural domination of the Hadrami *sada* was spearheaded by the so-called *Irshad* (Right Guidance) movement active in Southeast Asia (primarily in Java and Singapore).[278] Unlike the secularist, class-struggle rhetoric of the Yemeni Socialists of the 1970s and 1980s, the early twentieth-century Irshadi criticism of the Hadrami *sada* was articulated in religious terms, reflecting the reformist tendencies of the age, emanating from Egypt, where the influential reformist-modernist journal the *Beacon* (*al-Manar*) was published.[279] The Irshadi critics of the *sada*, who usually came from non-*sada* Hadrami families or the local Malay-speaking population, accused them of violating the principle of equality of all Muslims, clannish nepotism, and cultivating "idle superstitions" and "idolatrous practices" centered on the tombs of their ancestors.[280] The *sada*'s disregard for the principle of equality of all Muslims before God, according to the Irshadis, found its most dramatic expression in their marriage customs, which prohibited female members of the *sada* stratum (*sharifas*) from marrying men of non-*sada* background, whether Hadrami or not. The male *sada*, on the other hand, were (and still are) free to marry whomever they want(ed) with the parents' blessing. The dispute over this fraught issue was important enough to attract the attention of a leading Muslim reformer of the age, Muhammad Rashid Rida (d. 1354/1935).[281] He weighed in by ruling against what he considered the incorrect interpretation by the *sada* of the Islamic juridical principle of marriage parity (*kafa'a*).[282] In a *fatwa* published in *al-Manar*, Rashid Rida excoriated the Hadrami *sada* for their commitment to genealogical exclusivity, arguing that Muslims' relative excellence should be determined by their piety and moral character, not kinship.[283]

It is highly significant that the anti-*sada* polemical attacks originated in the Hadrami diaspora in Southeast Asia, especially in Java and Singapore.[284] In Hadramawt itself, whose society was socially and economically backward and intellectually conservative, the position of the *sada* as the privileged and indispensable purveyors of moral-ethical guidance and religious education for the local population remained unchallenged up until the triumph of the Yemeni leftists in 1968–69.[285] The leftists appropriated the Irshadi religiously inflected objections to the privileged status of the *sada*[286] but couched them in the rhetoric of the Marxian theory of social equality and proletarian struggle against what they labeled "parasitic feu-dal classes."[287] In the Marxist-Leninist nomenclature of the YSP, the *sada* families of Hadramawt fit neatly into this unenviable social category.

When the questioning of their privileged status started in the Southeast Asian Hadrami diaspora in the first decade of the twentieth century, the *sada* protested, but did not respond with a single voice. Some members of the Ba 'Alawi lineage accepted, at least partly, the Irshadi criticism and adopted a reformist, egalitarian stance promoted by their detractors.[288] A lack of alignment along kinship lines in this momentous dispute is further reflected in the fact that many conservative Hadramis of non-*sada* extrac-tion sided with the *sada* organization named the (Ba) 'Alawi League (*al-Rabita al-'Alawiyya*) against their non-*sada* detractors from Irshad.[289] The same is largely true of the more recent situation in Hadramawt and in the Hadrami diaspora around the Indian Ocean: the supporters and de-tractors of the *sada* do not fit neatly into prefabricated sociological and genealogical cubbyholes. Nevertheless, one can still discern some general tendencies in the social behavior of *sada* families as well as their ability to close ranks when attacked.

Dar al-Hadith versus Dar al-Mustafa: In Search of Authenticity

The resurgence of Islam as an ideological and social force in South Yemen in the aftermath of the collapse of the pro-Soviet regime and the unifica-tion of the country in 1990 has taken a variety of forms (see figure 6.4). Many variants of Salafi ideology, from the reformist-modernist one of the Muslim Brothers to the literalist and apolitical one of the *ahl al-hadith* movement of Shaykh Muqbil al-Wadi'i (d. 2001) of the Sa'da region of North Yemen,[290] had gained wide acceptance in many areas of Yemen with a partial exception of Hadramawt.[291] Here the positions of conservative, shrine-centered Islam proved to be particularly entrenched. The country's very landscape bears a vivid testimony to its prominence. Wherever one goes, one inevitably observes whitewashed domed shrines of God's friends (*awliya'*) and prophets (*anbiya'*). They dominate the Hadrami landscape, often competing with mosques in architectural elaboration and grandeur. The ritual calendar of the area is punctuated by seasonal pilgrimages (*hawl; ziyara*) to these shrines. Festive and colorful events, these pilgrim-ages draw hundreds, even thousands, of visitors from across the country and abroad.[292] Following the rapid collapse of the Socialist government of the country in 1990, the *sada* of Hadramawt became active promoters and

HADRAMAWT

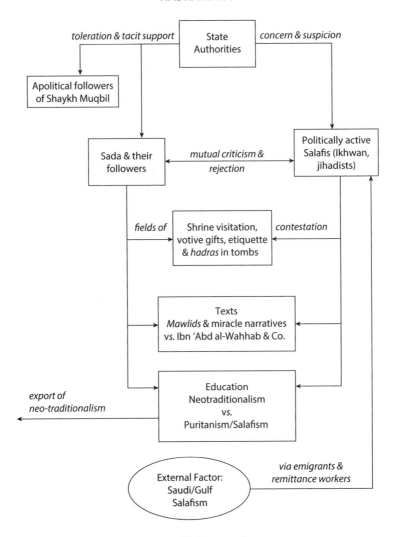

FIGURE 6.4. Hadramawt diagram

defenders the traditional religiosity that they presented as "authentic" in contradistinction to various versions of Salafism-Wahhabism that they declared to be a detrimental "innovation" (*bid'a*) in religion.[293] The result was truly impressive. Hadramawt's out-of-the-way, sleepy and dusty towns Tarim, al-Shihr, and Saywun have become a magnet for hundreds of pious visitors and avid students from all over the world.[294]

These obvious local advantages notwithstanding, the neo-traditionalist project of the *sada* had to compete with rival visions of Islam—mostly of a Salafi slant—and up until 1994, also with a revamped Socialist ideology

FIGURE 6.5. The Seven Domes of the town of 'Inat in Hadramawt, Yemen. One of the tombs contains the remains of Shaykh Abu Bakr b. (bin) Salim, ancestor of Habib 'Umar bin Hafiz (Hafidh) depicted on fig. 6.6. The photograph was kindly provided by Dr. Ismail Alatas of New York University.

that had survived the unification of the northern and southern parts of Yemen in 1990.[295] Interestingly, after the unification of the country the Socialist leadership of Yemen's southern part sought a rapprochement with the *sada* and their local followers, seeing in them a counterweight to the growing preponderance of the northerners, especially activist groups that espoused various versions of Salafi doctrine and practice.[296] Thus, the aforementioned Salafi preacher Muqbil al-Wadi'i accused the Socialist governor of Hadramawt of supporting the local Sufis (*sufiyyat Hadramawt*), while persecuting their Salafi-minded critics among the province's youth (*al-shabab*) who had called upon their opponents to "adhere to the [Holy] Book and the Sunna [of the Prophet]."[297]

The situation in the south was further complicated by the arrival of the political heavyweights from the country's north, namely, the ruling General Popular Congress and its ally-turned-rival, the Islamist "Reform" (*al-islah*) party. Both parties were eager to fill in the ideological vacuum left by the discredited Socialist rule and its Marxist-Leninist ideological foundations. The new political players made extensive use of religious rhetoric and slogans to rally the electorate and secure seats in the Yemeni Parliament in

Sanaa. In the ideological struggle among these various factions, Islamic education became a major focus of contestation. The *sada* families, which had either lived in exile or kept a low profile under Socialist rule, now saw in the ongoing religious resurgence an opportunity to restore their former privileged status in Hadrami society. Leaders of the *sada* considered religious education an important, if not the principal, means toward this goal.[298] Hadramawt's patriarchal, secluded, and religiously conservative society, which is relatively free from numerous "temptations" (*fitan*) and the "wickedness" (*fasad*) of modern urban life, has turned out to be a major selling point for avid seekers of Islamic authenticity who flocked to Hadramawt from both Muslim and Western countries.[299] The same, curiously, applies to the anti-Sufi, nonpolitical Salafi educational institutions of North Yemen that, too, have attracted "a certain number of foreign students who admire the 'authenticity' of [patriarchal] Yemen."[300]

Since the early 1990s several Islamic colleges run by Ba 'Alawi *sada* have sprung up in Hadramawt and elsewhere. Their main asset was their claim to revive and promote unalloyed, traditional religiosity, in which the *sada*'s vision of Islam generally and local history and culture in particular had an important role to play. It is noteworthy that this vision implicitly or explicitly ascribes the major cultural, economic, and religious achievements of Hadrami society to the members of certain *sada* families by portraying them as tireless social reformers, religious educators, and spiritual guides of not only of the Muslims of Hadramawt proper but also of Muslims worldwide.[301]

The most vivid example of a *sada*-sponsored educational effort was the establishment in 1993[302] of a neo-traditional *madrasa* in Tarim, the major spiritual center of the *sada*, located in the Hadrami hinterland. Known since 1997 as the House of the Elect One (*Dar al-Mustafa*),[303] it is headed by a charismatic *sayyid* preacher Habib 'Umar bin Hafiz. Son of a respected scholar of Tarim who is believed to have been kidnapped and executed by the secret police of the PDRY under the Socialists,[304] Habib 'Umar and his fellow instructors actively promote traditional Islamic education and ritual practices.[305] In Hadramawt, "traditional" implies observing the ritual calendar activities centered on the tombs of "righteous friends of God" (*al-awliya' al-salihun*)—most of whom come from the clans of the local *sada*—and those of the Arabian prophets, Hud, Salih, Hadun, and others.[306] Both types of the sacred sites and the ritual and educational activities associated with them are patronized by a number of the prominent and wealthy families of the Ba 'Alawi *sada*. As mentioned, under the Socialist regime, YSP's attempts to eradicate seasonal pilgrimages to the local shrines came to naught,[307] so upon his arrival from exile, the young *sayyid* Habib 'Umar b. (bin) Hafiz and his fellow *sada* scholars found the shrine-centered pattern of religious behavior of the local population still very much intact. All the enterprising *sada* had to do was to reinvigorate it through their patronage and by rendering it the centerpiece of Dar al-Mustafa's ritual and pedagogical activities.[308] Their efforts bore fruit. Since its foundation in 1997, Habib 'Umar's Islamic college has acquired a truly international reputation, attracting numerous students from East and South Africa, Yemen, Arab countries, South and Southeast Asia, and some Western countries (Britain, North America, France, Australia, and Italy). The female section of the *madrasa*, called the House of the Flower (*Dar al-Zahra*), houses around one hundred students.[309]

The Dar al-Mustafa curriculum features, in addition to the study of the classical Sufi works of al-Harith al-Muhasibi (d. 243/857),[310] Abu Talib al-Makki (d. 386/996),[311] Abu Hamid Muhammad al-Ghazali (d. 505/1111), 'Abd al-Qadir al-Jilani (d. 561/1166),[312] and 'Abdallah b. 'Alawi al-Haddad (d. 1132/1720),[313] a daily recitation of *mawlid* poetry, especially al-Busiri's *Qasidat al-burda*,[314] an internationally acclaimed example of the *mawlid* literary and devotional genre, as well as odes to the Prophet composed by local *sada*. Practically every day, Habib 'Umar and his students visit Tarim's famous cemetery Zanbal and the graveyards of the city's environs to recite litanies and homiletic poems inside the domed tombs of the *awliya'* buried therein or in the memorial mosques dedicated to and named after them. The annual pilgrimage to the grave of the Qur'anic prophet Hud[315] in Wadi Masila is performed with great pomp and videotaped, whereupon the footage is disseminated via local retail shops and Internet websites (see figure 5.1).[316] Organized and led by Habib 'Umar and his relatives from various respectable *sada* clans, the Hud pilgrimage[317] attracts large crowds from across Hadramawt and beyond, including, ironically, Saudi Arabia,[318] whose religious authorities vigorously condemn such events as expressions of idolatry (*shirk*). In short, Habib 'Umar and his numerous relatives of *sada* extraction (pl. *haba'ib*) associated with Dar al-Mustafa take the leading role in these and other devotional, educational, and missionary activities in Hadramawt. To distinguish themselves from the crowd, they wear a characteristic garb of Hadrami *sada* and accept token gestures of respect (such as the highly ritualized gesture of grabbing and kissing the hand of a *sayyid*)[319] from their disciples and other Muslims, who recognize their special status and authority (*jah*).

When questioned about their identity by an outsider, Habib 'Umar and his faculty and students are usually reluctant to explicitly recognize them-

FIGURE 6.6. Habib 'Umar bin Hafiz (Hafidh) of the Abu
Bakr b. Salim family of the *sada* in Hadramawt, Yemen.
This photograph, taken in 1999, is one of many circulated
in Hadramawt in the 1990s and 2000s. It was given to the
author by a street vendor as a talisman in Tarim,
Hadramawt, in November 1999.

selves as Sufis. Rather, they would speak of themselves as the restorers of
the traditional Hadrami Islam, the Islam of the great scholars and saints
of that Arabian country, whom they occasionally refer to as "[pious] ancestors" (*al-salaf*). In this sense, they certainly are "Salafis," albeit their definition of who exactly should be included into this category is at odds with
that of their Salafi critics, who have in mind Muhammad's first converts
and followers in Mecca and Medina.[320] In any event, the question of Sufism looms large on the intellectual horizon of the leaders of Dar al-
Mustafa. In an interview on May 14, 2009, published by alhaddad.org,
Habib 'Umar has defined Sufism as:

> The desire to purify the heart and perfect one's following of the Prophet
> Muhammad (Allah bless him and grant him peace). If that is what is
> meant by the word "Sufism," then its usage is only positive. We should
> not, however, let a word become a barrier preventing people from

knowing its true meaning. . . . Call it by another name if you do not like the word "Sufism": call it "Ihsan" or "knowledge of the inward" or "purification of the soul." Call it what you will, but the concept remains the same and we will not allow a mere word to become a cause of conflict and something, which prevents people from knowing the reality of the concept.[321]

When pressed, the teachers of Dar al-Mustafa might acknowledge the special merits of the method of the 'Alawiyya *tariqa(t)*. Named after the common ancestor of all local *sada* (who are known collectively as "Banu 'Alawi" or "Ba 'Alawi"), it combines two spiritual genealogies—that of the Shadhiliyya of North Africa and that of the Qadiriyya of Iraq.[322] However, most of the *sada* and their followers at Dar al-Mustafa would hasten to add that the 'Alawiyya spiritual method rests squarely on the Qur'an and Sunna and their elucidations by the foremost *sada* and non-*sada* Sunni scholars over the centuries.[323] Therefore, those Muslims who thoroughly implement the precepts of the Qur'an and Sunna in their lives are, in essence, following the method of the 'Alawiyya *tariqa(t)*.[324]

This is not how outsiders view the situation. Neutral observers refer to the followers of Habib 'Umar simply as "Sufis," while their detractors (who are quite numerous outside Tarim) denounce them as "grave-worshipping Sufis" (*al-quburiyun al-sufiyun*) and "[Sufi] purveyors of idle superstitions" (*ashab al-khurafat*).[325] The 'Alawiyya *tariqa*, in its turn, stands condemned by its opponents as a family affair whose heads covertly subjugate their non-*sada* membership to their will by forcing them to engage in heretical and outdated customs. The *sada* do this, so goes the opponents' argument, exclusively in order to preserve and justify their privileged social status in Hadramawt and beyond.[326]

The most vocal critics of Habib 'Umar describe themselves as "Salafis" (*al-da'wa al-salafiyya; salafiyya daw'iyya*).[327] Locally known as "supporters of [prophetic] *hadith*" (*ahl al-hadith*) or "supporters of the [Prophet's] Sunna" (*ahl al-sunna*), many of them are followers of the firebrand north Yemeni Shaykh Muqbil b. Hadi al-Wadi'i (d. 2001) of the Sa'da region in the northern part of the country.[328] The *ahl al-sunna* have their own religious institution called Dar al-Hadith, which has been functioning in the town of al-Dammaj, Sa'da, since the early 1980s. Home to almost one thousand students, including foreigners,[329] Muqbil's center at al-Dammaj may have given Habib 'Umar the idea to establish his own Dar al-Mustafa, possibly, as an educational alternative to the existing Dar al-Hadith. Be this as it may, both Dar al-Hadith[330] and Dar al-Mustafa have numerous branches across the country, including the port city of al-Shihr in Hadramawt,[331] which the author of this book visited in November 1999.[332] For their critics, the *ahl al-sunna*, are, of course, proponents of "Wahhabism"—an ideology that the *sada* and their followers denounce as alien to the spirit and letter of Hadrami and Yemeni Islam. It is even more suspect in the eyes of the locals because of its association with neighboring Saudi Arabia, both a geopolitical rival and a constant threat to Yemen's sovereignty and territorial integrity.[333]

Objectively speaking, Shaykh Muqbil, who received his education in Saudi Arabia under its foremost scholars (especially 'Abd al-'Aziz b. Baz and Nasir al-Din Muhammad al-Albani),[334] can be regarded as a Wahhabi, although his Wahhabism is rather unusual in its strict literalism and flat rejection of any form of political action.[335] Throughout his career, Muqbil continually railed against any political activity in the name of Islam, viewing it as a violation of Islam's original precepts, as he understood them. In particular, he went on record as a vocal critic of the Muslim Brotherhood: both its founding fathers (al-Banna and Qutb) and their recent followers, such as Muhammad al-Ghazali; al-Sha'rawi; Sa'id Hawwa;[336] 'Isam al-'Attar; 'Abd al-Hamid Kishk; Muhammad Surur Zayn al-'Abidin;[337] Hasan al-Turabi; and Muhammad Qutb, brother of Sayyid Qutb, who was executed by Nasser's regime in 1966.[338] Shaykh Muqbil, who was famous for his caustic and cantankerous temperament, jokingly dubbed the Muslim Brothers as *al-ikhwan al-muflisin*, that is, the "failed or bankrupt brothers."[339] Practically no modern Muslim scholar or Islamic movement of note has escaped Shaykh Muqbil's vitriolic condemnations, with the partial exception of Ibn 'Abd al-Wahhab (d. 1206/1792) and al-Shawkani (d. 1250/1834).[340] In general, Shaykh Muqbil's spirited tirades boil down to one principal theme—the ubiquitous presence of innovation (*bid'a*) in Muslim religious doctrine and practice. He was particularly concerned about the detrimental effect on the *umma* of the Shi'is, Sufis, communists, and "excommunicators" (*jama'at al-takfir*), namely, those puritanically minded Muslims who are prone to declare their fellow Muslims infidels for the slightest sin or slippage, for example, smoking tobacco.[341] He also rejected genealogically based claims to a special status in Yemeni society made by the *sada* and some other local kinship groups.[342] While calling on the Yemeni Muslims to cleanse their faith and practice of innovations and adopt the pious ways of the first Muslim *umma*, Shaykh Muqbil warned them against succumbing to the insidious erosion of Islam's moral-ethical values under the influence of Western secular ideologies and social practices.[343] In sum, Shaykh Muqbil saw his chief goal in forestalling the religious and moral decline of Muslim societies not through political participation or armed struggle (both of which he rejected),[344] but through inculcating in Muslim youth the "authentic" doctrines and practices of early (Salafi) Islam in a virtuous, sin-free environment.[345] Since the correct belief and virtuous way of life are enshrined in the prophetic Hadith, Muqbil named his educational institutions "houses [for the study] of Hadith" (sing. *dar al-hadith*).[346] In Muqbil's "educational fundamentalism" (*salafiyya 'ilmiyya*)[347] there is no place for the political action that is the preferred method of activist Salafis (*salafiyya munazzama* or *salafiyya harakiyya*), along the lines the Muslim Brothers and other Islamist movements (for example, Hizb al-Tahrir or Yemen's Islah). According to Shaykh Muqbil, the leaders of these movements and their misguided followers have succumbed to the grievous *bid'a* of mixing religion with politics. Their main mistake, he argued, is their desire to overthrow the incumbent rulers of their states who, corrupt and inefficient as they may be, are still nominally Muslim and therefore must be obeyed no matter what.[348] Basing himself on his apolitical principles, Shaykh Muqbil denounced Muslim reformers and modernists of the turn of the twentieth century, especially Muhammad 'Abdo and Muhammad Rashid Rida, as purveyors of detrimental innovations. In particular, their fascination with non-Islamic, Western values and institutions, such as parliament, pluralism, democracy, political parties, and electoral politics, was, according to Shaykh Muqbil, absolutely incompatible with the original teachings of the Qur'an and the Prophet's Sunna.[349] Sufis, too, did not escape Muqbil's condemnation for their alleged propensity to all manner of "heretical," "non-Islamic" beliefs and practices,[350] many of which have already been enumerated earlier in this chapter and need not be repeated here again.[351]

At stake in the Salafi-Sufi polemic in Yemen, represented respectively by Dar al-Hadith and Dar al-Mustafa, is the issue of authenticity. Each side claims to be uniquely and exclusively indigenous and authentic, while dismissing the opponent as a poacher intruding onto the religious hunting ground without a license, as it were.[352] For the Sufis, the Salafis-Wahhabis are the poachers who have brought with them onto the pristine soil of Yemen undesirable foreign (Saudi) implants. For the Salafis, on the contrary, Sufism is an alien good smuggled surreptitiously into the field of the pristine Islam of the pious ancestors (*al-salaf al-salih*) exemplified by the Prophet's Hadith. In this way, each of the two communities, which have extensive transnational connections and coteries of foreign students, seeks to position itself as the sole representative of the authentic Yemeni religion and by extension, nationhood as well. Their vigorous rivalry over religious and national authenticity casts doubt on Olivier Roy's fashionable theory of a transnational, "deterritorialized" Islam that is somehow "de-linked" from any specific national culture or history.[353] To succeed in spreading their teachings and practices, leaders of both the quietist Sufis of Dar al-Mustafa and the quietist Salafis of Dar al-Hadith[354] skillfully adapt to and make use of the local realities, beliefs, issues, fears, and expectations. Their overall strategy consists of outbidding the opponent in the competition for Yemeni authenticity. This strategy is essential to counter accusations of being foreign agents, of the West, Malaysia, or Indonesia in the case of Habib 'Umar's Sufis,[355] or of Saudi Arabia and its Wahhabism in the case of Shaykh Muqbil's Salafis.[356] Contrary to Roy's thesis regarding the ascendancy of what he calls "deterritorialized and deculturized Islam," for foreign Muslim students of both institutions, the attraction lies precisely in their deep embeddedness in the realities of local life and culture whose archaic, seemingly premodern nature exudes the air of Islamic authenticity. Again, *pace* Roy, this particular Muslim constituency is definitely interested in practicing a culturally specific, primeval, and even exotic Islam, not its abstract, deterritorialized, and deculturized distillation.

Following the unification of the two parts of Yemen in 1990, the northern leaders found it convenient to use the nascent Islamic (Islamist) movements and parties of the country in order to counter and discredit the residual secular ideology of the now defunct Socialist regime of the south.[357] On the eve of the first general elections in 1993, the regime of Sanaa blessed the creation of a motley religious-political coalition named "Reform" (*al-Islah*) whose main raison d'être was to divert votes from the southern Socialist leaders.[358] After the north militarily defeated the south in 1994, the active, politically involved Islah, which had made extensive use of Islamic slogans and rhetoric, became an unwanted rival to the President 'Ali 'Abdallah Salih and his party, the General Popular Congress (GPC). With the Socialist leadership in exile, the regime no longer needed the support of Islah's Islamically oriented membership.[359] Moreover, the president and his retinue were understandably apprehensive of the presence in the movement of Salafi war veterans (*al-salafiyya al-muqatila*), who had fought against the Soviets in Afghanistan and who had embraced the idea of "jihad without borders" against the world's superpowers and their Muslim backers.[360] The local jihadists' attacks on US military personnel stationed in Yemen and off the Yemeni coast created a major problem for the government of 'Ali 'Abdallah Salih that was keen on cooperating with the United States in return for economic assistance and international recognition.[361]

This cooperation became particularly close after the tragedy of September 11, 2001, when the Yemeni government accepted US troops and special operations units as part of the controversial "war on terror." Naturally, the government's actions caused a furor among the local Islamists, who threatened to take up arms against the "impious" Yemeni rulers, viewing them as agents of the "world's greatest oppressor of the Muslims."[362] To deflect this religion-based criticism of the jihadists and politically active Islamic parties generally, the country's leaders began to cultivate apolitical and quietist groups acting in the name of Islam. The two major local purveyors of "authentic Islamic education" fit the bill perfectly—the ultraconservative and quietist followers of Shaykh Muqbil, who staunchly opposed any involvement in politics, and the inwardly oriented devotees of Habib 'Umar bin Hafiz (Hafidh). Both groups had wide-ranging transnational connections[363] and placed a special emphasis on the "internal" (spiritual and moral-ethical) as opposed to the "external" (armed) jihad.[364] Thus, in a strange quirk of fate, the two ideologically incompatible and mutually hostile movements have found themselves in the Yemeni state's good books or, to put it differently, in the same (a)political camp.[365]

In the aftermath of the devastating civil war of 1994, during which a group of former South Yemeni political leaders attempted to secede from the north, the relations between Islah and Dar al-Mustafa developed in ways that the Yemeni government in Sanaa had not anticipated. Although many members of Islah were moderate Salafis (in line with his apolitical principles Shaykh Muqbil advised his followers against joining the ranks of this party), who viewed the activities of Dar al-Mustafa through the prism of the Salafi doctrine, that is, as "idle superstitions and grievous innovations," the two sides recognized that they had a common cause. Their shared goal was to re-Islamize the country's south with the view to eliminating vestiges of the atheist Socialist ideology that was still entrenched among the local elites. Despite Habib 'Umar's declared opposition to parties and electoral politics[366] (on this point he was in agreement with Shaykh Muqbil), there is evidence that Dar al-Mustafa's implicit support was essential in securing votes for the Islah party in inner regions of Hadramawt during the election of 1997 and afterward.[367] However, after Islah had opted out of the Yemeni government, the leaders of Dar al-Mustafa moved closely to the official government party, the GPC, eventually becoming its discreet but loyal ally in Hadramawt.[368]

It is noteworthy that, at some point, the leaders of Dar al-Mustafa also established good relations with the traditional opponents of Sufism, the

Zaydi al-Haqq party of the north, who in the past had shown themselves to be Sufism's implacable and occasionally violent persecutors.[369] The common ground was found in the two sides' shared conviction that the descendants of the Prophet are divinely chosen to provide religious guidance to their compatriots.[370] In short, both the Sunni *sada* of the south and the Shi'i *sada* of the north appealed to their common prophetic ancestry to overcome their long-standing doctrinal disagreements[371] for the sake of preserving Islam's role as the foundation of Yemeni society. All these facts demonstrate the political and diplomatic acumen of Habib 'Umar and his fellow *sada* at the helm of Dar al-Mustafa, who are not averse to making compromises with their opponents when it comes to implementing larger social and religious agendas. One such agenda, for the Ba 'Alawi *sada*, is to keep Hadramawt devout, socially and morally conservative, even patriarchal. This condition is a sine qua non for attracting to Hadramawt international students who seek a conservative type of Islamic piety uncontaminated by modern-day social, political, and cultural innovations. This goal is not unique to the denizens of Dar al-Mustafa. Tactical and doctrinal differences apart, it is also fully shared by the Salafis of Dar al-Hadith and the Zaydis of the al-Haqq party.

Who, then, are the principal opponents of Habib 'Umar and his followers in Hadramawt? They are not necessarily the adherents of Shaykh Muqbil, who, to our knowledge at least, has never had a large following in the province.[372] Rather, they are young men who have worked or studied in Saudi Arabia and the Gulf, where they imbibed the anti-Sufi and anti-saint message disseminated by local Salafi-Wahhabi preachers. On returning to Hadramawt, this fabled country of saints, they are sorely tempted to implement the famous Hanbali-Wahhabi precept of enjoying the good and forbidding the evil.[373] Hence, their verbal and occasionally physical attacks on what they regard as transgressions against the pure Islam of the pious ancestors. For the young repatriates steeped in Saudi Salafism, numerous tombs of Hadrami *awliya'* and the rituals associated with them epitomize the "non-Islamic" superstitions of "Sufi innovators and grave-worshippers" against whom the Saudi fundamentalist preachers never tire of railing.[374] As in the Northern Caucasus, these puritanically minded young Muslims demonstrate their protest against the status quo by refusing to attend the mosques of their "Sufi" opponents or to celebrate their "illicit" holidays (for example, *al-mawlid al-nabawi*; *al-isra' wa 'l-mi'raj*) out of fear of being contaminated by these "grievous innovations." The Salafi-trained youth believe that the only authentic, pure Islam is the one practiced in Saudi Arabia and the Arab Gulf states. It has assured, so they think, these Arabian countries the material prosperity that contrasts so sharply with Yemen's abject poverty.

Sufis and the State

In the Northern Caucasus, Yemen, and across the rest of the world, in conflicts between Sufi communities and their Salafi detractors, state authorities tend to side with the former.[375] While still in power, President 'Ali 'Abdallah Salih of Yemen demonstrated his approval of the activities of the Dar al-Mustafa compound in Tarim by paying several visits to it. Before his regime collapsed in 2012, the leaders of Dar al-Mustafa had enjoyed excellent working relations with the Yemeni ministry of the *awqaf*, and Habib 'Umar was generously granted time on the state TV and radio stations. He also served on several governmental committees, including one charged with the rehabilitation of Yemeni *mujahideen* returning from Afghanistan and other flash points.[376] One can hardly suspect the Yemeni regime of 'Ali 'Abdallah Salih of having a soft spot for Habib 'Umar's version Sufism or his educational project more generally. As with the majority of politicians, the Yemeni president and his retinue acted pragmatically in accordance with the principle of the lesser evil, which under the circumstances was to support the least politically active actors in society. In Dar al-Mustafa and Dar al-Hadith the regime's officials found a convenient counterweight to political activism and militancy in the name of Islam at the time when their cooperation with the US "war on terror" had exposed them to a vocal Islamist backlash.[377]

Rumors have it that the activities of Dar al-Mustafa were partly subsidized from the state coffers, although the accuracy of this information is impossible to ascertain, because of its potentially damaging impact on the educational project's reputation. In any event, whatever help Dar al-Mustafa may have been receiving from the Yemeni state before the Arab spring of 2011 is insignificant compared with the generous private donations from Indonesia, Malaysia, the UAE, Oman, and other countries of the Gulf, whose religious and political establishments have maintained close relations with the Dar al-Mustafa's leadership via its able emissary Habib 'Ali al-Jifri (b. 1971).[378]

In the educational institutions established by Habib 'Umar bin Hafiz and 'Ali al-Jifri and propagated by their followers in the East and in the West[379] we find a dynamic transnational religious movement that makes extensive use of the modern media and information technology to disseminate their message and to promote their version of Islam as uniquely primeval, authentic, yet open-minded. To the outside world the Dar al-Mustafa leadership projects itself as the moral-ethical bulwark against secularization and the attendant "moral decay," on the one hand, and, on the other, against the "hijacking" of Islam by "radical and extremist elements" who manipulate this religion of peace toward their destructive, inhumane ends.[380] Basically the same can be said about the Dar al-Hadith of the late Shaykh Muqbil and his successors in Yemen and abroad.[381] Their dissimilar religious ideals, which loom so large in analytic and media discourses about Islam, turn out to be of secondary importance after all. What matters is their (a)political stance.

Conclusions

In each Muslim society we have examined, the role of Sufism is determined by a complex interplay of social, political, and economic factors and actors, which makes any broad generalizations about it tenuous at best. What is abundantly clear is that Sufism—whatever phenomena and characteristics this notion may comprise in each particular case—is deeply embedded in the history, culture, and social and power relations of concrete Muslim societies. It cannot be properly understood in isolation from them. At the same time, Sufism is also distinct enough from non-Sufi versions of Islam and other Islamic movements to allow us to use this notion as an analytic tool. No matter how much we may be opposed to artificially detaching Sufism from Islam, actors on the ground have been doing this and will continue to do so in the foreseeable future. Thus, regardless of our personal preferences, we have no choice but "to follow the actors themselves."[382] If the actors' irrepressible drive to dichotomize Islam into Sufism and non-Sufism, while giving lip service to Islam's underlying unity, may appear contradictory to us, this is our problem, not theirs. After all, Islam and Sufism are full of paradoxes.

There are several features that the very different societies we have examined in this chapter seem to share. One is their transitional, unstable character. In the Caucasus as in Yemen, we have witnessed a momentous transition from one or the other version of political and ideological authoritarianism to a relative openness, pluralism, and ideological competition in the public sphere. Characteristic of this new sociopolitical condition is the emergence of the theretofore relatively inactive (dormant) actors that avail themselves of religious rhetoric to win the hearts and minds of various potential constituencies. The presence of choice is eminently important in that it creates what some Western researchers have described as "a religion market" with its rules of circulation, exchange, and marketing of the product for global consumption.[383] In the era of the Internet, domestic debates and rivalries often acquire long-ranging international repercussions. Rival parties promote disparate religious visions, agendas, and identities, appealing to the pristine purity and authenticity of Islam as represented by its pious ancestors or forebears (*al-salaf al-salih*). The identity of the ancestors, as has been shown, constitutes the crux of the disagreement among the disputants. Another feature that the Northern Caucasus and South Yemen have in common is their Soviet-Socialist past. In both cases the void created by the collapse of the Soviet Union and its ideological foundations led to a vigorous religious revival. As a result, the old communist clichés were replaced by religious ideologies with strong nationalist undertones. It is with these general considerations in mind that we will now summarize the conclusions that we have drawn for the vicissitudes of the Salafi-Sufi conflict in the Northern Caucasus and South Yemen (Hadramawt).

1. In both cases, the majority of Sufism's critics belong to the younger generation. While on the face of it the youth attack what they call "Sufism" or "traditional Islam" (the two are often rhetorically fused, rightly or wrongly) for their departure from the pristine, authentic Islam of its pious founders, they are driven by a conscious or unconscious desire to liberate themselves from the entrenched structures of power, loyalty, and authority. In the Northern Caucasus, these structures are represented by official Muslim scholars on the state payroll, who are usually affiliated with, and derive their authority from, a Sufi *silsila* or *wird*. Hence the conflation, in the minds of the critics, of Sufism with "what has gone wrong with Islam today." In addition to their desire to break away from the established networks of kinship and patronage, the Chechen and Daghestani Salafis consider their "pure" (*chistyi*) Islam of the *salaf al-salih* to be better suited for their ultimate goal: to join the imagined global *umma* unencumbered by the parochial conventions, rituals, and loyalties of their homeland.[384] In forging and promoting the notion of a pure, transnational Islam, the Salafis of the Northern Caucasus have acquired a powerful idiom to express their dissatisfaction with the status quo that has traditionally favored the older generation, while demanding unquestionable obedience of the younger one. We have observed a similar situation in

Hadramawt, although there the use of the egalitarian rhetoric of Salafism was fueled by the old popular resentment against the religious and social inequality based on genealogical claims of a number of the privileged *sada* families. The fact that the *sada* used a genealogy-based version of Sufism, the Ba ʿAlawiyya *tariqa(t)*, to support their claims made it a particularly convenient target of Salafi criticism.

2. Although discontent with the status quo can, in theory, be expressed by invoking a militant and activist stream within the Sufi tradition—this is true of Chechnya and Daghestan, but not of Hadramawt, where such tradition does not exist—the strident and pervasive criticism of Sufism by adherents of Salafism-Wahhabism in the past few decades has rendered the Sufi option unappealing to those who seek solutions to their problems in Islam. In a sense, Salafi-Wahhabi versions of Islamic ideology, at least at this historical stage, have turned out to be more effective, persuasive, and fashionable as a vehicle of protest, probably because of their simplicity, straightforward logic, and their modern, rationalist rejection of the miraculous and the fanciful, all of which resonates with the dominant intellectual attitudes of the present age.

3. In Hadramawt, Salafism derives its vitality from the country's proximity with and economic and political dependence on Saudi Arabia and the other Gulf states, in which the local version of Salafi-Wahhabi ideology is virtually unchallenged as long as renegade preachers do not use it to undermine the authority of the ruling family.[385] Many young men of Yemeni and Hadrami backgrounds are exposed to its tenets during their stay in these countries as remittance workers. By attending the often vitriolic sermons of Saudi and Gulf scholars they internalize the Wahhabi concepts of *tawhid*, *bidʿa*, and *shirk*, as well as the concomitant injunction to actively practice their religious convictions by condemning and fighting against "heretical" or "deviant" forms of Islamic doctrine and practice. On returning to their homeland, they immediately recognize numerous "deviations" from the principles of *tawhid* in the beliefs and practices of their "deluded" compatriots. What the young repatriates used to take for granted prior to their emigration to the Gulf now strikes them as a grievous heresy, or even outright unbelief (*kufr*). Very often they identify these deviations from the true Islamic creed as being "Sufi" in their origin or inspiration. In Hadramawt, when outsiders see the residents of

Dar al-Mustafa traveling to local shrines and memorial mosques in a fleet of cars chanting *mawlid* hymns, they almost invariably attribute their actions to their "Sufi" training at the hands of the "heretical" Ba 'Alawi *sada*.

4. In societies ravaged by war, social upheavals, and ideological transformations, Salafi-Wahhabi teachings become a particularly attractive option for disoriented youth. While in Yemen a quietist, Muqbilian version of Salafism gained popularity under the relative stability of 'Ali 'Abdallah Salih's regime, it has since been supplanted, at least in part, by the militant, politically oriented Salafism of the al-Qa'ida in the Arabian Peninsula (AQAP).[386] The country's recent and ongoing turmoil has favored the more radical elements, which the law enforcement units, secret police, and army had previously managed to hold in check. In Chechnya and Daghestan, too, the dire conditions brought about by the hostilities between the Chechen separatists and the Russian military have favored the most radical and jihad-oriented forms of Salafism (including terror against civilians). The fact that in the 1990s this militant trend of Salafism triumphed over its more moderate forms as well as over the traditional beliefs and practices of the Chechen Muslims, whether explicitly Sufi or not, can be attributed to the trauma and devastation of the war. Even today in Chechnya the cooperation between Russian federal authorities and the native power brokers associated with the local *wird*s (for example, the Kadyrov family) continues to breed resentment among mostly young men and women who have lost their relatives during the conflict and who are keen to exact revenge on the offenders. It is hardly surprising, despite the severities of Kadyrov's regime, that they occasionally adopt the jihadi version of Salafism-Wahhabism as their ideology and practice of choice.[387]

5. External factors and actors play an important role in sustaining tensions between various Sufi and Salafi versions of Islam. Conflicts between the two factions can be artificially cultivated or even deliberately induced by state authorities to weaken religious opposition to their rule. It is surprising to what extent both the Sufis and their Salafi opponents are penetrated and manipulated by state authorities and the state's secret agents.[388] In most cases, as we have already mentioned, the state chooses to cultivate a local Sufi community, viewing its members as a lesser evil, because of its assumed inward orientation and apolitical stance. Leaders of Sufi

communities, in their turn, often take advantage of their favorable treatment by the state in order to promote their disciples to positions of authority and, in so doing, to manipulate the state apparatus and its resources to their advantage.

6. In the case of external financial assistance, it is often the Salafis-Wahhabis who stand to benefit from the largesse of charitable foundations, most of which are based in the oil-rich states of the Gulf. The donors are naturally inclined to promote the version of Islam dominant in their own societies. One can even argue that in some cases "collective conversion" of activist religious groups to Salafism-Wahhabism is encouraged primarily by the promise of foreign financial assistance. Hence, the notion of "dollar Islam" that has been a stock in trade of the Russian media coverage of the troubles in the Northern Caucasus.[389] At the same time, the cordial relationships between Dar al-Mustafa and individuals and institutions in the Gulf are indicative of a relatively new tendency among the elites of the Salafi-Wahhabi states to support less politically active and vocal movements.[390] No more playing with fire, as it were. A quiet and almost invisible revival of Sufi teachings and movements in the Gulf area seems to indicate that they are no longer perceived by the authorities as a threat, especially in the light of the recent outbursts of Islamic militancy associated with home-grown Salafi groups of *mujahideen*.

7. It appears that individuals with a secular education are more prone to embrace the straightforward and seemingly rational teachings of Salafism. In Daghestan, for instance, an observer describes them as cell-phone-toting physicians, students, professors, businesspersons, and even former Komsomol functionaries.[391] However, this membership pattern may undergo drastic changes in times of armed conflicts, when the Salafi-Wahhabi recruitment pool becomes more inclusive and attracts elements from both the bottom and the top of the local social hierarchy.

8. As already discussed in chapter 2 of this book, a comprehensive and exhaustive definition of Sufism remains elusive. As we have seen, it depends largely on the position of the observer: what he or she recognizes or does not recognize as belonging to "Sufism" is usually determined by his or her intellectual background, group or class membership, professional goals and training, and personal life experiences.

9. In some Muslim communities of the Northern Caucasus, the concept of Sufism as a distinctive historical tradition within Islam has not yet taken shape. For instance, in Ingushetia uneducated men and women identify themselves not as followers of the abstraction called "Sufism" or even a concrete Sufi *tariqa(t)*, but rather as "spiritual children" of an authoritative spiritual guide, the *ustadh*. The fact that this *ustadh* happens to be the recipient of a certain Sufi spiritual pedigree (*silsila*)[392] is largely irrelevant to them. As already mentioned, loyalty is usually owed and given to a concrete *shaykh* or *ustadh*, not to Sufism as a whole.

10. The increasing (and now ubiquitous) use of this broad and elastic category to make sense out of certain practices, beliefs, and institutions appears to have been a largely unintended result of academic and theological studies of Sufism in the Muslim world and in the West. As we have seen, such academic and theological discourses often construe Sufism as a readily definable object as well as a self-sufficient and independent actor and factor operating freely in the societies and cultures in which it is embedded. When this reified theoretical construct leaves the narrow confines of theological seminaries or academic institutions and enters the public sphere, it acquires a life of its own. Once in the public sphere, this theological and academic abstraction begins to shape the ways in which ordinary Muslims think and speak of their faith and practice. In so doing they unwittingly contribute to metadiscourses on Sufism whose vicissitudes we have discussed earlier in this study. We have reason to believe that our own academic work has contributed to the popularization and use of such metadiscursive formations. A Russian translation of our book *Islamic Mysticism: A Short History*[393] has been recommended by the Supreme Council of the *ulama'* of the Russian Federation for study by Russia's Muslims.[394] One can only speculate how our present attempts to recontextualize and reimagine Sufism by placing it into the complex web of social relations and competing political interests will affect its perception by both its supporters and detractors.

Conclusion

*Believing, with Max Weber, that man is an animal suspended in webs of
significance he himself has spun, I take culture to be those webs.*

—CLIFFORD GEERTZ, *THE INTERPRETATION OF CULTURES*

IN THE COURSE OF OUR JOURNEY across time and space, we have made
several discoveries about Sufism and Islam as objects of knowledge. One
is that their history exhibits more continuity and less disruption than we
have previously admitted. The other is that they are products of collective
efforts and perspectives of both insiders and outsiders that are in dialogue
with each other. The combination of the inside and outside perspectives is
key to our understanding of Sufism as a historical phenomenon. In the
words of the late Patricia Crone, when "people see things from their own
perspective, much of what they say adds up to comforting ideas or outright
propaganda for themselves and the groups to which they belong." Furthermore, continues Crone, they "believe their own propaganda because they
cannot see that this is what it is: the bias is invisible because the angle
which produces it is felt as normal, not as a perspective peculiar to a specific group (you cannot see it unless you stand outside it)."[1] For the sake of
the accuracy of representation both insiders' and outsiders' perspectives
need to be combined. This combination may encourage at least some insiders to step back and evaluate their tradition and experience from a
broader, more comprehensive vantage point, thereby making them aware
of their affinity with similar traditions and experiences worldwide. Muslim
or not, outsiders' perspectives also help insiders to realize the normative
nature of the beliefs and practices they often take for granted. The entire
body of early Sufi literature is actually about convincing Muslims of the
correctness and legitimacy of the ascetic-mystical stream of Islam. By seek-

ing to convince others, one inevitably convinces oneself. Relationships between insider and outsider visions of Sufism in the modern age are more
complex than in premodern times, because outsiders now are not fellow
believers who are ready to give ear to Sufi arguments. Today, outsiders are
often armed with an enormous amount of relevant information about the
vicissitudes of various religions and their ascetic-mystical variants across
the globe. Access to this information and use of the modern analytic tools
may occasionally convince the outsiders of the superiority of their "scientific" vision of Sufism compared to the "devotional" one espoused by the
insiders. At the same time, for the academic outsiders who are lodged in
institutions producing highly valued scientific knowledge, their research
methodologies and analytic tools, such as "sociology," "anthropology," and
"discourse analysis" may become a religion of sorts. If they are not wise
enough to curb their academic hubris by taking seriously the insiders' perspective, they are likely to embarrass themselves as they did in failing, for
example, to make sense of the recent religious resurgence throughout the
globe[2] and in Muslim societies in particular or, for that matter, the Arab
spring of 2011 and its unexpected and confusing aftermath. In these and
similar events the much-lauded methods of social and political sciences
have demonstrated the powers of foresight and understanding that are
close to nil. This was truly a humbling and sobering experience, but has
anyone pursuing these academic professions taken heed?

As far as Sufism is concerned, its decline and even impending demise
was taken for granted by many Western outsiders in the first half of the
twentieth century,[3] but lo and behold, adapted to the new realities and
animated by modern communication technologies and social media, it is
now on the rise again. Real life will have many more surprises for academic
observers of human beliefs and practices, so a quantum of humility is the
best remedy from overconfidence in one's analytical and methodological
prowess. Nevertheless, as already mentioned in the introduction to this
book, objectively speaking, the understanding of Sufism by both insiders
and outsiders has grown more sophisticated and accurate over the past two
hundred years. The credit for this goes to both sides. This obvious fact
bodes well for Sufism and its students as long as they are aware that their
approach to the subject is not the only possible and correct one.

Al-Ghazali and many others have argued that rational investigation of
the world rarely if ever brings happiness and tranquility to the investigator,
whereas the knowledge and insight offered by ascetic-mystical convictions
and practices do. The veracity of this proposition is confirmed by Sufism's

abiding appeal to various constituencies inside and outside the Muslim world. After examining the historical development of Sufi metaphysics, gnoseology, pedagogy, and institutions, we can add that, for an outsider, this promise of Sufism is but a beautiful dream, beaconing temptingly from afar, but always elusive, never fulfilled.

In citing works in the notes, short titles have generally been used. Works frequently cited have been identified by the following abbreviations:

EI_2 *Encyclopedia of Islam*, 2nd ed. (Leiden: E. J. Brill, 1954–2004). http://referenceworks.brillonline.com/?fromBrillOnline=true.

EI_3 *Encyclopedia of Islam*, 3rd. ed. (Leiden: E. J. Brill, 2007). http://referenceworks.brillonline.com/?fromBrillOnline=true.

JRAS   *Journal of the Royal Asiatic Society*, London. http://royalasiaticsociety.org/journal/.

JSAI   *Jerusalem Studies in Arabic and Islam* (Jerusalem: Hebrew University of Jerusalem). http://www.hum.huji.ac.il/english/units.php?cat=859.

Q   The Qur'an. Two English translations (with occasional emendations) have been used: Arthur Arberry, trans., *The Koran Interpreted* (New York: Simon and Schuster, 1996), and Muhammad Asad, trans., *The Message of the Qur'an* (Gibraltar: Dar al-Andalus, 1980).

ZDMG   *Zeitschrift der Deutschen Morgenländischen Gesellschaft* (Berlin: Otto Harrassowitz). http://www.dmg-web.de/?page=6.

NOTES

Introduction

1. Following David Carr (1892–1982), Hayden White defines emplotment as "a product of an arbitrary imposition by the historian of a narrative *form* on what would otherwise be a non-narrative *content*. . . . As thus envisioned, historical narrative is a peculiar kind of discourse, the product of a process of verbal *figuration*," a creative reconfiguring of "stories about the same set of events" that use "the various *techniques* of narration, such as characterization, thematization and emplotment"; the function of emplotment in particular, argues White, is to give the original messiness and chaos of reality the coherence it does not, cannot possess; see Hayden White, *The Fiction of Narrative*, ed. Robert Doran (Baltimore: Johns Hopkins University Press, 2010), 279–82; cf. ibid., 273–92.

2. The word "Salafi" (a follower of the "pious ancestors of Islam" or *salaf*) is the preferred self-denomination of the so-called Muslim fundamentalists who usually reject Sufism as a blameworthy "innovation" in the bosom of Islam; their criticism of Sufism is discussed in the last chapter of this book.

3. A similar approach to the interaction of insider and outsider images of the prophet Muhammad is taken by Kecia Ali in her *Lives of Muhammad* (Cambridge, MA: Harvard University Press, 2014), 2–3 and 103–13.

4. Andreas Christmann, "Reclaiming Mysticism: Anti-Orientalism and the Construction of 'Islamic Sufism' in Postcolonial Egypt," in *Religion, Language, and Power*, ed. Nile Green and Mary Searle-Chatterjee (London: Routledge, 2008), 57; Christmann responds here to Richard King's critical assessment of the Western concepts of "Hindu mysticism" and "Buddhist mysticism" that will be discussed further on.

5. For a definition of "postmodern" pertinent to our discussion, see Keith Jenkins, *On "What Is History"? From Carr and Elton to Rorty and White* (London: Routledge, 1995), 6–10; according to Jenkins, hallmarks of "postmodernism" are suspicion of modernist-bourgeois metanarratives, of "certaintism," positivism, objectivism, and essentialism generally and of history writing in particular.

6. Jenkins, *On "What Is History"?*, 22.

7. As noted by Martin Heidegger (1889–1976); see Graham Harman, *Heidegger Explained: From Phenomenon to Thing* (Chicago: Open Court, 2007), 29.

8. Martin Heidegger tends to forefront negative aspects of this concept; in the case of the historians he would find fault with their single-minded absorption with external minutia of the world at the expense of recovering the all-important underlying roots of human existence, see ibid., 69–70 and 173–74.

9. Jenkins, *On "What Is History"?*, 23.

10. Harman, *Heidegger*, 32–35.

11. Jenkins, *On "What Is History"?*, 24.

12. Ibid., and Hayden White, *The Content of the Form* (Baltimore: Johns Hopkins University Press, 1987), 12.

13. Jenkins, *On "What Is History"?*, 25; this fact was readily recognized by Islamic thinkers, including Sayyid Qutb (1906–1966); see Roxanne Euben and Muhammad Qasim Zaman, eds., *Princeton Readings in Islamist Thought: Texts and Context from al-Banna to Bin Laden* (Princeton, NJ: Princeton University Press, 2009), 108–9.

14. Carl Ernst, "Preface to the Second Edition," in his *Eternal Garden: Mysticism, History, and Politics at a South Asian Sufi Center*, 2nd ed. with a new preface (Delhi: Oxford University Press, 2004), and Ernst, *The Shambhala Guide to Sufism* (Boston: Shambhala, 1997), 9 and 147; for Ernst's disagreement with Orientalist conceptualizations of Sufism see *Shambhala Guide*, 1–18; his statement about the "invented" nature of Sufism in Western Orientalist discourses is repeated by Robert Rozehnal in his *Islamic Sufism Unbound: Politics and Piety in Twenty-First-Century Pakistan* (New York: Palgrave Macmillan, 2007), 13. Interestingly, Rozehnal's entire work, in our opinion at least, shows the problematic nature of Ernst's idea that Western Orientalists are singularly responsible for "inventing Sufism." The Sufis examined in Rozehnal's book are as actively involved in the process of inventing and reinventing Sufism as any Orientalist has been and is. Furthermore, they widely use Western conceptualizations of Sufism to frame their own. Ernst's and Rozehnal's failure to acknowledge this fact cannot be explained by anything except the irresistible tendency among Western academics to see everything and everyone as "imagined constructs" purposefully created by various actors for critical postmodern scholars to discover and deconstruct. The fact that reductive, arbitrary, incomplete, or outright misleading definitions of Sufism abound in "native" Sufi literature (see, e.g., Reynold Nicholson, "A Historical Enquiry Concerning the Origin and Development of Sufism," *JRAS* [1906]: 303–48, and Ernst himself in his *Shambhala Guide*, 23) and that the much-reviled Orientalists often simply adapted these definitions to the languages and imagery of their respective Western audiences, in our view, absolves them of a deliberate invention or distortion imputed to them by Carl Ernst and his colleagues on the basis of the Saidian critique of Orientalism; on a related subject, see critical examinations of Western perceptions of Buddhism and Hinduism by Richard King in his *Orientalism and Religion* (London: Routledge, 1999); cf. Tomoko Masuzawa, *The Invention of World Religions* (Chicago: University of Chicago Press, 2005), 16–21 passim.

15. In the sense originally introduced by Heidegger and taken up and developed by Jacques Derrida (1930–2004), see Harman, *Heidegger*, 174; Umberto Eco, *The Limits of Interpretation* (Bloomington: Indiana University Press, 1994), 34–37 and 41.

16. For a critical evaluation of widespread and fashionable criticisms of a Western intellectual paradigm generally and its application to Islam and Muslim societies in particular see our review of Mohammad Salama, *Islam, Orientalism and Intellectual History: Modernity and the Politics of Exclusion since Ibn Khaldun* (London: I. B. Tauris, 2011), *Der Islam* 90, no. 1 (2013): 197–202; similar anti-Orientalist and anti-Western discourses are rife in Western academia and on the Internet; for a typical example see the verbose ruminations of Wael Hallaq in his "On Orientalism, Self-Consciousness, and History," *Islamic Law and Society* 18 (2011): 387–439, and Masuzawa, *Invention of World Religions*, 17–21 and part 2 passim; for Islam in particular see ibid., chapter 6.

17. As a typical example one can cite the seminal academic contributions to Sufi

studies by Reynold Nicholson (1868–1945) who has edited and made available to the reading public, both in the Muslim world and in the West, the major Sufi works from the tenth to thirteenth centuries CE; the fact that they are still being used by Western scholars as well as Muslims (Sufis and non-Sufis alike) today indicates that Nicholson's selection of these texts as representative of Sufi thought and ethos has been accepted by all those interested in the subject regardless of their personal backgrounds and convictions; on Nicholson's career see Arthur Arberry, *Oriental Essays: Portraits of Seven Scholars* (London: Allen and Unwin, 1960), chapter 5, titled "The Dervish"; Arberry himself was a worthy disciple of his mentor; see Arberry, chapter 6, "The Disciple." A great service to the field of Islamic studies has been rendered by the German scholars Helmut Ritter (1892–1971), Fritz Meier (1912–1998), and Richard Gramlich (1925–2006) as well as their Russian colleagues Vladimir Zhukovskii (1858–1918), Aleksandr Shmidt (1871–1939), and Evgenii Bertels (1890–1957). In France Sufism became known and appreciated largely thanks to the efforts of Louis Massignon (1883–1962), Marijan Molé (1924–1963), and Henry Corbin (1903–1978). Without the academic work of these and numerous other Orientalists our understanding of Sufism would have been incomparably poorer than it is.

18. For example, Georges Anawati's "Kalam" in Lindsay Jones, ed., *Encyclopedia of Religion* (Detroit, MI: Macmillan, 2005), 5059–69, and Richard Frank's "The Science of Kalam," *Arabic Science and Philosophy* 2 (1992): 7–37, faithfully reproduce Ibn Khaldun's (d. 808/1406) section on "Speculative theology" (*kalam*) in his *al-Muqaddima*; see Franz Rosenthal, trans., *Ibn Khaldun: The Muqaddimah; An Introduction to History*, 3 vols. (New York: Pantheon Books, 1958), 3: 34–75; for recasting images of the prophet Muhammad according to the changing demands and expectations of Western and Muslim audiences, see Ali, *Lives of Muhammad*, chapters 1–2 passim.

19. See, e.g., the entry on Abu 'l-Fazl 'Allami in *EI3* and Alexander Knysh, *Islam in Historical Perspective* (Upper Saddle River, NJ: Prentice Hall, 2011), 386, as well as the references quoted therein.

20. See chapter 1 of Ernst, *Shambhala Guide*; Christmann, "Reclaiming Mysticism," 58–64, and Alexander Knysh, "Historiography of Sufi Studies in the West and Russia," *Pis'mennye pamiatniki Vostoka (Written Monuments of the Orient)* 1, no. 4 (2006): 206–38.

21. See Ernst, *Shambhala Guide*, 8–18.

22. William Chittick, *The Sufi Path of Knowledge: Ibn al-'Arabi's Metaphysics of Imagination* (Albany: State University of New York Press, 1990), 361–64.

23. Ernst, *Shambhala Guide*, 16, and, more recently, Lloyd Ridgeon, "Mysticism in Medieval Islam," in *The Cambridge Companion to Sufism*, ed. Lloyd Ridgeon (Cambridge: Cambridge University Press, 2015), 125–26, 131, 147–49 passim.

24. King, *Orientalism*, 185.

25. For a typical modern example see Mohammad Hashim Kamali, *The Middle Path of Moderation in Islam* (Oxford: Oxford University Press, 2015), 115–22; premodern examples (culled from Sufi literature) are discussed in Alexander Knysh, *Islamic Mysticism: A Short History*, 2nd ed. (Leiden: E. J. Brill, 2010), 116–49.

26. Ernst, *Shambhala Guide*, 26–31.

27. Ernst's own *Shambhala Guide* is a laudable attempt to produce such an unbiased account; however, being a collection of essays and often illuminating observa-

tions, it is too cursory (or "tropical," to use Hayden White's terminology) to do justice to this vast and complex topic.

28. As argued in our "Historiography," most of the Western accounts of Sufism until recently were predominantly text-based.

29. An illuminating, if somewhat far-fetched, parallel can be drawn with Russian studies and Sovietology in Western countries; its doyens faithfully preserved and replicated the biases of the sources upon which they relied for their analysis, see, e.g., Susan Gross Solomon, ed., *Beyond Sovietology: Essays in Politics and History* (London: Routledge, 1993), and Michael Cox, ed., *Rethinking the Soviet Collapse: Sovietology, the Death of Communism and the New Russia* (London: Pinter, 1998).

30. Naturally, the choice by European scholars of texts representing a certain trend within Islam also reflected their own presuppositions about the norm or mainstream; for a recent attempt at creating a new normativity of Islam by means of a drastic re-examination of the Muslim intellectual tradition and its literary expressions, see Shahab Ahmed, *What Is Islam? The Importance of Being Islamic* (Princeton, NJ: Princeton University Press, 2016), passim.

31. Most notably by Talal Asad, Richard King, and Tomoko Masuzawa; for the invention of "Jewish religion" in the German Jewish context, see Leora Batnitzky, *How Judaism Became a Religion* (Princeton, NJ: Princeton University Press, 2011); with regard to Sufism, see Lloyd Ridgeon, "Mysticism in Medieval Islam," in *The Cambridge Companion to Sufism*, ed. Lloyd Ridgeon (Cambridge: Cambridge University Press, 2015), 125–49, and Itzchak Weismann, "Modernity from Within," in *Sufis and Salafis in the Contemporary Age*, ed. Lloyd Ridgeon (London: Bloomsbury, 2015), 9–31.

32. King, *Orientalism*, 35–41.

33. Ibid., 40 (quoting S. N. Balagangadhara).

34. Ibid., 20–28.

35. Ibid., passim; cf. Masuzawa, *Invention of World Religions*, passim.

36. For a detailed critical review of Said's arguments and the polemic that they have generated, see Daniel Varisco, *Reading Orientalism: Said and Unsaid* (Seattle: University of Washington Press, 2007).

37. As shown in Knysh, "Historiography," passim. For an abridged version see chapter 6. "Historiography of Sufi Studies in the West," in *Companion for the History of the Middle East*, ed. Youssef Choueiri (Oxford: Blackwell, 2005), 106–31; see also Alexander Knysh, "Sufism as an Explanatory Paradigm: The Issue of the Motivations of Sufi Movements in Russian and Western Historiography," *Die Welt des Islams* 42, no. 2 (2002): 139–73, and Knysh, *Islamic Mysticism*, 289–300; similar conclusions can be found in Christmann, "Reclaiming Mysticism," 59–60, and Knut Vikør, "Sufism and Colonialism," in *The Cambridge Companion to Sufism*, ed. Lloyd Ridgeon (Cambridge: Cambridge University Press, 2015), 212–32.

38. See Norman Daniel, *Islam and the West: The Making of an Image* (Oxford: Oneworld, 2003), passim, and Knysh, *Islam in Historical Perspective*, 365–72.

39. A fact completely ignored by Edward Said and his numerous followers; see Varisco, *Reading Orientalism*, 79–92, and 201–33, and Robert Irwin, *Dangerous Knowledge: Orientalism and Its Discontents* (Woodstock, NY: Overlook Press, 2008), 277–309.

40. Green and Searle-Chatterjee, "Introductory Essay," in Green and Searle-Chatterjee, *Religion, Language, and Power*, 3.

41. Irwin, *Dangerous Knowledge*, 298.

42. Knysh, "Historiography," 238; for a critical but balanced evaluation of the work of the major Islamologists of the first half of the twentieth century, see Jacques Waardenburg, *L'Islam dans le miroir de l'Occident* (Paris: Mouton, 1963).

43. See Knysh's review of Salama, *Islam*; for an instance of a problematic statement by today's postmodernist, anticolonial scholars of Islam, see Green and Searle-Chatterjee, "Introductory Essay," 10; here the authors treat the language as a self-sufficient and free actor ("[it] must conquer new lands and new tongues; it must see itself written and hear itself spoken")—something they would have never tolerated in the works of Orientalists, who did indeed often speak about "religion" or "Islam" in similar terms (namely, attributing agency to an abstraction).

44. Contrary to Carl Ernst, who uses this word to debunk Orientalism (*Shambhala Guide*, 9 passim), we see it as an admirable expression of the human desire to understand and learn from other religions and cultures.

45. King, *Orientalism*, 52; see also 49–50; for some pertinent warnings about the hubris of Western sociologists who assume that knowledge of social categories gives them "the impression of complete control over what is being surveyed," see Bruno Latour, *Reassembling the Social: An Introduction to Actor-Network Theory* (Oxford: Oxford University Press, 2005), 138 and 188.

46. Vincent Wimbush and Richard Valantasis, *Asceticism* (Oxford: Oxford University Press, 1999); Richard Valantasis, *The Making of the Self* (Eugene, OR: Cascade Books, 2008); Geoffrey Harpham, *The Ascetic Imperative in Culture and Criticism* (Chicago: University of Chicago Press, 1987), and Patrik Hagman, *The Asceticism of Isaac of Nineveh* (Oxford: Oxford University Press, 2010), 1–24.

47. In response to Richard King's call upon his colleagues to "transgress boundaries imposed by normative Western models of 'religion' . . . by interrogation and displacement of Western (Judeo-Christian/secular) paradigms of what 'religion' is" (quoted in Green and Searle-Chatterjee, *Religion, Language, and Power*, ix–x; originally stated in King, *Orientalism*, 210), a whole industry of deconstructions of the concept of "religion" has developed; for further references and a sympathetic overview, see Green and Searle-Chatterjee, *Religion, Language, and Power*, 1–23. The heuristic value of these self-referential and often repetitive "deconstructions" being in the eye of the beholder, their existence has to be acknowledged due their continuing presence in the field of Islamic studies and religious studies more generally.

48. Bernard McGinn, *The Foundations of Mysticism*, vol. 1 of *The Presence of God* (New York: Crossroad, 1991), 32–34 and 44–61; Paulina Remes, *Plotinus of Self: The Philosophy of the "We"* (Cambridge: Cambridge University Press, 2007), 5–6 and 23–33; Majid Fakhry, *A History of Islamic Philosophy*, 3rd ed. (New York: Columbia University Press, 2004), 21–23.

49. Green and Searle-Chatterjee, "Introductory Essay," 2, and the sources quoted therein.

50. Ahmed, *What Is Islam?*, passim.

51. Roy Rappaport, *Ritual and Religion in the Making of Humanity* (Cambridge:

Cambridge University Press, 1999), 24 and 33–37; see also Gavin Flood, *The Ascetic Self: Subjectivity, Memory, and Tradition* (Cambridge: Cambridge University Press, 2004), 218 and 222; Valantasis, *The Making of the Self*, 8–10.

52. Latour, *Reassembling the Social*, 37.

53. See Knysh, *Islam in Historical Perspective*, 4; for a recent example from Muslim theological discourse, see the introduction and discussion of the principle of "moderation" (*wasatiyya*) in Islam by Mohammad Hashim Kamali (b. 1944) in his *Middle Path of Moderation in Islam*.

54. This classification is based on Bruce Lincoln's discussion of the four major components of religion in his *Holy Terrors*, 2nd ed. (Chicago: University of Chicago Press, 2006), 5–7; I have added the fifth, which is subsumed in Lincoln's element 4, but which was not given a freestanding status in his classification; a more detailed structure of the notion "religion" that consists of seven dimensions was proposed by Ninian Smart (1927–2001); see his *Dimensions of the Sacred* (London: Harper Collins, 1996), 10–11 passim; cf. Ivan Strenski, *Thinking about Religion* (Oxford: Blackwell, 2006), 192.

55. The term "subjectivity" is widely used by many writers on asceticism and mysticism (e.g., Valantasis), although it is, to our mind, largely synonymous with "identity."

56. For an example of the former, see Ahmed, *What Is Islam?*, passim; examples of the latter are discussed in the last chapter of this book.

57. King, *Orientalism*, 49.

58. Ibid., 52.

59. See al-Ghazali's "Deliverance from Error," translated by Montgomery Watt in his *Faith and Practice of al-Ghazali*, 4th ed. (London: George Allen and Unwin, 1970), 55.

60. William James, *Varieties of Religious Experience* (London: Longmans, Green, 1928), 448.

61. We have addressed this issue in greater detail in an unpublished paper, "Islamic Studies and Islamic Religious Studies: Any Possibility for Reconciliation?" delivered at the Third International Conference "The World of Islam: History, Society, Culture," October 22–24, 2014, Moscow (sponsored by the Marjani Foundation).

62. See chapter 6.

63. Even more so because some Western scholars have argued that Marxism, nationalism, and other political movements and ideologies are but modern forms of religion; see, e.g., King, *Orientalism*, 14, and the references cited there.

64. For an alternative approach see Christopher Melchert, "The Transition from Asceticism to Mysticism at the Middle of the Ninth Century C.E.," *Studia Islamica* 83 (1996): 51–70. The constructed and culturally and socially determined character of the terms "mysticism" and "mystical" has been explored in great detail in numerous studies, most notably in Richard King's *Orientalism and Religion*; to avoid repetition we refer the reader to his investigations (see ibid., 7–34 passim). Because King's conclusions are based on his study of the non-Abrahamic religious traditions (Hinduism and Buddhism), they are only partially applicable to Islam, whose major non-Sufi spokesmen (e.g., al-Ash'ari, d. 935/936; Ibn al-Jawzi, d. 597/1201; Ibn Taymiyya, d. 728/1328; Ibn Khaldun, d. 808/1406) employed the notions of "mysticism" and "mystical experi-

ence" (under different Arabic names) that, as we shall find out, are not very different from the various modern Western conceptualizations of these phenomena.

65. Bryan Turner, *Weber and Islam* (London: Routledge and Kegan Paul, 1974), 171 and 138–39.

66. Max Weber, *The Sociology of Religion*, trans. Ephraim Fischoff (London: Methuen, 1965), 182 and 264–65.

67. E.g., Christopher Melchert, "The Transition," passim, and, somewhat less obviously, also Ahmet Karamustafa, *God's Unruly Friends* (Salt Lake City: University of Utah Press, 1994), 28–31, 36–39, and 90–102.

68. On this issue we are in full agreement with Bernd Radtke's scathing criticism of the asceticism-mysticism dichotomy that has been adopted by some Western Islamologists; see Radtke, *Neue kritische Gänge* (Utrecht: Houtsma, 2005); in a chapter titled "Von den hinderlichen Wirkungen der Extase und dem Wesen der Ignoranz," Radtke has furnished an ample textual evidence for the problematic nature of this dichotomy while simultaneously calling in doubt the usefulness of Weber's "ideal types" asceticism and mysticism when applied to Islamic phenomena; see, in particular, 257–59.

69. Weber, *Sociology of Religion*, 160–65; Hans Gerth and Charles Wright Mills, eds., *From Max Weber: Essays in Sociology* (London: Routledge and Kegan Paul, 1967), 290–92; Turner, *Weber and Islam*, 52–55 and 56–71; cf. Radtke, *Neue kritische Gänge*, 251, 253–54, 258–59, 281.

70. Such aspirations are routinely attributed to early ascetics-mystics by contemporary Muslim heresiographers; see Helmut Ritter, ed., *Maqalat al-islamiyyin*, ta'lif Abi al-Hasan 'Ali ibn Isma'il al-Ash'ari (Istanbul: Jam'iyat al-Mustashriqin al-Almaniyya, 1929), 289 and 438; Abu 'l-Hasan Muhammad al-Malati, *al-Tanbih wa 'l-radd 'ala ahl al-ahwa' wa 'l-bida'*, ed. Muhammad al-Kawthari (Baghdad: al-Muthanna; Beirut: Maktab al-ma'arif, 1968), 94–95; these and other passages from early heresiographical works are discussed by Bernd Radtke in his *Neue kritische Gänge*, 262–84, and his *Materialien zur alten islamischen Frömmigkeit* (Leiden: E. J. Brill, 2009), 89, 113–14, 116, 154–55, 162–63, 172–73; cf. Josef van Ess, *Theologie und Gesellschaft im 2. und 3. Jahrhundert Hidschra*, 6 vols. (Berlin: Walter de Gruyter, 1991), 1: 144; 2: 544–46; and 4: 278–88 and 411–15; for later Sufi views on experiencing paradisiacal visions and sensations in this life, see William Chittick, *Divine Love: Islamic Literature and the Path to God* (New Haven, CT: Yale University Press, 2013), 105–45.

71. For some pertinent examples from later Sufism, see Anna Akasoy, "What Is Philosophical Sufism?" in *In the Age of Averroes: Arabic Philosophy in the Sixth/ Twelfth Century*," ed. Peter Adamson (London; Turin: Warburg Institute; Nino Agarno Editore, 2011), 237–38; see our chapter "Sufi Commentary: Formative and Later Periods," in Mustafa Shah, ed., *Oxford Handbook of the Qur'an*, forthcoming.

72. McGinn, *The Foundations of Mysticism*, vol. 1 of *The Presence of God*, 24 passim; for some representative examples from later Western asceticism-mysticism, see McGinn, *The Flowering of Mysticism: Men and Women in the New Mysticism (1200–1350)* (New York: Crossroad, 1998), 82–87 and 99–112.

73. Harpham, *Ascetic Imperative in Culture and Criticism*, 59.

74. Ibid., xiv and xv.

75. Wimbush and Valantasis, *Asceticism*, 4–5.

76. Radtke, *Neue kritische Gänge*, 280.

77. Akasoy, "What Is Philosophical Sufism?," 237–38; cf. ibid., 234 note 27.

78. Discussed in chapter 5 of this book.

79. Akasoy, "What Is Philosophical Sufism?," 236.

80. Louis Massignon, *Essay on the Origins of the Technical Language of Islamic Mysticism*, trans. from the French with an introduction by Benjamin Clark (Notre Dame, IN: University of Notre Dame Press, 1997), 9, 56–57, and 208.

81. See our translation of al-Qushayri's *Epistle on Sufism* (Reading, UK; Garnet, 2007), passim, and Ahmet Karamustafa, *Sufism: The Formative Period* (Edinburgh: Edinburgh University Press, 2007), 88, quoting Abu Talib al-Makki (d. 386/996); however, Karamustafa himself, while showing sympathy for Christopher Melchert's dichotomy of "renunciant piety" of the ascetics (*zuhhad*) and the "mystical piety" of the Sufis, is vague on this point; see Karamustafa, *Sufism*, 6–7.

82. McGinn, *Foundations of Mysticism*, vol. 1 of *The Presence of God*, xiv.

83. McGinn, *Flowering of Mysticism*, 6–17.

84. Ibid., 25–30.

85. Vladimir Lossky, *The Mystical Theology of the Eastern Church* (London: James Clark, 1957), 13–14 and 246.

86. See, e.g., Hagman, *Asceticism of Isaac of Nineveh*, 13–16.

87. Patrik Hagman's excellent book, titled, misleadingly, *The Asceticism of Isaac of Nineveh*, shows an almost seamless fusion of ascetic praxis and mystical theology (i.e., mysticism) in the life and work of his hero, Isaac of Nineveh (fl. in the late seventh century CE).

88. Usually rendered in Arabic and other "Islamic" languages as *nafs* ("ego"; "self"); in contemporary biological terms, the *nafs* is but an assemblage of naturally programmed and inherited instincts geared to the survival of the human body; see, e.g., Richard Dawkins, *The Selfish Gene*, 40th anniversary ed. (Oxford: Oxford University Press, 2016), chapters 1, 4, and 5.

89. Valantasis, *Making of the Self*, 38, 40, 54, 113–15, 126–31, 211 passim; Hagman, *Asceticism of Isaac of Nineveh*, 10–11 and Harpham, *Ascetic Imperative in Culture and Criticism*, part I, chapters 1–4 passim.

90. Valantasis, *Making of the Self*, 39–42 and 55–57; for further references see the aforementioned four-volume study of Western mysticism by Bernard McGinn titled collectively *The Presence of God*.

91. Bernard McGinn defines mysticism as "a part and element of religion" as well as "a process or way of life" that attempts to express a direct consciousness of the presence of God; McGinn, *Foundations of Mysticism*, vol. 1 of *The Presence of God*, xv–xvi.

92. Dawkins, *Selfish Gene*, 1–14, 151–58 passim.

93. As with Hagman's book mentioned in note 46 above, Richard Valantasis's study of "ancient and modern asceticism" deals as much with ascetic practices as it does with mystical ("revelatory") metaphysics and construction of symbolic universes by ascetics-mystics he investigates; see, e.g., *Making of the Self*, 47, 55–56 passim.

94. McGinn, *Foundations of Mysticism*, vol. 1 of *The Presence of God*, xiii–xv; McGinn argues, among other things, that "the term 'mystical theology' antedated the

coining of the term 'mysticism' by over a millennium," xiv, which belies recent academic attempts to present "mysticism" ("la mystique") as an invention of seventeenth-century French mystics, especially Jean-Joseph Surin (1600–1665), ibid., 310; cf. xvi and 42–44; the widespread insistence, among Western academics, on the "invented" nature of the term "mysticism" is quite similar to Carl Ernst's idea about the "invention" of Sufism by European "Orientalists" that was mentioned earlier in our study.

95. See Knysh, *Islamic Mysticism*, 20.

96. David Margoliouth, trans., "The Devil's Delusion" (a partial translation of Ibn al-Jawzi's *Talbis Iblis*), in *Islamic Culture*, vol. 10 (1936), 352 and 357; Karamustafa, *God's Unruly Friends*, passim.

97. Megan Reid, *Law and Piety in Medieval Islam* (Cambridge: Cambridge University Press, 2013), passim.

98. Ibid., 1. While Reid's example cited here shows that in the figure of 'Abdallah b. Taymiyya (d. 727/1327), brother of the famous Ahmad b. Taymiyya (d. 728/1328), Sufism ("mystical insight," or *'irfan*) and ascetic practices (retreat, or *khalwa*) were organically combined, she, paradoxically, considers him a representative of ascetic piety (*zuhd*; *ta'abbud*) that, in her opinion, was somehow distinct from Sufism; ibid., 6–13, and note 11 on p. 6; for Reid's attempts to demonstrate that asceticism is somehow different from Sufism, see ibid., chapter 1.

99. The online version of all three editions of *EI* can be accessed at: http://referenceworks.brillonline.com/cluster/Encyclopaedia%20of%20Islam?s.num=0.

Chapter 1: How and Why Sufism Came to Be

1. As stated in one of the earliest extant Sufi treatises by Abu Nasr al-Sarraj (d. 378/988), "The teaching of the Sufis is supported and confirmed by compliance with the Book of God, may He be great and exalted, and following in the footsteps of the Messenger of God, may God bless and preserve him, as well as imitating the moral character traits of the Prophet's companions and those who came after them," al-Sarraj, *Kitab al-luma' fi l-tasawwuf*, ed. Reynold Nicholson (Leiden: E. J. Brill, 1914), 5; see also 1–2, 13, 16–17 passim; similar statements abound in Sufi literature; see, e.g., Alexander Knysh, trans., *Al-Qushayri's Epistle on Sufism* (Reading, UK: Garnet, 2007), 2–16.

2. Q 24:37; cf. 3:14–16; 5:54; 9:69, 16:96; 17:18–20; 18:7–8; 20:131; 28:60 and 83; 29:64; 31:33; 47:36; 52:13–17; 57:20–21; Louis Massignon, *Essay on the Origins of the Technical Language of Islamic Mysticism* (Notre Dame, IN: University of Notre Dame Press, 1997), 34–36 and 94–98; Alexander Knysh, *Islamic Mysticism: A Short History*, 2nd ed. (Leiden: E. J. Brill, 2010), 8–10; Leah Kinberg, "What Is Meant by 'Zuhd'?" *Studia Islamica* 41 (1985): 24–44.

3. For a helpful survey of Qur'anic passages relating to fear of God, see Erik Ohlander, "Fear of God (*taqwa*) in the Qur'an: Some Notes on Semantic Shift and Thematic Context," *Journal of Semitic Studies* 50 (2005): 137–52.

4. Q 57:27; the Qur'an refers, in all probability, to the Arabian, Syrian, and, somewhat less likely, Mesopotamian monks and recluses. Ignaz Goldziher, *Introduction to Islamic Theology* (Princeton, NJ: Princeton University Press, 1981), 129–30; Massignon, *Essay on the Origins of the Technical Language of Islamic Mysticism*, 101–4;

Paul Nwyia, *Un mystique prédicateur à la Qarawiyin de Fès Ibn 'Abbad de Ronda (1332–1390)* (Beirut: Imprimerie catholique, 1961), lii–liii note 1, and 231–32; Ofer Livne-Kafri, "Early Muslim Ascetics and the World of Christian Monasticism," *Jerusalem Studies in Arabic and Islam (JSAI)* 20 (1996): 105–29; Sara Sviri, "*Warahbaniyatan ibtada'ha*: An Analysis of Traditions concerning the Origin and Evaluation of Christian Mysticism," *JSAI* 13 (1990): 195–208.

5. Q 2:3–4; 5:55–56; 8:34; 9:71; Louise Marlow, "Friends and Friendship," *Encyclopedia of the Qur'an* (Leiden: E. J. Brill), online edition: http://referenceworks .brillonline.com/entries/encyclopaedia-of-the-quran. For a critical discussion of various possible translations of the terms *wali* and *awliya'* see Scott Kugle, *Rebel between Spirit and Law: Ahmad Zarruq, Sainthood, and Authority in Islam* (Bloomington: Indiana University Press, 2006), 27–33.

6. See, e.g., al-Harith al-Muhasibi, *Tawahhum: Rahlat al-insan ila 'alam al-akhira* (Cairo: Maktabat al-Qur'an, 1984), and Ibn Abi 'l-Dunya, *Dhikr al-mawt* ('Ajman: Maktabat al-furqan, 2002).

7. Q 10:62; for the parallel places see Q 2:62, 5:69, and 6:48. For discussions of various aspects of sainthood/friendship with God in Western academic literature, see Vincent Cornell, *Realm of the Saint* (Austin: University of Texas Press, 1998), xviii–xxi, 3–31, and 272–85; Carl Ernst, *The Shambhala Guide to Sufism* (Boston: Shambhala, 1997), 58–80; John Renard, *Friends of God* (Berkeley: University of California Press, 2008), chapter 2 passim; Robert Rozehnal, *Islamic Sufism Unbound: Politics and Piety in Twenty-First-Century Pakistan* (New York: Palgrave Macmillan, 2007), 42–44 passim; Kugle, *Rebel between Spirit and Law*, 27–33; Katherine Ewing, *Arguing Sainthood: Modernity, Psychoanalysis, and Islam* (Durham, NC: Duke University Press, 1997), 1–90.

8. Christopher Melchert, "Exaggerated Fear in the Early Islamic Renunciant Tradition," *Journal of the Royal Asiatic Society* 3, no. 3 (2011): 285.

9. For evidence supporting Sufi teachings and actions that medieval Sufi authors extracted from prophetic Hadith and commentaries on the Qur'an (*tafsir*), see Knysh, *Al-Qushayri's Epistle*, 268–73; also Bernd Radtke and John O'Kane, trans., *The Concept of Sainthood in Early Islamic Mysticism: Two Works by al-Hakim al-Tirmidhi* (Richmond, Surrey: Curzon Press, 1996), passim.

10. This is a common English translation of the Arabic term *nawafil*.

11. See, e.g., Gautier Juynboll, *Encyclopedia of Canonical Hadith* (Leiden: E. J. Brill, 2007); see "Index" under "the Prophet"; Massignon, *Essay on the Origins of the Technical Language of Islamic Mysticism*, 126 (quoting al-Hasan al-Basri, d. 110/728); Ernst, *Shambhala Guide*, 99.

12. Ernst, *Shambhala Guide*, 32–33.

13. Massignon, *Essay on the Origins of the Technical Language of Islamic Mysticism*, 94–98; Gerald Hawting, "Tahannuth," *EI2*, online edition: http://referenc eworks.brillonline.com.

14. Waki' b. al-Jarrah, *Al-Zuhd li-imam Waki'*, ed. 'Abd al-Rahman 'Abd al-Jabbar al-Faryawa'i (Medina: Maktabat al-Dar, 1984), 230.

15. Ibid., 242 passim, and Ibn Abi 'l-Dunya, *Al-Hamm wa-'l-huzn* (Cairo: Dar al-salam, 1991), passim; cf. Massignon, *Essay on the Origins of the Technical Language of Islamic Mysticism*, 98, 111, 126, and 165, and Nwyia, *Un mystique*, 226–30.

16. E.g., Abu Dharr al-Ghifari (d. 32/652), Abu 'l-Darda' (d. 18/639 or later) and

his wife Umm al-Darda' (?), Hudhayfa b. al-Yaman (d. 36/656), 'Imran b. al-Husayn al-Khuza'i (d. 52/672), 'Abdallah b. 'Amr b. al-'As (d. 65/685), 'Akkaf b. Wada al-Hilali (?), Mi'dad b. Yazid al-'Ijli (?), Goldziher, *Introduction*, 120–22; Scott Lucas, *Constructive Critics, Hadith Literature, and the Articulation of Sunni Islam* (Leiden: E. J. Brill, 2004), 296, and "Index" under the names of these individuals; Massignon, *Essay on the Origins of the Technical Language of Islamic Mysticism*, 111–19; cf. Christopher Melchert, "Asceticism," in *EI3*, online edition: http://referenceworks.brillonline.com; Tor Andrae, *In the Garden of Myrtles* (Albany: State University of New York Press, 1987), 9–10, and Knysh, *Islamic Mysticism*, 5–6.

17. For the praise by the Prophet and his companions of fear of God, frugality, humility, abstinence, and avoidance of passions, see the didactic books by the well-known moralist and ascetic Ibn Abi 'l-Dunya (d. 281/894), e.g., his *Kitab al-wara'*, ed. Bassam 'Abd al-Wahhab al-Jabi (Beirut: Dar Ibn Hazm, 2002); see also 'Abdallah b. al-Mubarak, *Kitab al-zuhd wa 'l-raqa'iq* (Alexandria: Dar al-salafiyya, 1998).

18. Max Weber, *The Sociology of Religion*, trans. Ephraim Fischoff (London: Methuen, 1965), 64–65, 132, 262–64; Hans Gerth and Charles Wright Mills, eds., *From Max Weber: Essays in Sociology* (London: Routledge and Kegan Paul, 1967), 287–92; Bryan Turner, *Weber and Islam* (London: Routledge and Kegan Paul, 1974), 54, 138, 140–41, and 171.

19. For parallel places, see Q 2:168; 5:88; 8:69; 16:114; 20:81.

20. Q 2:143; 5:66; 35:32.

21. Frederick Denny, "Umma," in *Encyclopedia of Islam*, 2nd ed., online edition: http://referenceworks.brillonline.com; for a book-size monograph on the subject of moderation, see Mohammad Hashim Kamali, *The Middle Path of Moderation in Islam: The Qur'anic Principle of Wasatiyya* (Oxford: Oxford University Press, 2015).

22. Goldziher, *Introduction*, 117–19.

23. Ibid., 122–23; Abdelwahab Bouhdiba, *Sexuality in Islam*, trans. from the French by Alan Sheridan (London: Saqi Books, 1998); for some notable exceptions see Megan Reid, *Law and Piety in Medieval Islam* (Cambridge: Cambridge University Press, 2013), 35–44, and Madeleine Farah, trans., *Marriage and Sexuality in Islam: A Translation of al-Ghazali's Book on the Etiquette of Marriage from the Ihya'* (Salt Lake City: University of Utah Press, 1984); for celibacy in Eastern Christianity before the rise of Islam, see Gilliam Clark, "Women and Asceticism in Late Antiquity: The Refusal of Status and Gender," in *Asceticism*, ed. Vincent Wimbush and Richard Valantasis (Oxford: Oxford University Press, 1998), 37–41.

24. Christopher Melchert, "The Interpretation of Three Qur'anic Terms (*Siyaha, Hikma,* and *Siddiq*) of Special Interest to the Early Renunciants," in *The Meaning of the Word: Lexicography and Qur'anic Exegesis*, ed. Stephen Burge (London: Oxford University Press, 2015), 89–116, especially 96; cf. Nwyia, *Un mystique*, 231.

25. For the role of poverty in the ascetic lifestyle of the late antique Christians of the Middle East and North Africa, see Clark, "Women and Asceticism," 35–37.

26. Goldziher, *Introduction*, 126.

27. E.g., 'Abd al-Rahman b. 'Awf (d. 32/652), al-Zubayr b. al-'Awwam (d. 36/656), Talha b. 'Ubaydallah (d. 36/656), and Khabbab b. al-Aratt (d. 37/657 or 39/659); see Goldziher, *Introduction*, 117–18 and the entries on these individuals in *Encyclopedia of Islam*, 2nd and 3rd eds.: http://referenceworks.brillonline.com.

28. Q 93:6–11.

29. Q 57:27: "And We put in the hearts of those who followed Jesus, compassion and mercy, and the monastic state (*rahbaniyya*); they instituted it (We did not prescribe it to them) only out of a desire to please God. Yet they observed not the same as it ought truly to have been observed. And We gave unto such of them as believed, their reward; but many of them have been doers of evil."

30. Abu Nu'aym al-Isbahani, *Hilyat al-awliya'*, 12 vols. (Beirut: Dar al-Kitab al-'Arabi, 1967), 1: 168; Goldziher, *Introduction*, 123 and 128; Massignon, *Essay on the Origins of the Technical Language of Islamic Mysticism*, 98–104; Livne-Kafri, "Early Muslim Ascetics," 107; Arend Wensinck, "Rahbaniyya," *EI2*, online edition: http:// referenceworks.brillonline.com.

31. Jon McGinnis and David Reisman, eds., *Classical Arabic Philosophy: An Anthology of Sources* (Indianapolis: Hackett Publishing House, 2007), 40–42; cf. Nwyia, *Un mystique*, 231, which discusses the criticism of Sufism voiced by an influential Andalusi jurist al-Shatibi, d. 790/1388.

32. Weber, *Sociology of Religion*, 263; for epistemological problems of Max Weber's conceptualizations of early Islam and Sufism, see Radtke, *Neue kritische Gänge*, 251, 253–54, 257–58, and 281–85; see also chapter 5 of this book.

33. On a pilgrimage or, according to Christopher Melchert, wandering "from place to place, worshipping," Melchert, "The Interpretation," 90.

34. Lamin Sanneh, "Gratitude and Ingratitude," in the *Encyclopedia of the Qur'an*, online edition: http://referenceworks.brillonline.com/entries/encyclopaedia-of-the -quran.

35. See also 4:95; 8:72; 9:88.

36. Goldziher, *Introduction*, 130; Nwyia, *Un mystique*, 231; and Melchert, "The Interpretation," passim.

37. See, e.g., Arthur Vööbus, *History of Asceticism in the Syrian Orient*, vol. 1 (Louvain: CorpusSCO, 1958), and Vööbus, *Syriac and Arabic Documents Regarding Legislation Relative to Syrian Asceticism* (Stockholm: Este, 1960); see also Nwyia, *Un mystique*, 41 note 2; Wimbush and Valantasis, *Asceticism*, passim; Patrik Hagman, *The Asceticism of Isaac of Nineveh* (Oxford: Oxford University Press, 2010), 25–51; Ora Limor and Guy Stroumsa, eds., *Christians and Christianity in the Holy Land: From the Origins to the Latin Kingdoms* (Brepols: Turnhout, 2006), passim. See also the numerous studies of Arab Christianity by Sydney Griffith.

38. See, e.g., Ibn al-Jawzi's "Devil's Delusion," trans. David Margoliouth and published as *Talbis Iblis (Delusion of the Devil)* by N. K. Singh (New Delhi: Kitab Bhavan, 2008); Nwyia, *Un mystique*, xxxiv–xxxvi, l, 226–27, and 229–31; for similar debates in early Christendom, see Peter Brown, *Through the Eye of a Needle* (Princeton, NJ: Princeton University Press, 2012), chapters 18 and 19 passim.

39. Marshall Hodgson, *The Venture of Islam: Conscience and History in a World Civilization*, 3 vols. (Chicago: University of Chicago Press, 1974), 1: 361–62; one should point out the problematic nature of the notion of "temperament"; Hodgson seems to have taken it to be one's natural psychological and intellectual predisposition rather than a product of one's cultural or social environment and upbringing.

40. "Piety," by which Hodgson understands a certain religious (as well as intellectual and spiritual) attitude and the practice resulting therefrom, is his major contribution to Islamic studies; for a critical examination of this concept and its legacy

today, see Shahab Ahmed, *What Is Islam? The Importance of Being Islamic* (Princeton, NJ: Princeton University Press, 2016), 158–65; 179, and 182.

41. Hodgson, *Venture of Islam*, 1: 72–79.

42. Ibid., 362.

43. Ibid., 394–95.

44. One should not forget, however, that Judaism has not been entirely alien to proselytizing; pre-Islamic Arabian inscriptions and Ethiopian chronicles mention the forceful conversion to Judaism of Christians by the Jewish king of Yemen, Dhu Nuwas (killed around 525 CE); see M. R. Al-Assouad's article "Dhu Nuwas" in *Encyclopedia of Islam*, 2nd ed., online edition: http://referenceworks.brillonline.com, and Glen Bowersock, *The Throne of Adulis: Red Sea Wars on the Eve of Islam* (Oxford: Oxford University Press, 2013), 78–105; for the proselytizing activities of Jewish merchants in the Caucasus, the Don Steppes, and the Volga region, see Richard Fry, *Ibn Fadlan's Journey to Russia* (Princeton, NJ: Markus Wiener, 2nd printing, 2006), 109–13.

45. Richard Finn, *Asceticism in the Graeco-Roman World* (Cambridge: Cambridge University Press, 2009), 34–57; Gershom Scholem, *Major Trends in Jewish Mysticism* (New York: Schocken Books, 1995), 1–79; Hodgson, *Venture of Islam*, 2: 202.

46. See a classical study of the subject by Vööbus, *History of Asceticism in the Syrian Orient*; for more recent studies see Wimbush and Valantasis, *Asceticism*; Valantasis, *Making of the Self*; and Hagman, *Asceticism of Isaac of Nineveh*. Note that, their titles notwithstanding, these studies deal as much with mysticism as with asceticism due to their authors' very broad definition of "asceticism" and the resultant tendency to place ascetic-mystical trends in Christianity under this broad rubric; for an opposite tendency, that is, to present various manifestations of asceticism as mysticism, see Bernard McGinn's four-volume series of studies titled *The Presence of God: A History of Western Christian Mysticism*.

47. Finn, *Asceticism*, 9–33, and John Pinsent, "Ascetic Moods in Greek and Latin Literature," in Wimbush and Valantasis, *Asceticism*, 211–19.

48. According to William McNeill, the famed proponent of the thesis of "the human web(s)," "People communicate information and use that information to guide their future behavior. They also communicate, or transfer, useful technologies, goods, crops, ideas, and much else"; John McNeill and William McNeill, *The Human Web: A Bird's-Eye View of World History* (New York: W. W. Norton, 2003), 3; a similar view of the evolution of the human race is taken by Jared Diamond in his *Guns, Germs, and Steel: The Fates of Human Societies* (New York: Norton, 2005), passim; in regard to the Muslim world, see Richard Eaton, "Islamic History as Global History," in *Islamic and European Expansion: The Forging of a Global Order*, ed. Michael Adas (Philadelphia: Temple University Press, 1993), 16–19.

49. See note 4 above, and Andrae, *In the Garden*, 8–9 passim; Margaret Smith, *Studies in Early Mysticism in the Near and Middle East* (London: Sheldon Press; New York: Macmillan, 1931), 249–50 and 124.

50. See the references in the previous note and Alexander Knysh, trans., *Al-Qushayri's Epistle*, "Index" under "Monk(s)."

51. Smith, *Studies in Early Mysticism*, 245.

52. For details see Alexander Knysh, "Historiography of Sufi Studies in the West

and Russia," *Pis'mennye pamiatniki Vostoka (Written Monuments of the Orient)* 1, no. 4 (2006): 227–28; we will have a chance to revisit this common explanation later on.

53. As shown convincingly, e.g., in Marijan Molé, *Les mystiques musulmans* (Paris: Presses Universitaires de France, 1965), 3–26.

54. For a tortuous and inconclusive discussion of the issue, see Nile Green, *Sufism: A Global History* (Chichester, UK: Wiley-Blackwell, 2012), 16–23.

55. For a classical formulation of this idea, see Massignon, *Essay on the Origins of the Technical Language of Islamic Mysticism*, 35–36, 45–72, and 94–98. For authoritative statements to this effect, see the works of S. H. Nasr, Carl Ernst, and William Chittick, to name but the most distinguished.

56. To use the title of Montgomery Watt's seminal book *The Majesty That Was Islam: The Islamic World, 66–1100* (New York: Praeger, 1974).

57. Carl Ernst, *Words of Ecstasy in Sufism* (Albany: State University of New York Press, 1985), 2, and Ernst, *Shambhala Guide*, 3–4 and 121; Nile Green's discussion of the issue obfuscates more than it reveals due precisely to his concern for "political correctness"; see Green, *Sufism*, 16–23.

58. Massignon, *Essay on the Origins of the Technical Language of Islamic Mysticism*, 73; a slightly different translation is given in Christmann, "Reclaiming Mysticism," 63.

59. Massignon, *Essay on the Origins of the Technical Language of Islamic Mysticism*, 35–36, 42–45, 50–52, 87–88, 95, etc., and Jacques Waardenburg, *L'Islam dans le miroir de l'Occident* (Paris: Mouton, 1963), 168, 172, 184, 204–7, 227, 257.

60. For a recent critical analysis of Massignon's overall approach to Islam in general and Sufism in particular, see Robert Irwin, *Dangerous Knowledge: Orientalism and Its Discontents* (Woodstock, NY: Overlook Press, 2006), "Index" under "Massignon, Louis."

61. Massignon, *Essay on the Origins of the Technical Language of Islamic Mysticism*, 94–98 passim; cf. Michael Sells, *Early Islamic Mysticism* (New York: Paulist Press, 1995), 19–56, and our entry "Sufism and the Qur'an" in *Encyclopedia of the Qur'an*, 6 vols., ed. Jane McAuliffe (Leiden: E. J. Brill, 2001–6), online edition: http://referenceworks.brillonline.com.

62. E.g., such important Sufi terms "[self-]annihilation and abiding [in God]" (*fana'/baqa'*), see Javid Mojaddedi, "Annihilation and Abiding in God," *EI3*; http://referenceworks.brillonline.com/entries/encyclopaedia-of-islam-3.

63. Andrae, *In the Garden*, 8; cf. Gabriel Said Reynolds, *The Qur'an and Its Biblical Subtext* (London: Routledge, 2010), 245–53 passim.

64. On this issue, see the recent studies by Angelika Neuwirth and Gabriel Said Reynolds.

65. Reynolds, *The Qur'an*, 51–54, 81–89, and 245–53.

66. Ibid., 257–58, and Harald Motzki, "Alternative Accounts of the Qur'an's Formation," in *The Cambridge Companion to the Qur'an*, ed. Jane McAuliffe (Cambridge: Cambridge University Press, 2006), 65–71; cf. Angelika Neuwirth, "Structural, Linguistic and Literary Features," ibid., 97–113.

67. See, e.g., Sharif Hazza' Sharif, *Naqd/tasawwuf: al-nass, al-kitab, al-tafkik* (Beirut: Dar al-Intishar al-'Arabi, 2008), 37–46; Seyyed Hossein Nasr, *Islamic Life*

and Thought (London: Allen and Unwin, 1981), 117–19; Reynolds, *The Qur'an*, 20–21, and Kevin van Bladel, *The Arabic Hermes: From Pagan Sage to Prophet of Science* (Oxford: Oxford University Press, 2009).

68. My use of the term "proto-Sufism" here is a gesture toward the recent efforts to posit discontinuity between the first Muslim ascetics and mystics and their Sufi successors who laid claim to their highly valued legacy; see, e.g., Green, *Sufism*, 15–16 and 23.

69. For parallels and affinities between Sufism and (ascetic-mystical) Christianity, see Ibrahim Basyuni, *Nash'at al-tasawwuf al-islami* (Cairo: Dar al-Ma'arif, 1969), 13–14; Maria Jaoudi, *Christian and Islamic Spirituality: Sharing a Journey* (New York: Paulist Press, 1993); Paul Oliver, *Mysticism: A Guide for the Perplexed* (London: Continuum, 2009); Llewellyn Vaughan-Lee, *The Prayer of the Heart in Christian and Sufi Mysticism* (Point Reyes, CA: Golden Sufi Center, 2012); Cheryl Urbanczyk, "Parallels between Sufism and Christianity," http://thesunnahway.wordpress.com/2011/01/04/parallels-between-sufism-and-christianity/; for Muslim views of the issue, see Elizabeth Sirriyeh, *Sufis and Anti-Sufis* (Richmond, Surrey: Curzon, 1999), 3–4; Ernst, *Shambhala Guide*, 3; 'Umar 'Abdallah Kamil, *Al-tasawwuf bayn al-ifrat wa 'l-tafrit* (Cairo: Dar Nahdat Misr, 2011), 122–27; Mustafa Bahu, *'Ulama' al-Maghrib wa muqawamatuhum li-bida' wa 'l-tasawwuf wa 'l-quburiyya wa 'l-mawasim*, 2nd ed. (Morocco: Jaridat al-Sabil, 2007), 137; 'Amir Hasan 'Amir, *Naqd al-tasawwuf* (Cairo: Al-Sawt al-'Ali, 2008), 164–65, 256–59 passim.

70. Vööbus, *History of Asceticism*, chapter 4.

71. Quoted in Knysh, "Historiography of Sufi Studies," 227.

72. For an attempt at deconstruction of Marx's famous adage, see Christopher Hitchens, *God Is Not Great: How Religion Poisons Everything* (New York: Twelve, 2007), 9–10.

73. Vööbus, *History of Asceticism*, v.

74. See Knysh, "Historiography of Sufi Studies," 228–29.

75. Massignon, *Essay on the Origins of the Technical Language of Islamic Mysticism*, 111–19; Knysh, *Islamic Mysticism*, 94–101.

76. Friedrich Engels, *The German Revolutions*, ed. Leonard Krieger (Chicago: University of Chicago Press, 1967), 34–35, and Engels, *Anti-Dühring* (New York: International Publishers, 1966), 26–29 and 344–45; Yuri Levada, *Sochineniia*, 5 vols. (Moscow: Karpov E. B., 2011), 1: 113–21 and 155–206.

77. Engels, *German Revolutions*, 36–38, and Levada, *Sochineniia*, 1: 181–87 and 191–92.

78. Goldziher, *Introduction*, 131–32, and Gerald Hawting, *The First Dynasty of Islam* (Carbondale: Southern Illinois University Press, 1987), 4–5, 51–52, 69–70, 76–81.

79. Engels, *German Revolutions*, 34, and Engels, *Anti-Dühring*, 344–45.

80. Goldziher, *Introduction*, 131–32.

81. Hodgson, *Venture of Islam*, 1: 247–79, and Knysh, *Islam in Historical Perspective*, 98–121.

82. For various types of ascetics-mystics in that age, see Knysh, *Islamic Mysticism*, 18–67.

83. See, e.g., Green, *Sufism*, 16–26; for an alternative account, see Radtke, *Neue kritische Gänge*, 257–59 and 283–85.

84. See Knysh, *Islamic Mysticism*, 116–49.

85. Bryan Turner, "Towards an Economic Model of Virtuoso Religion," in *Islamic Dilemmas: Reformers, Nationalists, and Industrialization*, ed. Ernest Gellner (Berlin: Mouton, 1985), 49–72, especially p. 49.

86. Shmuel Eisenstadt, ed., *Max Weber on Charisma and Institution Building* (Chicago: University of Chicago Press, 1968), passim.

87. See, e.g., Syeda Hameed, ed., *The Contemporary Relevance of Sufism* (New Delhi: Indian Council for Cultural Relations, 1993), especially the articles by Khaliq Ahmad Nizami, Mohammad Ishaq Khan, and Anwar Moazzam; cf. Ahmet Karamustafa, *God's Unruly Friends: Dervish Groups in the Islamic Later Middle Period* (Salt Lake City: University of Utah Press, 1994); Christopher Melchert, "Origins and Early Sufism," in *The Cambridge Companion to Sufism*, ed. Lloyd Ridgeon (Cambridge: Cambridge University Press, 2015), 13–18.

88. Elizabeth Clark, *Reading Renunciation: Asceticism and Scripture in Early Christianity* (Princeton, NJ: Princeton University Press, 1999), 22.

89. Ibid., 23, and Hagman, *Asceticism of Isaac of Nineveh*, 18.

90. Radtke, "Tasawwuf," in *EI2*, online edition: http://referenceworks.brillonline, and Radtke, *Neue kritische Gänge*, 284; curiously, Radtke never gives a definition of this term whose meaning is far from obvious; the same term is occasionally applied to Sufis by Ahmet Karamustafa ("the mediating *religiosi*"), who, too, never explains either its meaning or provenance; see *God's Unruly Friends*, 88.

91. See, e.g., http://www.newadvent.org/cathen/10579a.htm.

92. Radtke rejects Melchert's thesis (repeated recently by Nile Green in his *Sufism*, 20–22) about the distinctiveness of asceticism (*zuhd*) vis-à-vis mysticism (*tasawwuf*); see Radtke, *Neue kritische Gänge*, 258–59 and 284–85.

93. See Engels, *German Revolutions*, 34–39, and Engels, *Anti-Dühring*, 25; cf. Levada, *Sochineniia*, 1: 182–89 and 191–92.

94. To use the definition proposed by Robert Rozehnal in his *Islamic Sufism Unbound* (New York: Palgrave Macmillan, 2007), 227–28; Christopher Melchert has questioned Radtke's claims regarding "antinomianism and disrepute" of the (proto-) Sufis made by the latter in his entry "Tasawwuf," *EI2*, online edition: http://reference works.brillonline.com; see Melchert, "Basran Origins of Classical Sufism," *Der Islam* 82 (2005): 229.

95. To borrow a term introduced into Sufi studies by Christopher Melchert; see, e.g., Melchert, "The Interpretation," 89–116.

96. Eisenstadt, *Max Weber*, 248–78 and 279–93; Turner, "Towards an Economic Model," passim.

97. Eisenstadt, *Max Weber*, 248–78 and 279–93.

98. Turner, "Towards an Economic Model," 59–63.

99. *Baraka* is an Arabic word for "divine blessing" or "grace," although some Western scholars have occasionally translated it as "life-increasing force"; see, e.g., Julian Baldick, *Mystical Islam: An Introduction to Sufism* (London: I. B. Tauris, 1989), 144, 154, 203, and 205.

100. Turner, "Towards an Economic Model," 63.

101. The applicability of Max Weber's ideas, which are based on his examination of Calvinist Christianity, to the study of Sufism is called in doubt by Bernd Radtke in his *Neue kritische Gänge*, 251–60.

102. Turner, "Towards an Economic Model," 62; cf. Karamustafa, *God's Unruly Friends*, chapter 4 and pp. 86–91.

103. Knysh, *Islamic Mysticism*, 10–35, and Radtke, *Neue kritische Gänge*, 259–85, and Radtke, *Materialen*, passim.

104. On him, see Livnat Holtzman, "Ahmad b. Hanbal," *EI3*, online edition: http://referenceworks.brillonline.com.

105. Michael Cooperson, "Ahmad Ibn Hanbal and Bishr al-Hafi," *Studia Islamica* 86, no. 2 (1997): 71–101; Knysh, *Al-Qushayri's Epistle*, 130–31; Knysh, *Islamic Mysticism*, 44; and Christopher Melchert, "Early Renunciants as Hadith Transmitters," *Muslim World* 92, no. 3–4 (2002): 407–18.

106. Knysh, *Islamic Mysticism*, 99–101 and 140.

107. Radtke, *Neue kritische Gänge*, 284.

108. See the entries on these two "imams of great scholarship and piety" in the *EI2*, online edition: http://referenceworks.brillonline.com.

109. For details see Michael Bonner, *Aristocratic Violence and Holy War* (New Haven, CT: American Oriental Society, 1996), passim, and Knysh, *Islamic Mysticism*, 18–19.

110. As evidenced, for instance, by the Khariji poetry; see, e.g., Ihsan 'Abbas, ed., *Shi'r al-khawarij* (Beirut: Dar al-thaqafa, 1974), and Annie Higgins, "The Qur'anic Exchange of the Self in the Poetry of *Shurat* (*Khariji*) Political Identity, 37–132 A.H./657–750 A.D." (unpublished PhD thesis, University of Chicago, 2001) (available through ProQuest theses and dissertations online).

111. This perception of medieval Islamdom is finely captured in the titles of the influential monographs by Montgomery Watt, *The Majesty That Was Islam: The Islamic World 661–1100* (New York: Praeger, 1974); Tarif Khalidi, *Classical Arab Islam: The Culture and Heritage of the Golden Age* (Princeton, NJ: Darwin Press, 1985); and Maurice Lombard, *The Golden Age of Islam*, trans. Joan Spencer (Princeton, NJ: Markus Wiener Publishers, 2004).

112. Hodgson, *Venture of Islam*, 1: 364.

113. Ibid., 360 and 392–409.

114. As far as we can tell, Crone's ruminations are inspired, at least in part, by the debates in modern neurology and biology about the provenance and peculiar functions of the human brain; see, e.g., Richard Dawkins, *The Selfish Gene*, 40th anniversary ed. (Oxford: Oxford University Press, 2016), 75–78 and 372–75.

115. Clifford Geertz *Interpretation of Cultures* (New York: Basic Books, 1973), 5, 44–46, 89.

116. Patricia Crone, *Pre-Industrial Societies: Anatomy of the Pre-Modern World* (Oxford: Oneworld, 2003), 124–25; this statement is taken almost verbatim from Geertz, *Interpretation of Cultures*, 47–50.

117. Crone, *Pre-Industrial Societies*, 125.

118. Geoffrey Harpham, *The Ascetic Imperative in Culture and Criticism* (Chi-

cago: University of Chicago Press, 1987), xi–xii, and Richard Valantasis, *The Making of the Self: Ancient and Modern Asceticism* (Eugene, OR: Cascade Books, 2008), 35–37.

119. Valantasis, *Making of the Self*, 38 and 55–56.

120. Bruno Latour, *Reassembling the Social: An Introduction to the Actor-Network Theory* (Oxford: Oxford University Press, 2005), 31.

121. Hodgson, *Venture of Islam*, 1: 360–64 and 392–409.

122. This view of Sufism was taken by Hodgson and harks back to his influential concept of an internal dialogue, "response and counter-response," between and among various strands within the agglomeration of societies that he defined as "Islamic civilization"; Hodgson, *Venture of Islam*, 1: 79–83. For a more recent notion of Islam as a discursive, "polyphonic" formation, see Talal Asad, "The Idea of an Anthropology of Islam," Washington DC: Center for Contemporary Arab Studies at Georgetown University. Occasional Papers, Georgetown University, March 1986, 13–17, and Asad, *Genealogies of Religion* (Baltimore: Johns Hopkins University Press, 1993), 1–54 and 200–236.

123. Green, *Sufism*, 3, 8–10, 15–18, 42–43, 130 passim.

124. As defined, for example, by the great Sufi thinker Ibn (al-)'Arabi (d. 1240). In William Chittick's apt paraphrase: "The cosmos is God's imagination. He imagines everything other than Himself, but, in so doing, He gives all things a certain mode of real and seemingly independent existence"; see William Chittick, *The Sufi Path of Knowledge: Ibn al-'Arabi's Metaphysics of Imagination* (Albany: State University of New York Press, 1989), 16. According to Ibn (al-)'Arabi, we imagine God in ways that reflect our own individual predispositions rather than witnessing the impenetrable and unfathomable essence of God himself. He writes, "The True Reality [God] is that which His servant creates in his heart by means of rational enquiry or by following an authoritative precedent. This is the god of belief that varies according to the preparedness of each individual locus (i.e., human being) [for God's self-manifestation]"; Ibn (al-)'Arabi, *Fusus al-hikam*, ed. Abu 'l-'Ala 'Afifi (Beirut: Dar al-kitab al-'arabi, 1980), 225. It is in this sense that Ibn (al-)'Arabi describes our imagining of God, the world, and its phenomena as "a dream within dream" or "imagination within imagination," because we (and our imaginings of God) are, according to Ibn (al-)'Arabi, "imagined or dreamed" by God himself. Seen from this vantage point, we are but "figments" of God's all-encompassing, creative imagination, who imagine the reality outside ourselves by means of our relatively independent faculty of imagination.

125. The concept of "spiritual cosmology" will be examined in some detail in chapter 3 of this book.

126. Ernst, *Shambhala Guide*, 26–31.

127. For a comprehensive critical analysis of Edward Said's ideas and argumentative strategies, see Daniel Varisco, *Reading Orientalism: Said and Unsaid* (Seattle: University of Washington Press, 2007).

128. See Alexander Knysh, "Contextualizing the Sufi-Salafi Conflict (From the Northern Caucasus to Hadramawt)," *Middle Eastern Studies* 43, no. 4 (2007): 503–30; a detailed discussion of the conflict between the Salafi and Sufi visions of Islam and its sociopolitical underpinnings is provided in chapter 6 of this book.

129. See Alexander Knysh, "A Tale of Two Poets: Sufism in Yemen during the Ot-

toman Epoch," in *Le soufisme á l'époque ottoman*, ed. Rachida Chih and Catherine Mayeur-Jaouen (Cairo: IFAO, 2010), 337–68; Ahmed, *What Is Islam?*, 19–26, 79–80, 98–101, 350–53, 398–400, 517–19.

Chapter 2: What's in a Name?

1. Lloyd Ridgeon, "Introduction," in *Sufis and Salafis in the Contemporary Age*, ed. Lloyd Ridgeon (London: Bloomsbury, 2015), 1; cf. Ridgeon, "Mysticism in Medieval Sufism," in *The Cambridge Companion to Sufism*, ed. Lloyd Ridgeon (Cambridge: Cambridge University Press, 2015), 25–49 passim; Omid Safi, "Bargaining with *Baraka*: Persian Sufism, 'Mysticism,' and Pre-Modern Politics," *Muslim World* 90, no. 3–4 (2000): 259–87; for a critical summary of Sufism's definitions in academic and semiacademic contexts, see Sara Sviri, "Sufism: Reconsidering Terms, Definitions, and Processes in the Formative Period of Islamic Mysticism," in *Les maîtres soufis et leurs disciples*, ed. Geneviève Gobillot and Jean-Jacques Thibon (Beirut: IFPO, 2012), 17–34.

2. For a typical example of the latter see the chapter "Sufism (*tasawwuf*)" in al-Qushayri's "Epistle on Sufism"; Alexander Knysh, trans., *Al-Qushayri's Epistle on Sufism* (Reading, UK: Garnet, 2007), 288–92; as will be shown, these two types of definitions of Sufism are not as incompatible as they might appear. They often merge and feed off each other to cater to various doctrinal and ideological stances, either hidden or explicit.

3. Sviri, "Sufism," 18–20.

4. Graham Harman, *Heidegger Explained* (Chicago: Open Court, 2007), 29.

5. In reference to Islam and Sufism in particular, see Katherine Ewing, *Arguing Sainthood: Modernity, Psychoanalysis, and Islam* (Durham, NC: Duke University Press, 1997), 7–15.

6. Harman, *Heidegger Explained*, 32–33.

7. Carl Ernst, *The Shambhala Guide to Sufism* (Boston: Shambhala, 1997), 2–3; for a critical reexamination of some recent reconceptualizations of Sufism and of the terminological toolbox used by Western students of Sufism, see Sviri, "Sufism," 17–20 passim.

8. Shahab Ahmed, *What Is Islam? The Importance of Being Islamic* (Princeton, NJ: Princeton University Press, 2016), 19–31, 78–79, 92–97, 125–26, 286–90.

9. Henry Corbin himself preferred to use the term "esotericism" and its derivatives.

10. Henry Corbin, *En Islam iranien*, vol. 1, *Le Shi'isme duodécimain* (Paris: Gallimard, 1971), xi; cf. Matthijs van den Bos, *The Mystic Regimes: Sufism and the State in Iran; From the Late Qajar Era to the Islamic Republic* (Leiden: E. J. Brill, 2002), 45; see also Michael Fischer and Mehdi Abedi, *Debating Muslims* (Madison: University of Wisconsin Press, 1990), 119 and 452–54; passages from the latter work feature Ayatollah Khomeini's "poetic flirtations" with "antinomian" themes of wine and free love patterned on the scandalous utterings of the controversial Sunni mystic (al-) Husayn b. Mansur al-Hallaj, executed on charges of heresy in 309/922.

11. Bos, *Mystic Regimes*, 45.

12. Nasrollah Pourjavady, "Opposition to Sufism in Twelver Shiism," in *Islamic*

Mysticism Contested: Thirteen Centuries of Controversies and Polemics, ed. Frederick de Jong and Bernd Radtke (Leiden: E. J. Brill, 1999), 614.

13. For details on the impact of Ibn (al-)'Arabi's thought on the later Islamic intellectual tradition, see James Morris, "Ibn 'Arabi and His Interpreters," *Journal of the American Oriental Society* 106 (1986): 539–51, and 107 (1987): 101–19; for more recent references see Alexander Knysh and Ali Hussain, "Ibn al-'Arabi," *Oxford Bibliographies in Islamic Studies*, ed. John O. Voll. (New York: Oxford University Press, 2016): http://www.oxfordbibliographies.com/view/document/obo-9780195390155/obo-9780195390155-0206.xml?rskey=ApEPqk&result=62; whether or not Ibn (al-)'Arabi should be identified primarily and exclusively as "a Sufi" is doubted by William Chittick in his "Ibn Arabi," *The Stanford Encyclopedia of Philosophy* (spring 2014 ed.), Edward N. Zalta, ed., http://plato.stanford.edu/archives/spr2014/entries/ibn-arabi/; Chittick's misgivings apart, overall Ibn (al-)'Arabi's close association with Sufism from the beginning to the end of his career as thinker and writer is hardly in doubt.

14. Pourjavady, "Opposition to Sufism," 619–21, and Mangol Bayat, "Anti-Sufism in Iran," in Jong and Radtke, *Islamic Mysticism Contested*, 624 and 628.

15. In this particular case, the oppositional Iranian intellectual 'Abd al-Karim Soroush/Sorush (b. 1945), who now lives in exile in the West; see Bos, *Mystic Regimes*, 232–33.

16. Ibid., 235, and Martin van Bruinessen, "Sufism, 'Popular' Islam and the Encounter with Modernity," in *Islam and Modernity: Key Issues and Debates*, ed. Muhammad Khalid Masud, Armando Salvatore, and Martin van Bruinessen (Edinburgh: Edinburgh University Press, 2009), 143; a similar dichotomy between "sophisticated" philosophical Sufism and its "profane" or "quotidian" version current among the Sunnis was articulated, upon my request, by the renowned Iranian American scholar of Sufism S. H. Nasr during a seminar he held at the University of Michigan on September 17, 2015; Nasr basically reconfirmed the elitist, philosophically based view of Sufism that he had advanced earlier in his popular *Sufi Essays* (Albany: State University of New York Press, 1972), 13–14 and 105.

17. Richard Gramlich, *Die Schiitischen Derwischorden Persiens*, vol. 1 (Wiesbaden: Franz Steiner, 1965), 5 and 28–29.

18. Said Amir Arjomand, *The Shadow of God and the Hidden Imam* (Chicago: University of Chicago Press, 1984), 111; the meaning of "Sophi" in this context is moot and may refer to Shah 'Abbas's ancestor Shaykh Safi al-Din al-Ardabili (d. 735/1334), who was indeed a Sufi teacher; see Franz Babinger and Roger Savory, "Safi al-Din Ardabili," *EI2*, online edition: http://referenceworks.brillonline.com.

19. Arjomand, *Shadow of God*, 112–19 and 153–54.

20. Bos, *Mystic Regimes*, 51, citing the works of Said Amir Arjomand and Mangol Bayat, mentioned above.

21. Arjomand, *Shadow of God*, 147.

22. Ibid., 148; for definitions of *'irfan/'erfan* in Iranian Sufism of the Safavid epoch, see Richard Gramlich, *Die Schiitischen Derwischorden Persiens*, vol. 2 (Wiesbaden: Franz Steiner, 1976), notes 726 and 825.

23. Arjomand, *Shadow of God*, 147.

24. Ibid., 66–84.

25. Ibid., 149.

26. Ibid., 152 and 154–56, and Michael Fischer, *Iran: From Religious Dispute to Revolution* (Cambridge, MA: Harvard University Press, 1980), 140, 142, 144, and 146.

27. Arjomand, *Shadow of God*, 152 and 154–56; Bos, *Mystic Regimes*, 5; see also Kamil al-Shaibi, *Sufism and Shi'ism* (Surbiton, Surrey: LAAM, 1991), chapter 8; Kathryn Babayan, "Sufis, Dervishes, and Mullahs: The Controversy over Spiritual and Temporal Dominion in Seventeenth-Century Iran," *Pembroke Papers* 4 (1996): 117–38.

28. For the vicissitudes of Sufism under the Iranian dynasties, see al-Shaibi, *Sufism and Shi'ism*, chapters 6 and 8; Arjomand, *Shadow of God*, 109–19, 152–59, 243–44; al-Shaibi, "The Mujtahid of the Age and the Mulla-bashi," in *Authority and Political Culture in Shi'ism*, ed. Said Amir Arjomand (Albany: State University of New York Press, 1988), 84, 109, and 343; Bos, *Mystic Regimes*, 55–60; see also Bayat, "Anti-Sufism," 625; Pourjavady, "Opposition," 622–23; Knysh, *Islamic Mysticism*, 223.

29. Pourjavady, "Opposition," 621; for the more practical connotations of *hikma(t)* and ways to obtain it in the modern-day Iranian branches of the Ni'matullahiyya, see Gramlich, *Die Schiitischen*, 2: 412.

30. Arjomand, *Shadow of God*, 23, 148–50 passim.

31. Ibid., 153, quoting several seventeenth-century Iranian theological texts.

32. Bos, *Mystic Regimes*, 47–48, and Babayan, "Sufis, Dervishes, and Mullahs," 127–29 and 131–32.

33. Pourjavady, "Opposition," 619–21; Bos, *Mystic Regimes*, 46–50, and Alexander Knysh and Ali Hussain, "Ibn al-'Arabi," in *Oxford Bibliographies in Islamic Studies*, ed. by John O. Voll (New York: Oxford University Press, 2016): http://www.oxford bibliographies.com/view/document/obo-9780195390155/obo-9780195390155 -0206.xml?rskey=ApEPqk&result=62; see section "Ibn al-'Arabi in Shi'i Islam."

34. That Ibn (al-)'Arabi, the originator of these ideas, considered himself a Sufi is hardly in doubt. This is abundantly attested by his own writings; see, e.g., Ralph Austin, trans., *Sufis of Andalusia: The "Ruh al-quds" and "al-Durrat al-fakhira" of Ibn 'Arabi*, 2nd ed. (Berkeley: University of California Press, 1977), 50–59 passim. His magnum opus titled "The Meccan Revelations" (*al-Futuhat al-makkiya*) is another eloquent testimony to his identity as a Sufi master and thinker.

35. For later attribution of pole-hood and sainthood to leaders of Shi'i dervish groups (who usually claimed descent from the Prophet), see Gramlich, *Die Schiitischen*, 1: 1 and 5–6, and 2: 158–60.

36. Bos, *Mystic Regimes*, 235, and Bruinessen, "Sufism," 143.

37. Fischer, *Iran*, 28–30, 67–69, 139–46, 292, 294 passim. For further evidence see the webpage of the Institute of Islamic Studies at the University of Tehran: http:// ut.ac.ir/en/page/639/about-the-institute.

38. Fischer, *Iran*, 292 and 294.

39. See the seminal studies by Richard Gramlich, *Die Schiitische Derwischorden Persiens*, 3 vols. (Wiesbaden: Frantz Steiner, 1965–81), passim, and Bos, *Mystic Regimes*, passim; cf. Fischer, *Iran*, 139–46, 290, and 292.

40. As shown by Bos in his *Mystic Regimes*, chapter 1, see especially note 41 on p. 44.

41. Arjomand, *Shadow of God*, 23.

42. Ibid., and Nasr, *Sufi Essays*, 105.

43. Arjomand, *Shadow of God*, 23; cf. Fischer, *Iran*, 140–46; S. H. Nasr's numerous

writings on Sufism generally and Sufi philosophy in particular evince the same attitude; see, e.g., *Sufi Essays*, especially the chapter titled "Shi'ism and Sufism: Their Relationship in Essence and History," 104–22.

44. See Sviri, "Sufism," 19.

45. As argued by Ernst, *Shambhala Guide*, 1–31, and Safi, "Bargaining with *Baraka*," 259–87.

46. For a helpful "unpacking" of the notion of "philosophical Sufism" in both Muslim and Orientalist writings, see Anna Akasoy, "What Is Philosophical Sufism?" in *In the Age of Averroes: Arabic Philosophy in the Sixth/Twelfth Century*," ed. Peter Adamson (London; Turin: Warburg Institute; Nino Agarno Editore, 2011), 229–49.

47. See Chittick's article on Ibn (al-)'Arabi in *Stanford Encyclopedia of Philosophy*; online: http://plato.stanford.edu/entries/ibn-arabi/. Chittick's reluctance to identify the great mystical thinker as a Sufi par excellence is enthusiastically endorsed by the Russian historian of Islamic philosophy Andrei Smirnov in his *Ibn Arabi: Izbrannoe* ("Ibn 'Arabi: Selected Works") (Moscow: Iazyki slavianskoi kul'tury and OOO Sadra, 2014), 81; like Chittick, Smirnov wants to see Ibn (al-)'Arabi as a mouthpiece of a sophisticated "philosophical mysticism" first and foremost, ibid., 80.

48. Contrary to the evidence of Ibn (al-)'Arabi's own autobiographical and theological writings; see note 34 above.

49. Chittick's reluctance to apply the adjective "mystical" to Sufi metaphysics seems to be part of his philosophizing approach to the Sufi tradition; see, e.g., Sviri, "Sufism," 18–19, note 3.

50. See Carl Ernst, "Traditionalism, the Perennial Philosophy, and Islamic Studies," *Middle East Studies Association Bulletin* 28, no. 2 (1994): 176–81; available online: http://www.unc.edu/~cernst/Traditionalism.htm; cf. Mark Sedgwick, *Against the Modern World* (Oxford: Oxford University Press, 2004), part 1, p. 157.

51. As correctly pointed out by Carl Ernst in his *Shambhala Guide*, 8–18 and 147–49; the same observation was made earlier in Knysh, "Historiography of Islamic Studies," passim.

52. Ahmed, *What Is Islam?*, 350–54.

53. This conclusion is based on this author's own personal encounters with Sufis over the past thirty-five years of his academic career and, as such, should be judged subjective.

54. See, e.g., Edward Said, *Orientalism* (New York: Vintage Books, 1979), "Index" under "philology," and Ernst, *Shambhala Guide*, 8–18 and 169–73; Tomoko Masuzawa, *The Invention of World Religions* (Chicago: University of Chicago Press, 2005), chapters 5 and 7; Robert Rozehnal, *Islamic Sufism Unbound* (New York: Palgrave Macmillan, 2007), 13–14; Ali Mirsepassi and Tadd Fernée, *Islam, Democracy, and Cosmopolitanism: At Home and in the World* (Cambridge: Cambridge University Press, 2014), 142; cf. Varisco, *Reading Orientalism*, 40–43, 112–15 passim.

55. Of special interest to scholars are Sufi activities aimed at subduing the body to the rigors of "bodily regimes" or pedagogical uses of the body by Sufi masters (*shaykhs*), including gestures, postures, spatial positioning, and various other means of edification through equivocation.

56. See, e.g., Shahzad Bashir, *Sufi Bodies: Religion and Society in Medieval Islam* (New York: Columbia University Press, 2011), and Scott Kugle, *Sufis and Saints' Bod-

ies: Mysticism, Corporeality, and Sacred Power in Islam (Chapel Hill: University of North Carolina Press, 2007); cf. Vincent Cornell, *Realm of the Saint: Power and Authority in Moroccan Sufism* (Austin: University of Texas Press, 1998), xxix–xxxvi and 196–97.

57. For example, Robert Rozehnal's illuminating study of the Pakistani-Malaysian Sufi lineage named "Chishtiyya-Sabiriyya," although conducted as a field study, ends up focusing primarily on the brotherhood's textual production; see *Islamic Sufism Unbound*, passim; the same applies to Shahzad Bashir's examination of *Sufi Bodies* (see the previous note) and Vincent Cornell's sociological study of Moroccan Sufism; see his *Realm of the Saint*, 93–120 passim.

58. Sedgwick, *Against the Modern World*, 266.

59. James Morris, "Situating Islamic 'Mysticism': Between Written Tradition and Popular Spirituality," in *Mystics of the Book: Themes, Topics, and Typologies*, ed. R. A. Herrera (New York: Peter Lang, 1993), 293–334; see also Kugle, *Sufis and Saints' Bodies*, 12–14.

60. See, e.g., Ewing, *Arguing Sainthood*; Earle Waugh, *The Munshidin of Egypt: Their World and Their Song* (Columbia: University of South Carolina Press, 1989), Waugh, *Visionaries of Silence: The Reformist Sufi Order of the Demirdashiya al-Khalwatiya in Cairo* (Cairo: American University in Cairo Press, 2008); Ismail Alatas, "Aligning the Sunna and the Jama'a: The Religious Authority and Islamic Social Formation in Contemporary Central Java" (unpublished PhD thesis defended at the University of Michigan in February 2016).

61. For a typical example see Karin Jironet, *Sufi Mysticism into the West: The Life and Leadership of Hazrat Inayat Khan's Brothers: 1927–1967* (Leuven: Peeters, 2009), chapter 1 passim; cf. Sedgwick, *Against the Modern World*, passim; Ernst, "Traditionalism," passim; see also the numerous works of S. H. Nasr and William Chittick.

62. For a relevant firsthand observation in a German context, see Radtke, *Neue kritische Gänge*, 7; the designation of Sufism as "Islamic mysticism" has been challenged by a number of Western-trained academics, including Omid Safi, who, in turn, derives his inspiration from Richard King's *Orientalism and Religion* published in 1999; Omid Safi, "Bargaining with *Baraka*," 280–81.

63. Morris, "Situating," 307–8.

64. Radtke, *Neue kritische Gänge*, 1–25; Sviri, "Sufism," 18.

65. To rephrase the title of the influential comparative study of various regional manifestations of Sufism and Islam by Clifford Geertz, *Islam Observed: Religious Development in Morocco and Indonesia* (New Haven, CT: Yale University Press, 1968).

66. Morris, "Situating," 302–3.

67. See, e.g., Alexander Knysh, "The '*tariqa*' on a Landcruiser: The Resurgence of Sufism in Yemen," *Middle East Journal* 55, no. 3 (2001): 399–414. Likewise, in the premodern age, the initial perceptions of Ibn (al-)'Arabi by his contemporaries were based on his demeanor and oral statements rather than his texts. As time went on, Muslim scholars became more concerned with his written legacy and reoriented their attention to his metaphysical ideas and gnoseology; see Knysh, *Ibn 'Arabi in the Later Islamic Tradition: The Making of a Polemical Image in Medieval Islam* (Albany: State University of New York Press, 1999), chapter 1.

68. Cornell, *Realm of the Saint*, chapter 7.

69. To use the title of chapter 1 of Jironet, *Sufi Mysticism*, 1.

70. The alternative spelling/pronunciation is *wilaya*; with the exception of Vincent Cornell (*Realm of the Saint*, xvii–xxi passim), scholars of Islam and Sufism do not usually draw a semantic distinction between these two variants of the Arabic verbal noun.

71. Andrea Farshakh and Henry Corbin, quoted in Bos, *Mystic Regimes*, 46 note 5.

72. In addition to the aforementioned study of *walaya/wilaya* by Vincent Cornell, see also Bernd Radtke and John O'Kane, trans., *The Concept of Sainthood in Early Islamic Mysticism: Two Works by al-Hakim al-Tirmidhi* (Richmond, Surrey: Curzon, 1996); Michel Chodkiewicz, *Seal of the Saints: Prophethood and Sainthood in the Doctrine of Ibn 'Arabi*, trans. Liadain Sherrard (Cambridge: Islamic Texts Society, 1993), passim; John Renard, *Friends of God: Islamic Images of Piety, Commitment, and Servanthood* (Berkeley: University of California Press, 2008).

73. Gramlich, *Die Schiitischen*, 1: 1 and 5; Bos, *Mystic Regimes*, 46.

74. See, e.g., Knysh, *Al-Qushayri's Epistle*, 268–73, and Austin, *Sufis of Andalusia*, 79, 96–98, 114–16, 124–27 passim.

75. Pourjavady, "Opposition," 618–19, and Arjomand, *Shadow of God*, 147 and 172–73.

76. Gramlich, *Die Schiitischen*, 1: 5.

77. This is not to deny that many Sufi *awliya'* in Sunni Islam, such as al-Shadhili, al-Jazuli, Ahmad b. Idris, and many others, claimed descent from the Prophet's family; although not a prerequisite, this genealogical claim certainly enhanced their stature among their followers; see, e.g., Cornell, *Realm of the Saint*, xxv–xxix and 272–85.

78. Pourjavady, "Opposition," 618–19; Arjomand, *Shadow of God*, 147 and 172–73; and Bos, *Mystic Regimes*, 46.

79. Arjomand, *Shadow of God*, 147; for further discussions of Shi'i notions of *walaya* and their relations with Sunni-Sufi ones, see Gramlich, *Die Schiitischen*, 1: 1 and 5; 2: 158–81; Henry Corbin, *En Islam iranien*, vol. 3, *Les Fidèles d'amour Shî'isme et soufisme* (Paris: Gallimard, 1971–72), 149–355; Nasr, *Sufi Essays* (Albany: State University of New York Press, 1973), 104–20; cf. Mohammad Ali Amir-Moezzi, *The Spirituality of Shii Islam: Beliefs and Practices* (London: I. B. Tauris, 2011), chapter 7.

80. Gramlich, *Die Schiitischen*, 1: 5.

81. As shown in Bos, *Mystic Regimes*, 46–47 passim.

82. See, e.g., Shahzad Bashir, *Messianic Hopes and Mystical Visions: The Nurbakhshiyya between Medieval and Modern Islam* (Columbia: University of South Carolina Press, 2003), 35–41, and Knysh, *Islamic Mysticism*, 239–44.

83. Pourjavady, "Opposition," 618–19; Mohammad Ali Amir-Moezzi, *The Divine Guide in Early Shi'ism*, trans. David Streight (Albany: State University of New York Press, 1994), 159 passim; for the Nurbakhshiyya see Bashir, *Messianic Hopes*, 262–73 and 283–87.

84. Arjomand, *Shadow of God*, 112–19, 157–58, and 244; Bashir, *Messianic Hopes*, 285, and Al-Shaibi, *Sufism and Shi'ism*, chapter 8.

85. Arjomand, *Shadow of God*, 141–59; Bashir, *Messianic Hopes*, 284–85; al-Shaibi, *Sufism and Shi'ism*, 321–23.

86. Arjomand, *Shadow of God*, 141–59.

87. Spencer Trimingham, *The Sufi Orders in Islam*, with a new foreword by John Voll (Oxford: Oxford University Press, 1998), 250.

88. Ibid., 249.

89. Bruinessen, "Sufism," 125.

90. E.g., in the Kingdom of Saudi Arabia and Turkey, see ibid. Note, however, that the prohibition has not been strictly enforced of late; for a regional (Yemeni) manifestation of this ubiquitous phenomenon, see Alexander Knysh, "The Cult of Saints and Religious Reformism in Early Twentieth-Century Hadramawt," *New Arabian Studies* 4 (1997): 139–67.

91. We apologize for the pun.

92. For a typical array of arguments against "believers in the dead" (*quburiuyyn*), see Muhammad Memon, *Ibn Taimiya's Struggle against Popular Religion* (The Hague: Mouton, 1976), passim; Bernard Haykel, *Revival and Reform in Islam: The Legacy of Muhammad al-Shawkani* (Cambridge: Cambridge University Press, 2003), 130–38; see also Knysh, *Islam in Historical Perspective*, 237–38, 291–94, and 401–5, and Bernard Haykel, "Salafist Doctrine," in *Global Salafism: Islam's New Religious Movement*, ed. Roel Meijer (London: Hurst, 2009), 38–42.

93. See, e.g., Gino Schallenbergh, "Ibn Qayyim al-Jawziyya's Manipulation of Sufi Terms: Fear and Hope," in *Islamic Theology, Philosophy and Law: Debating Ibn Taymiyya and Ibn Qayyim al-Jawziyya*, ed. Birgit Krawietz and Georges Tamer (Berlin: Walter de Gruyter, 2013), 102–3 and 117–20.

94. Memon, *Ibn Taimiya's Struggle*, 24.

95. Ibid., 15–20, 47, 60–69, 77–78, and 83; Alina Kokoschka and Birgit Krawietz, "Appropriation of Ibn Taymiyya and Ibn Qayyim al-Jawziyya," in *Islamic Theology, Philosophy, and Law: Debating Ibn Taymiyya and Ibn Qayyim al-Jawziyya*, ed. Birgit Krawietz and Georges Tamer (Berlin: Walter de Gruyter, 2013); a similar position was espoused by Ibn Qayym al-Jawziyya; see Schallenbergh, "Ibn Qayym al-Jawziyya's Manipulation," 96–97.

96. For Ibn Taymiyya's understanding of "orthodox Sufism," see Th. Emil Homerin, "Ibn Taimiyah's *al-Sufiyah wa 'l-fuqara'*," *Arabica* 32, no. 2 (1985): 219–44; cf. the selective appropriation by Ibn Qayyim al-Jawziyya of Sufi concepts and terminology with a view to stripping them of their elitist character and making them available to the Muslim everyman; Schallenbergh, "Ibn Qayym al-Jawziyya's Manipulation," passim.

97. Schallenbergh, "Ibn Qayym al-Jawziyya's Manipulation," 96–97.

98. As acknowledged by Ibn Taymiyya himself; see Memon, *Ibn Taimiya's Struggle*, 66–69; cf. Trimingham, *Sufi Orders*, chapters 8 and 9 passim, and Knysh, *Islam in Historical Perspective*, 253–55, 291–93, and 418.

99. One recent study of al-Tirmidhi has shown that he himself took a negative view of the "wearers of wool" (that is, Sufis), both their woolen habit and their claim that poverty should take precedence over wealth; Sviri, "Sufism," 27 and 32; a similar conclusion was reached by my colleague Dr. Aiyub Palmer, who has written a doctoral dissertation on al-Tirmidhi and his concept of *walaya/wilaya*. Nevertheless, in the subsequent centuries, al-Tirmidhi's theory of *walaya/wilaya*, elaborated by a number of prominent Sufi thinkers (*shaykh*s), has become an integral and highly important part of the Sufi tradition.

100. For references see note 72 above.

101. Lit. "chains" connecting Sufi teachers (*shaykhs*) to the founders of their spiritual traditions all the way to the Prophet and his successors.

102. Memon, *Ibn Taimiya's Struggle*, 13–20, and Ernest Gellner, ed., *Islamic Dilemmas: Reformers, Nationalists, Industrialization* (Berlin: Mouton, 1995), chapters by Bryan Turner, Emanuel Marx, Paul Pascan, Kenneth Brown, Wim van Binsbergen, and Alexandre Popovic.

103. See, e.g., Peter Brown, *The Cult of the Saints: Its Rise and Function in Latin Christianity* (Chicago: University of Chicago Press, 1981), and Owen Chadwick, *The Early Reformation on the Continent* (Oxford: Oxford University Press, 2001), 208–10.

104. See, e.g., Kazuo Ohtsuka, "Sufi Shrine Culture," the entry "Sufism" in *The Oxford Encyclopedia of the Islamic World*, ed. John Voll, online edition: http://www.oxfordislamicstudies.com/article/opr/t236/e0759; Martin van Bruinessen, "Saints, Politicians, and Sufi Bureaucrats: Mysticism and Politics in Indonesia's New Order," in *Sufism and the "Modern" in Islam*, ed. Martin van Bruinessen and Julia Day Howell (London: I. B. Tauris, 2013), 92–112; Michael Laffan, *The Makings of Indonesian Islam* (Princeton, NJ: Princeton University Press, 2011), 178–89; Johannes Baljon, "Shah Waliullah and the Dargah," in *Muslim Shrines in India*, ed. Christian Troll (Delhi: Oxford University Press, 1989), 191–97 (some scholars, e.g., Marcia Hermansen, believe that the antisaint views were spuriously ascribed to Shah Wali Allah; a personal e-mail communication on March 6, 2016).

105. See Knysh, "Cult of Saints and Religious Reformism in Early Twentieth-Century Hadramawt," passim, and Gellner, *Islamic Dilemmas*, passim; cf. Husayn Muruwwa, *Al-Naza'at al-maddiyya fi 'l-falsafa al-'arabiyya-al-islamiyya*, 3 vols. (Beirut: Dar al-Farabi, 2002), 3: 214–16 and 225–26.

106. Elizabeth Sirriyeh, *Sufis and Anti-Sufis* (Richmond, Surrey: Curzon, 1999), 86–111; Bruinessen, "Sufism," 135–36, and Knysh, "Cult of Saints and Religious Reformism in Early Twentieth-Century Hadramawt," passim.

107. See, e.g., R. Po-chia Hsia, ed., *A Companion to the Reformation World* (Oxford: Blackwell, 2004), xv passim, and Chadwick, *Early Reformation*, 208–10.

108. For a very brief and accessible account, see, e.g., Bruce Lincoln, *Holy Terrors: Thinking about Religion after September 11*, 2nd ed. (Chicago: University of Chicago Press, 2006), 56–60; cf. Jose Casanova, *Public Religions in the Modern World* (Chicago: University of Chicago Press, 1994), 20–25; further literature on the subject is quoted in these two studies; cf. Talal Asad's critique of the validity of Enlightenment assumptions when applied to Muslim societies in his *Genealogies of Religion* (Baltimore: Johns Hopkins University Press, 1993), chapter 5.

109. In the nineteenth century, opposition to "grave worship" was not unique to the Wahhabis but was shared by some prominent Muslim scholars in neighboring Yemen, e.g., Muhammad al-Shawkani (d. 1250/1834); see Bernard Haykel, *Revival and Reform*, 130–38; for the Indian Subcontinent, see Claudia Preckel, "Screening Siddiq Hasan Khan's Library: The Use of Hanbali Literature in 19th-Century Bhopal," in *Islamic Theology, Philosophy, and Law: Debating Ibn Taymiyya and Ibn Qayyim al-Jawziyya*, ed. Birgit Krawietz and Georges Tamer (Berlin: Walter de Gruyter,

2013), 213–17; for the premodern antecedents see Schallenberg, "Ibn Qayyim al-Jawziyya's Manipulation," 96–97.

110. See Alexander Knysh, "The *'tariqa'* on a Landcruiser: The Resurgence of Sufi Movement in Yemen," *Middle East Journal* 55, no. 3 (2001): 399–414, and Knysh, "Contextualizing the Sufi-Salafi Conflict (From the Northern Caucasus to Hadramawt)," *Middle Eastern Studies* 43, no. 4 (2007): 503–30.

111. Memon, *Ibn Taimiya's Struggle*, vii.

112. Q 33:33, and William Shepard, "Ignorance." *Encyclopedia of the Qur'an*, online edition: http://referenceworks.brillonline.com/entries/encyclopaedia-of-the-quran/ignorance; cf. Charles Adams, *Islam and Modernism in Egypt* (New York: Russel and Russel, 1968), 161–64 and 188–89.

113. Knysh, "Contextualizing," passim.

114. See Knysh, "The *'tariqa'* on a Landcruiser."

115. For European parallels, see Casanova, *Public Religions*, 31.

116. Literally, "doing what is beautiful."

117. As argued, e.g., in Gavin Picken, *Spiritual Purification in Islam: The Life and Works of al-Muhasibi* (London: Routledge, 2011), passim, and Kamali, *Middle Path*, 120.

118. For a pertinent discussion of the dialectic of "private and public religions" in the modern age in non-Muslim contexts, see Casanova, *Public Religions*, 40–66.

119. See Edwin Calverley and Ian Netton, "Nafs," *EI2*, online edition: http://referenceworks.brillonline.com/; Marijan Molé, *Les mystiques musulmans* (Paris: Presses Universitaires de France, 1965), 10–26; Picken, *Spiritual Purification*, passim; Knysh, *Sufism*, 94–99, and "Index" under "Malamatiyya"; Sara Sviri, "Hakîm Tirmidhî and the Malâmatî Movement in Early Sufism," in *The Heritage of Sufism*, 2 vols., ed. Leonard Lewisohn (Oxford: Oneworld, 1999), 1: 583–613; Knysh, *Al-Qushayri's Epistle*, 109–10 passim.

120. Anna Akasoy has provided a critical examination of the academic constructions of "philosophical Sufism" in her "What Is Philosophical Sufism?" in *In the Age of Averroes: Arabic Philosophy in the Sixth/Twelfth Century*, ed. Peter Adamson (London: Warburg Institute, 2011), 229–49; it resonates, as already mentioned, with a similar approach adopted by Shi'i critics of Sufism, such as Muhammad Baqir Majlisi (d. 1110/1698); see Arjomand, *Shadow of God*, 152–54 and 156–59.

121. As demonstrated, e.g., by Bruinessen in his "Sufism," 132–40.

122. Ibid., 137–39.

123. Said, *Orientalism*, 38 (quoting a British Orientalist and a British colonial administrator); cf. Asad, *Genealogies of Religion*, chapter 5.

124. Waugh, *Visionaries*, 66.

125. Bruinessen, "Sufism," 135–40.

126. Talal Asad would probably disagree with this viewpoint (see chapter 5 of his *Genealogies of Religion*), but his own research is based on the findings of Western anthropology, not on Western studies of textual Islam.

127. Michel Foucault, *The Order of Things* (New York: Vintage Books, 1994), 52–53; Foucault, *The Archeology of Knowledge* (New York: Pantheon, 1972), 157–65.

128. Roman Loimeier, "Is There Something Like 'Protestant Islam'?" *Die Welt des*

Islams 45, no. 2 (2005): 247; cf. Ernest Gellner, *Muslim Society* (Cambridge: Cambridge University Press, 1982), passim.

129. Loimeier, "Is There Something," 246–47. The British-Czech sociologist Ernest Gellner (1925–1995) was one of the first to articulate this view in his *Saints of the Atlas* (Chicago: University of Chicago Press, 1969), and in his *Muslim Society*; building on Gellner's ideas, Dale Eickelman who, like Gellner, had studied Islam and Sufism in the Maghreb, introduced the notion (albeit without specific attention to Sufism) of "the Islamic Reformation"; see, e.g., "Inside the Islamic Reformation," *Wilson Quarterly* 22 (1988): 80–89, and Eickelman, "Print, Islam, and the Prospects for Civic Pluralism," *Journal of Islamic Studies* 8, no. 1 (1997): 43–62.

130. Gellner's parallels have since been challenged by his colleagues; see, e.g., Bruinessen, "Sufism," 139–40, and the literature cited therein.

131. Loimeier, "Is There Something," 217 note 2; for Muhammad Abdo's acquaintance with Western academic studies of religion, see Adams, *Islam and Modernism*, 95, 98, 167–68.

132. Loimeier, "Is There Something," 215.

133. Ibid., 218.

134. Rudolph Ware III, *The Walking Qur'an: Islamic Education, Embodied Knowledge, and History in West Africa* (Chapel Hill: University of North Carolina Press, 2014), 211.

135. Loimeier, "Is There Something," 218.

136. Samuli Schielke, "Hegemonic Encounters: Criticism of Saints' Day Festivals and the Formation of Modern Islam in Late 19th and Early 20th-Century Egypt," *Die Welt des Islams* 47 (2007): 319–55.

137. Fazlur Rahman, *Islam*, 2nd ed. (Chicago: University of Chicago Press, 1979), 206 and 239; Ira Lapidus, *A History of Islamic Societies* (Cambridge: Cambridge University Press, 1988), 257–58; Reinhard Schulze, *Islamischer Internationalismus im 20. Jahrhundert* (Leiden: E. J. Brill, 1990), 18–26; Schulze, "Was ist die islamische Aufklärung?" *Die Welt des Islams* 36, no. 3 (1996): 276–325; Schulze, "Hypothese einer islamischen Aufklärung," *ZDMG* 148 (1998): 83–110; for further references and criticism see Rex O'Fahey and Bernd Radtke, "Neo-Sufism Reconsidered," *Der Islam* 70, no. 1 (1993): 55–56, and Bernd Radtke, *Autochthone islamische Aufklärung im 18. Jahrhundert: Theoretische und filologische Bemerkungen* (Utrecht: Houtsma, 2000). The latter work is a line-by-line disproval of Schulze's thesis of the "autochthonous Islamic Enlightenment."

138. O'Fahey and Radtke, "Neo-Sufism," 71, which criticizes such assumptions; the "Islamic Enlightenment" thesis was articulated by Reinhard Schulze in the publications mentioned in the previous note; for a summary, see Muhammad Khalid Masud and Armando Salvatore, "Western Scholars of Islam on the Issue of Modernity," in Masud, Salvatore, and Bruinessen, *Islam and Modernity*, 48–50.

139. O'Fahey and Radtke, "Neo-Sufism," 55 and 61–64; for a more detailed, philological critique, see Radtke, *Autochtone*, passim; cf. Bruinessen, "Sufism," 125.

140. O'Fahey and Radtke, "Neo-Sufism," 73–81.

141. Radtke, *Autochtone*, 90–97.

142. O'Fahey and Radtke, "Neo-Sufism," 57–58; for India see Johannes Baljon,

"Shah Waliullah and the Dargah," in *Muslim Shrines in India*, ed. Christian Troll (Delhi: Oxford, 1989): 191–97.

143. Radtke, *Autochtone*, 40–50, and Bruinessen, "Sufism," 132–34.

144. Bruinessen, "Sufism," 135–38, which critically responds to Geertz's and Gellner's dichotomies of "scriptural"/"miracle-working" and "high"/"low" Islam; cf. ibid., 145.

145. http://plato.stanford.edu/entries/ibn-arabi/.

146. Ahmed, *What Is Islam?*, 10–26, 79–80, 94–97, 333, 357.

147. Anna Akasoy, "What Is Philosophical Sufism?," passim; for concrete examples see, e.g., Peter Adamson, *Philosophy in the Islamic World* (Oxford: Oxford University Press, 2016); S. H. Nasr and Oliver Leaman, eds., *History of Islamic Philosophy*, 2 vols. (London: Routledge, 1996); Ayman Shihadeh, ed., *Sufism and Theology* (Edinburgh: Edinburgh University Press, 2007); Tim Winter, ed., *The Cambridge Companion to Islamic Theology* (Cambridge: Cambridge University Press, 2008).

148. For concrete examples see Léon Gauthier, *Introduction à l'étude de la philosophie musulmane: L'esprit sémitique et l'esprit aryen, la philosophie grecque et la religion de l'Islâm* (Paris: E. Leroux, 1923); Richard Walzer, *Greek into Arabic: Essays on Islamic Philosophy* (Columbia: University of South Carolina Press, 1970); Georges Anawati, *Études de philosophie musulmane* (Paris: J. Vrin, 1974); Taufic Ibrahim and Arthur Sagadeev, *Classical Islamic Philosophy*, trans. from Russian by Campbell Creighton (Moscow: Progress Publishing, 1990); McGinnis and Reisman, *Classical Arabic Philosophy*; Oliver Leaman, *An Introduction to Classical Islamic Philosophy* (Cambridge: Cambridge University Press, 2002).

149. For details see Franz Rosenthal, "Ibn 'Arabi between 'Philosophy' and 'Mysticism,'" *Oriens* 31 (1988): 1–35.

150. As argued, e.g., in the classical work of Montgomery Watt, *Islamic Philosophy and Theology: An Extended Survey* (Edinburgh: Edinburgh University Press, 1985), chapter 7, "The Attraction of Greek Thought."

151. Noah Gardiner, "Forbidden Knowledge? Notes on the Production, Transmission, and Receptions of the Major Works of Ahmad al-Buni," *Journal of Arabic and Islamic Studies* 12 (2012): 81.

152. See Steven Katz, ed., *Mysticism and Language* (Oxford: Oxford University Press, 1992), passim, and Katz, *Mysticism and Sacred Scripture* (Oxford: Oxford University Press, 2000), 4.

153. These and other occult sciences in late medieval Islamic societies are discussed in detail in the unpublished PhD thesis of Dr. Noah Gardiner, "Esotericism in a Manuscript Culture: Ahmad al-Buni and His Readers through the Mamluk Period" (University of Michigan, 2014). The remainder of this section is based on Dr. Gardiner's findings; these and other Arabic terms for occult sciences (*'ulum al-ghayb*) in Islamic contexts are examined in detail in his thesis.

154. This term is used by some Western scholars of Islamic occultism, especially Noah Gardiner and Matthew Melvin-Koushki, to denote the knowledge and practical application of magical properties of the letters of the Arabic alphabet by the likes of Ahmad al-Buni.

155. See Gardiner, "Esotericism," 7, quoting the work of the German expert on the history of Islamic sciences Manfred Ullmann (b. 1931).

156. Ibid., quoting another German Arabist, Albert Dietrich (1912–2015).

157. See, e.g., Bruinessen, "Sufism," 125, which mentions Muslim reformers casti-gating in one breath "the attribution of miraculous powers to Sufi shaykhs and the traffic in magical objects such as amulets"; cf. ibid., 145, which questions this percep-tion by arguing that "orthodox ulama" also practiced "certain forms of magic" and that "the belief in miracles performed by saints is not a monopoly of the uneducated classes either."

158. Steven Katz, "Mystical Speech and Mystical Meaning," in *Mysticism and Lan-guage*, ed. Steven Katz (Oxford: Oxford University Press, 1992), 15–24; Katz, "Editor's Introduction," in *Mysticism and Sacred Scripture*, 4.

159. Pierre Lory, ed., *La science des lettres en Islam* (Paris: Éditions Dervy, 2004), and Pierre Lory and Jean-Charles Coulon, trans., *Talismans: Le soleil des connais-sances* (Paris: Orients éditions, 2013).

160. Jonathan Katz, *Dreams, Sufism, and Sainthood: The Visionary Career of Mu-hammad al-Zawawi* (Leiden: E. J. Brill, 1996), 109–17.

161. Matthew Melvin-Koushki, "The Quest for a Universal Science: The Occult Philosophy of Sa'in Al-Din Turka Isfahani (1369–1432) and Intellectual Millenarian-ism in Early Timurid Iran" (unpublished PhD diss., Yale University, 2012).

162. Gardiner, "Esotericism," 326–40; for Muhammad al-Zawawi, see note 160.

163. See, e.g., Gerhard Böwering and Yousef Casewit, eds., *A Qur'an Commentary by Ibn Barrajan (d. 536/1141)* (Leiden: E. J. Brill, 2016), 36.

164. Gardiner, "Esotericism," 239–40 and 334–35; for these Sufi personalities see Knysh, *Islamic Mysticism*, "Index."

165. Katz, "Mystical Speech," 18–20, and Katz, "Mysticism and the Interpretation of Sacred Scripture," in Katz, *Mysticism and Sacred Scripture*, 54–57; for al-Tirmidhi, see Aiyub Palmer, "The Social and Theoretical Dimensions of Sainthood in Early Islam: Al-Tirmidhi's Gnoseology and the Foundations of Sufi Social Praxis" (unpub-lished PhD diss., University of Michigan, 2015), chapter 5; for al-Tustari see Gerhard Böwering, *The Mystical Vision of Existence in Classical Islam* (Berlin: Walter de Gruyter, 1980), 11–18.

166. See Knysh, *Ibn 'Arabi*, 10–11, and "Index," under "*al-Futuhat al-makkiya*."

167. Denis Gril in Michel Chodkiewicz, eds., *The Meccan Revelations*, 2 vols. (New York: Pir Press, 2004), 2: 105–86. In this volume, Gril's original French translation of the Arabic text was translated into English.

168. Ibid., 107–8.

169. Noah Gardiner, "Forbidden Knowledge?," 87–88; on al-Mahdawi's role in Ibn (al-)'Arabi's Sufi training, see Austin, *Sufis*, "Index" under "al-Mahdawi," and Böwering and Casewit, *A Qur'an Commentary*, 18.

170. On al-Shadhili see Knysh, *Islamic Mysticism*, 207–12.

171. Ibn 'Ata' Allah al-Iskandari, *Lata'if al-minan*, ed. Khalid 'Abd al-Rahman al-'Akk (Damascus: Dar al-basha'ir, 1992), 120.

172. After his return from the Dar al-Mustafa compound in Hadramawt (on this institution see chapter 6 of this book) in the fall of 2013, Ali Hussain, a doctoral stu-dent at the University of Michigan, related a story of a blind and reclusive *sayyid* named 'Abd al-Mawla b. Tahir whose amulets written in scribbles on odd scraps of paper were in high demand among the students of the compound due to their per-

ceived miraculous powers; the circulation of these amulets among the students was condoned by the Sufi leaders of Dar al-Mustafa who alone were capable of deciphering them.

173. *Al-Kibrit al-ahmar* (lit. "the red sulfur"); this phrase serves as the title of one of Ibn 'Arabi's treatises; see Claude Addas, *Quest for the Red Sulphur: The Life of Ibn 'Arabi*, trans. from the French by Peter Kingsley (Cambridge: Islamic Texts Society, 1993).

174. According to the Central Asian Sufi master Najm al-Din Kubra (d. ca. 617/1220), "Our method (*tariq*) is the method of alchemy"; Julian Baldick, *Mystical Islam: An Introduction to Sufism* (London: I. B. Tauris, 1989), 80.

175. Böwering and Casewit, *A Qur'an Commentary*, 36

176. Ibid., 19–20.

177. Gardiner, "Esotericism," 299.

178. Gardiner, "Forbidden Knowledge?," 83.

179. See Momen, *Ibn Taimiya's Struggle*, part 2, and Knysh, *Ibn 'Arabi*, chapter 4.

180. Gardiner, "Esotericism," 297; I have slightly amended the translation.

181. Ibid. Gardiner relies on the conclusions reached by Yahia Michot in his " 'Misled and Misleading' . . . 'Yet Central in Their Intellectual Influence!': Ibn Taymiyya's Views on *Ikhwan al-Safa*," in *Epistles of the Brethren of Purity: The* Ikhwan Al-Safa' *and Their* Rasa'il; *An Introduction*, ed. Nader El-Bizri (Oxford: Oxford University Press, 2008), 139–89.

182. Gardiner, "Forbidden Knowledge?," 83.

183. See Knysh, *Ibn 'Arabi*, chapter 8.

184. Gardiner, "Esotericism," 302–4.

185. Ibid., 313, and Franz Rosenthal, trans., *Ibn Khaldun, The Muqaddimah: An Introduction to History* (New York: Pantheon, 1958), 3: 171–82.

186. Knysh, *Ibn 'Arabi*, 186–89.

187. Ibid., 189–97, and Gardiner, "Esotericism," 304.

188. Gardiner, "Esotericism," 311; on these Sufi thinkers see Knysh, *Ibn 'Arabi*; Morris, "Ibn 'Arabi and His Interpreters"; William Chittick, "*Wahdat al-wujud* in Islamic Thought," *Bulletin of the Henry Martyn Institute of Islamic Studies* 10 (January–March 1991): 7–27; Chittick, "Ibn 'Arabi and His School," in *Islamic Spirituality: Manifestations*, ed. S. H. Nasr (New York: Crossroad, 1991), 49–79; Michel Chodkiewicz, "The Diffusion of Ibn 'Arabi's Doctrine," *Journal of Muhyiddin Ibn 'Arabi Society* 9 (1991): 36–57; Éric Geoffroy, *Le soufisme en Égypte et en Syrie sous les derniers Mamelouks et les premiers Ottomans* (Damascus: Institut français de Damas, 1995); for a recent overview of the literature on the subject, see Knysh and Hussain, "Ibn al-'Arabi."

189. Knysh, *Ibn 'Arabi*, 184–97, and James Morris, "An Arab Machiavelli? Rhetoric, Philosophy, and Politics in Ibn Khaldun's Critique of Sufism," *Harvard Middle Eastern and Islamic Review* 8 (2009): 242.

190. Obviously, Hodgson's own ruminations here and throughout his *Venture of Islam* are marked by the male-centric presuppositions of his age.

191. Hodgson, *Venture of Islam*, 1: 27.

192. Foucault, *Archaeology of Knowledge*, chapters 1–7.

193. Whereas Marshall Hodgson has talked about dialogues of various cultures

and strands of "piety" within the Islamic tradition, Talal Asad envisioned Islam as a sum total of competing discursive formations, that is, as a "discursive religion" par excellence; see, respectively, *Venture of Islam*, 1: 71–95; and Asad, "Idea of an Anthropology," 13–17.

194. See chapter 6 of this book.

195. See Alexander Knysh, "Historiography of Sufi Studies in the West and Russia," *Pis'mennye pamiatniki Vostoka* (Written Monuments of the Orient) 1, no. 4 (2006): 238.

196. For details see Ivan Strenski, *Thinking about Religion* (Oxford: Blackwell, 2006), 260–63 and 269–73; cf. Adam Kuper, *Anthropology and Anthropologists: The British School in the Twentieth Century*, 4th ed. (New York: Routledge, 2015), chapters 1 and 2.

197. Ahmed, *What Is Islam?*, 109.

198. As discussed throughout Shahab Ahmed's book mentioned in the previous note.

Chapter 3: Discourses

1. For Sufism, see Nile Green, *Sufism: A Global History* (Chichester, UK: Wiley-Blackwell, 2012), 3–5 passim; see also our review of this book in *Journal of Sufi Studies* 3 (2014): 93–95.

2. Michel Foucault, *The Archaeology of Knowledge* (New York: Pantheon, 1972), 21.

3. Ibid., 22.

4. Despite his refusal to be seen as a structuralist, Foucault acknowledges, if only grindingly, his indebtedness to structuralism writ large; ibid., 15.

5. Ibid., 22.

6. In addition to Sufi allegorical-esoteric exegesis, scholars of the Qur'an also speak of its Shi'i and Isma'ili versions: see, e.g., Andrew Rippin, ed., *Blackwell Companion to the Qur'an* (Oxford: Blackwell, 2006), chapters 25 and 26.

7. E.g., Green, *Sufism*, 3 passim.

8. Foucault, *Archaeology of Knowledge*, 22–23.

9. For details, see Pierre Hadot, *Philosophy as a Way of Life*, ed. Arnold Davidson, trans. Michael Chase (Oxford: Blackwell, 1995), 26–30.

10. In his philosophical ruminations, Foucault has consistently encouraged this approach by speaking about "the living openness of history" and history as a process (*devenir*), "not [as] a system, but the hard work of freedom . . . which, in the end, breaks all bounds"; *Archeology of Knowledge*, 13.

11. For Hadith, also known as the Sunna of the Prophet, see Ian Richard Netton, *Islam, Christianity, and Tradition: A Comparative Exploration* (Edinburgh: Edinburgh University Press, 2006), 125–27, and Alexander Knysh, *Islam in Historical Perspective* (Upper Saddle River, NJ: Pearson, 2011), chapter 6.

12. Steven Katz, "Mysticism and Interpretation of Sacred Scripture," in *Mysticism and Sacred Scripture*, ed. Steven Katz (Oxford: Oxford University Press, 2000), 14; some comparisons between Sufi uses of the Scripture and those of their Abrahamic counterparts are drawn in chapter 4 of this book.

13. Katz, "Mysticism," 56.

14. For the rise of the "mystical language of Islam," see, e.g., Ignaz Goldziher, *Schools of Koranic Interpretation*, ed. and trans. Wolfgang Behn (Wiesbaden: Harrassowitz, 2006), 117, 160, and 165; Louis Massignon, *Essay on the Origins of the Technical Language of Islamic Mysticism* (Notre Dame, IN: University of Notre Dame Press, 1997), and Paul Nwyia, *Exégèse coranique et language mystique* (Beirut: Libraire Orientale, 1970).

15. Pierre Lory, *Les commentaires ésotériques du Coran d'après 'Abd al-Razzâq al-Qâshânî* (Paris: Les Deux Océans, 1980), 19, and our article "Sufism and the Qur'an," in *Encyclopedia of the Qur'an*, ed. Jane McAuliffe, online edition: http://referenceworks.brillonline.com. See also Netton, *Islam, Christianity, and Tradition*, 5–7 and 9–12; Katz, "Mysticism and Interpretation," 14, 17–23, 29–30, and 46–47.

16. Gerhard Böwering, *The Mystical Vision of Existence in Classical Islam: The Qur'anic Hermeneutics of the Sufi Sahl at-Tustari (d. 283/896)* (Berlin: Walter de Gruyter, 1980), 213; Steven Katz, "Mystical Speech and Mystical Meaning," in *Mysticism and Language*, ed. Steven Katz (Oxford: Oxford University Press, 1992), 23–24; Katz, "Mysticism and the Interpretation of Sacred Scripture," in *Mysticism and Sacred Scripture*, ed. Steven Katz (Oxford: Oxford University Press, 2000), 10–11.

17. Paul Nwyia, *Un mystique prédicateur à la Qarawiyin de Fès Ibn 'Abbad de Ronda (1332–1390)* (Beirut: Imprimerie catholique, 1961), 233.

18. On al-Khadir/Khidr, see Arent Wensinck, "Al-Khadir (al-Khidr)," *EI2*, online edition: http://referenceworks.brillonline.com; Netton, *Islam, Christianity, and Tradition*, 20–36, 134; William Chittick, *The Sufi Path of Knowledge: Ibn al-'Arabi's Metaphysics of Imagination* (Albany: State University of New York Press, 1989), see "Index" under "Khadir" and "Moses and Khadir"; Nwyia, *Un mystique*, 233.

19. For a list of Qur'anic passages commonly interpreted by Sufis, see Katz, "Mysticism," 10–11; some Sufi interpretations of Q 17:1 are analyzed in Nwyia, *Exégèse*, 97–99, and in chapter 1 of Michael Sells, *Early Islamic Mysticism* (New York: Paulist Press, 1996); for Jesus and Mary see Pierre Lory, *La science des lettres en islam* (Paris: Éditions Dervy, 2004), 140–42, cf. 117, 246, and 247; the verses dealing with al-Khadir, 'Isa, and Maryam are explored in detail in Kristin Zahra Sands, *Sufi Commentaries on the Qur'an in Classical Islam* (London: Routledge, 2005), chapters 8 and 9.

20. Böwering, *Mystical Vision*, 172; Lory, *La science*, 140; Chittick, *Sufi Path*, "Index" under "Moses"; Sells, *Early Islamic Mysticism*, 42, and Goldziher, *Schools*, 145; some exegetical elaborations on Moses's interactions with his Lord are discussed later in this chapter.

21. Böwering, *Mystical Vision*, 178 and 202.

22. Ibid., 202; cf. Ibn (al-)'Arabi's use of this verse in his *al-Futuhat al-makkiyya*, 1: 280, and Chittick, *Sufi Path*, 12, 154, 249, 330, 364, 365, and 376.

23. See, e.g., Nwyia, *Exégèse*, 95–97; Böwering, *Mystical Vision*, 149, and Chittick, *Sufi Path*, 196, 225, 326, 366, and 376.

24. Marshall Hodgson, *The Venture of Islam*, 3 vols. (Chicago: University of Chicago Press, 1974), 2: 233.

25. Ibid., 234.

26. Nwyia, *Exégèse*, 95–96; Böwering, *Mystical Vision*, 149–53, 157, 159–65, and 218; cf. Chittick, *Sufi Path*, 106–9 and 322–23.

27. Goldziher, *Schools*, 118.

28. See, e.g., Chittick, *Sufi Path*, 322–23.

29. E.g., Q 2:5, 2:38; 2:257; 2:262; 2:264, 3:170, 10:62; 43:70, 56:10–14, 59:9, etc.

30. Chittick, *Sufi Path*, "Index" under "friend (*wali*) of God."

31. As stated repeatedly in the Qur'anic commentary by the Iranian Sufi gnostic ('*arif*) Ruzbihan al-Baqli, *'Ara'is al-bayan fi haqa'iq al-Qur'an*, 3 vols. (Beirut: Dar al-kutub al-'ilmiyya, 1429/2008), 1: 54, 224–25, 303, 352–53, 362–63, 406–7 passim; al-Baqli, in his turn, quotes an array of early Sufi exegetes, such as Sahl al-Tustari (d. 283/896), whose views of the *awliya'* and *'arifun* are detailed in Böwering, *Mystical Vision*, 205, 231–41; the doctrine of "sainthood" (*walaya/wilaya*), systematically formulated for the first time by the Arab-Iranian mystic al-Hakim al-Tirmidhi (d. circa 295–300/907–912), rests on his creative interpretation of the Qur'anic references to *awliya'*; see Aiyub Palmer, "The Social and Theoretical Dimensions of Sainthood in Early Islam: Al-Tirmidhi's Gnoseology and the Foundations of Sufi Social Praxis" (PhD thesis, University of Michigan, 2015).

32. See, e.g., Gerhard Böwering and Yousef Casewit, eds., *A Qur'an Commentary by Ibn Barrajan (d. 536/1141)* (Leiden: E. J. Brill, 2016), 33–34.

33. Katz, "Mystical Speech," 19.

34. William Graham, *Divine Word and Prophetic Word in Early Islam* (The Hague: Mouton, 1977), passim; Knysh, *Islam in Historical Perspective*, 94–95.

35. For the role of *hadith qudsi* in Sufi exegesis, see Annemarie Schimmel, *And Muhammad Is His Messenger: The Veneration of the Prophet in Islamic Piety* (Chapel Hill: University of North Carolina Press, 1985), 116–17, and 240.

36. Chittick, *Sufi Path*, 325, and "Index of Hadiths and Sayings" on 437–39.

37. Ibid., 111 and 249.

38. Ibid., 344 and 411 note 6.

39. Ibid., and Schimmel, *And Muhammad*, 130–31 and 223–24.

40. Chittick, *Sufi Path*, 66, 126, 180, 204, etc.

41. Quoted in ibid., 239 and 405 note 2; cf. ibid., 245.

42. Ibid., passim; William Chittick, *The Self-Disclosure of God: Principles of Ibn al-'Arabi's Cosmology* (Albany: State University of New York Press, 1998); and Ralph Austin, trans., *Ibn al'Arabi: The Bezels of Wisdom* (New York: Paulist Press, 1980), passim.

43. Schimmel, *And Muhammad*, "Index of Prophetic Traditions," 345–46.

44. For uses of Hadith by non-Sufi exegetes, see Goldziher, *Schools*, 36–64; for Ibn (al-)'Arabi's uses of Hadith, see Su'ad al-Hakim, *al-Mu'jam al-sufi: Al-hikma fi hudud al-kalima* (Beirut: Dandara, 1401/1981), passim, and Chittick's studies quoted above and throughout the rest of this chapter; see also Austin, *Ibn al'Arabi*, passim.

45. See, e.g., Carl Ernst, *Words of Ecstasy in Sufism* (Albany: State University of New York Press, 1985), 1, and Netton, *Islam, Christianity, and Tradition*, 3; for further references see chapter 1 of the present book.

46. As discussed below in chapter 4; see also Katz, *Mysticism and Sacred Scripture*, chapters 1–7, and Deborah Green and Laura Lieber, eds., *Scriptural Exegesis: The Shapes of Culture and the Religious Imagination* (Oxford: Oxford University Press, 2009), passim.

47. As argued, e.g., in the works of Günter Lüling, Gabriel Said Reynolds, and

Angelika Neuwirth; see, e.g., Gabriel Said Reynolds, *The Qur'an in Its Historical Context* (London: Routledge, 2007), Reynolds, *The Qur'an and Its Biblical Subtext* (London: Routledge, 2010), and Reynolds, *New Perspectives on the Qur'an* (London: Routledge, 2011); Angelika Neuwirth, Nicolai Sinai, and Michael Marx, eds., *The Qur'an in Context: Historical and Literary Investigations into the Qur'anic Milieu* (Leiden: E. J. Brill 2010).

48. As discussed in chapter 1 of this book.

49. Goldziher, *Schools*, 87–88; Nwyia, *Exégèse*, 46–49; analyzed in detail in Böwering, *Mystical Vision*, 146–65.

50. See, e.g., Böwering, *Mystical Vision*, 153.

51. Purificación de la Torre, ed., *Ibn Barraŷan (m. 536/1141), Šarh asma' Allah al-husna* (Madrid: Consejo Superior de Investigaciones Cientícas, 2000), 417.

52. Böwering, *Mystical Vision*, 156.

53. Ibid., 149–53 passim; Alexander Knysh, *Islamic Mysticism: A Short History*, 2nd ed. (Leiden: E. J. Brill, 2010), 86–88; for parallels in Muslim (Neo-)Platonism outside the Sufi tradition proper, see Goldziher, *Schools*, 120–26, and Ian Richard Netton, *Muslim Neoplatonists: An Introduction to the Thought of the Brethren of Purity* (London: Routledge and Curzon, 2002), 41.

54. For a concise discussion of the various states and stages of evolution of the human soul (*nafs*), see Lory, *Les commentaires*, 83; for a more detailed account, see Böwering, *Mystical Vision*, 241–61; for a modern Sufi view, see Muhtar Holland, trans., *Sheikh Muzaffer Ozak al-Jarrahi, Irshad: Wisdom of a Sufi Master* (New York: Amity, 1988), 319–21.

55. Nwyia, *Exégèse*, 130–33 and 306–7, and Böwering, *Mystical Vision*, 160, 161, 167, 200–207, 245–46, 253, and so on.

56. E.g., Q 17:1, Q 53:1–18; 73; 74, 94:1–4, and 96; see also Netton, *Islam, Christianity, and Tradition*, 6–10.

57. Böwering, *Mystical Vision*, 158.

58. Q 2:143; 3:20 and 32; 4:59; 33:21, etc.; cf. John Burton, *An Introduction to the Hadith* (Edinburgh: Edinburgh University Press, 1994), 17–21; Tariq Ramadan, *In the Footsteps of the Prophet: Lessons from the Life of Muhammad* (Oxford: Oxford University Press, 2007), xii and 211–14; Carl Ernst, *Following Muhammad: Rethinking Islam in the Contemporary World* (Chapel Hill: University of North Carolina Press, 2003) passim.

59. For premodern criticism of allegorical-mystical interpretations of the Qur'an, see Abou Ishaq Ibrahim al-Shatibi, *Kitab al-I'tisam*, trans. Muhammed Mahdi Al-Sharif, 2 vols. (Beirut: Dar al-Kutub al-'Ilmiyya, 2012), 231–53; see also Böwering, *Mystical Vision*, 160, Goldziher, *Schools*, 141–42, and Alexander Knysh, *Ibn 'Arabi in the Later Islamic Tradition* (Albany: State University of New York Press, 1999), chapter 6 passim; for more general studies of anti-Sufi discourses and persecutions, see Carl Ernst, *Words of Ecstasy in Sufism* (Albany: State University of New York Press, 1985); Frederick de Jong and Bernd Radtke, eds., *Islamic Mysticism Contested* (Leiden: E. J. Brill, 1999), and Elizabeth Sirriyeh, *Sufis and Anti-Sufis* (Richmond, Surrey: Curzon, 1999).

60. As shown, e.g., in Chittick, *Sufi Path*, 231–52; cf. ibid., xv–xvi; see also Knysh, "Sufism and the Qur'an."

61. Goldziher, *Schools*, 142 (citing Ibn (al-)'Arabi's *al-Futuhat*, but without giving the exact reference); for similar statements see Ibn (al-)'Arabi, *al-Futuhat al-makkiyya*, 4 vols. (Beirut: Dar Sadir,1968), 1: 278–81.

62. For a discussion of such instances, see Knysh, *Ibn 'Arabi*, passim.

63. Goldziher, *Schools*, 116–19; Böwering, *Mystical Vision*, 135–42 passim; Carl Ernst, "Mystical Language and the Teaching Context in the Early Lexicons of Sufism," in *Mysticism and Language*, ed. Steven Katz, 186–90; Ernst, *Words of Ecstasy*, 1; Chittick, *Sufi Path*, 231–52 and 361–64.

64. Goldziher, *Schools*, 38–39.

65. Recent scholarship on Sufi exegesis has identified the author of these glosses as "Pseudo-Ja'far al-Sadiq," who "flourished in fourth/tenth century"; see, e.g., Martin Nguyen, *Sufi Master and Qur'an Teacher: Abu'l-Qasim al-Qushayri and the Lata'if al-Isharat* (Oxford: Oxford University Press, 2012), 94 and 182; Nguyen, in his turn, relies on Gerhard Böwering's "The Light Verse: Qur'anic Text and Sufi Interpretation," *Oriens* 36 (2001): 113–44, and Böwering, "The Major Sources of al-Sulami's Minor Qur'an Commentary," *Oriens* 35 (1996): 35–56; see also Böwering, *Mystical Vision*, 141–42.

66. Q 22:26.

67. Nwyia, *Exégèse*, 161–62.

68. See, e.g., his commentary on Q 7:143; 27:34; 8:24; and 7:160.

69. See, e.g., Knysh, "Sufism and the Qur'an"; Chittick, *Sufi Path*, xv–xvi, and "Index" under "*ma'rifa*"; and Chittick, *Divine Love: Islamic Literature and the Path to God* (New Haven, CT: Yale University Press, 2013), 229–32.

70. Goldziher, *Schools*, 57.

71. Nguyen, *Sufi Master*, 243; Chittick, *Divine Love*, 226–37, and Chittick, *Sufi Path*, 161, 215, 250, and 391 note 14; Chittick, "The School of Ibn 'Arabi," in *History of Islamic Philosophy*, 2 vols., ed. S. H. Nasr and Oliver Leaman (London: Routledge, 1996), 1: 518–19.

72. As discussed later on in this chapter.

73. Chittick, *Sufi Path*, 166 and 250–52.

74. Nwyia, *Exégèse*, 271–72, and Chittick, *Sufi Path*, 162–66 and 235–39.

75. Chittick, *Sufi Path*, 231–39, and Nwyia, *Exégèse*, 124 and 170.

76. Nwyia, *Exégèse*, 172–74; Chittick, *Divine Love*, 226–31, and Chittick, *Sufi Path*, 49–50, 132–34, 178, 357; see also Chittick, *The Self-Disclosure of God*, "Index" under "creation (*khalq*)" and "Real (*haqq*)."

77. For a short summary see Sands, *Sufi Commentaries*, 69–71; Nguyen, *Sufi Master*, "Index" under "al-Sulami," and Jean-Jacques Thibon, *L'oeuvre d'Abu 'Abd al-Rahman al-Sulami (325/937–412/1021) et la formation du soufisme* (Damascus: IFPO, 2009), 396–406.

78. As argued in Knysh, *Islamic Mysticism*, 13–16, 24–26, 99–101.

79. Nwyia, *Exégèse*, 156–60, and Böwering, *Mystical Vision*, 141–42.

80. See note 65 above.

81. Nguyen, *Sufi Master*, 172, 177, 189, 196.

82. Nwyia, *Exégèse*, 6, 14, 21, 110, 162, 275, etc.; Sands, *Sufi Commentaries*, 12–13; some present-day examples are examined later in this chapter.

83. See Nwyia, *Exégèse*, "Index" under these four terms, and Böwering, *Mystical Vision*, 138–41, where several versions of the levels of meaning are given.

84. Gerhard Böwering, ed., *Ziyadat haqa'iq al-tafsir li-Abi 'Abd al-Rahman al-Sulami* (Beirut: Dar al-Mashriq, 1995), 2, and Böwering, *Mystical Vision*, 138–51 and 160.

85. Goldziher, *Schools*, 117 and 137.

86. Ibn (al-)'Arabi, *al-Futuhat*, 1: 278–81 and 550–51; Sands, *Sufi Commentaries*, 10–11 passim; Nguyen, *Sufi Master*, 243; Chittick, *Sufi Path*, 231–52, and Chittick, *Divine Love*, 158–59 and 231–37.

87. See Alexander Knysh, trans., *Al-Qushayri's Epistle on Sufism* (Reading, UK: Garnet, 2007), xxv–xxvi.

88. On al-Junayd al-Baghdadi and his version of Sufism, see Knysh, *Islamic Mysticism*, 52–56.

89. Nguyen, *Sufi Master*, 3, 16, and 122–23; for an excellent analytic survey of al-Qushayri's oeuvre, see the PhD thesis of Francesco Chiabotti, "Entre soufisme et savoir islamique: L'oeuvre de 'Abd al-Karim al-Qushayri (376–465/ 986–1072)," (Université de Provence, Ecole doctorale 355, UFR arts, lettres, langues et sciences humaines, I, Aix-en-Provence: IREMAM, 2014).

90. Al-Ghazali's oeuvre is discussed later in this book.

91. Nguyen, *Sufi Master*, 1, 101, and 254.

92. For examples, see chapters 2 and 3 of our translation of *al-Qushayri's Epistle*.

93. Because the original manuscript has a lacuna here, Martin Nguyen suggests "adjudicates for" to fill it, which is as good a guess as any; Nguyen, *Sufi Master*, 257.

94. Martin Nguyen translates this phrase as "theologians," but, in my opinion, al-Qushayri refers here to the leaders of juridical schools who formulate the general principles of extracting legal decisions from the sacred texts and authoritative precedents.

95. Al-Qushayri, *Tafsir al-Qushayri al-masamma Lata'if al-isharat*, 3 vols., ed. 'Abd al-Latif Hasan 'Abd al-Rahman (Beirut: Dar al-kutub al-'ilmiyya, 1420/2000), 1: 452–53; my translation is slightly different from Martin Nguyen's in his *Sufi Master*, 257.

96. Al-Qushayri, *Tafsir*, 1: 11, 17–18, 20, 137–39, 164, 189, 252, 384 passim; Nguyen, *Sufi Master*, 61–62 and 249–50.

97. For a discussion of the Sufi path, see Knysh, *Islamic Mysticism*, 301–11.

98. Chiabotti, "Entre soufisme," 615–16.

99. The phrase "In the name of God, the Merciful, the Compassionate" that opens every sura of the Qur'an, except sura 9.

100. See, e.g., Katz, "Mysticism and the Interpretation," 54–55 and Katz, "Mystical Speech," passim.

101. Nguyen, *Sufi Master*, 129.

102. E.g., Q 7:11–15, 31–33, 35–36, 39–40.

103. His name begins with the letter *alif*.

104. Al-Qushayri, *Tafsir*, 1: 395.

105. Adam Kamesar, "Biblical Interpretation in Philo," in *The Cambridge Compan-

ion to Philo, ed. Adam Kamesar (Cambridge: Cambridge University Press, 2009), 72; cf. Katz, "Mystical Speech," 25–30, and Katz, "Mysticism and the Interpretation," 15–16; Philo's role in the shaping of Christian "mystical theology" is highlighted in Bernard McGinn, *The Foundations of Mysticism*, vol. 1 of *The Presence of God: A History of Western Christian Mysticism* (New York: Crossroad, 1991), 35–41; Yehud Liebes, "The Work of the Chariot and the Work of Creation as Mystical Teachings in Philo of Alexandria," in *Scriptural Exegesis: The Shapes of Culture and Religious Imagination*, ed. Deborah Green and Laura Lieber (Oxford: Oxford University Press, 2009), 105–20; for references to "Philonic methods" in Sufi exegesis, see Goldziher, *Schools*, 117, 125, 134, 136, 150, and 158.

106. Kamesar, "Biblical Interpretation," 77.

107. Carlos Lévy, "Philo's Ethics," in Kamesar, ed., *Cambridge Companion to Philo*, 161.

108. To borrow a term used by Hodgson in his *Venture of Islam*, 2: 230–34.

109. Knysh, *Al-Qushayri's Epistle*, 89–91, and Jawid Mojaddedi, "Annihilation and abiding in God," *EI3*, online edition: http://referenceworks.brillonline.com.

110. Al-Qushayri, *Tafsir*, 1: 352.

111. Nguyen, *Sufi Master*, 257–58, and Chiabotti, "Entre soufisme," especially "Troisième partie: Doctrine, transmission du savoir et pratique spirituelle," 437–515; cf. Goldziher, *Schools*, 162.

112. Annabel Keeler, *Sufi Hermeneutics: The Qur'an Commentary of Rashid al-Din Maybudi* (Oxford: Oxford University Press, 2006), 40, and Keeler, "Mystical Theology and the Traditionalist Hermeneutics of Maybudi's *Kashf al-Asrar*," in *Sufism and Theology*, ed. Ayman Shihadeh (Edinburgh: Edinburgh University Press, 2007), 15; for another recent study of Maybudi's exegesis, see Chittick, *Divine Love*.

113. Chittick, *Divine Love*, xvii–xviii.

114. Ibid., xix.

115. Keeler, "Mystical Theology," 14–15; Chittick, however, disagrees with Keeler and identifies al-Maybudi rather as "a master of the various fields of Islamic learning," who was "nothing if not eclectic in his approach"; Chittick, *Divine Love*, xvii.

116. Sands, *Sufi Commentaries*, 73; Chittick, *Divine Love*, xvi, and "Index" under "allusion" (*ishara*).

117. Keeler, *Sufi Hermeneutics*, 22, and Chittick, *Divine Love*, xix, 5, 25, 96, 143, 180, 241–42, 255–56, 261.

118. Keeler, *Sufi Hermeneutics*, 15, and Keeler, "Mystical Theology," 16–18 and 26; cf. Chittick, *Divine Love*, xvii.

119. Keeler, "Mystical Theology," 26.

120. For a detailed examination of the issue of *muhkamat/mutashabihat* and their respective interpreters and audiences, see Sands, *Sufi Commentaries*, chapter 2.

121. Keeler, *Sufi Hermeneutics*, 49; cf. 44; see also Chittick, *Divine Love*, 81, 172, 195–96, and 217–26.

122. Q 4:162.

123. Chittick, *Divine Love*, 219.

124. Ibid., 172, 217, 231–32, and 403–4.

125. Ibid., 73, 199–203, 302–3 passim.

126. Keeler, *Sufi Hermeneutics*, 43–44.

127. See Sands, *Sufi Commentaries*, chapter 2.

128. See note 115 above.

129. On him see Knysh, *Islamic Mysticism*, 140–49; whether or not he should be classified as a full-fledged Sufi has been disputed of late; see, e.g., Kenneth Garden, *The First Islamic Reviver: Abu Hamid al-Ghazali and His Revival of the Religious Sciences* (Oxford: Oxford University Press, 2014), 10 and 79–80 passim.

130. What follows is our summary and analysis of al-Ghazali, *Jawahir al-Qur'an*, ed. Muhammad Rashid Rida al-Qabbani (Beirut: Dar ihya' al-'ulum, 1985); see also an English translation of this work by Muhammad Abul Quasem, *The Jewels of the Qur'an* (London: Kegan Paul International, 1983).

131. Keeler, *Sufi Hermeneutics*, 45–48.

132. For a translation of the relevant passage, see Sands, *Sufi Commentaries*, 7.

133. That the popularity of this image is by no means unique to Sunni Sufism is attested by the following commentary of the Shi'i mystic Haydar Amuli (fl. in the mid-8th/14th century) on Q 3:102 that encourages the faithful to "fear God as He should be feared": "After a person has given it [fear of God] its due, so that the veil of plurality and dispersion has been removed from his heart, the rust of oppression and negligence has been cleansed from the mirror of his soul and it thereby has achieved the complete and perfect clarity of polishing and purity, [then] God Most High will pour upon it one of His lights, so that the eye of its insight is opened and the world of divine sovereignty and power (*'alam al-malakut wa 'l-jabarut*) is revealed to it, after which God will send down upon it from the heaven of His being and His grace, wisdom (*hikma*), gnosis, knowledge and true realities"; quoted in Sayyid Muhsin al-Tabrizi, "Introduction to the Second Edition" (*Muqaddimat al-tab'a al-thaniyya*), in Haydar b. 'Ali Amuli (Amoli), *Tafsir al-Muhit al-a'zam wa 'l-bahr al-hidamm*," 4 vols. (Qumm: al-Ma'had al-thaqafi nur 'ala nur, 1422 AH), vol. 1, Kaf.

134. Mentioned in Q 22:70 and 85:22.

135. For a similar idea in a modern Sufi discourse, see Holland, trans., *Sheikh Muzaffer Ozak*, 321–22.

136. The analysis that follows is based on our reading of al-Ghazali's *Mishkat al-anwar*, ed. Samih Dughaym (Beirut: Dar al-fikr al-lubnani, 1994).

137. See Knysh, *Islamic Mysticism*, 145–46; it is sometimes argued that al-Ghazali's *Ihya'* represents the first comprehensive program for moral-ethical renewal and reform of Sunni Islam based on philosophical premises; see, e.g., Garden, *First Islamic Reviver*, chapters 3–6.

138. Sands, *Sufi Commentaries*, 33–34.

139. Al-Ghazali, *Mishkat*, 58.

140. Carl Ernst, *Ruzbihan Baqli* (Richmond, Surrey: Curzon, 1996), ix; cf. Sands, *Sufi Commentaries*, 75.

141. E.g., Gerhard Böwering, "Sufi Hermeneutics in Medieval Islam," *Revue des Études Islamiques* 55–57 (1987–89): 239–328.

142. It is also occasionally cited as "The Revelations of the [All-]Merciful Concerning the Allusions of the Qur'an" (*Futuh al-rahman fi isharat al-Qur'an*).

143. Elizabeth Alexandrin, "Witnessing the Lights of the Heavenly Dominion:

Dreams, Visions, and the Mystical Exegesis of Shams al-Din al-Daylami," in *Dreams and Visions in Islamic Societies*, ed. Özgen Felek and Alexander Knysh (Albany: State University of New York Press, 2012), 216–18.

144. Böwering, "Sufi Hermeneutics," 270.

145. Ibid.

146. Alexandrin, "Witnessing the Lights," 220–21 and 226.

147. Ibid., 223–24.

148. Ibid., 220 and 226.

149. Ibid., 220.

150. Ibid., 221.

151. Carl Ernst, "Ruzbihan," *EI2*, online edition: http://referenceworks.brillonline .com; Ernst, *Ruzbihan*, 24–28 and 68–101.

152. Quoted in Sands, *Sufi Commentaries*, 75; cf. Ernst, *Ruzbihan*, x–xi.

153. Sands, *Sufi Commentaries*, 75.

154. Ernst, *Ruzbihan*, 51; for a long list of similarly bold and controversial statements, see ibid., chapter 2.

155. Q 12:22–32.

156. Ernst, *Ruzbihan*, 71.

157. Ibid., 68–70; quoting Q 12:100; 30:27; 41:53; 42:11; cf. Ernst, *Ruzbihan*, 73–76, quoting Q 19:17 and 7:172.

158. (Al-)Baqli, *'Ara'is*, 1: 353 and 363.

159. Ibid., 301.

160. See Knysh, *Islamic Mysticism*, 72–82, and the literature cited therein.

161. Ernst, *Ruzbihan*, 68.

162. On his legacy in Central Asia, see Devin Deweese, "Baba Kamal and Jandi and the Kubravi Tradition among the Turks of Central Asia," *Der Islam* 71 (1994): 58–94, and Deweese, *Studies on Sufism in Central Asia* (Farnham: Ashgate Variorum, 2012), "Index" under "Kubra."

163. Denis Gril, "'La lecture supérieure' du Coran selon ibn Barraġan," *Arabica* 47, no. 3 (2000): 510–22; the works of Michel Chodkiewicz; and Knysh, *Ibn 'Arabi in the Later Islamic Tradition: The Making of a Polemical Image in Medieval Islam* (Albany: State University of New York Press, 1999); an annotated bibliography on Ibn (al-)'Arabi and his legacy can be found in Alexander Knysh and Ali Hussain, "Ibn al-'Arabi," in *Oxford Bibliographies in Islamic Studies*, ed. John Voll (Oxford: Oxford University Press, 2016): http://www.oxfordbibliographies.com/view/document/obo-9780195 390155/obo-9780195390155-0206.xml?rskey=ApEPqk&result=62.

164. The biographer was Ibn al-Abbar (d. 658/1260); quoted in Böwering and Casewit, eds., *A Qur'an Commentary*, 8.

165. Torre, *Ibn Barraġan*, 19, of the Spanish text, note 1; for a detailed description of Ibn Barrajan's exegetical oeuvre, see Böwering and Casewit, *Qur'an Commentary*, 23–33.

166. Böwering and Casewit, *Qur'an Commentary*, 37.

167. Torre, *Ibn Barraġan*, 42.

168. Ibid., 11–12, of the Arabic text, and Gril, "La lecture," 516; cf. Denis McAuley, *Ibn 'Arabi's Mystical Poetics* (Oxford: Oxford University Press, 2012), 65. Note that Ibn

(al-)'Arabi uses the term *i'tibar* and its synonym *'ubur* throughout chapters 68–73 of his *al-Futuhat al-makkiyya*; see Chittick, *Sufi Path*, "Index" under "*'ubur*."

169. Böwering and Casewit, *Qur'an Commentary*, 39.

170. Ibid., 38.

171. Ibid., 41 and 43.

172. As discussed much earlier by the Sufi Sahl al-Tustari (d. 283/896) in his mystical *tafsir*; see Böwering, *Mystical Vision*, 147–53; cf. Böwering and Casewit, *Qur'an Commentary*, 41.

173. Böwering and Casewit, *Qur'an Commentary*, 41.

174. Ibid., 34 and 42.

175. Ibid., 34.

176. Torre, *Ibn Barrağan*, 26–29, 64, 298–99, 423–25, and 569, of the Arabic text.

177. For some parallels in Ibn (al-)'Arabi's *al-Futuhat*, see Chittick, *Sufi Path*, 107, 276, 339, 340, 348, 379.

178. Gril, "La lecture," 520–21.

179. Eco, *Limits*, 23 and 41.

180. Böwering and Casewit, *Qur'an Commentary*, 41–42.

181. Torre, *Ibn Barrağan*, 221, of the Arabic text.

182. Ibid., 523–28, of the Arabic text.

183. Ibid., 111–16, 397, 489, 560, and 566, of the Arabic text; the term is taken from Q 4:69.

184. Torre, *Ibn Barrağan*, 116, of the Arabic text.

185. The title of this work is sometimes rendered into English as "The Bezels of Wisdom" (as in the widely used 1980 translation of the *Fusus* by Ralph Austin).

186. Chittick, *Sufi Path*; Chittick, *Self-Disclosure*, "Index" under "veil"; Lory, *Les commentaires*, 149.

187. Q 17:110.

188. For Ibn (al-)'Arabi's doctrine of the divine essence and divine names, see Chittick, *Sufi Path*, 8–11, 36, 58–59, 62–67, 90–91, 337, 390 note 17, etc.; Chittick, *Self-Disclosure*, "Index" under "name."

189. Q 13:3.

190. *Al-Futuhat*, 2: 557; translated in Chittick, *Sufi Path*, 62.

191. For Ibn (al-)'Arabi's views of gnosis (*ma'rifa*) and gnostics (*'arifun*), see Chittick, *Sufi Path*, "Index" under "gnosis" and "gnostic(s)"; Chittick, *Self-Disclosure*, "Index" under "gnosis" (*ma'rifa*).

192. For Ibn (al-)'Arabi's definitions of *kashf* and *mukashafa* (which are more or less synonymous), see Chittick, *Sufi Path*, and Chittick, *Self-Disclosure*, "Index" under "unveiling."

193. *Al-Futuhat*, 1: 101.

194. Ibid.; for parallels with Jewish mysticism, see Katz, "Mystical Speech," 16–17.

195. Chittick, *Sufi Path*, 97, 127–32, and 205–6, and Chittick, *Self-Disclosure*, 69–72.

196. See the quote in the text and *Futuhat*, chapter 73, 2: 32; for further details see Chittick, *Self-Disclosure*, and Chittick, *Sufi Path*, "Index" under "names (*asma'*)."

197. See *al-Futuhat*, chapter 5, and Michel Chodkiewicz, ed., *The Meccan Revelations*, 2 vols. (New York: Pir Press, 2005), 2: 29–40.

198. Chittick, *Sufi Path*, 96–112, and Chittick, *Self-Disclosure*, 57–66.

199. Ibn (al-)ʿArabi, *al-Futuhat*, 2: 346 and 4: 60; translated in Chittick, *Sufi Path*, 241–42.

200. These two Arabic designations of Sufi gnostics are synonymous, Chittick, *Sufi Path*, 400 note 3.

201. This term may also denote "interpretation of dreams," a connotation that Ibn (al-)ʿArabi no doubt wants to play on.

202. Ibn (al-)ʿArabi, *al-Futuhat*, 3: 257; translated by Chittick, *Sufi Path*, 246–47.

203. See Knysh, *Ibn ʿArabi*, passim; Michel Chodkiewicz, *An Ocean without Shore: Ibn ʿArabi, the Book, and the Law* (Albany: State University of New York Press, 1993), 4, and Gerald Elmore, *Islamic Sainthood in the Fullness of Time: Ibn al-ʿArabi's Book of the Fabulous Gryphon* (Leiden: E. J. Brill, 1999), passim.

204. Ibn (al-)ʿArabi, *al-Futuhat*, 1: 150, and 2: 399–400; Katz, "Mysticism and the Interpretation," 22–23; Chittick, *Sufi Path*, 250–52; Ron Nettler, *Sufi Metaphysics and Qurʾanic Prophets: Ibn ʿArabi's Thought and Method in the Fusus al-hikam* (Cambridge: Islamic Texts Society, 2003), 29.

205. Ibn [(al-)ʿArabi, *Diwan Ibn ʿArabi* (Baghdad: Maktabat Muthanna, 1963), 136–79.

206. Ibn (al-)ʿArabi, *Fusus al-hikam*, ed. Abu 'l-ʿAla ʿAfifi (Beirut: Dar al-kitab al-ʿarabi, 1980), 123; our translation of this passage is different from Ralph Austin's; see *The Bezels*, 153.

207. Peter Bachmann, "Un commentaire mystique du Coran," *Arabica* 47, no. 3 (2000): 503.

208. McAuley, *Ibn ʿArabi's Mystical Poetics*, 160–99.

209. As, e.g., in the introduction to his *Ringstones of Wisdom*; see Ibn (al-)ʿArabi, *Fusus*, 47–48; for an English translation, see Austin, *The Bezels*, 45–46.

210. Denis Gril, "Le commentaire du verset de la lumière d'après Ibn ʿArabi," *Bulletin de l'Institut français d'archéologie orientale* 90 (1990): 180.

211. Nettler, *Sufi Metaphysics*, 13–14; cf. Hodgson, *Venture of Islam*, 2: 242–43.

212. Nettler, *Sufi Metaphysics*, 14.

213. To use the translation suggested by Denis McAuley in his *Ibn ʿArabi's Mystical Poetics*, 65.

214. Sands, *Sufi Commentaries*, 41; for Ibn (al-)ʿArabi's own statements to this effect, see Chittick, *Sufi Path*, 243–44.

215. Chittick, *Sufi Path*, 356–81.

216. As shown in Knysh, *Ibn ʿArabi*, chapters 4–6.

217. Q 7:148–55 and Q 20:85–94.

218. Ibn (al-)ʿArabi, *Fusus*, 192; Nettler, *Sufi Metaphysics*, 53.

219. Nettler, *Sufi Metaphysics*, 67; the emphasis is of the original.

220. Ibid., 94.

221. *Al-Futuhat*, 1: 31; on a selection of Ibn (al-)ʿArabi's statements about "direct tasting," which can be defined as an unmediated (revelatory) perception or insight, see Chittick, *Sufi Path*, and Chittick, *Self-Disclosure*, "Index" under "tasting (*dhawq*)."

222. Ibn (al-)ʿArabi, *Al-Futuhat*, 2: 24.

223. See, e.g., chapter 5, vol. 1, p. 102; chapter 73, vol. 2, pp. 20, 23, 35, and so on.

224. Ralph Austin, trans., *Sufis of Andalusia: The Ruh al-Quds and Al-Durat Al-Fakhirah of Ibn 'Arabi* (Sherborne, Gloucestershire: Beshara Publications, 1988), passim.

225. See chapters 1–68, vol. 1, pp. 47–239; chapter 73, vol. 2, pp. 1–139 passim.

226. For a summary of this book, see Richard Todd, *The Sufi Doctrine of Man: Sadr al-Din al-Qunawi's Metaphysical Anthropology* (Leiden: E. J. Brill, 2014), 31–32; our translation of this title is different from that proposed by Todd.

227. Ibid., 32–35; our translation is different from Todd's.

228. According to Richard Todd; see ibid., 1 and 30–31.

229. For an assessment of al-Qunawi's work in relation to that of Ibn (al-)'Arabi, see Todd, *Sufi Doctrine*, 45–51.

230. See Ibn Barrajan's exegesis analyzed in Böwering and Casewit, *Qur'an Commentary*, 29–45, and Ibn (al-)'Arabi's *al-Futuhat*, 1: 102 and *Fusus*, 48–50.

231. Al-Qunawi, *al-Tafsir al-sufi li 'l-Qur'an: I'jaz al-bayan fi ta'wil al-Qur'an*, ed. 'Abd al-Qadir Ahmad 'Ata (Cairo: Dar al-kutub al-haditha, 1969), 98; cf. Todd, *Sufi Doctrine*, 33, and Chittick, *Divine Love*, 107–10.

232. As recognized by Ibn (al-)'Arabi himself; see, e.g., *al-Fututat*, 1: 104.

233. Chittick, "The School," 1: 513.

234. Chittick has suggested that this term was coined by al-Qunawi (see ibid., 514), although the idea had no doubt been articulated by his teacher in the *Meccan Revelations*, as Chittick himself shows in his *Sufi Path*, 4–6, and "Index" under "*hadra.*"

235. According to Richard Todd, al-Qunawi had in mind the widely known Muslim concept of the five revealed books: the Torah, the Psalms, the Gospel, the Discernment (*al-furqan*, i.e., the legal-juridical verses of the Qur'an), and the Qur'an proper; Todd, *Sufi Doctrine*, 99 note 72.

236. Ibid., 98.

237. Chittick, *Sufi Path*, 5.

238. Todd, *Sufi Doctrine*, 98–101.

239. See Ibn (al-)'Arabi, *Fusus*, 90–91, quoting Sahl al-Tustari (d. 283/896).

240. Todd, *Sufi Doctrine*, 101–7.

241. See Chittick, "The School," 514.

242. Todd, *Sufi Doctrine*, 30–31.

243. Todd translates this term as "synoptic copy"; ibid., 33.

244. Ibid., 83–86.

245. Ibid., 95–98.

246. Ibid., 136, and chapter 6; the phrase "the lowest of the low" is taken from the Qur'an (95:5).

247. Todd, *Sufi Doctrine*, 61.

248. Ibid., 62; for further evidence of the impact that the *Epistles* had on the intellectual life of the Muslim thinkers of the age in al-Andalus and beyond, see Böwering and Casewit, *Qur'an Commentary*, 35; Michael Ebstein, *Mysticism and Philosophy in al-Andalus: Ibn Masarra, Ibn al-Arabi, and the Isma'ili Tradition* (Leiden: E. J. Brill, 2014), passim; cf. Netton, *Muslim Neoplatonists*, 33–52.

249. As argued by Chittick in "The School," 1: 511–14.

250. James Morris, "Ibn 'Arabi and His Interpreters," *Journal of the American Oriental Society* 106, no. 3 (1986): 751–52.

251. Pierre Lory, "'Abd al-Razzaq al-Kashani," *EI3*, online edition: http://refer enceworks.brillonline.com; Lory, *Les commentaires*, 8–9, 21, 26, 31, etc., and Sands, *Sufi Commentaries*, 42–44 and 76–77.

252. In his *Les commentaires* (31) Pierre Lory stresses the fact that al-Qashani's explication of Ibn (al-)'Arabi's ideas was in large part driven by pedagogical concerns in an age when Sufi books were usually read out loud and commented upon by *shaykh*s in the presence of their students (*murid*s); see also Böwering and Casewit, *Qur'an Commentary*, 36.

253. Lory, *Les commentaires*, 23–27, and Lory, "'Abd al-Razzaq al-Kashani"; McAuley, *Ibn 'Arabi's Mystical Poetics*, 65 notes 33 and 34; Sands, *Sufi Commentaries*, 76–77; Alan Godlas, "Sufism," in *The Blackwell Companion to the Quran*, ed. Andrew Rippin (Oxford: Blackwell, 2006), 356; originally published in Egypt in 1293/1876 (Cairo, Bulaq), al-Qashani's commentary was titled *Tafsir Muhyi 'l-Din Ibn 'Arabi*; this misattribution was reproduced in the subsequent editions of this influential work.

254. Lory, *Les commentaires*, 31.

255. Lory, "'Abd al-Razzaq al-Kashani."

256. Ibn 'Arabi, *Tafsir al-Qur'an al-karim*, 2 vols. (Beirut: Dar al-yaqza al-'arabiyya, 1968), 1: 4 (henceforth al-Qashani/Ibn 'Arabi, *Tafsir*), and Lory, *Les commentaires*, 14–15.

257. Lory, *Les commentaires*, 14–15; for a survey of the semantic field of the word *ta'wil* in the Sufi exegetical tradition, see "Index" in Sands, *Sufi Commentaries*; for a comparative perspective, see Katz, "Mysticism and Sacred Scripture," 18.

258. Chittick, *Sufi Path*, 243; cf. 199–202, and Chittick, *Self-Disclosure*, 18, 95, and 118.

259. Lory, *Les commentaires*, 12–15, 23, 34–38; in his popular "encyclopedia of Qur'anic sciences," Jalal al-Din al-Suyuti (d. 911/1505) associates *ta'wil* primarily, though not exclusively, with the ambiguous verses of the Qur'an; see *al-Itqan fi 'ulum al-Qur'an*, 5 vols. (Abu Dhabi: Mu'assasat al-nida', 1424/2003), 3: 485, 488, 497, 498, 500–501; for al-Suyuti's list of definitions of *ta'wil* see ibid., 4: 331–34.

260. Johannes Baljon, *Religion and Thought of Shah Wali Allah Dihlawi, 1703–1762* (Leiden: E. J. Brill, 1986), 141.

261. Al-Qashani/Ibn 'Arabi, *Tafsir*, 1: 4; Lory, *Les commentaires*, 15–16.

262. Named after the Saint Victor Abbey of Paris built in 1113.

263. See the entry "High of St. Victor" in F. L. Cross and E. A. Livingstone, eds., *The Oxford Dictionary of the Christian Church*, 3rd ed. (Oxford: Oxford University Press, 1997), 800.

264. Lory, *Les commentaires*, 33–34.

265. Hodgson, *Venture of Islam*, 2: 22, 224–27; Katz, *Mysticism and Language*, chapters 1 and 2 passim; McGinn, *Foundations of Mysticism*, 110–12; Todd, *Sufi Doctrine*, 3–5, 33, and 68.

266. Lory, *Les commentaires*, 34–38 and 67–68.

267. Al-Qashani (Ibn 'Arabi), *Tafsir*, 1: 5, and Lory, *Les commentaires*, 27–28.

268. Lory, *Le commentaires*, 31.

269. Ibid., 29.

270. Al-Qashani/Ibn ʿArabi, *Tafsir*, 1: 5 passim.

271. Lory, *Le commentaires*, 29–30.

272. Ibid., 30, 55, 63, 64; variations on this tripartite system abound with *malakut* occasionally placed above *jabarut* by some Sufi thinkers.

273. Lory, "ʿAbd al-Razzaq al-Kashani."

274. Al-Qashani (Ibn ʿArabi), *Tafsir*, 1: 705–6.

275. Lory, "ʿAbd al-Razzaq al-Kashani."

276. Cited in Katz, "Mysticism and Interpretation," 28.

277. Lory, *Les commentaires*, 31.

278. See, e.g., chapter 6 of Ahmed, *What Is Islam?*

279. For debates around this issue see, e.g., Armando Salvatore, *Islam and the Political Discourse of Modernity* (Reading, UK: Ithaca Press, 1998); Muhammad Khalid Masud, Armando Salvatore, and Martin van Bruinessen, eds., *Islam and Modernity: Key Issues and Debates* (Edinburgh: Edinburgh University Press, 2009); Ali Mirsepassi and Tadd Fernée, *Islam, Democracy, and Cosmopolitanism: At Home and in the World* (Cambridge: Cambridge University Press, 2014); Ahmed, *What Is Islam?*, chapter 6.

280. Günay Alpay Kut, "Ismaʿil Hakki," *EI2*, online edition: http://referenceworks .brillonline.com.

281. Bulent Rauf, trans., *Ismail Hakki's Bursevi's Translation and Commentary on Fusus al-Hikam*, 3 vols. (Oxford: Muhyiddin Ibn ʿArabi Society and Oxford University Press, 1986–89), 1: 6–20.

282. One of the preferred epithets of God in Sufi metaphysics and gnoseology; see Chittick, *Sufi Path*, 49, 132–33 passim; Chittick, *Self-Disclosure*, "Index of Arabic Words" under "*al-haqq*."

283. Ibn (al-)ʿArabi, *Fusus*, 103–5; for a remarkable restatement of this idea by a modern-day Western academic who seems to share it, see Chittick, *Divine Love*, 18–19.

284. Rauf, *Ismail Hakki's*, 1: 90–159, and 3: 521–62; Ismaʿil Haqqi b. Mustafa, *Kitab tafsir al-Qurʾan al-musamma bi-ruh al-bayan*, 4 vols. (Cairo: Bulaq, 1860), 1: 64–67; for Ibn (al-)ʿArabi's original ideas, see Austin, *The Bezels*, 34–38.

285. Ibn ʿArabi, *Fusus*, 50, and Austin, *The Bezels*, 51; note the pun based on the Arabic word *insan*.

286. For Ibn (al-)ʿArabi's original usage, see Chittick, *Sufi Path*, 83–88.

287. Rauf, *Ismail Hakki's*, 1: 20–28; originally articulated by Ibn (al-)ʿArabi in his *Fusus*, chapter 9, and Austin, *The Bezels*, 119–27; see also Chittick, *Sufi Path*, 112–24.

288. See Chittick, *Sufi Path*, chapters 2 and 3, and Chittick, "The School," passim.

289. Ismaʿil Haqqi, *Kitab tafsir al-Qurʾan*, 1: 7, 8, 9, 13, 14, 15, 17, 20, 23, 24, 25, 27, 31, 51, 53, 55, 59, 63, 64–65, 70 passim.

290. See, e.g., ibid., 23, 29, 31; for the Kubrawi school of thought and exegesis see the section that follows.

291. Ismaʿil Haqqi, *Kitab tafsir al-Qurʾan*, 25.

292. Note in particular such vintage Akbarian concepts as absolute oneness (*ahadiyya*), emanation (*fayd*), perfect man (*insan kamil*), bewilderment (*hayra*), divine presence (*hadra ilahiyya*), etc.; ibid., 7, 9, 17 passim.

293. Ibid., 16–17 and 61; Ibn (al-)'Arabi presents basically the same idea as reception by primordial images-souls of the divine effusion, or emanation (*al-fayd*), see *Fusus*, 49; for light imagery more generally see ibid., 101–13; Austin, *The Bezels*, 50 and chapter 8.

294. Isma'il Haqqi, *Kitab tafsir al-Qur'an*, 20–21 and 54; cf. Ibn (al-)'Arabi, *Fusus*, 124–26.

295. Ibn 'Ajiba, *Tafsir al-Fatiha al-kabir al-musamma bi 'l-Bahr al-madid*, ed. Bassam Muhammad Barud, 2 vols. (Abu Dhabi: al-Majma' al-Thaqafi, 1999), 1: 129–31; cf. Godlas, "Sufism," 358; the title of this commentary is rendered as "Immense Sea" in its recent partial translation by Mohamed Fouad Aresmouk and Michael Abdurrahman Fitzgerald; see *The Immense Ocean: "Al-Bahr al-Madid"; A Thirteenth-Century Quranic Commentary on the Chapters of the All-Merciful, the Event, and Iron* (Louisville, KY: Fons Vitae, 2009).

296. For devotional and liturgical purposes, the text of the Qur'an is divided into sixty "portions" (*ahzab*; sing. *hizb*). The *hizb* translated by Mohamed Fouad Aresmouk and Michael Abdurrahman Fitzgerald (see the previous note) begins with sura 55 (*al-Rahman*) and ends with sura 57 (*al-Hadid*), see p. xxiv of the "Introduction."

297. (Al-)Baqli's '*Ara'is al-bayan* is misidentified by Ibn 'Ajiba as belonging to one "al-Wartajibi" (apparently, the scribe or original owner of the manuscript of (al-)Baqli's work); see Kenneth Honerkamp, "Introduction" to *Immense Ocean*, xxi and xvi.

298. Ibid.

299. Ibn 'Ajiba, *Tafsir*, 1: 132.

300. Ibid., 133.

301. For Indonesia see Syed Muhammad Naguib Al-Attas, *The Mysticism of Hamza Fansuri* (Kuala Lumpur: University of Malaya Press, 1970) and Vladimir Braginsky, "Universe-Man-Text: The Sufi Concept of Literature," *Journal of the Humanities and Social Sciences of Southeast Asia* 149, no. 2 (1993): 201–25; for West Africa see Rudolph Ware, *The Walking Qur'an: Islamic Education, Embodied Knowledge, and History in West Africa* (Chapel Hill: University of North Carolina Press, 2014), and Zachary Wright, "Embodied Knowledge in West African Islam: Continuity and Change in the Gnostic Community of Shaykh Ibrahim Niasse" (unpublished PhD thesis, Northwestern University, 2010).

302. Reinhard Schulze, *Islamischer Internationalismus im 20. Jahrhundert: Untersuchungen zur Geschichte der Islamischen Weltliga* (Leiden: E. J. Brill, 1990), chapters 1–6.

303. Hodgson, *Venture of Islam*, 2: 334–35.

304. E.g., Böwering, "Sufi Hermeneutics," 257; Godlas, "Sufism," 355.

305. That is, "The Greatest Master" (*al-shaykh al-akbar*).

306. The sobriquet of Kubra is an abbreviation of the Qur'anic expression *al-tammat al-kubra*, "the major disaster," a nickname that Najm al-Din earned through his formidable polemical skills; see Hamid Algar, "Kubra," *EI2*, online edition: http://referenceworks.brillonline.com.

307. For details see Knysh, *Islamic Mysticism*, chapters 3–6; al-Ghazali's association with Sufism has been contested of late (unconvincingly, to our mind); see Garden, *First Muslim Reviver*, 10, 79–80 passim.

308. Jamal Elias, *The Throne Carrier of God: The Life and Thought of 'Ala' ad-*

Dawla as-Simnani (Albany: State University of New York Press, 1995), 205; cf. Godlas, "Sufism," 355.

309. Simnani's exegesis is discussed on pp. 107–10 of Elias's book *The Throne Carrier of God* (see the previous note).

310. Elias, *Throne Carrier*, 108.

311. That is, its legal content.

312. From the Greek "climb" or "ascent" upward; for uses of this term in Christian mysticism, see McGinn, *Foundations of Mysticism*, 112, and "Index" under "anagogy."

313. Elias, *Throne Carrier*, 108; for various uses of the term *matla'* or *muttala'* in Sufi contexts, see Böwering, *Mystical Vision*, 139–41, and Sands, *Sufi Commentaries*, chapter 1; the former translates *matla'* (in his reading) as "point of transcendence" or "point of ascent," while the latter renders this term (reading it as *muttala'*) as "lookout point."

314. A similar classification of knowers of the Qur'an is found in the early *tafsir* of Sahl al-Tustari (d. 283/896); see Böwering, *Mystical Vision*, 141; it may well have been the source of Simnani's classification.

315. Elias, *Throne Carrier*, 108.

316. On him see Claude Gilliot, " 'Abdallah b. 'Abbas," *Encyclopedia of Islam*, 3rd ed., online edition: http://referenceworks.brillonline.com/entries/encyclopaedia -of-islam-3.

317. Haydar-i Amuli, *Al-Muhit al-a'zam*, 1: 118–28, and ibid., "Introduction," "lam-ha" and "lam-waw."

318. Haydar-i Amuli, *Al-Muhit al-a'zam*, 1: 85.

319. See Sands, *Sufi Commentaries*, 4.

320. Muhsin al-Musawi al-Tabrizi, "Introduction," Haydar-i Amuli, *Al-Muhit al-a'zam*, 1: "kaf-za' " and "kaf-ha'. "

321. See, e.g., Said Arjomand, *The Shadow of God and the Hidden Imam* (Chicago: University of Chicago Press, 1984), 23, 149–51, and 155–57; Matthijs van den Bos, *Mystic Regimes: Sufism and the State in Iran; From the Late Qajar Era to the Islamic Republic* (Leiden: E.J. Brill, 2002), passim.

322. *Al-shaykh al-akbar* is, as already mentioned, an honorific epithet of Ibn (al-)'Arabi widely used by his followers.

323. Haydar-i Amul, *Al-Muhit al-a'zam*, 1: 22; also quoted in Sayyid Muhsin al-Musawi al-Tabrizi's "Introduction," "ya-alif."

324. For several alternative titles, see ibid., "ha' " and "ta'."

325. Ibid., "ya" and "ya-alif."

326. Haydar-i Amuli, *Al-Muhit al-a'zam*, 2: 71; cf. ibid., 410.

327. See, e.g., ibid., 1: 242–43, 341, 361, 408; 2: 411, 412–13; and 3: 102, 151, etc.

328. Ibn (al-)'Arabi, *al-Futuhat*, 3: 328–40, and Elmore, *Fabulous Gryphon*, 5–7, 253 notes 58 and 62; 525 note 104; 531–32 note 45; and 534; cf., however, ibid., 595; and Rauf, *Ismail Hakki's*, vol. 1, pp. 6–20.

329. Haydar-i Amuli, *Al-Muhit al-a'zam*, 2: 412–13.

330. Ibid., 2: 99.

331. Ibid.

332. Ibid., 97.

333. Ibid., 240–41.

334. "He [God] is the First and the Last, the Apparent/Evident and the Hidden/Concealed, and He has knowledge of all things."

335. Or "identity" (*'ayn*).

336. Haydar-i Amuli, *al-Muhit al-a'zam*, 1: 338.

337. Ibid., 290–91.

338. Ibid., 339 and 242.

339. Chittick, *Sufi Path*, 356–81.

340. Haydar-i Amuli, *al-Muhit al-a'zam*, 1: 101–2, 104–5, 109–10, 112–13, 339.

341. Ibid., 97; as shown in chapter 2, this term was a bone of contention between Sufis and Shi'i scholars.

342. Haydar-i Amuli, *al-Muhit al-a'zam*, 1: 205 and 338–39.

343. Ibid., 120.

344. Ibid., 121.

345. Knysh, *Islam in Historical Perspective*, 177.

346. Meir Bar-Asher, *Scripture and Exegesis in Early Imami Shiism* (Leiden: E. J. Brill, 1999), 93–101.

347. On the *rijal* see Knysh, *Islam in Historical Perspective*, 175–77.

348. William Shakespeare, *Hamlet*, Act 2, Scene 2.

349. For his biography, see the website of the Naqshbandi-Haqqani-Rabbani Sufi order of which he was the founder: http://www.naqshbandi.org/golden-chain/the-chain/shaykh-muhammad-nazim/.

350. Shaykh Nazim al-Haqqani's following from sixty-five nationalities is estimated at several million worldwide in Annabelle Böttcher, "Religious Authority in Transnational Sufi Networks: Shaykh Nazim al-Qubrusi al-Haqqani al-Naqshbandi," in *Speaking for Islam: Religious Authorities in Muslim Societies*, ed. Gudrun Krämer and Sabine Schmidtke (Leiden: E. J. Brill, 2006), 242; D. W. Damrel mentions some 60,000 followers of the *tariqa* in the United States, in his "Aspects of the Naqshbandi-Haqqani Order in North America," in *Sufism in the West*, ed. Jamal Malik and John Hinnels (London: Routledge, 2006), 118; see also Mark Sedgwick, *Western Sufism: From the Abbasids to the New Age* (New York: Oxford University Press, 2017), 247.

351. Marcia Hermansen, "In the Garden of American Sufi Movements: Hybrids and Perennials," in *New Trends and Developments in the World of Islam*, ed. Peter Clarke (London: Luzac Oriental, 1998), 155.

352. Ibid., 172 note 24; Böttcher, "Religious Authority," 245–46 and 248–49; cf. Sedgwick, *Western Sufism*, 196 and 247.

353. Ibn (al-)'Arabi's own views of the matter have been analyzed in Elmore, *Fabulous Gryphon*, passim; for Ibn Khaldun's scathing criticism of the Sufi millennialism of Ibn (al-)'Arabi and other North African and Andalusi Sufis, see Franz Rosenthal, trans., *Ibn Khaldun: The Muqaddimah; An Introduction to History* (New York: Pantheon, 1958), 2: 186–200.

354. For some recent studies of the *tariqa*, see Böttcher, "Religious Authority"; Damrel, "Aspects of the Naqshbandi-Haqqani Order"; Marcia Hermansen, "What's American about American Sufi Movements?" in *Sufism in Europe and North America*, ed. David Westerlund (London: Routledge, 2004), 51–52, and Veronika Tsibenko (Ivanova), "The Naqshbandi-Haqqani (Rabbani) Sufi Order: Contemporary Sufism of Neo-Ottoman Style," in *Sufism and the Muslim Spiritual Tradition: Texts, Institu-*

tions, Ideas, and Interpretations, ed. Alexander Knysh (St. Petersburg: Peterburgskoe vostokovedenie, 2015), 258–75 (in Russian with an English summary).

355. For a discussion of the *tariqa(t)*'s history and present-day following, see Hermansen, "In the Garden," 157–58, and the studies mentioned in the previous note.

356. https://www.facebook.com/DrNourKabbani and http://sufilive.com/.

357. Hermansen, "In the Garden," 163; Sedgwick, *Western Sufism*, 196 and 247; and Tsibenko, "Naqshbandi-Haqqani," 259–60.

358. See, e.g., http://www.nurmuhammad.com/Dwnlds/Tafsirs/TafsirIkhlas1.pdf. The file has no pagination.

359. http://ahlulbidahwalhawa.com/2013/06/03/exposing-hisham-kabbani-naqshabandi-sufi/. For a criticism of Shaykh Hisham's use of allegorical-esoteric interpretation of the Qur'an (*ta'wil*) see point 4.

360. For a harsh criticism of Shaykh Hisham's words and actions by the fellow Naqshbandi Sufi Shaykh 'Adnan Kabbani, see https://defendingthetruth.wordpress.com/2010/04/25/reutationofhishamkabbani/.

361. http://sufilive.com/; for Shaykh 'Adnan Kabbani's homilies and sermons, see https://shaykhadnan.wordpress.com/about/.

362. The discussion that follows is based on our reading of the websites mentioned in the previous notes and conversations with the followers of Shaykh Nazim and Shaykh Hisham, who reside in Michigan. One of them, "Muhammad," is a long-standing follower, whereas the other, "Khadija," is a relatively recent convert who joined the *tariqa(t)* in 2013. In addition to the oral conversations, we have used the notes "Khadija" had taken in 2013–15 during her meetings with Shaykh Hisham. Such study sessions, named *sohba(t)* (from the Arabic *suhba*, "companionship"), are readily available online at http://sufilive.com/ and https://www.youtube.com/user/sufilive.

363. This hyphenated title reflects the various iterations of the *tariqa(t)*'s name over several decades of its existence; see Tsibenko, "Naqshbandi-Haqqani," 259–63; as far as one can tell, the adjective "Nazimiyya" was added to the *tariqa(t)*'s name after the death of Shaykh Nazim in May 2014.

364. A transliteration of the Arabic *qudrat Allah*, i.e., "power of God."

365. http://sufismus-online.de/InterpretationOfQuran.

366. Abdullah Saeed, *Interpreting the Qur'an: Towards a Contemporary Approach* (London: Routledge, 2006), 22; this position is shared by the majority of liberal Muslims today; see Knysh, *Islam in Historical Perspective*, 458–60.

367. Saeed, *Interpreting the Qur'an*, 21.

368. Böttcher, "Religious Authority," 253–54.

369. E.g., *al-Baqara* (2), *Al 'Imran* (3), *al-Sajda* (32)—six in all (see also Q 29, 30, 31); on the mysterious letters, known as "openers of the suras," see Knysh, *Islam in Historical Perspective*, 75.

370. From the context, it appears that Shaykh Nazim refers here both to Western scholars (e.g., translators) of the Qur'an and fundamentalist Muslims, whom he styles "Wahabis" [*sic*].

371. http://sufismus-online.de/InterpretationOfQuran.

372. Ibid.

373. http://sufismus-online.de/LearnedMan; we have preserved intact the wording of the original.

374. Böttcher, "Religious Authority," 259.

375. His exegetical elaborations were transcribed and posted on the *tariqa(t)*'s website by an unknown follower or followers (hence some mistakes and inconsistencies characteristic of an oral narrative and nonprofessional transliteration). A podcast of the oral version of this oration is available at: http://sufilive.com/.

376. The transliteration is that of the original: http://www.nurmuhammad.com /Dwnlds/Tafsirs/TafsirIkhlas1.pdf.

377. That is, 'Abdallah Fa'iz (Faizi) al-Daghestani (d. 1973), the spiritual preceptor of both Shaykh Nazim and Shaykh Hisham.

378. Namely, Shaykh Muhammad Nazim (al-)Haqqani (now deceased), who was Shaykh Hisham Kabbani's father-in-law.

379. "S" may stand here for either "peace (*salam*) be upon him [i.e., the Prophet]" or for the ritual formula *salla llahu 'alayhi wa sallam* ("may God bless him and grant him [the Prophet] peace").

380. http://www.nurmuhammad.com/Dwnlds/Tafsirs/TafsirIkhlas1.pdf.

381. On him see Sedgwick, *Western Sufism*, 246–47.

382. Holland, *Sheikh Muzaffer Ozak*, 321–22.

383. Ibid., 517.

384. Ibid., 519.

385. Some translations of the Qur'an, including the one "Revised and Edited by The Presidency of Islamic Researchers, IFTA, Call and Guidance, Saudi Arabia," interpret the [greater] "knower" mentioned in the verse as being "God, the All-Knowing." Shaykh Hisham seems to be of opinion that it refers to members of the hierarchy of knowers generally, all the way to the Prophet and, ultimately, of course, to God himself.

386. What follows is a summary of the notes taken by "Khadija" during Shaykh Hisham's teaching sessions (*sohba(t)*s) in Fenton, Michigan, in 2013–14. "Khadija" has provided a preliminary analysis of Shaykh Hisham's epistemological statements that we will occasionally be quoting. In principle, such statements can be found in practically every Shaykh's discourse available on the web as well as in his numerous writings (eighty in all) available for purchase on amazon.com: http://www.amazon.com/s?ie =UTF8&page=1&rh=n%3A283155%2Cp_27%3AShaykh%20Muhammad%20 Hisham%20Kabbani.

387. Muhammad Hisham Kabbani, *Encyclopedia of Islamic Doctrine*, 7 vols. (Chicago: Kazi Publications, 1998), 3: 135 and 141.

388. For descriptions of miracles (*karamat*) ascribed to Shaykh Nazim by his followers see Böttcher, "Religious Authority," 254–55.

389. Shaykh Hisham renders this term as "disclosure."

390. Hisham Kabbani, *Encyclopedia*, 3: 137–38.

391. Usually translated as "the sincere" or "the truthful ones."

392. Based on "Khadija"'s notes and Hisham Kabbani, *Encyclopedia*, 3: 132.

393. The honorific title of the Naqshbandi spiritual genealogy or "chain" (*silsila*); see, e.g., http://www.naqshbandi.org/golden-chain/ and http://www.naqshbandi.org /golden-chain/the-chain/; Böttcher, "Religious Authority," 257.

394. "Our lord or master."

395. The reference is to Q 55:19–20.

396. "Khadija"'s notes; Hisham Kabbani, *The Hierarchy of Saints* (Fenton, MI: ISCA, Part 1, 2012), 6, and Böttcher, "Religious Authority," 252.

397. "Khadija"'s notes and https://www.youtube.com/watch?v=onYKoroHYLY; https://www.pinterest.com/pin/458663543270323835/; cf. Tsibenko, "Naqshbandi-Haqqani," 263–65; Shaykh Hisham praises Shaykh Nazim as "sultan, son of the sultan, son of the sultan, son of the sultan, up to the Prophet(s)"; http://sufismus-online.de/alqahhar.

398. http://www.nurmuhammad.com/Dwnlds/Tafsirs/tafsirnabatenthruthirteen.pdf; the file has no pagination; the emphasis is of the original.

399. http://www.nurmuhammad.com/Dwnlds/Tafsirs/tafsirnabatenthruthirteen.pdf. The correct Arabic spelling is *haqiqat al-jadhba,* meaning "the [true] reality of attraction"; the Shaykh alludes to the state of an irresistible attraction to God (or his elect friends) experienced by ordinary believers; cf. Böttcher, "Religious Authority," 252.

400. Namely, the Arab rulers of the oil-rich Gulf region.

401. http://www.nurmuhammad.com/Dwnlds/Tafsirs/tafsirsurahannaas.pdf; elsewhere Shaykh Nazim calls democracy "the religion of Ancient Greece" and a "Jewish stratagem"; Tsibenko, "Naqshbandi-Haqqani," 264.

402. http://www.sufismus-online.de/DemocracyIsDictatorship.

403. http://sufismus-online.de/BeRabbaniyin; the Qur'anic term chosen by Shaykh Nazim as the designation for his project of unifying the *umma* originally referred to, in all probability, Jewish rabbis, as one can construe from the context of the Qur'an (3:79 and 5:44) in which it appears; see Rudi Paret, *Der Koran: Kommentar und Konkordanz* (Stuttgart: W. Kohlhammer, 1971), 121–22, and the studies quoted therein.

404. For details, see Tsibenko, "Naqshbandi-Haqqani," 267–69.

405. http://www.sufismus-online.de/DemocracyIsDictatorship.

406. http://www.sufismus-online.de/SubjectS.

407. See Holland, *Sheikh Muzaffer Ozak,* 338–39; overall, Muzaffer Ozak's teachings collected in this volume exhibit no distinctly esoteric themes; based on the Qur'an, Sunna, and references to the actions of pious Muslims of old, his discourses appear to be thoroughly moralistic to the point of being pedestrian; one is likely to gain a similar impression after reading the meditations on the state of affairs in this world by another neo-Sufi leader, Fethullah Gülen (b. 1941), who, however, allocates much more space to Sufism in his pietistic sermons; see Gülen, *Toward a Global Civilization of Love and Tolerance* (Somerset, NJ: The Light, 2006); Gülen's interpretations of Sufism, articulated in his widely read *Key Concepts in the Practice of Sufism: Emerald Hills of the Heart* (Somerset, NJ: The Light, 2006), lie outside the purview of this book.

408. As detailed in Tsibenko, "Naqshbandi-Haqqani," 263–70.

409. That is, the (Neo-)Platonic "One": "Beyond all bodies is the soul's essence; beyond all souls, the intellectual principle; and beyond all intellectual substances, the One"; Eric Dodds, ed. and trans., *Proclus: The Elements of Theology* (Oxford: Clarendon Press, 1963), 23; cf. Chittick, *Sufi Path,* "Index" under *"ahad"* and *"wahid"*; for a comparative perspective, see Katz, "Mystical Speech," 24–32.

410. http://www.nurmuhammad.com/Dwnlds/Tafsirs/TafsirIkhlas1.pdf.

411. This life.

412. The future life, or hereafter.

413. http://www.nurmuhammad.com/Dwnlds/Tafsirs/TafsirIkhlas1.pdf; the correct transliteration of the Arabic phrase is *ma'rifat Allah* or *ma'rifat ullah.*

414. See, e.g., *al-Futuhat*, 2: 6–8.

415. According to Shaykh Hisham, the *qutb* is the servant of the supreme divine name *ahad* ("One"); see http://www.nurmuhammad.com/Dwnlds/Tafsirs/Tafsir Ikhlas1.pdf.

416. See, e.g., Chittick, *Sufi Path*, "Index," under *ahad*, *wahid*, and "presence(s)"; and the discussion of al-Qunawi's cosmology earlier in this chapter.

417. See, e.g., *Futuhat*, 1: 265; 2: 680; 3: 275, 279, and 421–29.

418. See Henrik Nyberg, ed., *Kleinere Schriften des Ibn al-'Arabi* (Leiden: E. J. Brill, 1919), and a Russian translation of this work (*Insha' al-dawa'ir*) in Alexander Knysh, trans., *Mekkanskie otkroveniia* (St. Petersburg: Peterburgskoe vostokovedenie, 1991), passim; see also the discussion of the use of the Ibn (al-)'Arabi–style diagrams by Haydar-i Amuli earlier in this chapter.

419. "*Sohbet* (*suhba*), close proximity and communication with the shaykh, which had always been an important element in spiritual guidance, became modernized in the form of seminars and lectures, which were also made available as video and audio recordings as well as in printed form"; Martin van Bruinessen, "Sufism, 'Popular' Islam, and the Encounter with Modernity," in *Islam and Modernity: Key Issues and Debates*, ed. Muhammad Khalid Masud, Armando Salvatore, and Martin van Bruinessen (Edinburgh: Edinburgh University Press, 2009), 142; for Shaykh Nazim's *sohbet*s more specifically, see Böttcher, "Religious Authority," 243 and 258.

420. Lit. "the most concealed."

421. "The Different Levels of the Heart." Mawlana Shaykh Hisham Kabbani; Sohba/Discourse—Gaithersburg, MD, USA; Recorded: Friday, February 27, 2015; at: http://sufilive.com/the-different-levels-of-the-heart-5810.html; see also Shaykh Hisham's commentary on verses 10–13 of sura 78, "The Tidings" (*al-Naba'*), published online at: http://www.nurmuhammad.com/pbuh/?p=1584.

422. He received a bachelor's degree in chemistry from the American University of Beirut, Lebanon; see http://www.simplyislam.com.sg/main/about/our-scholars /shaykh-hisham-kabbani/. According to Annabelle Böttcher's sources, Shaykh Nazim also studied chemistry at the University of Istanbul, "Religious Authority," 244.

423. God speaking of himself using the royal or majestic "We."

424. Shaykh Hisham refers to the divine fiat (*kun*; "Be!"), frequently mentioned in the Qur'an: "Surely His Command, when He wills a thing, is only to say to it: Be! (*kun*) and it is (*fa-yakun*)!" (36:82 and 2:117); for the parallel places in the Qur'an, see Paret, *Der Koran*, 27.

425. The transcript seems to be garbled here, reflecting the oral nature of the discourse. We have slightly changed the interrogative sentence to render it meaningful.

426. http://www.nurmuhammad.com/NaqshbandiSecrets/tafsirsurahnaba8 -9naqshbandi.htm.

427. For Muslim beliefs and practices associated with sleep, dreams, and waking visions, see Felek and Knysh, *Dreams and Visions*, passim.

428. That is, *awliya' Allah*, God's friends or "saints."

429. "Die before you die," a saying attributed to the Prophet; see, e.g., http://omid safi.religionnews.com/2014/01/27/need-die-now-die-die-braveheart-garth-brooks -living-now-according-prophet-muhammad/. For several related themes of death and

dreams in Ibn (al-)'Arabi's work, see Chittick, *Sufi Path*, 119–20, 231; this subject is also discussed in detail by Haydar-i Amuli in his *al-Muhit al-a'zam*, 3: 102–6. For a contemporary parallel, see Holland, *Sheikh Muzaffer Ozak*, 360–61.

430. The collective name for the companions of the prophet Muhammad.

431. Supplications or litanies, usually uttered by Sufis on a regular basis.

432. That is, *murid*, a disciple of a Sufi master.

433. http://www.nurmuhammad.com/NaqshbandiSecrets/tafsirsurahnaba8 -9naqshbandi.htm.

434. E.g., al-Tustari (d. 283/896) as described in Böwering, *Mystical Vision*, 135–37.

435. https://www.facebook.com/DrNourKabbani/info?tab=page_info.

436. The analysis that follows is based on a series of lectures delivered by Shaykh Nour to an audience of his father's followers at Fenton, Michigan, in November –December 2014; see: 1. http://sufilive.com/tafseer-of-surah-yusuf-part-1-5809.html; 2. http://sufilive.com/Tafseer-Surah-Yusuf-Part-2-5808.html; 3. http://sufilive.com /Tafseer-Sura-Yusuf-Part-3-5718.html.

437. Neither Potiphar nor Zulaykha are mentioned by name in the Qur'an itself. Their names are supplied by later Muslim exegetes who availed themselves of the so-called stories of the ancient Israelites (*al-isra'iliyyat*).

438. Q 12:31.

439. Recollection of God's name, either silent or loud, individual or collective, which is a common Sufi practice.

440. In Q 12:31 the women indeed compare Joseph to "a noble angel."

441. In elaborating on this image, Shaykh Nour likens the women to the human sensualities seeking gratification and the knives, somewhat facetiously, to Viagra.

442. Eco, *Limits*, 14.

443. Quoted in Eco, *Limits*, 8.

444. Ibid., 11.

445. Ibid., 18.

446. Ibid., 12.

447. Cf. Goethe's definition of allegory cited in the text.

448. Eco, *Limits*, 27–34.

449. Elmore, *Fabulous Gryphon*, 8–9, and James Morris, "At the End of Time: The Mahdi's Helpers," in *The Meccan Revelations*, 2 vols., ed. Michel Chodkiewicz (New York: Pir Press, 2005), 1: 68–69, 75–76, 82, 85–86, and 91.

450. See, e.g., debates around the legitimacy of Sufi *ta'wil* on the Internet; http:// www.al-islam.org/new-analysis-wahhabi-doctrines-muhammad-husayn-ibrahimi /allegorical-interpretation-ta%E2%80%99wil-qur%E2%80%99; http://quransmes sage.com/articles/mutashabih%20FM3.htm; http://www.apbif.org/exegese-et-tafsir /linterpretation-le-tawil-des-textes; http://www.shia-forum.de/index.php?/topic /58586-tafsir-tawil-hermeneutik-im-koran-quran-teil-1/; https://answers.yahoo .com/question/index?qid=20101024234916AAHHjg3; for a liberal Sunni view, see Mohammad Hashim Kamali, "The Interplay of Revelation and Reason in the Sha-riah," in *The Oxford History of Islam*, ed. John Esposito (Oxford: Oxford University Press, 1999), 107–54; for Wahhabi approaches to the Qur'an from the viewpoint of a

sympathetic observer, see Natana J. DeLong-Bas, *Wahhabi Islam: From Revival and Reform to Global Jihad* (Oxford: Oxford University Press, 2004), 96–101.

451. The importance of experiencing divine presence within the contexts of the history of Christian asceticism-mysticism has been emphasized by Bernard McGinn, who tellingly named his magisterial study of the subject *The Presence of God*.

452. Arthur Arberry, ed., *Muslim Saints and Mystics* (London: Routledge and Kegan Paul, 1983), 55; cf. ibid., 104, 154, 189, 240, 262, 270, and so on; similar stories abound in al-Qushayri's *Epistle on Sufism*; see our translation of this work into English.

453. For a comparative perspective, see Olivier Roy, *Holy Ignorance: When Religion and Culture Part Ways* (New York: Columbia University Press, 2010), "Index" under "born-again."

454. As suggested by John Wansbrough in his controversial *Quranic Studies: Sources and Methods of Scriptural Interpretation* (Oxford: Oxford University Press, 1977); cf. Goldziher, *Schools*, passim; for the Judaic exegetical tradition proper, see Kamesar, *Cambridge Companion*, and Green and Lieber, *Scriptural Exegesis*.

455. See, e.g., Gavin Flood, *The Truth Within: A History of Inwardness in Christianity, Hinduism, and Buddhism*. Oxford Scholarship Online: http://www.oxford scholarship.com/view/10.1093/acprof:oso/9780199684564.001.0001/acprof -9780199684564. January 2014, 87–91; the references are to the pages of the printed edition; see also McGinn, *Foundations of Mysticism*, passim, and Eco, *Limits*, chapters 1 and 2 passim; Eco, *The Role of the Reader: Explorations in the Semiotics of Texts* (Bloomington: Indiana University Press, 1979), 51.

456. To use William Chittick's neologism; see Chittick, *Imaginal Worlds: Ibn al-'Arabi and the Problem of Religious Diversity* (Albany: State University of New York Press, 1994).

457. Cf. Eco, *Limits*, 27.

458. See, e.g., his "Devil's Delusion" (*Talbis Iblis*), trans. David Margoliouth and published as *Talbis Iblis (Delusion of the Devil)* by N. K. Singh (New Delhi: Kitab Bhavan, 2008); cf. Böwering, *Mystical Vision*, 37–38.

459. Paul Nwyia, *Un mystique prédicateur à la Qarawiyin de Fès Ibn 'Abbad de Ronda (1332–1390)* (Beirut: Imprimerie catholique, 1961), xxxiv–xxxvi and l.

460. See Knysh, *Islamic Mysticism*, chapter 4.

461. Abou Ishaq Ibrahim Ibn Musa Al-Shatibi, *Kitab al-I'tisam*, trans. Mohammed Mahdi Al-Sharif (Beirut: Dar al-kutub al-'imliyya, 2012), 223–70.

462. See, e.g., al-Suyuti, *al-Itqan*, 4: 484–509; cf. Honerkamp, "Introduction," xvi–xvii.

463. Flood, *Truth Within*, 71.

464. This denomination is problematic and requires a detailed explanation, so we use it as a "shortcut" to describe Sufi communities that make use of modern information technologies, organizational patterns, and advertising methods to disseminate their teachings and to recruit new followers.

465. Hermansen, "In the Garden," 172 note 24; Hermansen's earlier observation has since been confirmed by the predictions of world-changing events by the recently deceased founder of the Naqshbandiyya-Haqqaniyya described in Tsibenko (Ivanova),

"The Naqshbandi-Haqqani"; for the notion of "religion/religious market," see Roy, *Holy Ignorance*, chapter 6.

Chapter 4: Sufism in Comparison: The Common Ferment of Hellenism

1. Gavin Flood, *The Truth Within: A History of Inwardness in Christianity, Hinduism, and Buddhism* (Oxford: Oxford University Press, 2013), 70.

2. Gerhard Böwering, *The Mystical Vision of Existence in Classical Islam: The Qur'anic Hermeneutics of the Sufi Sahl at-Tustari (d. 283/896)* (Berlin: Walter de Gruyter, 1980), 139–41.

3. As exemplified, e.g., by Proclus's writings that have been analyzed, among others, by Eric Dodds in his *Proclus, The Elements of Theology* (Oxford: Clarendon Press, 1963).

4. Quoted in Dodds, *Proclus*, xxxiii.

5. Barrie Fleet, trans. and comment., *Enneads of Plotinus, Ennead IV.8: On the Descent of the Soul into Bodies* (Las Vegas: Parmenides, 2012), 37–38.

6. Flood, *Truth Within*, 74.

7. Bernard McGinn, *The Foundations of Mysticism*, vol. 1 of *The Presence of God: A History of Western Christian Mysticism* (New York: Crossroad, 1991), 55–61; for the Muslim appropriation of this late antique intellectual legacy, see Majid Fakhry, *A History of Islamic Philosophy*, 3rd ed. (New York: Columbia University Press, 2004), 21–33; Ian Netton, *Muslim Neoplatonists: An Introduction to the Thought of the Brethren of Purity* (London: Routledge and Curzon, 2002); Peter Adamson, *Philosophy in the Islamic World: A History of Philosophy without Any Gaps*, vol. 3 (Oxford: Oxford University Press, 2016), 21–25, 30, 38, 100–101, 104, 131, 199, 291, 381–82, and 388–89; and Pierre Hadot, *Philosophy as a Way of Life*, ed. Arbold Davidson, trans. Michael Chase (Oxford: Blackwell, 1995), 126–40 and 269–70.

8. McGinn, *Foundations of Mysticism*, passim, and Flood, *Truth Within*, 70, 72, 74, 76, 85, and so on.

9. Fakhry, *History of Islamic Philosophy*, 21–33; for Judaism in the Muslim world, see Adamson, *Philosophy in the Islamic World*, 209–11 and 279–81.

10. McGinn, *Foundations of Mysticism*, 139–42 and 144–82; see also Adamson, *Philosophy in the Islamic World*, 17, 21, 22, and 30; Hadot, *Philosophy as a Way of Life*, 74, 128–29, 135–38.

11. McGinn, *Foundations of Mysticism*, 139–42 and 144–82; Flood, *Truth Within*, 70–73; Hadot, *Philosophy as a Way of Life*, 269–70 and 277–85; see also McGinn, *The Flowering of Mysticism: Men and Women in the New Mysticism, 1200–1350* (New York: Crossroad, 1998), chapter 2.

12. Lloyd Gerson, trans. and comment., *Plotinus, Ennead V.5. That the Intelligibles Are Not External to the Intellect and on the Good* (Las Vegas: Parmenides, 2013), 4; James Wilberding, trans. and comment., *Plotinus' Cosmology: A Study of Ennead ii.1 (40)* (Oxford: Oxford University Press, 2006), 70 passim; Paulina Remes, *Plotinus on Self: The Philosophy of the 'We'* (Cambridge: Cambridge University Press, 2007), 5–6; Bernard McGinn, *Flowering of Mysticism*, 46–47.

13. Adamson, *Philosophy in the Islamic World*, 198–200; 321–22, and 386–91.

14. Remes, *Plotinus*, 6.

15. Ibid., 78, and Marshall Hodgson, *The Venture of Islam: Conscience and History in a World Civilization*, 3 vols. (Chicago: University of Chicago Press, 1974), 2: 222–27.

16. William Chittick, *Divine Love: Islamic Literature and the Path to God* (New Haven, CT: Yale University Press, 2013), 108; Sam'ani was a major source of the exegetical work of al-Maybudi, whose exegesis was discussed in the previous chapter; ibid., xvii–xviii; for similar ideas in Ibn (al-)'Arabi's oeuvre, see William Chittick, *The Sufi Path of Knowledge: Ibn al-'Arabi's Metaphysics of Imagination* (Albany: State University of New York Press, 1989), 16–17.

17. Gerson, *Plotinus*, 5; cf. Hodgson, *Venture of Islam*, 1: 426 and 429.

18. That is, existing in the mind of God.

19. Fleet, *Enneads of Plotinus*, 16.

20. For a classical study of what western European scholars came to designate "Neoplatonism," see Philip Merlan, *From Plato to Neoplatonism*, 3rd ed. (The Hague: Nijhoff, 1968); for a critical review of the first edition by Giorgio De Santillana, see *Isis* 48, no. 3, George Sarton Memorial Issue (September 1957): 360–62.

21. Gerson, *Plotinus*, 6, and Hodgson, *Venture of Islam*, 1: 426 and 429.

22. Gerson, *Plotinus*, 7.

23. Ibid., and Wilberding, *Plotinus' Cosmology*, 52.

24. Fleet, *Enneads of Plotinus*, 23.

25. On the body-soul relations in (Neo-)Platonism, see Remes, *Plotinus*, 27–30 and 185–86; cf. Hadot, *Philosophy as a Way of Life*, 86–87 and 102–3.

26. Gerson, *Plotinus*, 8, and Remes, *Plotinus*, 25–27, 61–62, and 245.

27. Gerson, *Plotinus*, 7.

28. Fleet, *Enneads of Plotinus*, 29.

29. Ibid., 26.

30. Ibid., 31; cf. Hadot, *Philosophy as a Way of Life*, 207 and 212.

31. Fleet, *Enneads of Plotinus*, 33.

32. Ibid., 27.

33. Especially in his *Enneads*, *1.6*; McGinn, *Foundations of Mysticism*, 47.

34. Ibid., and the references cited there.

35. On *eros* in Socratic tradition and its later interpretations, see Hadot, *Philosophy as a Way of Life*, 160–65.

36. McGinn, *Foundations of Mysticism*, 48 and 166.

37. Ibid., 55; for the history of the concept, see Kevin Corrigan, " 'Solitary' Mysticism in Plotinus, Proclus, Gregory of Nyssa, and Pseudo-Dionysius," *Journal of Religion* 76, no. 1 (1996): 28–42; see also Hadot, *Philosophy as a Way of Life*, 238–48.

38. Fleet, *Enneads of Plotinus*, 38.

39. See also Carl Ernst, *Ruzbihan Baqli* (Richmond, Surrey: Curzon, 1996), and Alexander Knysh, *Ibn 'Arabi in the Later Islamic Tradition: The Making of a Polemical Image in Medieval Islam* (Albany: State University of New York Press, 1999).

40. Dodds, *Proclus*, xii.

41. Quoted in ibid.; see also Hadot, *Philosophy as a Way of Life*, 71–76.

42. Dodds, *Proclus*, xii.

43. As demonstrated, e.g., in Adamson, *Philosophy in the Islamic Word*, "Index" under "Plato and Platonism" and "Neoplatonism"; Hadot, *Philosophy as a Way of Life*, 127–40 and 269–70.

44. E.g., Flood, *Truth Within*, 71.

45. McGinn, *Foundations of Mysticism*, 171; cf. Hadot, *Philosophy as a Way of Life*, 182–83 and 238–48.

46. Flood, *Truth Within*, 71; cf. Hadot, *Philosophy as a Way of Life*, passim.

47. For the medieval Christian world, see McGinn, *Foundations of Mysticism*, 89–99 (specifically concerning "gnostic mysticism"); McGinn, *The Mystical Thought of Meister Eckhart* (New York: Herder and Herder, 2011), 14–19; McGinn, *Flowering of Mysticism*, 5–8, 102–3 and 108–9, 125–26, and so on.

48. McGinn, *Foundations of Mysticism*, 117–30, concerning Origen; cf. Hadot, *Philosophy as a Way of Life*, 72.

49. McGinn, *Foundations of Mysticism*, 100–102, concerning Justin, Irenaeus, and Clement of Alexandria; and 108–30, concerning Origen; Adamson, *Philosophy in the Islamic World*, 209–11 and 278–84, concerning Ibn Gabirol and the Kabbalists.

50. McGinn, *Foundations of Mysticism*, 101.

51. Ibid., 102, and Hadot, *Philosophy as a Way of Life*, 72 and 269–70.

52. McGinn, *Foundations of Mysticism*, 108; despite their shared commitment to Platonism, the two thinkers were mortal enemies on account of their incompatible religious allegiances; ibid., 130.

53. Ibid., 110.

54. Quoting the following passages from the New Testament as his proof texts: 1 Cor. 10:1–11; 2 Cor. 3:4–18; Gal. 4:21–31.

55. McGinn, *Foundations of Mysticism*, 112, and Hadot, *Philosophy as a Way of Life*, 71–76.

56. McGinn, *Foundations of Mysticism*; see also McGinn, *Mystical Thought*, 25–26.

57. Whereas Clement of Alexandria used the term "true gnostic" to designate the advanced spiritual seeker, Origen spoke of "the 'spiritual' (*pneumatikos*) or 'perfect' (*teleios*) Christian," see McGinn, *Foundations of Mysticism*, 124.

58. Translated and quoted in McGinn, *Foundations of Mysticism*, 116.

59. Quoted in ibid., 117.

60. Ibid., 118; significantly, Origen is sometimes described by students of his legacy as a "mystic of light."

61. E.g., Origen's image of the spiritual "exodus" can be compared to al-Qushayri's interpretations of jihad and the fast of Ramadan; the same applies to al-Qashani's interpretation of the Prophet's night journey and Moses's actions; the image of the Promised Land filled with light resembles the Sufi interpretations of the Light Verse; parallels can also be drawn with Shaykh Nour Kabbani's interpretation of the characters of sura "Joseph" (*Yusuf*) discussed in chapter 3 of the present book.

62. McGinn, *Foundations of Mysticism*, 122.

63. See, e.g., Chittick, *Divine Love*, and Chittick, *The Sufi Path of Love: The Spiritual Teachings of Rumi* (Albany: State University of New York Press, 1983), "Index" under "love" and "lover" (*'ashiq*); see also Franklin Lewis, *Rumi: Past and Present, East and West; The Life, Teaching, and Poetry of Jalal al-Din Rumi* (Oxford: One-

world, 2000), and Fatemeh Keshavarz, *Reading Mystical Lyric: The Case of Jalal al-Din Rumi* (Columbia: University of South Carolina Press, 1998).

64. McGinn, *Foundations of Mysticism*, 124, and Hadot, *Philosophy as a Way of Life*, 134.

65. McGinn, *Foundations of Mysticism*, 125.

66. Ibid.

67. Dodds, *Proclus*, xii, xvii–xviii, and xxx.

68. Hadot, *Philosophy as a Way of Life*, 74 and 128–29.

69. McGinn, *Foundations of Mysticism*, 159.

70. Ibid., 163.

71. Ibid., 161 and 163.

72. Dodds, *Proclus*, xxix–xxx, and Fakhry, *A History of Islamic Philosophy*, 21–33.

73. Dodds, *Proclus*, 164.

74. See, e.g., Annemarie Schimmel, *Mystical Dimensions of Islam* (Chapel Hill: University of North Carolina Press, 1975), 4 and 16, and "Index" under "Shari'ah," "Tariqah," and "Haqiqah"; Arthur Buehler, *Sufi Heirs of the Prophet: The Indian Naqshbandiyya and the Rise of the Mediating Sufi Shaykh* (Columbia: University of South Carolina Press, 1998), 4–10; Knysh, *Ibn 'Arabi*, 77–79; Shahab Ahmed, *What Is Islam? The Importance of Being Islamic* (Princeton, NJ: Princeton University Press, 2016), 21–26; Chittick, *Sufi Path*, 170–72; Chittick, *Divine Love*, 92–93, 135–36, 155–56, 163, 201–2.

75. McGinn, *Flowering of Mysticism*, 81.

76. McGinn, *Foundations of Mysticism*, 172.

77. McGinn, *Flowering of Mysticism*, 81; for parallels with Ibn (al-)'Arabi's concept of "the station of no station" (*maqam la maqam*) of the perfect gnostic, see Chittick, *Sufi Path*, 375–81.

78. Dionysius was not alone among Christian mystics in using the figure of Moses to explore "the loving *ecstasis* of the soul"; Moses's image was used by Thomas Gallus, who died at Ivrea, Piedmont, in 1246, as discussed in McGinn, *Flowering of Mysticism*, 81–83.

79. McGinn, *Foundations of Mysticism*, 166–67; for parallels with the Sufi cosmogony and gnoseology of Ibn (al-)'Arabi, see Chittick, *Sufi Path*, 66, 126, 180, 204, and 250.

80. McGinn, *Foundations of Mysticism*, 168.

81. Ibid., 170.

82. Chittick, *Sufi Path*, 3, and "Index" under "bewilderment (*hayra, tahayyur*)"; cf. ibid., 375–81; see also Chittick, *Divine Love*, 145, and "Index" under "bewilderment (*hayra*)."

83. McGinn, *Foundations of Mysticism*, 173.

84. Ibid., 174.

85. Chittick, *Sufi Path*, 3–4.

86. Ibid., 4, 27–30, 116, 199, 212–15, 238, 365–66, 370, and so on.

87. McGinn, *Foundations of Mysticism*, 159, 172–73, and McGinn, *Flowering of Mysticism*, 81; for a central role allotted to Moses by Ibn (al-)'Arabi and his followers in their discussions of "human theomorphism," see Chittick, *Sufi Path*, 28.

88. See above, note 78.

89. McGinn, *Flowering of Mysticism*, 81–83.

90. Ibid., 80

91. Ibid.

92. Ibid.

93. Ibid., 86.

94. [Neo]platonic origins of such adaptations are unmistakable; consider, e.g., the following two statements by the German Catholic mystic and poet Johann Scheffler (alias Johann Angelus Silesius, d. 1677): "I am God's Son, I am sitting at His right; His Spirit, Flesh and Blood, He can there recognize," and "What men have said of God, not yet suffices me, my life and light is One beyond divinity"; Maria Shrady, trans., *Angelus Silesius: The Cherubinic Wanderer* (New York: Paulist Press, 1986), 39.

95. McGinn, *Flowering of Mysticism*, 86–112; McGinn, *Foundations of Mysticism*, chapter 4; and Flood, *Truth Within*, 71–86.

96. Flood, *Truth Within*, 74.

97. Genesis 28:10–19.

98. Flood, *Truth Within*, 76–77.

99. E.g., Angelus Silesius's "Cherubinic Wanderer"; Shrady, *Angelus Silesius*, passim.

100. McGinn, *Flowering of Mysticism*, 83–84.

101. McGinn, *Mystical Thought*, 25–34.

102. Flood, *Truth Within*, 84.

103. *Al-Futuhat*, 1: 101; for parallels with Jewish mystical-kabbalistic theories, see Katz, "Mystical Speech," 16–17.

104. Eco, *Limits*, 24–32, and Kevin van Bladel, *The Arabic Hermes: From Pagan Sage to Prophet of Science* (Oxford: Oxford University Press, 2009). Van Bladel provides a helpful discussion of the ambiguity of this denomination in Arabic sources; see 17–22 and 121–63.

105. Arnold Toynbee, *An Historian's Approach to Religion*, 2nd ed. (Oxford: Oxford University Press, 1979), 117.

106. Ibid., chapter 9; cf. Van Bladel, *Arabic Hermes*, 196–233.

107. Toynbee, *Historian's Approach*, 126; Toynbee speaks here of both Christianity and Islam; see also Hadot, *Philosophy as a Way of Life*, 71–77.

108. As argued, e.g., by Shahab Ahmed in his *What Is Islam?*, 10–19, 97–99, 211–16, 256–57, 343–56, 516, and so on.

109. Diana Steigerwald, "Isma'ili *ta'wil*," in *Blackwell Companion to the Qur'an*, ed. Andrew Rippin (Oxford: Blackwell, 2006), 386–400, and Adamson, *Philosophy in the Islamic World*, "Index" under "Isma'ilism."

110. Regarding the "Brethren of Purity" (*ikhwan al-safa'*), see Ian Netton, *Muslim Neoplatonists: An Introduction to the Thought of the Brethren of Purity* (Richmond, Surrey: Curzon, 2002); Netton, *Islamic Philosophy and Theology: Critical Concepts in Islamic Thought*, vol. 3, *Aristotelianism and Neoplatonism* (London: Routledge, 2011); Michael Ebstein, *Mysticism and Philosophy in al-Andalus: Ibn Masarra, Ibn al-'Arabi and the Isma'ili Tradition* (Leiden: E. J. Brill, 2014), and Adamson, *Philosophy in the Islamic World*, 102–5.

111. For some recent studies, see Meir Bar-Asher, *Scripture and Exegesis in Early*

Imami Shiism (Leiden: E. J. Brill, 1999); Farhad Daftary, *The Isma'ilis: Their History and Doctrines* (Cambridge: Cambridge University Press, 1990), 239–51; Heinz Halm, *The Empire of the Mahdi*, trans. Michael Bonner (Leiden: E. J. Brill, 1996), 16–22; Paul Walker, *Early Philosophical Shiism: The Ismaili Neoplatonism of Abu Ya'qub al-Sijistani* (Cambridge: Cambridge University Press), 1993, and the numerous other studies by this author.

112. See, e.g., Alexander Knysh, *Islam in Historical Perspective* (Upper Saddle River, NJ: Pearson and Prentice Hall, 2011); 2nd printing, (London: Routledge, 2015), 276, and Aiyub Palmer, "The Social and Theoretical Dimensions of Sainthood in Early Islam: Al-Tirmidhi's Gnoseology and the Foundations of Sufi Social Praxis" (PhD diss., University of Michigan, 2015), chapter 1.

113. See chapter 2 of this book and Moojan Momen, *An Introduction to Shii Islam* (New Haven, CT: Yale University Press, 1985), "Index" under "*Wali* and *Walaya*"; cf. Daftary, *Isma'ilis*, 86–87.

114. Knysh, *Islam in Historical Perspective*, 168–71, and the sources cited therein.

115. See Alexander Knysh, *Islamic Mysticism: A Short History*, 2nd ed. (Leiden: E. J. Brill, 2010), chapters 8 and 9.

116. See, e.g., Katz, "Mystical Speech," and Katz, "Mysticism and Interpretation," passim.

117. Dmitri Gutas, *Greek Thought, Arabic Culture: The Graeco-Arabic Translation Movement in Baghdad and Early 'Abbasid Society (2nd–4th/8th–10th Centuries)* (London: Routledge, 1998); Richard Walzer, *Greek into Arabic: Essays on Islamic Philosophy* (Oxford: B. Cassirer, 1962), and Fakhry, *History of Islamic Philosophy*, 21–33.

118. For instance, the idea of the primordial covenant (7:172); the story of Moses and the unnamed servant of God in 18:65–82, and Moses's direct encounters and conversations with God, as depicted in Q 7:142–43 and 20:9–15; the Prophet's experiences mentioned in 17:1 and 53:1–18, 73, 74, and 96, and, last but not least, the famous Light Verse, 24:35 discussed earlier.

Chapter 5: Practices, Ethos, Communities, and Leaders

1. Our understanding of ethos is based in part on that articulated by Clifford Geertz in his *Interpretation of Cultures* (New York: Basic Books, 1975). According to Geertz, "Religious belief and ritual confront and mutually confirm one another; the ethos is made intellectually reasonable by being shown to represent a way of life implied by the actual state of affairs which the world view describes, and the world view is made emotionally acceptable by being presented as an image of an actual state of affairs of which such a way of life is an authentic expression. The demonstration of a meaningful relation between the values a people holds and the general order of existence within which its finds itself is an essential element in all religions, however those values or that order be conceived," ibid., 127.

2. Alexander Knysh, *Islamic Mysticism: A Short History*, 2nd ed. (Leiden: E. J. Brill, 2010), 99–101 and 116–18.

3. For some major studies of Sufi ethics (*adab*) and regiments, see Meir Kister, ed., *Kitab adab al-suhba by Abu 'Abd ar-Rahman as-Sulami* (Jerusalem: Israeli Oriental

Society, 1954); Fritz Meier, *Essays on Islamic Piety and Mysticism*, trans. John O'Kane, ed. Bernd Radtke (Leiden: E. J. Brill, 1999), 49–92 and 93–133; Menahem Milson, trans., *A Sufi Rule for Novices* (Cambridge, MA: Harvard University Press, 1975); Milson, ed., *Kitab adab al-muridin* (Jerusalem: Hebrew University of Jerusalem, 1978); Etan Kohlberg, ed., *Jawami' Adab al-Sufiyya and 'Uyub al-Nafs wa-Mudawatuha by Abu 'Abd al-Rahman al-Sulami* (Jerusalem: Israel Oriental Society, 1976); Bernd Radtke, R. Seán O'Fahey, and John O'Kane, "Two Sufi Treatises of Ahmad Ibn Idris," *Oriens* 35 (1996): 143–78 (for a list of Sufi rules of behavior see 146–47); Alexander Knysh, trans., *Al-Qushayri's Epistle on Sufism* (Reading, UK: Garnet, 2007); Elena Biagi, trans., *A Collection of Sufi Rules of Conduct [by] Abu 'Abd al-Rahman al-Sulami* (Cambridge: Islamic Texts Society, 2010); Montgomery Watt, *The Faith and Practice of al-Ghazali* (London: George Allen and Unwin, 1970); a large body of relevant Sufi texts has been rendered into German and annotated by Richard Gramlich; see also Erik Ohlander, "Adab, in Sufism," *Encyclopedia of Islam*, 3rd ed., online edition: http://referenceworks.brillonline.com, and *Ethics and Spirituality in Islam: Sufi* adab, ed. Francesco Chiabotti, Eve Feuillebois-Pierunek et al. (Leiden: E. J. Brill, 2017); relations between Sufi *adab* and *adab* as a literary genre and code of behavior of a cultivated individual (*adib*) from the 'Abbasid epoch are discussed in Seeger Bonebakker, "*Adab* and the Concept of *Belles-Lettres*," in *'Abbasid Belles-Lettres*, ed. Julia Ashtiany et al. (Cambridge: Cambridge University Press, 1990), 16–30.

4. See, e.g., al-Sarraj, *Kitab al-luma'*, ed. Kamil Mustafa al-Nihawandi (Beirut: Dar al-kutub al-'ilmiyya, 2001), which contains a section on "mistakes of the Sufis," pp. 362–76; similar sections and entire treatises were composed by such classical Sufi authors as al-Sulami (d. 412/1021) and al-Hujwiri (d. 465/1073 or 469/1077); our translation of al-Qushayri's (d. 465/1072) *Epistle on Sufism* features numerous "anti-examples," especially in the chapters dealing with practical matters, such as companionship, rules of travel, begging, listening to music, and so on; cf. Biagi, *Collection of Sufi Rules*, passim, and the other translations and studies mentioned in the previous note.

5. See, e.g., Ibn al-Jawzi's "Devil's Delusion," trans. David Margoliouth and published as *Talbis Iblis (Delusion of the Devil)* by N. K. Singh (New Delhi: Kitab Bhavan, 2008), and Paul Nwyia, *Un mystique prédicateur à la Qarawiyin de Fès Ibn 'Abbad de Ronda (1332–1390)* (Beirut: Imprimerie catholique, 1961), xxxiv–xxxvi and l; for further examples, see *Ethics and Spirituality in Islam*, passim.

6. See, e.g., the works of Earle Waugh, Rüdiger Seesemann, Rudolph Ware III, Isobel Jeffery-Street, Marcia Hermansen, and Suha Taji-Farouki, to name but a few.

7. For various shades of meaning and definitions of this term, see Elena Biagi's "Introduction" to her translation of al-Sulami's *Jawami' adab al-sufiyya* (*A Collection of Sufi Rules of Conduct*), xxiv–xxxiii; Shahab Ahmed, *What Is Islam? The Importance of Being Islamic* (Princeton, NJ: Princeton University Press, 2016), 229–30, 234–38, 380–81; Bonebakker, "*Adab*," passim, and *Sufi Ethics and Spirituality*, 1–61.

8. On *ikhlas* and its near synonym *sidq*, see Alexander Knysh, "Sidk," in *EI2*, online edition: http://referenceworks.brillonline.com.

9. *Hukm* ("judgment"); see Kohlberg, *Jawami' Adab al-Sufiyya*, 47, of the Arabic text, and note 8 in section 119; an alternative reading is *hilm* ("even-headedness, pa-

tience and/or indulgence"), which Biagi, who has preferred this reading, renders as "discernment," see Biagi, *Collection of Sufi Rules*, 83 note 243.

10. Kohlberg, *Jawami' Adab al-Sufiyya*, 39–40.

11. Knysh, *Al-Qushayri's Epistle*, 293; al-Qushayri does not specify which Ibn 'Ata' he is quoting here. This can be either Ahmad b. 'Ata' al-Adami, a companion of the controversial Sufi martyr al-Hallaj, who was beaten to death by the vizier's body guards in 309/921 or 922, or the Iranian ascetic-mystic Ahmad b. 'Ata' al-Rudhbari (d. 369/980).

12. Ibid.

13. Ibid.

14. For Christian parallels, see Thomas Owen, "Interiority and Christian Spiritual- ity," *Journal of Religion* 80, no. 1 (2000): 41–60.

15. Ibn Khaldun, *Shifa' al-sa'il wa-tahdhib al-masa'il*, ed. Muhammad Muti' al- Hafiz (Damascus: Dar al-fikr, 1996), 44; cf. 54 and 101–2; the idea of *fiqh al-zahir* and *fiqh al-batin* is not original to Ibn Khaldun; he may have borrowed it from al-Ghazali, see Nwyia, *Un mystique*, 226.

16. Nwyia, *Un mystique*, lii.

17. Ibn Khaldun, *Shifa'*, 45.

18. Nwyia, *Un mystique*, lii.

19. Biagi, *Collection of Sufi Rules*, xxxv–xxxvi; Ibn Khaldun, *Shifa'*, 48; Meier, *Es- says*, 51.

20. Al-Sulami, *Kitab al-tabaqat al-sufiyya*, ed. Johannes Pedersen (Leiden: E. J. Brill, 1960), 110; Meier, *Essays*, 204, and *Ethics and Spirituality in Islam*, 1.

21. That is, the fleeting spiritual condition in which the Sufi finds himself at any given moment in time; see Knysh, *al-Qushayri's Epistle*, 75–77; for pre-Islamic, Hel- lenic antecedents, see Pierre Hadot, *Philosophy as a Way of Life*, ed. Arnold Davidson, trans. Michael Chase (Oxford: Blackwell, 1995), 81–89, 208–10, and 217–37.

22. For a definition of the mystical state (*hal*), see Knysh, *al-Qushayri's Epistle*, 78–79.

23. For a definition of the mystical station (*maqam*), see ibid., 77–78.

24. Shihab al-Din 'Umar al-Suharawrdi, *'Awarif al-ma'arif*, 2 vols., ed. 'Abd al- Halim Mahmud and Mahmud b. al-Sharif (Cairo: Dar al-ma'arif, no date), 2: 208.

25. Alexander Knysh, "Sidk," *EI2*, online edition: http://referenceworks.brillon line.com.

26. Knysh, *Al-Qushayri's Epistle*, 129–33, 134–38, 178–88, 288–92, passim, and Leah Kinberg, "What Is Meant by Zuhd?" *Studia Islamica* 61 (1985): 27–44, especially 39–40.

27. This term also connotes "election" and can be rendered into English as "God's choicest ones."

28. Knysh, *Al-Qushayri's Epistle*, 281.

29. Ibid., 282; based on Q 35:15.

30. Al-Ghazali, *Ihya' 'ulum al-din*, 5 vols. (Cairo: al-Maktaba al-tijariyya al-kubra, 1960), 4: 190.

31. Ibn Khaldun defines this later Sufism as one focused on seeking divine unveil- ing (*mukashafa*) and revelation (*tajalli*); he considers it "an unusual (or strange) philosophical view" (*ra'y gharib faylasufi*) and believes that practitioners of this type

of Sufism are especially prone to allegorical interpretations of the Scripture; Ibn Khaldun, *Shifa'*, 106–7.

32. For al-Sulami, see Knysh, *Islamic Mysticism*, 125–27, and chapter 3 of the present book.

33. Nicholas Heer and Kenneth Honerkamp, trans., *Three Early Sufi Texts* (Louisville, KY: Fons Vitae, 2009), 138.

34. Ibid., 154; for *tawakkul*, see Benedikt Reinert, *Die Lehre vom tawakkul in der klassischen Sufik* (Berlin: Walter de Gruyter, 1968), passim.

35. Al-Ghazali, *Ihya' 'ulum al-din* 4: 190–91.

36. On the path to God.

37. Heer and Honerkamp, *Three Early*, 155.

38. This word is commonly translated as "student" or "disciple" (of a Sufi master); however, some Western and Western-trained scholars prefer to render it as "aspirant," "novice," "adept," and so on; for an example of the usage by the same scholar of several variant translations, see Ahmet Karamustafa, *Sufism: The Formative Period* (Berkeley: University of California Press, 2007), 116–27.

39. Often translated as "reliance on God"; very closely related to poverty, *tawakkul* is the subject of an exhaustive study by Reinert, *Die Lehre*, passim.

40. See the respective sections in chapter 3 of Knysh, *Al-Qushayri's Epistle*.

41. Ibid.

42. On him see Francesco Chiabotti, "Entre soufisme et savoir islamique: L'oeuvre de 'Abd al-Karim al-Qushayri (376–465/ 986–1072)," Université de Provence, Ecole doctorale 355, UFR arts, lettres, langues et sciences humaines (Aix-en-Provence: IRE-MAM, 2014), 42–59.

43. Knysh, *Al-Qushayri's Epistle*, 267; in this context "jealousy" carries the connotation of "zeal" or "zealousness."

44. Ibid., 268.

45. Ibid., 266.

46. On him see Knysh, *Islamic Mysticism*, 118–20.

47. A typical representative of this type of Muslim intellectual is al-Jahiz (d. 255/869); see Charles Pellat, *Le milieu baṣrien et la formation de Ǧaḥiẓ* (Paris: Librairie d'Amérique et d'Orient Adrien-Maisonneuve, 1953), and Pellat, "Al-Jahiz," in Ashtiany, *'Abbasid Belles-Lettres*, 78–95, especially 93.

48. For a discussion of the nature of the mystical "moment" in Sufism, see Knysh, *Al-Qushayri's Epistle*, 75–77.

49. Ibid., 295 (I have made some minor changes to my own translation of this passage); this tripartite classification is reproduced by Abu 'l-Najib 'Umar al-Suhrawardi (d. 563/1168) in his *Adab al-muridin*; see Milson, *Sufi Rule*, 36–37; cf. Ian Netton, "The Breath of Felicity: *Adab*, *Ahwal*, and *Maqamat* and Abu Najib al-Suhrawardi," in *Classical Persian Sufism: From Its Origins to Rumi*, ed. Leonard Lewisohn (Oxford: Oneworld, 1993), 468.

50. See, e.g., Ibn al-Jawzi, *Talbis Iblis*, ed. Hilmi b. Muhammad b. Isma'il al-Rashidi (Alexandria: al-Dar al-'alamiyya li-'l-nashr wa-al-tawzi', 2015), and its partial translation by David Margoliouth, edited by N. K. Singh (New Delhi: Kitab Bhavan, 2008).

51. Meier, *Essays*, 52–53, quoting 'Izz al-Din Mahmud-i Kashani (d. 735/1335), the

Persian commentator on Abu Hafs 'Umar al-Suhrawardi's (d. 632/1234) 'Awarif al-ma'arif, one of the most influential Sufi textbooks of all time.

52. Contrary to the assertions made in recent studies of Sufism by some Western scholars, as summarized by Simon Sorgenfrei in his "American Dervish: Making Mevlevism in the United States of America," a doctoral dissertation defended on June 7, 2013, and published by the University of Gothenburg Press (Göteborg, Sweden, 2013), 54–58 and 64–65; cf. Gilles Veinstein, "Avant-propos," in *Les Voies d'Allah*, ed. Alexandre Popovic and Gilles Veinstein (Paris: Fayard, 1996), 7.

53. Shaykh Muhammad Hisham Kabbani, *The Naqshbandi Sufi Way* (collector's ed.) (Chicago: Kazi Publications, 1995), 25–47, and Hisham Kabbani, *Classical Islam and the Naqshbandi Sufi Tradition* (Washington, DC: ISCA, 2004), 40.

54. Monastic rules and regulations.

55. Meier, *Essays*, 53; for similar parallels with Christian monastic rules, see Netton, "Breath of Felicity," 476–79; the validity of comparisons between monastic orders and Sufi *tariqa*s is questioned, albeit inconclusively, in Julian Baldick, *Mystical Islam: An Introduction to Sufism* (London: I. B. Tauris, 1989), 169–71.

56. As mentioned in the previous note, a similar parallel has been drawn by Ian Netton.

57. See, e.g., Baldick, *Mystical Islam*, 74 and 169–70.

58. Shmuel Eisenstadt, ed., *Max Weber on Charisma and Institution Building* (Chicago: University of Chicago Press, 1968), 252–93, and Max Weber, *The Sociology of Religion*, trans. Ephraim Fischoff (London: Methuen, 1965), 20–31, 35–45, 60–79, 80–94, 219–22; as will be shown in what follows, Weber's "routinization of charisma" thesis has certain limitations when applied to Sufi personalities and institutions.

59. See, e.g., Sorgenfrei, "American Dervish," 54–58 and 64–65, and the Western scholars' opinions quoted therein; in his influential deconstruction of the "Orientalist" discourse on Sufism, Carl Ernst refers explicitly to the writings of Sir William Jones, Sir John Malcolm, Lieutenant James William Graham, and Friedrich Tholuck, all of whom lived in the late eighteenth–early nineteenth centuries; since no "fresher" Orientalist works are mentioned, Ernst's reader may assume (incorrectly) that later scholars of Islam in the West uncritically accepted the ideas of their predecessors, which is definitely not the case; see, e.g., Alexander Knysh, "Historiography of Sufi Studies in the West and Russia" *Pis'mennye pamiatniki Vostoka* (*Written Monuments of the Orient*) 1, no. 4 (2006): 206–38.

60. See, e.g., the final sections of chapter 3 in our translation of *al-Qushayri's Epistle*.

61. Al-Ghazali, *Ihya' 'ulum al-din (The Book of Religious Learnings)*, trans. Alhaj Maulana Fazlul Karim, 3 vols., *The Book of Worship* (New Delhi: Islamic Book Services, 1991), 1: 134–37; al-Ghazali, vol. 3, *The Book of Destructive Evils*, 38–39 and 46–49; cf. Watt, *Faith and Practice*, 92–97, 133–38, and 143–52.

62. Kenneth Garden, *The First Islamic Reviver: Abu Hamid al-Ghazali and His Revival of Religious Sciences* (Oxford: Oxford University Press, 2014), 63–103; some of the author's conclusions regarding the role of Sufism in al-Ghazali's Weltanschauung are not entirely convincing (in our view at least).

63. As can be surmised from the chapters describing the virtues and actions that assure salvation to the believer (*munjiyat*); see *Ihya'*, 4: especially 191, 355–57; cf.

Watt, *Faith and Practice*, 54–55 and 60–63; Marshall Hodgson, *The Venture of Islam*, 3 vols. (Chicago: University of Chicago Press, 1974), 2: 187–92; cf. Garden, *First Islamic Reviver*, 98–101.

64. Meier, *Essays*, 63.

65. Nwyia, *Un mystique*, xliii, l, lvi, and 225–31; Ibn 'Abbad's treatment of al-Ghazali as a Sufi thinker par excellence belies Kenneth Garden's attempts to dissociate al-Ghazali from Sufism by portraying him as a philosopher par excellence; see Garden, *First Islamic Reviver*, 102 and 174; even if al-Ghazali was indeed a philosopher and *mutakallim*, as Garden claims throughout his book, he was definitely not seen as such by his followers, such as Ibn 'Abbad and his contemporaries.

66. A similar view of al-Ghazali's legacy was advocated by another Islamologist, Paul Nwyia, in his *Un mystique*, 225–31.

67. Meier, *Essays*, 63.

68. Ibid.; this opposition informs the entire work of Meagan Reid titled *Law and Piety in Medieval Islam* (Cambridge: Cambridge University Press, 2013), e.g., 1–20; cf. Andreas Christmann, "Reclaiming Mysticism: Anti-Orientalism and the Construction of 'Islamic Sufism' in Postcolonial Egypt," in *Religion, Language, and Power*, ed. Nile Green and Mary Searle-Chatterjee (London: Routledge, 2008), 61–62.

69. Ernst, *Shambhala Guide*, 11, and Robert Rozehnal, *Islamic Sufism Unbound: Politics and Piety in Twenty-First-Century Pakistan* (New York: Palgrave Macmillan, 2007), 13.

70. Quoted in Ernst, *Shambhala Guide*, 17.

71. Nwyia, *Un mystique*, chapter 6.

72. The first and now classical work of this genre, titled "The Book of Observance of What Is Due to God" (*Kitab al-ri'aya li-huquq Allah*), belongs to al-Harith al-Muhasibi (d. 243/857) of Baghdad; on him see Knysh, *Islamic Mysticism*, 43–48 and 50–51; for similar evidence from the medieval Maghrib, see Paul Nwyia, ed., *Ibn 'Abbad de Ronda (792/1390), Lettres de direction spirituelle* (Beirut: Dar El-Machreq, 1974), 28–43, of the Arabic text.

73. Seconded by Paul Nwyia; see note 66 above.

74. Umberto Eco, *The Limits of Interpretation* (Bloomington: Indiana University Press, 1990), 14.

75. Meier, *Essays*, 57, citing *Adab al-muridin* by the Central Asian founder of the Kubrawiyya Sufi order, Najm al-Din Kubra (d. circa 617/1220).

76. Meier, *Essays*, 60.

77. *Risala*, i.e., Muhammad's status as the messenger of God.

78. *Khilafa*, the status of Adam (and of human beings who have descended from him) as deputies (vicegerents) of God on earth.

79. *Imama*, i.e., the leadership of the community of the faithful.

80. Meier, *Essays*, 60–61.

81. For the variants of the Hadith, which are many, see http://www.sahihmuslim .com/sps/smm/sahihmuslim.cfm?scn=dspchaptersfull&ChapterID=889&BookID=24.

82. *Ihya' 'ulum al-din*, 1: 49.

83. Ibid., and Ignaz Goldziher, *Schools of Koranic Commentators*, ed. and trans. Wolfgang Behn (Wiesbaden: Harrassowitz, 2006), 150.

84. Goldziher, *Schools*, 150.

85. Ibid., 151–52.

86. As detailed, e.g., in Ibn Khaldun's *Shifa'*, e.g., 106 and 108–9, and in al-Shatibi's *Kitab al-i'tisam*, trans. Mohammed Mahdi Al-Sharif (Beirut: Dar al-kutub al-'ilmiyya, 2012), 188–92, 223–28, 238–53, and 309–13.

87. Ibn (al-)'Arabi, *al-Futuhat al-makkiyya*, 4 vols. (Beirut: Dar Sadir, 1968), 1: 334–35.

88. Ibn al-'Arabi's point is based on his interpretation of Q 58:7 and 50:16, as well as several *hadith qudsi*; see Goldziher, *Schools*, 156–57.

89. Ibn (al-)'Arabi, *al-Futuhat*, 1: 407.

90. Goldziher, *Schools*, 158; see also our discussion of Shaykh Nour's interpretation of sura "Yusuf" in chapter 3 of this book.

91. Ibn (al-)'Arabi, *al-Futuhat*, 1: 408; according to a popular belief (based on several prophetic sayings to this effect), God is always present with the believer during his or her prayer.

92. Ibn (al-)'Arabi, *al-Futuhat*, 1: 408.

93. Ibid., 521–25, and Goldziher, *Schools*, 158.

94. Ibn (al-)'Arabi, *al-Futuhat*, 1: 392; that each "station" (*maqam*) of the Sufi path has its *adab* is a common motif of Sufi literature that predates Ibn (al-)'Arabi; see Milson, *Sufi Rule*, 36; Netton, "Breath of Felicity," 470; al-Suhrawardi, *'Awarif*, 2: 208, and, more recently, Shaykh Muhammad Hisham Kabbani, *Classical Islam*, 40.

95. Ibn (al-)'Arabi, *al-Futuhat*, 1: 395; see also William Chittick, *The Self-Disclosure of God* (Albany: State University of New York Press, 1998), 263; Chittick, *The Sufi Path of Knowledge: Ibn al-'Arabi's Metaphysics of Imagination* (Albany: State University of New York Press, 1989), chapter 3.

96. Chittick, *Self-Disclosure*, 263.

97. Ibn (al-)'Arabi, *al-Futuhat*, 1: 395; a detailed discussion of the *barzakh* in Ibn (al-)'Arabi's work can be found in Henry Corbin, *The Creative Imagination in the Sufism of Ibn 'Arabi* (London: Routledge and K. Paul, 1970), and Salman Bashier, *Ibn al-'Arabi's Barzakh: The Concept of the Limit and the Relationship between God and the World* (Albany: State University of New York Press, 2004).

98. Ibn (al-)'Arabi, *al-Futuhat*, 1: 720.

99. Ibid., 712.

100. Clifford Geertz has argued that this is exactly the function of religious discourse and ritual; see *Interpretation of Cultures*, 131, and the epigraph to the present chapter.

101. Eco, *Limits*, 30.

102. Ibid., 35.

103. Ibid., 27–34.

104. Ibid.

105. See Alexander Knysh, *Ibn 'Arabi in the Later Islamic Tradition* (Albany: State University of New York Press, 1998), 9–10; cf. Michael Sells, "Ibn 'Arabi's 'Polished Mirror': Perspective Change and Meaning Event," *Studia Islamica* 67 (1988): 121–49, and James Morris, "How to Read the *Futuhat*: Ibn 'Arabi's Own Advice," in *Muhyiddin Ibn 'Arabi: A Commemorative Volume*, ed. Stephen Hirtenstein and Michael Tiernan (Brisbane: Element, 1993), 73–89.

106. See Ibn Khaldun, *Shifaʾ*, 105–12, and Knysh, *Ibn ʿArabi*, chapter 7.

107. See, e.g., Martin van Bruinessen, "Ahl-i Haqq," *EI3*, online edition: http://referenceworks.brillonline.com; on the interpenetration of Sufism and Ismaʿilism, see Farhad Daftary, *The Ismaʿilis: Their History and Doctrines* (Cambridge: Cambridge University Press, 1990), 453–55 and 469–70, and Michael Ebstein, *Mysticism and Philosophy in al-Andalus: Ibn Masarra, Ibn al-ʿArabi, and the Ismaʿili Tradition* (Leiden: E. J. Brill, 2014); on the Druze and the Hurufis, see respectively Daftary, *Ismaʿilis*, 195–200 and 455–56, and Orkhan Mir-Kasimov, *Words of Power: Hurufi Teachings between Shiʿism and Sufism in Medieval Islam* (London: I. B. Tauris, 2015).

108. Knysh, *Ibn ʿArabi*, 26 and 193; for a comprehensive study of the underlying affinity between Ibn (al-)ʿArabi's thought and North African Ismaʿilism, see Ebstein, *Mysticism and Philosophy*, 8–13 and 231–35.

109. For some creative uses of Ibn (al-)ʿArabi's ideas by contemporary Arab fiction writers, see Alexander Knysh, "Sufi Motifs in Contemporary Arabic Literature: The Case of Ibn ʿArabi," *Muslim World* 86, no. 1 (1996): 33–49.

110. For the *muhibbun* (lit. "those who love, or have affection for, somebody") and their relations with Sufi communities and Muslim society at large, see Netton, "Breath of Felicity," 457–82, especially 461, 463–65, and 480–82; Julian Baldick, *Mystical Islam: An Introduction to Sufism* (London: I. B. Tauris, 1989), 72; Milson, *Sufi Rule*, 18–19; cf. Florian Sobieroj, "Ibn Khafif's *Kitab al-Iqtisad* and Abu al-Najib al-Suhrawardi's *Adab al-Muridin*," *Journal of Semitic Studies* 93, no. 2 (1998): 327 and 234, and Knysh, *Islamic Mysticism*, 194–95.

111. Hodgson, *Venture of Islam*, 2: 206–10.

112. For details see the classical study of Spenser Trimingham, *Sufi Orders in Islam* (Oxford: Oxford University Press, 1998); Popovic and Veinstein, *Les orders mystiques*, chapter 8.

113. According to Ibn Khaldun, the bond between the Sufi master (*shaykh*) and his pupil (*tilmidh*) is built on a chain of spiritual inheritance that connects (*muttasila ila*) the duo to the Prophet; *Shifaʾ*, 157; cf. Meier, *Essays*, 202, and Shaykh Muhammad Hisham Kabbani, *Classical Islam and the Naqshbandi Sufi Tradition*, 2nd ed. (Washington, DC: ISCA, 2004), 25–26.

114. Meier, *Essays*, 189–219; Bernd Radtke, "Sufism in the 18th Century: An Attempt at a Provisional Appraisal," *Die Welt des Islams* 36, no. 3 (1996): 326–64; cf. Laury Silvers-Alario, "The Teaching Relationship in Early Sufism: A Reassessment of Fritz Meier's Definition of the *shaykh al-tarbiya* and the *shaykh al-taʿlim*," *Muslim World* 93 (January 2003): 69–97.

115. Hodgson, *Venture of Islam*, 2: 209–10.

116. Ibid., 201–54; Fritz Meier, "The Mystic Path," in *The World of Islam: Faith, People, Culture*, ed. Bernard Lewis (London: Thames and Hudson, 1976), 122–26.

117. Shaykh Hisham Kabbani, *Naqshbandi*, 25–26; cf. 30 and Hisham Kabbani, *Classical Islam*, 31–32.

118. Fritz Meier, "Soufisme et déclin culturel," in *Classicisme et déclin culturel dans l'histoire de l'Islam*, ed. Robert Brunschvig and Gustave von Grunebaum (Paris: Editions Besson Chantemerle, 1957), 232.

119. Hisham Kabbani, *Naqshbandi*, 33, and Hisham Kabbani, *Classical Islam*, 39.

120. Hisham Kabbani, *Classical Islam*, 39; Hisham Kabbani, *Naqshbandi*, 33–34;

cf. Hodgson, *Venture of Islam*, 2: 210; for the premodern period, see al-Ghazali, *Ihya'*, 2: 239; al-Suhrawardi, *'Awarif al-ma'arif*, chapter 52; Ibn (al-)'Arabi, *al-Futuhat*, 2: 264–66; John Renard, trans., *Ibn 'Abbad of Ronda, Letters on the Sufi Path* (New York: Paulist Press, 1986), 184–87; and Ibn Khaldun, *Shifa'*, passim.

121. In addition to Knysh, *Islamic Mysticism* (chapters 8 and 9), and Knysh, "A Tale of Two Poets: Sufism in Yemen during the Ottoman Epoch," in *Le soufisme à l'époque ottoman/Sufism in the Ottoman Era*, ed. Rachida Chih and Catherine Mayeur-Jaouen (Cairo: IFAO, 2010), 337–67; see also the studies of Spencer Triming-ham, Julian Baldick, Vincent Cornell, Carl Ernst, Mark Sedgwick, John Renard, Rob-ert Rozehnal, Scott Kugle, Erik Ohlander, Nile Green, and Ahmet Karamustafa as well and other contemporary scholars of Sufism.

122. Silvers-Alario, "The Teaching," 77–79.

123. Hodgson's discussion is more general in nature and examines what he calls *"piri-muridi* discipline" alongside other changes in Sufi teachings and practices over time; see *Venture of Islam*, 2: 206–54 and 455–67; 3: 159; Meier dedicates a special study to this subject published in his *Essays*, 189–219.

124. See, e.g., John Renard, trans., *Ibn 'Abbad of Ronda*, Letter 16 (184–94) and 148–50; for the Arabic text see, Paul Nwyia, ed., *Ibn 'Abbad de Ronda (792/1390), Lettres de direction spirituelle* (Beirut: Dar El-Machreq, 1986), 130–40 and 99–100.

125. Hodgson's debt to his intellectual predecessors and contemporaries is meticu-lously acknowledged in his footnotes.

126. E.g., Bernd Radtke, Ahmet Karamustafa, Christopher Melchert, Nile Green, Erik Ohlander, to name but a few.

127. Durkheim, e.g., averred, "Religion is as fundamentally social as our human nature. Therefore, theoretically there are as many religions as there are societies"; quoted in Ivan Strenski, *Religion in Relation: Method, Application, and Moral Loca-tion* (Columbia: University of South Carolina Press, 1993), 78; in a similar vein, Dur-kheim's nephew and follower, Mauss, argued, "Thanks to sociology, we can study [re-ligious facts] comparatively, while at the same time pushing as far as possible the detailed analyses which preserve the value of [religious facts]"; quoted in ibid., 86.

128. See, e.g., Syed Farid Alatas, *Applying Ibn Khaldun: The Recovery of a Lost Tradition in Sociology* (London: Routledge, 2014), 9 passim; Mohammad Salama, *Islam, Orientalism, and Intellectual History: Modernity and the Politics of Exclusion since Ibn Khaldun* (London: I. B. Tauris, 2011), 77–101; Shukri al-Mamani, *Ibn Khal-dun wa-'ilm al-ijtima' al-insani: 'ala darb bina' al-ma'rifa al-'ilmiyya wa-hadarat al-insan* (Sfax: Dar amal li 'l-nashr wa 'l-tawzi', 2010), passim; see also an online publication "Ibn Khaldun, Father of Social Sciences": http://www.whyislam.org /muslim-world/ibn-khaldun/.

129. Meier's concept of the two types of Sufi pedagogy and, respectively, of the two types of Sufi masters associated with them has been challenged, unconvincingly, in our opinion, by Laury Silvers-Alario in her "The Teaching." In particular, Silvers-Alario seems to have downplayed the fact that this dual categorization of master-teacher relation in Sufism was not Meier's, but was originally advanced by the popular Maghribi Sufi master Ibn 'Abbad al-Rundi (d. 792/1390), as Meier duly notes in his *Essays*, 190–92; al-Rundi, in his turn, was responding to a polemic about the necessity of the Sufi master for the *murid*'s progress that had originated in Granada in the middle of the fourteenth century CE; see Nwyia, *Un mystique*, l–liv, 55, 209–10.

130. Meier, *Essays*, 189–90.

131. This much can be deduced from the numerous writings of modern Sufi masters, including Shaykh Nazim Haqqani, Shaykh Muhammad Hisham Kabbani, and Shaykh Muzaffer Ozak.

132. As clearly stated, e.g., in Shihab al-Din 'Umar al-Suharawrdi, *'Awarif al-ma'arif*, 2: 206–16; cf. Radtke, "Sufism," 343–45, and Radtke, "The Eight Rules of al-Junayd," in *Reason and Inspiration in Islam: Theology, Philosophy, and Mysticism in Muslim Thought*, ed. Todd Lawson (London: I. B. Tauris, 2005), 492–95.

133. Ibn 'Abbad's (and Nwyia's) interpretation of the two types of Sufi masters was somewhat different; however, in the final account, they complement each other rather than being in opposition; see Nwyia, *Un mystique*, 55 and 209–10; Nwyia, *Ibn 'Abbad de Ronda*, 130–31, of the Arabic text and its English translation in Renard, *Ibn 'Abbad*, 184–87.

134. Who, as mentioned in note 129 above, draws upon the ideas of the Maghribi Sufi master Ibn 'Abbad al-Rundi (d. 792/1390); on him see Nwyia, *Un mystique*, passim.

135. Meier, *Essays*, 95; cf. Renard, *Ibn 'Abbad*, 185; cf. ibid., 125; concerning the control of food intake and spiritual exercises, see Ibn Khaldun, *Shifa'*, 85–86, and al-Ghazali, *Ihya'*, 2: 239.

136. Meier, *Essays*, 94–97 and 190–92; Ibn 'Abbad himself speaks of "the sixth century [AH]," Nwyia, *Ibn 'Abbad*, 100, which John Renard inexplicably translates as "the sixth generation," Nwyia, *Ibn 'Abbad*, 150; most but not all of the authorities cited by Ibn 'Abbad had died before 1000 CE (with the exception of al-Ghazali, who died in 505/1111, and al-Suhrawardi, who died in 632/1234).

137. E.g., al-Qushayri (d. 465/1072); see Knysh, *al-Qushayri's Epistle*, 2–4.

138. Renard, *Ibn 'Abbad*, 127–31, 148–50, 185–87, and 190.

139. Meier, *Essays*, 95–96 and 189–91; Meier's caveats are ignored by Laury Silvers-Alario in her critical reassessment of his classification of the types of Sufi masters; see "The Teaching," passim.

140. Fritz Meier, *Abu Sa'id-i Abu l-Hayr: Wirklicheit und Legende* (Teheran-Liège: Bibliothèque Pahlavi; Leiden: E. J. Brill, 1976), 359.

141. Renard, *Ibn 'Abbad*, 186–92; cf. Meier, *Essays*, 191.

142. See, e.g., Bernd Radtke, "Sufism," and Radtke, "Von Iran nach Westafrika: Zwei Quellen für al-Ḥaǧǧ 'Umars *Kitab Rimah Hizb ar-Rahim*: Zaynaddin al-Hwafi und Šamsaddin al-Madyani," *Die Welt des Islams* 35, no. 1 (1995): 37–69.

143. Ibn 'Abbad's works contain numerous references to the Sufi writings that he considered to be a "must read" for every Sufi; see, e.g., Renard, *Ibn 'Abbad*, 125–26, and Nwyia, *Un mystique*, 81–120 and 169–213.

144. For an illuminating parallel with monastic orders in Catholic Christianity, see Renard, *Ibn 'Abbad*, 45.

145. As discussed in al-Suhrawardi, *'Awarif al-ma'arif*, 2: 211–15 and 221–22, and Ibn Khaldun, *Shifa'*, 84–87; similar observations had been made by al-Ghazali in his *Ihya'*, 2: 238–39.

146. Meier, *Essays*, 196, quoting Abu Nasr al-Sarraj (d. 378/988); on Abu Nasr al-Sarraj, see Knysh, *Islamic Mysticism*, 118–20; in a similar vein, al-Ghazali argues that the exact timing and frequency of seclusion for a Sufi novice (*murid*) should be

determined by the *shaykh* in accordance with the novice's personal disposition, see *Ihya'*, 2: 239.

147. On Ibn Khaldun's general approach to Sufism and its various representatives, see Franz Rosenthal, trans., *Ibn Khaldun: The Muqaddimah* (New York: Pantheon, 1956), 3: 76–103, and chapter 7 of Knysh, *Ibn 'Arabi*, especially 184–96.

148. Knysh, *Ibn 'Arabi*, 186; for Baybarsiyya see Leonor Fernandes, "Baybarsiyya," *EI3*, online edition: http://referenceworks.brillonline.com.

149. Nwyia, *Un mystique*, l–li.

150. For the controversy concerning the authorship of "The Cure," see Nwyia, *Un mystique*, l–li note 4; Nwyia's conclusion that this work belongs to 'Abd al-Rahman Ibn Khaldun himself, not his father Muhammad (d. 749/1348), is persuasive.

151. *Shifa'*, 100–121 and 162–63; the content of this treatise, inasmuch as it is relevant to Ibn (al-)'Arabi, is summarized in Knysh, *Ibn 'Arabi*, 186–97.

152. Ibn Khaldun, *Shifa'*, 109–10; Knysh, *Ibn 'Arabi*, 192–93.

153. Nwyia, *Un mystique*, xlviii–liv, 55, and 209–11; Renard, *Ibn 'Abbad*, 24–26 and 184–88.

154. "A man of Sicily," who studied under eminent Sufi masters of Qayrawan, Tunis, and died in the late fourth/tenth century; see Renard, *Ibn 'Abbad*, 219 note 4, and Nwyia, *Un mystique*, 196.

155. Ibn Khaldun, *Shifa'*, 86–96, 102–4, 126.

156. See Knysh, *Ibn 'Arabi*, 190–97.

157. *Shifa'*, 106–21 and 162–63; the practices that Ibn Khaldun has in mind included thaumaturgic exercises aimed at influencing people and environment by means of magical powers of the letters and numbers; for details see Noah Gardiner, "Forbidden Knowledge? Notes on the Production, Transmission, and Receptions of the Major Works of Ahmad al-Buni," *Journal of Arabic and Islamic Studies* 12 (2012): 81–143; for Ibn Khaldun's attempt to trace the roots of philosophical Sufism to Isma'ili teachings, see Ebstein, *Mysticism and Philosophy*, 10–12.

158. *Shifa'*, 75–82 and 124–25, and Nwyia, *Un mystique*, lii.

159. *Shifa'*, 47, 97, 125, 132; here and in what follows Ibn Khaldun's argument is similar to that of Ibn 'Abbad's; see Renard, *Ibn 'Abbad*, 184–90.

160. *Shifa'*, 124–26.

161. Ibid., 84–87.

162. Nwyia, *Un mystique*, liii–liv.

163. Ibn Khaldun, *Shifa'*, 125 and 135.

164. Ibid., 126 and 135–38.

165. Ibid., 126; cf. Meier, *Essays*, 202.

166. Ibn Khaldun, *Shifa'*, 142.

167. Nwyia, *Un mystique*, liv, and Knysh, *Ibn 'Arabi*, 196.

168. *Shifa'*, 166; Nwyia, *Un mystique*, xlviii–lii, and Renard, *Ibn 'Abbad*, 25–27 and 184–91; for Abu Ishaq al-Shatibi's treatment of Sufism, see his *al-I'tisam*, ed. Abu 'Ubayda Mashur Al Sulayman, 4 vols. (Manama, Bahrain: Maktabat al-tawhid, 2000), 1: 147–66, 333–34, and 347–68; 2: 113 and 119–22; an English translation of this book was made by Mohammed Mahdi Al-Sharif (Beirut: Dar al-kutub al-'ilmiyya, 2012).

169. See the works of Bernd Radtke and John O'Kane quoted in the text.

170. The terms that Sufi authors often use, such as "exercises" (*riyadat*) or "exerting oneself" (*mujahadat*), seem to justify this comparison.

171. Al-Ghazali, *Ihya'*, 2: 239.

172. Ibn Khaldun, *Shifa'*, 158–60.

173. Al-Sarraj, *Kitab al-luma'*, 163–65; al-Suhrawardi, *'Awarif al-ma'arif*, 2: 212; Milson, *Sufi Rule*, 43; Meier, *Essays*, 196–97.

174. On this Sufi of Nishapur in Khurasan, who died in 373/984, see Knysh, *Al-Qushayri's Epistle*, "Index" 435, and Biagi, *Collection of Sufi Rules*, 136–37.

175. Cf. al-Suhrawardi, *'Awarif al-ma'arif*, 2: 212, and Nwyia, *Un mystique*, 55 and 211.

176. Literally, "elevate his dignity" (*ta'zim hurmatihi*).

177. Menahem Milson, ed., *Kitab adab al-muridin by Abu al-Najib 'Abd al-Qahir al-Suhrawardi (d. 563 H.)* (Jerusalem: Hebrew University of Jerusalem, 1978), 37; cf. Meier, *Essays*, 192–219, and Bernd Radtke, "Sufism," 336–37 and 342–45; Radtke, "Lehrer-Schüle-Enkel: Ahmad b. Idris, Muhammad 'Uthman al-Mirgani, Isma'il al-Wali," *Oriens* 32 (1992): 94–132; Bernd Radtke, Rex O'Fahey, and John O'Kane, "Two Sufi Treatises of Ahmad b. Idris," *Oriens* 35 (1996): 143–78.

178. On him see Erik Ohlander, *Sufism in an Age of Transition: 'Umar al-Suhrawardi and the Rise of Islamic Mystical Brotherhoods* (Leiden: E. J. Brill, 2008).

179. Al-Suhrawardi, *'Awarif al-ma'arif*, 2: 207.

180. Ohlander, *Sufism*, 200, quoting *'Awarif al-ma'arif*, 2: 236.

181. Quoted in Meier, *Essays*, 203.

182. Ohlander, *Sufism*, 202, quoting *'Awarif al-ma'arif*, 1: 258.

183. Bernd Radtke, *Adab al-muluk: Ein Handbuch zur islamischen Mystik aus dem 4./10. Jahrhundert* (Beirut: Beiruter Texte und Studien, Bd. 37, 1991), 30–34 and 36–39.

184. Ibn (al-)'Arabi, *al-Futuhat*, 2: 364–66.

185. Meier, *Essays*, 202.

186. Karamustafa, *Sufism*, 117, quoting several Sufi sources.

187. Radtke, O'Fahey, and O'Kane, "Two Sufi Treatises," 143; on him see Rex O'Fahey, *The Enigmatic Saint: Ahmad ibn Idris and the Idrisi Tradition* (Evanston, IL: Northwestern University Press, 1990).

188. Radtke, O'Fahey, and O'Kane, "Two Sufi Treatises," 148–49.

189. Hisham Kabbani, *Naqshbandi*, 28; Hisham Kabbani, *Classical Islam*, 31–36; cf. Holland, *Sheikh Muzaffer Ozak*, 65–67 and 546–50.

190. Al-Suhrawardi, *'Awarif*, 2: 208.

191. Silvers-Alario, "The Teaching," 85, citing Abu Nasr al-Sarraj, *Kitab al-luma'*.

192. Hisham Kabbani, *Naqshbandi*, 33.

193. Radtke, "Eight Rules," 495, and Radtke, "Sufism," 343–45.

194. Meier, *Essays*, 193–94, and Radtke, "Eight Rules," 495.

195. Ibn Khaldun, *Shifa'*, 35.

196. Hisham Kabbani, *Naqshbandi*, 33.

197. Ibn (al-)'Arabi, *al-Futuhat*, 2: 365–66.

198. On him see Francesco Chiabotti, "Entre soufsme et savoir islamique: L'oeuvre de 'Abd al-Karim al-Qushayri (376–465/ 986–1072)" (PhD thesis, Aix-Marseille Université, Aix-en-Provence, 2014), 42–56.

199. Knysh, *al-Qushayri's Epistle*, 305–6.

200. As pointed out, disapprovingly, by Ibn Khaldun in his *Shifa'*, 109, 119–21, and 162–63.

201. Meier, *Essays*, 197.

202. See "Introduction" and chapter 1.

203. As evidenced, e.g., by the telltale title of a book by the Spanish Islamologist and Catholic priest Miguel Asín Palacios (1871–1944), *El Islam cristianizado: Estudio del sufismo a través de las obras de Abenárabi de Murcia* (Madrid: Editorial Plutarco, 1931).

204. That is, the *shaykh*.

205. Knysh, *al-Qushayri's Epistle*, 303.

206. Ohlander, *Sufism*, 198–206.

207. Silvers-Alario, "The Teaching," 88–89.

208. Al-Suhrawardi, *'Awarif*, 2: 218.

209. Ibid., 218–22; cf. Silvers-Alario, "The Teaching," 81–82 and 88–89.

210. Meier, *Essays*, 197.

211. Ibid., 198–99; Silvers-Alario, on the other hand, insists that the *shaykh-murid* relationship is patterned consciously and deliberately on the Prophet's interactions with his companions, see "The Teaching," 79 passim.

212. As described in detail in Radtke, O'Fahey, and O'Kane, "Two Sufi Treatises," 153–60.

213. Ibid., 164–66; cf. Knysh, *al-Qushayri's Epistle*, 302–6; today, the rules of initiation, remembrance of God (*dhikr*), and seclusion (*khalwa*) are detailed in Hisham Kabbani's *Naqshbandi*, 39–47, and Hisham Kabbani, *Classical Islam*, 36–56

214. In the words of Meier, "the novitiate has become an initiation," *Essays*, 202.

215. For an illuminating discussion of this practice, see Meier, *Abu Sa'id*, 356–60.

216. Meier, *Essays*, 201.

217. See Radtke, "Sufism," passim; Radtke, "Lehrer," passim, and Radtke, "Von Iran nach Westafrika," passim.

218. Geertz, *Interpreting Cultures*, 118; cf. Geertz's statement cited in the epigraph to this chapter.

219. Ohlander, *Sufism*, 198–242.

220. *Pace* Ernst, *Shambhala Guide*, chapter 1, and King, *Orientalism*, chapter 1, both of whom argue that the concept of "mysticism" and "mystical" are post-Enlightenment Orientalist constructs that had not existed in premodern indigenous non-European societies.

221. Ahmet Karamustafa, *God's Unruly Friends: Dervish Groups in the Islamic Later Middle Period, 1200–1550* (Salt Lake City: University of Utah Press, 1994), passim.

222. E.g., Bruinessen, "Sufism," 140–41.

223. Shmuel Eisenstadt, ed., *Max Weber on Charisma and Institution Building* (Chicago: University of Chicago Press, 1968), 46–77, and Hans Gerth and Charles Wright Mills, *From Max Weber: Essays on Sociology* (Oxford: Oxford University Press, 1958), 245–64 and 267–301.

224. Bruce Lincoln, *Authority: Construction and Corrosion* (Chicago: University of Chicago Press, 1994), chapter 1.

225. As detailed in Bryan Turner's *Weber and Islam: A Critical Study* (London: Routledge and Kegan Paul, 1974), chapter 11 passim; cf. Armando Salvatore, "Tradition and Modernity within Islamic Civilization and the West," in Masud, Salvatore,

and Bruinessen, *Islam and Modernity*, 11; Muhammad Khalid Masud and Armando Salvatore, "Western Scholars of Islam on the Issue of Modernity," in ibid., 38, 40, and 43.

226. The text-based approach is represented by Ibn 'Abbad al-Rundi, while Ibn Khaldun combines textual data with his own observations in his *Shifa' al-sa'il*; both discuss transformations of the role of the Sufi *shaykh* over time.

227. Al-Qushayri's bemoaning of this decline in his *Epistle* (2–4) is echoed by countless other writers, Sufis and non-Sufis alike; Hodgson, *Venture of Islam*, 1: 445–55; Aziz al-Azmeh's disquisitions on the subject are as erudite as they are obscure, although still relevant; see Aziz al-Azmeh, *The Times of History* (Budapest: CEU Press, 2007), chapters 2, 3, 4, 5, and 7.

228. This theme runs like a red thread across the entire narrative of al-Shatibi's multivolume *al-I'tisam* as well as the works of Ibn Taymiyya and his students Ibn Qayym al-Jawziyya (d. 751/1350) and Ibn Kathir (d. 774/1373), indicating a distinctive "nostalgic" turn in fourteenth-century Islamdom.

229. For a variety of academic explanations of "Muslim decline," see Robert Brunschvig and Gustave von Grunebaum, eds., *Classicisme et déclin culturel dans l'histoire de l'Islam* (Paris: Éditions Besson Chantemerle, 1957); Gustave von Grunebaum, *Classical Islam: A History, 600–1258* (Chicago: Aldine, 1970), 191–201; Hodgson, *Venture of Islam*, 2: 450–62, and 3: 176–248; for a critical analysis of such explanations, see Masud and Salvatore, "Western Scholars," 40–43.

230. See, e.g., Knysh, *Islamic Mysticism*, chapters 8 and 9; Green, *Sufism*, passim.

231. *Sufism: An Account of the Mystics of Islam* (London: Allen and Unwin, 1950), chapter 11, "The Decay of Sufism"; and Fritz Meier, "Soufisme et déclin culturel," in Brunschvig and von Grunebaum, *Classicisme et déclin culturel*, 217–45.

232. We use the terminology of the contributors to the collective monograph *Classicisme et déclin culturel dans l'histoire de l'Islam*, passim; for a scathing criticism of this work that, however, offers nothing constructive in return, see al-Azmeh, *Times of History*, 47–61.

233. As shown in Hodgson, *Venture of Islam*, 2: 206–54 and 455–67; see also Hodgson, 3: "Index" under "Sufism"; for a more recent attempt to prove the underlying dynamism of Sufism's historical evolution in the recent centuries, see Green, *Sufism*, chapter 3.

234. Salvatore, "Tradition," 23–26; Masud and Salvatore, "Western Scholars of Islam," 38, 40, and 43.

235. For a general overview see Charles Pellat, "Manakib," *EI2*, online edition: http://referenceworks.brillonline.com/. For more recent examples, see Hisham Kabbani, *Naqshbandi*, 3–14, and *Classical Islam*, passim; these and other writings by the same author can be seen as an unconscious attempt to routinize charisma by associating it primarily, if not exclusively, with the Naqshbandi "Golden Chain of the Saints" (i.e., the Naqshbandi masters of the past) that connects its recent and current holders (Shaykh Nazim al-Haqqani, Shaykh Muhammad 'Adil al-Haqqani, Shaykh Muhammad Hisham Kabbani, and Shaykh Nour Kabbani) to the Prophet.

236. See, e.g., Meier, *Essays*; Bruinessen, "Sufism," 125–57; Bruinessen and Julia Day Howell, eds., *Sufism and the "Modern" in Islam* (London: I. B. Tauris, 2013); Ohlander, *Sufism*, passim; Itzchak Weismann, *The Naqshbandiyya: Orthodoxy and*

Activism in a Worldwide Sufi Tradition (Abingdon, UK: Routledge, 2007); Catharina Raudvere and Leif Stenberg, eds., *Sufism Today: Heritage and Tradition in the Global Community* (London: I. B. Tauris, 2009); Alexander Knysh et al., eds., *Sufizm i musul'manskaia dukhovnaia traditsiia* (*Sufism and the Muslim Spiritual Tradition*) (St. Petersburg: Peterburgskoe vostokovedenie, 2015).

237. Knysh, *Islamic Mysticism*, 299–300.

238. See, e.g., Meenakshi Khanna, "Visionaries of a Tariqa: The Uwaysi Sufis of Shahjahanabad," in *Dreams and Visions in Islamic Societies*, ed. Özgen Felek and Alexander Knysh (Albany: State University of New York Press, 2012), 273–96.

239. For a typical example of this academic attitude, see Nile Green and Mary Searle-Chatterjee, eds., *Religion, Language, and Power* (London: Routledge, 2008).

240. As one can observe firsthand in the videos posted on the websites of the Naqshbandiyya-Haqqaniyya and other international Sufi communities, e.g., the Ba 'Alawiyya; for links to videos see: https://en.wikipedia.org/wiki/Habib_Umar_bin _Hafiz and https://www.youtube.com/watch?v=6afElzXOm7Y (which contains further references to relevant online videos).

241. As will be shown in the final chapter of this book.

242. Ernst, *Sufism*, 8–18; the same can be said regarding al-Azmeh's ruminations about the "Orientalist [mis-]construction" of Islamic civilization; see his *The Times*, chapter 2.

243. As discussed in Masud and Salvatore, "Western Scholars," passim.

244. Bruinessen, "Sufism," 126–27, and Arberry, *Sufism*, 123.

245. Massignon, *Essay on the Origins of the Technical Language of Islamic Mysticism*, (Notre Dame, IN: University of Indiana Press, 1997), 213–14.

246. See Knysh, "Historiography," 225.

247. Hodgson, *Venture of Islam*, 2: 455–62.

248. E.g., Arberry's "dark ages" is an obvious reference to how post-Enlightenment thinkers viewed the European Middle Ages; Massignon, on the other hand, apparently refers to the idea of the penetration of early Christianity by Hellenic philosophical discourse and the resultant "distortion" of its original message; see, e.g., Arnold Toynbee, *An Historian's Approach to Religion* (Oxford: Oxford University Press, 1979), chapter 9.

249. Ivan Strenski, *Thinking about Religion: An Historical Introduction to Theories of Religion* (Oxford: Blackwell, 2006), 213.

250. Quoted in ibid.; for an authoritative articulation of this theory by one of its major advocates and practitioners, see Ninian Smart, *Concept and Empathy: Essays in the Study of Religion* (Houndmills, Basingstoke: Macmillan, 1986).

251. Strenski, *Thinking*, 212–13.

252. For a critical assessment of their views, see Knysh, "Historiography," 234–36.

253. Contrary to the thesis of Franz Rosenthal (1914–2003) who argued that Muslim historiography, at least before Ibn Khaldun, was not seriously interested in accounting for historical change and its context, preoccupied as it was with "the religio-political significance of certain events"; see Rosenthal, *A History of Muslim Historiography* (Leiden: E. J. Brill, 1968), 70 and 84; for further details see ibid., chapter 3.

254. See, e.g., Abdesselam Cheddadi, *Ibn Khaldûn: L'homme et le théoricien de la civilization* (Paris: Gallimard, 2006), passim.

255. See, e.g., the comments of al-Qushayri at the beginning of his *Epistle* bemoaning the moral and intellectual decline of Sufism in his age; Knysh, *al-Qushayri's Epistle*, 2–4; similar statements abound in early Sufi manuals and sayings of Sufi masters quoted therein.

256. As is abundantly obvious from Ibn Khaldun's accounts of the evolution of various trends of Muslim thought and practice; see Rosenthal, *Ibn Khaldun*, 3: chapter 4, especially sections 13, 14, 15, 16, 17, 27, and 30.

257. See, e.g., Talal Asad, *Genealogies of Religion* (Baltimore: Johns Hopkins University Press, 1993); Salvatore, *Islam*, 24–30; Richard King, *Orientalism and Religion* (London: Routledge, 1999), chapter 1, passim; Talal Asad, *Formation of the Secular: Christianity, Islam, Modernity* (Stanford, CA: Stanford University Press, 2003), chapters 6 and 7; and Tomoko Masuzawa, *The Invention of World Religions* (Chicago: University of Chicago Press, 2005), 14–21 passim.

258. Jonathan Z. Smith, *Imagining Religion: From Babylon to Jonestown* (Chicago: University of Chicago Press, 1982), ix; cf. King, *Orientalism*, 11.

259. Masuzawa, *Invention*, 16–18.

260. E.g., Ibn Battuta (d. 770/1368 or 779/1377); see Ross Dunn, trans., *The Adventures of Ibn Battuta: A Muslim Traveler of the 14th Century* (Berkeley: University of California Press, 2012).

261. See, e.g., Armando Salvatore, *Islam and the Political Discourse of Modernity* (Reading, UK: Ithaca Press, 1997); Masud, Salvatore, and Bruinessen, *Islam and Modernity*, passim; Bruce Lincoln, *Holy Terrors: Thinking about Religion after September 11* (Chicago: University of Chicago Press, 2006), chapter 4.

262. Addressed in detail in King, *Orientalism*, and Masuzawa, *Invention*.

263. Strenski, *Thinking*, 2; Talal Asad, *Genealogies of Religion*, passim; Salvatore, *Islam*, 23–32.

264. As surveyed, e.g., in Roy Harrisville, *Pandora's Box Opened: An Examination and Defense of Historical Critical Method and Its Master Practitioners* (Grand Rapids, MI: Eerdmans, 2014), 113–29 and 173–86.

265. For a famous (infamous) example see the works of John Wansbrough (1928–2002), especially his *Qur'anic Studies* (Oxford: Oxford University Press, 1977), and Wansbrough, *Sectarian Milieu* (Oxford: Oxford University Press, 1978).

266. In his valuable book, Ivan Strenski discusses contributions to socio-anthropological and comparative study of religions by Edward Tylor, William Robertson Smith, James Frazer, Bronislaw Malinowski, Mary Douglas, and Mircea Eliade.

267. Strenski, *Thinking*, 2; see also Jonathan Smith's statement quoted above.

268. As discussed in Ninian Smart's "Methods in My Life," in *The Craft of Religious Studies*, ed. Jonathan Stone (New York: St. Martin's Press, 1998), 18–35.

269. For references see the previous footnotes and Mohammad Salama, *Islam, Orientalism, and Intellectual History* (London: I. B. Tauris, 2011) and Alexander Knysh's review of this book in *Der Islam* 90, no. 1 (2013): 197–202.

270. In addition to Ibn Khaldun, a prominent example is Muhammad al-Shahrastani's *Book of Religions and Sects* (*Kitab al-milal wa 'l-nihal*); for a complete

and carefully annotated French translation, see Daniel Gimaret and Guy Monnot, trans., *Shahrastani, Livre des religions et des sects* (Paris: Peeters, 1986).

271. They are usually called "heresiographers" in Western academic studies, a term that presupposes that they represented some sort of official orthodoxy, which was not exactly the case.

272. For a selection of critical assessments of Sufism by Muslim doxographers, see Bernd Radtke, *Neue kritische Gänger* (Utrecht: Houtsma, 2005), 251–91, and Radtke, *Materielen für alten islamischen Frömmigkeit* (Leiden: E. J. Brill, 2009), passim.

273. As an example one can cite, e.g., Ibn Hazm's (d. 456/1064) discussion of various Christian theological teachings, sects, and the Trinitarian debates in his *al-Fisal fi 'l-milal wa-'l-ahwa' wa-'l-nihal*, ed. Ahmad Shams al-Din, 3 vols. (Beirut: Dar al-kutub al-'ilmiyya, 1999), 1: 251–334; for al-Biruni's (d. circa 442/1050) description of the Indian religions and societies, see Edward Sachau, trans., *Alberuni's India: An Account of the Religion, Philosophy, Literature, Geography, Chronology, Astronomy, Customs, Laws, and Astrology of India about A.D. 1030* (Delhi: S. Chand, 1964).

274. Strenski, *Thinking*, 3.

275. Ibid.

276. Smart, "Methods," 29–33; the same idea is often attributed to Max Müller (1823–1900).

277. These disciplines comprised philology, theology, psychology, anthropology, phenomenology, and sociology, as demonstrated in Strenski's seminal survey of the rise and evolution of "the study of religion" in western Europe; Strenski, *Thinking*, passim.

278. As documented in the now-classical study of Norman Daniel, *Islam and the West: The Making of an Image* (Oxford: Oneworld, 2003).

279. See Weber, *Sociology of Religion*, 166–83; for its application to the study of Sufism, see Christopher Melchert, "The Transition from Asceticism to Mysticism at the Middle of the Ninth Century C.E.," *Studia Islamica* 83, no. 1 (1996): 51–70; Bernd Radtke has criticized Melchert's use of Weberian concepts in his *Neue kritische Gänge*, 251–91, especially 285–86.

280. Eisenstadt, *Max Weber*, 268–83.

281. Weber, *Sociology*, 166–67; Eisenstadt, *Max Weber*, 277, and Gerth and Wright Mills, *From Max Weber*, 276–78 and 283; cf. Turner, *Weber*, 139, 145–47, and 172.

282. Weber, *Sociology*, 262–66; Weber, *Economy and Society*, 2 vols., ed. Guenther Roth and Claus Wittich, trans. Ephraim Fischoff (Berkeley: University of California Press, 1978), 2: 1166–67; Eisenstadt, *Max Weber*, 277, and Gerth and Wright Mills, *From Max Weber*, 269 and 284–85.

283. Gerth and Wright Mills, *From Max Weber*, 290–92; Weber, *Economy and Society*, 1166–67; and Turner, *Weber*, 138–44.

284. Weber, *Sociology*, 220–22; Weber, *The Protestant Ethic and the Spirit of Capitalism* (New York: Charles Scribner, 1976), 154; and Weber, *Economy and Society*, 1: 540, 544, 555–56.

285. Weber, *Sociology*, 182; Eisenstadt, *Max Weber*, 270–75; cf. Turner, *Weber*, 146–47.

286. Turner, *Weber*, 146–50; for a later Muslim thinker, Sayyid Qutb, see Oliver Carré, *Mysticism and Politics: A Critical Reading of* Fi Zilal al-Qur'an *by Sayyid Qutb*

(1906–1966) (Leiden: E. J. Brill, 2003), 87, 96–100, 173; cf. Ibrahim Abu-Rabiʻ, *Intellectual Origins of Islamic Resurgence in the Modern Arab World* (Albany: State University of New York Press, 1996), 155–62.

287. See, e.g., Weber, *Sociology*, 182, and Weber, *Protestant Ethic*, 154.

288. Knysh, *Islamic Mysticism*, 33–35, 44–46, and 94–101.

289. Al-Harith al-Muhasibi, *Al-Makasib wa ʼl-waraʻ wa ʼl-shubha* (Beirut: Muʼassasat al-kutub al-thaqafiyya, 1987), passim; Florian Sobieroj, *Ibn Ḥafīf aš-Šīrāzī, und seine Schrift zur Novizenerziehung* (Stuttgart: Franz Steiner, 1998), 481–82, of the Arabic text; al-Ghazali, *Ihyaʼ*, 4: 189–293; and Ohlander, *Sufism*, 175–79, which is a summary of the relevant passages from al-Suhrawardi's *ʻAwarif al-maʻrif.*

290. See, e.g., Adams, *Islam and Modernism*, 25, 31–33, and 161–64; Sahar Bazzaz, "Heresy and Politics in Nineteenth-Century Morocco," *Arab Studies Journal* 10–11, no. 2/1 (Fall 2002/Spring 2003): 67–86.

291. *Ihyaʼ*, 2: 238.

292. Ibid.

293. Ibn Khaldun, *Shifaʼ*, 81 and 97.

294. Lit. "mixing."

295. Ibn ʻAjiba, *al-Bahr al-madid*, 8 vols. (Beirut: Dar al-kutub al-ʻilmiyya, 2010), 5: 119.

296. Knysh, *Islamic Mysticism*, 94–101 and 207–34; see also Weismann, *Naqshbandiyya*; Elmer Douglas, trans., *The Mystical Teachings of al-Shadhili* (Albany: State University of New York Press, 1993); cf. Bruinessen and Howell, *Sufism*, passim.

297. As evidenced by Ibn Khaldun, who, as mentioned, calls Sufism a "[legal] path" (*shariʻa*) of its own (*Shifaʼ*, p. 126); in a similar vein, a contemporary French scholar juxtaposes Sufism with "the Islam of the canonical Law (shariʻa), of the theologians and jurists, of the mosques and muezzins, and Islamic institutions and sciences"; see Veinstein, "Avant-propos," in Popovic and Veinstein, *Les Voies d'Allah*, 7.

298. See Chittick, *Sufi Path*, "Index" under "He/not He (*huwa la huwa*)."

299. As evidenced, e.g., by Shaykh Muhammad Husham Kabbani's insistence that the true Sufi master be a gnostic (*ʻarif*), in addition to being proficient in the rites and legal requirements of exoteric Islam; see *Naqshbandi*, 27.

300. Ibid., 28–29.

301. As discussed, e.g., in an early Sufi manual by Abu ʼl-Najib ʻAbd al-Qahir al-Suhrawardi (d. 563/1168); see Milson, *Sufi Rule*, and Milson, Abu al-Najib ʻAbd al-Qahir al-Suhrawardi, *Kitab adab al-muridin*, passim.

302. See Radtke, "Von Iran," passim.

303. Ernst, *Shambhala Guide*, 1–31.

304. As implicitly acknowledged by Carl Ernst himself; see ibid., 2.

Chapter 6: Sufism's Recent Trajectories: What Lies behind the Sufi-Salafi Confrontation?

1. As discussed in chapters 2 and 4 of this book.

2. E.g., in eastern Turkestan (Xinjiang), India, Russia, the Balkans, West Africa, and, of course, Europe and the Americas; for general studies of the institutional reach of Sufism, see Alexandre Popovic and Gilles Veinstein, eds., *Les Voies d'Allah: Les or-*

dres mystiques dans l'islam des origines à aujourd'hui (Paris: Fayard, 1996), and Fritz Meier, "The Mystic Path," in *The World of Islam: Faith, People, Culture*, ed. Bernard Lewis, Richard Ettinghausen, Oleg Grabar et al. (London: Thames and Hudson, 1976), 117–40; for the Indonesian Archipelago, see Michael Laffan, *The Makings of Indonesian Islam* (Princeton, NJ: Princeton University Press, 2011), part 1, chapters 1 and 2; for the Indian subcontinent, see Richard Eaton, *The Sufis of Bijapur 1300–1700: Social Roles of Sufis in Medieval India* (Princeton, NJ: Princeton University Press, 1977); for a brief survey of various geographical regions, see Alexander Knysh, *Islamic Mysticism: A Short History*, 2nd ed. (Leiden: E. J. Brill, 2010), chapters 8 and 9.

3. See, e.g., Laffan, *Makings of Indonesian Islam*, part 4.

4. Sahar Bazzaz, "Heresy and Politics in Nineteenth-Century Morocco," *Arab Studies Journal* 10–11, no. 2/1 (Fall 2002/Spring 2003): 67–86; Samer Akkach, *Letters of a Sufi Scholar* (Leiden: E. J. Brill, 2010), 29–31; cf. Itzchak Weismann, *Taste of Modernity: Sufism, Salafiyya, and Arabism in Late Ottoman Damascus* (Leiden: E. J. Brill, 2001), passim.

5. See, e.g., Knut Vikør, *Sufi and Scholar on the Desert Edge: Muhammad b. 'Ali al-Sanusi and His Brotherhood* (London: Hurst, 1995),270–73; Alexander Knysh, "Shamil," in *EI2*, online edition: http://referenceworks.brillonline.com.

6. In addition to chapters 8 and 9 of Knysh, *Islamic Mysticism*, and Knysh, "Sufism," in *The New Cambridge History of Islam*, vol. 4, *Islamic Cultures and Societies to the End of the Eighteenth Century*, ed. Robert Irwin (Cambridge: Cambridge University Press, 2010), 60–104; see also Nehemia Levtzion and John Voll, eds., *Eighteenth-Century Renewal and Reform in Islam* (Syracuse, NY: Syracuse University Press, 1987), passim; Nile Green, *Sufism: A Global History* (Chichester, UK: Wiley-Blackwell, 2012), passim; Itzchak Weismann, "Sufism in the Age of Globalization," in *Cambridge Companion to Sufism*, ed. Lloyd Ridgeon (Cambridge: Cambridge University Press, 2015), 257–81.

7. Weismann, "Sufism," 261–62; Reinhard Schulze, *Islamischer Internationalismus in 20. Jahrhundert* (Leiden: E. J. Brill, 1990), "Index" under "Mystik."

8. See, e.g., Charles Adams, *Islam and Modernism in Egypt* (Oxford: Oxford University Press, 1933), 23–33; Frederick de Jong and Bernd Radtke, eds., *Islamic Mysticism Contested* (Leiden: E. J. Brill, 1999), and Elizabeth Sirriyeh, *Sufis and Anti-Sufis: The Defense, Rethinking, and Rejection of Sufism in the Modern World* (Richmond, Surrey: Curzon, 1999); Gudrun Krämer, *Hasan al-Banna* (Oxford: Oneworld, 2010), "Index" under "Sufism"; and Laffan, *Makings of Indonesian Islam*, 189 and chapter 10.

9. See Alexander Knysh, "Historiography of Sufi Studies in the West and Russia," *Pis'mennye pamiatniki Vostoka (Written Monuments of the Orient)* 1, no. 4 (2006): 206–38; in addition to the general studies of Sufism in the premodern and modern age cited earlier in the present book, see Martin van Bruinessen and Julia Day Howell, eds., *Sufism and the "Modern" in Islam* (London: I. B. Tauris, 2013); Lloyd Ridgeon, ed., *The Cambridge Companion to Sufism* (Cambridge: Cambridge University Press, 2015), and Ridgeon, ed., *Sufism and Salafis in the Modern Age* (London: Bloomsbury, 2015); for an important insider perspective see Éric Geoffroy, *Introduction to Sufism: The Inner Path of Islam* (Bloomington, IN: World Wisdom, 2010).

10. See Alexander Knysh, "Contextualizing the Sufi-Salafi Conflict (From the Northern Caucasus to Hadramawt)," *Middle Eastern Studies* 43, no. 4 (2007): 503–30.

11. Hayden White, *Tropics of Discourse: Essays in Cultural Criticism* (Baltimore: Johns Hopkins University Press, 1978), 1–21 and chapters 3–5, and 9; White, *The Content of the Form: Narrative Discourse and Historical Representation* (Baltimore: Johns Hopkins University Press, 1987), 47; White, *The Fiction of Narrative*, ed. Robert Doran (Baltimore: Johns Hopkins University Press, 2010), chapters 4 and 12.

12. Hodgson, *The Venture of Islam: Conscience and History in a World Civilization*, 3 vols. (Chicago: University of Chicago Press, 1974), 2: 201–22.

13. Cf. Hodgson, *Venture of Islam*, 2: 206.

14. For a critical overview of various concepts of rites and rituals in Western sociology and anthropology, see Talal Asad, *Genealogies of Religion* (Baltimore: Johns Hopkins University Press, 1995), 55–79; unfortunately, Asad gives short shrift to the community-building function of ritual, preoccupied as he is with its, in our view, less important roles; as a remedy to Asad's "blind spot," see Eric Hobsbawm and Terrence Ranger, eds., *The Invention of Tradition* (Cambridge: Cambridge University Press, 1997), passim.

15. Hodgson, *Venture of Islam*, 2: 212–13.

16. Ibid., 217.

17. For striking, haunting, live images of such occurrences in various parts of the Muslim world, see the documentary *I Am a Sufi, I Am a Muslim* (Princeton, NJ: Films for the Humanities and Sciences, 1994).

18. The tombs of the Qur'anic prophets Hud and Salih are objects of the massive seasonal pilgrimages mentioned in our studies of Hadramawt, South Yemen (see the next note); their connection with the [neo-]Sufi movement instituted by the local *sayyid* families is discussed later in this chapter.

19. For this phenomenon in South Arabia and Yemen, see Alexander Knysh, "The Cult of Saints in Hadramawt: An Overview," in *New Arabian Studies*, ed. R. B. Serjeant, R. L. Bidwell, and G. Rex Smith, vol. 1 (Exeter: Exeter University Press, 1993), 137–52; Knysh, "The Cult of Saints and Religious Reformism in Early Twentieth-Century Hadramawt," *New Arabian Studies* 4 (1997): 139–67; Knysh, "The Cult of Saints and Religious Reformism in Hadhramaut," in *Hadhrami Traders, Scholars, and Statesmen in the Indian Ocean, 1750s–1960s*, ed. Ulrike Freitag and William Clarence-Smith (Leiden: E. J. Brill, 1997), 199–216; for other regions see John Renard, *Friends of God: Islamic Images of Piety, Commitment, and Servanthood* (Berkeley: University of California Press, 2008); Christian Troll, *Muslim Shrines in India* (Oxford: Oxford University Press, 1989); Pnina Werbner and Helen Basu, eds., *Embodying Charisma* (London: Routledge, 1998); Pnina Werbner, *Pilgrims of Love: The Anthropology of a Global Sufi Cult* (Bloomington: Indiana University Press, 2003); Werbner, "Transnationalism and Regional Cults," in *The Cambridge Companion to Sufism*, ed. Lloyd Ridgeon (Cambridge: Cambridge University Press, 2015), 282–300.

20. Hodgson, *Venture of Islam*, 2: 217–18; for a recent example of the social ramifications of Sufi rites and rituals, see Earle Waugh, *Visionaries of Silence: The Reformist Sufi Order of the Demirdashiya al-Khalwatiya in Cairo* (Cairo: American University in Cairo Press, 2008), chapter 3.

21. See Alexander Knysh, *Islam in Historical Perspective* (Upper Saddle River, NJ: Pearson, 2011), 293; for concrete examples from Central Asia, see Elyor Karimov, *Kubraviiskii vakf XVII–XIX vv.: Pis'mennye istochniki po istorii sufiiskogo bratstva Kubraviia v Srednei Azii* (Tashkent: Fan, 2008), and Aidar Abuov, *Mirovozzrenie Khodzha Akhmeta Iasavi* (Astana: Mezhdunarodnyi tsentr kul'tur i religii, 2009).

22. Hodgson, *Venture of Islam*, 2: 218.

23. Knysh, *Islam in Historical Perspective*, 293; for concrete examples see the studies mentioned in the previous notes, and Knysh, *Islamic Mysticism*, chapters 8 and 9; cf. Green, *Sufism*, chapters 2, 3, and 4.

24. As an example one can mention the Moroccan *wali* and man of letters al-Hasan b. Mas'ud al-Yusi (d. 1102/1691), one of the protagonists of Clifford Geertz's influential *Islam Observed* (New Haven, CT: Yale University Press, 1968); for a criticism and correction of Geertz's reconstruction of al-Yusi's portrait, see Henry Munson, *Religion and Power in Morocco* (New Haven, CT: Yale University Press, 1993), 16–34; cf. Abdelfattah Killito, "al-Yusi," *EI2*, online edition: http://referenceworks.brillonline .com.

25. Vincent Cornell, *Realm of the Saint* (Austin: University of Texas Press, 1998), 273; see also Munson's *Religion and Power*, passim, and the studies of Maghribi societies by Dale Eickelman.

26. For a classical study see E. E. Evans-Pritchard, *The Sanusi of Cyrenaica* (Oxford: Clarendon Press, 1954); cf. Knysh, *Islam in Historical Perspective*, 293; for more details see Knysh, *Islamic Mysticism*, chapters 8 and 9; see also the studies mentioned in the previous notes.

27. Hodgson, *Venture of Islam*, 2: 217.

28. Ibid., 218.

29. Ibid.

30. Alexander Knysh, *Ibn 'Arabi in the Later Islamic Tradition: The Making of a Polemical Image in Medieval Islam* (Albany: State University of New York Press, 1999), 49–58.

31. Hodgson, *Venture of Islam*, 3: 159.

32. Knysh, *Islam in Historical Perspective*, 235–56, and Knysh, *Islamic Mysticism*, 173; see also ibid., chapters 8 and 9.

33. Hodgson's occasional references to a progressive decline and inflation of the originally pure and lofty Sufi values and practices may have been influenced by his colleagues' pessimistic perception of Sufism's overall evolution, as articulated by Arthur Arberry in his *Sufism: An Account of the Mystics of Islam* (London: Allen and Unwin, 1950), 119–20 and 124; cf. Weismann, "Sufism," 265; Hodgson, too, speaks of "vulgarization" and "corruption and localism" in later Sufism. However, he seems to have been of the opinion that it was the price its leaders had to pay for maintaining its "catholic" appeal; see Hodgson, *Venture of Islam*, 2: 218 and 455–62.

34. Hodgson, *Venture of Islam*, 3: 159.

35. Ibid., 2: 220.

36. Knysh, *Islamic Mysticism*, 1–2; Geoffroy, *Introduction*, 126–27 and 198–99; Bruinessen and Howell, *Sufism*, 6–7, and Ridgeon, *Sufis*, 11–17 passim; Wiesmann, "Sufism," 261–66; Martin van Bruinessen, "Sufism, 'Popular' Islam, and the Encounter with Modernity," in *Islam and Modernity*, ed. Muhammad Khalid Masud, Armando Salvatore, and Martin van Bruinessen (Edinburgh: Edinburgh University Press,

2009), 125–57; Sirriyeh, *Sufis and Anti-Sufis*; and Jong and Radtke, *Islamic Mysticism Contested*, passim.

37. Cf., Hodgson, *Venture of Islam*, 3: 159, and Geoffroy, *Introduction*, 198–99.

38. For a general introduction to the thought of Muslim reformers and modernizers, see Ibrahim Abu-Rabi', *Intellectual Origins of Islamic Resurgence in the Modern Arab World* (Albany: State University of New York Press, 1996); Charles Kurzman, *Modernist Islam, 1840–1940: A Sourcebook* (Oxford: Oxford University Press, 2002); Roxanne Eubin and Muhammad Qasim Zaman, eds., *Princeton Readings in Islamist Thought* (Princeton, NJ: Princeton University Press, 2009); see also Masud, Salvatore, and Bruinessen, *Islam and Modernity*; for an illuminating recent study of Turkey's version of modernism with special reference to the role of the printing press, see Brett Wilson, *Translating the Qur'an in an Age of Nationalism* (Oxford: Oxford University Press, 2014).

39. Laffan, *Makings of Indonesian Islam*, 177.

40. Ibid., 181.

41. On the founder of this popular Sufi brotherhood, see Rex O'Fahey, *Enigmatic Saint: Ahmad Ibn Idris and the Idrisi Tradition* (Evanston, IL: Northwestern University Press, 1990).

42. Laffan, *Makings of Indonesian Islam*, 184.

43. Bazzaz, "Heresy and Politics, 71–72.

44. Oliver Roy, *Globalized Islam: The Search for a New Ummah* (New York: Columbia University Press, 2004), 259–61; for examples from South Arabia in the early twentieth century, see Knysh, "Cult of Saints and Religious Reformism in Early Twentieth-Century Hadramawt."

45. For a concise overview, see Knysh, *Islam in Historical Perspective*, 253–56 and 398–455; Knysh "Cult of Saints and Religious Reformism in Early Twentieth-Century Hadramawt," passim; for a more detailed analysis, see Katherine Ewing, *Arguing Sainthood: Modernity, Psychoanalysis, and Islam* (Durham, NC: Duke University Press, 1997); Armando Salvatore, *Islam and the Political Discourse of Modernity* (Reading, UK: Ithaca Press, 1998); Itzchak Weismann, "Modernity from Within: Islamic Fundamentalism and Sufism," in *Sufis and Salafis in the Contemporary Age*, ed. Lloyd Ridgeon (London: Bloomsbury, 2015), 9–32; Weismann, "Sufism," passim.

46. Ibn al-Jawzi (d. 597/1201), *Talbis Iblis*, ed. Muhammad 'Abd al-Qadir al-Fadili (Beirut: al-Maktaba al-misriyya, 1999); and Alexander Knysh, "A Hanbali Criticism of Sufism (Ibn al-Jawzi's *Talbis Iblis*)," in *The Literary Heritage of Eastern Peoples*, part 1 (Moscow: Nauka, 1989), 170–75 (in Russian).

47. See chapter 4 of Knysh, *Ibn 'Arabi*, and the literature cited therein; cf. Muhammad Memon, *Ibn Taimiya's Struggle against Popular Religion* (The Hague: Mouton, 1976).

48. Knysh, *Ibn 'Arabi*, chapter 7.

49. Ibid., chapter 6 and 9, and Sirriyeh, *Sufis and Anti-Sufis*, chapter 1.

50. See, e.g., Steve Bruce, *God Is Dead: Secularization in the West* (Malden, MA: Blackwell, 2002).

51. Bruce Lincoln, *Holy Terrors: Thinking about Religion after September 11*, 2nd ed. (Chicago: University of Chicago Press, 2006), 54–61.

52. Describing their condition as "underdevelopment" is an expression of this au-

thor's personal stance, which may or may not be objective; this said, the author is ready to acknowledge that his native country, Russia, was also in the state of underdevelopment (albeit admittedly less profound) vis-à-vis western Europe in the nineteenth century as it is now. This, alas, is a historical and geopolitical fact, not an ideological postulate.

53. For an eloquent testimony to the dramatic mutual misunderstanding between Westernizing Muslim reformers of Egypt and the country's Muslim masses, see Adams, *Islam and Modernism*, 97–99.

54. For a recent typical attempt, see Mark Gould, "Toward a Theory of 'Islamist Movements,'" *Sociology of Islam* 2 (2014): 21–59.

55. See, e.g., Sirriyeh, *Sufis and Anti-Sufis*; Jong and Radtke, *Islamic Mysticism Contested*; Bruinessen and Howell, *Sufism and the "Modern"*; Ridgeon, *Sufis*.

56. For a discussion of the terminological nuances involved in the naming of movements launched in the name and on behalf of Islam in recent times, see Knysh, *Islam in Historical Perspective*, 424–26; Weismann, "Modernity from Within"; Ernst, *Shambhala Guide*, 211–15; Scott Kugle, *Sufis and Saints' Bodies: Mysticism, Corporeality, and Sacred Power in Islam* (Chapel Hill: University of North Carolina Press, 2007), 262–64; Geoffroy, *Introduction*, 136–49; and Roy, *Globalized Islam*, passim.

57. Roxanne Euben, *Enemy in the Mirror: Islamic Fundamentalism and the Limits of Modern Rationalism* (Princeton, NJ: Princeton University Press, 1999), 17–18; this definition is quoted approvingly by Itzchak Weismann, who seems to have missed its self-referential nature, see "Modernity from Within," 12.

58. Roy, *Globalized Islam*, passim; Roy, *Holy Ignorance: When Religion and Culture Part Ways*, trans. Ros Schwartz (New York: Columbia University Press, 2010), 80–81.

59. See, e.g., Roy, *Globalized Islam*, 68–69.

60. See, e.g., Salih b. Fawzan al-Fawzan, *'Aqidat al-tawhid* (Riyadh: Dar al-'asima, 1999), 12, 18, 90–91, 217, 224–30, 233, passim.

61. See, e.g., Gilles Kepel and Jean-Pierre Milelli, eds., *Al Qaeda in Its Own Words* (Cambridge, MA: Belknap Press of Harvard University Press, 2008); for the original Wahhabi position vis-à-vis the Shi'i community, see Michael Crawford, *Ibn 'Abd al-Wahhab* (London: Oneworld, 2014), 86–88.

62. As detailed in Knysh, *Islam in Historical Perspective*, chapters 23–25; Euben and Zaman, *Princeton Readings*, passim; Carré, *Mysticism and Politics*, passim; cf. Schulze, *Islamischer Internationalismus*, 356–85.

63. For a detailed and relatively balanced account of these dramatic events, see Enver Kisriev, *Islam i vlast' v Dagestane* (Moscow: OGI, 2004), chapter 7, especially 211–13; Kisriev, *Islam v Dagestane* (Moscow: Logos, 2007), 94–95; Michael Kemper, "Jihadism: The Discourse of the Caucasus Emirate," in *Islamic Authority and the Russian Language*, ed. Alfrid Bustanov and Michael Kemper (Amsterdam: Pegasus Oost-Europese Studies, 2012), 265–93; Vladimir Bobrovnikov, "Izobretenie islamskikh traditsii v dagestanskom kolkhoze," in *Dagestan i musul'manskii Vostok*, ed. Alikber Alikberov and Vladimir Bobrovnikov (Moscow: Izdatel'skii dom Marjani, 2010), 139–40; for a Daghestani perspective, see Kaflan Khanbabayev, "Sufiiskie sheikhi i ikh posledovateli v sovremennom Dagestane," in Alikberov and Bobrovnikov, *Dagestan*, 176; for a Chechen perspective, which is rather different from the Russian official one

as well as from that of the majority of Daghestanis, see Vakhit Akaev, *Sufiiskaia kul'tura na Severnom Kavkaze: Teoreticheskie i prakticheskie aspekty*, 2nd ed. (Grozny: Knizhnoe izdatel'stvo, 2011), 164–66 and 176–79; for the Russian "terrorism-prevention expert" Igor Dobaev of Rostov-on-the-Don and for his coauthors, this event represents another instance of the geopolitical meddling in the area of "the United States and its satellites"; Igor Dobaev et al., *Radikalizatsiia islama v Rossiiskoi Federatsii* (Moscow: TsSRIiP YuFU, 2013), 64–66, 75–76, 81–84, 236–37, and 293.

64. For such Salafi "boot camps" in the Northern Caucasus, see Kisriev, *Islam*, 163 and 209; Igor Dobaev and Vera Nemchina, *Novyi terrorizm v mire i na iuge Rossii* (Rostov-on-the-Don: RostIzdat, 2005), 166–67; some details concerning recruitment and mobilization of militant *jama'at*s in the region are discussed in Sergei Suschii, *Severnyi Kavkaz: Realii, problemy, perspektivy pervoi treti XXI veka* (Moscow: LENAND, 2013), 225–28 and chapter 6; Dobaev et al., *Radikalizatsiia*, 171–73; cf. Vakhit Akaev, *Sufizm i vakhkhabizm na Severnom Kavkaze* (Moscow: Institut etnologii i antropologii RAN, 1999), 12, 16–17.

65. Akhmet Yarlykapov, "Kredo vakhkhabita," *Vestnik Evrazii* 3, no. 10 (2000): 114–37.

66. For examples of the usage of this term, see Kisriev, *Islam*, 133, 139, and 208; Akaev, *Sufiiskaia kul'tura*, 169; Suschii, *Severnyi Kavkaz*, 225 and 227; Dobaev and Nemchina, *Novyi terrorizm*, 171.

67. See, e.g., Igor Dobaev, *Islamskii radikalizm: Genezis, evoliutsiia, praktika* (Rostov-Don: SKNTs V Sh, 2003), 334–35.

68. For this important notion of the Salafi worldview, see Roel Meijer, "Introduction," in *Global Salafism: Islam's New Religious Movement*, ed. Roel Meijer (London: Hurst, 2009), 5 and 13; see also ibid., "Glossary," ix.

69. Vladimir Bobrovnikov and Akhmet Yarlykapov, "Vakhkhabity Severnogo Kavkaza," in *Islam na territorii byvshei Rossiiskoi imperii*, fasc. 2, ed. Stanislav Prozorov (Moscow: Nauka, 1999), 22; one should point out that in the early 1990s, writings containing Salafi-Wahhabi creedal statements were published in great numbers by private presses in Moscow and the Muslim republics of the former Soviet Union and were readily available to the reading public. In the late 1990s these publications were denounced as "extremist literature" and officially banished from circulation in the public domain; Dobaev, *Islamskii radikalizm*, 150–60; Sergei Sedel'nikov, "Savelofiia," http://gazeta.ru/print/2004/04/20/oa_118491.shtml; Ali Kaiaev, "Podlezhat unichtozheniiu," http://www.kavkazcenter.com.russ/article.php?od+21654; Geraldine Fagan, "Russia: Increasing Crackdown on Muslim 'Extremist' Books," Forum 18 News Service, September 14, 2004; Akaev, *Sufiiskaia kul'tura*, 170–71.

70. A Russian translation of his *Kitab al-tawhid*, published in Makhachkala in 1997 as *Kniga yedinobozhiia* (i.e., "The Book of [Divine] Oneness"), gained a wide circulation in Daghestan in the subsequent decade; see, e.g., Akaev, *Sufizm*, 10 and 23 note 18.

71. On these Saudi scholars, see Nabil Mouline, *Les clercs de l'islam: Autorité religieuse et pouvoir politique en Arabie Saoudite, XVIIIᵉ–XXIᵉ siècle* (Paris: Presses Universitaires de France, 2011), 312–24, and Meijer, *Global Salafism*, "Index."

72. Akaev, *Sufiiskaia kul'tura*, 171; according to Akhmet Yarlykapov, in the 1990s "the religious market" of Daghestan and Chechnya was overflowing with "well written

and elegantly produced Wahhabi production," see Yarlykapov, *Islam u stepnykh nogaitsev* (Moscow: Institut etnografii i antropologii, 2008), 214.

73. See, e.g., al-Fawzan, *'Aqidat al-tawhid*, 21–32 and 220–39; cf. Kisriev, *Islam*, 105–10.

74. This article of the creed is directed against Muslims who promise to sacrifice an animal at the tomb of a Sufi *shaykh* or a prophet should their request or wish be granted; cf. Schulze, *Islamischer Internationalismus*, 390–91.

75. That is, the Ka'ba in the sanctuary of Mecca.

76. Cf. al-Fawzan, *'Aqidat al-tawhid*, 171–78.

77. Cf. ibid., 62–64 and 141–48.

78. Cf. ibid., 141–48 and 161.

79. Cf. ibid., 121–28; cf. Schulze, *Islamischer Internationalismus*, 391–92.

80. The "battlefield notes" follow closely the articles of a standard Salafi-Wahhabi creed penned by a major Saudi religious authority, Salih b. Fawzan b. 'Abdallah al-Fawzan (b. 1938); his Salafi-Wahhabi writings had been translated into Russian and circulated in Daghestan in the early 1990s by the Santlada publishing house to be banned in 1998; for an English translation of one of Salih b. Fawzan al-Fawzan's condemnations of "polytheism" (*shirk*), see http://www.greenlanemasjid.org/Uploads/Resources/Publications/4-Foundations-of-Shirk.pdf; for a similar list of the beliefs and practices that many Salafis consider to be a conspiracy to undermine the authentic Islam of the pious ancestors, see Schulze, *Islamischer Internationalismus*, 436.

81. Whether or not they are indeed part of Sufism is a matter of the observer's perspective and definition of Sufism, as shown in chapter 2 of this book.

82. This point is a restatement, in Russian, of the one made by the aforementioned Salih b. Fawzan al-Fawzan in his creed; see *'Aqidat al-tawhid*, 231–33; the same applies to every point in the "battlefield notes" that follows; for the *mawlid* and debates around its public performances, see H. Fuchs, Frederick de Jong, and Jan Knappert, "Mawlid or Mawlud," *EI2*, online edition: http://referenceworks.brillonline.com; cf. Schulze, *Islamischer Internationalismus*, 392.

83. The use of photographs of Sufi *shaykh*s by their followers (*murid*s) in some Sufi communities is discussed below.

84. Cf. al-Fawzan, *'Aqidat al-tawhid*, 236–37.

85. For the roots of these points in the original teaching of Muhammad b. 'Abd al-Wahhab, see Mouline, *Les clercs*, 85–89, and Crawford, *Ibn 'Abd al-Wahhab*, 83–86; these anti-Sufi points mirror closely the anti-Sufi discourses of the Daghestani Salafi leader Bagauddin (Baha' al-Din) Magomed (Muhammad) Kebedov (b. 1945), which he repeatedly enunciated in his public speeches and on the pages on the Daghestani press in the 1990s (before the anti-Wahhabi crackdown of 1998–99); see Kisriev, *Islam*, 140–42.

86. Or "the saved sect" (*al-firqa al-najiya*); to avoid the value-laden term "sect," which is routinely used to render this Arabic phrase into English, we have used the word "host."

87. For a parallel with al-Fawzan's Wahhabi creed, see al-Fawzan, *'Aqidat al-tawhid*, 12.

88. For some local definitions of *jama'at* (*dzhamaat* in Russian) in Daghestan, see Kisriev, *Islam*, chapters 5 and 6.

89. The Russian spelling of this Arabic term is *tarikat*; i.e., "Sufi brotherhood" or "order."

90. For parallels with the Salafi-Wahhabi creed of Salih b. Fawzan al-Fawzan, see his *'Aqidat al-tawhid*, 12, 18, 90, 117, 129–33, 141–49, 232–33, etc.

91. For a comprehensive study of the doctrine of "enjoining the good and prohibiting the evil," see Michael Cook, *Commanding Right and Forbidding Wrong in Islamic Thought* (Cambridge: Cambridge University Press, 2000).

92. See, e.g., Muhammad b. 'Abd al-Wahhab, *Kitab al-tawhid* (Cairo: Dar al-ma'arif, 1974); Muhammad b. 'Abd al-Wahhab, *Sharh masa'il al-jahiliyya li-shaykh al-islam Muhammad b. 'Abd al-Wahhab* (with a commentary by Salih b. Fawzan al-Fawzan), 2 vols. (Riyadh: Dar al-'asima, 2001), and al-Fawzan, *'Aqidat al-tawhid*; for Western accounts, see Crawford, *Ibn 'Abd al-Wahhab*, 24, 31, and 83–86, and Meijer, *Global Salafism*, passim.

93. For examples from Morocco, see Henry Munson, *Religion and Power in Morocco* (New Haven, CT: Yale University Press, 1993), 14–18, 78–79, 84–87, 153–54, and 163; for popular attitudes toward Sufism and brotherhoods in Morocco today, see Mohammed El Ayadi, Hasan Rachik, and Mohamed Tazy, *L'islam au quotidien* (Casablanca: Editions la Croisee des Chemins, 2013), 75–81, 111–18.

94. For Salafi-Wahhabi definitions of *bid'a*, see al-Fawzan, *'Aqidat al-tawhid*, 214–16; the author argues that there is no such thing as "good innovation" (*bid'a hasana*); all innovations are equally pernicious and should be avoided at any cost; ibid., 217–19; cf. Crawford, *Ibn 'Abd al-Wahhab*, 27, 81, 83, and 97, and Meijer, *Global Salafism*, "Index" under "*bid'a/bida'*"; cf. Schulze, *Islamischer Internationalismus*, Dritter Teil, passim.

95. As should have become evident by now, the "battlefield notes" follow closely the Salafi-Wahhabi doctrine as articulated, among others by Salih b. Fawzan al-Fawzan in his *'Aqidat al-tawhid*.

96. This statement is absent from Salih b. Fawzan al-Fawzan's *'Aqidat al-tawhid*, but it is a staple of Wahhabi polemical literature generally; see e.g., Crawford, *Ibn 'Abd al-Wahhab*, 84–85.

97. Knysh, *Ibn 'Arabi*, chapter 4; for refutations of Ibn (al-)'Arabi's teachings by a foremost Saudi scholar, Muhammad Nasir al-Din al-Albani (d. 1999), see Stéphane Lacroix, "Between Revolution and Apoliticism: Nasir al-Din al-Albani and His Impact on the Shaping of Contemporary Salafism," in Meijer, *Global Salafism*, 69; the fact that Ibn (al-)'Arabi is known at least to some Muslims in the Northern Caucasus is attested in Said-Afandi al-Chirkavi, *Majmu'at al-fawa'id: Sokrovischnitsa blagodatnykh znanii*, trans. from the Avar language into Russian (Makhachkala: Nurul irshad, 2010), 133–34, 142–43, and 366.

98. On him see Knysh, *Islamic Mysticism*, 72–82.

99. Knysh, *Ibn 'Arabi*, chapter 4.

100. See, e.g., Birgit Krawietz and Georges Tamer, eds., *Islamic Theology, Philosophy, and Law: Debating Ibn Taymiyya and Ibn Qayyim al-Jawziyya* (Berlin: Walter de Gruyter, 2013), passim.

101. As shown in chapter 2 of this book.

102. For the criticism of this practice in the original Salafi-Wahhabi creed, see al-Fawzan, *'Aqidat al-tawhid*, 231–34; for the wide popularity of *mawlid*s among the

Avars of Daghestan (and the Daghestanis generally), see Vladimir Bobrovnikov, *Voyage au pays des avars* (Paris: Éditions cartouche, 2011), 101–6; see also Yarlykapov, *Islam*, 216, and Kisriev, *Islam*, 111.

103. Called *'urs* in Arabic, this is a celebration of the saint's demise and posthumous marriage with his divine beloved; see, e.g., John Renard, *Friends of God: Islamic Images of Piety, Commitment, and Servanthood* (Berkeley: University of California Press, 2008) 210–11 and 313 note 47.

104. Yarlykapov, *Islam*, 216; Akaev, *Sufiiskaia kul'tura*, 168–70; and Kisriev, *Islam*, 111, 139–42, 148 passim; cf. Crawford, *Ibn 'Abd al-Wahhab*, 83.

105. For the view of permissibility (or otherwise) of photographs and their various uses, see al-Chirkavi, *Majmu'at al-fawa'id*, 64–72.

106. For details see al-Chirkavi, *Majmu'at al-fawa'id*, 317–72; cf. Kisriev, *Islam*, 102; for various connotations of this term and the practices associated with it within the Naqshbandiyya brotherhood outside the Caucasus, see Itzchak Weismann, *The Naqshbandiyya: Orthodoxy and Activism in a Worldwide Sufi Tradition* (London: Routledge, 2007), "Index" under "*rabita*."

107. Michael Kemper, "Khalidiyya Networks in Daghestan and the Question of Jihad," *Die Welt des Islams* 42, no. 1 (2002): 56; cf. al-Chirkavi, *Majmu'at al-fawa'id*, 71.

108. Today, *rabita* can be practiced virtually via the Internet; for a recent transformation of the concept of *rabita* in some contemporary Sufi-based communities of Turkey, see Ilshat Saetov, "'Dzhamatizatsiia' tarikatov v respublikanskoi Turtsii," in *Sufizm i musul'manskaia dukhovnaia traditsiia*, ed. Alexander Knysh et al. (St. Petersburg: Peterburgskoe vostokovedenie, 2015), 247; for a lengthy explanation of *rabita* by the foremost Sufi *shaykh* of Daghestan, Said-Afandi of Chirkey (discussed below), see al-Chirkavi, *Majmu'at al-fawa'id*, 317–72, and Michael Kemper, "The Discourse of Said-Afandi, Daghestan's Foremost Sufi Master," in Bustanov and Kemper, *Islamic Authority*, 191–93.

109. Before his assassination, this Sufi master presided over a Sufi *tariqat* that combines both Naqshbandi and Shadhili teachings; see, e.g., Khanbabayev, "Sufiiskie sheikhi," 165; Kisriev, *Islam*, 97–100 and 103–4; Kisriev, *Islam v Dagestane*, 72–73; a detailed discussion of Said-Afandi follows.

110. Kemper, "The Discourse," 210.

111. As attested by Said-Afandi himself, who claims to have experienced such a conversion; see ibid., 179–80; the three terms for the Sufi community mentioned here are often used interchangeably in the Northern Caucasus.

112. See, e.g., Kisriev, *Islam*, 116–20 and 127–28.

113. *Tarikatizm* and its followers *tarikatisty* (i.e., members of a Sufi *tariqa*) are derogatory terms applied by the Daghestani Salafis respectively to Sufism and its adherents; see Kisriev, *Islam*, chapters 4 and 5.

114. Dobaev et al., *Radikalizatsiia islama*, 233–34.

115. As stated, e.g., in the Saudi creed by Salih b. Fawzan al-Fawzan, *'Aqidat al-tawhid*, 121–23; this Saudi author, however, does not attribute such claims exclusively to Sufis.

116. Valerii Tishkov, *Obschestvo v vooruzhennom konflikte* (Moscow: Nauka, 2001), 340; for a 1989 newspaper publication in the Chechen language that contains

similar anti-Sufi accusations, see Akaev, *Sufiiskaia kul'tura*, 168, and Khanbabayev, "Sufiiskie sheikhi," 176.

117. E.g., praying in front of the body of the newly deceased, the distribution of alms (*sadaqa*) during funerals, performing *dhikr* in public, etc.; see Bobrovnikov, "Izobretenie," 139; Bobrovnikov, *Voyage*, 112–14; Kisriev, *Islam*, 145–49.

118. Kisriev, *Islam*, pp. 117–20, and Marat Shterin and Akhmet Yarlykapov, "Reconsidering Radicalisation and Terrorism: The New Muslims Movement in Kabardino-Balkaria and Its Path to Violence," *Religion, State, and Society* 39, no. 2–3 (2011): 311.

119. On him see al-Chirkavi, *Majmu'at al-fawa'id*, 253–54; Shterin and Yarlykapov, "Reconsidering,"311; Akaev, *Sufiiskaia kul'tura*, 155–56, 159, 164–65, and 173; Bobrovnikov and others also call him "Magomedov"; see Bobrovnikov, "Izobretenie," 140; cf. Khanbabayev, "Sufiiskie sheikhi," 176, and Kisriev, *Islam*, 139.

120. Dmitri Makarov, *Ofitsial'nyi i neofitsial'nyi islam v Dagestane* (Moscow: Tsentr strategicheskikh i politicheskikh issledovanii, 2000), 15; Akaev, *Sufiiskaia kul'tura*, 168; Alexander Knysh, "Islam and Arabic as the Rhetoric of Insurgency: The Case of the Caucasus Emirate," *Studies in Conflict and Terrorism* 35 (2012): 324–25; for a brief summary of the Sufi-Salafi tensions within the Avar ethnic community of Daghestan, see Bobrovnikov, *Voyage*, 107–15.

121. Kisriev, *Islam*, 141–42, and Kisriev, *Islam v Dagestane*, 88–89.

122. Kisriev, *Islam*, 141–42, and Kisriev, *Islam v Dagestane*, 89.

123. Kisriev, *Islam*, 103, 119, 147–49 passim.

124. This process culminated in the legislative decree "On the prohibition of Wahhabism and any other extremist activities on the territory of the Republic of Daghestan"; it was voted into law by the Daghestani Parliament on September 16, 1999; for details, see Kisriev, *Islam*, 152–54, and Dobaev et al., *Radikalizatsiia*, 236.

125. See, e.g., al-Chirkavi, *Majmu'at al-fawa'id*, 120–218; Kisriev, *Islam*, chapter 4 and 5; Kemper, "The Discourse," 175, 195, 215–17; Galina Yemelianova, "Sufism and Politics in the Northern Caucasus," *Nationalities Papers* 29, no. 4 (2001): 661–88; Dobaev, *Islamskii radikalizm*, 150–380, and Anna Zelkina, "The 'Wahhabis' of the Northern Caucasus vis-à-vis State and Society: The Case of Daghestan," in *The Caspian Region*, vol. 2, *The Caucasus*, ed. Moshe Gammer (London: Routledge, 2004), 146–78; Alexander Knysh "A Clear and Present Danger: Wahhabism as a Rhetorical Foil," *Die Welt des Islams* 44, no. 1 (2004): 3–26; cf. Akaev, *Sufiiskaia kul'tura*, 155–73, which stresses the differences between Daghestan and Chechnya in how their respective populations have coped with the "Salafi-Wahhabi challenge."

126. As documented in Kisriev, *Islam*, chapters 4 and 5; see, especially, 103–4 and 146–48.

127. Between 1991 and 2007 Chechnya's political leaders of secular inclinations, most of whom resided abroad, referred to Chechnya as "Republic of Ichkeria"; it was officially abolished by the Islamist Chechen emir Dokku Umarov (1964–2013) on October 31, 2007; see Knysh, "Islam and Arabic," 316.

128. For details see Akaev, *Sufizm*, 12–16.

129. For a list of the major Daghestani *shaykhs/ustadh*s today (eighteen in all) see Kisriev, *Islam v Dagestane*, 75–79.

130. On him see Kisriev, *Islam*, 103–4; Bobrovnikov, *Voyage*, 98 and 114; Akaev,

Sufiiskaia kul'tura, 128–29; Khanbabayev, "Sufiiskie sheikhi," 166–67 and 173–74; and a special study of this influential Sufi master by Michael Kemper, "The Discourse," 167–217; a short hagiographical account of Said-Afandi's life can be found in al-Chirkavi, *Majmu'at al-fawa'id*, 5–10.

131. See, e.g., al-Chirkavi, *Majmu'at al-fawa'id*, 120–218, and 427–28.

132. This has been a standard accusation leveled at the founder of the Hanbali legal-theological school, Ibn Hanbal (d. 241/855), by its opponents; the Wahhabis, being, at least nominally, members of this school, are seen by their opponents as being "guilty by association."

133. Kemper, "The Discourse," 206–7 and 216; al-Chirkavi, *Majmu'at al-fawa'id*, 217–18; Kisriev, *Islam*, 103, and Kisriev, *Islam v Dagestane*, 75.

134. Al-Chirkavi, *Majmu'at al-fawa'id*, 338–40.

135. Kemper, "The Discourse," 195 and 216–17; Kemper's translation of the Russian phrase *griaznaia smuta* neglects the meaning implied by the Arabic original; the Russian word *smuta* is the approximate equivalent of the Arabic *fitna* ("trial"; temptation")—a term laden with a considerable historical and theological baggage; see, e.g., Louis Gardet, "Fitna," *EI2*, online edition: http://referenceworks.brillonline .com.

136. Although some journalists have credited Said-Afandi with 300,000 followers (in a republic with the overall population of 2.91 million!), a more realistic figure, according to Kaflan Khanbabayev, is 10,000; what is important, argues Khanbabayev, is that many of Said-Afandi's *murid*s occupy positions of authority in the religious institutions and administration of the Republic of Daghestan; see Khanbabaev, "Sufiiskie sheikhi," 167, 173–74; Kisriev, *Islam v Dagestane*, 75.

137. Al-Chirkavi, *Majmu'at al-fawa'id*, 121–26; Khanbabaev, "Sufiiskie sheikhi," 216 and 217; Kisriev, *Islam*, 124 note 39; cf. Akaev, *Sufiiskaia kul'tura*, 128–29; the alleged British sponsorship of the Wahhabi movement has been grist to the mill of its critics almost since its very inception; see, e.g., *Confessions of a British Spy and British Enmity against Islam*, online edition: http://www.hakikatkitabevi.com/down load/english/14-ConfessionsOf%20ABritishSpy.pdf; its Russian version is widely available in Russian bookstores under the title *Priznaniia angliiskogo shpiona* ("Confessions of a British Spy"), 11th ed. (Istanbul: Waqf Ikhlas Publications, 2002); such accusations have been reproduced, in a subtler manner, by some academics, e.g., Hamid Algar in his *Wahhabism: A Critical Essay* (New York: Oneonta, 2002), 37–46.

138. Al-Chirkavi, *Majmu'at al-fawa'id*, 202–4, 220, 279–81, 288–89, 302, 338, and 340; Kisriev, *Islam*, 101–2; Kemper, "The Discourse," 194–206; cf. Khanbabaev, "Sufiiskie sheikhi," 165–67 and 177.

139. In his sermons and lectures Said-Afandi often stated that Sufi masters (*ustadh*s or *shaykh*s) "hold the keys to Paradise"; see, e.g., al-Chirkavi, *Majmu'at al-fawa'id*, 254–55.

140. All the more so, because Said-Afandi continually supports his statements by quotations from classical Sufi literature and individual Sufi teachers of old; see, e.g., al-Chirkavi, *Majmu'at al-fawa'id*, 248–72.

141. Al-Fawzan, *'Aqidat al-tawhid*, 21–32; Kisriev, *Islam*, 135–36 and 141; Khanbabayev, "Sufiiskie sheikhi," 176, and Bobrovnikov and Yarlykapov, "Vakhkhabity Severnogo Kavkaza."

142. Crawford, *Ibn ʿAbd al-Wahhab*, 12; Crawford, however, acknowledges that this rhetorical commitment to equality was offset by Ibn ʿAbd al-Wahhab's deep-seated suspicion of the populace's propensity to lapse into polytheism and sedition, which, in his view, requires the presence of a vigilant vanguard of "true monotheists" in the community to police and enforce the borders of "orthodoxy"; ibid., 105.

143. See, e.g., Jong and Radtke, *Islamic Mysticism Contested*, passim; Ridgeon, *Sufis and Salafis*, passim; for "Russian Islam," see Knysh, "Islam and Arabic," 324–25, and Knysh "A Clear and Present Danger"; Alfrid Bustanov, "Rafail' Valishin's 'Anti-Wahhabi' Sufi Traditionalism in Rural Western Siberia," in Bustanov and Kemper, *Islamic Authority*, 219–63.

144. For concise summaries, see Bobrovnikov, *Voyage*, 17–25, and Kemper, "Jihadism," 265–71; for details see Suschii, *Severnyi Kavkaz*, 91–104; Moshe Gammer and David Wasserstein, eds., *Daghestan and the World of Islam* (Helsinki: Finnish Academy of Science and Letters, 2006); Moshe Gammer, ed., *Ethno-Nationalism, Islam, and the State in the Caucasus: Post-Soviet Disorder* (London: Routledge, 2008); Enver Kisriev, "Societal Conflict-Generating Factors in Daghestan," in Gammer, *The Caspian Region*, vol. 2, *The Caucasus*, 107–21; Kisriev, *Islam*.

145. Kisriev, *Islam*, 45–46; the recent statistical data (which should be treated with caution) is given in Suschii, *Severnyi Kavkaz*, 16–37; Moshe Gammer, "Between Mecca and Moscow: Islam, Politics, and Political Islam in Chechnya and Daghestan," *Middle Eastern Studies* 41, no. 6 (2005): 834; Bobrovnikov, "Rural Muslims' Nationalism"; for a critical assessment of the "creation or invention of nations" by the Soviet authorities, see Adrienne Edgar's review article published in *Kritika: Explorations in Russian and Eurasian History* 3, no. 1 (2002): 182–90.

146. On the Kumyk-Avar and Kumyk-Dargin conflicts over the land, see Suschii, *Severnyi Kavkaz*, 98.

147. Suschii, *Severnyi Kavkaz*, 201–2; the recent de-Russification of the Daghestani cities is discussed in ibid., 57–70.

148. Bobrovnikov, "Izobretenie," 144; Anatolii Genko, "Arabskii iazyk i kavkazovedenie," *Trudy vtoroi sessii assotsiatsii arabistov 19–23 oktiabria 1937 g.*, vol. 36 (Moscow: Trudy Instituta vostokovedenia, 1941), 81–110; for the current linguistic situation in the region that is characterized by the continuing hegemony of the Russian language, see Suschii, *Severnyi Kavkaz*, 195–202.

149. Kisriev, *Islam v Dagestane*, passim; Kisriev, *Islam*, passim; Bobrovnikov, *Voyage*, 27–35, and Bobrovnikov, "Izobretenie," passim; Suschii, *Severnyi Kavkaz*, 218–24; Gammer and Wasserstein, *Daghestan*, passim; and Kemper, "The Discourse," 167–75; one should mention a relatively small Shiʿi community, centered on the coastal city of Derbent (Darband) on the Caspian Sea; Vladimir Bobrovnikov, *Musul'mane Severnogo Kavkaza: obychai, pravo, nasilie* (Moscow: Vostochnaia literatura, 2002), 82–84, and Alikber Alikberov, *Epokha klassicheskogo islama na Kavkaze* (Moscow: Vostochnaia literatura, 2003), 700 and 197–232.

150. For a concise summary, see Bobrovnikov, *Voyage*, 45–64; for further details and literature on the subject, see Alexander Knysh, "Shamil," and "al-Kabk (the Caucasus), section 3," *EI2*, online edition: http://referenceworks.brillonline.com.

151. Zh. Zh. Gakaev, V. A. Tishkov, and A. D. Yandarov, *Kul'tura Chechni i sovremennye problemy* (Moscow: Nauka, 2002), 354; Moshe Gammer, "The Road Not Taken: Daghestan and Chechen Independence," *Central Asian Survey* 24, no. 2 (2005):

97, and Gammer, *The Lone Wolf and the Bear: Three Centuries of Chechen Defiance of Russian State* (London: Hurst, 2006), 200–220. The late Moshe Gammer authored a comprehensive study of Shamil's insurgency and the Russo-Caucasus War titled *Muslim Resistance to the Tsar* (London: Frank Cass, 1994).

152. Kisriev, *Islam*, 36–39; Kemper, "Khalidiyya Networks," 49–51, and Timirlan Aitberov, Yusup Dadaev et al., *Vosstaniia dagestantsev i chechentsev v posleshamilevskuiu epokhu i imamat 1877 goda* (Makhachkala: Dagestanskii gosudarstvennyi universitet, 2001); Makhach Musaev, *Musul'manskoe dukhovenstvo 60–70-kh godov XIX veka i vosstanie 1877 goda v Dagestane* (Makhachkala: Dagestanskii nauchnyi tsentr, 2005), 102–44.

153. Kisriev, *Islam v Dagestane*, 32–38; Gammer, *Lone Wolf*, chapter 10; Bobrovnikov, *Voyage*, 65; Bobrovnikov, *Musul'mane*, 85–90; Bobrovnikov, "Izobretenie," passim; and Knysh, "al-Kabk."

154. The literature on the subject is too vast to be listed here. For a standard account see Terry Martin and Ronald Suny, eds., *A State of Nations: Empire and Nation-Making in the Age of Lenin and Stalin* (Oxford: Oxford University Press, 2001); for Russian dissident perspectives on the idea of a classless and internationalist "Soviet man," see Mikhail Heller, *Cogs in the Soviet Wheel: The Formation of Soviet Man* (London: Collins Harvill, 1988), and Aleksandr Zinovyev, *Homo Sovieticus*, trans. Charles Janson (London: Paladin, 1986).

155. For the disintegration of Soviet state structures and the spread of lawlessness and chaos in post-Soviet Daghestan and Chechnya, see Bobrovnikov, *Musul'mane*, 90–92, and Knysh, "Kabk"; for the Northern Caucasus as a whole, see Suschii, *Severnyi Kavkaz*, passim, and Georgi Derluguian, *Bourdieu's Admirer in the Caucasus* (Chicago: University of Chicago Press, 2005), chapter 7.

156. For an illuminating, albeit highly impressionistic and subjective summary, see Derluguian, *Bourdieu's Secret Admirer*.

157. For Chechen assessments of these dramatic events, see Akaev, *Sufiiskaia kul'tura*, 143–50 and 174–80, and Gakayev, Tishkov, and Yandarov, *Kul'tura Chechni*, 311–62; the views of the irredentist separatist opposition, currently based outside Russia, are represented by the website Kavkaz Center: http://www.kavkazcenter.com. Various versions of official Russian views of the conflict can be found in the books of Igor Dobaev and his collaborators quoted previously; cf. Suschii, *Severnyi Kavkaz*, 225–26.

158. For a doomsday prediction (one of many) regarding the impending demise of the Russian state as a result of the Russo-Chechen conflict, see Anatole Lieven's *Chechnya: Tombstone of Russian Power* (New Haven, CT: Yale University Press, 1998); luckily for the Caucasus and Russia, the author has since moved to "greener pastures," especially America and Pakistan, to exercise his power of foresight.

159. Roy, *Globalized Islam*, 44, 172, 179.

160. For details that are impossible to verify independently because of the aid's informal and secretive nature, see Gordon Hahn, *Russia's Islamic Threat* (New Haven, CT: Yale University Press, 2007), 36–38; Dobaev and Nemchina, *Novyi terrorizm*, 173–202.

161. Yarlykapov, *Islam*, 215; see also Robert Bruce Ware, "A Multitude of Evils: Mythology and Political Failure in Chechnya," in *Chechnya: From Past to Future*, ed.

Richard Sakwa (London: Anthem Press, 2005), 81–87; Hahn, *Russia's Islamic Threat*, passim.

162. Rus. "Imarat Kavkaz"; the ideological premises and rhetoric of the Islamic State in the Caucasus is analyzed in Knysh, "Islam and Arabic"; see also Hahn, *Russia's Islamic Threat*, 77–86; the official mouthpiece of the insurgency, as mentioned earlier, is Kavkaz Center, available online in several languages, including English at http://www.kavkazcenter.com. This website is banned in Russia as "extremist."

163. For a strictly negative portrayal of the Salafi-Wahhabi movement in Chechnya by a pro-Sufi Chechen academic, see Akaev, *Sufizm*, 8–16; for a somewhat more objective view that emphasizes close links between the Salafi-Wahhabis of Chechnya and Daghestan, see Kisriev, *Islam*, chapter 6; for a Westerner's perspective, see Hahn, *Russia's Islamic Threat*, chapter 2.

164. Hahn, *Russia's Islamic Threat*; Akaev, *Sufizm*, passim, and Gakayev, Tishkov, and Yandarov, *Kul'tura Chechni*, 330.

165. For a lively eyewitness account by a Western journalist, see Jonathan Littell, *Chechnia: God tretii*, trans. from French by B. Skuratov (Moscow: Ad Marginem Press, 2012), 81–90, and "Kadyrov: Sufizm dolzhen stat' al'ternativoi radikal'nym techeniam v islame," *RIA Novosti*, August 29, 2014, online edition: https://ria.ru/religion /20140829/1021948338.html; "Vsio upiraetsia v religiiu" March 11, 2016; Lenta.ru: https://lenta.ru/articles/2016/05/17/shahidov/.

166. Kisriev, *Islam*, 47; cf. Hahn, *Russia's Islamic Threat*, 100–102.

167. Kisriev, *Islam*, 45–46, and Hahn, *Russia's Islamic Threat*, 97–99.

168. Suschii, *Severnyi Kavkaz*, 91–92.

169. For details see the studies of Vladimir Bobrovnikov that have consistently emphasized a deep and lasting impact of Soviet ideology on all aspects of life of the Daghestani populations; in addition to the references already mentioned in the notes, see Bobrovnikov, " 'Ordinary Wahhabism' versus 'Ordinary Sufism': Filming Islam for Post-Soviet Young People," *Religion, State, Society* 39, no. 2–3 (2011): 281–301.

170. As eloquently demonstrated by Vladimir Bobrovnikov in his "Izobretenie"; cf. Kisriev, *Islam v Dagestane*, 40–43, and Hahn, *Russia's Islamic Threat*, 99–100.

171. For a Russian view of the situation that emphasizes Russia's critical mediatory and supervisory role in the region, see Suschii, *Severnyi Kavkaz*, 91–104.

172. Vladimir Bobrovnikov, "Rural Muslims' Nationalism in the Post-Soviet Caucasus: The Case of Daghestan"; Gammer, *The Caspian Region*, vol. 2, *The Caucasus*, 179–97; Kisriev, "Societal Conflict-Generating Factors"; Suschii, *Severnyi Kavkaz*, 97–104; Hahn, *Russia's Islamic Threat*, 100–102.

173. See Knysh, "Kabk."

174. Vladimir Bobrovnikov, "Arkheologiia stroitel'stva islamskikh traditsii v dagestanskom kolkhoze," *Ab Imperio* 3 (2004): 584–86; for a more recent restatement by the author of basically the same argument, see Bobrovnikov, "Izobretenie," passim.

175. Bobrovnikov, "Izobretenie," 134–38, and Kisriev, *Islam*, 50–51; for a similar situation in the western Caucasus (Circassia), especially in the Republic of Kabardino-Balkaria, see Shtetin and Yarlykapov, "Reconsidering," 312.

176. Kisriev, *Islam*, 132.

177. Ibid., 136–46.

178. For a recent study of this influential Daghestani Sufi scholar, see Shamil Shikhaliev, "Agiografichesko-biograficheskie sochineniia dagestanskikh sheikhov Shu'ayba al-Bagini i Khasana al-Kakhi," in Knysh et al., *Sufizm i musul'manskaia dukhovnaia traditsiia*, 70–91.

179. Kisriev, *Islam*, 100.

180. Bobrovnikov, *Voyage*, 99–101, and Bobrovnikov, "Izobretenie," 139; cf. al-Chirkavi, *Majmu'at al-fawa'id*, 279–82, 298, 380–89.

181. See, e.g., Hahn, *Russia's Islamic Threat*, 24, 26, 100, and 104.

182. A local name for the Sufi community headed by a revered master (*ustadh*; *shaykh*); for explanations, connotations, and synonyms, see al-Chirkavi, *Majmu'at al-fawa'id*, 274–362.

183. E.g., Said-Afandi used to insist that one is incapable of taming one's lower soul (*nafs*) and wining God's pleasure without the guidance of a qualified Sufi *ustadh*; see Kisriev, *Islam*, 101–2.

184. Galina Khizrieva, "'Islam,' 'musul'mane,' 'gosudarstvo' v rossiiskom islamovedenii," *Ab Imperio* 3 (2004): 413–38; Kisriev, *Islam v Dagestane*, 72–79; Bobrovnikov, "Arkheologiia," 583–84; cf. Kemper, "Khalidiyya Networks," 58–59 and 66–68.

185. See, e.g., Gammer, *Muslim Resistance*, 39–46; Gammer, *Lone Wolf*, passim; Anna Zelkina, *In Quest for God and Freedom: Sufi Responses to the Russian Advance in the Northern Caucasus* (London: Hurst, 2000), 47–51 and 100–134.

186. Musaev, *Musul'manskoe dukhovenstvo*, 123–26; Akaev, *Sufiiskaia kul'tura*, 105–6; note that Enver Kisriev in his *Islam*, 28–32 and 94–98, downplays the role of Sufism in these anti-Russian uprisings.

187. His full name in Arabic documents was al-Hajji Uzun Khayr al-Salti; a personal communication by the Daghestani scholar Shamil Shikhaliyev, June 2, 2016; in line with his pacifistic stance, Said-Afandi called in doubt Uzun Hajji's Sufi credentials; see al-Chirkavi, *Majmu'at al-fawa'id*, 290–91.

188. Kisriev, *Islam*, 38–39, 49–52, and 66–71; Akaev, *Sufizm*, 5; Akaev, *Sufiiskaia kul'tura*, 110–11; Marie Bennigsen-Broxup, "The Last Ghazawat," in *The North Caucasus Barrier: The Russian Advance towards the Muslim World*, ed. Marie Bennigsen-Broxup (New York: St. Martin's Press, 1994), 112–45, and Marie Bennigsen-Broxup, "After the Putsch, 1991," in ibid., 219–40; cf. Knysh, "al-Kabk."

189. Vakhit Akaev, *Sheikh Kunta-Khadzhi. Zhizn' i uchenie* (Grozny: Ichkeriia, 1994), 31–35, and Akaev, *Sufiiskaia kul'tura*, 105.

190. Akaev, *Sheikh*, 30–32; Akaev, *Sufizm*, 5; Akaev, *Sufiiskaia kul'tura*, 84–85.

191. On the movement launched by the followers of Kunta Hajji, see Akaev, *Sheikh*, passim; Akaev, *Sufiiskaia kul'tura*, 86–108, and Dzhul'ietta Meskhidze, "Kunta-khadzhzhi," in *Islam na territorii byvshei Rossiiskoi imperii. Entsiklodedicheskii slovar'*, ed. Stanislav Prozorov (Moscow: Nauka, 1998), fasc. 1, 61–62.

192. The Soviet authorities allowed the exiled peoples, including Chechens and Ingush, to return to their homeland only in 1957; see Akaev, *Sufizm*, 6–7, and Akaev, *Sufiiskaia kul'tura*, 119–20.

193. Knysh, "Sufism as an Explanatory Paradigm: The Issue of the Motivations of Sufi Resistance Movements in Western and Russian Scholarship," *Die Welt des Islams* 42, no. 2 (2002): 139–73.

194. Knut Vikør, *Sufi and Scholar on the Desert Edge: Muhammad b. 'Ali al-Sanusi*

and His Brotherhood (London: Hurst, 1995); Vikør, "Sufism and Colonialism," in Ridgeon, *Cambridge Companion*, 217–22; Jean Louis Triaud, *La légende noire de Sanûsiyya*, 2 vols. (Paris: Éditions de la maison des sciences d'homme, 1995), and Bernard Simiti, *Le Dar-El-Kouti: Empire oubanguien de Senoussi (1890–1911)* (Paris: Harmattan, 2013).

195. See Knysh, *Islamic Mysticism*, 249–64.

196. E.g., al-Chirkavi makes mention of Shamwil (Shamil) only in connection with his military campaign against the Russians (*ghazawat*), never as a Sufi teacher or authority in his own right; see *Majmu'at al-fawa'id*, 286–89.

197. In the Northern Caucasus, this word is often used as a synonym of jihad.

198. Gammer, *Muslim Resistance*, 40, 49–50, 69, 71, and 238–39; Kemper, "Khalidiyya Networks," 44; Zelkina, *In Quest*, 105–20 and 141–44; Akaev, *Sufizm*, 4–5; Akaev, *Sufiiskaia kul'tura*, 72–73; and Kisriev, *Islam*, 30; cf. al-Chirkavi, *Majmu'at al-fawa'id*, 92.

199. As shown, unwittingly, by Zelkina herself, who has failed to draw appropriate conclusions from the disjuncture between the Naqshbandi moral-ethical precepts and the involvement of some of its members in military-political activities; see Zelkina, *In Quest*, 108–20 and 212–14.

200. As expounded in Jamal al-Din al-Ghazighumuqi's treatise *al-Adab al-mardiya*; see its Russian translation in *Adabul'-marziia (Pravila dostodolzhnykh prilichii)*, *Sbornik svedenii o kavkazskikh gortsakh*, vol. 2 (1869), 1–21 (separate pagination).

201. As claimed by Zelkina throughout her entire book; see also Gammer, *Muslim Resistance*, 238–40.

202. Knysh, "Sufism as an Explanatory Paradigm," 148–54 and 160–61, and Knysh, "Historiography of Sufi Studies," 214–17.

203. Knysh, *Islam in Historical Perspective*, 253–54; Naveed Hussain, "Are Sufis Essentially Non-Violent?," *Express Tribune*, January 18, 2011: http://tribune.com.pk/story/105628/are-sufis-essentially-non-violent/; Mark Woodward, Muhammad Sani Umar, Inayah Rohmaniyah, and Mariani Yahya, "Salafi Violence and Sufi Tolerance? Rethinking Conventional Wisdom," *Perspectives on Terrorism* 7, no. 6 (2013): http://www.terrorismanalysts.com/pt/index.php/pot/article/view/311/html; Muhammad Ashraf Padikkal, "Sufism in India Today," *Huffington Post*, August 9, 2016, online: http://www.huffingtonpost.in/entry/sufism-in-india-today_b_11384348; Ashraf Thachar, "Religious Sermons to Resist the Islamic State Threat to Humanity," *Café Dessensus Everyday*, February 20, 2016, online: https://cafedissensusblog.com/2016/02/20/religious-sermons-to-resist-the-islamic-state-threat-to-humanity/.

204. For an official exposition of this doctrine, see M. S. Junusov, M. M. Skibitsky, and I. P. Tsameryan, *The Theory and Practice of Proletarian Internationalism* (Moscow: Progress Publishers, 1976); for a critical Western view articulated in the aftermath of the collapse of the Soviet Union, see Daniel Orlovsky, ed., *Beyond Soviet Studies* (Washington, DC: WWICS and Johns Hopkins University Press, 1995), part 2: "Nationalism and National Identities."

205. For an insider discussion of the vicissitudes of the Sufi *tariqats* of the Northern Caucasus and their relations with one another, see al-Chirkavi, *Majmu'at al-fawa'id*, 218–389.

206. The author learned this firsthand in the 1970s as a student of the Arabic language and literature at the Oriental Department (*vostochnyi fakultet*) of the Leningrad State University where approximately one-fourth of his classmates came from Daghestan or Chechnya-Ingushetia.

207. The Arabic for "room"; examples of informal and often semiclandestine transmission of religious learning are given in al-Chirkavi, *Majmu'at al-fawa'id*, 8, 104–5, 230–31, 304–7, and 342–43.

208. Kisriev, *Islam*, 69–71, and al-Chirkavi, *Majmu'at al-fawa'id*, passim.

209. See, e.g., Gilles Kepel, *Jihad: The Trail of Political Islam* (London: I. B. Tauris, 2002), part 1, "Expansion."

210. Kisriev, *Islam*, 114–18.

211. Ibid., 69.

212. Ibid., 70, 76–78, and 88; cf. Dobaev et al., *Radikalizatsiia*, 170–71, 233–35, and 274; for the western Caucasus, which witnessed the rise of a similar "new Muslim" movement, see Shterin and Yarlykapov, "Reconsidering," passim.

213. Dobaev et al., *Radikalizatsiia*, 273–76; Shterin and Yarlykapov, "Reconsidering," 314–15; for details see also the studies of Kisriev, Akaev, Khanbabaev, Dobaev, and Bobrovnikov mentioned in the notes to this chapter; they represent a spectrum of views regarding the "new Muslims" ranging from a strict and unequivocal condemnation (Dobaev and Akaev) to a more balanced attempt to understand the epistemological and sociopolitical roots of the phenomenon in question (Kisriev, Bobrovnikov, Shterin, and Yarlykapov).

214. Derluguian, *Bourdieu's Secret Admirer*, chapter 7.

215. Kisriev, *Islam*, chapter 2.

216. Akaev, *Sufizm*, 11–12; Dobaev, *Radikalizatsiia*, 238 and 292; Dobaev and Nemchina, *Novyi terrorizm*, 173–202; Shterin and Yarlykapov, "Reconsidering," 311 and 322 note 8.

217. For the global outreach of Salafi-Wahhabi creeds over the past few decades, see Meijer, *Global Salafism*, passim.

218. Kisriev, *Islam*, 87–91.

219. Ibid., and chapter 4; see also Bobrovnikov and Yarlykapov, "Vakhkhabity," 19–20; cf. Meijer, "Introduction," in Meijer, *Global Salafism*, 13–15.

220. Ibid., 13.

221. Al-Chirkavi, *Majmu'at al-fawa'id*, 427–28; Akaev, *Sufizm*, 8–16, and Kisriev, *Islam*, chapter 6; Yarlykapov, *Islam*, 214–17; cf. Dobaev and Nemchina, *Novyi terrorizm*, 173–202.

222. For Daghestan see Kisriev, *Islam*, chapter 2, and Kisriev, *Islam v Dagestane*, 102–3 and 118; for Chechnya see Akaev, *Sufiiskaia kul'tura*, 146–50.

223. Kisriev, *Islam*, chapter 2; over the past decade, the former luster of democracy has faded considerably among the populations of the former Soviet Union for reasons that should not detain us here.

224. Gammer, "Road Not Taken," 97.

225. Akaev, *Sufiiskaia kul'tura*, 147–48; cf. Gammer, "Between Mecca and Moscow," 834; the anti-Russian attitudes of the Chechen leadership can be explained, at least in part, by the trauma of the 1944 exile to Kazakhstan where many of current and former Chechen intellectuals and field commanders (or their parents) were born.

226. As detailed in Akaev, *Sufizm*, 7–8; Akaev, *Sheikh*, 108–10; and Kisriev, *Islam*, chapter 6.

227. For an analysis of various forms of solidarity in Chechnya and Ingushetia, see Ekaterina Sokirianskaia, "Families and Clans in Ingushetia and Chechnya," *Central Asian Survey* 24, no. 4 (2005): 453–67; cf. Kimitaka Matsuzato and Magomed-Rasul Ibragimov, "Islamic Politics at the Sub-Regional Level in Dagestan," *Europe-Asia Studies* 57, no. 5 (2005): 753–79.

228. Listed in Kisriev, *Islam v Dagestane*, 79; only one *shaykh* on the list, Ma-gomedkhabib (Muhammad Habib) Ramazanov (b. 1947) belongs to a local branch of the Qadiriyya brotherhood founded by Shaykh Kunta Hajji Kishiev mentioned above; for details see Akaev, *Sheikh*, passim.

229. As Enver Kisriev has shown in his *Islam v Dagestane*, 102–3, the officialdom of the Republic of Daghestan, including its chief *mufti* Sa'id Muhammad (Saidma-gomed) Abubakarov (assassinated on August 21, 1998), were loyal followers of Said-Afandi.

230. Yemelianova, "Sufism and Politics," 669.

231. For Said-Afandi's partisan position on the issue of the legitimacy of the two branches of the *tariqat*, see al-Chirkavi, *Majmu'at al-fawa'id*, 286–95 and 310–11.

232. Kemper, "Khalidiyya Networks," 50–51; cf. Musaev, *Musul'manskoe duk-hovenstvo*, 119 and 122–27.

233. Musaev, *Musul'manskoe dukhovenstvo*, 117–19; for a dissenting view see Kis-riev, *Islam*, 98.

234. His official name in Russian documents was "Saifulla-kadi Bashlarov" (1853–1920); for details of his biography, see al-Chirkavi, *Majmu'at al-fawa'id*, 310–11; Kis-riev, *Islam*, 97–99.

235. Ibid., and Kemper, "Khalidiyya Networks," 52–68.

236. As evidenced by Said-Afandi's own admonitions addressed to his *murids*, see al-Chirkavi, *Majmu'at al-fawa'id*, 91–94 and 210–18.

237. Ibid., 310–11.

238. Ibid.; see also Kemper, "Khalidiyya Networks," 65–66, and Kisriev, *Islam*, 97.

239. For details of their human resources policy, see Kisriev, *Islam v Dagestane*, 102–3; Kisriev, *Islam*, 103; Matsuzato and Ibragimov, "Islamic Politics," passim.

240. Kisriev, *Islam*, 150–54 and chapter 6; Knysh, "A Clear and Present Danger," passim; and Darion Rhodes, "Salafist-Takfiri Jihadism: The Ideology of the Caucasus Emirate," March 9, 2014; online: https://www.ict.org.il/Article/132/Salafist-Takfiri%20Jihadism%20the%20Ideology%20of%20the%20Caucasus%20Emirate; for a pro-Sufi view of these developments by a Chechen academic, see Akaev, *Sufiiskaia kul'tura*, 156–66; for an official Russian viewpoint, see Dobaev, *Islamskii radikalizm*, 342–45; cf. Roy, *Globalized Islam*, 71.

241. Gakayev, Tishkov, and Yandarov, *Kul'tura Chechni*, 327–28; Zelkina, "The 'Wahhabis,'" 159–64; and Roy, *Globalized Islam*, 286.

242. Some observers hold them responsible for the retaliatory bombings of several apartment complexes in Moscow and south Russia in the fall of 1999; see, e.g., Gakayev, Tishkov, and Yandarov, *Kul'tura Chechni*, 352; Akaev, *Sufiiskaia kul'tura*, 166; Ware, "Mythology," 90–96; activities of the anti-Russian Islamic resistance in the Caucasus have been documented in Stephen Blank, ed., *Russia's Homegrown Insur-*

gency: Jihad in the North Caucasus (Carlisle, PA: Strategic Studies Institute, 2012), and Hahn, *Russia's Islamic Threat*, chapters 2 and 4.

243. It should be pointed out that some Chechen field commanders chose to side with the Russian federal troops against the Chechen "Wahhabis"; see Gakayev, Tishkov, and Yandarov, *Kul'tura Chechni*, 330.

244. See, e.g., "V Karachaevo-Cherkesii zaderzhali vakhkhabita s bombami i literaturoi," Lenta.RU, http:///lenta.ru/voijna/2003/08boevik/.

245. Knysh, "Islam and Arabic," passim.

246. Akaev, *Sheikh Kunta Khadzhi*, 108–10.

247. See Knysh, "al-Kabk."

248. See, e.g., Elise Giuliano, "Islamic Identity and Political Mobilization in Russia: Chechnya and Dagestan Compared," *Nationalism and Ethnic Politics* 11 (2005): 210–12.

249. Roy, *Globalized Islam*, 258–62.

250. For details see Knysh, "A Clear and Present Danger," and Tom Parfitt, "The Battle for the Soul of Chechnya," *The Guardian*, November 22, 2007: http://www.theguardian.com/world/2007/nov/22/chechnya.tomparfitt. For the Salafi doctrinal position in regard to the cult saints outside the Northern Caucasus, see Knysh, "Cult of Saints and Religious Reformism in Early Twentieth-Century Hadramawt"; Laurent Bonnefoy, *Salafism in Yemen: Transnationalism and Religious Identity* (New York: Columbia University Press, 2011), 45 and 47.

251. Akaev, "Religious-Political Conflict in the Chechen Republic of Ichkeria," *Central Asia and the Caucasus*, online edition: http://www.ca-c.org/dataeng/05.akaev.shtml; cf. Akaev, *Sufizm*, 10–11; for a picture of the shrine see Knysh et al., *Sufizm*.

252. Akaev, *Sufizm*, 13, and Giuliano, "Islamic Identity," 210–11.

253. Yemelianova, "Sufism and Politics," 681.

254. One hundred fighters, according to some reports; see, e.g., Vakhitov, *Sufizm*, 12–13; cf. Kisriev, *Islam*, 178, who estimates the casualties to have been between fifty and a hundred fighters.

255. See, e.g., https://lenta.ru/articles/2016/05/17/shahidov/ and http://ria.ru/religion/20140829/1021948338.html.

256. Roy, *Globalized Islam*, 69.

257. Littell, *Chechnia*, 10 and 81–90; for a Russian semiofficial perspective, see Aleksei Malashenko, *Kak vybirali v Chechne* (Moscow: Carnegie Endowment for International Peace, 2006); for a Chechen view, see Akaev, *Sufiiskaia kul'tura*, 181–95, and https://lenta.ru/articles/2016/05/17/shahidov/; for a sampling of Western views, see http://www.thedailybeast.com/articles/2015/06/04/moscow-is-turning-on-chechnya-s-ruthless-kadyrov.html (American); and http://www.bbc.com/russian/russia/2012/09/120918_kadyrov_chechnya (British).

258. See, e.g., an anonymous feature published on the website of *Radio Free Europe/Radio Liberty*: "Kadyrov's 'Chechen Sufism' Accommodates Christmas Trees, 'Holy Water' " http://www.rferl.org/content/kadyrovs_chechen_sufism_accomodates_christmas_trees_holy_water/24453480.html; Parfitt, "Battle for the Soul of Chechnya"; for the opinion of Ramzan Kadyrov himself, see http://ria.ru/religion/2014 0829/1021948338.html.

259. Parfitt, "Battle for the Soul of Chechnya," and C. J. Chivers, "A Whirling Sufi Revival with Unclear Implications," *New York Times*, May 24, 2005: http://www.nytimes.com/2006/05/24/world/europe/24grozny.html?_r=0; Andrei Smirnov, "Kadyrov Turns to Zikrism to Legitimize His Rule," *Jamestown Foundation, North Caucasus Analysis* 8, no. 11 (2007): http://www.jamestown.org/single/?no_cache =1&tx_ttnews%5Btt_news%5D=3487#.VfSMWFVVhBc.

260. Knysh, "al-Kabk"; for a contemporary Chechen perspective on Kunta Hajji, see the works of Vakhit Akaev cited in the notes to this chapter.

261. Knysh, "al-Kabk," and Akaev, *Sheikh*, 59–68.

262. Akaev, *Sheikh*, 79–98.

263. Gammer, "Islam," 839; cf. Zelkina, "The 'Wahhabis'" 159; for Said-Afandi's own detailed denunciation of the Salafi–Wahhabi teachings and practices, see al-Chirkavi, *Majmu'at al-fawa'id*, 185–219 passim.

264. See, e.g., Paul Dresch, *A History of Modern Yemen* (Cambridge: Cambridge University Press, 2000), chapters 5 and 6.

265. Alexander Knysh, "The *'tariqa'* on a Landcruiser: The Resurgence of Sufism in Yemen," *Middle East Journal* 55, no. 3 (2001): 406.

266. For historical overviews of religious and social life in Hadramawt and South Arabia, see Alexander Knysh, "A Tale of Two Poets: Sufism in Yemen during the Ottoman Epoch," in *Le soufisme à l'epoque ottomane/Sufism in the Ottoman Era*, ed. Rachida Chih and Catherine Mayeur-Jaouen (Cairo: IFAO, 2010), 337–67; Knysh, "The Cult of Saints in Hadramawt: An Overview," *New Arabian Studies* 1 (1993): 137–52; Knysh, "The Cult of Saints and Religious Reformism in Early Twentieth-Century Hadramawt," *New Arabian Studies* 4 (1997), 139–67.

267. As it happens, the Yemeni Socialists had a point; see a quotation from Michael Gilsenan's book cited below; Laurent Bonnefoy also considers the sayyids of Hadramawt, collectively, to have been "a mainstay of British colonial administration until 1967," *Salafism*, 83; cf. Dresch, *A History*, 36–41 and 122–23; Linda Boxberger, *On the Edge of Empire: Hadhramawt, Emigration, and the Indian Ocean, 1880s–1930s* (Albany: State University of New York Press, 2002), 233–40 and 244.

268. Literally, "lords" or "masters"; the Arabic singular is *sayyid*; for a pioneering study of this family-based stratum of South Arabian society, see Robert Serjeant, *The Sayyids of Hadramawt* (Cambridge: Cambridge University Press, 1957); Serjeant, *Prose and Poetry from Hadramawt* (London: Taylor's Foreign Press, 1951), passim; for further references, see Knysh, "Cult of Saints and Religious Reformism in Early Twentieth-Century Hadramawt," 149–52, and Boxberger, *On the Edge*, 19–24, 198–207, and 233–40.

269. For a poignant firsthand account of the privileged role of the *sada* in Hadrami society under British rule (and the resentment it elicited among ordinary Muslims of the country), see Michael Gilsenan, *Recognizing Islam: Religion and Society in the Modern Middle East* (London: I. B. Tauris, 2000), 9–11; cf. Dresch, *A History*, 36–37 and 39–41, and Boxberger, *On the Edge*, passim.

270. See, e.g., Boxberger, *On the Edge*, 19–24 and 159–80; Anne Bang, *Sufis and Scholars of the Sea: Family Networks in East Africa, 1860–1925* (London: Routledge-Curzon, 2003); Bang, *Islamic Sufi Networks in the Western Indian Ocean (c. 1880–*

1940): Ripples of Reform (Leiden: E. J. Brill, 2014), 29–32 passim; see also Eng Seng Ho, *The Graves of Tarim: Genealogy and Mobility across the Indian Ocean* (Berkeley: University of California Press, 2006), passim.

271. Gilsenan, *Recognizing*, 11.

272. Dresch, *A History*, 108–18.

273. Ibid., 120–23.

274. To use the term introduced by Abdalla Bujra in his *The Politics of Stratification: A Study of Political Change in a South Arabian Town* (Oxford: Clarendon Press, 1971).

275. Abu Bakr al-ʿAdani al-Mashhur, *Al-Khuruj min al-daʾira al-hamraʾ* (Aden: Ribat al-tarbiyya al-islamiyya, 2002), passim; cf. Dresch, *A History*, 122.

276. See, e.g., Alexander Knysh, "The *Sada* in History: A Critical Essay on Hadrami Historiography," *Journal of the Royal Asiatic Society* 9, no. 2 (1999): 215–22; Knysh, "The Cult of Saints and Religious Reformism in Hadhramaut," in *Hadhrami Traders, Scholars, and Statesmen in the Indian Ocean, 1750s–1960s*, ed. Ulrike Freitag and William Clarence-Smith (Leiden: E. J. Brill, 1997), 199–216; Knysh, "The *tariqa*.'"

277. Dresch, *A History*, 39–41.

278. Ibid., 39–41 and 50; Boxberger, *On the Edge*, 53–62; and our studies mentioned in note 276; for a recent discussion and further references, see Laffan, *Makings of Indonesian Islam*, chapters 10, 11, and 12.

279. Laffan, *Makings of Indonesian Islam*, 183–89.

280. Ibid., 220; Dresch, *A History*, 39–41.

281. On the role of Muhammad Rashid Rida and his *al-Manar* in the Hadrami diaspora in Indonesia, see Boxberger, *On the Edge*, 53 and 61, and Laffan, *Makings of Indonesian Islam*, 187–89 and 220–22; on Muhammad Rashid Rida himself, see the classical study of Charles Adams, *Islam and Modernism in Egypt* (Oxford: Oxford University Press, 1933), chapters 8 and 9.

282. For details, see Knysh, "Cult of Saints and Religious Reformism in Early Twentieth-Century Hadramawt," 199–216; Natalie Mobini-Kesheh, "Islamic Modernism in Colonial Java," in Freitag and Clarence-Smith, *Hadhrami Traders*, 231–48, and Boxberger, *On the Edge*, 17, 20, 54–55, 58.

283. Citing Q 49:13.

284. Boxberger, *On the Edge*, 53–61.

285. Ibid., 62.

286. Dresch, *A History*, 39.

287. Ibid., 122–23.

288. Knysh, "Cult of Saints and Religious Reformism in Early Twentieth-Century Hadramawt," 150.

289. Boxberger, *On the Edge*, 56–60.

290. On him see Bonnefoy, *Salafism*, 87–88, and Meijer, *Global Salafism*, "Index" under "al-Wadiʿi."

291. Bonnefoy, *Salafism*, 81–84 and 229–35; we do not discuss here the recent developments, especially the activities of the al-Qaʿida in the Arabian Peninsula (AQAP) following the forced resignation from his office of the longtime Yemeni president ʿAli ʿAbdallah Salih in February 2012. The situation in Hadramawt has been one of turmoil and anarchy ever since and would require a special analysis that is now

impossible to undertake because of the continuing hostilities in the country and a lack of accurate information from the region; see, e.g., William McCants, *The ISIS Apocalypse* (New York: St. Martin's Press, 2015), 47–71. For a reaction to these events on the part of the leaders of Hadramawt's Islamic college Dar al-Mustafa, discussed below, see: http://muwasala.org/prophetic-guidance-in-times-of-tribulation/.

292. Boxberger, *On the Edge*, 151–159; the author attended a number of such events in 1986–1989 and 1999.

293. For details see Knysh, "Cult of Saints and Religious Reformism in Early Twentieth-Century Hadramawt" and "The '*tariqa*.'"

294. For a historical overview of these and other Hadrami towns, see Boxberger, *On the Edge*, chapters 3 and 4; the recent developments in Tarim have been documented in Knysh, "The '*tariqa*,'" and Amira Kotb, "La Tarîqa Ba 'Alawiyya et le développement d'un réseau soufi transnational" (master's thesis, Aix-Marseille III, Institut d'Etudes Politiques, Université Paul Sezanne, 2003–4); for insider accounts of the *sada* educational project, see Amin Buxton, *Imams of the Valley* (Western Cape, South Africa: Dar al-Turath al-Islami Publishing House, 2012), and Mustafa al-Badawi, *Sufi Sage of Arabia: Imam 'Abdallah ibn 'Alawi al-Haddad* (Louisville KY: Fons Vitae, 2005); cf. Bonnefoy, *Salafism*, 146–47.

295. Kotb, "La Tarîqa," 73, and Bonnefoy, *Salafism*, 229–35.

296. Franck Mermier, "L'islam politique au Yémen ou la 'Tradition' contre les 'traditions,'" *Monde arabe: Magreb-Machrek* 155 (January–March 1997): 15–16; cf. Kotb, "La Tarîqa," 71–72.

297. 'Abd al-Rahman Muqbil b. Hadi al-Wadi'i, *Gharat al-ashrita 'ala ahl al-jahl wa 'l-safsata*, 2 vols. (Cairo: Dar al-haramayn, 1998), 2: 253.

298. For a historical overview of the *sada* role in establishing, maintaining, and reforming the region's educational system, see Boxberger, *On the Edge*, 159–80.

299. Our observations regarding the educational strategy of the *sada* in Hadramawt are based on our own field notes and conversations with those who had studied under their guidance.

300. Bonnefoy, *Salafism*, 147.

301. See Knysh, "The *Sada* in History"; Knysh, "Cult of Saints and Religious Reformism in Early Twentieth-Century Hadramawt"; cf. Ho, *Graves of Tarim*, passim, and Mobini-Kesheh, "Islamic Modernism in Colonial Java," passim.

302. According to the Wikipedia page of Dar al-Mustafa, the *madrasa* was established in 1993; it was upgraded to the status of a college "with a campus" and dormitory in 1997; see: https://en.wikipedia.org/wiki/Dar_al-Mustafa.

303. *Mustafa*, "the elect one," is one of the honorific epithets of the Prophet.

304. Bonnefoy, *Salafism*, 146–47 note 17.

305. For details see Knysh, "The '*tariqa*,'" 406–8.

306. See, e.g., Muqbil b. Hadi al-Wadi'i, *Gharat al-ashrita*, 2: 249–50.

307. Knysh, "The Cult of Saints in Hadramawt: An Overview," passim.

308. Knysh, "The '*tariqa*,'" passim.

309. The numbers of male students (around 1,500 in 2003–4) given by Kotb in her "La Tarîqa," 38–42, seem to be vastly exaggerated; according to a student who stayed at Dar al-Mustafa in the summer of 2013, the overall population of the compound was around 300, although there were, in his words, "a lot more at the various branches in

Tarim, 'Enat ('Inat), Sey'oun (Saywun), etc." The Dar al-Mustafa's Wikipedia page mentions 270 students in 2007 and 700 students in 2009, see https://en.wikipedia .org/wiki/Dar_al-Mustafa.

310. On him see Knysh, *Islamic Mysticism*, 43–48, and Gavin Picken, *Spiritual Purification in Islam: The Life and Works of al-Muhasibi* (London: Routledge, 2011).

311. On him see Knysh, *Islamic Mysticism*, 121–23.

312. Ibid., 179–86; for a list of authoritative Sufi masters of old cited by the educators of Dar al-Mustafa, see the section "Our Methodology" at: http://muwasala.org /prophetic-guidance-in-times-of-tribulation/; cf. http://tarim.shifa.net.au/wp-content /uploads/2012/10/Dar-al-Mustafa-Curriculum.pdf.

313. On him, see Ismail Alatas, " 'Abdallah b. 'Alawi al-Haddad," *EI3*, online edition: http://referenceworks.brillonline.com/entries/encyclopaedia-of-islam-3; for an image of this Hadrami saint propagated by the leaders of Dar al-Mustafa, see al-Badawi, *Sufi Sage of Arabia*.

314. On Sharaf al-Din Muhammad al-Busiri (d. between 694 and 696/1294 and 1297), see Th. Emil Homerin, "al-Busiri," *EI3*, online edition: http://referenceworks .brillonline.com.

315. This Arabian prophet who is the subject of sura 11 of the Qur'an; for a recent study of the pilgrimage, see Marianus Hundhammer, *Prophetenverehrung im Hadramaut: Die Ziyara nach Qabr Hud aus diachroner und synchroner Perspektive* (Berlin: Schwarz, 2010).

316. See http://tarim.shifa.net.au; for a now slightly out-of-date list of these websites, see Kotb, "La Tarîqa," 130; videos of the annual pilgrimages to the shrine of the prophet Hud performed by Habib 'Umar and his followers are posted on YouTube; see, e.g., https://www.youtube.com/watch?v=Fvr2pHoFfOw and https://www.you tube.com/watch?v=ZZMgRNRtpkQ.

317. In Arabic: *ziyarat qabr nabi Allah Hud*; for a brief account of the rites and social functions of the Hud pilgrimage and the role of the *sada* therein, see Boxberger, *On the Edge*, 156–59 and Hundhammer, *Prophetenverehrung im Hadramaut*; there are numerous brochures in Arabic that detail the stages and rituals of the pilgrimage.

318. As was evident from the Saudi license plates of the cars parked outside the shrine that this author observed firsthand in November 1999.

319. See, e.g., Dresch, *A History*, 122; Gilsenan, *Recognizing Islam*, 10–11; Boxberger, *On the Edge*, 23.

320. Knysh, "The '*tariqa*,'" 409–12, and Bonnefoy, *Salafism*, 236–37.

321. http://www.alhaddad.org/blog/?p=943; the same position is restated on May 1, 2013, at http://muwasala.org/responding-to-critics-of-sufism/.

322. Knysh, "The *sada*," 220, and Ismail Alatas, "(al-)'Alawiyya (in Hadramawt)," *EI3*, online edition: http://referenceworks.brillonline.com; for the Internet presence, see https://en.wikipedia.org/wiki/Ba_%27Alawiyya and https://www.facebook.com /LaVoieBaAlawi/?ref=py_c.

323. http://muwasala.org/responding-to-critics-of-sufism/ and a video interview with Habib 'Umar posted at https://www.youtube.com/watch?v=pDtxSzFS3zg.

324. See Alatas, "(al-)'Alawiyya," and Alatas, " 'Abdallah b. 'Umar ibn Yahya and the Dissemination of the Tariqa 'Alawiyya in the Early Nineteenth Century Indonesian

Archipelago," in *Orders and Itineraries: Buddhist, Islamic, and Christian Networks in Southern Asia, c. 900–1900*, ed. Michael Feener and Ann Blackburn (under review with University of Hawai'i Press); see also Alatas, "'They are the Inheritors of the Prophet': Discourses on the Ahl al-Bayt and Religious Authority among the Ba 'Alawi in Modern Indonesia," in *Shi'ism in Southeast Asia: 'Alid Piety and Sectarian Construction*, ed. Michael Feener and Chiara Formichi (London: Hurst, 2015), 139–64. We express our deep gratitude to Dr. Alatas for sharing with us the drafts of these valuable publications.

325. See, e.g., Bonnefoy, *Salafism*, 149–50.

326. Ibid., 60–61, 230–31; cf. Ho, *Graves of Tarim*, 9.

327. Bonnefoy, *Salafism*, 44–47, 52–53, 152–55 passim.

328. François Burgat and Muhammad Sbitli, "Les Salafis au Yémen ou la modernisation malgré tout," *Chroniques yéménites* 10 (2002): online: http://cy.revues.org/document137.html; for a more recent, and detailed, study of this movement, see Bonnefoy, *Salafism*, 54–61 passim.

329. Bonnefoy, *Salafism*, 144–45 and 275–76.

330. Ibid., 59–60, 237–48 passim.

331. Burgat and Sbitli, "Les Salafis," 50 note 94.

332. For details see Knysh, "The '*tariqa*,'" passim.

333. Ibid., 403, and Bonnefoy, *Salafism*, chapter 6 passim; that the fears of the Yemenis are not unfounded is attested by the aggressive actions of the Saudi leadership toward Yemen over the past several years, including the devastating military campaign against a faction of Yemeni Shi'is (al-Hawthiyya) prosecuted by the Kingdom's military in coalition with a number of allies.

334. They are quoted throughout Shaykh Muqbil's *Gharat al-ashrita*; see also Burgat and Sbitli, "Les Salafis," 8, and Bonnefoy, *Salafism*, 55–56; on these two Saudi scholars, see Stéphane Lacroix, "Between Revolution and Apoliticism: Nasir al-Din al-Albani and His Impact on the Shaping of Contemporary Salafism," in Meijer, *Global Salafism*, 58–80.

335. Bonnefoy, *Salafism*, 52–53, 61–62, 69, 168, and chapter 2 passim.

336. On him see Itzchak Weismann, "Sufi Fundamentalism between India and the Middle East," in Bruinessen and Howell, *Sufism*, 115–28, especially 119–21.

337. According to Bonnefoy, this Saudi scholar of Syrian origin "mixed the teachings of Hasan al-Banna and Sayyid Qutb with Salafi literalism," for which he was expelled from Saudi Arabia to the United Kingdom in 1984; *Salafism*, 67.

338. Burgat and Sbitli, "Les Salafis," 14, and Bonnefoy, *Salafism*, 52–53.

339. Muqbil b. Hadi al-Wadi'i, *Gharat al-ashrita*, 1: 125, 127, 130, 195, 197, 260–61 passim; Burgat and Sbitli, "Les Salafis," 13; Bonnefoy translates this Arabic phrase as "ruined bothers," see *Salafism*, 238.

340. Burgat and Sbitli, "Les Salafis," 18–20; cf. Bonnefoy, *Salafism*, 243–45; concerning Muhammad al-Shawkani of Yemen see Bernard Haykel, *Revival and Reform in Islam: The Legacy of Muhammad al-Shawkani* (Cambridge: Cambridge University Press, 2003).

341. Muqbil b. Hadi al-Wadi'i, *Gharat al-ashrita*, 2: 139 and 294; cf. 1: 121–33.

342. Ibid., 1: 326–30.

343. Ibid., 1: 351–64, and 2: 137–42.

344. Ibid., 1: 197–99.

345. Bonnefoy, *Salafism*, 59.

346. Ibid., 54, 57, 71, 81–82 and 288.

347. Ibid., 44.

348. Muqbil b. Hadi al-Wadiʻi, *Gharat al-ashrita*, 1: 259–264; Bonnefoy, *Salafism*, 88–97 and 105–6 (concerning the "impious Yemeni constitution"). A similar position is advocated by the Daghestani Sufi Said-Afandi, discussed earlier in this chapter; see al-Chirkavi, *Majmuʻat al-fawaʼid*, 88–94.

349. Muqbil b. Hadi al-Wadiʻi, *Gharat al-ashrita*, 1: 42, 84–86; 133, 156–57, and 260; Bonnefoy, *Salafism*, 61–69 and 88–90.

350. Muqbil b. Hadi al-Wadiʻi, *Gharat al-ashrita*, 1: 132, 156–57; 2: 195–97; 249–50, and 253; Bonnefoy, *Salafism*, 229–37.

351. For a detailed explanation of Shaykh Muqbil's positions on various controversial issues, see his *Gharat al-ashrita*, passim.

352. Bonnefoy, *Salafism*, chapter 6.

353. Roy, *Globalized Islam*, chapter 7 and 8 passim, and Roy, *Holy Ignorance*, chapter 4.

354. Bonnefoy, *Salafism*, 224.

355. See, e.g., Muqbil b. Hadi al-Wadiʻi, *Gharat al-ashrita*, 2: 253.

356. Bonnefoy, *Salafism*, chapter 6 passim.

357. Ibid., 24–25, and chapter 7 passim; Shaykh Muqbil's *Gharat al-ashrita* brims with references to Communism and Communist rulers of South Yemen.

358. For a perceptive discussion of the role of the Islah party in Yemeni politics in the early 1990s, see Paul Dresch and Bernard Haykel, "Stereotypes and Political Styles: Islamists and Tribesfolk in Yemen," *IJMES* 27, no. 4 (1995): 405–31.

359. For the changing relationship between GPC and Islah, see ibid., and Bonnefoy, *Salafism*, 24–25.

360. See Knysh, *Islam in Historical Perspective*, chapter 25.

361. Burgat and Sbitli, "Les Salafis," 27–30.

362. Fawaz Gerges, *The Far Enemy: Why Jihad Went Global*, new ed. (Cambridge: Cambridge University Press, 2009), 178–84; William McCants, *The ISIS Apocalypse* (New York: St. Martin's Press, 2015), chapter 3.

363. Bonnefoy, *Salafism*, 233.

364. Muqbil b. Hadi al-Wadiʻi, *Gharat al-ashrita*, 1: 249–56; http://muwasala.org /prophetic-guidance-in-times-of-tribulation/.

365. Bonnefoy, *Salafism*, 262–64.

366. As is evident from his statement issued in the aftermath of the collapse of the central Yemeni government precipitated by the insurgency led by the Zaydi-Huthi (al-Huthiyya or al-Hawthiyya) movement originating in the Saʻda mountains; see http://muwasala.org/prophetic-guidance-in-times-of-tribulation/.

367. Kotb, "La Tarîqa," 76–77.

368. Bonnefoy, *Salafism*, 232.

369. E.g., the Zaydi rulers of Saʻda had destroyed the shrine of the great Sufi scholar and *wali* Ahmad b. ʻAlwan (d. 665/1266) in Yafrus (near Taʻizz); for the Zaydi-Sufi relations in the north of the country, see Muhammad Ali Aziz, *Religion and Mys-*

ticism in Early Islam: Theology and Sufism in Yemen (London: I. B. Tauris, 2011), chapter 8.

370. Kotb, "La Tarîqa," 77–78.

371. Wilferd Madelung, "Zaydi Attitudes to Sufism," in Jong and Radtke, *Islamic Mysticism Contested*, 124–44.

372. Bonnefoy, *Salafism*, 229–37.

373. Ibid., 53, and Michael Cook, *Commanding Good and Forbidding Wrong in Islamic Thought* (Cambridge: Cambridge University Press, 2000), part 2, "The Hanbalites."

374. As detailed in the author's articles cited earlier in this chapter.

375. Bonnefoy, *Salafism*, 232–33.

376. Kotb, "La Tarîqa," 114–15.

377. Bonnefoy, *Salafism*, 262.

378. Kotb, "La Tarîqa," 96; 'Ali al-Jifri (b. 1971) is a Saudi-born scholar of Yemeni ancestry who was instrumental in establishing Dar al-Mustafa in Tarim and in making it part of a transnational educational network stretching from Yemen to Indonesia and all the way to California; see http://www.alhabibali.com/en/biography/, and Bonnefoy, *Salafism*, xii, 146–47 note 17, and 262.

379. As detailed in a Wikipedia entry; see https://en.wikipedia.org/wiki/Habib _Umar_bin_Hafiz; and in 'Ali al-Jifri's online biography: http://www.alhabibali.com /en/biography/.

380. For Habib 'Umar's ecumenical message of peace, love, and reconciliation with the other monotheistic faiths, see his widely advertised speech at the University of Cambridge: http://www.acommonword.com/downloads-and-translations/. For his rejection of terrorism in the name of Islam, see "Issues of Controversy: Interview with Al-Habib Umar bin Hafiz," May 14, 2009, available online at: http://www.alhaddad .org/blog/?p=943; his books are available at Amazon.com: http://www.amazon.co .uk/Books-Al-Habib-Umar-bin-Hafiz/s?ie=UTF8&page=1&rh=n%3A266239%2Cp _27%3AAl-Habib%20Umar%20bin%20Hafiz.

381. Such as, e.g., Abu 'l-Hasan al-Ma'ribi (b. 1958), an Egyptian-born Salafi preacher who had studied under Shaykh Muqbil and later established a Dar al-Hadith near the town of Ma'rib in North Yemen, see Bonnefoy, *Salafism*, xiii, and "Index" under "al-Ma'ribi."

382. To quote Bruno Latour's advice in his *Reassembling the Social: An Introduction to Actor Network Theory* (Oxford: Oxford University Press, 2005), 11–12.

383. Roy, *Holy Ignorance*, chapter 6, and the literature cited therein; Roy also speaks here of "deterritorialization of the local," "de-ethnicization of religion," and "deculturation," however, as we have pointed out earlier, these concepts are problematic, especially when applied to Yemen where religiously motivated actors or actors using Islamic rhetoric are so keen to prove their local authenticity. It seems that Roy's concepts are more germane to the experiences of Muslims living in Western societies, although this, too, is debatable, because many seekers of authenticity come to Yemen from the West.

384. Here Roy's concepts of "deterritorialization," "de-ethnicization," or "deculturation" seem to be more relevant than in the case of Yemen, but, then again, the Dagh-

estanis and Chechens are a minority in the predominantly non-Muslim Russian state, which seems to confirm the suggestion we have made in the previous note.

385. As documented in Bonnefoy, *Salafism*, passim; Meijer, *Global Salafism*, passim, and Bernard Haykel, Thomas Hegghammer, and Stéphane Lacroix, eds., *Saudi Arabia in Transition: Insights on Social, Political, Economic and Religious Change* (Cambridge: Cambridge University Press, 2015), part 3.

386. For a brief journalistic account of the AQAP and its offspring, Ansar al-Shari'a, see McCants, *The ISIS*, 47–71; the ideological agenda of AQAP is represented by the online journal (currently suppressed) titled *Sada al-Malahim* (*Echoes of Epic Battles*).

387. As discussed in Knysh, "A Clear and Present Danger"; cf. Littell, *Chechnia*, 91–125.

388. Burgat and Sbitli, "Les Salafis," 37–38.

389. Tishkov, *Obschestvo*, 339–49; cf. al-Chirkavi, *Majmu'at al-fawa'id*, 427–28.

390. Muhammad Al-Zekri, "The Religious Encounter between Sufis and Salafis: The Issue of Identity" (PhD thesis, University of Exeter, England, 2004).

391. Gammer, "Islam," 836.

392. The Kunta Hajji branch of the Qadiriyya in this case.

393. Published by the Dilya Publishing House in St. Petersburg (2004).

394. "Spisok bogoslovskikh i inykh trudov, izdannykh v RF i rekomendovannykh Sovetom Ulemov k prochteniiu i izucheniiu"; online: http://www.interfax-religion.ru /islam/?act=documents&div=101.

Conclusion

1. Patricia Crone, *Pre-Industrial Societies: Anatomy of the Pre-Modern World* (Oxford: Oneworld, 2003), 136.

2. In the 1950s–1970s, many Western academics adhered to the so-called modernization theory that predicted a gradual demise of religion as a motivating and ideological factor across the globe; for a classical application of this theory to Muslim societies, see Manfred Halpern, *The Politics of Social Change in the Middle East and North Africa* (Princeton, NJ: Princeton University Press, 1963), and Daniel Lerner, *The Passing of Traditional Society: Modernizing the Middle East* (Glencoe, IL: Collier-Macmillan, 1964); for a criticism of the modernization theory and its proponents, see Armando Salvatore, *Islam and the Political Discourse of Modernity* (Reading, UK: Ithaca Press, 1997), 125–29.

3. Alexander Knysh, *Islamic Mysticism: A Short History*, 2nd ed. (Leiden, E. J. Brill, 2010), 1–2.

'Abbas, Ihsan, ed. *Shi'r al-khawarij*. Beirut: Dar al-thaqafa, 1974.

Abu Rabi', Ibrahim. *Intellectual Origins of Islamic Resurgence in the Modern Arab World*. Albany: State University of New York Press, 1996.

Abul Quasem, Muhammad, trans. *The Jewels of the Qur'an*. London: Kegan Paul International, 1983.

Abuov, Aidar. *Mirovozzrenie Khodzha Ahmeta Iasavi*. Astana: Mezhdunarodnyi tsentr kul'tur i religii, 2009.

Adams, Charles. *Islam and Modernism in Egypt*. Oxford: Oxford University Press, 1933.

Adamson, Peter, ed. *In the Age of Averroes: Arabic Philosophy in the Sixth/Twelfth Century*. London; Turin: Warburg Institute; Nino Agarno Editore, 2011.

———. *Philosophy in the Islamic World*. Oxford: Oxford University Press, 2016.

Addas, Claude. *Quest for the Red Sulphur: The Life of Ibn 'Arabi*. Translated by Peter Kingsley. Cambridge: Islamic Texts Society, 1993.

Ahmed, Shahab. *What Is Islam? The Importance of Being Islamic*. Princeton, NJ: Princeton University Press, 2016.

Aitberov, Timirlan, Yusup Dadaev, et al. *Vosstaniia dagestantsev i chechntsev v posle-shamilevskuiu epokhu i imamat 1877 goda*. Makhachkala: Dagestanskii gosudarstvennyi universitet, 2001.

Akaev, Vakhit. *Sheikh Kunta-Khadzhi: Zhizn' i uchenie*. Grozny: Ichkeriia, 1994.

———. *Sufiiskaia kul'tura na Severnom Kavkaze: Teoreticheskie i prakticheskie aspekty*. 2nd ed. Grozny: Knizhnoe izdatel'stvo, 2011.

———. *Sufizm i vakhkhabizm na Severnom Kavkaze*. Moscow: Institut etnologii i antropologii RAN, 1999.

Akasoy, Anna. "What Is Philosophical Sufism?" In *In the Age of Averroes: Arabic Philosophy in the Sixth/Twelfth Century*, edited by Peter Adamson. London; Turin: Warburg Institute; Nino Agarno Editore, 2011.

Akkach, Samer. *Letters of a Sufi Scholar*. Leiden: E. J. Brill, 2010.

Alatas, Farid, Syed. *Applying Ibn Khaldun: The Recovery of a Lost Tradition in Sociology*. London: Routledge, 2014.

Alatas, Ismail Fajrie. "Aligning the Sunna and the Jama'a: The Religious Authority and Islamic Social Formation in Contemporary Central Java." PhD diss., University of Michigan, 2016.

Alatas, Ismail Fajrie. "'Abdallah b. 'Umar ibn Yahya and the Dissemination of the Tariqa 'Alawiyya in the Early Nineteenth Century Indonesian Archipelago." In *Orders and Itineraries: Buddhist, Islamic, and Christian Networks in Southern Asia, c. 900–1900*, edited by Michael Feener and Ann Blackburn. Under review with University of Hawai'i Press.

———. "'They Are the Inheritors of the Prophet': Discourses on the Ahl al-Bayt and Religious Authority among the Ba 'Alawi in Modern Indonesia." In *Shi'ism in*

Southeast Asia: 'Alid Piety and Sectarian Construction, edited by Michael Feener and Chiara Formichi, 139–64. London: Hurst, 2015.

Alexandrin, Elizabeth. "Witnessing the Lights of the Heavenly Dominion: Dreams, Visions, and the Mystical Exegesis of Shams al-Din al-Daylami." In *Dreams and Visions in Islamic Societies*, edited by Özgen Felek and Alexander Knysh, 215–32. Albany: State University of New York Press, 2012.

Algar, Hamid. *Wahhabism: A Critical Essay*. New York: Oneonta, 2002.

Ali, Kecia. *Lives of Muhammad*. Cambridge, MA: Harvard University Press, 2014.

Alikberov, Alikber. *Epokha klassicheskogo islama na Kavkaze*. Moscow: Vostochnaia literatura, 2003.

'Amir, 'Amir Hasan. *Naqd al-tasawwuf*. Cairo: Al-Sawt al-'Ali, 2008.

Amir-Moezzi, Mohammad Ali. *The Divine Guide in Early Shi'ism*. Translated by David Streight. Albany: State University of New York Press, 1994.

———. *The Spirituality of Shii Islam: Beliefs and Practices*. London: I. B. Tauris, 2011.

Amuli [Amoli], Haydar b. 'Ali. *Tafsir al-Muhit al-a'zam wa 'l-bahr al-hidamm*. Edited by Sayyid Muhsin al-Tabrizi. 4 vols. Qumm: al-Ma'had al-thaqafi nur 'ala nur, 1422.

Anawati, Georges. *Études de philosophie musulmane*. Paris: J. Vrin, 1974.

———. "Kalam." In *Encyclopedia of Religion*, edited by Lindsay Jones, 5059–69. Detroit: Macmillan, 2005.

Andrae, Tor. *In the Garden of Myrtles*. Albany: State University of New York Press, 1987.

Arberry, Arthur. *Oriental Essays: Portraits of Seven Scholars*. London: Allen and Unwin, 1960.

———. *Sufism: An Account of the Mystics of Islam*. London: Unwin Hyman, 1950.

Arberry, Arthur, ed. *Muslim Saints and Mystics: Episodes from the Tadhikirat al-auliya ("Memorial of the Saints") by Farid al-Din Attar*. London: Routledge and Kegan Paul, 1983.

Aresmouk, Mohamed Fouad, and Michael Abdurrahman Fitzgerald. *The Immense Ocean: "Al- Bahr al-Madid"; A Thirteenth Century Quranic Commentary on the Chapters of the All-Merciful, the Event, and Iron*. Louisville, KY: Fons Vitae, 2009.

Arjomand, Said Amir. "The Mujtahid of the Age and the Mulla-bashi." In *Authority and Political Culture in Sufism*, edited by Said Amir Arjomand. Albany: State University of New York Press, 1988.

———. *The Shadow of God and the Hidden Imam*. Chicago: University of Chicago Press, 1984.

Asad, Talal. *Formations of the Secular: Christianity, Islam, Modernity*. Stanford, CA: Stanford University Press, 2003.

———. *Genealogies of Religion*. Baltimore: Johns Hopkins University Press, 1993.

———. "The Idea of an Anthropology of Islam." Washington, DC: Center for Contemporary Arab Studies at Georgetown University. Occasional Papers, Georgetown University, March 1986.

Al-Attas, Muhammad Naguib, Syed. *The Mysticism of Hamza Fansuri*. Kuala Lumpur: University of Malaya Press, 1970.

Austin, Ralph, trans. *Ibn al'Arabi. The Bezels of Wisdom*. New York: Paulist Press, 1980.

———. *The Sufis of Andalusia: The Ruh al-Quds and Al-Durat Al-Fakhirah of Ibn 'Arabi*. Sherborne, Gloucestershire: Beshara Publications, 1988.

Aziz, Muhammad Ali. *Religion and Mysticism in Early Islam: Theology and Sufism in Yemen.* London: I. B. Tauris, 2011.

al-Azmeh, Aziz. *The Times of History.* Budapest: CEU Press, 2007.

Babayan, Kathryn. "Sufis, Dervishes, and Mullahs: The Controversy over Spiritual and Temporal Dominion in Seventeenth-Century Iran." *Pembroke Papers* 4 (1996): 117–38.

Bachmann, Peter. "Un commentaire mystique du Coran." *Arabica* 47, no. 3 (2000): 503–9.

al-Badawi, Mustafa. *Sufi Sage of Arabia: Imam 'Abdallah ibn 'Alawi al-Haddad.* Louisville, KY: Fons Vitae, 2005.

Bahu, Mustafa. *'Ulama' al-Maghrib wa muqawamatuhum li-bida' wa 'l-tasawwuf wa 'l-quburiyya wa 'l-mawasim.* 2nd ed. Morocco: Jaridat al-Sabil, 2007.

Baldick, Julian. *Mystical Islam: An Introduction to Sufism.* London: I. B. Tauris, 1989.

Baljon, Johannes. *Religion and Thought of Shah Wali Allah Dihlawi, 1703–1762.* Leiden: E. J. Brill, 1986.

———. "Shah Waliullah and the Dargah." In *Muslim Shrines in India,* edited by Christian Troll, 191–97. Delhi: Oxford University Press, 1989.

Bang, Anne. *Islamic Sufi Networks in the Western Indian Ocean (c. 1880–1940): Ripples of Reform.* Leiden: E. J. Brill, 2014.

———. *Sufis and Scholars of the Sea: Family Networks in East Africa, 1860–1925.* London: Routledge-Curzon, 2003.

al-Baqli, Ruzbihan. *'Ara'is al-bayan fi haqa'iq al-Qur'an.* 3 vols. Beirut: Dar al-kutub al-'ilmiyya, 1429/2008.

Bar-Asher, Meir. *Scripture and Exegesis in Early Imami Shiism.* Leiden: E. J. Brill, 1999.

Bashier, Salman. *Ibn al-'Arabi's Barzakh: The Concept of the Limit and the Relationship between God and the World.* Albany: State University of New York Press, 2004.

Bashir, Shahzad. *Messianic Hopes and Mystical Visions: The Nurbakhshiyya between Medieval and Modern Islam.* Columbia: University of South Carolina Press, 2003.

———. *Sufi Bodies: Religion and Society in Medieval Islam.* New York: Columbia University Press, 2011.

Basyuni, Ibrahim. *Nash'at al-tasawwuf al-islami.* Cairo: Dar al-Ma'arif, 1969.

Batnitzky, Leora. *How Judaism Became a Religion.* Princeton, NJ: Princeton University Press, 2011.

Bayat, Mangol. "Anti-Sufism in Iran." In *Islamic Mysticism Contested: Thirteen Centuries of Controversies and Polemics,* edited by Frederick de Jong and Bernd Radtke, 624–38. Leiden: E. J. Brill, 1999.

Bazzaz, Sahar. "Heresy and Politics in Nineteenth-Century Morocco." *Arab Studies Journal* 10/11, no. 2/1 (Fall 2002/Spring 2003): 67–86.

Bennigsen-Broxup, Marie. "After the Putsch, 1991." In *The North Caucasus Barrier: The Russian Advance towards the Muslim World,* edited by Marie Bennigsen-Broxup, 219–40. New York: St. Martin's Press, 1994.

———. "The Last Ghazawat." In *The North Caucasus Barrier: The Russian Advance towards the Muslim World,* edited by Marie Bennigsen-Broxup, 112–45. New York: St. Martin's Press, 1994.

Biagi, Elena, trans. *A Collection of Sufi Rules of Conduct [by] Abu 'Abd al-Rahman al-Sulami*. Cambridge: Islamic Texts Society, 2010.

Blank, Stephen, ed. *Russia's Homegrown Insurgency: Jihad in the North Caucasus*. Carlisle, PA: Strategic Studies Institute, 2012.

Bobrovnikov, Vladimir. "Arkheologiia stroitel'stva islamskikh traditsii v dagestanskom kolkhoze." *Ab Imperio* 3 (2004): 563–93.

———. "Izobretenie islamskikh traditsii v dagestanskom kolkhoze." In *Dagestan i musul'manskii Vostok*, edited by Alikber Alikberov and Vladimir Bobrovnikov, 125–49. Moscow: Izdatel'skii dom Marjani, 2010.

———. *Musul'mane Severnogo Kavkaza: Obychai, pravo, nasilie*. Moscow: Vostochnaia literatura, 2002.

———. "'Ordinary Wahhabism' versus 'Ordinary Sufism': Filming Islam for Post-Soviet Young People." *Religion, State, Society* 39, no. 2–3 (2011): 281–301.

———. "Rural Muslims' Nationalism in the Post-Soviet Caucasus: The Case of Daghestan." In *The Caspian Region*. Vol. 2, *The Caucasus*, edited by Moshe Gammer, 179–97. London: Routledge, 2004.

Bobrovnikov, Vladimir, and Akhmet Yarlykapov. "Vakhkhabity Severnogo Kavkaza." In *Islam na territorii byvshei Rossiiskoi imperii*, fasc. 2, edited by Stanislav Prozorov, 19–23. Moscow: Nauka, 1999.

Bonebakker, Seeger. "*Adab* and the Concept of *Belles-Lettres*." In *'Abbasid Belles-Lettres*, edited by Julia Ashtiany et al., 16–30. Cambridge: Cambridge University Press, 1990.

Bonnefoy, Laurent. *Salafism in Yemen: Transnationalism and Religious Identity*. New York: Columbia University Press, 2011.

Bonner, Michael. *Aristocratic Violence and Holy War*. New Haven, CT: American Oriental Society, 1996.

Bos, Matthijs van den. *The Mystic Regimes: Sufism and the State in Iran; From the Late Qajar Era to the Islamic Republic*. Leiden: E. J. Brill, 2002.

Böttcher, Annabelle. "Religious Authority in Transnational Sufi Networks: Shaykh Nazim al-Qubrusi al-Haqqani al-Naqshbandi." In *Speaking for Islam: Religious Authorities in Muslim Societies*, edited by Gudrun Krämer and Sabine Schmidtke, 241–68. Leiden: E. J. Brill, 2006.

Bouhdiba, Abdelwahab. *Sexuality in Islam*. Translated by Alan Sheridan. London: Saqi Books, 1998.

Böwering, Gerhard. "The Light Verse: Qur'anic Text and Sufi Interpretation." *Oriens* 36 (2001): 113–44.

———. "The Major Sources of al-Sulami's Minor Qur'an Commentary." *Oriens* 35 (1996): 35–56.

———. *The Mystical Vision of Existence in Classical Islam: The Qur'anic Hermeneutics of the Sufi Sahl at-Tustari (d. 283/896)*. Berlin: Walter de Gruyter, 1980.

———. "Sufi Hermeneutics in Medieval Islam." *Revue des Études Islamiques* 55–57 (1987–89): 239–328.

Böwering, Gerhard, ed. *Ziyadat haqa'iq al-tafsir li-Abi 'Abd al-Rahman al-Sulami*. Beirut: Dar al-Mashriq, 1995.

Böwering, Gerhard, and Yousef Casewit, eds. *A Qur'an Commentary by Ibn Barrajan (d. 536/1141)*. Leiden: E. J. Brill, 2016.

Bowersock, Glen. *The Throne of Adulis: Red Sea Wars on the Eve of Islam.* Oxford: Oxford University Press, 2013.

Boxberger, Linda. *On the Edge of Empire: Hadhramawt, Emigration, and the Indian Ocean, 1880s-1930s.* Albany: State University of New York Press, 2002.

Braginsky, Vladimir. "Universe-Man-Text: The Sufi Concept of Literature." *Journal of the Humanities and Social Sciences of Southeast Asia* 149, no. 2 (1993): 201–25.

Brown, Peter. *The Cult of the Saints: Its Rise and Function in Latin Christianity.* Chicago: University of Chicago Press, 1981.

———. *Through the Eye of a Needle.* Princeton, NJ: Princeton University Press, 2012.

Bruce, Steve. *God Is Dead: Secularization in the West.* Oxford: Blackwell, 2002.

Bruinessen, Martin, van. "Saints, Politicians, and Sufi Bureaucrats: Mysticism and Politics in Indonesia's New Order." In *Sufism and the "Modern" in Islam,* edited by Martin van Bruinessen and Julia Day Howell, 92–112. London: I. B. Tauris, 2013.

———. "Sufism, 'Popular' Islam, and the Encounter with Modernity." In *Islam and Modernity: Key Issues and Debates,* edited by Muhammad Khalid Masud, Armando Salvatore and Martin van Bruinessen, 125–57. Edinburgh: Edinburgh University Press, 2009.

Bruinessen, Martin van, and Julia Day Howell, eds. *Sufism and the "Modern" in Islam.* London: I. B. Tauris, 2013.

Brunschvig, Robert, and Gustave von Grunebaum, eds. *Classicisme et déclin culturel dans l'histoire de l'Islam.* Paris: Éditions Besson Chantemerle, 1957.

Bujra, Abdalla. *The Politics of Stratification: A Study of Political Change in a South Arabian Town.* Oxford: Clarendon Press, 1971.

Burgat, François, and Muhammad Sbitli. "Les Salafis au Yémen ou la modernisation malgré tout." *Chroniques yéménites* 10 (2002): online edition.

Buehler, Arthur. *Sufi Heirs of the Prophet: The Indian Naqshbandiyya and the Rise of the Mediating Sufi Shaykh.* Columbia: University of South Carolina Press, 1998.

Burton, John. *An Introduction to the Hadith.* Edinburgh: Edinburgh University Press, 1994.

Bustanov, Alfrid. "Rafail' Valishin's 'Anti-Wahhabi' Sufi Traditionalism in Rural Western Siberia." In *Islamic Authority and the Russian Language,* edited by Alfrid Bustanov and Michael Kemper, 219–63. Amsterdam: Pegasus Oost-Europese Studies, 2012.

Buxton, Amin. *Imams of the Valley.* Western Cape, South Africa: Dar al-Turath al-Islami Publishing House, 2012.

Carré, Oliver. *Mysticism and Politics: A Critical Reading of Fi Zilal al-Qur'an by Sayyid Qutb (1906-1966).* Leiden: E. J. Brill, 2003.

Casanova, Jose. *Public Religions in the Modern World.* Chicago: University of Chicago Press, 1994.

Chadwick, Owen. *The Early Reformation on the Continent.* Oxford: Oxford University Press, 2001.

Cheddadi, Abdesselam. *Ibn Khaldûn: L'homme et le théoricien de la civilization.* Paris: Gallimard, 2006.

Chiabotti, Francesco. "Entre soufisme et savoir islamique: L'oeuvre de 'Abd al-Karim al-Qushayri (376-465/986-1072)." PhD diss., Université de Provence, Ecole doctorale 355, UFR arts, lettres, langues et sciences humaines, i Aix-en-Provence: IREMAM, 2014.

Chiabotti, Francesco, Eve Feuillebois-Pierunek et al., eds. *Ethics and Spirituality in Islam: Sufi adab*. Leiden: E. J. Brill, 2017.

al-Chirkavi, Said-Afandi. *Majmu'at al-fawa'id: Sokrovischnitsa blagodatnykh znanii*. Translated from the Avar language. Makhachkala: Nurul irshad, 2010.

Chittick, William. *Divine Love: Islamic Literature and the Path to God*. New Haven, CT: Yale University Press, 2013.

———. "Ibn Arabi." In *The Stanford Encyclopedia of Philosophy*, spring 2014 edition, edited by Edward N. Zalta. Online edition: http://plato.stanford.edu/archives /spr2014/entries/ibn-arabi/.

———. "Ibn 'Arabi and His School." In *Islamic Spirituality: Manifestations*, edited by S. H. Nasr, 49–79. New York: Crossroad, 1991.

———. *Imaginal Worlds: Ibn al-'Arabi and the Problem of Religious Diversity*. Albany: State University of New York Press, 1994.

———. "The School of Ibn 'Arabi." In *History of Islamic Philosophy*, edited by S. H. Nasr and Oliver Leaman, 2 vols., 1: 510–23. London: Routledge, 1996.

———. *The Self-Disclosure of God: Principles of Ibn al-'Arabi's Cosmology*. Albany: State University of New York Press, 1998.

———. *The Sufi Path of Knowledge: Ibn al-'Arabi's Metaphysics of Imagination*. Albany: State University of New York Press, 1989.

———. *The Sufi Path of Love: The Spiritual Teachings of Rumi*. Albany: State University of New York Press, 1983.

———. "*Wahdat al-wujud* in Islamic Thought." *Bulletin of the Henry Martyn Institute of Islamic Studies* 10 (January–March 1991): 7–27.

Chivers, C. J. "A Whirling Sufi Revival with Unclear Implications." *New York Times*, May 24, 2005.

Chodkiewicz, Michel. "The Diffusion of Ibn 'Arabi's Doctrine." *Journal of Muhyiddin Ibn 'Arabi Society* 9 (1991): 36–57.

———. *An Ocean without Shore: Ibn 'Arabi, the Book, and the Law*. Albany: State University of New York Press, 1993.

———. *Seal of the Saints: Prophethood and Sainthood in the Doctrine of Ibn 'Arabi*. Translated by Liadain Sherrard. Cambridge: Islamic Texts Society, 1993.

Chodkiewicz, Michel, ed. *The Meccan Revelations*. 2 vols. New York: Pir Press, 2005.

Choueiri, Youssef. *Companion for the History of the Middle East*. Oxford: Blackwell, 2005.

Christmann, Andreas. "Reclaiming Mysticism: Anti-Orientalism and the Construction of 'Islamic Sufism' in Post-Colonial Egypt." In *Religion, Language, and Power*, edited by Nile Green and Mary Searle-Chatterjee, 58–64. London: Routledge, 2008.

Clark, Elizabeth. *Reading Renunciation: Asceticism and Scripture in Early Christianity*. Princeton, NJ: Princeton University Press, 1999.

Clark, Gilliam. "Women and Asceticism in Late Antiquity: The Refusal of Status and Gender." In *Asceticism*, edited by Vincent Wimbush and Richard Valantasis, 37–41. Oxford: Oxford University Press, 1998.

Cook, Michael. *Commanding Right and Forbidding Wrong in Islamic Thought*. Cambridge: Cambridge University Press, 2000.

Cooperson, Michael. "Ahmad Ibn Hanbal and Bishr al-Hafi." *Studia Islamica* 86, no. 2 (1997): 71–101.

Corbin, Henry. *The Creative Imagination in the Sufism of Ibn 'Arabi*. London: Routledge and K. Paul, 1970.

———. *En Islam iranien*. Vol. 1, *Le Shi'isme duodécimain*. Paris: Gallimard, 1971.

———. *En Islam iranien*. Vol. 3, *Les Fidèles d'amour Shi'isme et soufisme*. Paris: Gallimard, 1971–72.

Cornell, Vincent. *Realm of the Saint: Power and Authority in Moroccan Sufism*. Austin: University of Texas Press, 1998.

Corrigan, Kevin. " 'Solitary' Mysticism in Plotinus, Proclus, Gregory of Nyssa, and Pseudo-Dionysius." *Journal of Religion* 76, no. 1 (1996): 28–42.

Cox, Michael, ed. *Rethinking the Soviet Collapse: Sovietology, the Death of Communism, and the New Russia*. London: Pinter, 1998.

Crawford, Michael. *Ibn 'Abd al-Wahhab*. London: Oneworld, 2014.

Crone, Patricia. *Pre-Industrial Societies: Anatomy of the Pre-Modern World*. Oxford: Oneworld, 2003.

Cross, F. L., and E. A. Livingstone, eds. *The Oxford Dictionary of the Christian Church*. 3rd ed. Oxford: Oxford University Press, 1997.

Daftary, Farhad. *The Isma'ilis: Their History and Doctrines*. Cambridge: Cambridge University Press, 1990.

Damrel, D. W. "Aspects of the Naqshbandi-Haqqani Order in North America." In *Sufism in the West*, edited by Jamal Malik and John Hinnels, 115–26. London: Routledge, 2006.

Daniel, Norman. *Islam and the West: The Making of an Image*. Oxford: Oneworld, 2003.

Dawkins, Richard. *The Selfish Gene*. 40th anniversary ed. Oxford: Oxford University Press, 2016.

DeLong-Bas, Natana J. *Wahhabi Islam: From Revival and Reform to Global Jihad*. Oxford: Oxford University Press, 2004.

Derluguian, Georgi. *Bourdieu's Admirer in the Caucasus*. Chicago: University of Chicago Press, 2005.

De Santillana, Giorgio. Review of Philip Merlan, *From Plato to Neoplatonism*. 3rd ed. The Hague: Nijhoff, 1968. *Isis*, 48, no. 3, George Sarton Memorial Issue (1957): 360–62.

Deweese, Devin. "Baba Kamal and Jandi and the Kubravi Tradition among the Turks of Central Asia." *Der Islam* 71 (1994): 58–94.

———. *Studies on Sufism in Central Asia*. Farnham: Ashgate Variorum, 2012.

Diamond, Jared. *Guns, Germs, and Steel: The Fates of Human Societies*. New York: Norton, 2005.

Dobaev, Igor. *Islamskii radikalizm: Genezis, evoliutsiia, praktika*. Rostov-Don: SKNTs V. Sh., 2003.

Dobaev, Igor, et al. *Radikalizatsiia islama v Rossiiskoi Federatsii*. Moscow: TsSRIiP YuFU, 2013.

Dobaev, Igor, and Vera Nemchina. *Novyi terrorizm v mire i na iuge Rossii*. Rostov-on-the-Don: RostIzdat, 2005.

Dodds, Eric, ed. and trans. *Proclus: The Elements of Theology*. Oxford: Clarendon Press, 1963.

Douglas, Elmer, trans. *The Mystical Teachings of al-Shadhili*. Albany: State University of New York Press, 1993.

Dresch, Paul. *A History of Modern Yemen*. Cambridge: Cambridge University Press, 2000.

Dresch, Paul, and Bernard Haykel. "Stereotypes and Political Styles: Islamists and Tribesfolk in Yemen." *IJMES* 27, no. 4 (1995): 405–31.

Dunn, Ross, trans. *The Adventures of Ibn Battuta, a Muslim Traveler of the 14th Century*. Berkeley: University of California Press, 2012.

Eaton, Richard. "Islamic History as Global History." In *Islamic and European Expansion: The Forging of a Global Order*, edited by Michael Adas, 1–36. Philadelphia: Temple University Press, 1993.

———. *The Sufis of Bijapur, 1300–1700: Social Roles of Sufis in Medieval India*. Princeton, NJ: Princeton University Press, 1977.

Ebstein, Michael. *Mysticism and Philosophy in al-Andalus: Ibn Masarra, Ibn al-'Arabi, and the Isma'ili Tradition*. Leiden: E. J. Brill, 2014.

Eco, Umberto. *The Limits of Interpretation*. Bloomington: Indiana University Press, 1994.

———. *The Name of the Rose*. Translated by William Weaver. London: Picador in association with Secker and Warburg, 1984.

———. *The Role of the Reader: Explorations in the Semiotics of Texts*. Bloomington: Indiana University Press, 1979.

Eickelman, Dale. "Inside the Islamic Reformation." *Wilson Quarterly* 22 (1988): 80–89.

———. "Print, Islam, and the Prospects for Civic Pluralism." *Journal of Islamic Studies* 8, no. 1 (1997): 43–62.

Eisenstadt, Shmuel, ed. *Max Weber on Charisma and Institution Building*. Chicago: University of Chicago Press, 1968.

El Ayadi, Mohammed, Hasan Rachik, and Mohamed Tazy. *L'islam au quotidien*. Casablanca: Editions la Croisee des Chemins, 2013.

El-Bizri, Nader, ed. *Epistles of the Brethren of Purity: The Ikhwan Al-Safa' and Their Rasa'il; An Introduction*. Oxford: Oxford University Press, 2008.

Elias, Jamal. *The Throne Carrier of God: The Life and Thought of 'Ala' ad-Dawla as-Simnani*. Albany: State University of New York Press, 1995.

Elmore, Gerald. *Islamic Sainthood in the Fullness of Time: Ibn al-'Arabi's Book of the Fabulous Gryphon*. Leiden: E. J. Brill, 1999.

Engels, Friedrich. *Anti-Dühring*. New York: International Publishers, 1966.

———. *The German Revolutions*. Edited by Leonard Krieger. Chicago: University of Chicago Press, 1967.

Ernst, Carl. *Eternal Garden: Mysticism, History, and Politics at a South Asian Sufi Center*. 2nd ed. Delhi: Oxford University Press, 2004.

———. *Following Muhammad: Rethinking Islam in the Contemporary World*. Chapel Hill: University of North Carolina Press, 2003.

———. "Mystical Language and the Teaching Context in the Early Lexicons of Sufism." In *Mysticism and Language*, edited by Steven Katz, 186–90. Oxford: Oxford University Press, 1992.

———. *Ruzbihan Baqli*. Richmond, Surrey: Curzon, 1996.

———. *The Shambhala Guide to Sufism*. Boston: Shambhala, 1997.

———. "Traditionalism, the Perennial Philosophy, and Islamic Studies." *Middle East Studies Association Bulletin* 28, no. 2 (1994): 176–81.

———. *Words of Ecstasy in Sufism*. Albany: State University of New York Press, 1985.

Eubin, Roxanne. *Enemy in the Mirror: Islamic Fundamentalism and the Limits of Modern Rationalism*. Princeton, NJ: Princeton University Press, 1999.

Eubin, Roxanne, and Muhammad Qasim Zaman, eds. *Princeton Readings in Islamist Thought: Texts and Context from al-Banna to Bin Laden*. Princeton, NJ: Princeton University Press, 2009.

Evans-Pritchard, E. E. *The Sanusi of Cyrenaica*. Oxford: Clarendon Press, 1954.

Ewing, Katherine. *Arguing Sainthood: Modernity, Psychoanalysis, and Islam*. Durham, NC: Duke University Press, 1997.

Fakhry, Majid. *A History of Islamic Philosophy*. 3rd ed. New York: Columbia University Press, 2004.

Farah, Madeleine, trans. *Marriage and Sexuality in Islam: A Translation of al-Ghazali's Book on the Etiquette of Marriage from the Ihya'*. Salt Lake City: University of Utah Press, 1984.

al-Fawzan, Salih b. Fawzan. *'Aqidat al-tawhid*. Riyadh: Dar al-'asima, 1999.

Fazlul Karim, Alhaj Maulana, trans. Al-Ghazali, *Ihya' 'ulum al-din (The Book of Religious Learnings)*. Vol. 1, *The Book of Worship*. New Delhi: Islamic Book Services, 1991.

———. Al-Ghazali, *Ihya' 'ulum al-din (The Book of Religious Learnings)*. Vol. 3, *The Book of Destructive Evils*. New Delhi: Islamic Book Services, 1991.

Finn, Richard. *Asceticism in the Graeco-Roman World*. Cambridge: Cambridge University Press, 2009.

Fischer, Michael. *Iran: From Religious Dispute to Revolution*. Cambridge, MA: Harvard University Press, 1980.

Fischer, Michael, and Mehdi Abedi. *Debating Muslims*. Madison: University of Wisconsin Press, 1990.

Fleet, Barrie, trans. and comment. *Enneads of Plotinus, Ennead IV.8: On the Descent of the Soul into Bodies*. Las Vegas: Parmenides, 2012.

Flood, Gavin. *The Ascetic Self: Subjectivity, Memory, and Tradition*. Cambridge: Cambridge University Press, 2004.

———. *The Truth Within: A History of Inwardness in Christianity, Hinduism, and Buddhism*. Oxford: Oxford University Press, 2013.

Foucault, Michel. *The Archaeology of Knowledge*. New York: Pantheon, 1972.

———. *The Order of Things*. New York: Vintage Books, 1994.

Frank, Richard. "The Science of Kalam." *Arabic Science and Philosophy* 2 (1992): 7–37.

Fry, Richard. *Ibn Fadlan's Journey to Russia*. Princeton, NJ: Markus Wiener, 2nd printing, 2006.

Gakayev, Zh. Zh., Tishkov, V. A., and A. D. Yandarov. *Kul'tura Chechni: Istoriia i sovremennye problemy*. Moscow: Nauka, 2002.

Gammer, Moshe. "Between Mecca and Moscow: Islam, Politics, and Political Islam in Chechnya and Daghestan." *Middle Eastern Studies* 41, no. 6 (2005): 833–48.

———. *The Lone Wolf and the Bear: Three Centuries of Chechen Defiance of Russian State*. London: Hurst, 2006.

———. *Muslim Resistance to the Tsar*. London: Frank Cass, 1994.

———. "The Road Not Taken: Daghestan and Chechen Independence." *Central Asian Survey* 24, no. 2 (2005): 97–108.

Gammer, Moshe, and David Wasserstein, eds. *Daghestan and the World of Islam*. Helsinki: Finnish Academy of Science and Letters, 2006.

———. *Ethno-Nationalism, Islam, and the State in the Caucasus: Post-Soviet Disorder*. London: Routledge, 2008.

Garden, Kenneth. *The First Islamic Reviver: Abu Hamid al-Ghazali and His Revival of the Religious Sciences*. Oxford: Oxford University Press, 2014.

Gardiner, Noah. "Esotericism in a Manuscript Culture: Ahmad al-Buni and His Readers through the Mamluk Period." PhD diss., University of Michigan, 2014.

———. "Forbidden Knowledge? Notes on the Production, Transmission, and Receptions of the Major Works of Ahmad al-Buni." *Journal of Arabic and Islamic Studies* 12 (2012): 81–143.

Gauthier, Léon. *Introduction à l'étude de la philosophie musulmane: L'esprit sémitique et l'esprit aryen, la philosophie grecque et la religion de l'Islâm*. Paris: E. Leroux, 1923.

Geertz, Clifford. *Interpretation of Cultures*. New York: Basic Books, 1973.

———. *Islam Observed: Religious Development in Morocco and Indonesia*. New Haven, CT: Yale University Press, 1968.

Gellner, Ernest. *Muslim Society*. Cambridge: Cambridge University Press, 1982.

———. *Saints of the Atlas*. Chicago: University of Chicago Press, 1969.

Gellner, Ernest, ed. *Islamic Dilemmas: Reformers, Nationalists, Industrialization*. Berlin: Mouton, 1995.

Genko, Anatolii. "Arabskii iazyk i kavkazovedenie." *Trudy vtoroi sessii assotsiatsii arabistov 19–23 oktiabria 1937 g.* Moscow: Trudy Instituta vostokovedenia, vol. 36 (1941): 81–110.

Geoffroy, Éric. *Introduction to Sufism: The Inner Path of Islam*. Bloomington, IN: World Wisdom, 2010.

———. *Le soufisme en Égypte et en Syrie sous les derniers Mamelouks et les premiers Ottomans*. Damascus: Institut français de Damas, 1995.

Gerges, Fawaz. *The Far Enemy: Why Jihad Went Global*. New ed. Cambridge: Cambridge University Press, 2009.

Gerson, Lloyd, trans. and comment. *Plotinus, Ennead V.5., That the Intelligibles Are Not External to the Intellect and on the Good*. Las Vegas: Parmenides, 2013.

Gerth, Hans, and Charles Wright Mills, eds. *From Max Weber: Essays in Sociology*. London: Routledge and Kegan Paul, 1967.

Al-Ghazali. *Ihya' 'ulum al-din*. 5 vols. Cairo: al-Maktaba al-tijariyya al-kubra, 1960.

———. *Jawahir al-Qur'an*. Edited by Muhammad Rashid Rida al-Qabbani. Beirut: Dar ihya' al-'ulum, 1985.

———. *Mishkat al-anwar*. Edited by Samih Dughaym. Beirut: Dar al-fikr al-lubnani, 1994.

Gilsenan, Michael. *Recognizing Islam: Religion and Society in the Modern Middle East*. London: I. B. Tauris, 2000.

Gimaret, Daniel, and Guy Monnot, trans. *Shahrastani, Livre des religions et des sects*. Paris: Peeters, 1986.

Giuliano, Elise. "Islamic Identity and Political Mobilization in Russia: Chechnya and Dagestan Compared." *Nationalism and Ethnic Politics* 11, no. 2 (2005): 195–220.

Godlas, Alan. "Sufism." In *The Blackwell Companion to the Quran*, edited by Andrew Rippin. Malden, MA: Blackwell, 2006.

Goldziher, Ignaz. *Introduction to Islamic Theology*. Princeton, NJ: Princeton University Press, 1981.

———. *Schools of Koranic Commentators*. Edited and translated by Wolfgang Behn. Wiesbaden: Harrassowitz, 2006.

Gould, Mark. "Toward a Theory of 'Islamist Movements.'" *Sociology of Islam* 2 (2014): 21–59.

Graham, William. *Divine Word and Prophetic Word in Early Islam*. The Hague: Mouton, 1977.

Gramlich, Richard. *Die Schiitischen Derwischorden Persiens*. 3 vols. Wiesbaden: Franz Steiner, 1965–76.

Green, Nile. *Sufism: A Global History*. Chichester, UK: Wiley-Blackwell, 2012.

Green, Nile, and Mary Searle-Chatterjee, eds. *Religion, Language, and Power*. London: Routledge, 2008.

Gril, Denis. "Le commentaire du verset de la lumière d'après Ibn 'Arabi." *Bulletin de l'Institut francais d'archéologie orientale* 90 (1990): 179–87.

———. "'La lecture supérieure' du Coran selon ibn Barraǧan." *Arabica* 47, no. 3 (2000): 510–22.

Gross Solomon, Susan, ed. *Beyond Sovietology: Essays in Politics and History*. London: Routledge, 1993.

Gülen, Fethullah. *Key Concepts in the Practice of Sufism: Emerald Hills of the Heart*. Somerset, NJ: The Light, 2006.

———. *Toward a Global Civilization of Love and Tolerance*. Somerset, NJ: The Light, 2006.

Gutas, Dmitri. *Greek Thought, Arabic Culture: The Graeco-Arabic Translation Movement in Baghdad and Early 'Abbasid Society (2nd–4th/8th–10th Centuries)*. London: Routledge, 1998.

Hadot, Pierre. *Philosophy as a Way of Life*, ed. Arnold Davidson, trans. Michael Chase, Oxford: Blackwell, 1995.

Hagman, Patrik. *The Asceticism of Isaac of Nineveh*. Oxford: Oxford University Press, 2010.

Hahn, Gordon. *Russia's Islamic Threat*. New Haven, CT: Yale University Press, 2007.

al-Hakim, Su'ad. *al-Mu'jam al-sufi: Al-hikma fi hudud al-kalima*. Beirut: Dandara. 1401/1981.

Hallaq, Wael. "On Orientalism, Self-Consciousness, and History." *Islamic Law and Society* 18 (2011): 387–439.

Halm, Heinz. *The Empire of the Mahdi*. Translated by Michael Bonner. Leiden: E. J. Brill, 1996.

Halpern, Manfred. *The Politics of Social Change in the Middle East and North Africa.* Princeton, NJ: Princeton University Press, 1963.

Hameed, Syeda, ed. *The Contemporary Relevance of Sufism.* New Delhi: Indian Council for Cultural Relations, 1993.

Harman, Graham. *Heidegger Explained: From Phenomenon to Thing.* Chicago: Open Court, 2007.

Harpham, Geoffrey. *The Ascetic Imperative in Culture and Criticism.* Chicago: University of Chicago Press, 1987.

Harrisville, Roy. *Pandora's Box Opened: An Examination and Defense of Historical Critical Method and Its Master Practitioners.* Grand Rapids, MI: Eerdmans, 2014.

Hawting, Gerald. *The First Dynasty of Islam.* Carbondale: Southern Illinois University Press, 1987.

Haykel, Bernard. *Revival and Reform in Islam: The Legacy of Muhammad al-Shawkani.* Cambridge: Cambridge University Press, 2003.

———. "Salafist Doctrine." In *Global Salafism: Islam's New Religious Movement,* edited by Roel Meijer, 33–57. London: Hurst, 2009.

Haykel, Bernard, Thomas Hegghammer, and Stéphane Lacroix, eds. *Saudi Arabia in Transition: Insights on Social, Political, Economic, and Religious Change.* Cambridge: Cambridge University Press, 2015.

Hazza' Sharif, Sharif. *Naqd/tasawwuf: al-nass, al-kitab, al-tafkik.* Beirut: Dar al-intishar al-'arabi, 2008.

Heer, Nicholas, and Kenneth Honerkamp, trans. *Three Early Sufi Texts.* Louisville, KY: Fons Vitae, 2009.

Heller, Mikhail. *Cogs in the Soviet Wheel: The Formation of Soviet Man.* London: Collins Harvill, 1988.

Hermansen, Marcia. "In the Garden of American Sufi Movements: Hybrids and Perennials." In *New Trends and Developments in the World of Islam,* edited by Peter Clarke, 155–78. London: Luzac Oriental, 1998.

———. "What's American about American Sufi Movements?" In *Sufism in Europe and North America,* edited by David Westerlund, 36–63. London: Routledge, 2004.

Higgins, Annie. "The Qur'anic Exchange of the Self in the Poetry of *Shurat (Khariji)* Political Identity, 37–132 A.H./657–750 A.D." PhD diss., University of Chicago, 2001; available through ProQuest theses and dissertations online.

Hisham Kabbani, Muhammad. *Classical Islam and the Naqshbandi Sufi Tradition.* 2nd ed. Washington, DC: ISCA, 2004.

———. *Encyclopedia of Islamic Doctrine.* 7 vols. Chicago: Kazi Publications, 1998.

———. *The Hierarchy of Saints.* Fenton, MI: ISCA, part 1, 2012.

———. *The Naqshbandi Sufi Way.* Collector's ed. Chicago: Kazi Publications, 1995.

Hitchens, Christopher. *God Is Not Great: How Religion Poisons Everything.* New York: Twelve, 2007.

Ho, Eng Seng. *The Graves of Tarim: Genealogy and Mobility across the Indian Ocean.* Berkeley: University of California Press, 2006.

Hobsbawm, Eric, and Terrence Ranger, eds. *The Invention of Tradition.* Cambridge: Cambridge University Press, 1997.

Hodgson, Marshall. *The Venture of Islam: Conscience and History in a World Civilization.* 3 vols. Chicago: University of Chicago Press, 1974.

Holland, Muhtar, trans. *Sheikh Muzaffer Ozak al-Jarrahi, Irshad: Wisdom of a Sufi Master*. New York: Amity, 1988.

Homerin, Th. Emil. "Ibn Taimiyah's *al-Sufiyah wa 'l-fuqara'*." *Arabica* 32, no. 2 (1985): 219–44.

Howell, Julia Day, and Martin van Bruinessen, eds. *Sufism and the "Modern" in Islam*. London: I. B. Tauris, 2013.

Hsia, R. Po-chia, ed. *A Companion to the Reformation World*. Oxford: Blackwell, 2004.

Hundhammer, Marianus. *Prophetenverehrung im Hadramaut: Die Ziyara nach Qabr Hud aus diachroner und synchroner Perspektive*. Berlin: Schwarz, 2010.

Hussain, Naveed. "Are Sufis Essentially Non-Violent?" *Express Tribune*, January 18, 2011.

Ibn 'Abd al-Wahhab, Muhammad. *Kitab al-tawhid*. Cairo: Dar al-ma'arif, 1974.

———. *Sharh masa'il al-jahiliyya li-shaykh al-islam Muhammad b. 'Abd al-Wahhab* (with a commentary by Salih b. Fawzan al-Fawzan). 2 vols. Riyadh: Dar al-'asima, 2001.

Ibn Abi 'l-Dunya. *Dhikr al-mawt*. 'Ajman: Maktabat al-furqan, 2002.

———. *Al-Hamm wa-al-huzn*. Cairo: Dar al-salam, 1991.

———. *Kitab al-wara'*. Edited by Bassam 'Abd al-Wahhab al-Jabi. Beirut: Dar Ibn Hazm, 2002.

Ibn 'Ajiba. *Al-Bahr al-madid*. 8 vols. Beirut: Dar al-kutub al-'ilmiyya, 2010.

———. *Tafsir al-Fatiha al-kabir al-musamma bi 'l-Bahr al-madid*. Edited by Bassam Muhammad Barud. 2 vols. Abu Dhabi: al-Majma' al-Thaqafi, 1999.

Ibn [al-]'Arabi. *Diwan ibn 'Arabi*. Baghdad: Maktabat Muthanna, 1963.

———. *Fusus al-hikam*. Edited by Abu 'l-'Ala 'Afifi. Beirut: Dar al-kitab al-'arabi, 1980.

Ibn 'Arabi. *Tafsir al-Qur'an al-karim*. 2 vols. Beirut: Dar al-yaqza al-'arabiyya, 1968.

Ibn Hazm. *Al-Fisal fi 'l-milal wa-'l-ahwa' wa-'l-nihal*. 3 vols. Edited by Ahmad Shams al-Din. Beirut: Dar al-kutub al-'ilmiyya, 1999.

Ibn al-Jarrah, Waki'. *Al-Zuhd li-imam Waki'*. Edited by 'Abd al-Rahman 'Abd al-Jabbar al-Faryawa'i. Medina: Maktabat al-Dar, 1984.

Ibn al-Jawzi. "Devil's Delusion." Translated by David Margoliouth. Published as *Talbis Iblis (Delusion of the Devil)* by N. K. Singh. New Delhi: Kitab Bhavan, 2008.

———. *Talbis Iblis*. Edited by Muhammad 'Abd al-Qadir al-Fadili. Beirut: al-Maktaba al-misriyya, 1999.

Ibn Khaldun. *Shifa' al-sa'il wa tahdhib al-masa'il*. Edited by Muhammad Muti' al-Hafiz. Damascus: Dar al-fikr, 1996.

Ibrahim, Taufic, and Arthur Sagadeev. *Classical Islamic Philosophy*. Translated by Campbell Creighton. Moscow: Progress Publishing, 1990.

Irwin, Robert. *Dangerous Knowledge: Orientalism and Its Discontents*. Woodstock, NY: Overlook Press, 2006.

al-Isbahani, Abu Nu'aym. *Hilyat al-awliya'*. 12 vols. Beirut: Dar al-kutub al-'arabi, 1967.

al-Iskandari, Ibn 'Ata' Allah. *Lata'if al-minan*. Edited by Khalid 'Abd al-Rahman al-'Akk. Damascus: Dar al-basha'ir, 1992.

Isma'il Haqqi b. Mustafa. *Kitab tafsir al-Qur'an al-musamma bi-ruh al-bayan*. 4 vols. Cairo: Bulaq, 1860.

James, William. *Varieties of Religious Experience*. New York: Longmans, 1925.

Jaoudi, Maria. *Christian and Islamic Spirituality: Sharing a Journey*. New York: Paulist Press, 1993.

Jenkins, Keith. *On "What Is History"? From Carr and Elton to Rorty and White*. London: Routledge, 1995.

Jironet, Karin. *Sufi Mysticism into the West: The Life and Leadership of Hazrat Inayat Khan's Brothers: 1927–1967*. Leuven: Peeters, 2009.

Jong, Frederick de, and Bernd Radtke, eds. *Islamic Mysticism Contested: Thirteen Centuries of Controversies and Polemics*. Leiden: E. J. Brill, 1999.

Junusov, M. S., M. M. Skibitsky, and I. P. Tsameryan. *The Theory and Practice of Proletarian Internationalism*. Moscow: Progress Publishers, 1976.

Juynboll, Gautier. *Encyclopedia of Canonical Hadith*. Leiden: E. J. Brill, 2007.

Kamali, Mohammad Hashim. "The Interplay of Revelation and Reason in the Shariah." In *The Oxford History of Islam*, edited by John Esposito, 107–54. Oxford: Oxford University Press, 1999.

———. *The Middle Path of Moderation in Islam: The Qur'anic Principle of Wasatiyya*. Oxford: Oxford University Press, 2015.

Kamesar, Adam. "Biblical Interpretation in Philo." In *The Cambridge Companion to Philo*, edited by Adam Kamesar, 65–94. Cambridge: Cambridge University Press, 2009.

Kamil, 'Umar 'Abdallah. *Al-tasawwuf bayn al-ifrat wa 'l-tafrit*. Cairo: Dar nahdat Misr, 2011.

Karamustafa, Ahmet. *God's Unruly Friends: Dervish Groups in the Islamic Later Middle Period, 1200–1550*. Salt Lake City: University of Utah Press, 1994.

———. *Sufism: The Formative Period*. Edinburgh: Edinburgh University Press, 2007.

Karimov, Elyor. *Kubraviiskii vakf XVII–XIX vv.: pis'mennye istochniki po istorii sufiiskogo bratstva Kubraviia v Srednei Azii*. Tashkent: Fan, 2008.

Katz, Jonathan. *Dreams, Sufism, and Sainthood: The Visionary Career of Muhammad al-Zawawi*. Leiden: E. J. Brill, 1996.

Katz, Steven. "Mystical Speech and Mystical Meaning." In *Mysticism and Language*, edited by Steven Katz, 3–41. Oxford: Oxford University Press, 1992.

———. "Mysticism and the Interpretation of Sacred Scripture." In *Mysticism and Sacred Scripture*, edited by Steven Katz, 7–67. Oxford: Oxford University Press, 2000.

Katz, Steven, ed. *Mysticism and Language*. Oxford: Oxford University Press, 1992.

———. *Mysticism and Sacred Scripture*. Oxford: Oxford University Press, 2000.

Keeler, Annabel. "Mystical Theology and the Traditionalist Hermeneutics of Maybudi's *Kashf al-Asrar*." In *Sufism and Theology*, edited by Ayman Shihadeh, 15–30. Edinburgh: Edinburgh University Press, 2007.

———. *Sufi Hermeneutics: The Qur'an Commentary of Rashid al-Din Maybudi*. Oxford: Oxford University Press, 2006.

Kemper, Michael. "The Discourse of Said-Afandi, Daghestan's Foremost Sufi Master." In *Islamic Authority and the Russian Language*, edited by Alfrid Bustanov and Michael Kemper, 167–217. Amsterdam: Pegasus Oost-Europese Studies, 2012.

———. "Jihadism: The Discourse of the Caucasus Emirate." In *Islamic Authority and the Russian Language*, edited by Alfrid Bustanov and Michael Kemper, 265–93. Amsterdam: Pegasus Oost-Europese Studies, vol. 19, 2012.

———. "Khalidiyya Networks in Daghestan and the Question of *Jihad.*" *Die Welt des Islams* 42, no. 1 (2002): 41–71.

Kepel, Gilles. *Jihad: The Trail of Political Islam.* London: I. B. Tauris, 2002.

Kepel, Gilles, and Jean-Pierre Milelli, eds. *Al Qaeda in Its Own Words.* Cambridge, MA: Belknap Press of Harvard University Press, 2008.

Keshavarz, Fatemeh. *Reading Mystical Lyric: The Case of Jalal al-Din Rumi.* Columbia: University of South Carolina Press, 1998.

Khalidi, Tarif. *Classical Arab Islam: The Culture and Heritage of the Golden Age.* Princeton, NJ: Darwin Press, 1985.

Khanbabayev, Kaflan. "Sufiiskie sheikhi i ikh posledovateli v sovremennom Dagestane." In *Dagestan i musul'manskii Vostok,* edited by Alikber Alikberov and Vladimir Bobrovnikov, 165–78. Moscow: Izdatel'skii dom Marjani, 2010.

Khanna, Meenakshi. "Visionaries of a Tariqa: The Uwaysi Sufis of Shahjahanabad." In *Dreams and Visions in Islamic Societies,* edited by Özgen Felek and Alexander Knysh, 273–96. Albany: State University of New York Press, 2012.

Khizrieva, Galina. " 'Islam,' 'musul'mane,' 'gosudarstvo' v rossiiskom islamovedenii." *Ab Imperio* 3 (2004): 413–38.

Kinberg, Leah. "What Is Meant by 'Zuhd'?" *Studia Islamica* 41 (1985): 24–44.

King, Richard. *Orientalism and Religion.* London: Routledge, 1999.

Kisriev, Enver. *Islam i vlast' v Dagestane.* Moscow: OGI, 2004.

———. *Islam v Dagestane.* Moscow: Logos, 2007.

———. "Societal Conflict-Generating Factors in Daghestan." In *The Caspian Region.* Vol. 2, *The Caucasus,* edited by Moshe Gammer, 107–21. London: Routledge, 2004.

Kister, Meir, ed. *Kitab adab al-suhba by Abu 'Abd ar-Rahman as-Sulami.* Jerusalem: Israeli Oriental Society, 1954.

Knysh, Alexander. "A Clear and Present Danger: Wahhabism as a Rhetorical Foil." *Die Welt des Islams* 44, no. 1 (2004): 3–26.

———. "Contextualizing the Sufi-Salafi Conflict (From the Northern Caucasus to Hadramawt)." *Middle Eastern Studies* 43, no. 4 (2007): 503–30.

———. "The Cult of Saints and Religious Reformism in Early Twentieth-Century Hadramawt." *New Arabian Studies* 4 (1997): 139–67.

———. "The Cult of Saints and Religious Reformism in Hadhramaut." In *Hadhrami Traders, Scholars, and Statesmen in the Indian Ocean, 1750s–1960s,* edited by Ulrike Freitag and William Clarence-Smith, 199–216. Leiden: E. J. Brill, 1997.

———. "The Cult of Saints in Hadramawt: An Overview." *New Arabian Studies* 1 (1993): 137–52.

———. "A Hanbali Criticism of Sufism (Ibn al-Jawzi's *Talbis Iblis*)." In *The Literary Heritage of Eastern Peoples.* Part 1, 170–75. Moscow: Nauka, 1989 (in Russian).

———. "Historiography of Sufi Studies in the West and Russia." *Pis'mennye pamiatniki Vostoka (Written Monuments of the Orient)* 1, no. 4 (2006): 206–38.

———. *Ibn 'Arabi in the Later Islamic Tradition: The Making of a Polemical Image in Medieval Islam.* Albany: State University of New York Press, 1999.

———. "Islam and Arabic as the Rhetoric of Insurgency: The Case of the Caucasus Emirate." *Studies in Conflict and Terrorism* 35 (2012): 315–37.

———. *Islam in Historical Perspective.* Upper Saddle River, NJ: Pearson and Prentice Hall, 2011; 2nd printing, London: Routledge, 2015.

———. *Islamic Mysticism: A Short History*. 2nd ed. Leiden: E. J. Brill, 2010.

———. Review of Mohammad R. Salama. *Islam, Orientalism, and Intellectual History: Modernity and the Politics of Exclusion since Ibn Khaldun*. London: I. B. Tauris, 2011. *Der Islam* 90, no. 1 (2013): 197–202.

———. Review of Nile Green. *Sufism: A Global History*. Chichester, UK: Wiley-Blackwell, 2012. *Journal of Sufi Studies* 3 (2014): 93–95.

———. "The *sada* in History: A Critical Essay on Hadrami Historiography." *Journal of the Royal Asiatic Society* 9, no. 2 (1999): 215–22.

———. "Sufi Commentary: Formative and Later Periods." Edited by Mustafa Shah. *Oxford Handbook of the Qur'an*. Forthcoming.

———. "Sufi Motifs in Contemporary Arabic Literature: The Case of Ibn 'Arabi." *Muslim World* 86, no. 1 (1996); 33–49.

———. "Sufism." In *The New Cambridge History of Islam*. Vol. 4, *Islamic Cultures and Societies to the End of the Eighteenth Century*, edited by Robert Irwin, 60–104. Cambridge: Cambridge University Press, 2010.

———. "Sufism as an Explanatory Paradigm: The Issue of the Motivations of Sufi Resistance Movements in Western and Russian Scholarship." *Die Welt des Islams* 42, no. 2 (2002): 139–73.

———. "A Tale of Two Poets: Sufism in Yemen during the Ottoman Epoch." In *Le soufisme á l'époque ottoman*, edited by Rachida Chih and Catherine Mayeur-Jaouen, 337–68. Cairo: IFAO, 2010.

———. "The *tariqa* on a Landcruiser: The Resurgence of Sufism in Yemen." *Middle East Journal* 55, no. 3 (2001): 399–414.

Knysh, Alexander, trans. *Mekkanskie otkroveniia*. St. Petersburg: Peterburgskoe vostokovedenie, 1991.

———. *Al-Qushayri's Epistle on Sufism*. Reading, UK: Garnet, 2007.

Knysh, Alexander et al., eds. *Sufizm i musul'manskaia dukhovnaia traditsiia*. St. Petersburg: Peterburgskoe vostokovedenie, 2015.

Knysh, Alexander, and Ali Hussain. "Ibn al-'Arabi." In *Oxford Bibliographies in Islamic Studies*, edited by John O. Voll. New York: Oxford University Press, 2016 (electronic publication).

Kohlberg, Etan, ed. *Jawami'Adab al-Sufiyya and 'Uyub al-Nafs wa-Mudawatuha by Abu 'Abd al-Rahman al-Sulami*. Jerusalem: Israel Oriental Society, 1976.

Kotb, Amira. "La Tarîqa Ba 'Alawiyya et le développement d'un réseau soufi transnational." Master's thesis, Aix-Marseille III: Institut d'Etudes Politiques, Université Paul Sezanne, 2003–4.

Krämer, Gudrun. *Hasan al-Banna*. Oxford: Oneworld, 2010.

Krawietz, Birgit, and Georges Tamer, eds. *Islamic Theology, Philosophy, and Law: Debating Ibn Taymiyya and Ibn Qayyim al-Jawziyya*. Berlin: Walter de Gruyter, 2013.

Kugle, Scott. *Rebel between Spirit and Law: Ahmad Zarruq, Sainthood, and Authority in Islam*. Bloomington: Indiana University Press, 2006.

———. *Sufis and Saints' Bodies: Mysticism, Corporeality, and Sacred Power in Islam*. Chapel Hill: University of North Carolina Press, 2007.

Kuper, Adam. *Anthropology and Anthropologists: The British School in the Twentieth Century*. 4th ed. New York: Routledge, 2015.

Kurzman, Charles. *Modernist Islam, 1840–1940: A Sourcebook*. Oxford: Oxford University Press, 2002.

Lacroix, Stéphane. "Between Revolution and Apoliticism: Nasir al-Din al-Albani and His Impact on the Shaping of Contemporary Salafism." In *Global Salafism: Islam's New Religious Movement*, edited by Roel Meijer, 58–80. London: Hurst, 2009.

Laffan, Michael. *The Makings of Indonesian Islam*. Princeton, NJ: Princeton University Press, 2011.

Lapidus, Ira. *A History of Islamic Societies*. Cambridge: Cambridge University Press, 1988.

Latour, Bruno. *Reassembling the Social: An Introduction to Actor-Network Theory*. Oxford: Oxford University Press, 2005.

Leaman, Oliver. *An Introduction to Classical Islamic Philosophy*. Cambridge: Cambridge University Press, 2002.

Lerner, Daniel. *The Passing of Traditional Society: Modernizing the Middle East*. Glencoe, IL: Collier-Macmillan, 1964.

Levada, Yuri. *Sochineniia*. 5 vols. Moscow: Karpov E. B., 2011.

Levtzion, Nehemia, and John Voll, eds. *Eighteenth-Century Renewal and Reform in Islam*. Syracuse, NY: Syracuse University Press, 1987.

Lévy, Carlos. "Philo's Ethics." In *The Cambridge Companion to Philo.*, edited by Adam Kamesar, 146–74. Cambridge: Cambridge University Press, 2009.

Lewis, Franklin. *Rumi: Past and Present, East and West: The Life, Teaching, and Poetry of Jalal al-Din Rumi*. Oxford: Oneworld, 2000.

Liebes, Yehud. "The Work of the Chariot and the Work of Creation as Mystical Teachings in Philo of Alexandria." In *Scriptural Exegesis: The Shapes of Culture and Religious Imagination*, edited by Deborah Green and Laura Lieber, 105–20. Oxford: Oxford University Press, 2009.

Lieven, Anatole. *Chechnya: Tombstone of Russian Power*. New Haven, CT: Yale University Press, 1998.

Limor, Ora, and Guy G. Stroumsa, eds. *Christians and Christianity in the Holy Land: From the Origins to the Latin Kingdoms*. Brepols: Turnhout, 2006.

Lincoln, Bruce. *Authority: Construction and Corrosion*. Chicago: University of Chicago Press, 1994.

———. *Holy Terrors: Thinking about Religion after September 11*. 2nd ed. Chicago: University of Chicago Press, 2006.

Littell, Jonathan. *Chechnia: God tretii*. Translated from French by B. Skuratov. Moscow: Ad Marginem Press, 2012.

Livne-Kafri, Ofer. "Early Muslim Ascetics and the World of Christian Monasticism." *Jerusalem Studies in Arabic and Islam (JSAI)* 20 (1996): 105–29.

Loimeier, Roman. "Is There Something Like 'Protestant Islam'?" *Die Welt des Islams* 45, no. 2 (2005): 216–54.

Lombard, Maurice. *The Golden Age of Islam*. Translated by Joan Spencer. Princeton, NJ: Markus Wiener, 2004.

Lory, Pierre. *Les commentaires ésotériques du Coran d'après 'Abd al-Razzâq al-Qâshânî*. Paris: Les Deux Océans, 1980.

Lory, Pierre, ed. *La science des lettres en Islam*. Paris: Éditions Dervy, 2004.

Lory, Pierre, and Jean-Charles Coulon, trans. *Talismans: Le soleil des connaissances.* Paris: Orients éditions, 2013.

Lossky, Vladimir. *The Mystical Theology of the Eastern Church.* London: James Clark, 1957.

Lucas, Scott. *Constructive Critics, Hadith Literature, and the Articulation of Sunni Islam.* Leiden: E. J. Brill, 2004.

Madelung, Wilferd. "Zaydi Attitudes to Sufism." In *Islamic Mysticism Contested: Thirteen Centuries of Controversies and Polemics,* edited by Frederick de Jong and Bernd Radtke, 124–44. Leiden: E. J. Brill, 1999.

Makarov, Dmitri. *Ofitsial'nyi in neofitsial'nyi islam v Dagestane.* Moscow: Tsentr strategicheskikh i politicheskikh issledovanii, 2000.

Malashenko, Aleksei. *Kak vybirali v Chechne.* Moscow: Carnegie Endowment for International Peace, 2006.

al-Malati, Abu 'l-Hasan Muhammad. *Al-Tanbih wa 'l-radd 'ala ahl al-ahwa' wa 'l-bida'.* Edited by Muhammad al-Kawthari. Baghdad: al-Muthanna and Beirut: Maktab al-ma'arif, 1968.

al-Mamani, Shukri. *Ibn Khaldun wa-'ilm al-ijtima' al-insani: 'ala darb bina' al-ma'rifa al- 'ilmiyya wa-hadarat al-insan.* Sfax: Dar amal li 'l-nashr wa 'l-tawzi', 2010.

Martin, Terry, and Ronald Suny, eds. *A State of Nations: Empire and Nation-Making in the Age of Lenin and Stalin.* Oxford: Oxford University Press, 2001.

al-Mashhur, Abu Bakr al-'Adani. *Al-Khuruj min al-da'ira al-hamra'.* Aden: Ribat al-tarbiyya al-islamiyya, 2002.

Massignon, Louis. *Essay on the Origins of the Technical Language of Islamic Mysticism.* Notre Dame, IN: University of Notre Dame Press, 1997.

Masud, Muhammad Khalid, and Armando Salvatore. "Western Scholars of Islam on the Issue of Modernity." In *Islam and Modernity: Key Issues and Debates,* edited by Muhammad Khalid Masud, Armando Salvatore, and Martin van Bruinessen, 36–53. Edinburgh: Edinburgh University Press, 2009.

Masud, Muhammad Khalid, Armando Salvatore, and Martin van Bruinessen, eds. *Islam and Modernity: Key Issues and Debates.* Edinburgh: Edinburgh University Press, 2009.

Masuzawa, Tomoko. *The Invention of World Religions; or, How European Universalism Was Preserved in the Language of Pluralism.* Chicago: University of Chicago Press, 2005.

Matsuzato, Kimitaka, and Magomed-Rasul Ibragimov. "Islamic Politics at the Sub-Regional Level in Dagestan." *Europe-Asia Studies* 57, no. 5 (2005): 753–79.

McAuley, Denis. *Ibn 'Arabi's Mystical Poetics.* Oxford: Oxford University Press, 2012.

McCants, William. *The ISIS Apocalypse.* New York: St. Martin's Press, 2015.

McGinn, Bernard. *The Flowering of Mysticism: Men and Women in the New Mysticism, 1200–1350.* New York: Crossroad, 1998.

——. *The Foundations of Mysticism.* Vol. 1 of *The Presence of God: A History of Western Christian Mysticism.* New York: Crossroad, 1991.

——. *The Mystical Thought of Meister Eckhart.* New York: Herder and Herder, 2011.

McGinnis, Jon, and David Reisman, eds. and trans. *Classical Arabic Philosophy: An Anthology of Sources*. Indianapolis, IN: Hackett, 2007.

McNeill, John, and William McNeill. *The Human Web: A Bird's-Eye View of World History*. New York: W. W. Norton, 2003.

Meier, Fritz. *Abu Sa'id-i Abu l-Hayr: Wirklicheit und Legende*. Teheran-Liège: Bibliothèque Pahlavi; Leiden: E. J. Brill, 1976.

———. *Essays on Islamic Piety and Mysticism*. Translated by John O'Kane. Edited by Bernd Radtke. Leiden: E. J. Brill, 1999.

———. "The Mystic Path." In *The World of Islam: Faith, People, Culture*, edited by Bernard Lewis, 117–28. London: Thames and Hudson, 1976.

———. "Soufisme et déclin culturel." In *Classicisme et déclin culturel dans l'histoire de l'Islam*, edited by Robert Brunschvig and Gustave von Grunebaum, 217–41. Paris: Éditions Besson Chantemerle, 1957.

Meijer, Roel, ed. *Global Salafism: Islam's New Religious Movement*. London: Hurst, 2009.

Melchert, Christopher. "Basran Origins of Classical Sufism." *Der Islam* 82 (2005): 221–40.

———. "Early Renunciants as Hadith Transmitters." *Muslim World* 92, no. 3–4 (2002): 407–18.

———. "Exaggerated Fear in the Early Islamic Renunciant Tradition." *Journal of the Royal Asiatic Society* 3, no. 3 (2011): 283–300.

———. "The Interpretation of Three Qur'anic Terms (*Siyaha, Hikma,* and *Siddiq*) of Special Interest to the Early Renunciants." In *The Meaning of the Word: Lexicography and Qur'anic Exegesis*, edited by Stephen Burge, 89–116. London: Oxford University Press, 2015.

———. "Origins and Early Sufism." In *The Cambridge Companion to Sufism*, edited by Lloyd Ridgeon, 3–23. Cambridge: Cambridge University Press, 2015.

———. "The Transition from Asceticism to Mysticism at the Middle of the Ninth Century C.E." *Studia Islamica* 83 (1996): 51–70.

Melvin-Koushki, Matthew. "The Quest for a Universal Science: The Occult Philosophy of Sa'in Al-Din Turka Isfahani (1369–1432) and Intellectual Millenarianism in Early Timurid Iran." PhD diss., Yale University, 2012.

Memon, Muhammad. *Ibn Taimiya's Struggle against Popular Religion*. The Hague: Mouton, 1976.

Merlan, Philip. *From Plato to Neoplatonism*. 3rd ed. The Hague: Nijhoff, 1968.

Mermier, Franck. "L'islam politique au Yémen ou la 'Tradition' contre les 'traditions.'" *Monde arabe: Magreb-Machrek* 155 (January–March 1997): 6–19.

Meskhidze, Dzhul'ietta. "Kunta-khadzhzhi." In *Islam na territorii byvshei Rossiiskoi imperii: Entsiklodedicheskii slovar'*, edited by Stanislav Prozorov, 61–62. Moscow: Nauka, 1998, fasc. 1.

Milson, Menahem, ed. *Kitab adab al-muridin by Abu al-Najib 'Abd al-Qahir al-Suhrawardi (d. 563 H.)*. Jerusalem: Hebrew University of Jerusalem, 1978.

Milson, Menahem, trans. *A Sufi Rule for Novices*. Cambridge, MA: Harvard University Press, 1975.

Mir-Kasimov, Orkhan. *Words of Power: Hurufi Teachings between Shi'ism and Sufism in Medieval Islam*. London: I. B. Tauris, 2015.

Mirsepassi, Ali, and Tadd Fernée. *Islam, Democracy, and Cosmopolitanism: At Home and in the World.* Cambridge: Cambridge University Press, 2014.

Mobini-Kesheh, Natalie. "Islamic Modernism in Colonial Java." In *Hadhrami Traders, Scholars, and Statesmen in the Indian Ocean, 1750s–1960s,* edited by Ulrike Freitag and William Clarence-Smith, 231–48. Leiden: E. J. Brill, 1997.

Molé, Marijan. *Les mystiques musulmans.* Paris: Presses Universitaires de France, 1965.

Momen, Moojan. *An Introduction to Shii Islam.* New Haven, CT: Yale University Press, 1985.

Morris, James. "An Arab Machiavelli? Rhetoric, Philosophy, and Politics in Ibn Khaldun's Critique of Sufism." *Harvard Middle Eastern and Islamic Review* 8 (2009): 242–91.

———. "At the End of Time: The Mahdi's Helpers." In *The Meccan Revelations,* 2 vols., edited by Michel Chodkiewicz, 1: 65–92. New York: Pir Press, 2005.

———. "How to Read the *Futuhat*: Ibn 'Arabi's Own Advice." In *Muhyiddin Ibn 'Arabi: A Commemorative Volume,* edited by Stephen Hirtenstein and Michael Tiernan, 73–89. Brisbane: Element, 1993.

———. "Ibn 'Arabi and His Interpreters." *Journal of the American Oriental Society* 106 (1986): 539–51, and 107 (1987): 101–19.

———. "Situating Islamic 'Mysticism': Between Written Tradition and Popular Spirituality." In *Mystics of the Book: Themes, Topics, and Typologies,* edited by Robert Herrera, 293–334. New York: Peter Lang, 1993.

Motzki, Harald. "Alternative Accounts of the Qur'an's Formation." In *The Cambridge Companion to the Qur'an,* edited by Jane McAuliffe, 65–71. Cambridge: Cambridge University Press, 2006.

Mouline, Nabile. *Les clercs de l'islam: Autorité religieuse et pouvoir politique en Arabie Saoudite, XVIIIᵉ–XXIᵉ siècle.* Paris: Presses Universitaires de France, 2011.

al-Mubarak, 'Abdallah Ibn. *Kitab al-zuhd wa 'l-raqa'iq.* Alexandria: Dar al-salafiyya, 1998.

al-Muhasibi, al-Harith. *Al-Makasib wa 'l-wara' wa 'l-shubha.* Beirut: Mu'assasat al-kutub al-thaqafiyya, 1987.

al-Muhasibi, al-Harith. *Tawahhum: Rahlat al-insan ila 'alam al-akhira.* Cairo: Maktabat al-Qur'an, 1984.

Munson, Henry. *Religion and Power in Morocco.* New Haven, CT: Yale University Press, 1993.

Muruwwa, Husayn. *Al-Naza'at al-maddiyya fi 'l-falsafa al-'arabiyya-al-islamiyya.* 3 vols. Beirut: Dar al-Farabi, 2002.

Musaev, Makhach. *Musul'manskoe dukhovenstvo 60–70-kh godov XIX veka i vosstanie 1877 goda v Dagestane.* Makhachkala: Dagestanskii nauchnyi tsentr, 2005.

Nasr, Seyyed Hossein. *Islamic Life and Thought.* London: Allen and Unwin, 1981.

———. *Sufi Essays.* Albany: State University of New York Press, 1972.

Nasr, Seyyed Hossein, and Oliver Leaman, eds. *History of Islamic Philosophy.* 2 vols. London: Routledge, 1996.

Nettler, Ron. *Sufi Metaphysics and Qur'anic Prophets: Ibn 'Arabi's Thought and Method in the Fusus al-hikam.* Cambridge: Islamic Texts Society, 2003.

Netton, Ian Richard. "The Breath of Felicity: *Adab, Ahwal,* and *Maqamat* and Abu

Najib al-Suhrawardi." In *Classical Persian Sufism: From Its Origins to Rumi*, edited by Leonard Lewisohn, 457–82. Oxford: Oneworld, 1999.

———. *Islam, Christianity, and Tradition: A Comparative Exploration*. Edinburgh: Edinburgh University Press, 2006.

———. *Muslim Neoplatonists: An Introduction to the Thought of the Brethren of Purity*. London: Routledge and Curzon, 2002.

Netton, Ian Richard, ed. *Islamic Philosophy and Theology: Critical Concepts in Islamic Thought*. Vol. 3, *Aristotelianism and Neoplatonism*. London: Routledge, 2011.

Neuwirth, Angelika. "Structural, Linguistic, and Literary Features." In *The Cambridge Companion to the Qur'an*, edited by Jane McAuliffe, 97–113. Cambridge: Cambridge University Press, 2006.

Neuwirth, Angelika, Nicolai Sinai, and Michael Marx, eds. *The Qur'an in Context: Historical and Literary Investigations into the Qur'anic Milieu*. Leiden: E. J. Brill, 2010.

Nguyen, Martin. *Sufi Master and Qur'an Teacher: Abu'l-Qasim al-Qushayri and the Lata'if al-Isharat*. Oxford: Oxford University Press, 2012.

Nicholson, Reynold. "A Historical Enquiry concerning the Origin and Development of Sufism." *Journal of the Royal Asiatic Society* (1906): 303–48.

Nwyia, Paul. *Exégèse coranique et language mystique*. Beirut: Libraire Orientale, 1970.

———. *Un mystique prédicateur à la Qarawiyin de Fès Ibn 'Abbad de Ronda (1332–1390)*. Beirut: Imprimerie catholique, 1961.

Nwyia, Paul, ed. *Ibn 'Abbad de Ronda (792/1390), Lettres de direction spirituelle*. Beirut: Dar El-Machreq, 1986.

Nyberg, Henrik, ed. *Kleinere Schriften des Ibn al-'Arabi*. Leiden: E. J. Brill, 1919.

O'Fahey, Rex. *The Enigmatic Saint: Ahmad ibn Idris and the Idrisi Tradition*. Evanston, IL: Northwestern University Press, 1990.

O'Fahey, Rex, and Bernd Radtke. "Neo-Sufism Reconsidered." *Der Islam* 70, no. 1 (1993): 52–87.

Ohlander, Erik. "Fear of God (*taqwa*) in the Qur'an: Some Notes on Semantic Shift and Thematic Context." *Journal of Semitic Studies* 50 (2005): 137–52.

———. *Sufism in an Age of Transition: 'Umar al-Suhrawardi and the Rise of Islamic Mystical Brotherhoods*. Leiden: E. J. Brill, 2008.

Oliver, Paul. *Mysticism: A Guide for the Perplexed*. London: Continuum, 2009.

Orlovsky, Daniel, ed. *Beyond Soviet Studies*. Washington, DC: Woodrow Wilson Center Press and Johns Hopkins University Press, 1995.

Owen, Thomas. "Interiority and Christian Spirituality." *Journal of Religion* 80, no. 1 (2000): 41–60.

Palacios, Miguel Asín. *El Islam cristianizado: Estudio del sufismo a través de las obras de Abenárabi de Murcia*. Madrid: Editorial Plutarco, 1931.

Palmer, Aiyub. "The Social and Theoretical Dimensions of Sainthood in Early Islam: Al-Tirmidhi's Gnoseology and the Foundations of Sufi Social Praxis." PhD diss., University of Michigan, 2015.

Paret, Rudi. *Der Koran Kommentar und Konkordanz*. Stuttgart: W. Kohlhammer, 1971.

Parfitt, Tom. "The Battle for the Soul of Chechnya." *The Guardian*, November 22, 2007.

Pellat, Charles. "Al-Jahiz." In *'Abbasid Belles-Lettres*, edited by Julia Ashtiany et al., 78–95. Cambridge: Cambridge University Press, 1990.

———. *Le milieu baṣrien et la formation de Ǧaḥiẓ*. Paris: Librairie d'Amérique et d'Orient Adrien-Maisonneuve, 1953.

Picken, Gavin. *Spiritual Purification in Islam: The Life and Works of al-Muhasibi*. London: Routledge, 2011.

Pinsent, John. "Ascetic Moods in Greek and Latin Literature." In *Asceticism*, edited by Vincent Wimbush and Richard Valantasis, 211–19. Oxford: Oxford University Press, 1999.

Popovic, Alexandre, and Gilles Veinstein, eds. *Les Voies d'Allah: Les ordres mystiques dans l'islam des origines à aujourd'hui*. Paris: Fayard, 1996.

Pourjavady, Nasrollah. "Opposition to Sufism in Twelver Shiism." In *Islamic Mysticism Contested: Thirteen Centuries of Controversies and Polemics*, edited by Frederick de Jong and Bernd Radtke, 614–23. Leiden: E. J. Brill, 1999.

Preckel, Claudia. "Screening Siddiq Hasan Khan's Library: The Use of Hanbali Literature in 19th-Century Bhopal." In *Islamic Theology, Philosophy, and Law: Debating Ibn Taymiyya and Ibn Qayyim al-Jawziyya*, edited by Birgit Krawietz and Georges Tamer, 162–219. Berlin: Walter de Gruyter, 2013.

Al-Qunawi. *al-Tafsir al-sufi li 'l-Qur'an: I'jaz al-bayan fi ta'wil al-Qur'an*. Edited by 'Abd al-Qadir Ahmad 'Ata. Cairo: Dar al-kutub al-haditha, 1969.

Al-Qushayri. *Tafsir al-Qushayri al-masamma Lata'if al-isharat*. 3 vols. Edited by 'Abd al-Latif Hasan 'Abd al-Rahman. Beirut: Dar al-kutub al-'ilmiyya, 1420/2000.

Radtke, Bernd. *Adab al-muluk: Ein Handbuch zur islamischen Mystik aus dem 4./10. Jahrhundert*. Beirut: Beiruter Texte und Studien, 1991.

———. *Autochthone islamische Aufklärung im 18. Jahrhundert: Theoretische und filologische Bemerkungen*. Utrecht: Houtsma, 2000.

———. "The Eight Rules of al-Junayd: A General Overview of the Genesis and Development of Islamic Dervish Orders." In *Reason and Inspiration in Islam: Theology, Philosophy, and Mysticism in Muslim Thought*, edited by Todd Lawson, 490–502. London: I. B. Tauris; New York: St. Martin's Press, 2005.

———. "Lehrer-Schüle-Enkel: Ahmad b. Idris, Muhammad 'Uthman al-Mirgani, Isma'il al-Wali." *Oriens* 32 (1992): 94–132.

———. *Materialien zur alten islamischen Frömmigkeit*. Leiden: E. J. Brill, 2009.

———. *Neue kritische Gänge*. Utrecht: Houtsma, 2005.

———. "Sufism in the 18th Century: An Attempt at a Provisional Appraisal." *Die Welt des Islams* 36, no. 3 (1996): 326–64.

———. "Von Iran nach Westafrika: Zwei Quellen für al-Ḥaǧǧ 'Umars *Kitab Rimah Hizb ar-rahim*: Zaynaddin al-Hwafi und Šamsaddin al-Madyani." *Die Welt des Islams* 35, no. 1 (1995): 37–69.

Radtke, Bernd, Rex O'Fahey, and John O'Kane. "Two Sufi Treatises of Ahmad Ibn Idris." *Oriens* 35 (1996): 143–78.

Radtke, Bernd, and John O'Kane, trans. *The Concept of Sainthood in Early Islamic Mysticism: Two Works by al-Hakim al-Tirmidhi*. Richmond, Surrey: Curzon Press, 1996.

Rahman, Fazlur. *Islam*. 2nd ed. Chicago: University of Chicago Press, 1979.

Ramadan, Tariq. *In the Footsteps of the Prophet: Lessons from the Life of Muhammad.* Oxford: Oxford University Press, 2007.

Rappaport, Roy. *Ritual and Religion in the Making of Humanity.* Cambridge: Cambridge University Press, 1999.

Raudvere, Catharina, and Leif Stenberg, eds. *Sufism Today: Heritage and Tradition in the Global Community.* London: I. B. Tauris, 2009.

Rauf, Bulent, trans. *Ismail Hakki's Bursevi's Translation and Commentary on Fusus al-Hikam.* 3 vols. Oxford: Muhyiddin Ibn 'Arabi Society and Oxford University Press, 1986–89.

Reid, Megan. *Law and Piety in Medieval Islam.* Cambridge: Cambridge University Press, 2013.

Reinert, Benedikt. *Die lehre vom tawakkul in der klassischen Sufik.* Berlin: Walter de Gruyter, 1968.

Remes, Paulina. *Plotinus of Self: The Philosophy of the "We."* Cambridge: Cambridge University Press, 2007.

Renard, John. *Friends of God: Islamic Images of Piety, Commitment, and Servanthood.* Berkeley: University of California Press, 2008.

Reynolds, Gabriel Said. *New Perspectives on the Qur'an.* London: Routledge, 2011.

———. *The Qur'an and Its Biblical Subtext.* London: Routledge, 2010.

———. *The Qur'an in Its Historical Context.* London: Routledge, 2007.

Ridgeon, Lloyd. "Mysticism in Medieval Islam." In *The Cambridge Companion to Sufism,* edited by Lloyd Ridgeon, 125–49. Cambridge: Cambridge University Press, 2015.

Ridgeon, Lloyd, ed. *The Cambridge Companion to Sufism.* Cambridge: Cambridge University Press, 2015.

———. *Sufis and Salafis in the Contemporary Age.* London: Bloomsbury Academic, 2015.

Rippin, Andrew, ed. *Blackwell Companion to the Qur'an.* Oxford: Blackwell, 2006.

Ritter, Helmut, ed. *Maqalat al-islamiyyin.* Ta'lif Abi al-Hasan 'Ali ibn Isma'il al-Ash'ari. Istanbul: Jam'iyat al-Mustashriqin al-Almaniyya, 1929.

Rosenthal, Franz. *A History of Muslim Historiography.* Leiden: E. J. Brill, 1968.

———. "Ibn 'Arabi between 'Philosophy' and 'Mysticism.'" *Oriens* 31 (1988): 1–35.

———. *Man versus Society in Medieval Islam.* Leiden: E. J. Brill, 2015.

Rosenthal, Franz, trans. *Ibn Khaldun: The Muqaddimah; An Introduction to History.* 3 vols. New York: Pantheon, 1958.

Roy, Olivier. *Globalized Islam: The Search for a New Ummah.* New York: Columbia University Press, 2004.

———. *Holy Ignorance: When Religion and Culture Part Ways.* Translated by Ros Schwartz. New York: Columbia University Press, 2010.

Rozehnal, Robert. *Islamic Sufism Unbound: Politics and Piety in Twenty-First-Century Pakistan.* New York: Palgrave Macmillan, 2007.

Sachau, Edward, trans. *Alberuni's India: An Account of the Religion, Philosophy, Literature, Geography, Chronology, Astronomy, Customs, Laws, and Astrology of India about A.D. 1030.* Delhi: S. Chand, 1964.

Saeed, Abdullah. *Interpreting the Qur'an: Towards a Contemporary Approach.* London: Routledge, 2006.

Saetov, Ilshat. "'Dzhamatizatsiia' tarikatov v respublikanskoi Turtsii." In *Sufizm i musul'manskaia dukhovnaia traditsiia*, edited by Alexander Knysh et al., 240–57. St. Petersburg: Peterburgskoe vostokovedenie, 2015.

Safi, Omid. "Bargaining with *Baraka*: Persian Sufism, 'Mysticism,' and Pre-Modern Politics." *Muslim World* 90 (September 2000): 259–87.

Said, Edward. *Orientalism*. New York: Vintage Books, 1979.

Salama, Mohammad. *Islam, Orientalism, and Intellectual History*. London: I. B. Tauris, 2011.

Salvatore, Armando. *Islam and the Political Discourse of Modernity*. Reading, UK: Ithaca Press, 1998.

———. "Tradition and Modernity within Islamic Civilization and the West." In *Islam and Modernity: Key Issues and Debates*, edited by Muhammad Khalid Masud, Armando Salvatore, and Martin van Bruinessen, 3–35. Edinburgh: Edinburgh University Press, 2009.

Sands, Kristin Zahra. *Sufi Commentaries on the Qur'an in Classical Islam*. London: Routledge, 2005.

al-Sarraj. *Kitab al-luma'*. Edited by Kamil Mustafa al-Nihawandi. Beirut: Dar al-kutub al-'ilmiyya, 2001.

———. *Kitab al-luma' fi l-tasawwuf*. Edited by Reynold Nicholson. Leiden: E. J. Brill, 1914.

Schallenbergh, Gino. "Ibn Qayyim al-Jawziyya's Manipulation of Sufi Terms: Fear and Hope." In *Islamic Theology, Philosophy, and Law: Debating Ibn Taymiyya and Ibn Qayyim al-Jawziyya*, edited by Birgit Krawietz and Georges Tamer, 94–122. Berlin: Walter de Gruyter, 2013.

Schielke, Samuli. "Hegemonic Encounters: Criticism of Saints' Day Festivals and the Formation of Modern Islam in Late 19th and Early 20th-Century Egypt." *Die Welt des Islams* 47 (2007): 319–55.

Schimmel, Annemarie. *And Muhammad Is His Messenger: The Veneration of the Prophet in Islamic Piety*. Chapel Hill: University of North Carolina Press, 1985.

———. *Mystical Dimensions of Islam*. Chapel Hill: University of North Carolina Press, 1975.

Scholem, Gershom. *Major Trends in Jewish Mysticism*. New York: Schocken Books, 1995.

Schulze, Reinhard. "Hypothese einer islamischen Aufklärung." *ZDMG* 148 (1998): 83–110.

———. *Islamischer Internationalismus im 20. Jahrhundert*. Leiden: E. J. Brill, 1990.

———. "Was ist die islamische Aufklärung?" *Die Welt des Islams* 36, no. 3 (1996): 276–325.

Sedgwick, Mark. *Against the Modern World*. Oxford: Oxford University Press, 2004.

———. *Western Sufism: From the Abbasids to the New Age*. Oxford: Oxford University Press, 2017.

Sells, Michael. *Early Islamic Mysticism*. New York: Paulist Press, 1994.

———. "Ibn 'Arabi's 'Polished Mirror': Perspective Change and Meaning Event." *Studia Islamica* 67 (1988): 121–49.

Serjeant, Robert. *Prose and Poetry from Hadramawt*. London: Taylor's Foreign Press, 1951.

——. *The Sayyids of Hadramawt*. Cambridge: Cambridge University Press, 1957.

al-Shaibi, Kamil. *Sufism and Shi'ism*. Surbiton, Surrey: LAAM, 1991.

al-Shatibi, Abou Ishaq Ibrahim. *Kitab al-I'tisam*. Translated by Muhammed Mahdi Al-Sharif. 2 vols. Beirut: Dar al-Kutub al-'Ilmiyya, 2012.

al-Shatibi, Abu Ishaq. *Al-I'tisam*. Edited by Abu 'Ubayda Mashur Al Sulayman. 4 vols. Manama, Bahrain: Maktabat al-tawhid, 2000.

Shihadeh, Ayman, ed. *Sufism and Theology*. Edinburgh: Edinburgh University Press, 2007.

Shikhaliev, Shamil. "Agiografichesko-biograficheskie sochineniia dagestanskikh sheikhov Shu'ayba al-Bagini i Khasana al-Kakhi." In *Sufizm i musul'manskaia dukhovnaia traditsiia*, edited by Alexander Knysh et al., 70–91. St. Petersburg: Peterburgskoe vostokovedenie, 2015.

Shrady, Maria, trans. *Angelus Silesius: The Cherubinic Wanderer*. New York: Paulist Press, 1986.

Shterin, Marat, and Akhmet Yarlykapov. "Reconsidering Radicalisation and Terrorism: The New Muslims Movement in Kabardino-Balkaria and Its Path to Violence." *Religion, State, and Society* 39, no. 2–3 (2011): 311.

Silvers-Alario, Laury. "The Teaching Relationship in Early Sufism: A Reassessment of Fritz Meier's Definition of the *shaykh al-tarbiya* and the *shaykh al-ta'lim*." *Muslim World* 93 (January 2003): 69–97.

Simiti, Bernard. *Le Dar-El-Kouti: Empire oubanguien de Senoussi (1890–1911)*. Paris: Harmattan, 2013.

Sirriyeh, Elizabeth. *Sufis and Anti-Sufis: The Defense, Rethinking, and Rejection of Sufism in the Modern World*. Richmond, Surrey: Curzon, 1999.

Smart, Ninian. *Concept and Empathy: Essays in the Study of Religion*. Houndmills, Basingstoke: Macmillan, 1986.

——. *Dimensions of the Sacred*. London: Harper Collins, 1996.

——. "Methods in My Life." In *The Craft of Religious Studies*, edited by Jonathan Stone, 18–35. New York: St. Martin's Press, 1998.

Smirnov, Andrei. *Ibn Arabi: Izbrannoe* ("Ibn 'Arabi: Selected Works"). Moscow: Iazyki slavianskoi kul'tury and OOO Sadra, 2014.

Smirnov, Andrei. "Kadyrov Turns to Zikrism to Legitimize His Rule." *Jamestown Foundation, North Caucasus Analysis* 8, no. 11 (2007): online publication.

Smith, Jonathan Z. *Imagining Religion: From Babylon to Jonestown*. Chicago: University of Chicago Press, 1982.

Smith, Margaret. *Studies in Early Mysticism in the Near and Middle East*. London: Sheldon Press, 1931.

Sobieroj, Florian. *Ibn Ḫafīf aš-Šīrazi und seine Schrift zur Novizenerziehung*. Stuttgart: Franz Steiner, 1998.

——. "Ibn Khafif's *Kitab al-Iqtisad* and Abu al-Najib al-Suhrawardi's *Adab al-Muridin*." *Journal of Semitic Studies* 93, no. 2 (1998): 327–45.

Sokirianskaia, Ekaterina. "Families and Clans in Ingushetia and Chechnya." *Central Asian Survey* 24, no. 4 (2005): 453–67.

Sorgenfrei, Simon. *American Dervish: Making Mevlevism in the United States of America*. Göteborg, Sweden: University of Gothenburg Press, 2013.

Steigerwald, Diana. "Isma'ili *ta'wil*." In *Blackwell Companion to the Qur'an*, edited by Andrew Rippin, 386–400. Oxford: Blackwell, 2006.

Strenski, Ivan. *Thinking about Religion: An Historical Introduction to Theories of Religion*. Oxford: Blackwell, 2006.

———. *Religion in Relation: Method, Application, and Moral Location*. Columbia: University of South Carolina Press, 1993.

al-Suhrawardi, Shihab al-Din 'Umar. *'Awarif al-ma'arif*. 2 vols. Edited by 'Abd al-Halim Mahmud and Mahmud b. al-Sharif. Cairo: Dar al-ma'arif, 1971.

al-Sulami. *Kitab al-tabaqat al-sufiyya*. Edited by Johannes Pedersen. Leiden: E. J. Brill, 1960.

Suschii, Sergei. *Severnyi Kavkaz: Realii, problemy, perspektivy pervoi treti XXI veka*. Moscow: LENAND, 2013.

Sviri, Sara. "Hakîm Tirmidhî and the Malâmatî Movement in Early Sufism." In *The Heritage of Sufism*, 2 vols., edited by Leonard Lewisohn, 1: 583–613. Oxford: Oneworld, 1999.

———. "Sufism: Reconsidering Terms, Definitions, and Processes in the Formative Period of Islamic Mysticism." In *Les maîtres soufis et leurs disciples*, edited by Geneviève Gobillot and Jean-Jacques Thibon, 17–34. Beirut: IFPO, 2012.

———. "*Wa-rahbaniyatan ibtada'ha*: An Analysis of Traditions concerning the Origin and Evaluation of Christian Mysticism." *JSAI* 13 (1990): 195–208.

Thibon, Jean-Jacques. *L'oeuvre d'Abu 'Abd al-Rahman al-Sulami (325/937–412/1021) et la formation du soufisme*. Damascus: IFPO, 2009.

Tishkov, Valerii. *Obschestvo v vooruzhennom konflikte*. Moscow: Nauka, 2001.

Todd, Richard. *The Sufi Doctrine of Man: Sadr al-Din al-Qunawi's Metaphysical Anthropology*. Leiden: E. J. Brill, 2014.

Torre, Purificación de la, ed. *Ibn Barraŷan (m. 536/1141), Šarh asma' Allah al-husna*. Madrid: Consejo Superior de Investigaciones Cientícas, 2000.

Toynbee, Arnold. *An Historian's Approach to Religion*. 2nd ed. Oxford: Oxford University Press, 1979.

Triaud, Jean Louis. *La légende noire de Sanûsiyya*. 2 vols. Paris: Éditions de la maison des sciences d'homme, 1995.

Trimingham, Spencer. *The Sufi Orders in Islam*. With a new foreword by John Voll. Oxford: Oxford University Press, 1998.

Troll, Christian, ed. *Muslim Shrines in India*. Oxford: Oxford University Press, 1989.

Tsibenko (Ivanova), Veronika. "The Naqshbandi-Haqqani (Rabbani) Sufi Order: Contemporary Sufism of Neo-Ottoman Style." In *Sufizm i musul'manskaia dukhovnaia traditsiia (Sufism and the Muslim Spiritual Tradition)*, edited by Alexander Knysh et al., 258–75. St. Petersburg: Peterburgskoe vostokovedenie, 2015.

Turner, Bryan. "Towards an Economic Model of Virtuoso Religion." In *Islamic Dilemmas: Reformers, Nationalists, and Industrialization*, edited by Ernest Gellner, 49–72. Berlin: Mouton, 1985.

———. *Weber and Islam: A Critical Study*. London: Routledge and Kegan Paul, 1974.

Valantasis, Richard. *The Making of the Self: Ancient and Modern Asceticism*. Eugene, OR: Cascade Books, 2008.

van Bladel, Kevin. *The Arabic Hermes: From Pagan Sage to Prophet of Science*. Oxford: Oxford University Press, 2009.

van Ess, Josef. *Theologie und Gesellschaft im 2. und 3. Jahrhundert Hidschra*. 6 vols. Berlin: Walter de Gruyter, 1991.

Varisco, Daniel. *Reading Orientalism: Said and Unsaid*. Seattle: University of Washington Press, 2007.

Vaughan-Lee, Llewellyn. *The Prayer of the Heart in Christian and Sufi Mysticism*. Point Reyes, CA: Golden Sufi Center, 2012.

Veinstein, Gilles. "Avant-propos." In *Les Voies d'Allah*, edited by Alexandre Popovic and Gilles Veinstein. Paris: Fayard, 1996.

Vikør, Knut. *Sufi and Scholar on the Desert Edge: Muhammad b. 'Ali al-Sanusi and His Brotherhood*. London: Hurst, 1995.

———. "Sufism and Colonialism." In *The Cambridge Companion to Sufism*, edited by Lloyd Ridgeon, 212–32. Cambridge: Cambridge University Press, 2015.

von Grunebaum, Gustave. *Classical Islam: A History, 600–1258*. Chicago: Aldine, 1970.

Vööbus, Arthur. *History of Asceticism in the Syrian Orient*. Vol. 1. Louvain: CorpusSCO, 1958.

———. *Syriac and Arabic Documents Regarding Legislation Relative to Syrian Asceticism*. Stockholm: Este, 1960.

Waardenburg, Jacques. *L'Islam dans le miroir de l'Occident*. Paris: Mouton, 1963.

al-Wadi'i, 'Abd al-Rahman Muqbil b. Hadi. *Gharat al-ashrita 'ala ahl al-jahl wa 'l-safsata*. 2 vols. Cairo: Dar al-haramayn, 1998.

Walker, Paul E. *Early Philosophical Shiism: The Ismaili Neoplatonism of Abu Ya'qub al- Sijistani*. Cambridge: Cambridge University Press, 1993.

Walzer, Richard. *Greek into Arabic: Essays on Islamic Philosophy*. Columbia: University of South Carolina Press, 1970.

Wansbrough, John. *Quranic Studies: Sources and Methods of Scriptural Interpretation*. Oxford: Oxford University Press, 1977.

———. *Sectarian Milieu*. Oxford: Oxford University Press, 1978.

Ware, Robert Bruce. "A Multitude of Evils: Mythology and Political Failure in Chechnya." In *Chechnya: From Past to Future*, edited by Richard Sakwa, 81–87. London, Anthem Press, 2005.

Ware, Rudolph, III. *The Walking Qur'an: Islamic Education, Embodied Knowledge, and History in West Africa*. Chapel Hill: University of North Carolina Press, 2014.

Watt, Montgomery. *Faith and Practice of al-Ghazali*. 4th ed. London: George Allen and Unwin, 1970.

———. *Islamic Philosophy and Theology: An Extended Survey*. Edinburgh: Edinburgh University Press, 1985.

———. *The Majesty That Was Islam: The Islamic World, 661–1100*. New York: Praeger, 1974.

Waugh, Earle. *The Munshidin of Egypt: Their World and Their Song*. Columbia: University of South Carolina Press, 1989.

———. *Visionaries of Silence: The Reformist Sufi Order of the Demirdashiya al-Khalwatiya in Cairo*. Cairo: American University in Cairo Press, 2008.

Weber, Max. *The Protestant Ethic and the Spirit of Capitalism*. New York: Charles Scribner, 1976.

———. *The Sociology of Religion*. Translated by Ephraim Fischoff. London: Methuen, 1965.

Weismann, Itzchak. "Modernity from Within: Islamic Fundamentalism and Sufism." In *Sufis and Salafis in the Contemporary Age*, edited by Lloyd Ridgeon, 9–32. London: Bloomsbury, 2015.

——. *The Naqshbandiyya: Orthodoxy and Activism in a Worldwide Sufi Tradition.* Abingdon, Oxon: Routledge, 2007.

——. "Sufism in the Age of Globalization." In *The Cambridge Companion to Sufism*, edited by Lloyd Ridgeon, 257–81. Cambridge: Cambridge University Press, 2015.

——. *Taste of Modernity: Sufism, Salafiyya, and Arabism in Late Ottoman Damascus.* Leiden: E. J. Brill, 2001.

Werbner, Pnina. *Pilgrims of Love: The Anthropology of a Global Sufi Cult.* Bloomington: Indiana University Press, 2003.

——. "Transnationalism and Regional Cults." In *The Cambridge Companion to Sufism*, edited by Lloyd Ridgeon, 282–300. Cambridge: Cambridge University Press, 2015.

Werbner, Pnina, and Helen Basu, eds. *Embodying Charisma.* London: Routledge, 1998.

Wilberding, James, trans. and comment. *Plotinus' Cosmology: A Study of Ennead ii.1 (40).* Oxford: Oxford University Press, 2006.

Wilson, Brett. *Translating the Qur'an in an Age of Nationalism.* Oxford: Oxford University Press, 2014.

Wimbush, Vincent, and Richard Valantasis. *Asceticism.* Oxford: Oxford University Press, 1999.

Winter, Tim, ed. *The Cambridge Companion to Islamic Theology.* Cambridge: Cambridge University Press, 2008.

White, Hayden. *The Content of the Form: Narrative Discourse and Historical Representation.* Baltimore: Johns Hopkins University Press, 1987.

——. *The Fiction of the Narrative.* Edited by Robert Doran. Baltimore: Johns Hopkins University Press, 2010.

——. *Tropics of Discourse: Essays in Cultural Criticism.* Baltimore: Johns Hopkins University Press, 1978.

Woodward, Mark; Muhammad Sani Umar, Inayah Rohmaniyah, and Mariani Yahya. "Salafi Violence and Sufi Tolerance? Rethinking Conventional Wisdom." *Perspectives on Terrorism* 7, no. 6 (2013): 58–78.

Wright, Zachary. "Embodied Knowledge in West African Islam: Continuity and Change in the Gnostic Community of Shaykh Ibrahim Niasse." PhD diss., Northwestern University, 2010.

Yarlykapov, Akhmet. *Islam u stepnykh nogaitsev.* Moscow: Institut etnograffi i antropologii, 2008.

——. "Kredo vakhkhabita." *Vestnik Evrazii* 3, no. 10 (2000): 114–37.

Yemelianova, Galina. "Sufism and Politics in the Northern Caucasus." *Nationalities Papers* 29, no. 4 (2001): 661–88.

Zarrabi-Zadeh, Saeed. *Practical Mysticism in Islam and Christianity: A Comparative Study of Jalal al-Din Rumi and Meister Eckhart.* New York: Routledge, 2016.

Al-Zekri, Muhammad. "The Religious Encounter between Sufis and Salafis: The Issue of Identity." PhD diss., University of Exeter, England, 2004.

Zelkina, Anna. *In Quest for God and Freedom: Sufi Responses to the Russian Advance in the Northern Caucasus.* London: Hurst, 2000.

———. "The 'Wahhabis' of the Northern Caucasus vis-à-vis State and Society: The Case of Daghestan." In *The Caspian Region.* Vol. 2, *The Caucasus*, edited by Moshe Gammer, 146–78. London: Routledge, 2004.

Zinovyev, Aleksandr. *Homo Sovieticus.* Translated by Charles Janson. London: Paladin, 1986.

A NOTE ON THE TYPE

THIS BOOK has been composed in Miller, a Scotch Roman typeface designed by Matthew Carter and first released by Font Bureau in 1997. It resembles Monticello, the typeface developed for The Papers of Thomas Jefferson in the 1940s by C. H. Griffith and P. J. Conkwright and reinterpreted in digital form by Carter in 2003.

Pleasant Jefferson ("P. J.") Conkwright (1905–1986) was Typographer at Princeton University Press from 1939 to 1970. He was an acclaimed book designer and AIGA Medalist.

The ornament used throughout this book was designed by Pierre Simon Fournier (1712–1768) and was a favorite of Conkwright's, used in his design of the *Princeton University Library Chronicle*.